Clinical Assessment of Voice

About the Author

Robert Thayer Sataloff, MD, DMA, who has organized this volume especially for speech-language pathology students and clinicians who are new to the field of voice care, is Chairman of the Department of Otolaryngology-Head and Neck Surgery at the Graduate Hospital in Philadelphia and Professor of Otolaryngology-Head and Neck Surgery at Jefferson Medical College, Thomas Jefferson University. He is President-Elect of the American Laryngeal Association; Chairman of the Speech, Voice and Swallowing Committee of the American Academy of Otolaryngology-Head and Neck Surgery; and Chairman of Board of Directors of the Voice Foundation and the American Institute for Voice and Ear Research. A prolific author, Dr. Sataloff has contributed to more than 500 publications, including 23 textbooks. Dr. Sataloff is also Editor-in-Chief of the *Journal of Voice* and the *Ear, Nose and Throat Journal*.

Clinical Assessment of Voice

Robert Thayer Sataloff, MD, DMA

Plural Publishing, Inc.
San Diego Oxford

MW

PLURAL PUBLISHING
5521 Ruffin Road
San Diego, CA 92123

e-mail: info@pluralpublishing.com
Web site: http://www.pluralpublishing.com

49 Bath Street
Abingdon, Oxfordshire OX14 1EA
United Kingdom

Clinical Assessment of Voice is one of three student editions prepared for speech-language pathology students and clinicians who are new to the field of voice care from selected chapters of the third edition of *Professional Voice: The Science and Art of Clinical Care* to provide relevant information in an affordable format.

Typeset in 10/12 Palatino by So Cal Graphics

ISBN 1-59756-039-1

Library of Congress Control Number: 2005905963

5/8/06

Contents

Foreword

Dr. Robert Sataloff was a professional singer and singing teacher before he began his medical career. His dedication to voice stems from his personal love and active involvement in singing and vocal pedagogy. His medical and scientific interests in the voice developed during his residency as his musical colleagues solicited his medical advice. Much to his surprise, he learned that there was not much written about the medical and scientific aspects of the voice, especially about the singer's voice. While completing his fellowship in otology, neurotology, and skull base surgery, his interest in voice grew to a point that he chose to pursue the study of voice with such a force that he has become the most prolific writer of voice books for laryngologists, speech-language pathologists and voice teachers. In 1977, he began attending the meetings of the Voice Foundation in New York City and became more and more interested in the voice and its relation to the field of otolaryngology. With the support and influence of people such as Drs. Wilbur J. Gould, Friederic Brodnitz, Hans von Leden, and Paul Moore, among others, he combined his love for the voice and his medical practice into a well-known center for the care of professional singers and other vocal performers from all over the world. His clinical practice and pursuit of knowledge led him to publish his first paper on professional singers in 1981 entitled, "Professional Singers: The Science and Art of Clinical Care" and the first chapter on modern voice care in an otolaryngology textbook in 1986. He eventually became Chairman of the Board of Directors of the Voice Foundation in 1989 where he has since championed the need for interdisciplinary voice care through the annual Symposium on Care of the Professional Voice sponsored by the Voice Foundation and the monthly publication of the *Journal of Voice* of which he is currently Editor-in-Chief

Gifted as a surgeon and skilled in the art of expression, whether it be through his singing or his lecturing, Dr. Sataloff has taken the humble beginnings of the Voice Foundation and has made its influence felt around the world by physicians, speech-language pathologists, singing teachers, and vocal performers of all types from reggae to opera and from rap poets to the highest profile public speakers. In addition, Dr. Sataloff has trained many of the most influential laryngologists who specialize in the care of the professional voice. A cursory review of any program from the Voice Foundation's Symposium on Care of the Professional Voice attests to his influence in all aspects of voice care.

In *Clinical Assessment of Voice*, one of three student editions derived from chapters selected for speech-language pathology students and clinicians from the third edition of *Professonal Voice: The Science and Art of Clinical Care*, Dr. Sataloff brings together professionals with an interdisciplinary philosophy of voice care that he has espoused since joining his father in practice on Pine Street in Philadelphia. He was joined by a speech pathologist in1980 and added a singing voice specialist to his practice in 1981. Since then, he has been joined in his practice by a psychologist, a nurse with a special interest in singing, and laryngology colleagues.

Clinical Assessment of Voice includes chapters written by otolaryngologists, an acting teacher, world-class surgeons, speech-language pathologists, a singing teacher, a nurse and a psychologist. In fact, this volume mirrors his clinical practice.

Throughout this book, we are reminded of the interdisciplinary care that is required in the assessment of voice disorders. All aspects of voice assessment are presented in a coherent fashion. Starting with an extensive case history and following with the physical examination, the objective documentation in the voice laboratory, and the latest diagnostic imaging with laryngeal computed tomography and strobovideolaryngoscopy, the chapters delineate the possible diagnoses and treatment approaches that currently represent the state of the art in assessment of voice disorders.

For the practicing otolaryngologist and speech-language pathologist, *Clinical Assessment of Voice* is an essential guide for understanding the techniques for proper diagnosis and for organizing a plan of treatment for patients with voice disorders. For singers and performers, knowledge of the clinical voice assessment process is presented in a manner that allows them to determine what level of assessment they should pursue in search of the most current treatment.

Every effort has been made to maintain style and continuity throughout the book. Dr. Sataloff is the author or co-author of 11 of the 15 chapters in this book. *Clinical Assessment of Voice* brings together the generous knowledge of renowned colleagues, merged with the continuity of a seasoned editor, making this book not only a classic in voice diagnostics but an enjoyable book to read and understand the marvelous complexity of the human organ known as the voice.

Thomas Murry, PhD
New York, NY

Preface

Clinical Assessment of Voice is part of a five-book student edition of selected chapters from the third edition of *Professional Voice: The Science and Art of Clinical Care*. That compendium fills nearly 2000 pages, including 160 chapters and numerous appendices, and it is not practical for routine use by students. However, *Professional Voice* was intended to be valuable to not only laryngologists, but also to speech-language pathologists, voice teachers, performers, students, and anyone else interested in the human voice. *Clinical Assessment of Voice* and other volumes of the student edition were prepared to make relevant information available to students in a convenient and affordable form, suitable for classroom use as well as for reference.

Chapter 1 reviews the information sought when taking a history on a patient with a voice complaint, and it includes introductory information on the meaning of many of the abnormal symptoms that patients reported. **Chapter 2** provides insights into specific information that should be added when evaluating actors with voice complaints. **Chapter 3** introduces the concepts and techniques used in physical examination of voice patients. **Chapter 4** includes not only basic concepts of laboratory evaluation, but also the authors' most recent practices regarding instrumentation and test protocols. The chapter also includes more recent measurement of cepstral peak prominence. **Chapter 5** on laryngeal electromyography includes clinical and technical information on this increasingly important test. **Chapter 6** reviews Dr. Eiji Yanagisawa's techniques for laryngeal photography, including all of the specifics readers require to replicate his success. **Chapter 7** reviews remarkable developments in computed tomography technology that were developed in France to provide color images that might almost be mistaken for histologic sections. It represents the state-of-the-art in imaging. **Chapter 8** introduces concepts of validated assessment of quality of life. **Chapter 9** provides a brief overview of common medical diagnoses and treatments of patients with voice disorders, reducing information that occupies entire chapters in *Professional Voice* to a paragraph or two. **Chapter 10** covers various aspects of psychological assessment and treatment of patients with voice disorders.

Chapter 11 reviews many of the neurological disorders that may affect the voice. **Chapter 12**, on vocal fold paresis and paralysis, includes the latest concepts in diagnosis and treatment, as well as discussions of laryngeal reinnervation and laryngeal pacemakers. **Chapter 13** not only reviews the most current literature on spasmodic dysphonia, but also specifies our current practices regarding clinical and laboratory diagnosis and treatment. **Chapter 14** describes many of the structural abnormalities that may afflict the larynx and helps the student understand the differences between lesions such as nodules, cysts, and polyps. **Chapter 15** includes discussions of impairment, disability and handicap; proposals for equitable disability calculation including case examples; and the role of voice care professionals in medical-legal matters.

Every effort has been made to maintain style and continuity throughout the book. Although the interdisciplinary expertise of numerous authors has been invaluable in the preparation of this text, contributions have been edited carefully, where necessary, to maintain consistency of linguistic style and complexity. I have written or coauthored 11 of the 15 chapters and made every effort to preserve the concept and continuity of a single-author text with generous input from colleagues, rather than an edited text with numerous authors each writing independently. This paradigm was used in a conscious effort to minimize repetition and provide consistent reading from cover to cover. All of us who were involved with the preparation of this book hope that readers will find it not only informative but also enjoyable to read.

Robert T. Sataloff, MD, DMA

Contributors

Mona M. Abaza, MD
Assistant Professor
Department of Otolaryngology-Head and Neck Surgery
University of Colorado
Denver, Colorado

Jean Abitbol, MD
Ancien Chef de Clinique
Faculty of Medicine of Paris
Oto-Rhino-Laryngologiste
Phoniatrie—Chirurgie
Paris, France

Patrick Abitbol, MD
Faculty of Medicine of Paris
Oto-Rhino-Laryngologiste
Paris, France

Joseph Anticaglia, MD
Ear, Nose, and Throat Associates of New York
Flushing, New York

Michael S. Benninger, MD
Chair, Department of Otolaryngology-Head and Neck Surgery
Henry Ford Hospital and Medical Centers
Detroit, Michigan

Albert Castro, MD
Radiologue
Directeur Centre d'Imagerie Médicale Numérisér Monceau
Paris, France

Daniel A. Deems, MD, PhD
University ENT Associates
Sarasota, Florida

Brian P. Driscoll, MD
Ear, Nose, Throat, and Plastic Surgery Associates
Attending Otolaryngologist
Florida Hospital
Orlando, Florida

Glendon M. Gardner, MD
Department of Otolaryngology-Head and Neck Surgery
Department of Neurology
Henry Ford Hospital
Detroit, Michigan

Rodolphe Gombergh, MD
Radiologue, Directeur du Centre d'Imagerie Médicale Numérisér Monceau
Paris, France

Reena Gupta, MD
Resident Physician, Class of 2008
Department of Otolaryngology-Head and Neck Surgery
New York University School of Medicine
New York, New York

Mary J. Hawkshaw, BSN, RN, CORLN
Otolaryngologic Nurse Clinician
Executive Director
American Institute for Voice and Ear Research
Philadelphia, Pennsylvania

Yolanda D. Heman-Ackah, MD
Assistant Professor, Department of Otolaryngology-Head and Neck Surgery
Jefferson Medical College
Thomas Jefferson University
Philadelphia, Pennsylvania

Reinhardt J. Heuer, PhD
Professor, Department of Communication Sciences and Disorders
College of Allied Health Professionals
Temple University
Consulting Scientist
American Institute for Voice and Ear Research
Philadelphia, Pennsylvania

Barbara H. Jacobson, PhD
Division of Speech-Language Sciences and Disorders
Department of Neurology
Henry Ford Hospital
Detroit, Michigan

Steven H. Levy, MD, PhD
Medical Director
Psych Arts Center
Research Associate, American Institute for Voice and Ear Research
Philadelphia, Pennsylvania

Heidi Mandel, PhD
Podiatry Resident
Podiatric College of Medicine
Temple University
Philadelphia, Pennsylvania

Steven Mandel, MD
Clinical Professor of Neurology
Thomas Jefferson University
Philadelphia, Pennsylvania

Ramon Mañon-Espaillat, MD
Clinical Associate Professor of Neurology
Thomas Jefferson University
Philadelphia, Pennsylvania

Bonnie N. Raphael, PhD
Professor and Head of the Professional Actor Training Program
Center of Dramatic Art
University of North Carolina at Chapel Hill
Chapel Hill, North Carolina

Deborah Caputo Rosen, RN, PhD
Medical Psychologist and Director of Health Outreach
External Affairs and Communications
Temple University Health System
Philadelphia, Pennsylvania
Adjunct Professor
Department of Counseling and Human Relations
College of Education
Villanova University
Villanova, Pennsylvania

Adam D. Rubin, MD
Department of Otolaryngology-Head and Neck Surgery
Lake Shore ENT
St. Clear Shores, Michigan

Robert Thayer Sataloff, MD, DMA
Professor
Department of Otolaryngology-Head and Neck Surgery
Thomas Jefferson University
Chairman, Department of Otolaryngology-Head and Neck Surgery
The Graduate Hospital
Chairman, Board of Directors
The Voice Foundation
Faculty, Academy of Vocal Arts
Faculty, The Curtis Institute of Music
Chairman, American Institute for Voice and Ear Research
Philadelphia, Pennsylvania

H. Steven Sims, MD
Clinical Fellow in Laryngology and Care of the Professional Voice
Department of Otolaryngology
Vanderbilt University Medical Center
Nashville, Tennessee

Eiji Yanagisawa, MD, FACS
Clinical Professor of Otolaryngology
Yale University School of Medicine
Attending Otolaryngologist, Yale-New Haven Hospital
Attending Otolaryngologist, Hospital of Saint Raphael
New Haven, Connecticut

Acknowledgments

I am indebted to the many distinguished colleagues who collaborated in writing this book. Their friendship and wisdom are appreciated greatly. I also remain indebted to the many friends and colleagues who have helped develop the field of voice over the last few decades, particularly the late Wilbur James Gould.

As always, I cannot express sufficient thanks to Mary J. Hawkshaw, RN, BSN for her tireless editorial assistance, proofreading, and scholarly contributions. Without her help, many of my books would still be unfinished. I am also indebted to Helen Caputo and Beth V. Luby for their tireless, painstaking preparation of the manuscript and for the many errors they found and corrected and to my associates Joseph Sataloff, MD, DSc, Karen M. Lyons, MD, and Yolanda D. Heman-Ackah, MD. Without their collaboration, excellent patient care, and tolerance of my many academic distractions and absences, writing would be much more difficult. In addition, I am indebted to Sandy Doyle from Plural Publishing Company, Inc. who has done a truly superb job editing this book and preparing it for publication.

My greatest gratitude goes to my wife Dahlia M. Sataloff, MD, and sons Ben and John who patiently allow me to spend so many of my evenings, weekends, and vacations writing.

Dedication

To my wife Dahlia Sataloff, MD, my sons Benjamin Harmon Sataloff and Johnathan Brandon Sataloff, my parents Joseph Sataloff, MD and Ruth Sataloff, and my friend and editorial assistant Mary J. Hawkshaw RN, BSN, for their unfailing patience and support

and

To Wilbur James Gould, MD, friend, scholar, educator, and founder of the Voice Foundation, who devoted his life to improving, understanding, and caring for the human voice.

and

To Howell S. Zulick, my voice teacher for twenty-nine years and an inspiration for life.

and

To Walter P. Work, Charles J. Krause, and Malcolm D. Graham, the professors who trained me and cultivated the love for academic medicine inspired by my father and for which he wisely sent me to Ann Arbor.

1

Patient History

Robert Thayer Sataloff, Mary J. Hawkshaw, and Joseph Anticaglia

A comprehensive history and physical examination usually reveals the cause of voice dysfunction. Effective history taking and physical examination depend on a practical understanding of the anatomy and physiology of voice production.[1-3] Because dysfunction in virtually any body system may affect phonation, medical inquiry must be comprehensive. The current standard of care for all voice patients evolved from advances inspired by medical problems of voice professionals such as singers and actors. Even minor problems may be particularly symptomatic in singers and actors, because of the extreme demands they place on their voices. However, a great many other patients are voice professionals. They include teachers, sales people, attorneys, clergy, physicians, politicians, telephone receptionists, and anyone else whose ability to earn a living is impaired in the presence of voice dysfunction. Because good voice quality is so important in our society, the majority of our patients are voice professionals; and all patients should be treated as such.

The scope of inquiry and examination for most voice patients is similar to that required for singers and actors, except that performing voice professionals have unique needs, which require additional history and examination. Questions must be added regarding performance commitments, professional status and voice goals, the amount and nature of voice training, the performance environment, rehearsal practices, abusive habits during speech and singing, and many other matters. Such supplementary information is essential to proper treatment selection and patient counseling of singers and actors. However, analogous factors must also be taken into account for stockbrokers, factory shop foremen, elementary school teachers, homemakers with several noisy children, and many others. Physicians familiar with the management of these challenging patients are well equipped to evaluate all patients with voice complaints.

Patient History

Obtaining extensive historical background information is necessary for thorough evaluation of the voice patient, and the otolaryngologist who sees voice patients (especially singers) only occasionally cannot reasonably be expected to remember all the pertinent questions. Although some laryngologists consider a lengthy inquisition helpful in establishing rapport, many of us who see a substantial number of voice patients each day within a busy practice need a thorough but less time-consuming alternative. A history questionnaire can be extremely helpful in documenting all of the necessary information, helping the patient sort out and articulate his or her problems, and saving the clinician time recording information. The author has developed a questionnaire[4] that has proven helpful (see Appendix IA). The patient is asked to complete the relevant portions of the form at home prior to his or her office visit or in the waiting room before seeing the doctor. A similar form has been developed for voice patients who are not singers (see Appendix IB).

No history questionnaire is a substitute for direct, penetrating questioning by the physician. However, the direction of most useful inquiry can be determined from a glance at questionnaire, obviating the need for extensive writing, which permits the physician greater eye contact with the patient and facilitates rapid establishment of the close rapport and confidence that are so important in treating voice patients. The physician is also able to supplement initial impressions and historical information from the questionnaire with seemingly leisurely conversation during the physical examination. The use of the history questionnaire has added substantially to the efficiency, consistent thoroughness, and ease of managing these delightful, but often complex, patients. A similar set of questions is also used by the speech-language pathologist with new patients and by many enlightened singing teachers when assessing new students.

How Old Are You?

Serious vocal endeavor may start in childhood and continue throughout a lifetime. As the vocal mechanism undergoes normal maturation, the voice changes. The optimal time to begin serious vocal training is controversial. For many years, most singing teachers advocated delay of vocal training and serious singing until near puberty in the female and after puberty and voice stabilization in the male. However, in a child with earnest vocal aspirations and potential, starting specialized training early in childhood is reasonable. Initial instruction should teach the child to vocalize without straining and to avoid all forms of voice abuse. It should not permit premature indulgence in operatic bravado. Most experts agree that taxing voice use and singing during puberty should be minimized or avoided altogether, particularly by the male. Voice maturation (attainment of stable adult vocal quality) may occur at any age from the early teenage years to the fourth decade of life. The dangerous tendency for young singers to attempt to sound older than their vocal years frequently causes vocal dysfunction.

All components of voice production are subject to normal aging. Abdominal and general muscular tone frequently decrease, lungs lose elasticity, the thorax loses its distensibility, the mucosa of the vocal tract atrophies, mucous secretions change character and quantity, nerve endings are reduced in number, and psychoneurologic functions change. Moreover, the larynx itself loses muscle tone and bulk and may show depletion of submucosal ground substance in the vocal folds. The laryngeal cartilages ossify, and the joints may become arthritic and stiff. Hormonal influence is altered. Vocal range, intensity, and quality all may be modified. Vocal fold atrophy may be the most striking alteration. The clinical effects of aging seem more pronounced in female singers, although vocal fold histologic changes may be more prominent in males. Excellent male singers occasionally extend their careers into their 70s or beyond.[5,6] However, some degree of breathiness, decreased range, and other evidence of aging should be expected in elderly voices. Nevertheless, many of the changes we typically associate with elderly singers (wobble, flat pitch) are due to lack of conditioning, rather than inevitable changes of biological aging. These aesthetically undesirable concomitants of aging often can be reversed.

What Is Your Voice Problem?

Careful questioning as to the onset of vocal problems is needed to separate acute from chronic dysfunction. Often an upper respiratory tract infection will send a patient to the physician's office; but penetrating inquiry, especially in singers and actors, may reveal a chronic vocal problem that is the patient's real concern. Identifying acute and chronic problems before beginning therapy is important so that both patient and physician may have realistic expectations and make optimal therapeutic selections.

The specific nature of the vocal complaint can provide a great deal of information. Just as dizzy patients rarely walk into the physician's office complaining of "rotary vertigo," voice patients may be unable to articulate their symptoms without guidance. They may use the term hoarseness to describe a variety of conditions that the physician must separate. Hoarseness is a coarse or scratchy sound that is most often associated with abnormalities of the leading edge of the vocal folds such as laryngitis or mass lesions. Breathiness is a vocal quality characterized by excessive loss of air during vocalization. In some cases, it is due to improper technique. However, any condition that prevents full approximation of the vocal folds can be responsible. Possible causes include vocal fold paralysis, a mass lesion separating the leading edges of the vocal folds, arthritis of the cricoarytenoid joint, arytenoid dislocation, scarring of the vibratory margin, senile vocal fold atrophy (presbyphonia), psychogenic dysphonia, malingering, and other conditions.

Fatigue of the voice is inability to continue to speak or sing for extended periods without change in vocal quality and/or control. The voice may show fatigue by becoming hoarse, losing range, changing timbre, breaking into different registers, or exhibiting other uncontrolled aberrations. A well-trained singer should be able to sing for several hours without vocal fatigue.

Voice fatigue may occur through more than one mechanism. Most of the time, it is assumed to be due to muscle fatigue. This is often the case in patients who have voice fatigue associated with muscle tension dysphonia. The mechanism is most likely to be peripheral muscle fatigue and due to chemical changes (or depletion) in the muscle fibers. "Muscle fatigue" may also occur on a central (neurological) basis. This mechanism is common in certain neuropathic disorders, such as some patients with multiple sclerosis; may occur with myasthenia gravis (actually neuromuscular junction pathology); or may be associated with paresis from various causes. However, the voice may also fatigue due to changes in the vibratory margin of the vocal fold. This phenomenon may be described as "lamina propria" fatigue. It, too, may be related to chemical or fluid changes in the lamina propria or cellular damage associated with conditions such as phonotrauma and dehydration. Excessive voice use, suboptimal tissue environment (eg, dehydration, effects of pollution, etc), lack of sufficient time of recovery between phonatory stresses, and genetic or structural tissue weaknesses that predispose to injury or delayed recovery from trauma all may be associated with lamina propria fatigue.

Although it has not been proven, this author (RTS) suspects that fatigue may also be related to the linearity of vocal fold vibrations. The principles behind this belief are discussed in *Voice Science*.[7] However, briefly, voices have linear and nonlinear (chaotic) characteristics. As the voice becomes more trained, vibrations become more symmetrical; and the system becomes more linear. In many pathologic voices, the nonlinear components appear to become more prominent. If a voice is highly linear, slight changes in the vibratory margin may have little effect on the output of the system. However, if the system has substantial nonlinearity due to vocal fold pathology, poor tissue environment, or other causes, slight changes in the tissue (slight swelling, drying, surface cell damage) may cause substantial changes in the acoustic output of the system (the butterfly effect), causing vocal quality changes and fatigue much more quickly with much smaller changes in initial condition in more linear vocal systems.

Fatigue is often caused by misuse of abdominal and neck musculature or oversinging, singing too loudly, or too long. However, we must remember that vocal fatigue also may be a sign not only of general tiredness or vocal abuse (sometimes secondary to structural lesions or glottal closure problems), but also of serious illnesses such as myasthenia gravis. So, the importance of this complaint should not be understated.

Volume disturbance may manifest as inability to sing loudly or inability to sing softly. Each voice has its own dynamic range. Within the course of training, singers learn to sing more loudly by singing more efficiently. They also learn to sing softly, a more difficult task, through years of laborious practice. Actors and other trained speakers go through similar training. Most volume problems are secondary to intrinsic limitations of the voice or technical errors in voice use, although hormonal changes, aging, and neurologic disease are other causes. Superior laryngeal nerve paralysis impairs the ability to speak or sing loudly. This is a frequently unrecognized consequence of herpes infection (cold sores) and Lyme disease and may be precipitated by any viral upper respiratory tract infection.

Most highly trained singers require only about 10 minutes to half an hour to "warm up the voice." Prolonged warm-up time, especially in the morning, is most often caused by reflux laryngitis. Tickling or choking during singing is most often a symptom of an abnormality of the vocal fold's leading edge. The symptom of tickling or choking should contraindicate singing until the vocal folds have been examined. Pain while singing can indicate vocal fold lesions, laryngeal joint arthritis, infection, or gastric acid reflux irritation of the arytenoid region. However, pain is much more commonly caused by voice abuse with excessive muscular activity in the neck rather than an acute abnormality on the leading edge of a vocal fold. In the absence of other symptoms, these patients do not generally require immediate cessation of singing pending medical examination. However, sudden onset of pain (usually sharp pain) while singing may be associated with a mucosal tear or a vocal fold hemorrhage and warrants voice conservation pending laryngeal examination.

Do You Have Any Pressing Voice Commitments?

If a singer or professional speaker (eg, actor, politician) seeks treatment at the end of a busy performance season and has no pressing engagements, management of the voice problem should be relatively conservative and designed to insure long-term protection of the larynx, the most delicate part of the vocal mechanism. However, the physician and patient rarely have this luxury. Most often, the voice professional needs treatment within a week of an important engagement and sometimes within less than a day. Younger singers fall ill shortly before performances, not because of hypochondria or coincidence, but rather because of the immense physical and emotional stress of the preperformance period. The singer is frequently working harder and singing longer hours than usual. Moreover, he or she may be under particular pressure to learn new material and to perform well for a new audience. The singer may also be sleeping less than usual because of additional time spent rehearsing or because of the discomforts of a strange city. Seasoned professionals make their living by performing regularly, sometimes several times a week. Consequently, any time they get sick is likely to precede a performance. Caring for voice complaints in these situations requires highly skilled judgment and bold management.

Tell Me About Your Vocal Career, Long-Term Goals, and the Importance of Your Voice Quality and Upcoming Commitments

To choose a treatment program, the physician must understand the importance of the patient's voice and his or her long-term career plans, the importance of the upcoming vocal commitment, and the consequences of canceling the engagement. Injudicious prescription of voice rest can be almost as damaging to a vocal career as injudicious performance. For example, although a singer's voice is usually his or her most important commodity, other factors distinguish the few successful artists from the multitude of less successful singers with equally good voices. These include musicianship, reliability, and "professionalism." Canceling a concert at the last minute may seriously damage a performer's reputation. Reliability is especially critical early in a singer's career. Moreover, an expert singer often can modify a performance to decrease the strain on his or her voice. No singer should be allowed to perform in a manner that will permit serious injury to the vocal folds; but in the frequent borderline cases, the condition of the larynx must be weighed against other factors affecting the singer as an artist.

How Much Voice Training Have You Had?

Establishing how long a singer or actor has been performing seriously is important, especially if his or her active performance career predates the beginning of vocal training. Active untrained singers and actors frequently develop undesirable techniques that are difficult to modify. Extensive voice use without training or premature training with inappropriate repertoire may underlie persistent vocal difficulties later in life. The number of years a performer has been training his or her voice may be a fair index of vocal proficiency. A person who has studied voice for 1 or 2 years is somewhat more likely to have gross technical difficulties than is someone who has been studying for 20 years. However, if training has been intermittent or discontinued, technical problems are common, especially among singers. In addition, methods of technical voice use vary among voice teachers. Hence, a student who has had many teachers in a relatively brief period of time commonly has numerous technical insecurities or deficiencies that may be responsible for vocal dysfunction. This is especially true if the singer has changed to a new teacher within the preceding year. The physician must be careful not to criticize the patient's current voice teacher in such circumstances. It often takes years of expert instruction to correct bad habits.

All people speak more often than they sing, yet most singers report little speech training. Even if a singer uses the voice flawlessly while practicing and performing, voice abuse at other times can cause damage that affects singing.

Under What Kinds of Conditions Do You Use Your Voice?

The Lombard effect is the tendency to increase vocal intensity in response to increased background noise. A well-trained singer learns to compensate for this tendency and to avoid singing at unsafe volumes. Singers of classical music usually have such training and frequently perform with only a piano, a situation in which the balance can be controlled well. However, singers performing in large halls, with orchestras, or in operas early in their careers tend to oversing and strain their voices. Similar problems occur during outdoor concerts because of the lack of auditory feedback. This phenomenon is seen even more among "pop" singers. Pop singers are in a uniquely difficult position; often, despite little vocal training, they enjoy great artistic and financial success and endure extremely stressful demands on their time and voices. They are required to sing in large halls or outdoor arenas not designed for musical performance, amid smoke and other environmental irritants, accompanied by extremely loud background music. One frequently neglected key to survival for these singers is the proper use of monitor speakers. These direct the sound of the singer's voice toward the singer on the stage and provide auditory feedback. Determining whether the pop singer uses monitor speakers and whether they are loud enough for the singer to hear is important.

Amateur singers are often no less serious about their music than are professionals, but generally they have less ability to compensate technically for illness or other physical impairment. Rarely does an amateur suffer a great loss from postponing a performance or permitting someone to sing in his or her place. In most cases, the amateur singer's best interest is served through conservative management directed at long-term maintenance of good vocal health.

A great many of the singers who seek physicians' advice are primarily choral singers. They often are enthusiastic amateurs, untrained but dedicated to their musical recreation. They should be handled as amateur solo singers, educated specifically about the Lombard effect, and cautioned to avoid the excessive volume so common in a choral environment. One good way for a singer to monitor loudness is to cup a hand to his or her ear. This adds about 6 dB[8] to the singer's perception of his or her own voice and can be a very helpful guide in noisy surroundings. Young professional singers are often hired to augment amateur choruses. Feeling that the professional quartet has been hired to "lead" the rest of the choir, they often make the mistake of trying to accomplish that goal by singing louder than others in their sections. These singers should be advised to lead their section by singing each line as if they were soloists giving a voice lesson to the people standing next to them and as if there were a microphone in front of them recording their choral performance for their voice teacher. This approach usually not only preserves the voice but also produces a better choral sound.

How Much Do You Practice and Exercise Your Voice? How, When, and Where Do You Use Your Voice?

Vocal exercise is as essential to the vocalist as exercise and conditioning of other muscle systems is to the athlete. Proper vocal practice incorporates scales and specific exercises designed to maintain and develop the vocal apparatus. Simply acting or singing songs and giving performances without routine studious concentration on vocal technique is not adequate for the vocal performer. The physician should know whether the vocalist practices daily, whether he or she practices at the same time daily, and how long the practice lasts. Actors generally practice and warm up their voices for 10 to 30 minutes daily, although more time is recommended. Most serious singers practice for at least 1 to 2 hours per day. If a singer routinely practices in the late afternoon or evening but frequently performs in the morning (religious services, school classes, teaching voice, choir rehearsals, etc), one should inquire into the warm-up procedures preceding such performances as well as cooldown procedures after voice use. Singing "cold," especially early in the morning, may result in the use of minor muscular alterations to compensate for vocal insecurity produced by inadequate preparation. Such crutches can result in voice dysfunction. Similar problems may result from instances of voice use other than formal singing. School teachers, telephone receptionists, sales people, and others who speak extensively also often derive great benefit from 5 or 10 minutes of vocalization of scales first thing in the morning. Although singers rarely practice their scales too long, they frequently perform or rehearse excessively. This is especially true immediately before a major concert or audition, when physicians are most likely to see acute problems. When a singer has hoarseness and vocal fatigue and has been practicing a new role for 14 hours a day for the last 3 weeks, no simple prescription will solve the problem. However, a treatment regimen can usually be designed to carry the performer safely through his or her musical obligations.

The physician should be aware of common habits and environments that are often associated with abusive voice behavior and should ask about them routinely. Screaming at sporting events and at children is among the most common. Extensive voice use in noisy environments also tends to be abusive. These include noisy rooms, cars, airplanes, sports facilities, and other locations where background noise or acoustic design impairs auditory feedback. Dry, dusty surroundings may alter vocal fold secretions through dehydration or contact irritation, altering voice function. Activities such as cheerleading, teaching, choral conducting, amateur singing, and frequent communication with hearing-impaired persons are likely to be associated with voice abuse, as is extensive professional voice use without formal training. The physician should inquire into the patient's routine voice use and should specifically ask about any activities that frequently lead to voice change such as hoarseness or discomfort in the neck or throat. Laryngologists should ask specifically about other activities that may be abusive to the vocal folds such as weight lifting, aerobics, and the playing of some wind instruments.

Are You Aware of Misusing or Abusing Your Voice During Singing?

A detailed discussion of vocal technique in singing is beyond the scope of this chapter but is discussed in other chapters. The most common technical errors involve excessive muscle tension in the tongue, neck, and larynx; inadequate abdominal support; and excessive volume. Inadequate preparation can be a devastating source of voice abuse and may result from limited practice, limited rehearsal of a difficult piece, or limited vocal training for a given role. The latter error is tragically common. In some situations, voice teachers are at fault; and both the singer and teacher must resist the impulse to "show off" the voice in works that are either too difficult for the singer's level of training or simply not suited to the singer's voice. Singers are habitually unhappy with the limitations of their voices. At some time or another, most baritones wish they were tenors and walk around proving they can sing high Cs in "Vesti la giubba." Singers with other vocal ranges have similar fantasies. Attempts to make the voice something that it is not, or at least that it is not yet, frequently are harmful.

Are You Aware of Misusing or Abusing Your Voice During Speaking?

Common patterns of voice abuse and misuse will not be discussed in detail in this chapter. They are covered elsewhere in this book. Voice abuse and/or misuse should be suspected particularly in patients who complain of voice fatigue associated with voice use, whose voices are worse at the end of a working day or week, and in any patient who is chronically hoarse. Technical errors in voice use may be the primary etiology of a voice complaint, or it may develop secondarily due to a patient's effort to compensate for voice disturbance from another cause.

Dissociation of one's speaking and singing voices is probably the most common cause of voice abuse problems in excellent singers. Too frequently, all of the expert training in support, muscle control, and projection is not applied to a singers' speaking voice. Unfortunately, the resultant voice strain affects the singing voice as well as the speaking voice. Such damage is especially likely to occur in noisy rooms and in cars, where the background noise is louder than it seems. Backstage greetings after a lengthy performance can be particularly devastating. The singer usually is exhausted and distracted; the environment is often dusty and dry; and generally a noisy crowd is present. Similar conditions prevail at postperformance parties where smoking and alcohol worsen matters. These situations should be avoided by any singer with vocal problems and should be controlled through awareness at other times.

Three particularly abusive and potentially damaging vocal activities are worthy of note. *Cheerleading* requires extensive screaming under the worst possible physical and environmental circumstances. It is a highly undesirable activity for anyone considering serious vocal endeavor. This is a common conflict in younger singers because the teenager who is the high school choir soloist often is also student council president, yearbook editor, captain of the cheerleaders, and so on.

Conducting, particularly choral conducting, can also be deleterious. An enthusiastic conductor, especially of an amateur group, frequently sings all four parts intermittently, at volumes louder than the entire choir, during lengthy rehearsals. Conducting is a common avocation among singers but must be done with expert technique and special precautions to prevent voice injury. Hoarseness or loss of soft voice control after conducting a rehearsal or concert suggests voice abuse during conducting. The patient should be instructed to record his or her voice throughout the vocal range singing long notes at dynamics from soft to loud to soft. Recordings should be made prior to rehearsal and following rehearsal. If the voice has lost range, control, or quality during the rehearsal, voice abuse has occurred. A similar test can be used for patients who sing in choirs, teach voice, or perform other potentially abusive vocal activities. Such problems in conductors can generally be managed by additional training in conducting techniques and by voice training, including warm-up and cooldown exercises.

Teaching singing may also be hazardous to vocal health. It can be done safely but requires skill and thought. Most teachers teach while seated at the piano. Late in a long, hard day, this posture is not conducive to maintenance of optimal abdominal and back support. Usually, teachers work with students continually positioned to the right or left of the keyboard. This may require the teacher to turn his or her neck at a particularly sharp angle, especially when teaching at an upright piano. Teachers also often demonstrate vocal works in their students' vocal ranges rather than their own, illustrating bad as well as good technique. If a singing teacher is hoarse or has neck discomfort, or his or her soft singing control deteriorates at the end of a teaching day (assuming that the teacher warms up before beginning to teach voice lessons), voice abuse should be suspected. Helpful modifications include teaching with a grand piano, sitting slightly sideways on the piano bench, or alternating student position to the right and left of the piano to facilitate better neck alignment. Retaining an accompanist so that the teacher can stand rather than teach from sitting behind a piano and many other helpful modifications are possible.

Do You Have Pain When You Talk or Sing?

Odynophonia, or pain caused by phonation, can be a disturbing symptom. It is not uncommon, but relatively little has been written or discussed on this subject. A detailed review of odynophonia is beyond the scope of this publication. However, laryngologists should be familiar with the diagnosis and treatment of at least a few of the most common causes, as discussed *Professional Voice: The Science and Art of Clinical Care.*[9]

What Kind of Physical Condition Are You In?

Phonation is an athletic activity that requires good conditioning and coordinated interaction of numerous physical functions. Maladies of any part of the body may be reflected in the voice. Failure to maintain good abdominal muscle tone and respiratory endurance through exercise is particularly harmful, because deficiencies in these areas undermine the power source of the voice. Patients generally attempt to compensate for such weaknesses by using inappropriate muscle groups, particularly in the neck, causing vocal dysfunction. Similar problems may occur in the well-conditioned vocalist in states of fatigue. These are compounded by mucosal changes that accompany excessively long hours of hard work. Such problems may be seen even in the best singers shortly before important performances in the height of the concert season.

A popular but untrue myth holds that great opera singers must be obese. However, the vivacious, gregarious personality that often distinguishes the great performer seems to be accompanied frequently by a propensity for excess, especially culinary excess. This excess is as undesirable in the vocalist as it is in most other athletic artists, and it should be prevented from the start of one's vocal career. Appropriate and attractive body weight has always been valued in the pop music world and is becoming particularly important in the opera world as this formerly theater-based art form moves to television and film media. However, attempts at weight reduction in an established speaker or singer are a different matter. The vocal mechanism is a finely tuned, complex instrument and is exquisitely sensitive to minor changes. Substantial fluctuations in weight frequently cause deleterious alterations of the voice, although they are usually temporary. Weight reduction programs for people concerned about their voices must be monitored carefully and designed to reduce weight in small increments over long periods. A history of sudden recent weight change may be responsible for almost any vocal complaint.

Have You Noted Voice or Bodily Weakness, Tremor, Fatigue, or Loss of Control?

Even minor neurological disorders may be extremely disruptive to vocal function. Specific questions should be asked to rule out neuromuscular and neurological diseases such as myasthenia gravis, Parkinson's disease, tremors, other movement disorders, spasmodic dysphonia, multiple sclerosis, central nervous system neoplasm, and other serious maladies that may be present with voice complaints.

Do You Have Allergy or Cold Symptoms?

Acute upper respiratory tract infection causes inflammation of the mucosa, alters mucosal secretions, and makes the mucosa more vulnerable to injury. Coughing and throat clearing are particularly traumatic vocal activities and may worsen or provoke hoarseness associated with a cold. Postnasal drip and allergy may produce the same response. Infectious sinusitis is associated with discharge and diffuse mucosal inflammation, resulting in similar problems, and may actually alter the sound of a voice, especially the patient's own perception of his or her voice. Futile attempts to compensate for disease of the supraglottic vocal tract in an effort to return the sound to normal frequently result in laryngeal strain. The expert singer or speaker should compensate by monitoring technique by tactile rather than by auditory feedback, or singing "by feel" rather than "by ear."

Do You Have Breathing Problems, Especially After Exercise?

Voice patients usually volunteer information about upper respiratory tract infections and postnasal drip, but the relevance of other maladies may not be obvious to them. Consequently the physician must seek out pertinent history.

Respiratory problems are especially important in voice patients. Even mild respiratory dysfunction may adversely affect the power source of the voice.[10] Occult asthma may be particularly troublesome.[11] A complete respiratory history should be obtained in most patients with voice complaints, and pulmonary function testing is often advisable.

Have You Been Exposed to Environmental Irritants?

Any mucosal irritant can disrupt the delicate vocal mechanism. Allergies to dust and mold are aggravated commonly during rehearsals and performances in concert halls, especially older theaters and concert halls, because of numerous curtains, backstage trappings, and dressing room facilities that are rarely cleaned thoroughly. Nasal obstruction and erythematous conjunctivae suggest generalized mucosal irritation. The drying effects of cold air and dry heat may also affect mucosal secretions, leading to decreased lubrication, a "scratchy" voice, and tickling cough. These symptoms may be minimized by nasal breathing, which allows inspired air to be filtered, warmed, and humidified. Nasal breathing, whenever possible, rather than mouth breathing, is proper vocal technique. While the performer is backstage between appearances or during rehearsals, inhalation of dust and other irritants may be controlled by wearing a protective mask, such as those used by carpenters, or a surgical mask that does not contain fiberglass. This is especially helpful when sets are being constructed in the rehearsal area.

A history of recent travel suggests other sources of mucosal irritation. The air in airplanes is extremely dry, and airplanes are noisy.[12] One must be careful to avoid talking loudly and to maintain good hydration and nasal breathing during air travel. Environmental changes can also be disruptive. Las Vegas is infamous for the mucosal irritation caused by its dry atmosphere and smoke-filled rooms. In fact, the resultant complex of hoarseness, vocal "tickle," and fatigue is referred to as "Las Vegas voice." A history of recent travel should also suggest jet lag and generalized fatigue, which may be potent detriments to good vocal function.

Environmental pollution is responsible for the presence of toxic substances and conditions encountered daily. Inhalation of toxic pollutants may affect the voice adversely by direct laryngeal injury, by causing pulmonary dysfunction that results in voice maladies, or through impairments elsewhere in the vocal tract. Ingested substances, especially those that have neurolaryngologic effects may also adversely affect the voice. Nonchemical environmental pollutants such as noise can cause voice abnormalities, as well. Laryngologists should be familiar with the laryngologic effects of the numerous potentially irritating substances and conditions found in the environment. We must also be familiar with special pollution problems encountered by performers. Numerous materials used by artists to create sculptures, drawings, and theatrical sets are toxic and have adverse voice effects. In addition, performers are exposed routinely to chemicals encountered through stage smoke, and pyrotechnic effects, as discussed in *Professional Voice*.[13] Although it is clear that some of the "special effects" result in serious laryngologic consequences, much additional study is need to clarify the nature and scope of these occupational problems.

Do You Smoke, Live with a Smoker, or Work Around Smoke?

The effects of smoking on voice performance were reviewed recently in the *Journal of Singing*,[14] and that review is recapitulated here.

Smoking tobacco is the number one cause of preventable death in the United States as well as a leading cause of heart disease, stroke, emphysema, and cancer. The Centers for Disease Control (CDC) attributes approximately 442,000 premature (shortened life expectancy) deaths annually in the United States to smoking, which is more than the combined incidence of deaths caused by highway accidents, fires, murders, illegal drugs, suicides and AIDS[15] (Fig 1–1).

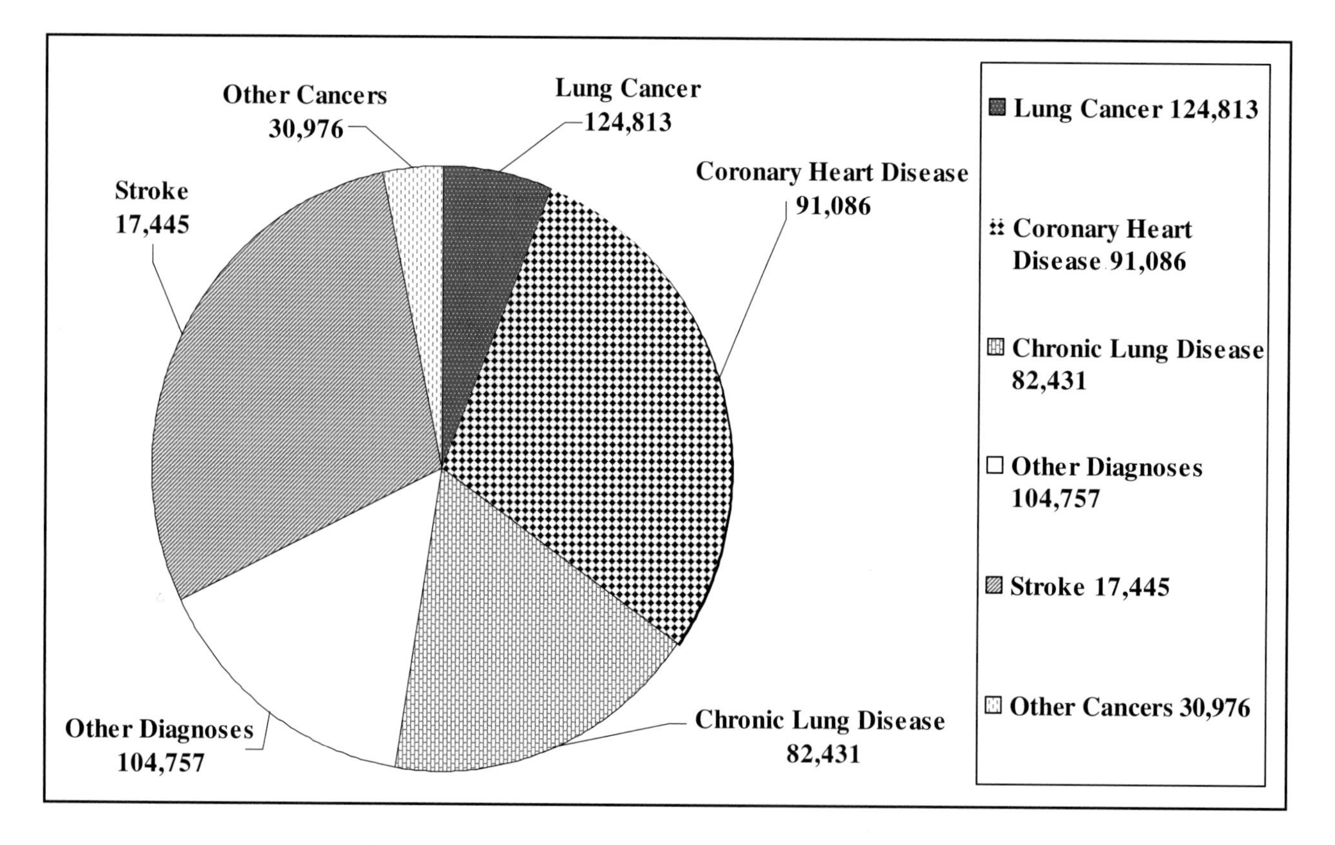

Fig 1–1. Average annual number of deaths attributable to cigarette smoking, 1995–1999.

Approximately 4 million deaths per year worldwide result from smoking; and if this trend continues, by the year 2030 this figure will increase to about 10 million deaths globally.[16] In addition to causing life-threatening diseases, smoking impairs a great many body systems, including the vocal tract. Harmful consequences of smoking or being exposed to smoke influence voice performance adversely.

Singers need good vocal health to perform well. Smoking tobacco can irritate the mucosal covering of the vocal folds, causing redness and chronic inflammation, and can have the same effects on the mucosal linings of the lungs, trachea, nasopharynx (behind the nose and throat), and mouth. In other words, the components of voice production: the generator, the oscillator, the resonator, and the articulators all can be compromised by the harmful effects of tobacco use. The onset of effects from smoking may be immediate or delayed.

Individuals who have allergies and/or asthma are usually more sensitive to cigarette smoke with the potential for an immediate adverse reaction involving the lungs, larynx, nasal cavities, and/or eyes. Chronic use of tobacco, or exposure to it, can cause the toxic chemicals in tobacco to accumulate in the body damaging the delicate linings of the vocal tract, as well as the lungs, heart, and circulatory system.

The lungs are critical components of the power source of the vocal tract. They help generate an airstream that is directed superiorly through the trachea toward the undersurface of the vocal folds. The vocal folds respond to the increase in subglottic pressure by producing sounds of variable intensities and frequencies. The number of times per second the vocal folds vibrate influences the pitch, and the amplitude of the mucosal wave influences the loudness of the sound. The sound produced by the vibration (oscillation) of the vocal folds passes upward through the oral cavity and nasopharynx where it resonates, giving the voice its richness and timbre; and eventually it is articulated by the mouth, teeth, lips, and tongue into speech or song.

Any condition that adversely affects lung function, such as chronic exposure to smoke or uncontrolled asthma, can contribute to dysphonia by impairing the strength, endurance and consistency of the airstream responsible for establishing vocal fold oscillation. Any lesion that compromises vocal fold vibration and glottic closure can cause hoarseness and breathiness. Inflammation of the cover layer of the vocal folds and/or the mucosal lining of the nose, sinuses, and oral or nasopharyngeal cavities can affect the quality and clarity of the voice.

Tobacco smoke can damage the lungs' parenchyma and the exchange of air through respiration. Cigarette manufacturers add hundreds of ingredients to their tobacco products to improve taste, to make smoking seem milder and easier to inhale and to prolong burning and shelf life.[17] More than 3000 chemical compounds have been identified in tobacco smoke, and more than 60 of these compounds are carcinogens.[18]

The tobacco plant, *Nicotiana tabacum*, is grown for its leaves, which can be smoked, chewed, or sniffed with various effects. The nicotine in tobacco is the addictive component and rivals crack cocaine in its ability to enslave its users. Most smokers want to stop; yet only a small percentage are successful in quitting cigarettes; and the majority who quit relapse into smoking once again.[19] Tars and carbon monoxide are among the disease-causing components in tobacco products. The tar in cigarettes exposes the individual to a greater risk of bronchitis, emphysema, and lung cancer. These chemicals affect the entire vocal tract as well as the cardiovascular system (Table 1–1).

Cigarette smoke in the lungs can lead also to increased vascularity, edema, and excess mucous production, as well as epithelial tissue and cellular changes. The toxic agents in cigarette smoke have been associated with an increase in the number and severity of asthma attacks, chronic bronchitis, emphysema, and lung cancer, all of which can interfere with the lungs' ability to generate the stream of air needed for voice production.

Chronic bronchitis due to smoking has been associated with an increase in the number of goblet (mucous) cells, an increase in the size (hyperplasia) of the mucous-secreting glands, and a decrease in the number of ciliated cells, the cells used to clean the lungs. Chronic cough and sputum production are seen more commonly in smokers compared to nonsmokers. Also, the heat and chemicals of unfiltered cigarette and marijuana smoke are especially irritating to the lungs and larynx.

An important component of voice quality is the symmetrical, unencumbered vibration of the true vocal folds. Anything that prevents the epithelium covering the vocal folds from vibrating or affects the loose connective tissue under the epithelium (in the superficial layer of the lamina propria known as Reinke's space) can cause dysphonia. Cigarette smoking can cause the epithelium of the true vocal folds to become red, swollen, develop whitish discolorations (leukoplakia), undergo chronic inflammatory changes, or develop squamous metaplasia or dysplasia (tissue changes from normal to a potentially malignant state).

In chronic smokers, the voice may become husky due to the accumulation of fluid in Reinke's space (Reinke's edema). These alterations in structure can interfere with voice production by changing the bio-

Table 1–1. Chemical Additives Found in Tobacco and Commercial Products.

Tobacco Chemical Additives	***Also Found In***
Acetic acid	vinegar; hair dye
Acetone	nail polish remover
Ammonia	floor cleaner, toilet cleaner
Arsenic	poison
Benzene	a leukemia-producing agent in rubber cement
Butane	cigarette lighter fluid
Cadmium	batteries, some oil paints
Carbon monoxide	car exhaust
DDT	insecticides
Ethanol	alcohol
Formaldehyde	embalming fluid, fabric, lab animals
Hexamine	barbecue lighter
Hydrazine	jet fuel, rocket fuel
Hydrogen cyanide	gas chamber poison
Methane	swamp gas
Methanol	rocket fuel
Naphthalene	explosives, mothballs, paints
Nickel	electroplating
Nicotine	insecticides
Nitrobenzene	gasoline additive
Nitrous oxide phenols	disinfectant
Phenol	disinfectants, plastics
Polonium-210	a radioactive substance
Stearic acid	candle wax
Styrene	insulation materials
Toluene	industrial solvent, embalmer's glue
Vinyl chloride	plastic manufacturing; garbage bags

mechanics of the vocal folds and their vibratory characteristics. In severe cases, cancer can deform and paralyze the vocal folds.

Vocal misuse often follows in an attempt to compensate for dysphonia and an altered self-perception of one's voice. The voice may feel weak, breathy, raspy or strained. There may be loss of range, vocal breaks, long warm-up time, and fatigue. The throat may feel raw, achy, or tight. As the voice becomes unreliable, bad habits increase as the individual struggles harder and harder to compensate vocally.

As selected sound waves move upward, from the larynx towards and through the pharynx, nasopharynx, mouth, and nose (the resonators), sounds gain a unique richness and timbre. Exposing the pharynx to cigarette smoke aggravates the linings of the oropharynx, mouth, nasopharynx, sinuses, and nasal cavities. The resulting erythema, swelling, and inflammation predispose one to nasal congestion and increased mucous production. With nasal congestion and impaired mucosal function, there may be predisposition to sinusitis and pharyngitis, in which the voice may become hyponasal, the sinuses achy, and the throat painful.

Although relatively rare in the United States, cancer of the nasopharynx has been associated with cigarette smoking,[20] and one of the presenting symptoms is unilateral hearing loss due to fluid in the middle ear caused by eustachian tube obstruction from the cancer. Smoking-induced cancers of the oral cavity, pharynx, larynx and lung are common throughout the world, including in the United States.

The palate, tongue, cheeks, lips, and teeth articulate the sound modified by the resonators into speech. Cigarette, cigar, or pipe smoking can cause a "black hairy tongue," precancerous oral lesions (leukoplakia), and/or cancer of the tongue and lips.[21] Any irritation that causes burning or inflammation of the oral mucosa can affect phonation; and all tobacco products are capable of causing these effects.

Smokeless "Spit" tobacco is highly addictive, and users who dip 8 to 10 times a day may get the same nicotine exposure as those who smoke 1½ to 2 packs of cigarettes per day.[22] Smokeless tobacco has been associated with gingivitis, cheek carcinoma, and cancer of the larynx and hypopharynx.

Exposure to environmental tobacco smoke (ETS), also called secondhand smoke, sidestream smoke, or passive smoke, accounts for an estimated 3000 lung cancer deaths, and approximately 35,000 deaths in the United States from heart disease in nonsmoking adults.[23]

Secondhand smoke is the "passive" inhalation of tobacco smoke from environmental sources such as smoke given off by pipes, cigars, cigarettes (sidestream), or the smoke exhaled from the lungs of smokers and inhaled by other people (mainstream). This passive smoke contains a mixture of thousands of chemicals some of which are known to cause cancer. The National Institutes of Health (NIH) lists ETS as a "known" carcinogen, and the more you are exposed to secondhand smoke, the greater your risk.[24]

Infants and young children are affected particularly by secondhand smoke with increased incidences of otitis media (ear infections), bronchitis, and pneumonia. If small children are exposed to secondhand smoke, the child's resulting illness can have a stressful effect on the parent who frequently catches the child's illness. Both the illness and the stress of caring for the sick child may interfere with voice performance. People who are exposed routinely to secondhand smoke are at risk for lung cancer, heart disease, respiratory infection, and an increased number of asthma attacks.[25]

There is an intricate relationship between the lungs, larynx, pharynx, nose, and mouth in the production of speech and song. Smoking can have deleterious effects on any part of the vocal tract, causing the respiratory system to lose power, damaging the vibratory margins of the vocal folds, and detracting from the richness and beauty of a voice.

The deleterious effects of tobacco smoke on mucosa are indisputable. Anyone concerned about the health of his or her voice should not smoke. Smoking causes erythema, mild edema, and generalized inflammation throughout the vocal tract. Both smoke itself and the heat of the cigarette appear to be important. Marijuana produces a particularly irritating, unfiltered smoke that is inhaled directly, causing considerable mucosal response. Voice patients who refuse to stop smoking marijuana should at least be advised to use a water pipe to cool and partially filter the smoke. Some vocalists are required to perform in smoke-filled environments and may suffer the same effects as the smokers themselves. In some theaters, it is possible to place fans upstage or direct the ventilation system so as to create a gentle draft toward the audience, clearing the smoke away from the stage. "Smoke eaters" installed in some theaters are also helpful.

Do Any Foods Seem to Affect Your Voice?

Various foods are said to affect the voice. Traditionally, singers avoid milk and ice cream before performances. In many people, these foods seem to increase the amount and viscosity of mucosal secretions. Allergy and casein have been implicated, but no satisfactory explanation has been established. In some cases, restriction of these foods from the diet before a voice performance may be helpful. Chocolate may have the same effect and should be viewed similarly. Chocolate also contains caffeine, which may aggravate reflux or cause tremor. Voice patients should be asked about eating nuts. This is important not only because some people experience effects similar to those produced by milk products and chocolate, but also because they are extremely irritating if aspirated. The irritation produced by aspiration of even a small organic foreign body may be severe and impossible to correct rapidly enough to permit performance. Highly spiced foods may also cause mucosal irritation. In addition, they seem to aggravate reflux laryngitis. Coffee and other beverages containing caffeine also aggravate gastric reflux and may promote dehydration and/or alter secretions and necessitate frequent throat clearing in some people. Fad diets, especially rapid weight reducing diets, are notorious for causing voice problems. Lemon juice and herbal teas are considered beneficial to the voice. Both may act as demulcents, thinning secretions, and may very well be helpful. Eating a full meal before a speaking or singing engagement may interfere with abdominal support or may aggravate upright reflux of gastric juice during abdominal muscle contraction.

Do You Have Morning Hoarseness, Bad Breath, Excessive Phlegm, a Lump in Your Throat, or Heartburn?

Reflux laryngitis is especially common among singers and trained speakers because of the high intra-abdominal pressure associated with proper support and because of lifestyle. Singers frequently perform at night. Many vocalists refrain from eating before performances, because a full stomach can compromise effective abdominal support. They typically compensate by eating heartily at postperformance gatherings late at night and then going to bed with a full stomach. Chronic irritation of arytenoid and vocal fold mucosa by reflux of gastric secretions may occasionally be associated with dyspepsia or pyrosis. However, the key features of this malady are bitter taste and halitosis on awakening in the morning, a dry or "coated" mouth, often a scratchy sore throat or a feeling of a "lump in the throat," hoarseness, and the need for prolonged vocal warm-up. The physician must be alert to these symptoms and ask about them routinely; otherwise, the diagnosis will often be overlooked; because people who have had this problem for many years or a lifetime do not even realize it is abnormal

Do You Have Trouble with Your Bowels or Belly?

Any condition that alters abdominal function, such as muscle spasm, constipation, or diarrhea, interferes with support and may result in a voice complaint. These symptoms may accompany infection, anxiety, various gastroenterological diseases, and other maladies.

Are You Under Particular Stress or in Therapy?

The human voice is an exquisitely sensitive messenger of emotion. Highly trained voice professionals learn to control the effects of anxiety and other emotional stress on their voices under ordinary circumstances. However, in some instances, this training may break down or a performer may be inadequately prepared to control the voice under specific stressful conditions. Preperformance anxiety is the most common example; but insecurity, depression, and other emotional disturbances are also generally reflected in the voice. Anxiety reactions are mediated in part through the autonomic nervous system and result in a dry mouth, cold clammy skin, and thick secretions. These reactions are normal, and good vocal training coupled with assurance that no abnormality or disease is present generally overcomes them. However, long-term, poorly compensated emotional stress and exogenous stress (from agents, producers, teachers, parents, etc) may cause substantial vocal dysfunction and result in permanent limitations of the vocal apparatus. These conditions must be diagnosed and treated expertly. Hypochondriasis is uncommon among professional singers, despite popular opinion to the contrary.

Recent publications have highlighted the complexity and importance of psychological factors associated with voice disorders.[26] A comprehensive discussion of this subject is also presented in chapter 10. It is important for the physician to recognize that psychological problems may not only cause voice disorders, but they may also delay recovery from voice disorders that were entirely organic in etiology. Professional voice users, especially singers, have enormous psychological investment and personality identification associated with their voices. A condition that causes voice loss or permanent injury often evokes the same powerful psychological responses seen following death of a loved one. This process may be initiated even when physical recovery is complete if an incident (injury or surgery) has made the vocalist realize that voice loss is possible. Such a "brush with death" can have profound emotional consequences in some patients. It is essential for laryngologists to be aware of these powerful factors and manage them properly if optimal therapeutic results are to be achieved expeditiously.

Do You Have Problems Controlling Your Weight? Are You Excessively Tired? Are You Cold When Other People Are Warm?

Endocrine problems warrant special attention. The human voice is extremely sensitive to endocrinological changes. Many of these are reflected in alterations of fluid content of the lamina propria just beneath the laryngeal mucosa. This causes alterations in the bulk and shape of the vocal folds and results in voice change. Hypothyroidism[27-31] is a well-recognized cause of such voice disorders, although the mechanism is not fully understood. Hoarseness, vocal fatigue, muffling of the voice, loss of range, and a sensation of a lump in the throat may be present even with mild hypothyroidism. Even when thyroid function test results are within the low normal range, this diagnosis should be entertained, especially if thyroid-stimulating hormone levels are in the high normal range or are elevated. Thyrotoxicosis may result in similar voice disturbance.[28]

Do You Have Menstrual Irregularity, Cyclical Voice Changes Associated with Menses, Recent Menopause, or Other Hormonal Changes or Problems?

Voice changes associated with sex hormones are encountered commonly in clinical practice and have been investigated more thoroughly than have other hormonal changes.[32,33] Although a correlation appears to exist between sex hormone levels and depth of male voices (higher testosterone and lower estradiol levels in basses than in tenors),[32] the most important hormonal considerations in males occur during or are related to puberty,[34,35] as discussed in *Professional Voice*.[36] Voice problems related to sex hormones are more common in female singers.[37-53] They are also reviewed in *Professional Voice*.[36]

Do You Have Jaw Joint or Other Dental Problems?

Dental disease, especially temporomandibular joint (TMJ) dysfunction, introduces muscle tension in the head and neck, which is transmitted to the larynx directly through the muscular attachments between the mandible and the hyoid bone and indirectly as generalized increased muscle tension. These problems often result in decreased range, vocal fatigue, and change in the quality or placement of a voice. Such tension often is accompanied by excess tongue muscle activity, especially pulling of the tongue posteriorly. This hyperfunctional behavior acts through hyoid attachments to disrupt the balance between the intrinsic and extrinsic laryngeal musculature. TMJ problems are also problematic for wind instrumentalists and some string players, including violinists. In some cases, the problems may actually be caused by instrumental technique. The history should always include information about musical activities, including instruments other than the voice.

Do You or Your Blood Relatives Have Hearing Loss?

Hearing loss is often overlooked as a source of vocal problems. Auditory feedback is fundamental to speaking and singing. Interference with this control mechanism may result in altered vocal production, particularly if the person is unaware of the hearing loss. Distortion, particularly pitch distortion (diplacusis) may also pose serious problems for the singer. This appears to be due not only to aesthetic difficulties in matching pitch, but also to vocal strain that accompanies pitch shifts.[54]

In addition to determining whether the patient has hearing loss, inquiry should also be made about hearing impairment occurring in family members, roommates, and other close associates. Speaking loudly to people who are hard-of-hearing can cause substantial, chronic vocal strain. This possibility should be investigated routinely when evaluating voice patients.

Have You Suffered Whiplash or Other Bodily Injury?

Various bodily injuries outside the confines of the vocal tract may have profound effects on the voice. Whiplash, for example, commonly causes changes in technique, with consequent voice fatigue, loss of range, difficulty singing softly, and other problems. These problems derive from the neck muscle spasm, abnormal neck posturing secondary to pain, and consequent hyperfunctional voice use. Lumbar, abdominal, head, chest, supraglottic, and extremity injuries may also affect vocal technique and be responsible for the dysphonia that prompted the voice patient to seek medical attention.

Did You Undergo Any Surgery Prior to the Onset of Your Voice Problems?

A history of laryngeal surgery in a voice patient is a matter of great concern. It is important to establish exactly why the surgery was done, by whom it was done, whether intubation was necessary, and whether voice therapy was instituted pre- or postoperatively if the lesion was associated with voice abuse (vocal nodules). If the vocal dysfunction that sent the patient to the physician's office dates from the immediate postoperative period, surgical trauma must be suspected.

Otolaryngologists frequently are asked about the effects of tonsillectomy on the voice. Singers especially may consult the physician after tonsillectomy and complain of vocal dysfunction. Certainly removal of tonsils can alter the voice.[55,56] Tonsillectomy changes the configuration of the supraglottic vocal tract. In addition, scarring alters pharyngeal muscle function, which is trained meticulously in the professional singer. Singers must be warned that they may have permanent voice changes after tonsillectomy; however, these changes can be minimized by dissecting in the proper plane to lessen scarring. The singer's voice generally requires 3 to 6 months to stabilize or return to normal after surgery, although it is generally safe to begin limited singing within 2 to 4 weeks following surgery. As with any procedure for which general anesthesia may be needed, the anesthesiologist should be advised preoperatively that the patient is a professional singer. Intubation and extubation should be performed with great care, and the use of nonirritating plastic rather than rubber or ribbed metal endotracheal tubes is preferred. Use of a laryngeal mask may be advisable for selected procedures for mechanical reasons; but this device is often not ideal for tonsillectomy; and it can cause laryngeal injury such as arytenoid dislocation.

Surgery of the neck, such as thyroidectomy, may result in permanent alterations in the vocal mechanism through scarring of the extrinsic laryngeal musculature. The cervical (strap) muscles are important in maintaining laryngeal position and stability of the laryngeal skeleton; and they should be retracted rather than divided whenever possible. A history of recurrent or superior laryngeal nerve injury may explain a hoarse, breathy, or weak voice. However, in rare cases, even a singer can compensate for recurrent laryngeal nerve paralysis and have a nearly normal voice.

Thoracic and abdominal surgery interfere with respiratory and abdominal support. After these procedures, singing and projected speaking should be prohibited until pain has subsided and healing has occurred sufficiently to allow normal support. Abdominal exercises should be instituted before resumption of vocalizing. Singing and speaking without proper support are often worse for the voice than not using the voice for performance at all.

Other surgical procedures may be important factors if they necessitate intubation or if they affect the musculoskeletal system so that the person has to change stance or balance. For example, balancing on one foot after leg surgery may decrease the effectiveness of the support mechanism.

What Medications and Other Substances Do You Use?

A history of alcohol abuse suggests the probability of poor vocal technique. Intoxication results in incoordination and decreased awareness, which undermine vocal discipline designed to optimize and protect the voice. The effect of small amounts of alcohol is controversial. Although many experts oppose its use because of its vasodilatory effect and consequent mucosal alteration, many people do not seem to be adversely affected by small amounts of alcohol such as a glass of wine with a meal. However, some people have mild sensitivities to certain wines or beers. Patients who develop nasal congestion and rhinorrhea after drinking beer, for example, should be made aware that they probably have a mild allergy to that particular beverage and should avoid it before voice commitments.

Patients frequently acquire antihistamines to help control "postnasal drip" or other symptoms. The drying effect of antihistamines may result in decreased vocal fold lubrication, increased throat clearing, and irritability leading to frequent coughing. Antihistamines may be helpful to some voice patients, but they must be used with caution.

When a voice patient seeking the attention of a physician is already taking antibiotics, it is important to find out the dose and the prescribing physician, if any, as well as whether the patient frequently treats himself or herself with inadequate courses of antibiotics often supplied by colleagues. Singers, actors, and other speakers sometimes have a "sore throat" shortly before important vocal presentations and start themselves on inappropriate antibiotic therapy, which they generally discontinue after their performance.

Diuretics are also popular among some performers. They are often prescribed by gynecologists at the vocalist's request to help deplete excess water in the premenstrual period. They are not effective in this scenario, because they cannot diurese the protein-bound water in the laryngeal ground substance. Unsupervised use of these drugs may cause dehydration and consequent mucosal dryness.

Hormone use, especially use of oral contraceptives, must be mentioned specifically during the physician's inquiry. Women frequently do not mention them routinely when asked whether they are taking any medication. Vitamins are also frequently not mentioned. Most vitamin therapy seems to have little effect on the voice. However, high-dose vitamin C (5 to 6 g/day), which some people use to prevent upper respiratory tract infections, seems to act as a mild diuretic and may lead to dehydration and xerophonia.[57]

Cocaine use is common, especially among pop musicians. This drug can be extremely irritating to the nasal mucosa, causes marked vasoconstriction, and may alter the sensorium, resulting in decreased voice control and a tendency toward vocal abuse.

Many pain medications (including aspirin and ibuprofen), psychotropic medications, and many others may be responsible for a voice complaint. So far, no adverse vocal effects have been reported with selective COX-2 inhibiting anti-inflammatory medications (which do not promote bleeding, as do other nonsteroid anti-inflammatory medicines and aspirin), such as selecoxib (Celebrex, Pfizer Inc, New York, NY) and valdecoxib (Bextra, Pharmacia Corp, New York, NY). The effects of other new medications such as sildenafil citrate (Viagra, Pfizer Inc, New York) and medications used to induce abortion remain unstudied and unknown; but it seems plausible that such medication may affect voice function, at least temporarily. Laryngologists must be familiar with the laryngologic effects of the many substances ingested medically and recreationally. These are reviewed elsewhere in this book and in other literature.

References

1. Sataloff RT. Professional singers: the science and art of clinical care. *Am J Otolaryngol.* 1981;2:251–266.
2. Sataloff RT. The human voice. *Sci Am.* 1992;267:108–115.
3. Sundberg J. *The Science of the Singing Voice.* DeKalb, Ill: Northern Illinois University Press; 1987:1–194.
4. Sataloff RT. Efficient history taking in professional singers. *Laryngoscope.* 1984;94:1111–1114.
5. Ackermann R, Pfau W. [Gerontology studies on the susceptibility to voice disorders in professional speakers. *Folia Phoniatr* (Basel). 1974;26:95–99.
6. von Leden H. Speech and hearing problems in the geriatric patient. *J Am Geriatr Soc.* 1977;25:422–426.
7. Bhatia R, Hawkshaw MJ, Sataloff RT. Chaos in voice research. In: Sataloff RT. *Voice Science.* San Diego, Calif: Plural Publishing; 2005:203–212.
8. Schiff M. Comment. Presented at the Seventh Symposium on Care of the Professional Voice; June 15–16, 1978; The Juilliard School, New York, NY.
9. Sataloff RT. Common infections, inflammations, and other conditions. In: Sataloff RT. *Professional Voice: The Science and Art of Clinical Care.* San Diego, Calif: Plural Publishing Inc; 2005:807–814.
10. Spiegel JR, Cohn JR, Sataloff RT, et al. Respiratory function in singers: medical assessment, diagnoses, treatments. *J Voice.* 1988;2:40–50.
11. Cohn JR, Sataloff RT, Spiegel JR, et al. Airway reactivity-induced asthma in singers (ARIAS). *J Voice.* 1991;5:332–337.
12. Feder RJ. The professional voice and airline flight. *Otolaryngol Head Neck Surg.* 1984;92:251–254.
13. Sataloff RT. *Professional Voice: The Science and Art of Clinical Care.* San Diego, Calif: Plural Publishing Inc; 2005: 729–756.
14. Anticaglia A, Hawkshaw M, Sataloff RT. The effects of smoking on voice performance. *J Singing.* 2004;60:161–167.
15. Center for Disease Control (CDC). Annual smoking-attributable mortality, years of potential life lost, and economic costs, United States—1995–1999. *Morbidity & Mortality Weekly Report (MMWR).* 2002;51(14):300–303.
16. World Health Organization. *World Health Report 1999.* Geneva, Switzerland: WHO; 1999.
17. United States Department of Health and Human Services, (USDHHS). *Tobacco Products Fact Sheet, 2000.* Washington, DC: Government Printing Office; 2000.
18. National Cancer Institute. Environmental tobacco smoke. Fact sheet 3.9; 1999. Available at: http//cis.nci.nih.gov/fact/3_9htm
19. Centers for Disease Control and Prevention. Cigarette smoking among adults—United States, 1993. *Morbidity & Mortality Weekly Report (MMWR).* 1994;3:925–929.
20. Chow WH, McLaughlin JK, Hrubec Z, et al. Tobacco use and nasopharyngeal carcinoma in a cohort of US veterans. *Int J Cancer.* 1993;55(4):538–540.
21. Casiglia J, Woo, SB. A comprehensive view of oral cancer. *Gen Dent.* 2001;49(1):72–82
22. Centers for Disease Control. Determination of nicotine, pH and moisture content of six U.S. commercial moist snuff products. *Mortality & Morbidity Weekly Review (MMWR).* 1999;48 (19):398.
23. American Cancer Society. *Cancer Facts and Figures 2002.* Atlanta, Ga: ACS; 2002.
24. US Dept Health and Human Services, Public Health Service, National Toxicology Program (NTP). *Report on Carcinogens.* 10th ed. 2002. Available at: http://ehp.niehs.nih.gov/roc/toc10.html.
25. Academy of Pediatrics, Committee on Environmental Health. Environmental tobacco smoke: a hazard to children. *Pediatrics.*1997;99(4): 639–642.
26. Rosen DC, Sataloff RT. *Psychology of Voice Disorders.* San Diego, Calif: Singular Publishing Group; 1997:1–261.
27. Gupta OP, Bhatia PL, Agarwal MK, et al. Nasal pharyngeal and laryngeal manifestations of hypothyroidism. *Ear Nose Throat J.* 1977;56:10–21.
28. Malinsky M, Chevrie-Muller, Cerceau N. Etude clinique et electrophysiologique des alterations de la voix au cours des thyrotoxioses. *Ann Endocrinol* (Paris). 1977;38: 171–172.
29. Michelsson K, Sirvio P. Cry analysis in congenital hypothyroidism. *Folia Phoniatr* (Basel). 1976;28:40–47.
30. Ritter FN. The effect of hypothyroidism on the larynx of the rat. *Ann Otol Rhinol Laryngol.* 1964;67:404–416.
31. Ritter FN. Endocrinology. In: Paparella M, Shumrick D, eds. *Otolaryngology.* Vol I. Philadelphia, Pa: Saunders; 1973:727–734.
32. Meuser W, Nieschlag E. [Sex hormones and depth of voice in the male.] *Dtsch Med Wochenschr.*1977:102: 261–264.
33. Schiff M. The influence of estrogens on connective tissue. In: Asboe-Hansen G, ed. *Hormones and Connective Tissue.* Coopenhagen, Denmark: Munksgaard Press; 1967:282–341.
34. Brodnitz F. The age of the castrato voice. *J Speech Hear Disord.* 1975;40:291–295.
35. Brodnitz F. Hormones and the human voice. *Bull N Y Acad Med.* 1971;47:183–191.
36. Sataloff RT, Linville SE. The effects of age on voice. In: Sataloff RT. *Professional Voice: The Science and Art of Clinical Care.* San Diego, Calif: Plural Publishing Inc; 2005: 497–512.
37. Carroll C. Personal communication with Dr. Hans von Leden; 1992; Arizona State University at Tempe.
38. van Gelder L. Psychosomatic aspects of endocrine disorders of the voice. *J Commun Disord.* 1974;7:257–262.
39. Lacina O. Der Einfluss der Menstruation auf die Stimme der Sangerinnen. *Folia Phoniatr* (Basel). 1968;20:13–24.
40. Wendler J. [The influence of menstruation on the voice of the female singer.] *Folia Phoniatr* (Basel). 1972;24: 259–277.

41. Brodnitz F. Medical care preventive therapy (panel). In: Lawrence VL, ed. *Transcripts of the Seventh Annual Symposium. Care of the Professional Voice.* New York, NY: The Voice Foundation; 1978;3:86.
42. Dordain M. Etude Statistique de l'influence des contraceptifs hormonaux sur la voix. *Folia Phoniatr* (Basel). 1972;24:86–96.
43. Pahn J, Goretzlehner G. [Voice changes following the use of oral contraceptives.] *Zentralbl Gynakol.* 1978;100: 341–346.
44. Schiff M. "The pill" in otolaryngology. *Trans Am Acad Ophthalmol Otolaryngol.* 1968;72:76–84.
45. von Deuster CV. [Irreversible vocal changes in pregnancy.] *HNO.* 1977;25:430–432.
46. Flach M, Schwickardi H, Simen R. Welchen Einfluss haben Menstruation and Schwangerschaft auf die augsgebildete Gesangsstimme? *Folia Phoniatr* (Basel). 1968; 21:199–210.
47. Arndt HJ. Stimmstorungen nach Behandlung mit Androgenen und anabolen Hormonen. *Munch Med Wochenschr.* 1974;116:1715–1720.
48. Bourdial J. Les troubles de la voix provoques par la therapeutique hormonale androgene. *Ann Otolaryngol Chir Cervicofac.* 1970;87:725–734.
49. Damsté PH. Virilization of the voice due to the use of anabolic steroids. *Ned Tijdschr Geneeskd.* 1963;107:891–892.
50. Damsté PH. Voice changes in adult women caused by virilizing agents. *J Speech Hear Disord.* 1967;32:126–132.
51. Saez S, Sakai F. Recepteurs d'androgenes: mise en evidence dans la fraction cytosolique de muqueuse normale et d'epitheliomas pharyngolarynges humains. *C R Acad Sci Hebd Seances Acad Sci D.* 1975;280:935–938.
52. Vuorenkoski V, Lenko HL, Tjernlund P, et al. Fundamental voice frequency during normal and abnormal growth, and after androgen treatment. *Arch Dis Child.* 1978;53:201–209.
53. Imre V. Hormonell bedingte Stimmstorungen. *Folia Phoniatr* (Basel). 1968;20:394–404.
54. Sundberg J, Prame E, Iwarsson J. Replicability and accuracy of pitch patterns in professional singers. In: Davis PJ, Fletcher NH, eds. *Vocal Fold Physiology: Controlling Chaos and Complexity.* San Diego, Calif: Singular Publishing Group Inc; 1996:291–306.
55. Gould WJ, Alberti PW, Brodnitz F, Hirano M. Medical care preventive therapy. [Panel.] In: Lawrence VL, ed. *Transcripts of the Seventh Annual Symposium. Care of the Professional Voice.* New York, NY: The Voice Foundation; 1978;3:74–76.
56. Wallner LJ, Hill BJ, Waldrop W, Monroe C. Voice changes following adenotonsillectomy. *Laryngoscope.* 1968;78:1410–1418.
57. Lawrence VL. Medical care for professional voice (panel). In: Lawrence VL, ed. *Transcripts from the Annual Symposium. Care of the Professional Voice.* New York, NY: The Voice Foundation; 1978;3:17–18.

2

Special Considerations Relating to Members of the Acting Profession

Bonnie N. Raphael

Individuals who act for a living are a breed unto themselves. Many of the same attributes that make them exciting and electric onstage—high levels of habitual energy; ability to bring to the surface and communicate a large range of strong emotions; high degree of sensitivity, awareness, and concentration—make them susceptible to functional voice difficulties. Moreover, because so many of them rely on their vocal capabilities to do their work, any interference with their vocal effectiveness can be both frightening and highly intimidating.

Physicians and speech-language pathologists who work with actors must augment their standard patient histories to include additional questions relevant to both diagnosis and treatment. For example, many actors find they must supplement their income with "survival jobs"; in addition to whatever acting they are doing, many work as waiters and waitresses, taxicab drivers, receptionists, part-time teachers or babysitters, tour guides, or sales personnel. When a stage actor is a member of the national actors' union (Actors' Equity Association, or Equity), then he or she can be called in for up to 8 hours of rehearsal per day, 6 days a week. (This does not include time spent learning lines; taking classes in singing, dancing, dialects, acting, fencing, and the like; research the actor may have to do on a particular role; etc). Non-union stage actors may be working even longer hours for less money *and* may be holding down another job at the same time in order to make ends meet. Furthermore, the vast majority of working stage and film actors are hired for one show or one film at a time. Even as they rehearse and perform in their current projects, part of their energies must be devoted to finding their next employment.

It is important to ascertain what kind of acting each actor is doing—proscenium stage, theatre in-the-round, camera work (television and film), voiceover work (often requiring a number of different voices in quick succession), cabaret or club work, musical acting or "straight" performance, demanding character work, and so on. It is also important to find out whether the actor has been trained vocally or has learned how to use the voice by watching other actors and engaging in self-directed trial and error.

When an actor describes his or her symptoms to a physician or voice therapist, he or she may do so in a deceptively beautiful voice. As a result, the physician or speech-language pathologist may suspect either hypochondria or pre-opening night nervousness instead of understanding that many actors know their voices well enough and are sensitive enough to the sound and sensation of their voices to be the first to know that something is wrong. In a questionnaire study conducted at the Denver Center for the Performing Arts, a significant number of professional actors considered the following factors indicative of voice malfunction: general physical fatigue, throat fatigue, tightness or constriction, strain or tension, a greater awareness of the voice and the mechanism, greater effort needed to produce and sustain voice, reduction in functional pitch range, and greater difficulty in producing higher pitches.[1] Such factors may not be immediately discernible to anyone but the actor. For these reasons the criteria according to which the voice is evaluated need to be different for the actor than for the average voice patient.

A number of special circumstances make the work and lifestyle of actors particularly conducive to the development of voice difficulties:

1. Professional actors work hard and long. As stated earlier, a professional actor who is an Equity member is expected to work an 8-hour day during rehearsals (with one or two 10-out-of-12-hour days during technical rehearsals) and could conceivably be rehearsing his or her next show during the day in a different location while performing a current show in the evenings. Actors who are doing workshop productions just to be seen by potential agents and producers or who are working at non-union theaters will be paid very little, if anything at all, and are typically holding down other work at the same time.

2. Professional actors often engage in a great deal of travel and in a series of temporary living arrangements. Many will be "jobbed in" for the run of a single show. Many will use their one day off per week to travel from the theater at which they are employed to a number of different places for auditions for their next jobs. This lifestyle often necessitates living in hotels or rooming houses. A number of actors who are members of touring companies will appear night after night in single performances in different theaters and travel by bus all day to their next destination. Temperature, relative humidity, altitude, irritants, allergens, and the like are ongoing possibilities as a result.

3. Every actor must adjust vocal production to meet the particular needs of a number of different performance spaces. Theaters can range in size from that of a 99-seat proscenium house to a 2,500-seat stadium or even larger. Certain theaters are wonderfully designed to provide acoustics quite salutary to the speaking voice, whereas others provide absolute nightmares for even the best-trained actor. Projection of the voice is a concept that involves certain absolutes and a large number of variables that are related to different playing spaces. Furthermore, many actors change rehearsal spaces, change theaters during the run of a show, or even tour extensively, making these adjustments far more frequent. Technical skill at such changes is essential to the maintenance of good vocal production.

4. Many actors have personalities that a physician or speech-language pathologist might describe as volatile or emotional. In addition to a habitual energy level that is quite high by most standards, actors perform roles that very frequently involve out-of-the-ordinary life experiences. Plays are most typically written about people in crisis or transition. Actors are trained to get in touch with their emotions, to give over to the "given circumstances" of the plays in which they appear. (In *Macbeth,* for example, young Malcolm discovers that his wife and children have been murdered . . . In *The Winter's Tale* Leontes believes that his wife is having an affair with his very dear friend . . . In *King Lear,* the title character makes his final entrance howling, with the body of his daughter in his arms . . .) Simulating this broad range of emotions may produce volatility and vulnerability not only onstage but offstage as well.

5. The vocal demands made on actors' voices can be abusive. Even basic, no frills acting frequently necessitates vocal production that explores a wider than usual range—in terms of loudness, pitch, rhythm, and vocal quality. When one adds to this the demands of characterization (ie, the character being played by the actor may age during the course of the play from early 20s to late 70s; the character may be suffering from any number of illnesses, disabilities, or psychological aberrations; the actor may be playing two or three or more characters in the same show), the term "transformational actor" or "vocal athlete" becomes aptly descriptive. To create the illusion of illness or duress or high emotion, the actor may modify breathing or tighten the shoulders and jaw or constrict the voice, any of which may be harmful to the vocal mechanism. In addition, within the given circumstances of the play, the actor may be required to laugh hysterically or sob or scream or shriek or cough or choke or even "die." Although trained and experienced actors may be able to do this with relative impunity, there is a price to be paid for this extraordinary behavior. Last but certainly not least, many times, the actor is doing this work over a great deal of aural competition—there may be thunder in the background, a storm raging, music playing underneath spoken dialogue, the sounds of swords hitting shields or battle cries, the march of an approaching army—or even the constant hum and vibration of a theater's ventilation system—the siren of a passing ambulance—the roar of a passing airplane. The actor must find a way to ensure that his or her voice is dominant and the competition remains background to the ear of the audience. Not surprisingly, in the study previously cited,[1] actors reported that the three factors most consistently contributing to vocal strain and fatigue are long working hours, screaming or shouting onstage, and having to speak over high levels of background noise and/or music.

6. A series of potential occupational hazards complicate the actor's work even further. The wearing of certain costumes may restrict the actor's physical mobility so much that vocal production is affected. For example, ruffs, high collars, and heavy capes can produce difficulties, as can artificial beards and artificial moustaches, which are glued to the actor's skin. Actors may be asked to wear half or even full masks while they speak. They may be wearing makeup that limits facial mobility (eg, artificial scars) or prosthetic devices (to change the look of the teeth or jawline), that make projection and articulation more difficult. Similarly,

the scene may call for the presence of large amounts of onstage smoke or fog, which the actor inhales before and while he or she performs. Add to this the ever-present stage dust (in the canvas on the flats, in the curtains, and in the costumes), and the ongoing use of various sprays (to hold the hair in place, to set the makeup, to keep the costumes stain- and static-free) and it is clear that the hazards are ongoing and plentiful.

7. There is tremendous competition in the acting profession. Actors benefit greatly from being known as cooperative, professional, willing to go the extra mile. Typically, the actor has a real desire to please—an agent, a director, a critic—that will make him or her reticent to "take it easy" during rehearsals or performances. Many fear they will lose their jobs if they refuse to scream or to smoke a cigarette onstage or to shout over unfair competition. Most do not feel they are in a sufficiently secure position professionally to make demands or even requests for any modification of stage business.

8. The actor who has achieved success or popularity has done so by selling an image very closely connected with an identifiable vocal sound. Even if he or she knows that the sound is not ideal from a physiological or an aesthetic point of view, giving it up may be perceived as career-threatening, foolhardy, or professional suicide. A physician or speech-language pathologist must be clear and communicative with actor-patients, while at the same time being extremely aware of the ramifications of any significant vocal change in that individual.

Many actors will not seek the services of an otolaryngologist or a speech-language pathologist except as a last resort. They would rather tough it out or wait for this "cold" to pass. Consequently and unfortunately, this often means that they do not set foot in the office until the damage is already quite severe and the poor habits deeply entrenched.

Physicians and speech-language pathologists whom actors admire most are those who know about the exigencies of the actor's life and really care about the actor as both a patient and a performer. Such physicians and speech-language pathologists will take the time to come see the actor in action, on location whenever possible. Such physicians and speech-language pathologists will recommend treatment and/or therapy that makes sense to the actor and is compatible with and achievable within the confines of his or her professional needs and lifestyle. Such physicians and speech-language pathologists will communicate with actors in a voice that sounds as if they, too, value a good, healthy, projectable sound, and in a language that the actor can understand and embrace rather than fear and reject. Such physicians and speech-language pathologists show both an interest in and a willingness to work directly with theatre and film teachers, coaches, and directors. Results can be astounding and "dramatic," but only if the actor is a willing contributor to the healing process rather than a frightened and intimidated victim of medical jargonese, inflexibility, insensitivity, or ignorance. Fortunately, with the rapid advance of voice medicine, more and more interested and specially trained physicians and speech-language pathologists are undergoing specialized training, and major improvements in quality of care are beginning to take place.

References

1. Raphael BN, Scherer RC. Repertory actors' perceptions of the voice in relation to various professional conditions. In: Lawrence V, ed. *Transcripts of the Fourteenth Symposium: Care of the Professional Voice*. New York, NY: The Voice Foundation; 1985:124–130.

3

Physical Examination

Robert Thayer Sataloff

Physical Examination

A detailed history frequently reveals the cause of a voice problem even before a physical examination is performed. However, a comprehensive physical examination, often including objective assessment of voice function, also is essential.[1-3] In response to feedback from readers of the previous editions, this chapter has been expanded to include a brief overview of objective voice assessment and other subjects covered more comprehensively in subsequent chapters. This overview is provided here for the reader's convenience.

Physical examination must include a thorough ear, nose, and throat evaluation and assessment of general physical condition. A patient who is extremely obese or appears fatigued, agitated, emotionally stressed, or otherwise generally ill has an increased potential for voice dysfunction. This could be due to any number of factors: altered abdominal support, loss of fine motor control of laryngeal muscles, decreased bulk of the submucosal vocal fold ground substance, change in the character of mucosal secretions, or other similar mechanisms. Any physical condition that impairs the normal function of the abdominal musculature is suspect as a cause for dysphonia. Some conditions, such as pregnancy, are obvious; however, a sprained ankle or broken leg that requires a singer or actor to balance in an unaccustomed posture may distract him or her from maintaining good abdominal support and thereby result in voice dysfunction. A tremorous neurological disorder, endocrine disturbances such as thyroid dysfunction or menopause, the aging process, and other systemic conditions also may alter the voice. The physician must remember that maladies of almost any body system may result in voice dysfunction, and the doctor must remain alert for conditions outside the head and neck. If the patient uses his or her voice professionally for singing, acting, or other vocally demanding professions, physical examination should also include assessment of the patient during typical professional vocal tasks. For example, a singer should be asked to sing. Evaluation techniques for assessing performance are described in greater detail elsewhere in this book.

Complete Ear, Nose, and Throat Examination

Examination of the ears must include assessment of hearing acuity. Even a relatively slight hearing loss may result in voice strain as a singer tries to balance his or her vocal intensity with that of associate performers. Similar effects are encountered among speakers, but they are less prominent in the early stages of hearing loss. This is especially true of hearing losses acquired after vocal training has been completed. The effect is most pronounced with sensorineural hearing loss. Diplacusis, distortion of pitch perception, makes vocal strain even worse. With conductive hearing loss, singers tend to sing more softly than appropriate rather than too loudly; and this is less harmful.

During an ear, nose, and throat examination, the conjunctivae and sclerae should be observed routinely for erythema that suggests allergy or irritation, for pallor that suggests anemia, and for other abnormalities such as jaundice. These observations may reveal the problem reflected in the vocal tract even before the larynx is visualized. Hearing loss in a spouse may be problematic as well if the voice professional strains vocally to communicate.

The nose should be assessed for patency of the nasal airway, character of the nasal mucosa, and nature of secretions, if any. A patient who is unable to breathe through the nose because of anatomic obstruction is forced to breathe unfiltered, unhumidified air through the mouth. Pale gray allergic mucosa or swollen infected mucosa in the nose suggests abnormal mucosa elsewhere in the respiratory tract.

Examination of the oral cavity should include careful attention to the tonsils and lymphoid tissue in the posterior pharyngeal wall, as well as to the mucosa. Diffuse lymphoid hypertrophy associated with a complaint of "scratchy" voice and irritative cough may indicate infection. The amount and viscosity of mucosal and salivary secretions also should be noted. Xerostomia is particularly important. The presence of scalloping of the lateral aspects of the tongue should be noted. This finding is caused commonly by tongue thrust and may be associated with inappropriate tongue tension and muscle tension dysphonia. Dental examination should focus not only on oral hygiene but also on the presence of wear facets suggestive of bruxism. Bruxism is a clue to excessive tension and may be associated with dysfunction of the temporomandibular joints, which should also be assessed routinely. Thinning of the enamel of the central incisors in a normal or underweight patient may be a clue to bulimia. However, it may also result from excessive ingestion of lemons, which some singers eat to help thin their secretions.

The neck should be examined for masses, restriction of movement, excess muscle tension and/or spasm, and scars from prior neck surgery or trauma. Laryngeal vertical mobility is also important. For example, tilting of the larynx produced by partial fixation of cervical muscles cut during previous surgery may produce voice dysfunction, as may fixation of the trachea to overlying neck skin. Particular attention should be paid to the thyroid gland. Examination of posterior neck muscles and range of motion should not be neglected. The cranial nerves should also be examined. Diminished fifth nerve sensation, diminished gag reflex, palatal deviation, or other mild cranial nerve deficits may indicate cranial polyneuropathy. Postviral, infectious neuropathies may involve the superior laryngeal nerve(s) and cause weakness of the vocal fold muscle secondary to decreased neural function resulting in ineffective compensatory efforts in attempts to overcome diminished neural input, fatigability, and loss of range and projection of the voice. The recurrent laryngeal nerve is also affected in some cases. More serious neurologic disease may also be associated with such symptoms and signs.

Laryngeal Examination

Examination of the larynx begins when the singer or other voice patient enters the physician's office. The range, ease, volume, and quality of the speaking voice should be noted. If the examination is not being conducted in the patient's native language, the physician should be sure to listen to a sample of the patient's mother tongue, as well. Voice use is often different under the strain or habits of foreign language use. Rating scales used to describe of the speaking voice more consistent may be helpful.[4,5] The classification proposed by the Japanese Society of Logopedics and Phoniatrics is one of the most widely used. It is known commonly as the GRBAS Voice Rating Scale and is discussed below in the section on psychoacoustic evaluation.[6]

Physicians are not usually experts in voice classification. However, physicians should at least be able to discriminate substantial differences in range and timbre, such as between bass and tenor or alto and soprano. Although the correlation between speaking and singing voices is not perfect, a speaker with a low, comfortable bass voice who reports that he is a tenor may be misclassified and singing inappropriate roles with consequent voice strain. This judgment should be deferred to an expert, but the observation should lead the physician to make the appropriate referral. Excessive volume or obvious strain during speaking clearly indicates that voice abuse is present and may be contributing to the patient's singing complaint. The speaking voice can be evaluated more consistently and accurately using standardized reading passages (Appendix IIA); and such assessments are performed routinely by speech-language pathologists, phoniatricians, and sometimes by laryngologists.

Any patient with a voice complaint should be examined by indirect laryngoscopy at least (Fig 3–1A). It is not possible to judge voice range, quality, or other vocal attributes by inspection of the vocal folds. However, the presence or absence of nodules, mass lesions, contact ulcers, hemorrhage, erythema, paralysis, arytenoid erythema (reflux), and other anatomic abnormalities must be established. Erythema and edema of the laryngeal surface of the epiglottis is seen often in association with muscle tension dysphonia and with frequent coughing or clearing of the throat. It is caused by direct trauma from the arytenoids during these maneuvers. The mirror or a laryngeal telescope often provides a better view of the posterior portion of the endolarynx than is obtained with flexible endoscopy. Stroboscopic examination adds substantially to diagnostic abilities (Fig 3–1B), as discussed below. Another occasionally helpful adjunct is the operating microscope. Magnification allows visualization of small mucosal disruptions and hemorrhages that may be significant but overlooked otherwise. This technique also allows photography of the larynx with a microscope camera. Magnification may also be achieved through magnifying laryngeal mirrors or by wearing loupes. Loupes usually provide a clearer image than do most of the magnifying mirrors available.

A laryngeal telescope may be combined with a stroboscope to provide excellent visualization of the vocal folds and related structures. The author usually uses a 70-degree laryngeal telescope, although 90-degree telescopes are required for some patients. The combi-

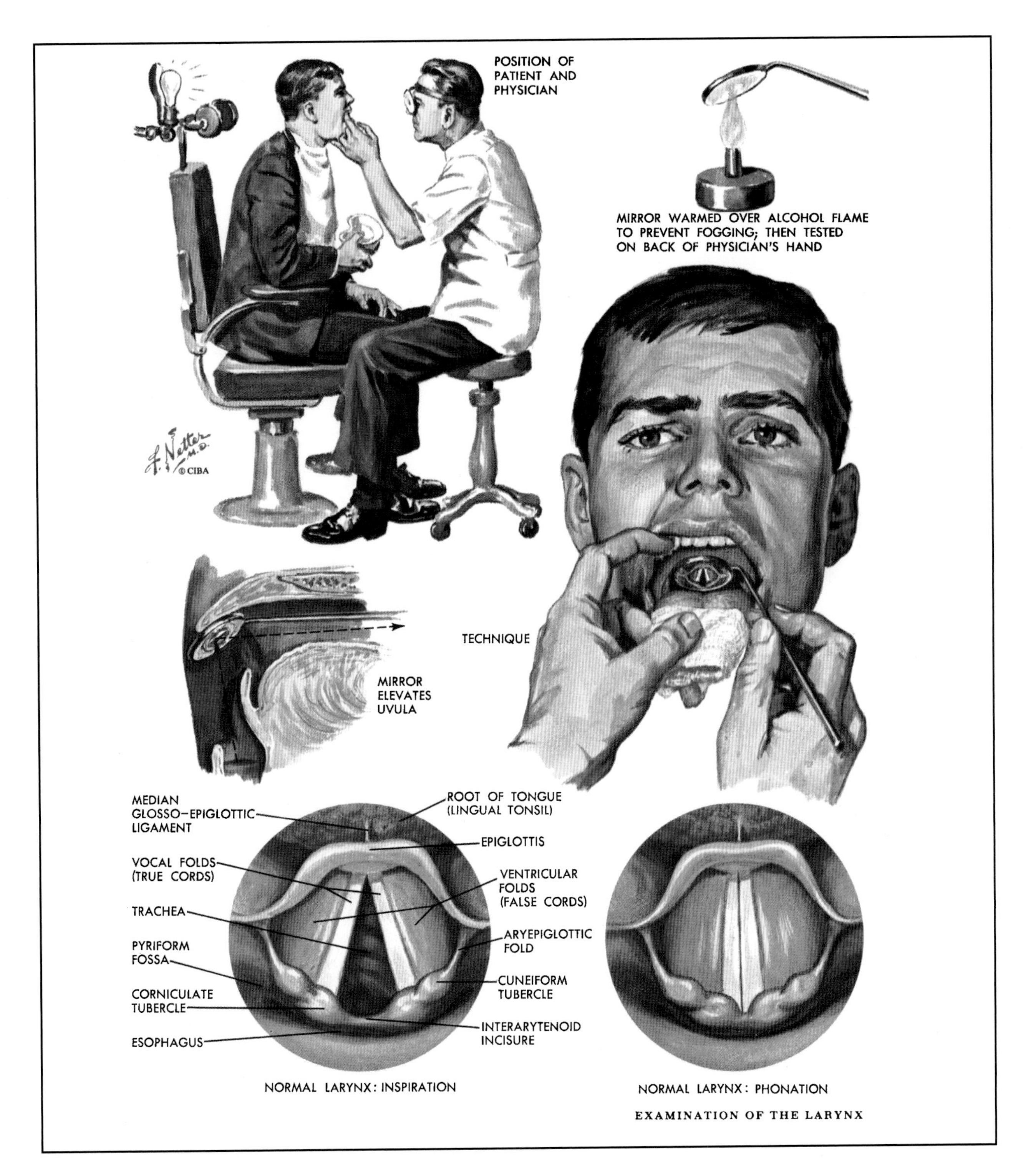

Fig 3–1. A. Traditional laryngeal examination. The laryngologist uses a warmed mirror to visualize the vocal fold indirectly. The tongue is grasped between the thumb and third finger. The thumb is placed as far posteriorly as possible in the middle third of the tongue (farther back than illustrated). The grip optimizes tongue depression and rotation. If the third finger is held firmly against the lower teeth and used to pivot rather than pull, discomfort along the frenulum can be avoided. The mirror is placed against the soft palate while the patient phonates on the vowel /i/. Placing the mirror during the phonation decreases the tendency to gag, and the vowel /i/ puts the larynx in the best position for visualization. (From the Larynx, *Clinical Symposia*, New Jersey: CIBA Pharmaceutical Company, 1964;16(3): Plate VI. Copyright 1964. Icon Learning Systems, LLC, a subsidiary of MediMedia USA Inc. Reprinted with permission from Icon Learning Systems, LLC, illustrated by Frank H. Netter, MD. All rights reserved.) *(continued)*

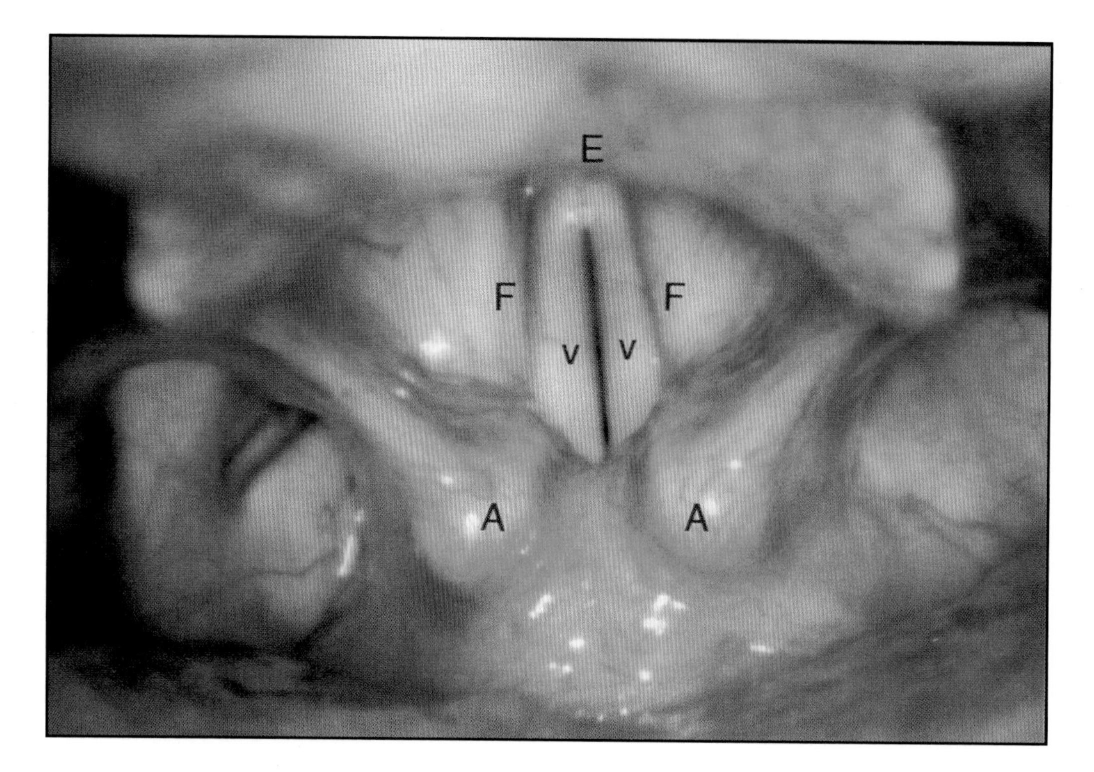

Fig 3–1. *(continued)* **B.** Photograph of normal larynx showing the true vocal folds (V), false vocal folds (F), arytenoids (A), and epiglottis (E).

nation of a telescope and stroboscope provides optimal magnification and optical quality for assessment of vocal fold vibration. However, it is generally performed with the tongue in a fixed position; and the nature of the examination does not permit assessment of the larynx during normal phonatory gestures.

Flexible fiberoptic laryngoscopy can be performed as an office procedure and allows inspection of the vocal folds in patients whose vocal folds are difficult to visualize indirectly. In addition, it permits observation of the vocal mechanism in a more natural posture than does indirect laryngoscopy, permitting sophisticated dynamic voice assessment. In the hands of an experienced endoscopist, this method may provide a great deal of information about both speaking and singing techniques. The combination of a fiberoptic laryngoscope with a laryngeal stroboscope may be especially useful. This system permits magnification, photography, and detailed inspection of vocal fold motion. Sophisticated systems that permit flexible or rigid fiberoptic strobovideolaryngoscopy are currently available commercially. They are invaluable assets for routine clinical use. The video system also provides a permanent record, permitting reassessment, comparison over time, and easy consultation. A refinement not currently available commercially is stereoscopic fiberoptic laryngoscopy, which is accomplished by placing a laryngoscope through each nostril, fastening the two together in the pharynx, and observing the larynx through the eyepieces.[7] This method allows visualization of laryngeal motion in three dimensions. However, it is used primarily in a research setting.

Rigid endoscopy under general anesthesia may be reserved for the rare patient whose vocal folds cannot be assessed adequately by other means or for patients who need surgical procedures to remove or biopsy laryngeal lesions. In many cases, this can be done with local anesthesia, avoiding the need for intubation and the traumatic coughing and vomiting that may occur even after general anesthesia administered by mask. Coughing after general anesthesia can be minimized by using topical anesthesia in the larynx and trachea. However, topical anesthetics act as severe mucosal irritants in a small number of patients. They may also predispose the patient to aspiration in the postoperative period. If a patient has had difficulty with a topical anesthetic administered in the office, it should not be used in the operating room. When used in general anesthesia cases, topical anesthetics should usually be applied at the end of the procedure. Thus, if inflammation occurs, it will not interfere with performance of microsurgery. Postoperative duration of anesthesia is also optimized. The author has had the least difficulty with 4% Xylocaine.

Objective Tests

Reliable, valid, objective analysis of the voice is extremely important and is an essential part of a comprehensive physical examination.[2] It is as valuable to the laryngologist as audiometry is to the otologist.[8,9] Familiarity with some of the measures and technological advances currently available is helpful. This information is covered in greater detail in chapter 4 but is included here as a brief overview for the convenience of the reader.

Strobovideolaryngoscopy

Integrity of the vibratory margin of the vocal fold is essential for the complex motion required to produce good vocal quality. Under continuous light, the vocal folds vibrate approximately 250 times per second while phonating at middle C. Naturally, the human eye cannot discern the necessary details during such rapid motion. The vibratory margin may be assessed through high-speed photography, strobovideolaryngoscopy, high-speed video, videokymography, electroglottography (EGG), or photoglottography. Strobovideolaryngoscopy provides the necessary clinical information in a practical fashion. Stroboscopic light allows routine slow-motion evaluation of the mucosal cover layer of the leading edge of the vocal fold. This state-of-the-art physical examination permits detection of vibratory asymmetries, structural abnormalities, small masses, submucosal scars, and other conditions that are invisible under ordinary light.[10-11] Documentation of the procedure by coupling stroboscopic light with the video camera allows later re-evaluation by the laryngologist or other health care providers.

Stroboscopy does not provide a true slow-motion image, as is obtained through high-speed photography. The stroboscope actually illuminates different points on consecutive vocal fold waves, each of which is retained on the retina for 0.2 seconds. The stroboscopically lighted portions of the successive waves are fused visually, thus the examiner is actually evaluating simulated cycles of phonation. The slow-motion effect is created by having the stroboscopic light desynchronized with the frequency of vocal fold vibration by approximately 2 Hertz. When vocal fold vibration and the stroboscope are synchronized exactly, the vocal folds appear to stand still, rather than move in slow motion. In most instances, this approximation of slow motion provides all of the clinical information necessary. Our routine stroboscopy protocol is described elsewhere[11] and in chapter 4. We use a modification of the standardized method of subjective assessment of strobovideolaryngoscopic images, as proposed by Hirano et al.[12,13] Characteristics evaluated include the fundamental frequency, the symmetry of movements, periodicity, glottic closure, the amplitude of vibration, the mucosal wave, the presence of nonvibrating portions of the vocal fold, and other unusual findings. With practice, perceptual judgments of stroboscopic images provide a great deal of information. However, it is easy for an inexperienced observer to draw unwarranted conclusions because of normal variations in vibration. Vibrations depend upon fundamental frequency, intensity, and vocal register. For example, failure of glottic closure occurs normally in falsetto phonation. Consequently, it is important to note these characteristics and to examine each voice under a variety of conditions.

Other Techniques to Examine Vocal Fold Vibration

Other techniques to examine vocal fold vibration include ultrahigh-speed photography, EGG, photoelectroglottography and ultrasound glottography, and most recently videokymography[14] and high-speed video (digital or analog). Ultrahigh-speed photography provides images that are in true slow motion, rather than simulated. High-speed video offers similar advantages without most of the disadvantages of high-speed motion pictures. Videokymography offers high speed imaging of a single line along the vocal fold. EGG uses two electrodes placed on the skin of the neck above the thyroid laminae. It traces the opening and closing of the glottis and can be compared with stroboscopic images.[15] EGG allows objective determination of the presence or absence of glottal vibrations and easy determination of the fundamental period of vibration and is reproducible. It reflects the glottal condition more accurately during its closed phase. Photo- electroglottography and ultrasound glottography are less useful clinically.[16]

Measures of Phonatory Ability

Objective measures of phonatory ability are easy to use, readily available to the laryngologist, helpful in treatment of professional vocalists with specific voice disorders, and quite useful in assessing the results of surgical therapies. Maximum phonation time is measured with a stopwatch. The patient is instructed to sustain the vowel /ɑ/ for as long as possible after deep inspiration, vocalizing at a comfortable frequency and intensity. The frequency and intensity may be determined and controlled by an inexpensive frequency analyzer and sound level meter. The test is repeated three times, and the greatest value is recorded. Normal values have been determined.[16] Frequency range of phonation is recorded in semitones and documents the vocal range from the lowest note in the modal register (excluding vocal fry) to the highest falsetto note. This is the physiologic frequency range of phonation and disregards quality. The musical frequency range of phonation measures lowest to highest notes of musically acceptable quality. Tests for maximum phonation time, frequency ranges, and many of the other parameters discussed later (including spectrographic analysis) may be preserved on a tape recorder or digitized and stored for analysis at a convenient future time and used for pre- and post-treatment comparisons. Recordings should be made in a standardized, consistent fashion.

Frequency limits of vocal register also may be measured. The registers are (from low to high) vocal fry, chest, mid, head, and falsetto. However, classification of registers is controversial, and many other classifications are used. Although the classification listed above is common among musicians, at present, most voice scientists prefer to classify registers as pulse, modal, and loft. Overlap of frequency among registers occurs routinely.

Testing the speaking fundamental frequency often reveals excessively low pitch, an abnormality associated with chronic voice abuse and development of vocal nodules. This parameter may be followed objectively throughout a course of voice therapy. Intensity range of phonation (IRP) has proven a less useful measure than frequency range. It varies with fundamental frequency (which should be recorded) and is greatest in the middle frequency range. It is recorded in sound pressure level (SPL) re: 0.0002 microbar. For normal adults who are not professional vocalists, measuring at a single fundamental frequency, IRP averages 54.8 dB for males and 51 dB for females.[17] Alterations of intensity are common in voice disorders, although IRP is not the most sensitive test to detect them. Information from these tests may be combined in a fundamental frequency-intensity profile,[16] also called a phonetogram.

Glottal efficiency (ratio of the acoustic power at the level of the glottis to subglottal power) provides useful information but is not clinically practical because measuring acoustic power at the level of the glottis is difficult. Subglottic power is the product of subglottal pressure and airflow rate. These can be determined clinically. Various alternative measures of glottic efficiency have been proposed, including the ratio of radiated acoustic power to subglottal power,[18] airflow intensity profile,[19] and ratio of the root mean square value of the AC component to the mean volume velocity (DC component).[20] Although glottal efficiency is of great interest, none of these tests is used in routine clinical circumstances.

Aerodynamic Measures

Traditional pulmonary function testing provides the most readily accessible measure of respiratory function. The most common parameters measured include: (1) tidal volume, the volume of air that enters the lungs during inspiration and leaves during expiration in normal breathing; (2) functional residual capacity, the volume of air remaining in the lungs at the end of inspiration during normal breathing, which can be divided into expiratory reserve volume (maximal additional volume that can be exhaled) and residual volume (the volume of air remaining in the lungs at the end of maximal exhalation); (3) inspiratory capacity, the maximal volume of air that can be inhaled starting at the functional residual capacity; (4) total lung capacity, the volume of air in the lungs following maximal inspiration; (5) vital capacity, the maximal volume of air that can be exhaled from the lungs following maximal inspiration; (6) forced vital capacity, the rate of airflow with rapid, forceful expiration from total lung capacity to residual volume; (7) FEV1, the forced expiratory volume in 1 second; (8) FEV3, the forced expiratory volume in 3 seconds; (9) maximal mid-expiratory flow, the mean rate of airflow over the middle half of the forced vital capacity (between 25% and 75% of the forced vital capacity).

For singers and professional speakers with an abnormality caused by voice abuse, abnormal pulmonary function tests may confirm deficiencies in aerobic conditioning or reveal previously unrecognized asthma.[21] Flow glottography with computer inverse filtering is also a practical and valuable diagnostic for assessing flow at the vocal fold level, evaluating the voice source, and imaging the results of the balance between adductory forces and subglottal pressure.[22] It also has therapeutic value as a biofeedback tool. The spirometer, readily available for pulmonary function testing, can also be used for measuring airflow during phonation.Air volume is measured by the use of a mask fitted tightly over the face or by phonating into a mouthpiece while wearing a nose clamp. Measurements may be made using a spirometer, pneumotachograph, or hot-wire anemometer. The normal values for mean flow rate under habitual phonation, with changes in intensity or register, and under various pathologic circumstances were determined in the 1970s.[16] Normal values are available for both adults and children. Mean flow rate also can be measured and is a clinically useful parameter to follow during treatment for vocal nodules, recurrent laryngeal nerve paralysis, spasmodic dysphonia, and other conditions.

Glottal resistance cannot be measured directly, but it can be calculated from the mean flow rate and mean subglottal pressure. Normal glottal resistance is 20 to 100 dyne seconds/cm^5 at low and medium pitches and 150 dyne seconds/cm^5 at high pitches.[18] The normal values for subglottal pressure under various healthy and pathologic voice conditions have also been determined by numerous investigators.[16] The phonation quotient is the vital capacity divided by the maximum phonation time. It has been shown to correlate closely with maximum flow rate[23] and is a more convenient measure. Normative data determined by various authors have been published.[16] The phonation quotient provides an objective measure of the effects of treatment and is particularly useful in cases of recurrent laryngeal nerve paralysis and mass lesions of the vocal folds, including nodules.

Acoustic Analysis

Acoustic analysis equipment can determine frequency, intensity, harmonic spectrum, cycle to cycle perturbations in frequency (jitter), cycle-to -cycle perturbations in amplitude (shimmer), harmonics-to-noise ratios, breathiness index, and many other parameters. The DSP Sona-Graph Sound Analyzer Model 5500 (Kay Elemetrics, Lincoln Park, NJ) is an integrated voice analysis system. It is equipped for sound spectrography capabilities. Spectrography provides a visual record of the voice. The acoustic signal is depicted using time (x axis), frequency (y axis), and intensity (z axis), shading of light versus dark. Using the band pass filters, generalizations about quality, pitch, and loudness can be made. These observations are used in formulating the voice therapy treatment plan. Formant structure and strength can be determined using the narrow-band filters, of which a variety of configurations are possible. In clinical settings in which singers and other professional voice users are evaluated and treated routinely, this feature is extremely valuable. A sophisticated voice analysis program (an optional program) may be combined with the Sona-Graph and is an especially valuable addition to the clinical laboratory. The voice analysis program (Computer Speech Lab, Kay Elemetrics, Lincoln Park, NJ) measures speaking fundamental frequency, frequency perturbation (jitter), amplitude perturbation (shimmer), harmonics-to-noise ratio, and provides many other useful values. An electroglottograph may be used in conjunction with the Sona-Graph to provide some of these voicing parameters. Examining the EGG waveform alone is possible with this setup, but its clinical usefulness has not yet been established. An important feature of the Sona-Graph is the long-term average (LTA) spectral capability, which permits analysis of longer voice samples (30-90 seconds). The LTA analyzes only voiced speech segments, and may be useful in screening for hoarse or breathy voices. In addition, computer interface capabilities (also an optional program) have solved many data storage and file maintenance problems.

In analyzing acoustic signals, the microphone should be placed at the level of the mouth or positioned in or over the trachea, although intratracheal recordings are used for research purposes only. The position should be standardized in each office or laboratory.[24] Various techniques are being developed to improve the usefulness of acoustic analysis. Because of the enormous amount of information carried in the acoustic signal, further refinements in objective acoustic analysis should prove particularly valuable to the clinician.

Laryngeal Electromyography

Electromyography (EMG) requires an electrode system, an amplifier, an oscilloscope, a loudspeaker, and a recording system.[25] Electrodes are placed transcutaneously into laryngeal muscles. EMG can be extremely valuable in confirming cases of vocal fold paresis, differentiating paralysis from arytenoid dislocation, distinguishing recurrent laryngeal nerve paralysis from combined recurrent and superior nerve paralysis, diagnosing other more subtle neurolaryngological pathology, and documenting functional voice disorders and malingering. It is also recommended for needle localization when using botulinum toxin for treatment of spasmodic dysphonia and other conditions.

Psychoacoustic Evaluation

Because the human ear and brain are the most sensitive and complex analyzers of sound currently available, many researchers have tried to standardize and quantify psychoacoustic evaluation. Unfortunately, even definitions of basic terms such as hoarseness and breathiness are still controversial. Psychoacoustic evaluation protocols and interpretations are not standardized. Consequently, although subjective psychoacoustic analysis of voice is of great value to individual skilled clinicians, it remains generally unsatisfactory for comparing research among laboratories or for reporting clinical results.

The GRBAS scale[6] helps standardize perceptual analysis for clinical purposes. It rates the voice on a scale from 0 to 3, with regard to grade, roughness, asthenia, breathiness, and strain. Grade 0 is normal; 1 is slightly abnormal; 2 is moderately abnormal; and 3 is extremely abnormal. Grade refers to the degree of hoarseness or voice abnormality. Roughness refers to the acoustic/auditory impression of irregularity of vibration and corresponds with gear and shimmer. Asthenic evaluation assesses weakness or lack of power and corresponds to vocal intensity and energy in higher harmonics. Breathiness refers to the acoustic/auditory impression of air leakage and corresponds to turbulence. Strain refers to the acoustic/auditory impression of hyperfunction and may be related to fundamental frequency, noise in the high-frequency range, and energy in higher harmonics. For example, a patient's voice might be graded as G2, R2, B1, A1, S2.

Outcome Assessment

Measuring the impact of a voice disorder has always been challenging. However, recent advances have begun to address this problem. Validated instruments such as the Voice Handicap Index (VHI)[26] are currently in clinical use, and are likely to be utilized widely in future years. Chapter 8 reviews current trends and future directions in measuring voice treatment outcomes.

Voice Impairment and Disability

Quantifying voice impairment and assigning a disability rating (percentage of whole person) remain controversial. This subject is still not addressed comprehensively even in the most recent editions (2001, 5th ed) of the American Medical Association's *Guides to the Evaluation of Permanent Impairment* (The Guides).The Guides still do not take into account the person's profession when calculating disability. Alternative approaches have been proposed,[27] and advances in this complex arena are anticipated over the next few years. This subject is discussed in greater detail in chapter 15.

Evaluation of the Singing Voice

The physician must be careful not to exceed the limits of his or her expertise especially in caring for singers. However, if voice abuse or technical error is suspected, or if a difficult judgment must be reached on whether to allow a sick singer to perform, a brief observation of the patient's singing may provide invaluable information. This is accomplished best by asking the singer to stand and sing scales either in the examining room or in the soundproof audiology booth. Similar maneuvers may be used for professional speakers, including actors (who can vocalize and recite lines), clergy and politicians (who can deliver sermons and speeches), and virtually all other voice patients. The singer's stance should be balanced, with the weight slightly forward. The knees should be bent slightly and the shoulders, torso, and neck should be relaxed. The singer should inhale through the nose whenever possible allowing filtration, warming, and humidification of inspired air. In general, the chest should be expanded, but most of the active breathing is abdominal. The chest should not rise substantially with each inspiration, and the supraclavicular musculature should not be involved obviously in inspiration. Shoulders and neck muscles should not be tensed even with deep inspiration. Abdominal musculature should be contracted shortly before the initiation of the tone. This may be evaluated visually or by palpation (Fig 3–2). Muscles of the neck and face should be

Fig 3–2. Bimanual palpation of the support mechanism. The singer should expand posteriorly and anteriorly with inspiration. Muscles should tighten prior to onset of the sung tone.

relaxed. Economy is a basic principle of all art forms. Wasted energy and motion and muscle tension are incorrect and usually deleterious.

The singer should be instructed to sing a scale (a five-note scale is usually sufficient) on the vowel /ɑ/, beginning on any comfortable note. Technical errors are usually most obvious as contraction of muscles in the neck and chin, retraction of the lower lip, retraction of the tongue, or tightening of the muscles of mastication. The singer's mouth should be open widely but comfortably. When singing /ɑ/, the singer's tongue should rest in a neutral position with the tip of the tongue lying against the back of the singer's mandibular incisors. If the tongue pulls back or demonstrates obvious muscular activity as the singer performs the scales, improper voice use can be confirmed on the basis of positive evidence (Fig 3–3). The position of the larynx should not vary substantially with pitch changes. Rising of the larynx with ascending pitch is evidence of technical dysfunction. This examination also gives the physician an opportunity to observe any dramatic differences between the qualities and ranges of the patient's speaking voice and the singing voice. A physical examination summary form has proven helpful in organization and documentation[3] (Appendix IIB).

Remembering the admonition not to exceed his or her expertise, the physician who examines many singers often can glean valuable information from a brief attempt to modify an obvious technical error. For example, deciding whether to allow a singer with mild or moderate laryngitis to perform is often difficult. On

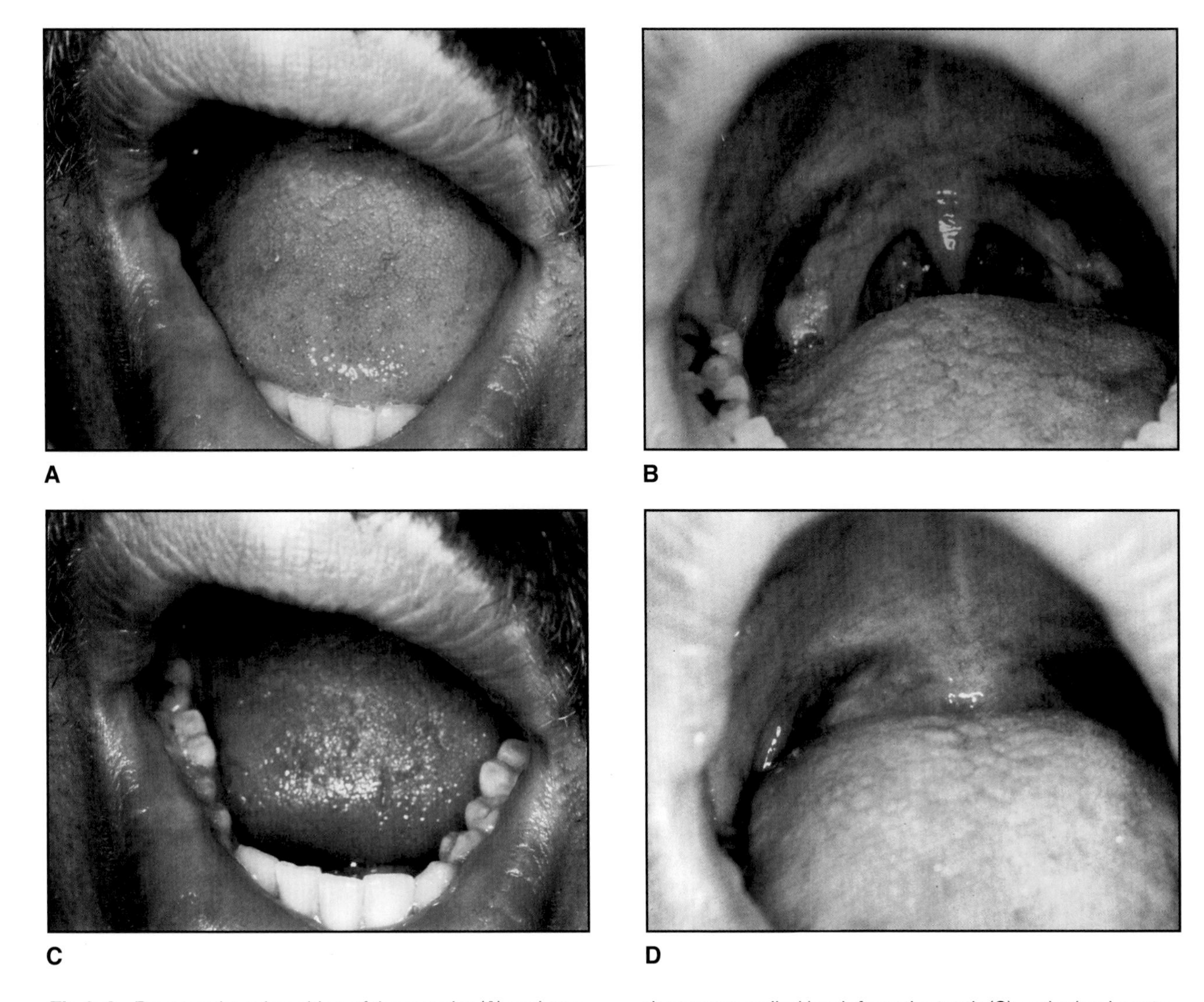

Fig 3–3. Proper relaxed position of the anterior (**A**) and posterior (**B**) portions of the tongue. Common improper use of the tongue pulled back from the teeth (**C**) and raised posteriorly (**D**).

the one hand, an expert singer has technical skills that allow him or her to compensate safely. On the other hand, if a singer does not sing with correct technique and does not have the discipline to modify volume, technique, and repertoire as necessary, the risk of vocal injury may be increased substantially even by mild inflammation of the vocal folds. In borderline circumstances, observation of the singer's technique may greatly help the physician in making a judgment.

If the singer's technique appears flawless, the physician may feel somewhat more secure in allowing the singer to proceed with performance commitments. More commonly, even good singers demonstrate technical errors when experiencing voice difficulties. In a vain effort to compensate for dysfunction at the vocal fold level, singers often modify their technique in the neck and supraglottic vocal tract. In the good singer, this usually means going from good technique to bad technique. The most common error involves pulling back the tongue and tightening the cervical muscles. Although this increased muscular activity gives the singer the illusion of making the voice more secure, this technical maladjustment undermines vocal efficiency and increases vocal strain. The physician may ask the singer to hold the top note of a five-note scale; while the note is being held, the singer may simply be told, "Relax your tongue." At the same time the physician points to the singer's abdominal musculature. Most good singers immediately correct to good technique. If they do, and if upcoming performances are particularly important, the singer may be able to perform with a reminder that meticulous technique is essential. The singer should be advised to "sing by feel rather than by ear," to consult his or her voice teacher, and conserve the voice except when it is absolutely necessary to use it. If a singer is unable to correct from bad technique to good technique promptly, especially if he or she uses excessive muscle tension in the neck and ineffective abdominal support, it is generally safer not to perform with even a mild vocal fold abnormality. With increased experience and training, the laryngologist may make other observations that aid in providing appropriate treatment recommendations for singer patients. Once these skills have been mastered for the care of singers, applying them to other patients is relatively easy, so long as the laryngologist takes the time to understand the demands of the individual's professional, avocational, and recreational vocal activities.

If treatment is to be instituted, making at least a tape recording of the voice is advisable in most cases and essential before any surgical intervention. The author routinely uses strobovideolaryngoscopy for diagnosis and documentation in virtually all cases as well as many of the objective measures discussed. Pretreatment testing is extremely helpful clinically and medicolegally.

Additional Examinations

A general physical examination should be performed whenever the patient's systemic health is questionable. Debilitating conditions such as mononucleosis may be noticed first by the singer as vocal fatigue. A neurologic assessment may be particularly revealing. The physician must be careful not to overlook dysarthrias and dysphonias, which are characteristic of movement disorders and of serious neurologic disease. Dysarthria is a defect in rhythm, enunciation, and articulation that usually results from neuromuscular impairment or weakness such as may occur after a stroke. It may be seen with oral deformities or illness, as well. Dysphonia is an abnormality of vocalization usually caused by problems at the laryngeal level.

Physicians should be familiar with the six types of dysarthria, their symptoms, and their importance.[28,29] Flaccid dysarthria occurs in lower motor neuron or primary muscle disorders such as myasthenia gravis and tumors or strokes involving the brainstem nuclei. Spastic dysarthria occurs in upper motor neuron disorders (pseudobulbar palsy) such as multiple strokes and cerebral palsy. Ataxic dysarthria is seen with cerebellar disease, alcohol intoxication, and multiple sclerosis. Hypokinetic dysarthria accompanies Parkinson's disease. Hyperkinetic dysarthria may be spasmodic, as in Gilles de la Tourette's disease, or dystonic, as in chorea and cerebral palsy. Mixed dysarthria occurs in amyotrophic lateral sclerosis (ALS) or Lou Gehrig's disease. The preceding classification actually combines dysphonic and dysarthric characteristics but is very useful clinically. The value of a comprehensive neurolaryngologic evaluation[30] cannot be overstated. More specific details of voice changes associated with neurologic dysfunction and their localizing value are available in chapter 11.[2,32]

It is extremely valuable for the laryngologist to assemble an arts-medicine team that includes not only a speech-language pathologist, singing voice specialist, acting voice specialist, and voice scientist, but also medical colleagues in other disciplines. Collaboration with an expert neurologist, pulmonologist, endocrinologist, psychologist, psychiatrist, internist, physiatrist, and others with special knowledge of, and interest in, voice disorders is invaluable in caring for patients with voice disorders. Such interdisciplinary teams have not only changed the standard of care in voice evaluation and treatment, but are also largely responsible for the rapid and productive growth of voice as a subspecialty.

References

1. Sataloff RT. Professional singers: the science and art of clinical care. *Am J Otolaryngol*. 1981;2:251–266.
2. Rubin JS, Sataloff RT, Korovin GS. *Diagnosis and Treatment of Voice Disorders*. 2nd ed. Clifton Park, NY: Delmar Thomson Learning; 2003:137–284.
3. Sataloff RT. The professional voice: part II, physical examination. *J Voice*. 1987;1:91–201.
4. Fuazawa T, Blaugrund SM, El-Assuooty A, Gould WJ. Acoustic analysis of hoarse voice: a preliminary report. *J Voice*. 1988;2(2):127–131.
5. Gelfer M. Perceptual attributes of voice: development and use of rating scales. *J Voice*. 1988;2(4):320–326.
6. Hirano M. *Clinical Examination of the Voice*. New York, NY: Springer-Verlag; 1981:83–84.
7. Fujimura O. Stereo-fiberoptic laryngeal observation. *J Acoust Soc Am*. 1979;65:70–72.
8. Sataloff RT, Spiegel JR, Carroll LM, Darby KS, Hawkshaw MJ, Rulnick RK. The clinical voice laboratory: practical design and clinical application. *J Voice*. 1990;4: 264–279.
9. Sataloff RT, Heuer RH, Hoover C, Baroody MM. Laboratory assessment of voice. In: Gould WJ, Sataloff RT, Spiegel JR. *Voice Surgery*. St. Louis, Mo: Mosby; 1993: 203–216.
10. Sataloff RT, Spiegel JR, Carroll LM, Schiebel BR, Darby KS, Rulnick RK. (1988) Strobovideolaryngoscopy in professional voice users: results and clinical value. *J Voice*. 1986;1:359–364.
11. Sataloff RT, Spiegel JR, Hawkshaw MJ. Strobovideolaryngoscopy: results and clinical value. *Ann Otol Rhinol Laryngol*. 1991;100:725–727.
12. Bless D, Hirano M, Feder RJ. Video stroboscopic evaluation of the larynx. *Ear Nose Throat J*. 1987;66:289–296.
13. Hirano M. Phonosurgery: basic and clinical investigations. *Otologia* (Fukuoka). 1975;21:239–442.
14. Svec J, Shutte H. Videokymography: high-speed line scanning of vocal fold vibration. *J Voice*. 1996;10:201–205.
15. Leclure FLE, Brocaar ME, Verscheeure J. Electroglottography and its relation to glottal activity. *Folia Phoniatr* (Basel). 1975;27:215–224.
16. Hirano M. *Clinical Examination of the Voice*. New York: Springer-Verlag; 1981:25–27, 85–98.
17. Coleman RJ, Mabis JH, Hinson JK. Fundamental frequency sound pressure level profiles of adult male and female voices. *J Speech Hear Res*. 1977;20:197–204.
18. Isshiki N. Regulatory mechanism of voice intensity variation. *J Speech Hear Res*. 1964;7:17–29.
19. Saito S. Phonosurgery: basic study on the mechanisms of phonation and endolaryngeal microsurgery. *Otologia* (Fukuoka). 1977;23:171–384.
20. Isshiki N. Functional surgery of the larynx. In: *Report of the 78th Annual Convention of the Oto-Rhino-Laryngological Society of Japan*. Fukuoka: Kyoto University; 1977.
21. Cohn JR, Sataloff RT, Spiegel JR, Fish JE, Kennedy K. Airway reactivity-induced asthma in singers (ARIAS). *J Voice*. 1991;5:332–337.
22. Sundberg J. *The Science of the Singing Voice*. Dekalb, Ill: Northern Illinois University Press; 1987:11, 66, 77–89.
23. Hirano M, Koike Y, von Leden H. Maximum phonation time and air usage during phonation. *Folia Phoniatr* (Basel). 1968;20:185–201.
24. Price DB, Sataloff RT. A simple technique for consistent microphone placement in voice recording. *J Voice*. 1988; 2:206–207.
25. Sataloff RT, Mandel S, Mañon-Espaillat R, et al. *Laryngeal Electromyography*. Clifton Park, NY: Delmar Thomson Learning; 2003:1–128.
26. Benninger MS, Gardner GM, Jacobson BH, Grywalski C. New dimensions in measuring voice treatment outcomes. In: Sataloff RT. *Professional Voice: The Science and Art of Clinical Care*. 2nd ed. San Diego, Calif: Singular Publishing Group, Inc; 1997:789–794.
27. Sataloff RT. Voice and speech impairment and disability. In: Sataloff RT. *Professional Voice: The Science and Art of Clinical Care*. 2nd ed. San Diego, Calif: Singular Publishing Group, Inc; 1997:795–801.
28. Darley FL, Aronson AE, Brown JR. Differential diagnostic of patterns of dysarthria. *J Speech Hear Res*. 1969;12(2): 246–249.
29. Darley FL, Aronson AE, Brown JR. Clusters of deviant speech dimensions in the dysarthrias. *J Speech Hear Res*. 1969;12(3):462–496.
30. Rosenfield DB. Neurolaryngology. *Ear Nose Throat J*. 1987;66:323–326.
31. Raphael BN, Sataloff RT. Increasing vocal effectiveness. In: Sataloff RT. *Professional Voice: Science and Art of Clinical Care*. 2nd ed. San Diego, Calif: Singular Publishing Group, Inc; 1997;721–730.

4

The Clinical Voice Laboratory

Reinhardt J. Heuer, Mary J. Hawkshaw, and Robert Thayer Sataloff

A battery of tests that allows reliable, valid, objective assessment of subtle changes in voice function, a "meter of the voice," is needed. Because convenient instrumentation is still being developed, appropriate equipment is not yet in routine use by many otolaryngologists. Nevertheless, a rapidly increasing number of institutions and private offices are developing clinical voice laboratories. Such sophistication is necessary not only to treat professional voice users, but also in nonprofessional voice patients to assess the results of laryngeal surgery, treatments for spasmodic dysphonia and other conditions, and to help diagnose the many systemic diseases associated with voice change. The otolaryngologic community has recognized in the past several years that reporting that a patient's "voice is better" without objective measures is as unsatisfactory as reporting that a patient's "hearing is better" without an audiogram. Nevertheless, the otolaryngologists who wish to establish a state-of-the-art voice laboratory are hard pressed to know how to start.

Our clinical voice laboratory includes an ever-changing list of instrumentation, but it has been in constant use and evolution for more than two decades. Colleagues frequently request a written description of our system of patient care, as well as a list of the instrumentation we use. This chapter is written to fill that request; however, it is presented with important reservations, which the reader is urged to bear in mind. First, we have not solved the problem of developing an ideal voice laboratory. We are involved constantly in experimentation to assess the validity and reliability of the equipment we use and to explore new and better ways to accomplish desired tasks. Consequently, by the time this book is printed, certain details will undoubtedly be obsolete. Second, this chapter should not be misconstrued as a commercial endorsement for any specific manufacturer. In some cases, at the time of writing, certain companies produce equipment that is clearly superior to their competitors'. However, in this rapidly changing area of technology, competing companies are likely to produce even better equipment soon. The reader is encouraged to investigate the latest developments before purchasing equipment. In addition, some of the equipment we use is selected on the basis of personal preference, rather than unequivocal advantage. In our hands, the equipment described works well. In many cases, we have supplied manufacturers' names and model numbers for the convenience of colleagues trying to generate an equipment list as a starting point toward the development of a voice laboratory.

Purposes of a Clinical Voice Laboratory

During the past 25 years, there have been substantial improvements in medical care of voice patients. Nevertheless, this new subspecialty is in a period of rapid evolution, and much remains to be learned. Although voice laboratories can be designed exclusively for clinical diagnosis, or exclusively for basic research, we believe that a good clinical voice laboratory serves both functions. At present, some laboratory procedures clearly provide invaluable diagnostic information that cannot be obtained easily in any other way (eg, strobovideolaryngoscopy and pulmonary function testing). Other measures are somewhat helpful diagnostically and are particularly useful for following and documenting the results of the treatment (eg, laryngeal airflow and some acoustic analyses). The value of some other tests remains to be determined. In structuring our clinical voice laboratory and protocols, we have attempted not only to optimize patient diagnosis and treatment, but also to gather research data that will allow development of better technology and even more sophisticated patient care in the future.

As valuable as they are, voice laboratories are still somewhat cumbersome. We undoubtedly gather more information than we need. However, in this way, we hope to be able to determine which information is most valuable, reliable, and clinically important. For example, ongoing intrasubject variability studies are in progress for several measures while the value of others has been established. Still other measures have been found not useful and deleted from our protocol. Eventually, this combination of clinical and research analysis should lead to the development of a simple, less time-consuming, less expensive clinical voice laboratory that will be as valuable to the general otolaryngologist as an audiometer. Progress has been made in this regard since the first and second editions of this book were published, as discussed below.

Examination Sequence

Ideally, the clinical voice laboratory team should include a laryngologist, speech-language pathologist, singing voice specialist, acting-voice specialist, psychologist, nurse, and voice scientist. Daily clinical use of the voice laboratory is understood best when viewed in the context of total voice-patient management. When a patient with a voice complaint enters our office, the patient is asked to complete a specialized history questionnaire. If the patient is not seen emergently, the questionnaire has been mailed to the patient and completed in advance of the visit. Separate questionnaires are used for singers and nonsingers (Appendixes IA and IB). In most cases, the patient proceeds from the waiting room to the physician's examination room or has a history taken by a nurse or assistant and is then brought to the laryngologist. We have tried other systems, such as having the patient examined first by another member of the voice care team, but alternate approaches have not been as satisfactory in our hands.

The laryngologist reviews the questionnaire, supplements it with a complete history often started by the nurse-clinician or physician assistant, and performs a physical examination, as described in previous publications[1] and in chapter 3. At this point, the larynx is visualized with a mirror using continuous light. Generally, this is done using a head mirror or Keeler video headlight. This device provides excellent light and visualization, even though the light source is centered over the bridge of the nose rather than being concentric with the line of sight. The video headlight permits easy, excellent video documentation of nasal and oral findings, mouth and tongue movement during speech and singing, and a fair indirect laryngeal image. It is also extremely valuable as a teaching aid for patients, residents, and visitors. Two monitors are used, one behind the patient and one behind the physician. These monitors allow the patient and other observers to see clearly whatever the examining laryngologist sees. Showing intranasal, oral, and hypopharyngeal lesions to patients in this manner facilitates explanations of the physician's findings and is especially helpful when abnormalities requiring surgery are encountered. In addition, clinical findings can be easily transferred to the chart through use of a video printer.

The physician also performs a limited evaluation of the speaking voice and singing voice, which is documented on a laryngeal examination form[1] (Appendix IIb). When indicated, strobovideolaryngoscopy is performed next. If the patient requires topical anesthetic, it is applied usually in the physician's examination room. This determination is made during laryngeal mirror examination. The patient is then escorted to the special procedures room by a nurse, assistant, speech-language pathologist, or singing voice specialist and is prepared for examination. After being brought into the room, the patient is seated comfortably, and the electroglottography (EGG) leads and laryngeal microphone are positioned. Proper function of all cameras (larynx, face, EGG) and other equipment is confirmed. During this brief interval, the team member with the voice patient explains the procedure again, allays any patient concerns or fears, and has an opportunity to observe behavior or gather information that may not have been volunteered in the physician's presence. The laryngologist then proceeds to the stroboscopy room and performs the strobovideolaryngoscopy with at least one other member of the team present. Ideally, the speech-language pathologist and singing voice specialist who will be involved in the patient's treatment are both present. We have found it helpful to use a small room for strobovideolaryngoscopy. A room 10′ × 8′ is more than sufficient (Fig 4–1). This small size allows the physician and assistant (usually the nurse clinician) to maintain contact with the patient and still have easy access to all equipment during the procedure. Although larger rooms are more elegant, we found a small room much easier to work in. In addition, the room must be quiet enough so that no extraneous noises are picked up by the recording microphone.

Following strobovideolaryngoscopy, the physician provides the voice team with his preliminary impres-

Fig 4–1. A. Special procedures room containing a stroboscope and monitor (a), examination chair (b), specially modified microscope (c), camera for facial photography (d), endoscopic camera (e), and cabinet housing electronic equipment (f). This setup has been replaced and simplified with a Kay Elemetrics system, as discussed later in this chapter. The older arrangement is included for the benefit of colleagues who still use noncomputerized stroboscopy systems. *(continued)*

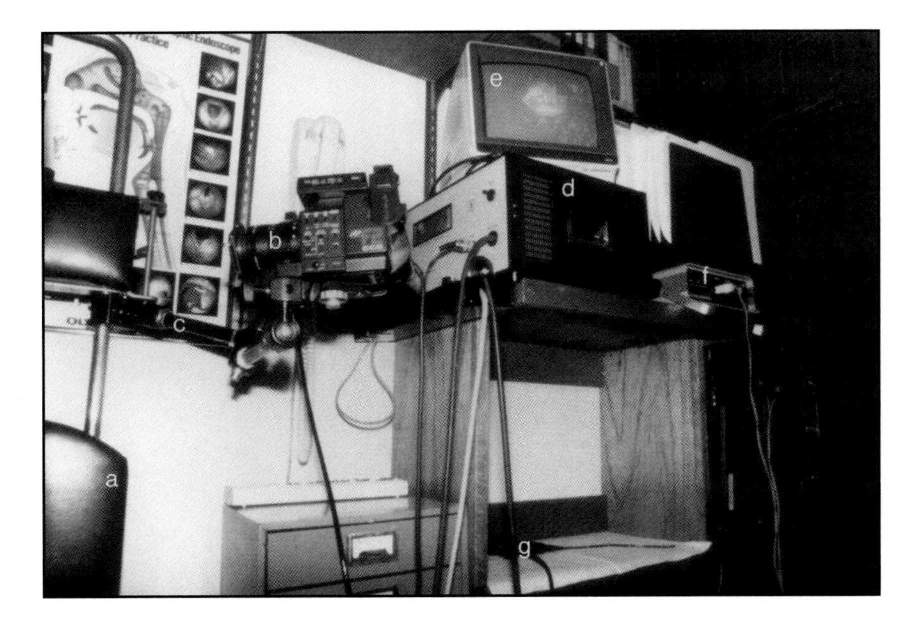

Fig 4–1. (*(continued)* **B.** Closer view of the examining area showing a portion of the examination chair (a), the camera for endoscopy (b), suspended on a magic arm (c), a Bruel & Kjäer stroboscope (d), the monitor viewed by the physician (e), the laryngograph (f), and an Olympus ENFL-3 flexible fiberoptic laryngoscope (g). In our current system, all of this equipment has been replaced with technologically superior instrumentation including a much smaller camera. However, if cost is a factor, good images can still be obtained with older style equipment. *(continued)*

Fig 4–1. *(continued)* **C.** Contents of the electronic storage cabinet facing the examining chair as pictured in Fig 4–1A. This figure shows the overall layout for orientation. Equipment is a specified in Figs 4–1D and E. *(continued)*

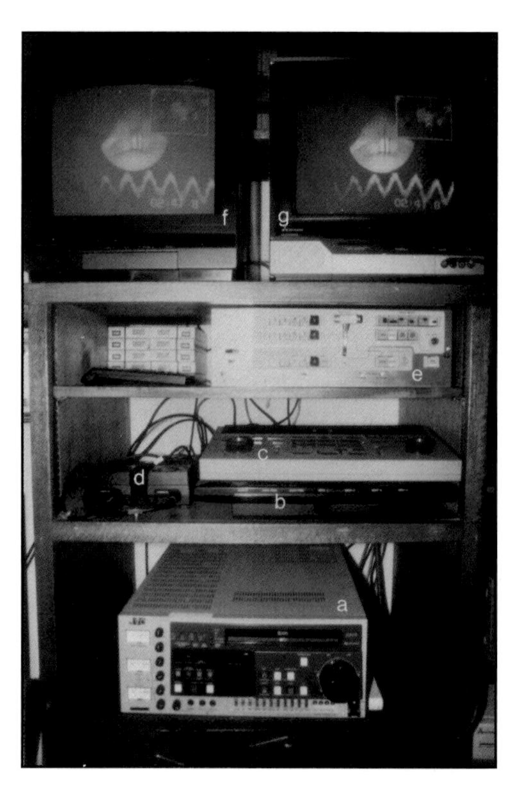

Fig 4–1. *(continued)* **D.** Equipment directly opposite the examining chair and within easy reach of the endoscopist includes a super VHS recorder (a), multivision (b), editor/controller that links the super VHS recorder with copying decks (c), power sources for cameras (d), special effects generator (e), monitor for the super VHS master deck (f), and monitor for the output of the editing deck (g). These monitors face the patient and may be switched off without disturbing the rest of the system. *(continued)*

Fig 4–1 *(continued)* **E.** The right section of the electronic equipment cabinet contains the primary copy deck in the editing system, which is linked to the master tape recorder through the controller (a), a second VHS recorder so that the two copies can be made simultaneously (b), a 3/4-inch video for copying (lower shelf, not shown), a black and white video printer (f), a character generator (g), two video switchers for multiple camera inputs (h), a hand-held video camera (i), and an oscilloscope (j), a Genlock camera to record the oscilloscope display of the electroglottograph (EGG) (k), the wall-mounted camera for facial video (l), and a laryngeal model used for patient education (m). In our current arrangement, the editing system has been moved to a separate room.

sions and assures the other members that it is medically safe to proceed with the rest of the examination (some of which is vocally stressful). In selected instances, it is also helpful to present these preliminary impressions to the patient while reviewing the strobovideolaryngoscopy tape. When the physician's examination has been completed, the evaluation is continued by the speech-language pathologist, voice technologist, or singing voice specialist.

The next step is object voice analysis. This is performed in a separate room that should be at least 10′ × 10′ in size. When possible, a larger room is preferable (Fig 4–2). The room should be very quiet or should incorporate a soundproof booth. The voice laboratory

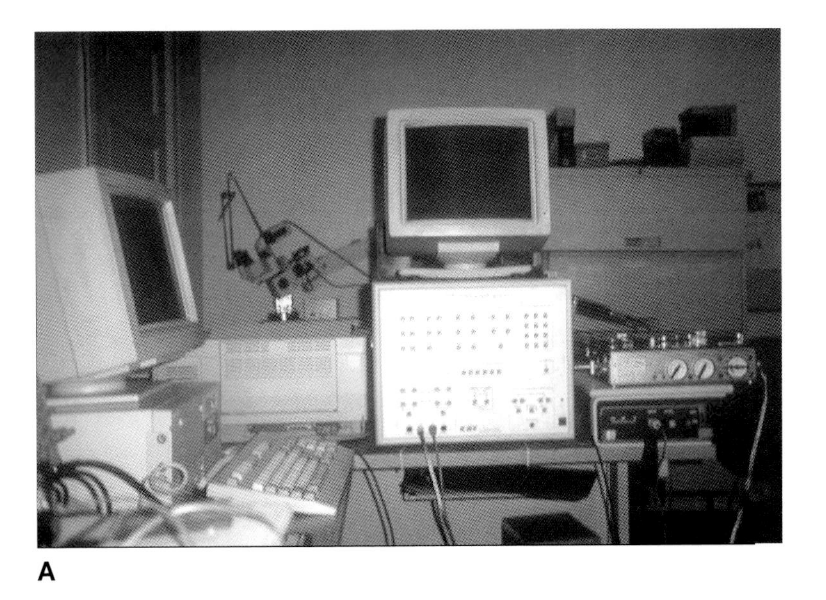

A

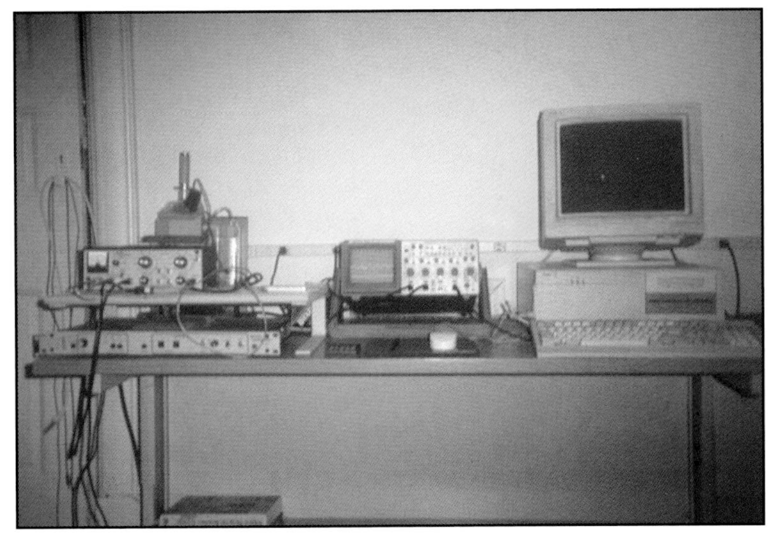

B

Fig 4–2. A. The voice laboratory at the time of the second edition of this book contained a DSP 5500 Sona-Graph™ (*center*), Nagra tape recorder (*right above*), EGG (*right below*), and Pentium chip computer (*left*) with CSL 50, database software, and printer. **B.** The computer at the right above is the same computer seen at the left in Fig 4–2A. The additional equipment on this workstation at 90 degrees to the Sona-Graph workstation pictured above includes a digital storage oscilloscope (*center*) and an inverse filter and flow glottography equipment (*left*) for use with a Rothenberg mask. *(continued)*

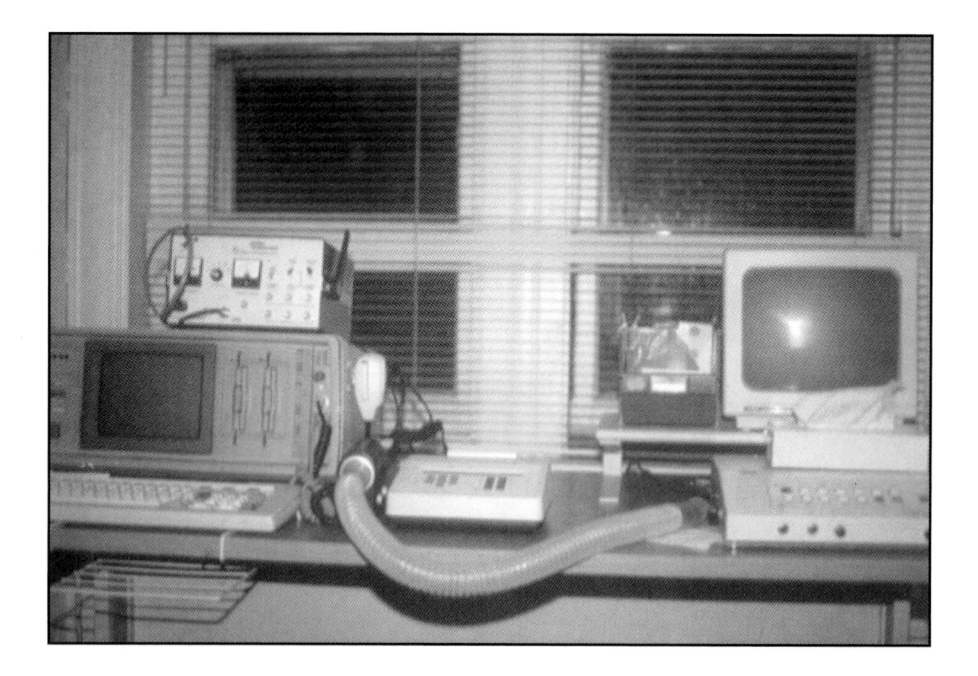

Fig 4–2 *(continued)* **C.** In the same room are (*far to the right*) a Kay 6087 PC Visi-Pitch™, Rothenberg EGG (*above left*), Tamarac pulmonary function machine, and PM 100 Pitch Analyzer. Some of this equipment is still in use; and this arrangement proved satisfactory for several years. However, changes were made to improve the system as recently as 2001, as reviewed elsewhere in this chapter.

includes equipment for measures of respiratory function, phonatory function, and acoustic analysis. It is essential that this be separate from the strobovideolaryngoscopy room, speech-language pathology treatment rooms (Fig. 4–3), and singing and acting voice studios (Fig. 4–4). Otherwise, it will interrupt patient flow and interfere with efficient treatment. Noise from other patients working with speech and singing specialists will also interfere frequently with laboratory recordings or audiological testing unless a proper layout is used. Following objective voice analysis, the patient undergoes a 1-hour evaluation by the speech-language pathologist, and a 1-hour evaluation by the singing voice specialist. In some cases, 1-hour evaluations by the acting voice trainer and/or psychologist and a psychiatrist are also included. Laryngeal EMG is commonly needed, as well. The findings of the voice team are documented in several reports. There is a separate report for strobovideolaryngoscopy. Other objective voice analysis is organized in a clinical voice laboratory report. Sample documents are included in Appendix III. At the conclusion of the examination, the team members share their findings and prepare comprehensive reports. The laryngologist provides the patient with a comprehensive letter and specific treatment plan. A summary report is sent to the referring physician or other voice specialist (speech-language pathologist, voice teacher), including copies of all internal reports and a videotape of the strobovideolaryngoscopy.

Objective Voice Measures

Measures of vocal function may be divided into six categories: (a) Assessment of vibratory function gives us information about the leading edge of the vocal fold. (b) Aerodynamic measures reveal the ability of the lungs and abdomen to provide power to the voice, and the ability of the glottis to release air efficiently. (c) Measures of phonatory function quantify the limits of vocal frequency, intensity, and duration. (d) Acoustic analysis detects and documents numerous subtleties in the vocal signal. (e) Laryngeal electromyography may confirm the presence or absence of appropriate neuromuscular function. (f) Psychoacoustic evaluation is difficult to quantify. However, the human ear and brain are still the best equipment we have available; and we have attempted to increase the validity of our team's psychoacoustic assessments so that perceptual evaluation can become more consistent and useful.

Assessment of Vibration

Integrity of the vibratory margin of the vocal fold is essential for the complex motion required to produce

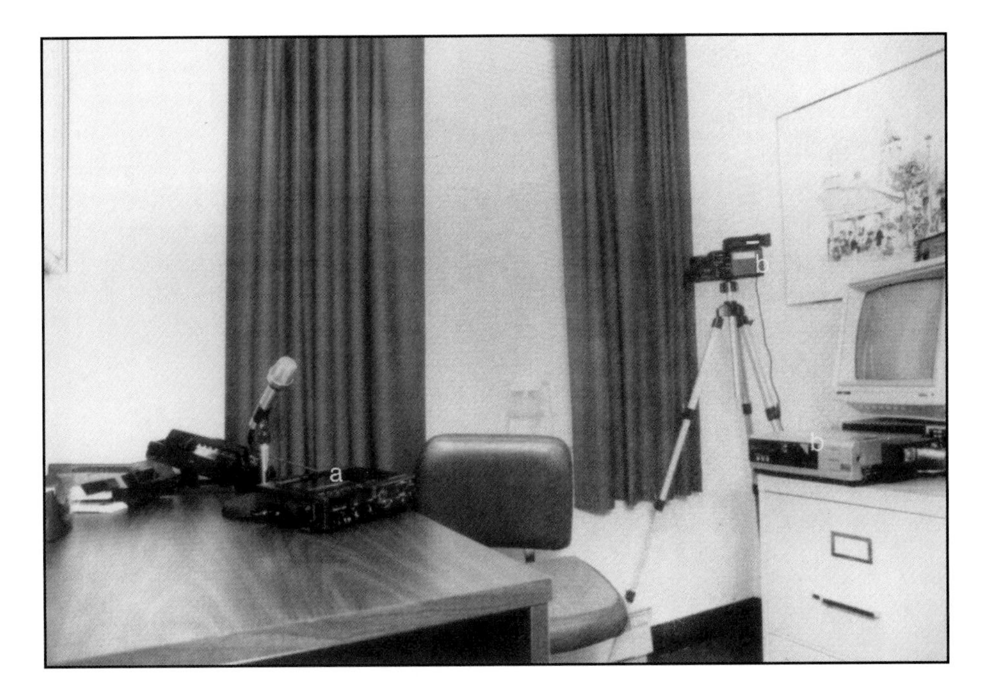

Fig 4–3. The speech-language pathology office is equipped with both audio (a) and video (b) equipment.

good vocal quality. Under continuous light, the vocal folds vibrate approximately 250 times per second while phonating at middle C. Naturally, the human eye cannot discern necessary details during such rapid motion. Assessment of the vibratory margin may be performed through high-speed photography, strobovideolaryngoscopy, electroglottography, photoglottography, videokymography, or high-speed video. Strobovideolaryngoscopy provides the necessary clinical information in the most practical fashion, but a combination of techniques should be used.

Strobovideolaryngoscopy

Strobovideolaryngoscopy is the single most important technological advance in diagnostic laryngology with the possible exception of the flexible fiberoptic laryngoscope. Stroboscopic light allows routine, slow motion evaluation of the mucosal cover layer of the leading edge of the vocal fold. Vocal fold vibration is complex (Fig 4–5). This improved physical examination permits detection of vibratory asymmetries, structural abnormalities, small masses, submucosal scars, and other conditions that are invisible under ordinary light.[2,3] For example, in a patient with a poor voice following laryngeal surgery and a "normal-looking larynx," stroboscopic light reveals adynamic segments that explain the problem even to a untrained observer (such as the patient). In addition, it also permits differentiation between cysts and nodules, allowing better treatment planning and prognostic predictions. Stroboscopy does not provide a true slow motion image, as obtained through high-speed photography (Fig 4–6) or high-speed video. The stroboscope actually illuminates different points on consecutive vocal folds waves, each of which is retained on the retina for 0.2 sec. The stroboscopically lighted portions of the successive waves are fused visually. The slow motion effect is created by having the stroboscopic light desynchronized with the frequency of vocal fold vibration by approximately 2 Hz. When vocal fold vibration and the stroboscope are synchronized exactly, the vocal folds appear to stand still, rather than moving in slow motion (Fig 4–7). In most instances, this approximation of slow motion provides all the clinical information necessary; but in some patients, videokymography or high-speed video may be needed.

The stroboscope is also extremely sensitive in detecting changes caused by fixation from small laryngeal neoplasms in patients who are being followed for leukoplakia or following laryngeal irradiation. Coupling stroboscopic light with the video camera allows later re-evaluation by the laryngologist, or by other physicians. A relatively standardized method of subjective assessment of videostroboscopic pictures is in wide clinical use,[4-6] allowing comparison of results among various physicians and investigators. Charac-

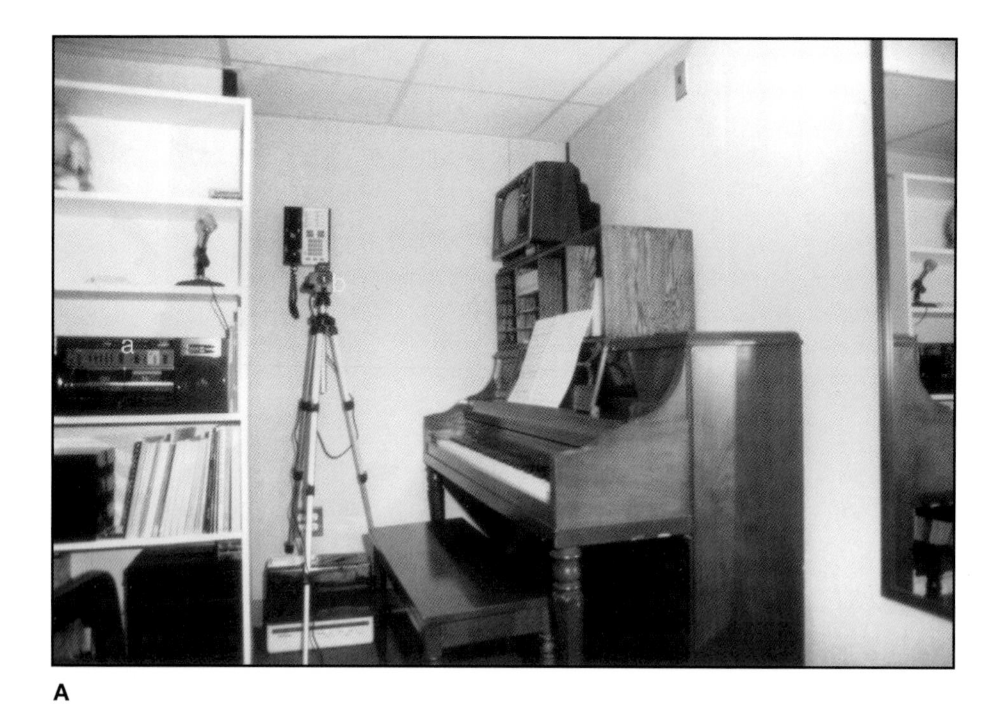

A

B

Fig 4–4. A. The voice studio should also be equipped with audio (a) and video equipment (b), in addition to a piano. The audio and video equipment need not be fancy or expensive, but they should be utilized. **B.** The room used by the acting-voice trainer should be large enough to permit the patient to move about, to lie on the floor comfortably, and to accomplish the kinds of exercises utilized in acting voice training. It is also advisable to have a piano in the room so that acting and singing training can be combined easily when appropriate for a patient/performer's needs. It is helpful for this room to be equipped with audio and video recording devices.

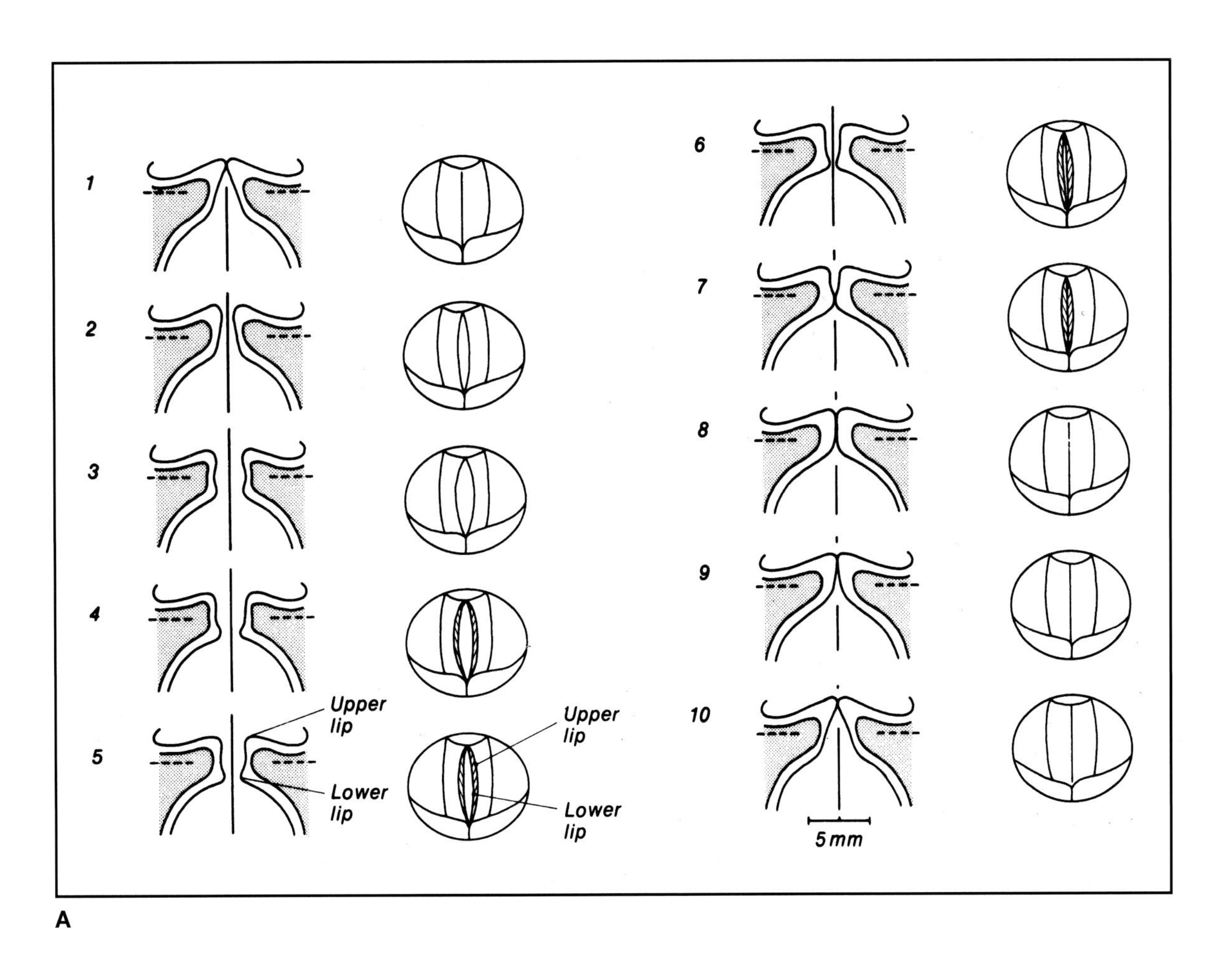

Fig 4–5. A. Frontal view (*left*) and view from above (*right*) illustrating the normal pattern of vocal vibration. The vocal fold closes and opens from the inferior aspect of the vibratory margin upward. (From Hirano M. *Clinical Examination of the Voice*. New York, NY: Springer-Verlag; 1981;44, with permission.) *(continued)*

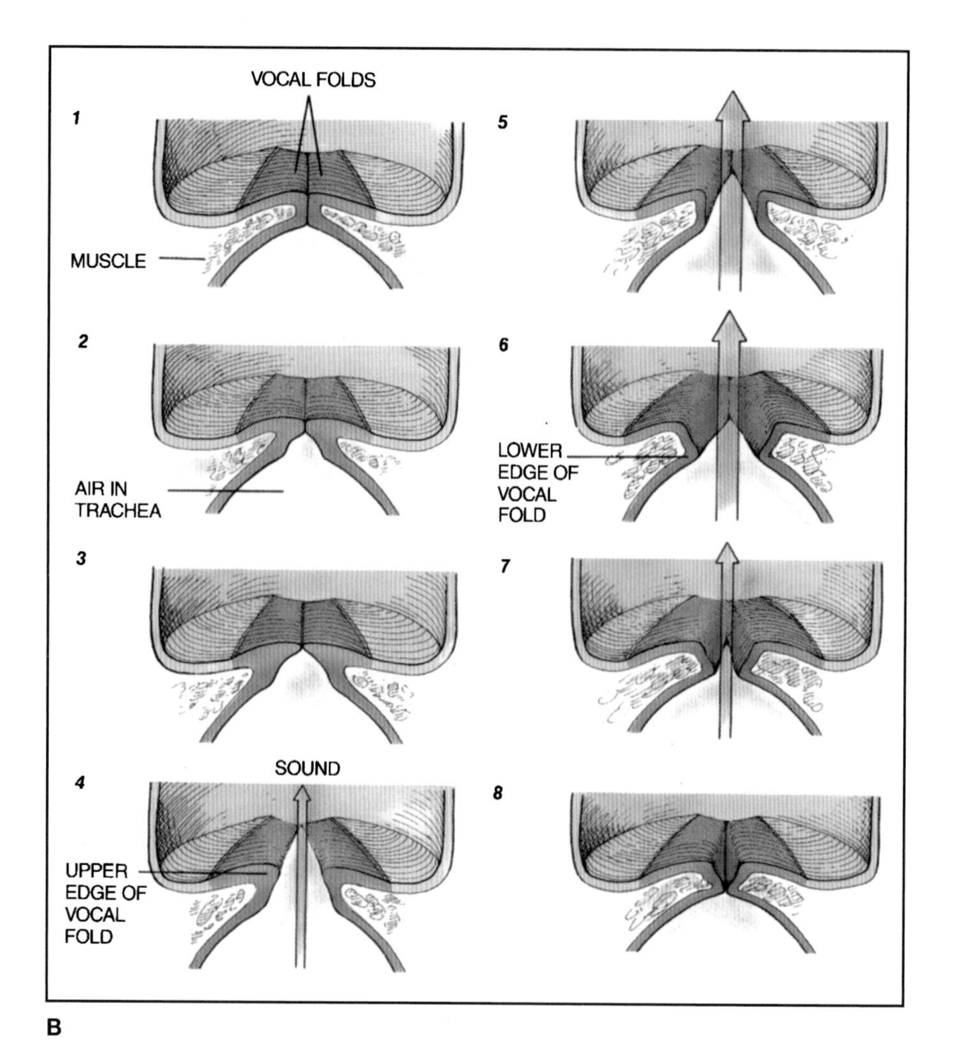

B

Fig 4–5. *(continued)* **B.** Vibration of the vocal folds is shown in a more three-dimensional vertical cross-section through the middle part of the vocal folds, during the production of a single sound. The perspective is from the front of the larynx. Before the process starts (1), the folds are together. They separate as air is forced upward through the trachea (2-7) and then come together again as the sound ceases (8). (From Sataloff RT. The human voice. *Sci Am.* 1992;267(6):108-115, with permission).

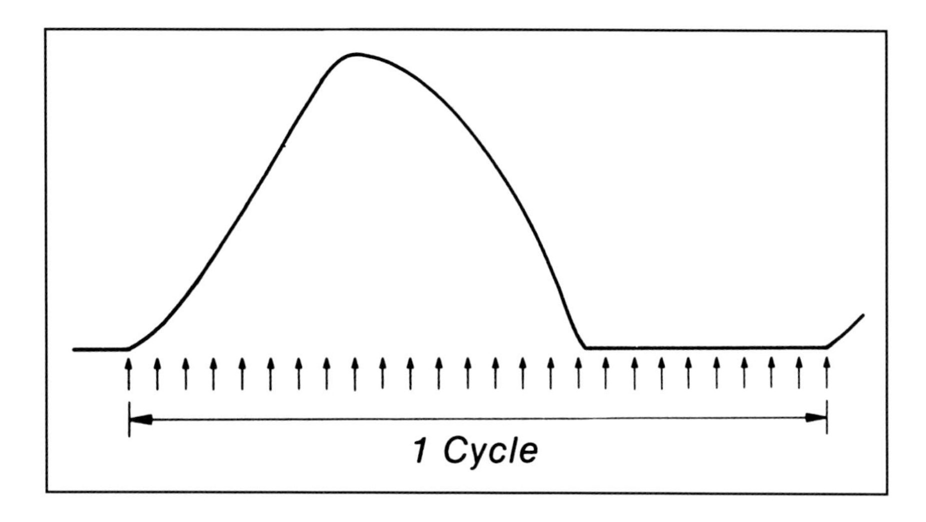

Fig 4–6. The principle of ultra high speed photography and high speed video. Numerous images are taken during each vibratory cycle. This technique is a true slow motion representation of each vocal fold vibration. (From Hirano M. *Clinical Examination of the Voice.* New York, NY: Springer-Verlag; 1981;55, with permission.)

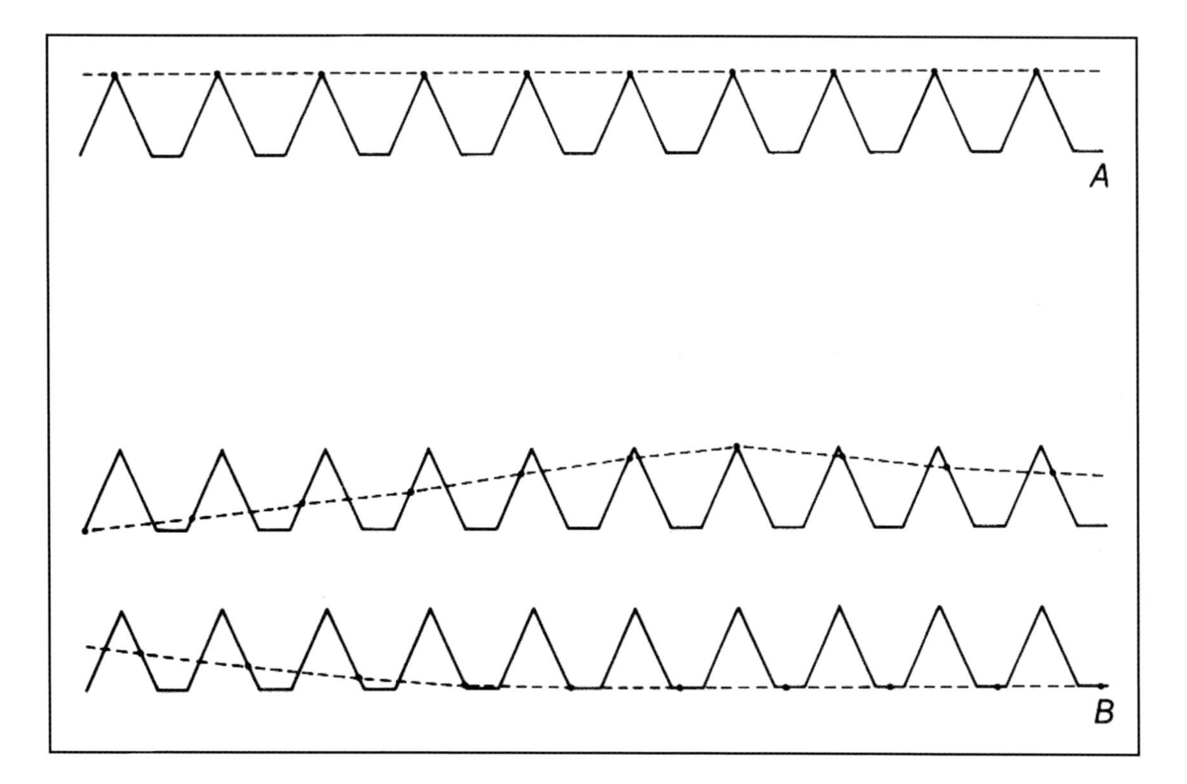

Fig 4–7. The principle of stroboscopy. The stroboscopic light illuminates portions of successive cycles. The eye fuses the illuminated points into an illusion of slow motion. If the stroboscope is synchronized with vocal fold vibration (**A**), a similar point is illuminated on each successive cycle and the vocal fold appears to stand still. If slightly desynchronized (**B**), each cycle is illuminated at a slightly different point, and the slow motion effect is created. (From Hirano M. *Clinical Examination of the Voice*. New York, NY: Springer-Verlag; 1981:49, with permission.)

teristics assessed include fundamental frequency, symmetry of bilateral movements, periodicity, glottal closure, amplitude, mucosal wave, the presence of nonvibrating portions, and other unusual findings (such as a tiny polyp).

Laryngeal stroboscopy is not a new technique. However, poor light limited its use for many years. Recent improvements in laryngeal stroboscopes and low-light cameras have provided instrumentation that is practical for clinical use. When necessary, it can be supplemented with other techniques, as discussed below. Stroboscopic light was used initially to evaluate the larynx in 1878.[7] Since that time, many investigators have recommended the technique and numerous equipment designs have been tried, only some of which are referenced in this chapter.[8-102] Stroboscopy has been used much more widely in Europe and Japan than in the United States. Various shortcomings prevented its routine inclusion in the otolaryngologist's office. For many years, the only equipment available was expensive and cumbersome; and it provided insufficient illumination. In addition, there was no easy way to record the images. In the 1980s, technological improvements resulted in stroboscopes that provide light bright enough to produce acceptable video recordings through a flexible fiberoptic naso-laryngoscope utilizing inexpensive video equipment. In the past several years, such equipment has been used routinely by a growing number of laryngologists who specialize in voice disorders.

From 1985 through 1994 we used the equipment pictured in Figure 4–1 with minor modifications. Numerous cameras, special effects generators, and other devices developed for use in conjunction with this equipment are discussed in the first edition of this book.[101] During the time between the first and the second editions, we switched to improved Panasonic SVHS cameras, a Panasonic SVHS special effects generator, and made other modifications. However, the details are not being discussed in this edition because we are currently using our Bruel and Kjäer stroboscopes only rarely. They still incorporate multiple-camera imaging systems that permit simultaneous display of at least three images. These are usually the larynx, face, and electroglottography (EGG). However, the video headlight may be used to add detailed views of the oral cavity.

In early 1995, we began using the Kay Elemetrics Model RLS 9100 as our primary strobovideolaryngoscopy system (Fig 4–8). This elegantly packaged system provides many advantages, including excellent light. The stroboscopy bulb in some systems has to be changed at the factory. The Kay Elemetric bulb can be changed by the physician's office staff. This can be an important advantage, especially in offices that have only one stroboscope. Perhaps more important, however, are the major technological advances provided by the Kay system. In the early system that we used from 1995 until 1998, the model RLS 9100 stroboscope is integrated into a package that includes a computer-controlled video system, computer, monitor, EGG, and videoprinter. Images are automatically digitized for storage and individual frame acquisition, and are recorded simultaneously on SVHS videotape. Cleverly, the Kay engineers have put the camera under video control so that each video frame captures only one image. This eliminates the problem of variability in brightness and sharpness from frame to frame encountered on all previous systems, and it results in a much crisper video. In addition, the digitalization and computer storage capabilities permit direct transmittal of individual images to film for preparation of slides and to an optional analysis program that allows digital assessment of glottal area and other parameters of the stroboscopic images. The Kay system provides many other convenient capabilities (Figs 4–9 through 4–13).

Since 1999, we have used the latest Kay System Model (RLS9100B, Fig 4–8C). This system is entirely digital; and it records to disk, eliminating the need for videotapes. It is still possible to copy examinations onto videotape for the convenience of patients or referring doctors or for visualization in the operating room. The digital system has many advantages, including the ability to access previous examinations almost instantaneously, and the ability to display them on a split screen so that they can be compared easily with the current examination. In addition it has a built-in program for generating reports, and many other useful features.

Our routine stroboscopy protocol has been described in previous publications.[2,3] In virtually all cases, we evaluate patients with both flexible and rigid endoscopes at the time of initial assessment. We routinely use either an Olympus ENF-P3 or ENF-L3. The ENF-L3 is large (4.3 mm) and more frequently requires topical nasal anesthesia. It is also quite expensive. However, it provides extraordinarily good images through a flexible endoscope, permitting high-resolution examination of nearly all patients. For children, and the small number of patients who cannot tolerate the ENF-L3, the ENF-P3 is quite satisfactory. The flexible laryngoscope permits evaluation and documentation of laryngeal motion during natural speech tasks, without tongue restriction. This allows assessment of laryngeal posture during speech and singing, fairly good assessment of vibratory margin activity during normal phonatory activities, and good

Fig 4–8. A. Kay Elemetrics Model RSL 9100 with computer and other options, as provided by the manufacturer. **B.** The Kay Elemetrics system as modified in our laboratory to permit the use of multiple cameras, with simultaneous image display, under computer control. **C.** Kay Elemetrics Model RLS9100B, which is designed without a video recorder. Although the unit is designed with one camera, we modified it for use with two endoscopic cameras (one for flexible and one for rigid endoscopy) and a third camera to image the patient's face. We sometimes add a fourth camera attached to a video headlight to image the oral cavity and larynx simultaneously. The cameras are controlled through a special effects generator, which can be seen partially at the bottom of the equipment rack. The video machine on the shelf above the Kay equipment is used to create copy tapes.

assessment of laryngeal motion during numerous tasks such as whistling, rapid speech repetition, and others. We have the patient repeat the spoken and sung maneuvers in his native language, if it is not English. We also determine how much time he speaks his native language versus foreign languages; and we try to determine visually under what circumstances his voice production appears best. Laryngeal telescopes provide better optical images and higher resolution; and they are used routinely for detailed assessment of vibratory margin motion. We generally use a 70° telescope although we also have 90° telescopes available, because a few patients find them easier to tolerate.

Our protocol begins with flexible fiberoptic laryngoscopy. The patient is asked to state his or her name and the date of the examination. He or she is asked then to count from 1 to 10, to count again from 1 to 10 in a higher pitched voice, and to repeat these maneuvers in his or her native language, if it is not English. These maneuvers, and those discussed in the rest of this paragraph, are designed to evaluate laryngeal biomechanics. This is accomplished best by fiberoptic laryngoscopy. If there is supraglottic compression and the vocal folds are difficult to visualize during spontaneous phonation, but supraglottic posture becomes normal and vocal folds are seen easily when counting at a slightly higher pitch, then the observer has evidence that patient phonates habitually at a pitch that is lower than desirable. This information is helpful to the speech-language pathologist in planning treatment. It should be noted that simply advising the patient to try to raise his or her pitch is inadequate, as is therapy that

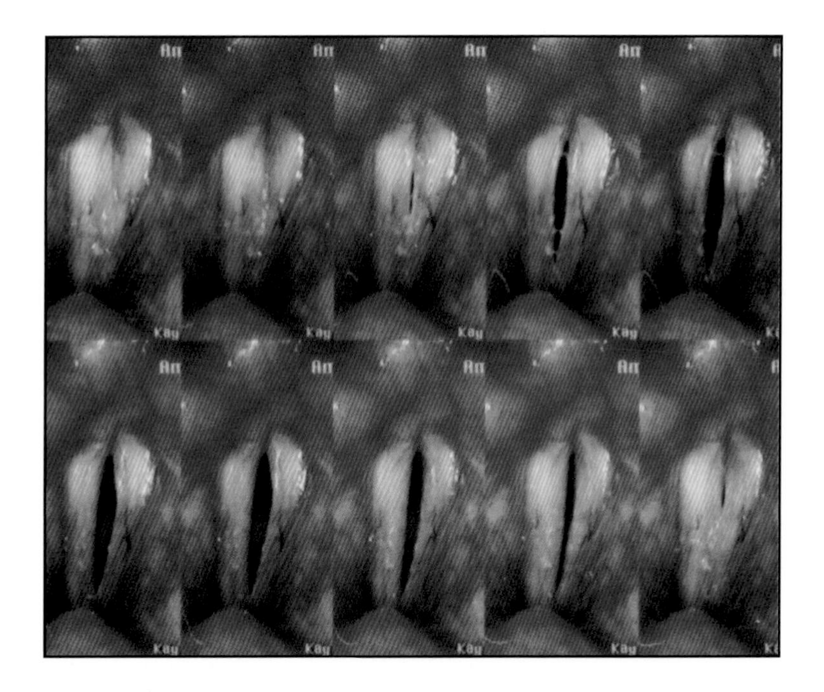

Fig 4–9. Videoprint from the Kay Elemetrics stroboscopy system. This special feature automatically captures the vocal folds at 36° intervals and prints 10 images (360°), simulating the behavior of a complete glottic cycle. This feature can be very helpful in illustrating asymmetries.

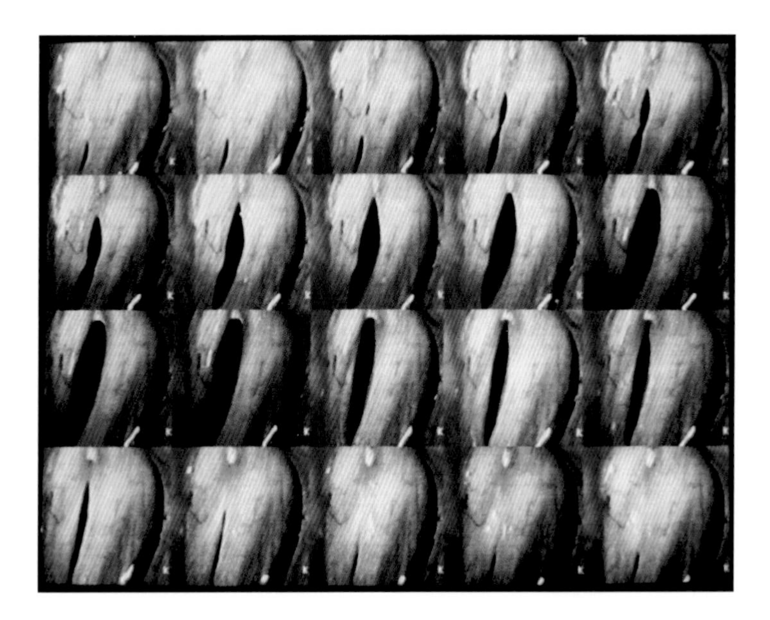

Fig 4–10 The computer can also provide automatically images at 18° intervals, printing 20 images to simulate the behavior of a complete glottic cycle in greater detail.

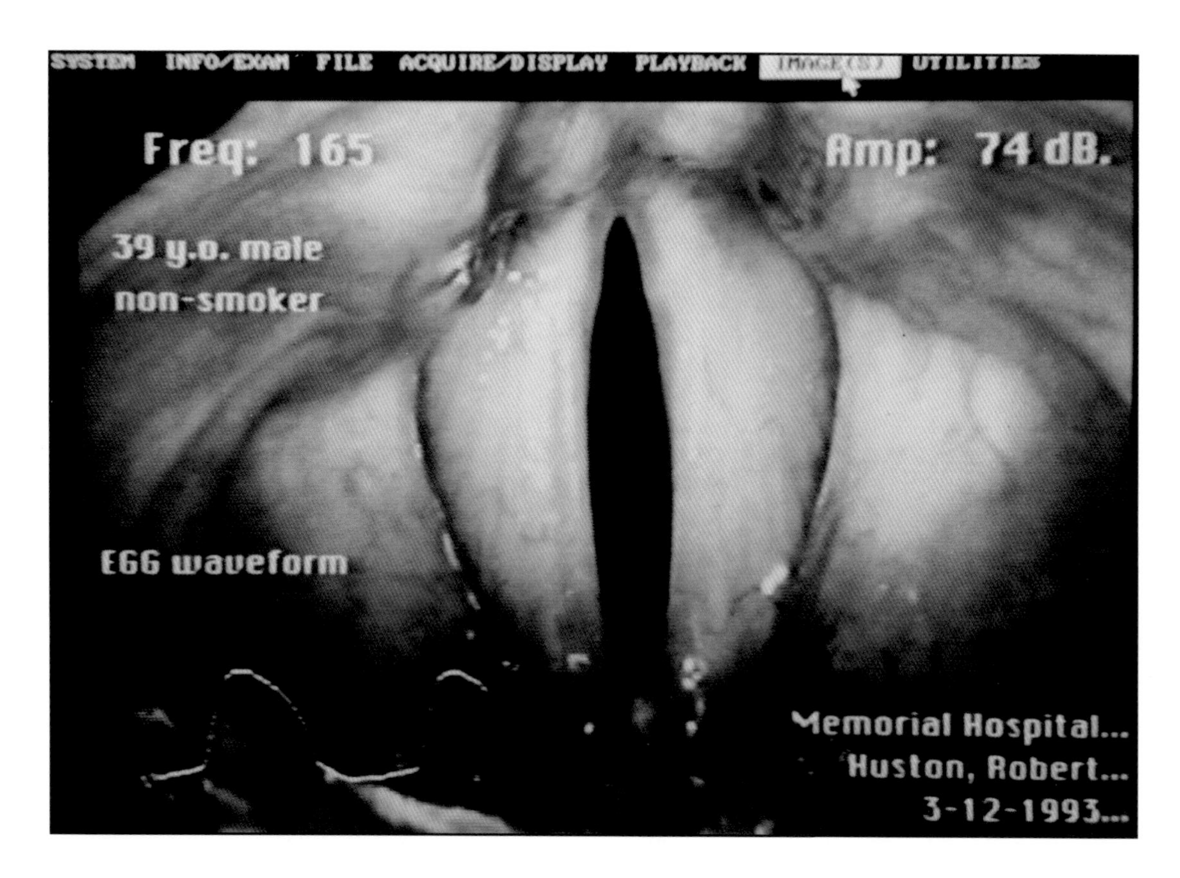

Fig 4–11. The computer capabilities allow labeling of videoprints and automatically provide superimposed EGG display.

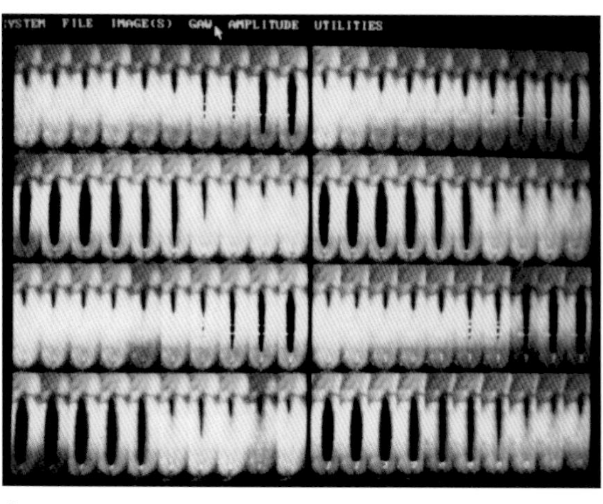

A

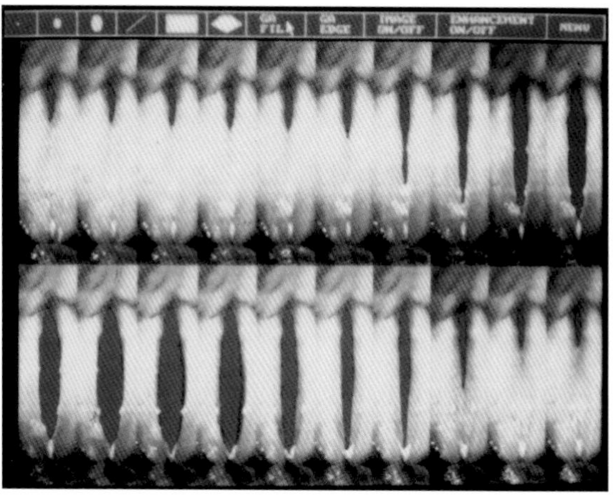

B

Fig 4–12. A. In the digital analysis program, 80 images representing 4 complete glottic cycles are taken from a stroboscopy recording. **B.** An edge detection algorithm such as the one shown above is used to calculate the area of the glottis and fill it with a contrasting color. The automatic selections can be modified by the user using the computer mouse.

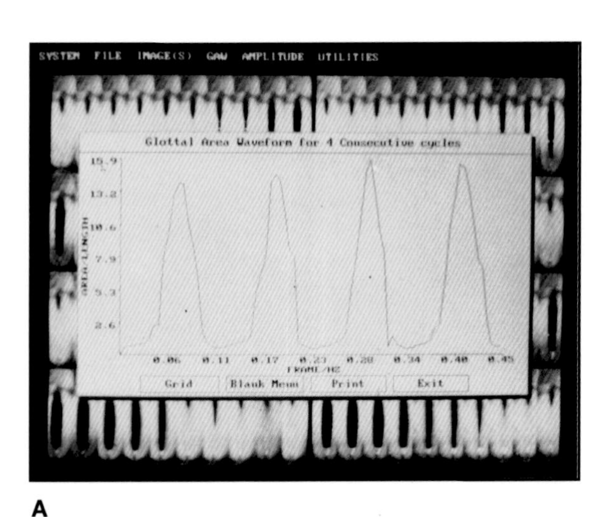

A

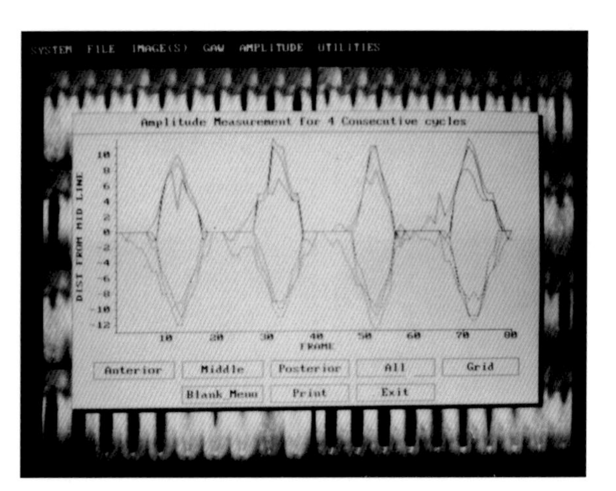

B

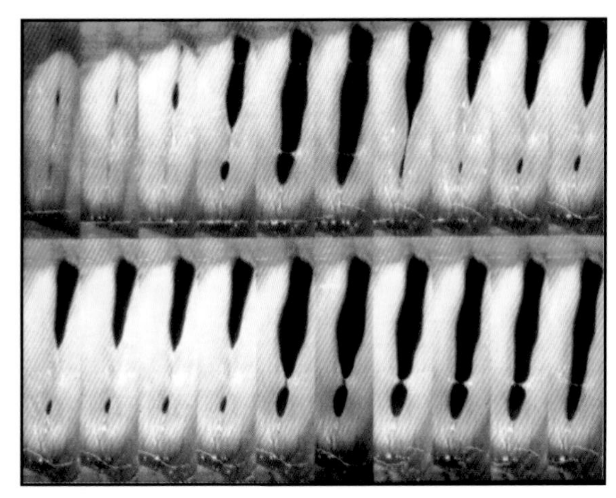

C

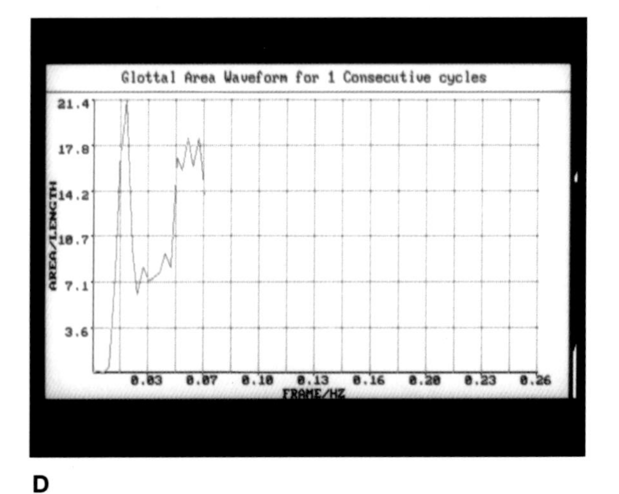

D

Fig 4–13. A. The digital analysis program allows determination of the glottal area waveform (GAW) as shown above. This is a graphic representation of glottal area changes during 4 cycles of phonation. **B.** An amplitude/symmetry waveform (A/SW) may be even more useful. This represents the excursion at three locations (anterior, middle, and posterior) of each vocal fold during the glottal cycle. These are plotted as mirror images and permit assessment of each vocal fold separately, as well as comparison of one vocal fold with the other. **C.** Twenty images, representing one glottic cycle, in a patient with vocal fold cysts. **D.** Glottal area waveform of same glottic cycle. *(continued)*

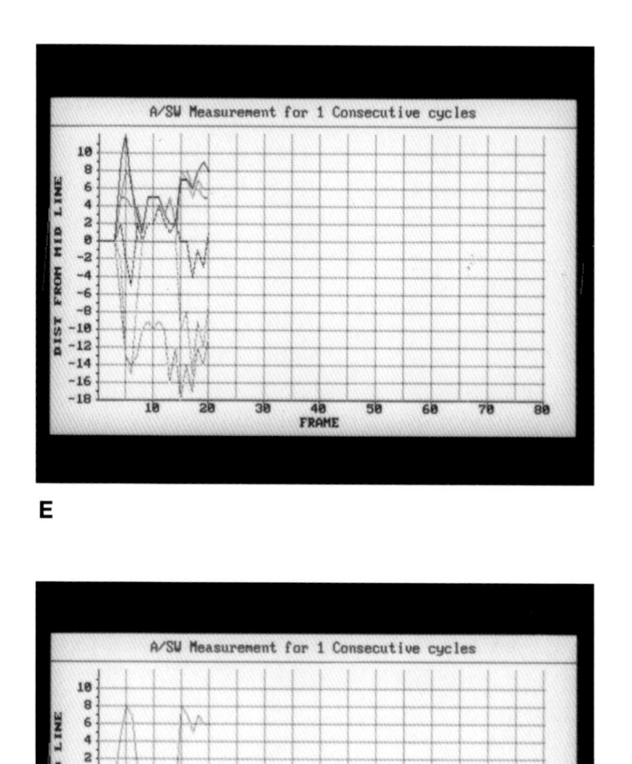

E

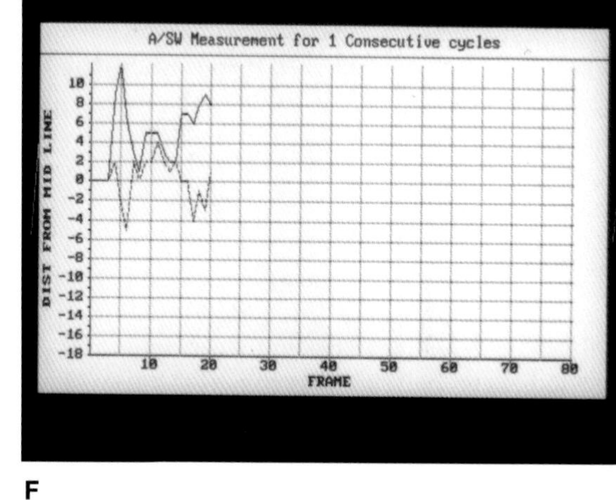

F

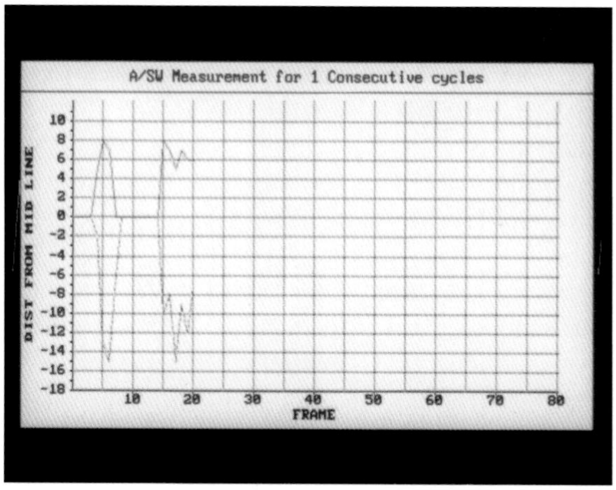

G

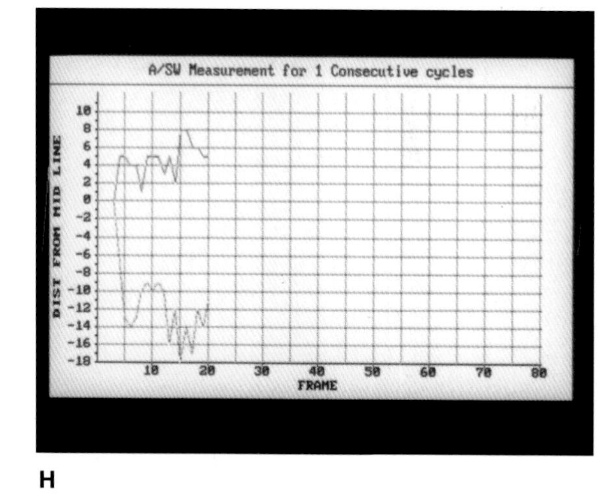

H

Fig 4–13. *(continued)* **E.** Amplitude/symmetry waveform of the same glottic cycle. **F.** A/SW measurement for anterior portion of the vocal fold, graphed separately.**G.** A/SW measurement for middle portion. **H.** A/SW measurement for posterior portion.

uses attainment of "optimal pitch" as the primary focus of voice modification. However, when expert therapy has been completed (as described elsewhere in this book), laryngeal appearance during speech (and habitual pitch) improves in most cases. Biomechanical assessment also includes other maneuvers to assess techniques of voice use and to identify even subtle movement disorders such as mild superior laryngeal nerve paresis, which may underlie other voice problems and must be detected in order to plan optimal treatment. The patient is asked to whistle "Yankee Doodle," to slide slowly from lowest to highest pitch and then to slide down; to sniff several times; to alternate rapidly a sniff with the vowel /i/ several times; to repeat several times /i/-/hi/-/i/-hi/-/i/-hi/; to repeat /pɑ/-/tɑ/-/kɑ/ several times; to sing "Happy Birthday"; to sing a song or scale, or to speak lines, to demonstrate the patient's problem, if possible; and to sustain /i/. Strobovideolaryngoscopy is performed initially with a flexible laryngoscope. The findings are not as detailed as those obtained later with the rigid telescope, but they are helpful for several reasons. First, they permit visualization of vocal fold motion with the larynx in normal posture, rather than with the tongue protruded and being held. Second, they provide a more accurate assessment of posterior glottic opening than can be obtained during rigid endoscopy. We have observed this phenomenon, as have Sodersten and Lindestad.[102,104] However, it should be remembered that an open posterior glottic chink is not necessarily abnormal. Third, in the rare patient whose gag reflex or anatomy precludes visualization with a telescope, flexible images may be the only stroboscopic views that can be obtained. Flexible stroboscopic images are obtained with the vocal folds moving at the usual simulated, slow speed created by the stroboscope, at slower speed, and with the stroboscopic light adjusted so that the vocal fold should appear to stand still (to test periodicity). The flexible laryngoscope is removed when this portion of the examination has been completed and a rigid laryngoscope is used. The patient is asked to phonate /i/ at various frequencies and intensities. The tip of the stroboscope is brought as close to the vocal folds as possible, usually within the laryngeal inlet. With an appropriate size camera lens, the vocal folds should fill the monitor screen. The vocal folds should be observed not only at a 90° angle from directly above the larynx, but also tangentially with the stroboscope moved to each side and angled toward the vibratory margin. This maneuver provides a better three-dimensional perspective of the vocal fold edge.

We use a standardized method of subjective assessment of strobovideolaryngoscopic images, as proposed by Hirano et al.[4-6] Characteristics that are evaluated include fundamental frequency, symmetry of movements, periodicity, glottic closure, amplitude of vibration, mucosal wave, and the presence of nonvibrating portions of the vocal fold. Other unusual findings such as subgottal cysts or sulcus vocalis may also be observed. In addition, objective frame-by-frame computer analysis is possible with inexpensive computer equipment or the analysis system built into the Kay Elemetrics stroboscopy system software.

With practice, perceptual judgments of stroboscopic images provide a great deal of information. However, it is easy for the inexperienced observer to draw unwarranted conclusions because of normal variations in vibration. Vibrations depend on fundamental frequency, intensity, and vocal register (Fig 4–14). For example, failure of glottic closure occurs normally in falsetto phonation. So, if patients are examined only during phonation on a high-pitched /i/ (as is done during routine indirect laryngoscopy with a mirror) everyone will have failure of glottic closure. Consequently, it is important to be familiar with the physiologic variation in vocal fold behavior and to examine each voice under a variety of conditions. Fundamental frequency can be influenced by various vocal fold parameters. For example, *fundamental frequency* is increased with increasing vocal fold tension or stiffness, increased subglottal pressure, or a shortened length of vibrating vocal fold. Fundamental frequency (F_0) is decreased as vocal fold mass increases. More unusual normal variations may also be seen, even in advanced voice professionals.[103,104]

Symmetry is assessed by observing both vocal folds simultaneously. In a trained voice, they are mirror images, opening with the same lateral excursions (symmetry of amplitude) and mirror-image waves

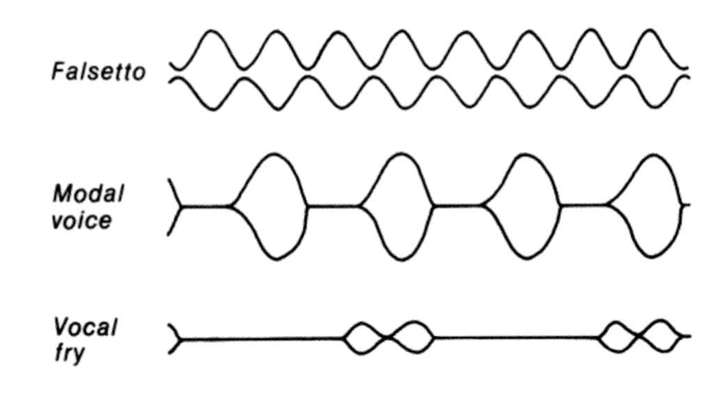

Fig 4–14. The normal vibratory pattern of vocal folds. (From Hirano M. *Clinical Examination of the Voice*. New York, NY: Springer-Verlag; 1981:48, with permission.)

(symmetry of phase). In untrained voices, phase asymmetry is common. Clinically significant asymmetries may be due to differences between vocal folds in position, tension, elasticity, viscosity, shape, mass, or other mechanical properties.

Periodicity refers to the regularity of successive vibrations. Regular periodicity requires balanced control of the expiratory force and the mechanical characteristics of the vocal folds. Irregular periodicity may be caused by inability to maintain a steady expiratory stream of air, inability to sustain steady laryngeal muscle contraction (as in neuromuscular disease), and marked differences in the mechanical properties of the vocal folds. Periodicity is assessed by locking the stroboscope in phase with vocal fold vibration. This should result in the vocal folds appearing to stand still. If they move, vibration is aperiodic. Failure of glottic closure may be due to vocal fold paresis or paralysis, an irregular vocal fold edge, a mass (or masses) separating the vocal fold edges, stiffness of a vibratory margin, cricoarytenoid joint dysfunction, falsetto singing, psychogenic dysphonia, and other causes. It is helpful to describe failures of glottic closure more specifically. They may be complete or incomplete, consistent or intermittent, and may involve a posterior glottic chink, specific small portion of the vocal folds, or as much as the entire vocal fold.

Amplitude of vibration and mucosal wave characteristics are assessed looking at the vocal folds one at a time. Small amplitude is associated with short vibrating segments of vocal fold, increased stiffness, increased mass, and vocal fold masses or other mechanical obstacles to vocal fold motion. Amplitude is increased by increasing subglottal pressure, such as occurs with loud phonation. Amplitude is not generally affected very much by soft masses such as cysts and nodules. The mucosal wave is affected by many factors. It is diminished by dryness, scar, mucosal stiffness or edema, epithelial hyperplasia, masses, dehydration, and falsetto phonation. It also varies with pitch. The mucosal wave is also increased with loud phonation (increased subglottal pressure) and altered by hypofunctional or hyperfunctional voice technique. If there is an area of stiffness on the vocal fold, this will impede the traveling mucosal wave. This situation is encountered with small scars, some mass lesions, and sulcus vocalis.

Nonvibrating (adynamic) *segments* are often signs of serious vocal fold injury involving scar that obliterates the complex anatomy of the lamina propria and mucosa. Adynamic segments are seen only under stroboscopic light or in high speed imaging techniques. They are found typically on vocal folds that have undergone previous surgery, hemorrhage, or other trauma. Often the vocal folds look "normal" under continuous light, but the voice is hoarse and breathy. The reason is obvious when the adynamic segment is revealed under stroboscopic light. Adynamic segments may occur also in association with invasive malignancies and may be ominous signs when encountered within an area of leukoplakia. Hypodynamic segments may also occur temporarily, as seen sometimes in acute vocal fold hemorrhage with submucosal hematoma.

Recalling that strobovideolaryngoscopy provides an illusion of slow motion but does not actually image every cycle, simultaneous EGG display supplies potentially valuable additional information on each vibratory event. In our older systems, the stroboscope and an oscilloscope are synchronized by connecting the output at the back of the Bruel and Kjäer stroboscope to the external trigger input of the oscilloscope, as described by Karnell.[105] The EGG display and synchronization are built into the Kay Elemetrics system. We use the Fourcin Laryngographs available through Kay Elemetrics with all stroboscopes. For objective voice assessment we also use a Rothenberg EGG. The EGG he designed has two sensors on each side of the larynx in a vertical array, instead of just one. This arrangement has resulted in noticeable improvements in EGG recordings.[106]

Strobovideolaryngoscopy is so valuable that only the expense, and perhaps the size and portability of stroboscope units, have delayed its use in every otolaryngology office. Some of these disadvantages may be overcome by a new device that is not available commercially yet, but which the author (RTS) has seen in prototype. Using light-emitting diodes (LEDs), Marcus Hess from Hamburg, Germany has developed a new illumination source that makes stroboscopy possible in a portable, self-contained, entirely hand-held device. Tiny LEDs clipped onto the tip of a rigid endoscope provide sufficient illumination of the larynx for stroboscopic examination. LEDs are advantageous because they are small, bright, shock and water resistant, and very inexpensive. The LEDs and electronic stroboscopy control unit may be driven by the same battery power source. If this device is brought to market and works as well as the prototype appeared to work, it may be possible to carry the device in a pocket or medical bag for easy use during hospital consultations, backstage at a theater, or in multiple examination rooms. Although it is unlikely to replace highly sophisticated, computer-based strobovideolaryngoscopy systems for definitive assessment, it will potentially provide a useful additional tool for the busy laryngologist in special circumstances, and an affordable stroboscope for otolaryngologists who have not been able to acquire a stroboscopy system, so far.

Strobovideolaryngoscopy is the most common technique for assessing vocal fold vibration in clinical use, but it has limitations. It works well with patients whose vocal folds vibrate in a periodic or pseudo-periodic fashion. However, it is not optimal for assessment of aperiodic vibration because the frequency detection system of the stroboscope cannot track rapid, irregular changes effectively. Stroboscopy also can give an incorrect impression when the vocal folds are producing more than one periodic source, as in some cases of diplophonia. Because of these limitations, which are based in the technology of strobovideolaryngoscopy, examination of some voice problems is troublesome. These include some cases of severe hoarseness, diplophonia, voice breaks, vocal tremor, and other problems. It is also difficult to examine the vocal folds in patients who have very short phonation times. This was even more troublesome using the first version of Bruel and Kjäer stroboscope in which the frequency-tracking system required approximately one second to engage. This was improved to approximately 0.1 second. Nevertheless, short phonation times can make stroboscopy challenging, and sometimes misleading. Because of the tracking problems that impair the ability of stroboscopy to image voice breaks clearly, register transitions cannot be assessed definitively using strobovideolaryngoscopy. Most of these problems do not exist with high-speed motion pictures. However, although high-speed film was used effectively to study vocal fold behavior, the cumbersome equipment and delay in processing make it impractical for clinical use.[107] Newer techniques such as videokymography and high-speed video are promising additions to the clinical voice armamentarium.

Videokymography

Videokymography (VKG) uses a line scanning camera to visualize the vocal folds. One disadvantage is the camera scans a single line on the vocal fold, rather than the entire vocal fold. So, the images illustrate only one point on the vocal fold, although they do so in considerable detail. However, two-dimensional spatial resolution is lost, and there is no coordination between the visual image and an auditory signal as one obtains during the strobovideolaryngoscopy. Videokymography acquires nearly 8,000 frames per second. The images we see are influenced by the fact that each video frame contains 512 lines, and video acquires 30 frames per second. The images from the VKG are displayed on the monitor, with time dimension in the vertical axis. Time scrolls vertically at 144 line images per half frame. A monitor frame covers a time interval of 18.4 milliseconds. In the VKG system currently available as an option with the Kay Elemetrics stroboscope, the camera can record vibrations of a single point along both vocal folds at a rate of 7,812.5 images per second, as compared with the 50 images per second recorded on standard videotape. VKG images are in black and white.

VKG is relatively new technology. It was introduced in 1984 by Gall.[108] However, it was not until 1996 that it was developed by Svec and Schutte into a system that was practical for clinical purposes.[109,110] Their system is incorporated with the Kay equipment. It uses a continuous light source that allows identification of the line of interest along the vocal fold. The change from normal to high-speed VKG mode is controlled with a foot switch. The clinical value of VKG was reported in 1998,[111] and its use has been increasing slowly. The author (RTS) has found VKG to be a useful addition to strobovideolaryngoscopy in selected cases. It permits detailed evaluation of vibratory abnormalities that cannot be analyzed by strobovideolaryngoscopy. It is useful in assessing the effects of scar and outcomes of surgical treatment of scar, the presence of subharmonic vibrations, double or triple vocal fold openings in a single glottal cycle, irregular vocal fold vibrations, and other abnormalities. Although each VKG image is limited to a single line along the vocal fold, VKG images can be acquired at multiple positions, thus providing a meaningful sample of vibratory detail throughout the length of the vocal fold. Although VKG lacks spatial resolution, when combined with strobovideolaryngoscopy useful additional information can be obtained. In some cases, even better information can be obtained with high-speed video; but videokymography equipment is substantially less expensive than high-speed video equipment.

High-Speed Video

The many investigators who used high-speed motion picture technology after it was introduced by Von Leden et al[107] showed that high-speed imaging provided extremely useful, detailed information about vocal fold function even under difficult circumstances such as in aperiodic voices, dichotic phonation, and vocal fry. In order to try to reacquire this information in a more practical fashion, high-speed digital imaging was introduced in 1987.[112] Recently, equipment has been improved; and high-speed video is now available commercially and is practical (although expensive) as an option with the Kay Elemetrics Stroboscopy System. Images are in black and white; and, like VKG and high-speed motion pictures, no sound is linked with the images. At the camera's slower recording rate of about 2,000 frames per second, image resolution is reasonably good. At its upper limit of about 4,000 frames per second, additional information may be acquired, but the images become somewhat blurry. The amount of time during which images are captured is adjustable, but 2 seconds are usually sufficient. Images are played back at approximately 15 frames per second. Thus, a 2-second acquisition requires approximately 4.44 minutes to view. This limits its convenience for routine clinical use, but it is manageable for special clinical problems and for research. In addition, a specific area can be identified on the initial video frame and analyzed using digitally generated VKG, created from the high-speed film. This interesting technology essentially allows digital VKG to be obtained without losing spatial resolution or watching the entire video display; but the information obtained is less detailed than that acquired from true VKG, because of the difference in frames per second of acquisition (2,000 versus 8,000). Hess, Hertegard, Eysholdt, and other authors have reported on the usefulness of high-speed video.[113-115] Woo has shown that digital high-speed video is useful in a variety of situations. He has used this method to study normal onset and offset of vocal fold oscillation; to analyze diplophonia; to study vocal fold tension, stiffness, mass, and other parameters in greater detail; and for other purposes.[116] Recently, Larsson et al explored a combined high-speed, acoustic kymographic analysis package, concluding that combining such information appears promising for separating and specifying different voice quality such as diplophonia and vocal tremor.[117] They believe that this will have both clinical and research value and speculate that combining such information should be helpful for improving specifications of the terminology of different voice qualities. We anticipate that high-speed video will play an increasing role in clinical practice as more information is acquired and as equipment becomes less costly.

Other Techniques to Examine Vocal Fold Vibration

Electroglottography (EGG) uses two electrodes on the skin of the neck above the thyroid laminae. A weak, high-frequency current is passed through the larynx from one electrode to the other. Opening and closing of the vocal folds varies the transverse electric voltage in phase with vocal fold vibration. The resultant voltage tracing is called an electroglottogram. It traces the opening and closing of the glottis, and can be correlated with stroboscopic images (Fig 4–15).[118] Electroglottography allows objective determination of the presence or absence of glottal vibration, and is reproducible. It reflects the glottal condition more accurately during its closed phase, and quantitative interpretation of the glottal condition is possible. We use electroglottography routinely. Photoelectroglottography and ultrasound glottography are less useful clinically, and are described in Hirano's invaluable book *Clinical Examination of the Voice*[119] and other literature.[120]

Inverse filtering provides an estimate of glottal airflow produced during an acoustic speech signal, or from airflow related to breathing. The signal from sustained sound is passed through filters designed to "cancel out" the main resonance of the vocal tract. Eliminating the resonance characteristics provides a representation of the voice source as a glottal volume velocity waveform known as a flow glottogram. Essentially, the flow glottogram plots transglottal airflow in milliliters per second against time. When the vocal folds are closed, the air stream is reduced and/or stops. When the vocal folds open, the air stream increases, peaks, and decreases when the glottis closes. The flow glottogram can be evaluated with measures similar to those used for the electroglottographic waveform. The EGG gives information primarily about the closed glottis. The flow glottogram describes primarily the open glottis. Generating synchronized signals from both modalities provides a useful representation of glottal activity. In addition, the flow glottogram allows assessment of pressed, breathy, and flow phonation. This instrumentation has proven extremely useful for documentation of improvement and for biofeedback during voice therapy. Photoglottography can also be used to assess the open glottis.

Aerodynamic Measures

Traditional *pulmonary function testing* provides the most readily accessible measure of respiratory function. The most common parameters measured include: (a) *tidal volume* (the volume of air that enters the lungs during inspiration and leaves during expiration in normal breathing); (b) *functional residual capacity* (the volume of air remaining in the lungs at the end of inspiration during normal breathing), which may be divided into *expiratory reserve volume*

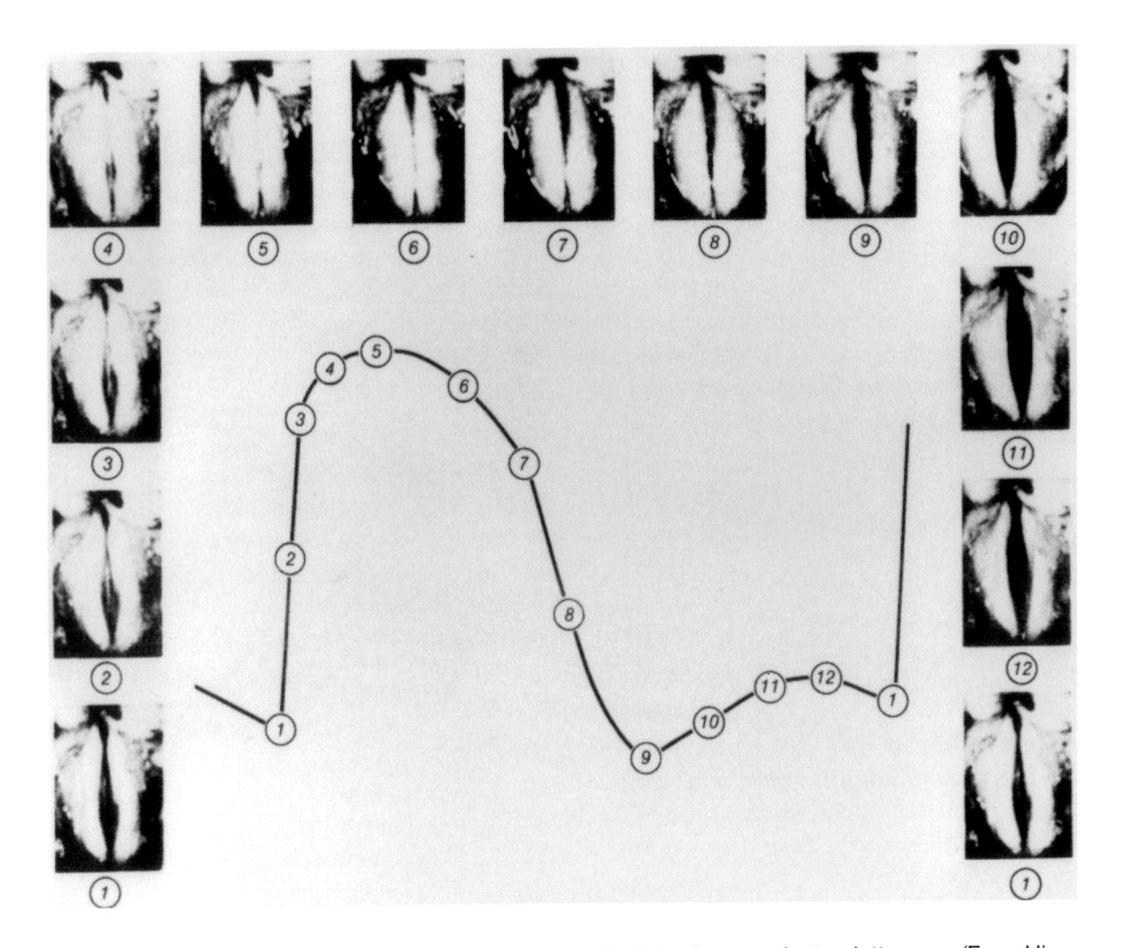

Fig 4–15. Correlation between stroboscopic images and points along an electroglottogram. (From Hirano M. *Clinical Examination of the Voice.* New York, NY: Springer-Verlag; 1981:57, with permission; originally appearing in Leclure.[118])

(maximal additional volume that can be exhaled) and residual volume (the volume of air remaining in the lungs at the end of maximal exhalation); (c) *inspiratory capacity* (the maximal volume of air that can be inhaled starting at the functional residual capacity); (d) *total lung capacity* (the volume of air in the lungs following maximal inspiration); (e) *vital capacity* (the maximal volume of air that can be exhaled from the lungs following the maximal inspiration); (f) *forced vital capacity* (the rate of airflow with rapid, forceful expiration from total lung capacity to residual volume); (g) FEV_1 (the forced expiratory volume in 1 sec); (h) FEV_3 (the forced expiratory volume in 3 sec); and (i) *maximal midexpiratory flow* (the mean rate of airflow over the middle half of the forced vital capacity [between 25% and 75% of the forced vital capacity]).

Testing before and after bronchodilator therapy may help establish a diagnosis of asthma. In most established singers, routine pulmonary function testing is not helpful. However, in singers and professional speakers with voice complaints, abnormal pulmonary function tests may conform deficiencies in aerobic conditioning or may reveal previously unrecognized asthma. Either condition can undermine the power source of the voice and cause voice dysfunction. Testing before and after a vigorous 1-hour singing lesson can also be diagnostically revealing. Pulmonary function should not deteriorate substantially following singing. If there is a change, especially in the midexpiratory flow rates, asthma should be suspected. Even in the absence of routine pulmonary function test abnormalities, if asthma is suspected, a methacholine challenge test should be performed by a pulmonologist. Even mild or moderate obstructive pulmonary disease may have substantial deleterious effects on the voice; and asthma may be present and clinically significant in a professional voice user even in the absence of obvious wheezing.

The *spirometer*, readily available for pulmonary function testing, can be used for measuring airflow during phonation. However, it does not allow simultaneous display of acoustic signals, and its frequency response is poor. A *pneumotachograph* consists of a laminar air resistor, a differential pressure transducer and an amplifying and recording system. It allows measurement of airflow and simultaneous recording of other signals when coupled with a polygraph. A *hot-wire anemometer* allows determination of airflow velocity by measuring the electrical drop across the hot wire. Modern hotwire anemometers containing electrical feedback circuitry that maintains the temperature of the hot wire provide a flat frequency response up to 1 kHz and are useful clinically.[112]

The four parameters traditionally measured in analyzing the aerodynamic performance of a voice include *subglottal pressure* (Psub), *supraglottal pressure* (Psup), *glottal impedance*, and *volume velocity of airflow at the glottis*. These parameters and their rapid variations can be measured under laboratory circumstances. Clinically, their mean value is usually determined as follows:

$$P_{sub} - P_{sup} = MFR \times GR$$

Where MFR is the mean (root mean square) flow rate and GR is the mean (root mean square) glottal resistance.

When vocalizing the open vowel /ɑ/, the supraglottic pressure equals the atmospheric pressure, reducing the equation to

$$P_{sub} = MFR \times GR$$

The *mean flow rate* is calculated by dividing the total volume of air used during phonation by the duration of phonation. The subject phonates at a comfortable pitch and loudness either over a determined period of time or for a maximum sustained period of phonation. *Air volume* is measured by the use of a mask fitted tightly over the face or by phonating into a mouthpiece while wearing a nose clamp. Measurements may be made using a spiromoter, pneumotachograph, or hot-wire anemometer. The normal values for mean flow rate under habitual phonation, with changes in intensity or register, and under various pathologic circumstances have been determined.[117] Normal values are available for both adults and children. Mean flow rate is a clinically useful parameter for vocal nodules, laryngeal nerve paralysis, spasmodic dysphonia, and other conditions.

Glottal resistance cannot be measured directly but can be calculated from the mean flow rate and mean subglottal pressure. Normal glottal resistance is 20 to 100 dyne sec/cm^5 at low and medium pitches and 150 dyne sec/cm^5 at high pitches.[122] *Subglottal pressure* is less useful clinically, because it requires an invasive procedure for accurate measurement. It may be determined by tracheal puncture, transglottal catheter, or measurement through a tracheostoma using a transducer. Subglottal pressure may be approximated using an esophageal balloon. *Intratracheal pressure*, which is roughly equal to subglottal pressure, is transmitted to the balloon through the trachea. However, measured changes in the esophageal balloon are affected by intraesophageal pressure, which is dependent on lung volume. Therefore, estimates of subglottal pressure using this technique are valid only under specific, controlled circumstances. The normal values for subglottal pressure under various healthy and pathologic voice conditions have also been determined by numerous investigations.[119]

The *phonation quotient* is the vital capacity divided by the maximum phonation time. It has been shown to correlate closely with maximum flow rate[121] and is a more convenient measure. Normative data determined by various authors have been published.[119] The phonation quotient provides an objective measure of the effects of treatment and is particularly useful in cases of recurrent laryngeal nerve paralysis and mass lesions of the vocal folds, including nodules.

Laryngeal airflow is measured while the patient sustains the vowel /ɑ/. Simultaneous recordings of frequency and intensity are helpful. A stopwatch is used to measure the time in seconds. The mean flow rate is calculated as airflow volume divided by time. As a measure of glottal efficiency, we expect in normal nonprofessional voice users a mean flow rate of approximately 100 mL/sec in males and 92 mL/sec in females.[119] Expectations are somewhat different in professional singers.[122] We evaluate these data in conjunction with s/z ratios. Other useful techniques include flow glottography using a mask and inverse filter as discussed above, and modifications of body plethysmography.

Measures of Phonatory Ability

Objective measures of phonatory ability are among the easiest and most readily available for the laryngologist, helpful in treating professional vocalists with specific voice disorders, and useful in assessing the results of surgical therapies. *Maximum phonation* time is measured using a stopwatch. The patient is instructed to sustain the vowel /ɑ/ for as long as possible following deep inspiration, vocalizing at a comfortable pitch and loudness. In selected cases, frequency and intensity may be controlled using an inexpensive frequency analyzer and sound level meter. The test is repeated three times, and the greatest value is recorded. Normal values have been determined for nonprofessional voice users.[119] We use normal values of approximately 34 sec for males and 26 sec for females. Normal values for professional singers differ somewhat from those for untrained speakers. *Frequency range of phonation* is measured in Hertz and converted to semitones, recording the vocal range from the lowest note in the modal register (excluding vocal fry) to the highest falsetto note. *Physiological frequency range of phonation* (PFRP) disregards the quality of the voice. In nonprofessional voice users, we accept approximately 36 semitones for males and 35 semitones for females as normal. The *musical frequency range of phonation* (MFRP) measures the lowest to highest musically acceptable notes. We have found normal MFRP to be 35 semitones for professional singers.

Tests for maximum phonation time, frequency range, and many of the other parameters discussed below (including spectrographic analysis) may be preserved on a tape recorder for analysis at a later time and used for pre- and post-treatment comparisons. High quality tape recorders and microphones are essential to avoid equipment noise or distortion. Frequency limits of *vocal register* may also be measured. The registers are (from low to high) vocal fry, chest, mid, head, falsetto, and whistle, as discussed in previous chapters, although register classification is controversial and some reduce the classification to vocal fry, modal, and loft. Overlap of frequency among registers occurs routinely. Testing the *speaking fundamental frequency* frequently reveals excessively low pitch, an abnormality associated with chronic voice abuse and misuse and development of vocal nodules. This parameter may be followed objectively throughout a course of voice therapy. "Normal" must be determined on an individual basis; however, expected approximate normal values are 120 Hz for males and 225 Hz for females, and they vary with age and misuse. Normative values for vocal fundamental frequency in children have been established.[123] *Intensity range of phonation* (IRP) has proved a less useful measure than frequency range. It varies with fundamental frequency (which should be recorded) and is greatest in the middle frequency range. It is recorded in sound pressure level (SPL) relative to 0.0002 microbar. For normal adults who are not professional vocalists, measuring at a single, fundamental frequency, IRP averages 54.8 dB for males and 51 dB for females. Alterations of intensity are common in voice disorders, although IRP is not the most sensitive test to detect them.

Information from the above tests may be combined in the *frequency-intensity profile*[124] (Fig 4–16). The maximum and minimum sound level that can be produced at different fundamental frequencies are plotted to provide the frequency-intensity profile. The resultant graph is called a *phonetogram* and may be helpful in describing the status of the voice. *Glottal efficiency* (the ratio of the acoustic power at the level of the glottis to subglottal power) provides useful informa-

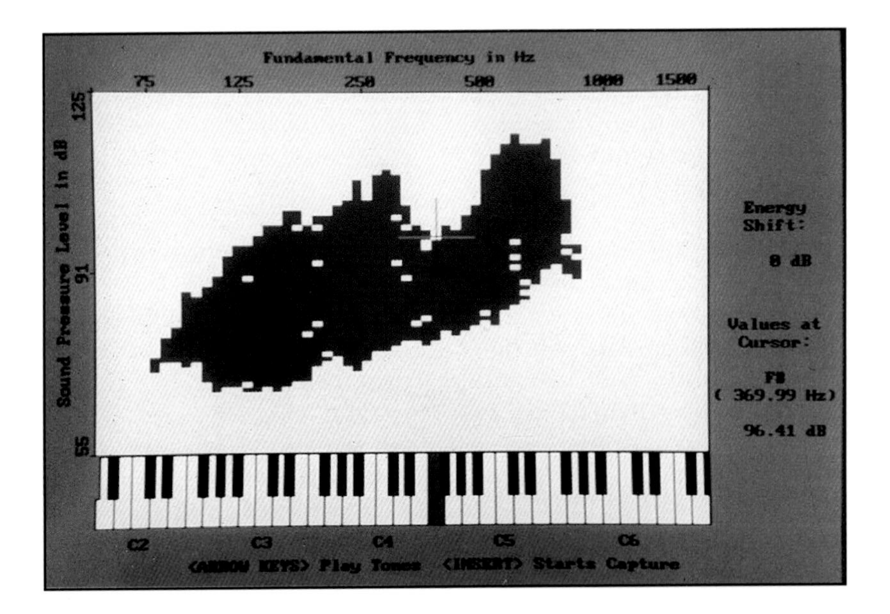

Fig 4–16. Typical phonetogram (fundamental frequency-intensity profile), obtained through an optional program for the Kay Elemetrics CSL 50.

tion but is not clinically practical because it is difficult to measure acoustic power at the level of the glottis. *Subglottic power* is the product of subglottal pressure and *airflow rate*. These can be determined clinically. Various alternative measures of glottic efficiency have been proposed including the *ratio of radiated acoustic power to subglottal power*,[125] *airflow-intensity profile*,[126] and ratio of the root mean square value of the AC component.[127] Although glottal efficiency is of great interest, none of these tests is particularly helpful under routine clinical circumstances.

Acoustic Analysis

Acoustic analysis of voice signals is both promising and disappointing. The skilled laryngologist, speech-language pathologist, musician, or other trained listener frequently infers a great deal of valid information from the sound of the voice. Available equipment is still not as good as our hearing, but equipment makes acoustic signals easy to quantify and study. At present, although acoustic analysis has become increasingly useful, we still use more equipment and devote more time to each voice patient than is practical for most laryngologists. We are currently involved in studies of intrasubject variability in all of the tests we do,[128] as well as validity studies comparing tests on different equipment and from different laboratories. We anticipate rapid technological evolution particularly in this section of the voice laboratory. The tape recorder is an essential tool of the voice team. The patient's voice should be recorded under controlled, repeatable circumstances. High-quality microphones should be used. The microphone is held at a fixed distance from the mouth. The validity and reliability of voice analysis depend on consistent recording technique from subject to subject, and from one recording session to the next. Microphone placement is critical. The intensity of sound varies in proportion to the square of the distance from the sound source. We have overcome variability in our voice laboratory by using a microphone holder. Like previously proposed devices, it is imperfect; but we feel it has been more satisfactory than methods described previously. We are currently using a harmonica holder[129] (Hohner International) that can be purchased inexpensively from a music supply house (Fig 4–17). A microphone attached to a headband would be equally satisfactory. However, the microphone should not be fixed on a microphone stand because this method tends to elicit an unnatural neck or jaw posture in some patients. It also permits excessive variability with slight patient motion. The microphone is placed 4 inches from the mouth for all recordings. Like other methods for maintaining constant distance between the sound source and microphone, the harmonica holder or headband device involves compromises. However, we have found them preferable to the compromises of other devices.

Probably the most widely used instrument for acoustic analysis in the United States is the Visi-Pitch™, sold by Kay Elemetrics. We have used the Visi-Pitch™ 6087PC. This instrument is an analog fundamental frequency and intensity analyzer specially designed for ease of use in clinical practice. It provides a computer display of both fundamental frequency (F_0) and relative intensity over time. A digital readout is used with cursors to determine the exact fundamental frequency of points on the screen's display and averages between the selected points. A summary of the acoustic analysis is given through a two-page report, which may be saved in file management, on a diskette, or sent to a printer for hard copy. The Visi-

Fig 4–17. Hohner International harmonica holder with Beyer dynamic undirectional microphone positioned for routine voice recording.

Pitch™ allows the statistical results of the segment between two cursors to be analyzed and summarized. It can both store and display in real time the extracted pitch contour and intensity curves. This statistical analysis calculates average fundamental frequency, extended fundamental frequency, average intensity, frequency perturbation, pitch range, and other useful parameters. Intensity and analog F_0 outputs are provided for optional chart recording. The Visi-Pitch™ is used in our practice to analyze short segments of prerecorded tapes for fundamental frequency, relative intensity, perturbation, voiced/unvoiced percentages, and for measurement of physiological low and high frequencies. Numerous segments of /ɑ/ are measured before computation of mean fundamental frequency, mean perturbation (Koike formula), and percent voicing.

Spectrography has been readily available for many years. Traditionally, a spectrograph has displayed the frequency and harmonic spectrum of a short sample of voice, and visually recorded noise. In addition to routine spectrographs, other equipment exists to analyze longer voice samples. Long-time-average-spectrography (LTAS) devices analyze spectral distribution of speech amplitude levels over time,[130] providing additional information.

The Kay Elemetrics DSP Sona-Graph™ (Model 5500) is an integrated voice analysis system that we have found particularly helpful. It is equipped especially for speech spectrography capabilities. Spectrography provides a visual record of the voice. The acoustic signal is depicted using time (x axis), frequency (y axis), and intensity (z axis, shading of light versus dark). Using the band-pass filters, generalizations about quality, pitch, and loudness can be made. These observations are used in formulating the voice therapy treatment plan. Format structure and strength can be determined using the narrow-band filters, of which a variety of configurations are possible. In clinical settings where singers and other professional voice users are routinely evaluated and treated, this feature is extremely valuable. A sophisticated voice analysis program (an optional program) has made the Sona-Graph™ an especially valuable addition to the clinical laboratory. The voice analysis program measures speaking fundamental frequency, frequency perturbation (jitter), amplitude perturbation (shimmer), and the harmonics-to-noise ratio. An electroglottograph (EGG) is used in conjunction with the Sona-Graph™ to provide these voicing parameters. Examining the EGG waveform alone is possible with this setup, but its clinical usefulness has not been established. An important feature of the Sona-Graph™ is the long-time average (LTA) spectral capability. This allows for analyzing longer voice samples. The LTA analyzes only voiced speech segments, and may be useful in screening for hoarse or breathy voices. In addition, computer interface capabilities (also an optional program) have solved many data storage and file maintenance problems. It is possible to digitize the acoustic and glottographic analog waveforms for storage on disk and later analysis on the Sona-Graph™ or through PC computer software programs such as Keithley ASYST, C-Speech, or CSL (Kay).

The KAY CSL50 (Computerized Speech Lab) has been the most valuable tool for acoustic analysis in our laboratory for several years. CSL is a highly flexible and versatile set of computer programs. It provides a convenient graphic summary of the parameters measured (Fig 4–18). It also has a satellite of ancillary programs, including MDVP (MultiDimension Voicing Profile), VP2 (Visi-Pitch 2), and an EGG Processing Program, which are extremely powerful and useful in obtaining objective voice data. Coupled with fast Pentium chip computer, the MDVP program significantly reduces the time involved in obtaining acoustic measures from patients. The data obtained from MDVP program are comparable with those obtained by the Kay 5500 and the first generation Visi-Pitch.

Measures of cepstral peak prominence have been added to our protocol since the year 2000. The value of cepstral peak prominence has been highlighted by Heman-Ackah et al.[131,132] Measures of cepstral peak prominence (CPP) appear to be more reliable predictors of dysphonia and breathiness than many of the measures we have used traditionally such as jitter, shimmer, and noise-to-harmonic ratio. A cepstrum is a Fourier transformation of a voice spectrum. As described by Heman-Ackah et al,[132] the spectrum is thought of as a complex waveform that is the summation of many smaller component sine waves. Each of the sine waves also has an amplitude and a "frequency." To avoid confusion in terminology, the "frequency" of each of the component waves of the spectrum is renamed quefrency.[133,134] Quefrency is the frequency of the frequency in the power spectrum (the unit of measure is cycles/frequency, which is seconds). When the amplitude of each of the component waves of the spectrum is graphed as a function of quefrency, the cepstrum is produced; and the resultant Fourier transformation has taken the information in the spectrum (the frequency domain) and transformed it to a time (quefrency) domain. The predominant peak in the cepstrum is the fundamental period of the spectrum. The fundamental period is the quefrency ("frequency") of the dominant sine wave of the complex wave termed the spectrum, just as the fundamental frequency is the frequency of the dominant sine wave

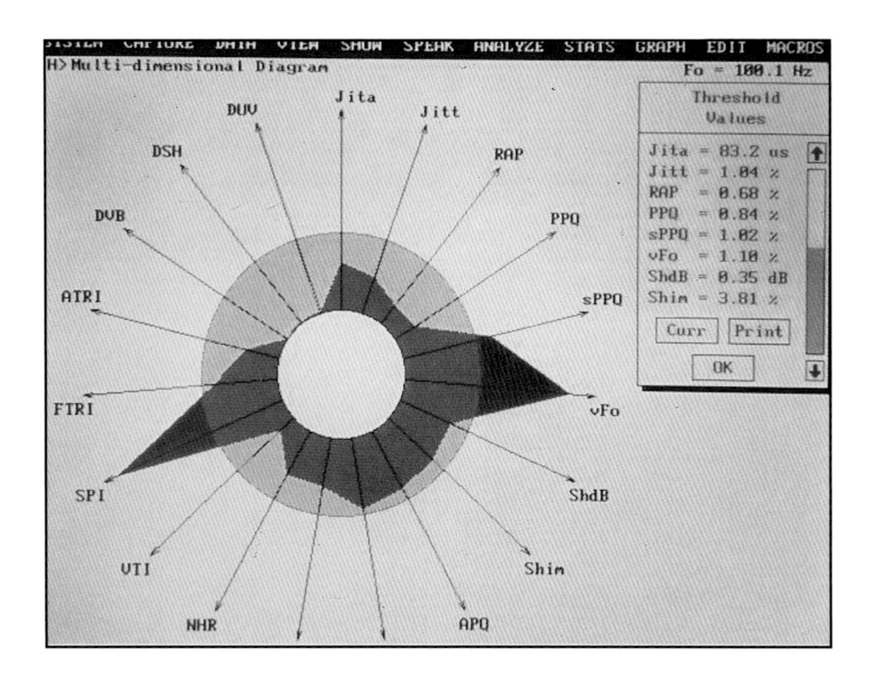

Fig. 4–18. Typical CSL printout showing acoustic measures obtained from a spoken prolonged /ɑ/ vowel. They include: average fundamental frequency; absolute jitter (Jita); jitter percent (Jitt); relative average perturbation (RAP); pitch perturbation quotient (PPQ); smoothed PPQ (sPPQ); fundamental frequency variation (v_{FO}); shimmer in dB (ShdB); shimmer percent (Shim); amplitude perturbation quotient (APQ); smoothed APQ (sAPQ); peak amplitude variation (vAm); noise to harmonic ration (NHR); voice turbulence index (VTI); soft phonation index (SPI); F_0 tremor intensity index (FTRI); amplitude tremor intensity index (ATRI); degree of voice breaks (DVB); degree of subharmonics (DSH), degree of voiceless (DUV); number of voice breaks (NVB); number of subharmonic segments (NSH); number of unvoiced segments (NUV); number of segments computed (SEG); and total pitch periods detected (PER). It is convenient to note that each quadrant of the multidimensional diagram groups related measures. Measures in the right upper quadrant relate to fundamental frequency perturbation. In the right lower quadrant, measures reflect amplitude perturbation. Three measures in the left lower quadrant are noise-related: noise/harmonic ratio (NHR), voice turbulence index (VTI), and soft phonation index (SPI). Tremor measures, F_0 tremor intensity (FTRI) and amplitude tremor intensity index (ATRI), are located in the middle of the left side of the diagram. The measures in the left upper quadrant reflect phonatory and aerodynamic function of the vocal folds: degree of voice breaks (DVB), degree of subharmonics (DSH), and degree of voiceless (DUV).

of the complex wave termed the voice signal. The smaller amplitude peaks in the cepstrum are called hamonics.[133,134] A highly periodic voice signal will have a strong peak at the fundamental frequency and at multiples of the fundamental frequency in the voice spectrum. These peaks will occur at a regular interval. This interval corresponds to the fundamental period of the cepstrum. Thus, a large amplitude peak is seen at the fundamental period.

An aperiodic or weakly periodic voice signal will have multiple similar amplitude peaks in the voice spectrum at many frequencies, without any definite pattern or defined intervals. A weakly periodic signal will produce a very low amplitude cepstral peak. The cepstrum of an aperiodic signal will demonstrate multiple similar amplitude peaks at many quefrencies.

The cepstral peak is the peak in the cepstrum with the highest amplitude. When a linear regression line that represents the average sound energy is drawn through the cepstrum, the distance from the cepstral peak to this linear regression line is termed the cepstral peak prominence (CPP). This linear regression line is drawn to normalize for variability in amplitude of phonation from one person to another.[135,136] Without this linear regression line, a speaker with a weakly periodic voice who is talking at 70 dB will produce a cepstral peak that is greater in absolute amplitude than a speaker with a very periodic voice who is talking at 50 dB because of the loudness of phonation rather than because of the prominence of the peak. Thus, the addition of the linear regression line allows one to determine the magnitude of the cepstral peak in relation to the amplitude of phonation and allows comparison from one testing situation to another. A highly periodic voice signal will have a large-amplitude cepstral peak prominence, and a weakly periodic or aperiodic voice signal will have a low-amplitude cepstral peak prominence.

Although the idea of the cepstrum was first introduced by Noll in 1964, the lack of high-speed computers made calculating the cepstrum cumbersome and time-consuming.[133,134] In 1994, Hillenbrand et al developed an automated method of calculating the cepstrum using the high-speed capabilities of modern computers.[135] In addition, the concept of the linear regression line was added as a means of normalizing the measure for purposes of comparison; and the use of cepstral peak prominence was introduced.[135] A smoothing feature was added to the cepstral peak prominence measure smoothing (CPPS) in 1996 in which the individual cepstra are averaged over a given number of frames.[136]

Both CPP and CPPS were shown to be reliable indicators of breathiness in two separate samples of 20 voice signals that were analyzed perceptually with regard to the quality of breathiness.[135,136] Subsequently, in a sample of 38 dysphonic voices, it was found that CPPS reflected overall dysphonia most strongly, although it continued to correlate well with breathiness.[132] These earlier studies were limited by small samples and few patients with voice pathology. Heman-Ackah et al addressed that problem by analyzing 281 consecutive patients who presented for objective voice analysis during 1999 in the senior author's (RTS) practice.[131] Based on the substantial sample of patients with a variety of voice abnormalities, they determined that CPPS-s (for speech) and CPPS-/ɑ/ (for a sustained vowel) are good predictors of dysphonia. Overall, CPPS-s has better sensitivity, specificity, and positive and negative predictive values than measures of jitter, shimmer, and noise-to-harmonic ratio. CPPS-s and CPPS-/ɑ/ are fast and easy to use and rely merely on the transfer into the CPP program of acoustic signals captured in computerized speech laboratory (Kay Elemetrics, Lincoln Park, NJ) CSL. CPPS-s and CPPS-/ɑ/ are reliable measures that should become routine for objective voice analysis.

Usefulness and interpretation of many of the acoustic measures discussed above should be self-evident. Various voice disorders may be accompanied by decreased range, intensity, and stability. Acoustic measures allow us to recognize and document such deviations from normal. In addition, they permit quantitative assessment of vocal progress during and following treatment. In order to compare various forms of voice therapy, medications, and different surgical techniques, we need as much objective information as possible about the degree and nature of voice improvement. Restoring or increasing vocal range and intensity, decreasing perturbation, and restoring normal harmonic patterns are important measures of therapeutic success. Because the sound of the voice is usually the patient's primary concern, acoustic analysis provides especially relevant information assessing and modifying nonsurgical and surgical treatments.

Current Voice Laboratory Protocol

Introduction

At the time of this writing, our standard voice laboratory examination protocol has been streamlined somewhat, and recent changes have been made in equipment and information management.

Careful attention to recording techniques and equipment is essential to ensure production of good quality recordings. Baken and Orlikoff[137] and Butler and Napora[138] have provided useful overviews of recording mediums and voice signal storage. The consensus points to careful data collection and a reliable storage medium as the cornerstones for accurate and reproducible voice analysis.

With computer technology changing so rapidly, there is a need to review new software systems for the benefit of the current users and for the developers who service the voice science community. Some research exists in this area, but the need for a systematic evaluation of these programs has not been met.[139-144] Although we provide the reader with our current preferences and practices as a practical convenience, our instrumentation and protocols change frequently. The reader is encouraged to investigate the latest technological advances before designing his or her clinical voice laboratory.

For recording and storing the voice signal, we presently use the TASCAM (DA-P1) portable digital/audio tape recorder (DAT) (TEAC Corporation, Montebello, Calif). Signal contamination for frequency perturbation values is consistently minimal with digital recorders (0.05%-0.10%).[137,145] The DAT recorder is very similar to a cassette recorder except that the analog voice signal is digitized and recorded on tape. The voice signal can be transferred via a digital connector directly to a computer for data analysis. A headset condenser microphone (Kay model 4302) is used with a mouth-to-microphone distance of 30 cm. Head-mounted microphones have the advantage of keeping a fixed position with respect to the speaker and are even more effective than the harmonica holders we used to use. Closer placement (less than 30 cm) may subject the microphone to air turbulence created by the plosive sounds. The TASCAM has an XLR (analog input) (TEAC Corporation, Montebello, Calif) microphone line input (with phantom power) that is designed to accept a broad range of signal levels from –60 dB to +4 dB. Recordings are made in a quiet room. Noise levels in the rooms are checked periodically and should be less than 50 dB at low frequencies.

Depending on the size of the tape, up to 4 hours of high quality signal can be recorded. The TASCAM is the size of a notebook and operates from batteries or AC line source, and it is capable of recording at multiple sampling rates of 48 kHz, 44.1 kHz, and 32 kHz. The frequency response ranges from 20 Hz to 20 kHz. Signal-to-noise ratio is better than 92 dB, and the dynamic range is better than 93 dB. In addition to a full complement of useful recording features, other advantages of the TASCAM DAT include amount of storage and portability. An abundance of material can be collected and stored, and clinicians can obtain pre- and posttherapy and surgical acoustic data both in the voice laboratory and off site.

The majority of voice analysis in our laboratory is conducted using the Computerized Speech Laboratory Windows software (Kay Elemetrics, Lincoln Park, NJ) loaded on a Dell Pentium III 933 GX MiniTower. The Sound Blaster Audigy Platinum (Creative Technology Ltd, USA) soundcard provides sufficiently high quality digital audio signal processing.

Protocol

Measures of mean fundamental frequency, standard deviation, and dBSPL are collected from a spoken monologue (name, date, and age) and a reading sample (Marvin Williams passage, Appendix IIA) by the patient. Data are analyzed using the Multi Dimensional Voice Program (MDVP) (Kay Elemetrics, Lincoln Park, NJ) and computerized speech lab (CSL) Core Program and a sound level meter. Calculations for cepstral peak prominence (CPP) are accomplished using additional software and the first sentence from the Marvin Williams passage (approximately 3 seconds). CPP analysis isolates the fundamental frequency while simultaneously revealing important characteristics of the vocal tract filter function.

Measurements of dBSPL intensity, signal typing (Yanagihara hoarseness ratings, discussed below), mean fundamental frequency, standard deviation, noise perturbation (jitter, shimmer, noise-to-harmonic ratio), and CPP are collected via the sustained vowel /ɑ/. CSL programs used include CSL Core Program Energy, CSL Spectrogram, and MDVP. Fundamental frequency phonational range is collected by asking patients to produce the highest and then the lowest sounds they can, or by using a singing scale progressing upward and downward in a stepwise pattern. Ranges are expressed in semitones. Analysis takes place using the CSL Core Program using cursors to track one cycle at the lowest and the highest frequency using the semitone conversion (39.86*log [F2/F1] 39.86*log [1754/141]).

Laryngeal efficiency measures (s/z ratio) are obtained using a stopwatch. The patient repeats the phonatory task twice, and the longest duration is recorded. For maximum vowel duration /ɑ/, the patient is instructed to take a deep breath and sustain the vowel /ɑ/ as long as possible at a comfortable pitch and loudness level. The task is repeated three times, and the longest duration is recorded.

The Voice Range Profile (VRP), or phonetogram, can be obtained in a therapy room with only a keyboard (or a pitch pipe) and a sound level meter to record vocal intensity or by using a CLS VRP program. We presently use the phonetogram for vocalists to help track register transitions, vocal "fach," and pathology. The vocalist produces the softest and loudest notes on pitches C, E, G, and A, respectively, until the entire range is sampled. The greatest range of intensity is usually found in the middle of the frequency range. Vocal intensity can have a range of 20 to 30 dB. At the extreme ends of the range, the intensity ranges are restricted. It must be understood that the VRP is not a complete representation of what the singer can and cannot do. However, by documenting changes in vocal intensity and fundamental frequency ranges, guidelines for voice training and treatment may be developed; and progress can be documented.

Classification of Signal Type

In 1995, Titze proposed that voice signals be classified into three major categories.[146] Classification distinguishes the qualitative differences among voice signals and aids in selecting the best measures for clinical assessment in an evaluating the validity of voice data. His classifications are:

Type I: Periodic or nearly periodic signals that display no qualitative changes during the time interval to be analyzed. If modulating frequencies or subharmonics are present, their energies are in order of magnitude below the energy of the fundamental frequency. For type I signals, perturbation analysis (jitter, shimmer, and noise-to harmonic ratio is reliable).

Type II: Signals with qualitative changes (bifurcations) in the segment to be analyzed or signals with subharmonic frequencies or modulating frequencies whose energies approach the energy of the fundamental frequency. In these signals, there is no obvious, single fundamental frequency throughout the segment. For type II, visual signals, visual displays such as spectrograms and phase portraits for next-cycle-parameters contours are most useful for understanding the physical characteristics of the oscillating system. Perturbations are unreliable.

Type III: Voice signals with no apparent periodic structure. For type III voice signals, perceptual ratings are most useful for clinical purposes.

Although this classification scheme has not been accepted universally, it is useful in highlighting potential pitfalls in voice analysis. Equipment currently available in voice laboratories has many limitations; and it is essential to select methods of analysis that will provide, valid, reliable measures of a given voice signal. If appropriate precautions are not followed and, for example, perturbation analysis is performed on a patient with a profoundly disordered voice producing a type III signal, meaningless numbers will be generated. Such data may be worse than no measures at all and may mislead clinicians trying to design therapy or assess outcomes.

Yanagihara Hoarseness Ratings

Spectrograms image the properties of the voice source (vibratory characteristics of the vocal folds) and filter system (resonators or vocal tract). Spectrograms can be useful clinically for analyzing and tracking changes in the spectral characteristics of the voice signal over time (or severity of dysphonia). A spectrogram of an abnormal voice displays greater noise and less energy in the harmonics of the signal than is seen in the spectrogram of a normal voice. Wideband spectrography is useful in identifying levels of noise in the voice signal. Although resolution of individual harmonics is sacrificed with wideband analysis, identification of the formant frequencies is easier. On this basis, in 1967, Yanagihara[147] proposed classification of hoarseness into four types. These four types can also be related to the vibratory pattern of the vocal folds and the mean airflow.[148]

Type I: The regular harmonic components are mixed with the noise component chiefly in the formant region of the vowels.

Type II: The noise components in the second formants of /e/ and /i/ predominate over the harmonic components, and slight additional noise components appear in the high frequency region above 3000 Hz in the vowels of /e/ and /i/

Type III: The second formants of /e/ and /i/ are totally replaced by noise components, and the additional noise components above 3 kHz further intensify their energy and expand their range.

Type IV: The second formants of /ɑ/, /e/, and /i/ are replaced by noise components, and even the first formants of all the vowels often lose their periodic components which are supplemented by noise components. In addition, more intensive high frequency components are present.

Laryngeal Electromyography

Electromyography (EMG) requires an electrode system, an amplifier, an oscilloscope, a loudspeaker, and a recording system. Electrodes are inserted into laryngeal muscles. Either a needle electrode or a hooked-wire electrode may be used.

Laryngeal electromyography has proven to be an extremely valuable technique in assessment of complex voice disorders. It is discussed in detail in chapter 5.

Laryngeal Evoked Brainstem Response

Laryngeal evoked brainstem response (LBR) is a relatively new technique that shows promise for neurolaryngologic diagnostic purposes. The test assesses a laryngeal reflex, which includes the internal branch of the superior laryngeal nerve, laryngeal loci in the brainstem, and recurrent and superior laryngeal nerves. Impulses from the superior laryngeal nerve pass through the nucleus of the tractus solitarius, the nucleus ambiguus, the nucleus of the vagus nerve, the retrofacial nucleus, and the nucleus of the reticular reformation. When the superior laryngeal nerve is stimulated electrically on one side, there are ipsilateral and bilateral adductor responses. Ludlow[149] showed an R1 and R2 response in the thyroarytenoid muscle after stimulation of the superior laryngeal nerve. R1 occurs bilaterally at 66 to 70 msec. This indicates that R2 is a polysynaptic bilateral response.

Clinically, LBR can be performed with an appropriate ABR device using equipment similar to that used for facial electroneuronography. The superior laryngeal nerve is stimulated using a bipolar surface electrode placed between the greater cornu of the hyoid bone and the superior cornu of the thyroid cartilage. Hooked wire electrodes can also be used instead of surface electrodes. Special techniques are necessary to refine the response, and LBR technique is still under development. At present, most of the information available about LBR is based on research in cats, although Yin et al have reported results of LBR in 7 normal adult humans.[149-154] In the future, we anticipate greater sophistication of LBR technique, and increasing recognition of its clinical value.

Photography

From a practical standpoint, most laryngeal photography in the office is performed using a laryngeal telescope and the video printer connected with the strobovideolaryngoscope. This provides high-quality images (especially with the Kay Elemetrics Digital Strobe System) suitable for clinical documentation and for publication. Even higher quality images can be obtained using the laryngeal telescope coupled to a 35-mm camera. Fast film (ASA 800–1000) and a good automatic winder are used. The patient is asked to breath or to phonate (depending on the image desired). Photography can be performed under continuous light or stroboscopic light. If an image is desired during phonation, the author (RTS) usually has the patient sustain phonation and rapidly acquires one- to three-dozen pictures. This is inefficient with regard to film, but it usually results in several high-quality pictures of the area desired. In the operating room, images can be acquired either through the video camera and printer or using a 35 mm camera, either through the microscope or through fiberoptic rods (Karl Storz, Culver City, Calif). Photographs using a 35-mm camera through a 10 mm, 0° or 4 mm, 70° Storz rod are superb. Many other techniques for vocal fold photography have been described since Thomas French acquired the first successful laryngeal photographs in 1882; and these are reviewed in chapter 6.

Imaging

Sophisticated imaging has enhanced greatly our ability to recognize the cause of many voice problems. CT scanning and MR imaging are currently the two most important and widely used modalities. Details of imaging techniques will not be discussed in this book. Physicians caring for patients with voice problems should be familiar with the latest information in the radiologic literature, should demand the highest quality CT and MR studies, and should be familiar with special techniques such as three-dimensional (3-D) CT (Fig 4–19), which may be extremely helpful under some circumstances. In addition to the 3-D imaging techniques that are available in most facilities, a new, extremely sophisticated 3-D CT imaging technique has been developed and is presented in chapter 7.

Psychoacoustic Evaluation

Many researchers have tried to quantify and standardize psychoacoustic evaluation of the voice. Unfortunately, even definitions of such basic terms as hoarseness and breathiness are still controversial. Standardization of psychoacoustic evaluation protocol and interpretation does not exist. Therefore, although subjective psychoacoustic analysis of the voice is of great value to the skilled clinician, it remains generally unsatisfactory for comparing research among laboratories or for reporting clinical results. Nevertheless, recognizing that the human ear and brain are still our best tools, we try to optimize the validity and usefulness of our psychoacoustic observations.

Psychoacoustic evaluation is performed independently by at least three examiners, and their findings are compared. The first evaluation is performed by the physician who records his auditory observations of specific aspects of spoken and sung voice on the laryngeal examination form. Following strobovideolaryngoscopy and objective voice analysis, the speech-language pathologist performs an examination and prepares a report describing vocal quality, vocal habits (such as harsh glottal attacks), resonance, use of vocal fry, audible and visible tension, and so on. The speech-language pathologist's office is equipped with a tape recorder and video recording so that observations can be reviewed with the patient and other members of the team. In addition, a 1-hour evaluation is performed by the singing voice specialist whose office is equipped with a piano, tape recorder, and video camera. The singing voice specialist also provides a written analysis of voice quality, habits, and techniques of voice production. At the conclusion of these evaluations, the findings of the examiners are compared; and discrepancies are resolved by reviewing tapes of the examinations. In selected cases, a similar examination is performed by the acting-voice specialist. Although this system does not solve the need for quantitative psychoacoustic analysis, it has proven useful and thorough for clinical purposes.

The GRBAS scale remains the most widely used and convenient method for rating voice quality. It was pro-

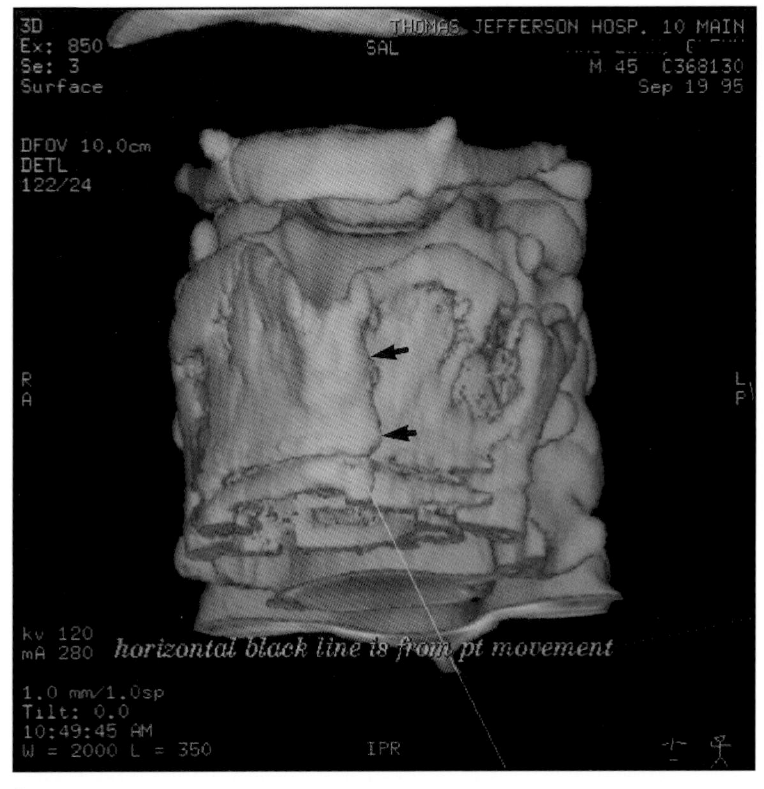

Fig 4–19. A. Three-dimensional CT of larynx, AP view illustrating vertical fracture (*arrows*). *(continued)*

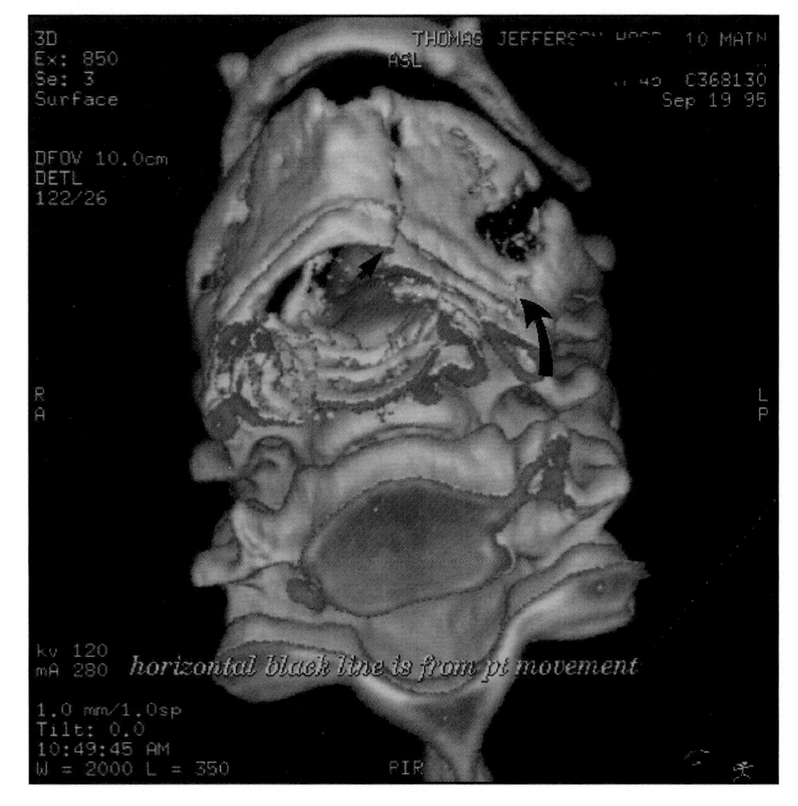

B

Fig 4–19. *(continued)* **B.** The same larynx, titled by the computer, showing that an intact right hemi-larynx overlaps the fractured side (*arrow*) and showing more clearly a posterior partial fracture (*curved arrow*). *(continued)*

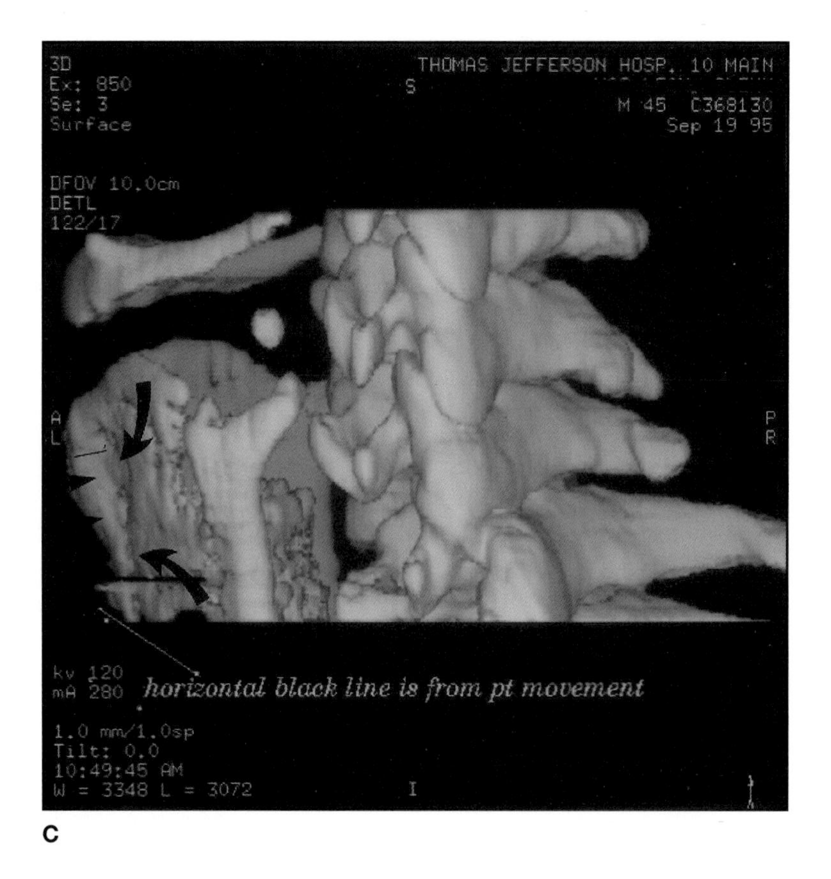

C

Fig 4–19. *(continued)* **C.** Oblique orientation of the CT of the same larynx clearly showing the left thyroid lamina (*curved arrows*) depressed below the edge (*straight arrows*) of the normal portion of the thyroid cartilage.

posed by the Committee for Phonatory Function Tests of the Japan Society of Logopedics and Phonatrics.[119] This scale is summarized in Table 4–1. Grade (G), roughness (R), Breathiness (B), Asthenic quality (A), and Strain (S) are assessed on a 4-point scale from 0 (normal) to 4 (extreme). A normal voice would be rated at G0, R0, B0, A0, S0. A patient struggling to compensate for recurrent laryngeal nerve paralysis might be rated at G1, R2, B3, A3, S2.

Collation of Results

After the laryngologist has completed the examination, reviewed test results, and received the opinions and recommendations of all team members, the physician provides the patient with the diagnosis (or diagnoses) and treatment plan. Regardless of whether the treatment involves medication, surgery, voice therapy, specialized singing training, or referral to other medical specialists, the laryngologist has primary responsibility for directing and coordinating treatment. In general, most patients with voice abnormalities benefit from comprehensive care involving all members of the clinical voice laboratory team. Such medically supervised collaborative intervention optimizes not only initial clinical care, but also long-term follow-up and acquisition of research data. All members of the clinical voice laboratory team must be expert and committed to high quality voice care, but the importance of a well-informed, active, dedicated physician to the successful establishment of a clinical voice laboratory cannot be overemphasized.

Conclusion

Although the ideal clinical voice laboratory has not yet been defined, systematic use of instrumentation has become invaluable in state-of-the-art care of the voice. In establishing a new voice laboratory, an effort should be made to address each of the categories of vocal function. A laryngostroboscope to assess vibratory function is virtually essential. If funds are limited

Table 4–1. GRBAS Voice Rating Scale.

GRADE: degree of hoarseness or voice abnormality

0	1	2	3
Normal	Slight	Moderate	Extreme

ROUGHNESS: auditory/acoustic impression of irregularity of vibration (jitter and shimmer)

0	1	2	3
Normal	Slight	Moderate	Extreme

BREATHINESS: auditory/acoustic impression of degree of air leakage (related to turbulence)

0	1	2	3
Normal	Slight	Moderate	Extreme

ASTHENIC: weakness or lack of power (related to vocal intensity and energy in higher harmonics)

0	1	2	3
Normal	Slight	Moderate	Extreme

STRAIN: auditory/acoustic impression of hyperfunction (related to fundamental frequency, noise in high-frequency range, and energy in higher harmonics)

0	1	2	3
Normal	Slight	Moderate	Extreme

Check for presence of the following:

❏ tremor ❏ pitch variation ❏ loudness variation

❏ voice interruption ❏ other: specify ______________

initially, most of the aerodynamic measures can be performed in a pulmonologist's office or hospital's pulmonary function laboratory. Phonatory function measurements require extremely inexpensive equipment that can be obtained at a neighborhood electronics store. Equipment for acoustic analysis is important, useful, and elegant and should be included as soon as possible. However, if funds to purchase such equipment are not available initially, at least a high quality microphone and tape recorder should be acquired. Arrangements usually can be made with other voice laboratories to analyze these recordings as needed, so long as appropriate, standardized recording techniques and protocols are used. Laryngeal electromyography can be referred to a neurologist or neurophysiologist trained (usually by the laryngologist) in laryngeal electrode placement or laryngeal EMG may be performed by the laryngologist. Once a team has begun using even a minimally equipped voice laboratory regularly, its value becomes clear, and additional equipment can be added as dictated by need and resources.

References

1. Sataloff RT. The professional voice. II: Physical examination. *J Voice*. 1987;1(2):191–201.
2. Sataloff RT, Spiegel JR, Carroll LM, et al. Strobovideolaryngoscopy in professional voice users: results and clinical value. *J Voice*. 1988;1(4):359–364.
3. Sataloff RT. Strobovideolaryngoscopy in professional voice users: results and clinical value. *Ann Otol Rhinol Laryngol*. 1991;1a(9):725–727.
4. Hirano M. Phonosurgery. Basic and clinical investigations. *Otologia (Fukuoka)*. 1975;21:239–442.
5. Bless D, Hirano M, Feder RJ. Video stroboscopic evaluation of the larynx. *Ear Nose Throat J*. 1987;66(7):289–296.
6. Hirano M, Bless D. *Videostroboscopic Examination of the Larynx*. San Diego, Calif: Singular Publishing Group; 1993.
7. Oertel MJ. Das laryngoskopische untersuchung. *Arch Laryngol Rhinol (Berl)*. 1895;3:1–16
8. Aberti PW. The diagnostic role of laryngeal stroboscopy. *Otolaryngol Clin North Am*. 1978;11(2)(June): 347–354.
9. Barth V, Pilorget J. La stroboscopie laryngee. *Rev Laryngol Otol Rhinol (Bord)*. 1983;104(4):359–364.
10. Beck J, Schoenhaerl E. The significance of stroboscopy for the diagnosis of functional voice disorders. *Arch Ohr Nas Kehlkopfheilk*. 1959;175:449–452.
11. Bekbulatov GT. Stroboskopiia v otsenke funktsional'nugo vosstanovleniia golosovogo apparata posle operatsii na golosovykh sladkakh. *Vestn Otorinolaring*. 1969;31: 52–54.
12. Bohme G. The efficacy of electrotherapy in laryngeal diseases as shown in the stroboscopic picture. *Laryngol Rhinol Otol* (Stuttgart). 1965;44(7):481–488.
13. Boudin G, Duron B, Ossart M, Abitol J. Electromyographie larynge technique—premiers resultats. *J Fr Otorhinolaryngol*. 1984;33(1):46–48.

14. Brewer DW, McCall G. Visible laryngeal changes during voice therapy: fiberoptic study. *Ann Otol Rhinol Laryngol.* 1974;83:423–427.
15. Cammann RJ, Pahn J, Rother U. Diagnostik der N.—laryngeus—superior—parese. *Folia Phoniatr* (Basel). 1976;28(6):349–353.
16. Chaplin Vl, I lakovleva II. Stroboskopiia detei kapelly mal'chikov. *Nov Med Tekhn.* 1964;2:41–44.
17. Cornut G, Bouchayer M, Parent F. Value of videostroboscopy in indicating phonosurgery. *Acta Otorhinolaryngol Belg.* 1986;40(2):436–442.
18. Croft TA. Failure of visual estimation of motion under strobe. *Nature.* 1971;231(5302):397.
19. Eigler G, Podzuweit G, Weiland H. New microphone controlled stroboscope with flashlights for study of vocal cord vibrations. *Ztschr Laryng Rhin Otol.* 1953; 32(Jan):40–45.
20. Ernst R. Stroboscopic studies in professional speakers. *HNO.* 1960;8(March 31):170–174.
21. Ernst R. The stroboscopic recognition of functional voice disorders by means of singing and speaking stress. *Arch Ohr Nas Kehlkopfheilk.* 1959;175:452–455.
22. Ertt S, Stein L. History of motorless laryngostroboscopy. *Monatschr f Ohrenh.* 1936;70(Dec):1463–1464.
23. Fex S, Elmqvist D. Endemic recurrent laryngeal nerve paresis: correlation between EMG and stroboscopic findings. *Acta Otolaryngol* (Stockh). 1973;75(4):368–369.
24. Fulgenicio MS. Laryngeal stroboscopy. *AMB Rev Assoc Med Bras.* 1978;24(1):17–18.
25. Gerull G, Gesen M, Mrowinski D, Rudolph N. Laryngeal stroboscopy using a scanning microphone. *HNO.* 1972;20(12):369.
26. Gould WI. The clinical voice laboratory—clinical application of voice research. *Ann Otol Rhinol Laryngol.* 1984; 93(4 Pt 1):346–350.
27. Gould WJ, Kojima H, Lambiase A. A technique for stroboscopic examination of the vocal folds using fiberoptics. *Arch Otolaryngol.* 1979;105(5):258.
28. Greiner GF, Dillenschneider E, Conraux C. Stroboscopic and sonographic aspects of the traumatic larynx. *J Fr Ororhinolaryngol.* 1968;17(3):237–241.
29. Haas, E, Bildstein P. The significance of stroboscopy in the early diagnosis of vocal fold cancer. *Laryngol Rhinol Otol* (Stuttgart). 1974;53(3):169–172.
30. Hala B, Honty L. Cinematography of vocal cords by means of stroboscope and great speed. *Otolaryng Slavica.* 1931;3(Jan):1–12.
31. Hollien H, Coleman R, Moore P. Stroboscopic laminography of the larynx during phonation. *Acta Otolaryngol* (Stockh). 1968;65(Jan–Feb):209–251.
32. Honjo I, Isshiki N. Laryngoscopic and voice characteristics of aged persons. *Arch Otolaryngol.* 1980;106(3)(Mar): 149–150.
33. Husson R. Principal facts of vocal physiology and pathology gained by laryngostroboscopy. *Rev de Laryng.* 1936;57(Dec):1132–1145.
34. Husson R. Stroboscopic study of reflex modifications of vibration of vocal cords produced by experimental stimulations of auditory and trigeminal nerves. *C R Hebd Seances Acad Sci.* 1951;232(Mar 19):1247–1249.
35. Kallen LA. Laryngostroboscopy in the practice of otolaryngology. *Arch Otolaryngol.* 1932;16:791–807.
36. Kallen LA, Polin HS. A physiological stroboscope. *Science.* 1934;80:592.
37. Kitzing P. Stroboscopy—a pertinent laryngological examination. *Otolaryngology.* 1985;14(3)(Jun):151–175.
38. Koike Y. Diagnosis of voice disorders. *Nippon Jihiinkoka Gakkai Kaiho.* 1979;82(11)(Nov):1434–1437.
39. Krauhulec L. Importance of stroboscopy in laryngology. *Cesk Otolaryngol.* 1970;19(1):29–31.
40. Kristensen HK, Zilstorff-Pedersen K. Synchrono-electrostroboscopic examination of the vocal cords. *Nord Med.* 1982;68(July 19):927–929.
41. Leitao FB, Morgati AP, Elisabetsky M, Mantoanelli JB. Stroboscopy control of phonetic sound before and after tracheal intubation. *Rev Bras Anesthesiol.* 1968;18(2):182.
42. Luchsinger R. Stroboscopic symptomatology. *Pract Otorhinolaryngol.* 1948;10:209–214.
43. MacKay DM. Fragmentation of binocular fusion in stroboscopic illumination. *Nature.* 1970;227(257):518.
44. Maliutin EN. Stroboscopic phenomena in vocal students. *Russk Klin.* 1930;13:681–691.
45. Mareev VM, Papshitsky YA. Stroboscopy in hyperplastic and tumour processes of the larynx. *Vestn Otorinolaryingol.* 1972;34:71–75.
46. Mareev VM, Papshitskii IA. Stroboskopiia pri giperplasticheskikh I opukhdevykh protsessakh gortani. *Vestn Otorinolaringol.* 1973;76(April):495–500.
46. McKelvie WB. Stroboscope using grid-controlled neon tube, "strobotron." *J Laryngol Otol.* 1944;59(Dec):464–465.
47. Merriman JS. Stroboscopic photography as a research instrument. *Res Quart Am Assoc Health Phys Ed.* 1977; 48(3):628–631.
48. Milner M, Brennan PK, Wilberforce CB. Stroboscopic Polaroid photography in clinical studies of human locomotion. *S Afr Med J.* 1973;47(22):948–950.
49. Minnigerode B. The defiguration phenomenon in motion perception and its effect on stroboscopic laryngoscopy. *Laryngol Rhinol Otol* (Stuttgart). 1967;101(1): 33–38.
50. Moore DM, Berle S, Hanson DG, Ward PH. Videostroboscopy of the canine larynx: the effects of asymmetric laryngeal tension. *Laryngoscope.* 1987;97(5):543–553.
51. Morrison MD. A clinical voice laboratory: videotape and stroboscopic instrumentation. *Otolaryngol Head Neck Surg.* 1984;92(4)(Aug):487–488.
52. Musehold A. Stroboskopische und photographische studien uber die stellung der stimmlippen im brust-und falsett-register. *Arch Laryngol Rhinol* (Berl). 1898;7:1–21.
53. Oertel MJ. Ueber eine neue laryngostroboscopische untersuchungsmethode. *Munchen Med Woknschr.* 1895; 42:233–236.
54. Padovan IF, Christman NT, Hamilton LH, Darling RJ. Indirect microlaryngostrocopy. *Laryngoscope.* 1973;83: 2035–2041.
55. Pakhmilevich AG. Elektonnaia laringostroboskopicheskaia Kartina prinektrorykh. *Vestn Otorhinolaringol.* 1981;5(Sept–Oct):58–62.

56. Pantiukhin VP. Stroboscopy in patients after laryngectomy. *Vestn Otorhynolaringol.* 1961;23(May–Jun):69–73.
57. Pearlman HB. Laryngeal stroboscopy. *Ann Otol Rhinol Laryngol.* 1945;54(Mar):159–165.
58. Powell LS. Laryngostroboscope. *Arch Otolaryngol.* 1934;19(June):708–710.
59. Powell LS. The laryngo-stroboscope in clinical examination. *Eye Ear Nose Throat Monthly.* 1935;14:265.
60. Raes J, Lebrun Y, Clement P. Videostroboscopy of the larynx. *Acta Otorhinolaryngol Belg.* 1986;40(2):421–425.
61. Rohrs M. Untersuchungen uber das schwingungsverhalten der stimmlippen in verschiedenen registerbereichen mit unterschiedlichen stroboskipischen techniken. *Folia Phoniatr* (Basel). 1985;37(3–4):113–118.
62. Russell GO, Tuttle CH. Color movies of vocal cord action aid in diagnosis. *Laryngoscope.* 1930;40(Aug): 549–552.
63. Saito S, Fukuda H, Kitahara S, Kowawa N. Stroboscopic observation of vocal fold vibration with fiberoptics. *Folia Phoniatr* (Basel). 1978;30(4):241–244.
64. Salivon LG, Kirina NI. Stroboscopy in malignant tumors of the larynx in the postradiation period. *Zhurnal Ushnykh, no sovkh i Gorlovykh Boleznei* (Kiev). 1972;32(2):74–76.
65. Sawashima M, Hirose H. New laryngoscopic technique by use of fiberoptics. *J Acoust Soc Am.* 1968;43:168–169.
66. Schlosshauer B, Timcke R. Stroboscopic studies in hemilaryngectomized patients. *Arch Ohren-Nasen-u-Kehlkopfh.* 1956;168:404–413.
67. Schonharl E. *Die stroboskopie in der praktischen laryngologie.* Stuttgart, Germany: Georg Thieme Verlag; 1960.
68. Schonharl E. Significance of laryngostroboscopy for practicing otorhinolaryngologists. *Ztschr Laryng Rhin Otol.* 1952;31(July–Aug):383–386.
69. Schonharl E. Stroboscopic study in myxedema. *Arch Ohren-Nasen-u Kehlkopfh.* 1954;165:633–635.
70. Schonharl E. New stroboscope with automatic regulation of frequency and recent results of its application to study of vocal cord vibrations in dysphonias of various origins. *Rev Laryn.* 1956;77(suppl)(May):476–481.
71 Sedlackova E. Stroboscopic data in relation to the development of voice in children. *Folia Phoniatr.* 1961;13:81–92.
72. Segre R. Vocal nodules as revealed by stroboscope. *Valsalva.* 1933;9(May):380–389.
73. Silberman HD, Wilf H, Tucker JA. Flexible fiberoptic nasopharyngolaryngoscope. *Ann Otol Rhinol Laryngol.* 1976;85:640–645.
74. Stern H. Study of larynx and of voice by means of stroboscopic moving picture. *Monatschr f Ohrenh.* 1935;69 (June):648–652.
75. Szentesi DI. Stroboscopic electron mirror microscopy at frequencies up to 100 MHz. *J Phys Sci Instr.* 1972;5(6): 563–567.
76. Tarneaud J. Study of larynx and of voice by stroboscopy. *Clinique* (Paris). 1933;28[Nov(A)]:337–341.
77. Tobin HA. Office fiberoptic laryngeal photography. *Otorhinolaryngol Head Neck Surg.* 1980;88:172–173.
78. Tischner H. Vocal cord stroboscopy with automatic adjustment of frequency. *Arch Ohren-Nasen-u Kehlkopfh.* 1955;167:254–529.
79. Von Leden H. The electric synchron-stroboscope: its value for the practicing laryngologist. *Ann Otol Rhinol Laryngol.* 1961;70:881–893.
80. Voronina EM, Shtumer YF. Strobofaradizator. *Zhur ush nos i gorl hoky.* 1939;16:258–263.
81. Watanabe H, Shin T, Matsuo K, et al. A new computer-analyzing system for clinical use with the strobovideoscope. *Arch Otolaryngol Head Neck Surg.* 1986;112(9) 978–981.
82. Welsh AR. The practical and economic value of flexible system laryngoscopy. *J Laryngol Otol.* 1982;96:1125–1129.
83. Wendler J. Significance of the strength of the voice in stroboscopic examination. *Folia Phoniatr* (Basel). 1967; 19(2):73–88.
84. Wendler J, Seidner W, Halbedl G, et al. Tele-Mikrostroboskopie. *Folia Phonatr* (Basel). 1973;25:281–287.
85. West R. A view of the larynx through a new stroboscope. *Q J Speech.* 1935;21:355.
86. White JF, Knight RE. Office videofiberoptic laryngoscopy. *Laryngoscope.* 1984;94(9):1166–1169.
87. Williams GT, Farquharson IM, Anthony J. Fiberoptic laryngoscopy in the assessment of laryngeal disorders. *J Laryngol Otol.* 1975;89:299–316.
88. Wilson FB, Kudryk WH, Sych JA. The development of flexible fiberoptic video nasendoscopy (FFVN)—clinical-teaching-research applications. *Asha.* 1986;28(11)(Nov): 25–30.
89. Winckel F. Improved stroboscopic technic for examination. *Arch Ohren-Nasen-u Kehlkopfh.* 1954;165:582–586.
90. Witton TH. An introduction to the fiberoptic laryngoscope. *Can Anesth Soc J.* 1981;28:475–478.
91. Yana D. Stroboscopy of the larynx: apropos of a new stroboscope; the stroborama type L.6. *Ann Otolaryngol Chir Cervicofac.* 1969;86(9):589–592.
92. Yanagisawa E. Office telescopic photography of the larynx. *Ann Otol Rhinol Laryngol.* 1982;91:354–358.
93. Yanagisawa E, Owens TW, Strothers G, Honda K. Videolaryngoscopy: a comparison of fiberoptic and telescopic documentation. *Ann Otol Rhinol Laryngol.* 1983; 92(5 Pt 1):430–436.
94. Yanagisawa E. Videolaryngoscopy using a low cost home video system color camera. *J Biol Photogr.* 1984 52(2):9–14.
95. Yanagisawa E, Sullivano J, Carlson RD. Simultaneous video imaging of lip and vocal cord movements for videographic documentation of laryngeal function. *J Biol Photogr.* 1986;54(3)(Jul):107–109.
96. Yoshida Y, Koiwa S, Amano M. Comparison between the original and modified NLA methods in stroboscopic laryngomicrosurgery. *Jpn J Anesthesiol.* 1976;25(5): 497–501.
97. Yoshida Y, Hirano M, Nakajima T. An improved model of laryngo-stroboscope. *Otolaryngology* (Tokyo). 1977;49: 663–669.
98. Yoshida Y, Hirano M, Nakajima T. A videotape recording system for laryngostroboscopy. *J Jpn Bronchoesophagol Soc.* 1979;30:1–5.
99. Yoshida Y, Hirano M, Yoshida T, Tateishi O. Strobofibrescopic colour video recording of vocal fold vibration. *J Laryngol Otol.* 1985;99(8):795–800.

100. Young KA, Atkins JP Jr, Keane WM, Rowe LD. The role of the voice science center in the otorhinolaryngology practice. *Trans Pa Acad Ophthalmol Otolaryngol*. 1982; 35(2)(Fall):141–144.
101. Sataloff RT: *Professional Voice: The Science and Art of Clinical Care*. New York: Raven Press; 1991:111–120.
102. Heman-Ackah YD, Dean C, Sataloff RT. Strobovideolaryngoscopic findings in singing teachers. *J Voice*. 2002;16(1):81–86.
103. Elias ME, Sataloff RT, Rosen DC, et al. Normal strobovideolaryngoscopy: variability in healthy singers. *J Voice*. 1997;11:104–107.
104. Sodersten M, Lindestad PA. A comparison of vocal fold closure in rigid telescopic and flexible fiberoptic laryngostroboscopy. *Acta Otolaryngol* (Stockh). 1992; 112:144–150.
105. Karnell MP. Synchronized videostroboscopy and electroglottography. *J Voice*. 1989;3(1):68–75.
106. Staloff RT: *Professional Voice: The Science and Art of Clinical Care*. New York Raven Press; 1991:101–140.
107. Von Leden H, Moore P, Timcke R. Laryngeal vibrations: measurements of the glottic wave: Part 3. The pathologic larynx. *Arch Otolaryngol*. 1960;71:16–35.
108. Gall V. Strip kymography of the glottis. *Arch Otorhinolaryngol*. 1984;240:287–293.
109. Svec JG, Schutte HK. Videokymography: high-speed line canning of vocal fold vibration. *J Voice*. 1996;10: 201–205.
110. Schutte HK, Svec JG, Sram F. Videokymography: research and clinical application of videokymography. *Log Phon Vocol*. 1998;22:152–156..
111. Schutte HK, Svec JG, Sram F. First results of clinical application videokymography. *Laryngoscope*. 1998;108: 1206–1210.
112. Honda R Kiritani S, Imagawa H, Hirose KS, In: Baer T, Sasaki C, Harris KS, eds. *Laryngeal Function in Phonation and Respiration*. San Diego Calif: College-Hill Press; 1987:485–491.
113. Hess MM, Gross M. High-speed, light-intensified digital imaging of vocal fold vibrations in high optical resolution via indirect microlaryngoscopy. *Ann Otol Rhinol Laryngol*. 1993;102:502–507.
114. Hertegard S, Lindestad PA. Vocal fold vibrations studied during phonation with high-speed video imaging. Stockholm, Sweden: Karolinska Institute, Huddinge University Hospital Phoniatric and Logepedic Progress Report; 1994;9:33–40.
115. Eysholdt U, Tigges M, Wittenberg T, Proschel U. Direct evaluation of high-speed recordings of vocal fold vibrations. *Folia Phoniatr Logop*. 1996;48:163–170.
116. Colton RH, Woo P: Measuring vocal fold function. In: Rubin JS, Sataloff RT, Korovin GS, eds. *Diagnosis and Treatment of Voice Disorders*. 2nd ed. Clifton Park, NY: Delmar Thomson Learning; 2003.
117. Larsson H, Hertegard S, Lindestad PA, Hammarberg B. Vocal fold vibrations: high-speed imaging, kymography, and acoustic analysis: a preliminary report. *Laryngoscope*. 2000;110:2117–2122.
118. Leclure FLE, Broccar ME, Verschuure J. Elecroglottography and its relation to glottal activity. *Folia Phoniatr*. 1975;27:215–224.
119. Hirano M. *Clinical Examination of the Voice*. New York: Springer-Verlag; 1981:1–98.
120. Gould WJ, Sataloff RT, Spiegel JR: *Voice Surgery*. St. Louis: Mosby-Year Book; 1993.
121. Hirano M, Koike Y, von Leden H. Maximum phonation time and air usage during phonation. *Folia Phoniatr*. 1968;20:185–201.
122 Carroll LM, Sataloff RT, Heuer RJ, Spiegel JR, Radionoff SL, Cohn JR. Respiratory and glottal efficiency measures in normal classically trained singers. *J Voice*. 1996; 10(2):139–145.
123. Robb MP, Saxman JH. Developmental trends in vocal fundamental frequency of young children. *J Speech Hear Res*. 1985;28:421–427.
124. Coleman RJ, Mabis JH, Hinson JK. Fundamental frequency-sound pressure level profiles of adult male and female voices. *J Speech Hear Res*. 1977;20:197–204.
125. Isshiki N. Regulatory mechanism of voice intensity variation. *J Speech Hear Res*. 1964;7:17–29.
126. Saito S. Phonosurgery, basic study on the mechanism of phonation and endolaryngeal microsurgery. *Otologia* (Fukuoka). 1977;23 (suppl 1):171–384.
127. Isshiki N. Functional surgery of the larynx (official report of the 78th annual convention of the Oto-Rhino-Laryngological Society of Japan, Fukuoka), Kyoto University, 1977.
128. Bough ID Jr, Heuer RJ, Sataloff RT, et al. Intrasubject variability of objective voice measures. *J Voice*. 1996; 10(2):166–174.
129. Price DB, Sataloff RT. Technical note: a simple technique for consistent microphone placement in voice recording. *J Voice*. 1988;2(3)206–207.
130. Frokjaer-Jenson B, Prytz S. Registration of voice quality. *Bruel & Kjäer Rev*. 1976;3:3–17.
131. Heman-Ackah YD, Heuer RJ, Michael DD, et al. Cepstral peak prominence: a more reliable measure of dysphonia. *Ann Otol Rhinol Laryngol*. 2003;112:324–333.
132. Heman-Ackah YD, Michael DD, Goding GS Jr. The relationship between cepstral peak prominence and selected parameters of dysphonia. *J Voice*. 2002;16: 20–27.
133. Noll AM. Short-time spectrum and "cepstrum" techniques for vocal-pitch detection. *J Acoust Soc Am*. 1964; 36:296–302.
134. Noll AM. Cepstrum pitch determination. *J Acoust Soc Am*. 1967;41:293–309.
135. Hillenbrand J, Cleveland RA, Erickson RL. Acoustic correlates of breathy voice quality. *J Speech Hear Res*. 1994;37:769–778.
136. Hillenbrand J, Houde RA. Acoustic correlates of breathy voice quality: dysphonic voices and continuous speech. *J Speech Hear Res*. 1996;39:311–321.
137. Baken RJ, Orlikoff RF. *Clinical Measurements of Speech and Voice*. San Diego, Calif: Singular Publishing Group; 2000:53–90.

138. Butler JP, Napora LS. The voice history, examination and testing. In: Colton RH, Casper JK, eds. *Understanding Voice Problems*. Baltimore, Md: Williams and Wilkins; 1996: 165–210.
139. Winholtz WS, Titze IR. Suitability of minidisc (MD) recordings for voice perturbation analysis. *J Voice*. 1998;12(2):138–142.
140. Bielamowicz S, Kineman J, Gerralt BR, et al. Comparison of voice analysis systems for perturbation measurement. *J Speech Hear Res*. 1996;39(1):126–134.
141. Read C, Buder EH, Kent RD. Speech analysis systems: a survey. *J Speech Hear Res*. 1990;33(2):363–374.
142. Karnell MP, Scherer RS, Fischer LB. Comparison of acoustic voice perturbation measures among three independent voice laboratories. *J Speech Hear Res*. 1991; 34(4):781–790.
143. Perkell JS, Holmberg EB, Hillman RE. A system for signal processing and data extraction for aerodynamic, acoustic and electroglottographic signals in the study of voice production. *J Acoust Soc Am*. 1991;89(4 Pt1): 1777–1781.
144. Berke GS, Hanson DG, Trapp TK, et al Office-based system for voice analysis. *Arch Otolaryngol Head Neck Surg*. 1989;115(1):74–77.
145. Jiang J, Lin E, Hanson DG. Effect of tape recording on perturbation measures. *J Speech Lang Hear Res*. 1998; 41(5):1031–1041.
146. Titze IR. *Workshop on Acoustic Voice Analysis: Summary Statement*. Denver, Colo: National Center for Voice and Speech; 1995:18–23, 26.
147. Yanagihara N. Significance of harmonic changes and noise components in hoarseness. *J Speech Hear Res*. 1967;10:531–541.
148. Hirano M. *Clinical Examination of Voice*. Wien/New York: Springer-Verlag; 1981:73.
149. Ludlow CL, Van Pelt FV, Koda J. Characteristics of late responses to superior laryngeal nerve stimulation in humans. *Ann Otol Rhinol Laryngol*. 1992;101:127–134.
150. Kim YH, Hong WP, Kim KM, Kim HY. Superior laryngeal nerve brain stem evoked response in the cat. *Ann Otol Rhinol Laryngol*. 1997;106:101–108.
151. Lalakea ML, Anonsen CK, Hannley M. Laryngeal brainstem evoked response: a developmental study. *Laryngoscope*. 1990;100:294–301.
152. Anonsen CK, Lalakea ML, Hannley M. Laryngeal brain stem evoked response. *Ann Otol Rhinol Laryngol*. 1989; 98:677–683.
153. Fukuyama T, Umezaki T, Shin T. Origin of laryngeal sensory-evoked potentials (LSEPs) in the cat. *Brain Res Bull*. 1993;31:381–392.
154. Yin SS, Qiu WW, Stucker FJ, et al.. Laryngeal evoked brainstem response in humans: a preliminary study. *Laryngoscope*. 1997;107:1261–1266.

5

Laryngeal Electromyography

Robert Thayer Sataloff, Steven Mandel, Ramon Mañon-Espaillat, Yolanda D. Heman-Ackah, and Mona M. Abaza

Electromyography (EMG) evaluates the integrity of the motor system by recording action potentials (electrical activity) generated in the muscle fibers. EMG is particularly useful for evaluating disorders affecting the lower motor neurons, peripheral nerves, neuromuscular junctions, and muscles. EMG should be considered an extension of the physical examination rather than solely a laboratory procedure. Following a thorough and careful examination of the patient, the muscles to be evaluated by EMG are selected prior to beginning the study. Also, abnormalities detected by EMG should be interpreted within the context of the clinical impressions. For interested readers, other texts provide a comprehensive presentation of EMG in the diagnosis and treatment of the neurological disorders.[1-3]

Basic Neurophysiology

The interior of a muscle or nerve cell is electrically negative with respect to its exterior. This electrical potential difference is called the resting membrane potential. In muscles, it is on the order of –90 millivolts; for lower motor neurons, it is about –70 millivolts. This resting membrane potential reflects the difference in ionic concentration that exists across the cell membrane and the selective permeability of the cell membrane. The intracellular and interstitial fluids are in osmotic and electrical equilibrium with each other; however, the distribution of the ions between the two compartments is unequal. The intracellular compartment has a high concentration of potassium, whereas the extracellular compartment has a high concentration of sodium and chloride. This inequality of ionic concentration is maintained by an active energy-dependent transport mechanism. With the application of an appropriate stimulus, nerves and muscles generate action potentials. The action potential is a fast and transient reversal of the membrane potential caused by a temporary change in membrane permeability. This action potential is propagated along the fiber without decrement. In order to generate the propagating action potential, the membrane must be depolarized to a minimum level known as the membrane threshold potential.[4,5]

The motor unit consists of a single lower motor neuron and the muscle fibers that it innervates. Therefore, it includes the cell body of the lower motor neuron in the spinal cord, its axon with its terminal arborization, the neuromuscular junctions, and all the muscle fibers innervated by them (Fig 5–1). The innervation ratio of the muscle is the ratio of the total number of muscle fibers to the total number of motor axons supplying them. The innervation ratio in small muscles such as the laryngeal muscles, external rectus, tensor tympani, and platysma muscles is approximately 25:1, as compared to the innervation ratio of the medial head of the gastrocnemius (a large muscle), which is approximately 1700:1. Muscles with low innervation ratios typically are required to perform finely graded movements, as opposed to muscles with high innervation ratios, which typically are involved in coarser activity. The individual muscle fibers that belong to a given motor unit are scattered diffusely in the muscles without grouping.[6]

Based on histochemical characteristics, there are two types of muscle fibers. Type 1 fibers are rich in mitochondrial oxidative enzymes but poor in myofib-

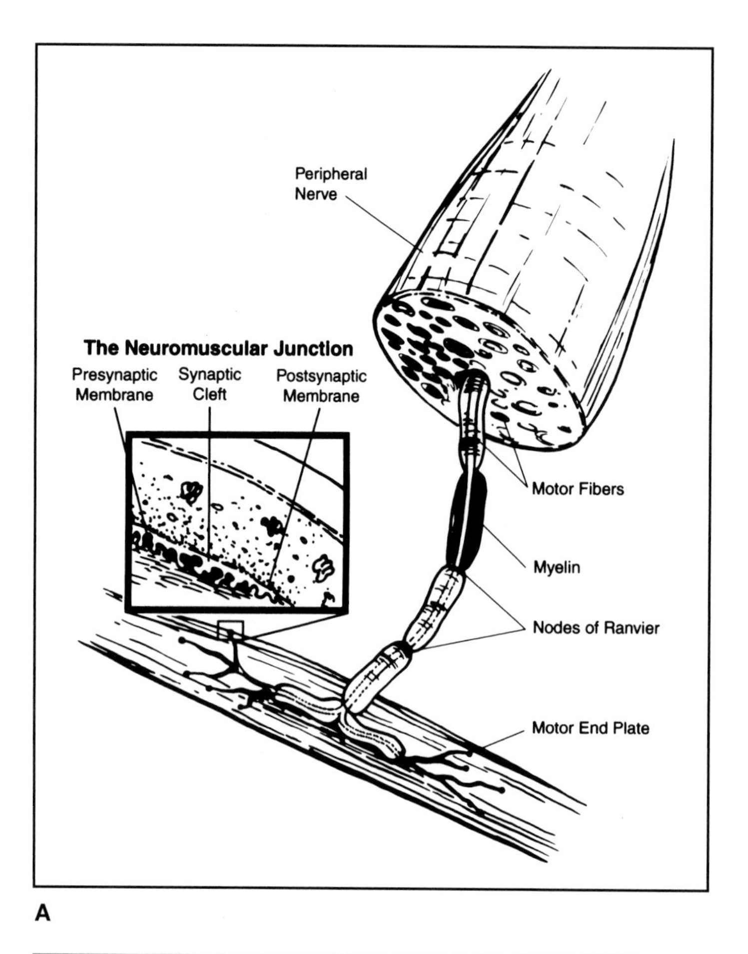

A

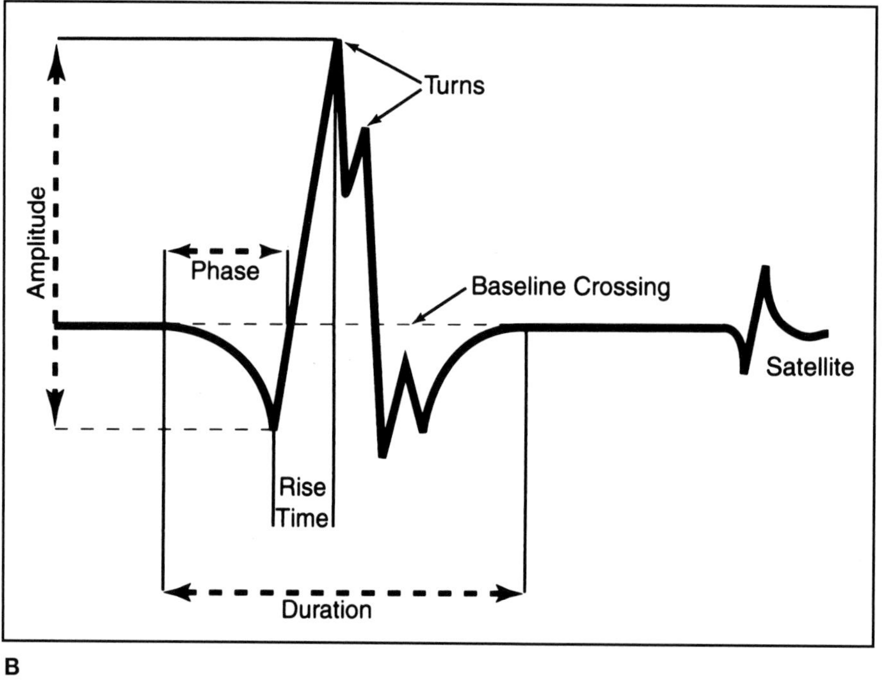

B

Fig 5–1. A. A motor unit. **B.** Components of the action potential generated from a motor unit.

rillar adenosine triphosphatase (ATPase); whereas for Type 2 fibers, the reverse is true. The muscle fibers of an individual motor unit are all of the same histochemical type. The lower motor neuron has trophic influence on the muscle fiber so that a muscle fiber may change its histochemical characteristics when reinnervated by another motor unit. Type 1 muscle fibers are best suited for producing low intensity tension for a long time. Type 2 fibers are best suited for generating high tension for a short time[7] (Table 5–1).

In the spinal cord, smaller motor neurons innervate Type 1 fibers and large motor neurons innervate Type 2 fibers (Table 5–2). Smaller motor neurons are typically activated at low muscle tension; therefore, they are the first ones to be observed during the electromyographic evaluation. Large motor neurons are recruited during high muscle tension and are, therefore, seen during maximal muscle contraction. Small motor neurons fire at a lower rate, typically less than 20 Hz; large motor neurons are capable of firing at rates as high as 100 Hz. With aging there is a significant loss of motor neurons in the anterior horn cells. This causes an increase in the innervational ratio of the surviving units.[8]

Table 5–1. Properties of Muscle Component of the Motor Unit.

Properties	*Type S Motor Unit*	*Type FR Motor Unit*	*Type FF Motor Unit*
Capillary supply	Extensive	Extensive	Sparse
Contractile properties			
Resistance to fatigue during repetitive stimulation	High	Moderate	Low
Stimulation rate for fused tetanic contraction	Low	High	High
Twitch response	Slow	Fast	Fast
Twitch and tetanus tensions	Small	Moderate	Large
Histochemical type	1	2A	2B
Reactivity with histochemical stains for			
Mitochondrial oxidative enzymes	High	Moderate to High	Low
Myofibrillar ATPase	Low	High	High
Phosphorylase	Low	High	High

Table 5–2. Properties of Motor Neuron Component of the Motor Unit.

Properties	*Type S Motor Unit*	*Type FR Motor Unit*	*Type FF Motor Unit*
Duration of after-hyperpolarization	Long	Short	Long
Firing pattern during activity			
Firing frequency	About 20 Hz	Up to 100 Hz	Up to 100 Hz
Firing pattern	Continuous	Bursts	Bursts
Intensity of stimulation required for activation	Low	Moderate	High
Power of accommodation	Low	Moderate	High
Size	Small	Moderately large	Large

The Electrodiagnostic Apparatus

Bioelectrical potentials from the muscles and / or nerves being examined are detected by an active recording electrode connected to a differential amplifier with a typical common mode rejection ratio of 100,000:1 and a high input impedance of at least 100 kΩ. The frequencies of muscle action potentials range between 2 Hz and 10,000 kHz; and the frequency band of the electromyography machine is typically set at 10 Hz to 10,000 kHz. The reference electrode is also connected to the amplifier. The signal of interest is measured as the potential difference between the active and reference electrode. The patient must be grounded to reduce the risk of electrical injury and 60 Hz interference. The electrodiagnostic signal is displayed on a cathode ray oscilloscope in real time and can be heard through a loudspeaker. The amplified signal can then be monitored visually and acoustically. The signal can be stored permanently on magnetic tape, a computer disk, or paper. In addition to the qualitative analysis used most commonly, quantitative EMG assessment is also possible. In modern systems the amplifier signal is also connected to an analog-to-digital converter, a microprocessor, and a video monitor for a digital display of the signal. This permits rapid mathematical manipulation of the raw data.

In addition, an electrical stimulator is incorporated into the system so that it is connected to the microprocessor and the oscilloscope and can trigger the recording system when stimulation is provided. The ability of an amplifier to reject common mode signals is indicated by its common mode rejection ratio (CMRR). The higher the ratio, the greater the ability of the amplifier is to reject common mode potentials. In clinical electromyography, amplifiers with a CMRR of 10,000 are preferred, which means that unequal potential differences between the two inputs of the amplifier will be amplified 10,000 times more than potentials equal to both inputs.[9,10]

In most EMG laboratories, sophisticated, multichannel systems are utilized. Several excellent systems are available commercially. They have many advantages, including permitting simultaneous, multi-channel recording; but EMG systems are fairly expensive. For otolaryngologists who plan to utilize laryngeal electromyography for needle guidance when injecting botulinum toxin or for occasional diagnostic purposes, less expensive, conveniently portable systems are now available (Fig 5–2). The device utilized by the author (RTS) for this purpose is manufactured by Xomed (Jacksonville, Fla). In its basic form, this EMG unit provides only auditory information and single channel recording; but it can be connected to the computer to provide a visual display. Such compact devices are also valuable for bedside, inpatient testing of patients with laryngeal trauma to help differentiate between arytenoid injury and vocal fold paralysis; they are especially convenient during evenings and weekends when formal EMG laboratory facilities may not be available. Another cost-effective option for otolaryngologists is use of the auditory brainstem evoked response (ABR) audiometer already found in many offices. Most ABR units can be used (sometimes with minor modifications) for single-channel EMG. However, although such devices are used for specific, clinically important purposes, they are utilized in addition to, not in place of, a sophisticated, multi-channel EMG system for diagnostic testing.

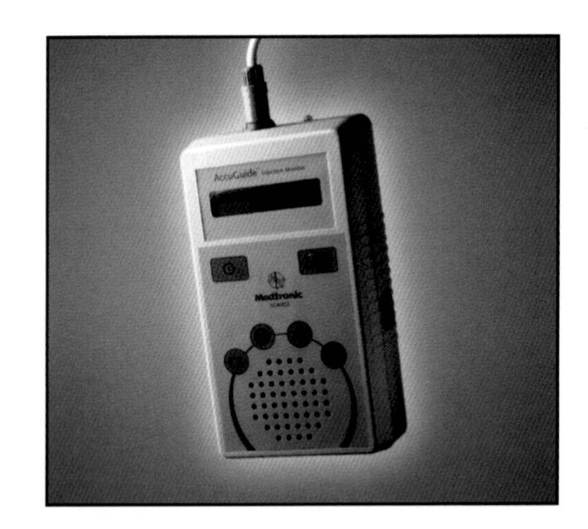

Fig 5–2. Portable, cost-effective, single channel EMG device (Medtronics-Xomed, Jacksonville, Fla).

The flow of current in biological tissues occurs as a result of the movement of ions; in electronic systems, it is due to the movements of electrons. The conversion of ionic activity into electron movements occurs at the electrode-tissue interface. Electrodes usually are made of a metal that is a good conductor of electricity. Surface and needle electrodes are used in electromyography. Surface electrodes are placed on the skin or mucosa and do not penetrate the surface. Although they are noninvasive, they are the least selective type of electrode. Surface electrodes are used in the study of nerve conduction velocity and neuromuscular transmission. The potential that is recorded represents the sum of all individual potentials produced by the nerve or muscle fibers that are activated. These electrodes are not suitable for recording details of electrical events associated with individual motor units. Typically, surface electrodes consist of a metal disk with a diameter of 0.5 to 2.5 cm.

There are several types of needle electrodes–monopolar, bipolar, concentric, hooked wire and single fiber (Fig 5–3). The monopolar needle electrode is a solid stainless steel needle that is insulated except at its tip. The recording area from this electrode is circular.

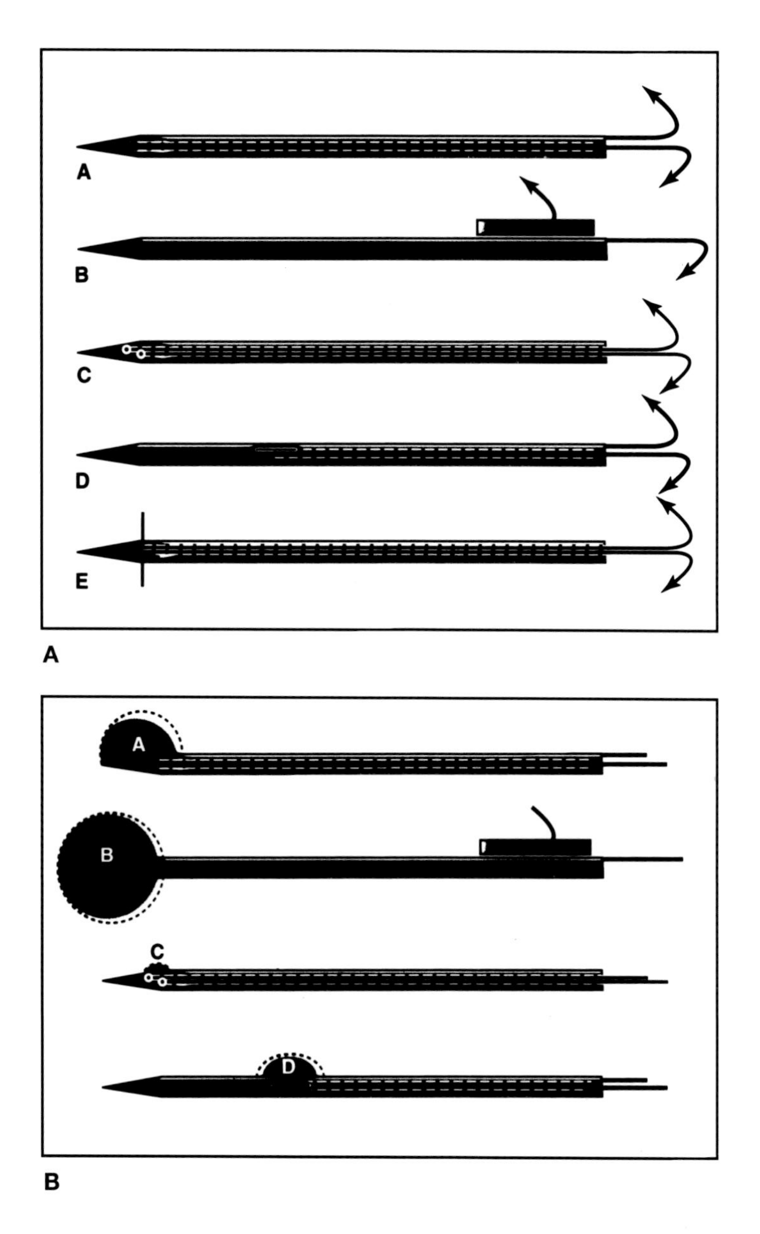

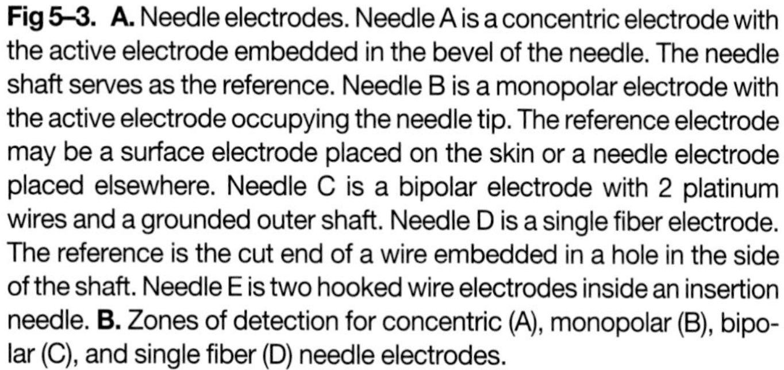

Fig 5–3. A. Needle electrodes. Needle A is a concentric electrode with the active electrode embedded in the bevel of the needle. The needle shaft serves as the reference. Needle B is a monopolar electrode with the active electrode occupying the needle tip. The reference electrode may be a surface electrode placed on the skin or a needle electrode placed elsewhere. Needle C is a bipolar electrode with 2 platinum wires and a grounded outer shaft. Needle D is a single fiber electrode. The reference is the cut end of a wire embedded in a hole in the side of the shaft. Needle E is two hooked wire electrodes inside an insertion needle. **B.** Zones of detection for concentric (A), monopolar (B), bipolar (C), and single fiber (D) needle electrodes.

Therefore, potentials tend to be larger and longer, and have more phases than those recorded with concentric needle electrodes. This is because more muscle fibers are within the zone of detection, and there is less cancellation due to potentials being recorded from the canula of the electrode. The reference electrode is at a remote location on the body and may be a surface electrode.

The *concentric needle electrode* consists of a hollow steel needle through which runs a silver, steel, or platinum wire that is insulated fully except at the tip. The potential difference between the outer shaft of the needle and the tip of its contained wire is measured by connecting it to one side of the differential amplifier. Because the electrode cannula acts as a shield, the electrode has directional recording characteristics controlled by the angle and position of the bevel. Therefore, simple rotation of the electrode may alter significantly the configuration of the motor units.

The *bipolar electrode* is a hollow needle containing two platinum wires, each of which is insulated except at its tip. The outer shaft is grounded and the two internal wires are each connected to one side of the differential amplifier so that the potential difference is measured. The restricted recording range of this electrode makes it unsatisfactory for many routine clinical purposes. The potentials are shorter and lower in voltage than those recorded with concentric needle electrodes.[11]

Hooked wire electrodes are completely insulated except at the tip, which is hooked. A needle is used to insert the electrode. When the needle is withdrawn, the hook on the end of the wire acts as a barb, stabilizing the position of the electrode in the muscle. Obviously, the electrodes cannot be repositioned once they have been placed, but they bend easily and can thus be withdrawn without difficulty. Hooked wire electrodes are extremely well tolerated and can be left in place for long periods of time (hours, or even days).

Safety Considerations

Current may leak from the electrodiagnostic system due to capacity coupling. This leakage current may lead to death or injury in a patient by causing ventricular fibrillation. To minimize the risk of this complication, every patient must be grounded. Also, the leakage current from the instrument should not exceed 10 microamperes.[12]

Basic Components of EMG Examination

The details of an EMG examination are discussed below. Discussion of insertional activity, spontaneous activity, minimal and maximal voluntary contraction, and other aspects of EMG examination and interpretation is applicable generally to EMG performed in the larynx and elsewhere in the body, as well.

Insertional Activity

Insertional activity is the electrical signal that is produced as the needle is introduced into the muscle. Normally, insertion of the needle causes bursts of electrical activity. These should last no more than several hundred milliseconds. This burst of electrical activity results from the fact that the needle itself has some electrical energy that, when placed near the muscle membrane, causes a relative change in the surrounding electrical energy. If the electrical charges surrounding the muscle membrane are unstable, such as occurs during early nerve and muscle injuries, the insertional activity will be increased. With late nerve and muscle injuries, healing sometimes results in replacement of normal muscle with scar tissue or fat, which insulates the remaining muscle fibers and causes a decrease in the insertional activity.

Spontaneous Activity

Spontaneous activity refers to the presence of electrical activity in a resting muscle; and under normal conditions, there should be no spontaneous electrical activity at rest. Electrical activity arises from neural impulses that signal the muscle to contract.

Spontaneous electrical activity occurs in a severely denervated muscle with unstable electrical charges. The presence of spontaneous activity implies that the muscle is degenerating and / or that the nerve has been injured and that the process that caused the injury is ongoing. This is true in muscles throughout the body, including those in the larynx.[13,14] Spontaneous activity usually begins 2 to 3 weeks after denervation has occurred because it takes a while for the nerve to degenerate to a degree that results in absence of electrical impulses from the nerve to the muscle. This degree of denervation occurs only with severe nerve injury, and the presence of spontaneous activity indicates a worse prognosis for recovery. Once regeneration begins, the muscle begins to receive electrical impulses from the regenerating nerve, and the spontaneous activity ceases.

Waveform Morphology

Waveform morphology refers to the shape, amplitude, and duration of the motor unit potentials, which are the electrical signals captured by EMG. The normal motor unit potential is biphasic; that is, it has an upward positive spike and a downward negative spike. It also has an amplitude of 200 to 500 microvolts and a duration of about 5 to 6 milliseconds. The amplitude of the motor unit potential reflects the number and the strength of the muscle fibers innervated by one nerve ending. The duration of the motor unit potential reflects the velocity of the neural input, which is influenced by the insulation of the nerve. Nerves that are insulated well and have an intact and functioning sheath are able to transmit electrical impulses faster than those that are not, as electrical impulses are then transmitted from one node of Ranvier to another. The shape of the motor unit potential reflects changes in the electrical activity of the muscle membrane. Under normal circumstances, this is biphasic.

The waveform morphology of the motor unit potential provides information regarding likelihood of recovery. After injury, the nerve goes through a process of denervation followed by regeneration. The length of time that denervation and regeneration occur can vary from one situation to another and can last for periods of weeks to months each. What determines how much a nerve will denervate or regenerate is not known. During denervation, there is no neural input into the muscle; and thus, no abnormal waveforms are produced. Abnormal motor unit potential morphologies are produced during the period of regeneration.

During the early phases of regeneration, tiny nerves begin to course back into the muscles that have atrophied during the period of time that they were denervated. Early in regrowth, the insulation of the nerve is decreased. The combination of the tiny, minimally insulated nerves and the weak muscle fibers produces electrical signals on the EMG that are seen as motor unit potentials that have small amplitudes, long durations, and polyphasic shapes. These waveforms are sometimes referred to as nascent units; they imply the presence of a recent nerve injury.

As the regeneration progresses, the nerves become healthier and better insulated through regrowth of their sheaths; and the muscle fibers become stronger and gain more mass. Not all of the nerve fibers regenerate. Those that do branch more than before the injury to innervate as many muscle fibers that lack innervation as possible. The motor unit potentials that are produced as a result of this ongoing regeneration have greater amplitudes than normal, are polyphasic, and have a prolonged duration. These motor unit potentials are usually described as being polyphasic or as giant polyphasic potentials; their presence implies an old nerve injury.

If the nerve is uninjured and the muscle is damaged, the morphology of the motor unit potential is different. The nerve is intact and functioning well, so the duration of the motor unit potential is normal. The electrical charges in the muscle membrane are abnormal, resulting in a polyphasic shape. The amplitude, which reflects the decreased muscle mass and force of contraction, is decreased.

Recruitment

Recruitment refers to the serial activation of motor units during increased voluntary muscle contraction. Normally, as the intensity of the muscle contraction increases, the motor units have increased activity and new motor units are "recruited" to maintain the strength of the contraction. This is seen on EMG as an increase in the number and density of motor unit potentials. Thus, recruitment reflects the degree of innervation, which is a reflection of the number of active nerve fibers of a given muscle.

Common Abnormal EMG Findings

Increased insertional activity occurs when the burst of electrical potential produced by insertion or movement of the needle electrode in the muscle lasts more than several hundred milliseconds. This is an indication of muscle membrane instability that occurs in both myopathic and neurogenic processes. Finding reduced insertional activity indicates loss of muscle fiber and replacement of it by fibrotic tissue or lipoid degeneration. This is observed in end-stage myopathic and some neuropathic processes.

At rest, different kinds of abnormal spontaneous activity can be observed. *Fibrillation potentials* (Fig 5–4) are spontaneous single fiber muscle action potentials typically with amplitudes of several hundred microvolts and durations of less than 2 milliseconds, firing regularly at 1 to 50 Hz. They can occur spontaneously or with movement of the needle. Typically, these potentials have a biphasic or triphasic appearance with an initial positive deflection. This abnormality is seen more commonly when denervation has occurred. Rarely, it can be seen in myopathic processes, as well. A positive sharp wave is characterized by a large positive deflection of several hundred microvolts lasting less than 2 milliseconds, followed by a negative deflection of 10 to 30 milliseconds and regular firing at 1 to 50 Hz. Fibrillation potentials and positive sharp waves usually occur together and produce very characteristic noises on the loudspeaker, allowing identification of these potentials even without looking at the oscilloscope screen. It takes approximately 2 to 3 weeks after denervation occurs to observe fibrillation potentials or positive sharp waves. After a nerve injury, the presence of fibrillations and positive sharp waves indicates denervation and axonal loss.

Complex repetitive discharges (Fig 5–5) occur when a group of muscle fibers discharges repetitively in near synchrony though ephaptic activation. These discharges typically have an abrupt onset and cessation and a bizarre configuration. The discharge rate is anywhere between 5 and 100 Hz, with an amplitude of 100 microvolts (μV) to 1 millivolt (mV). This abnormality indicates chronicity, and it can be observed in both neuropathic and myopathic processes.

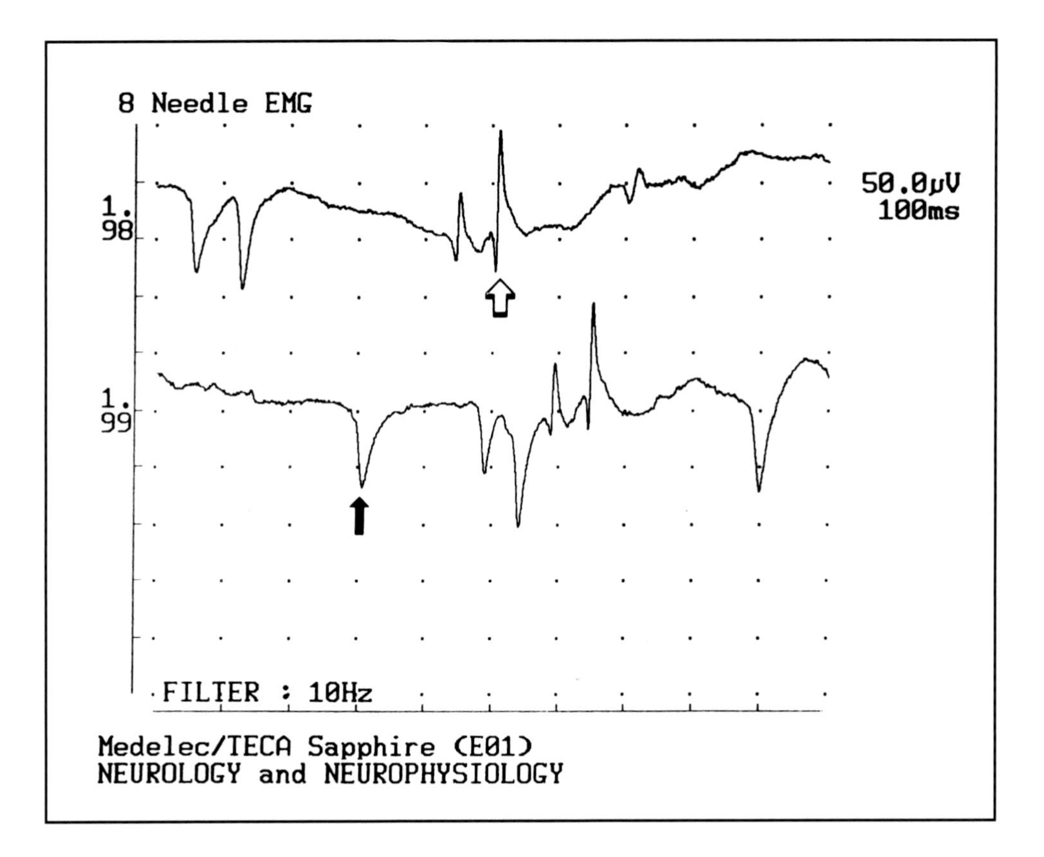

Fig 5–4. Fibrillation potentials (*solid arrow*) and positive sharp wave recorded from the right thyroarytenoid muscle in a patient with recurrent laryngeal neuropathy.

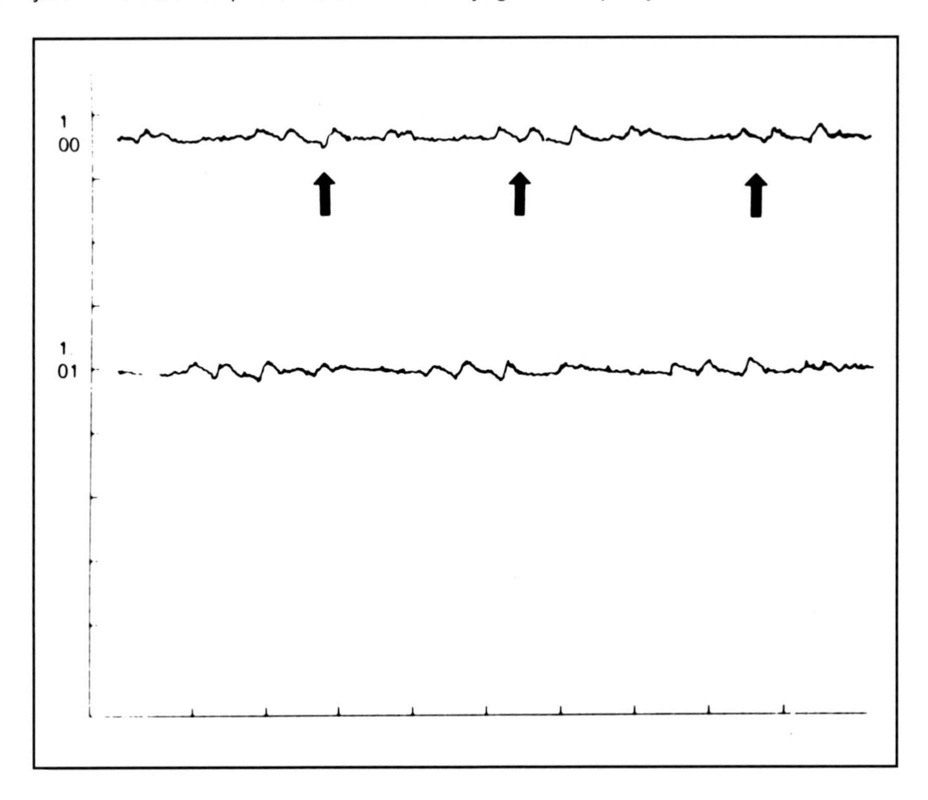

Fig 5–5. Low amplitude complex repetitive discharges (*arrows*) recorded from the right thyroarytenoid muscle in a patient with recurrent laryngeal neuropathy.

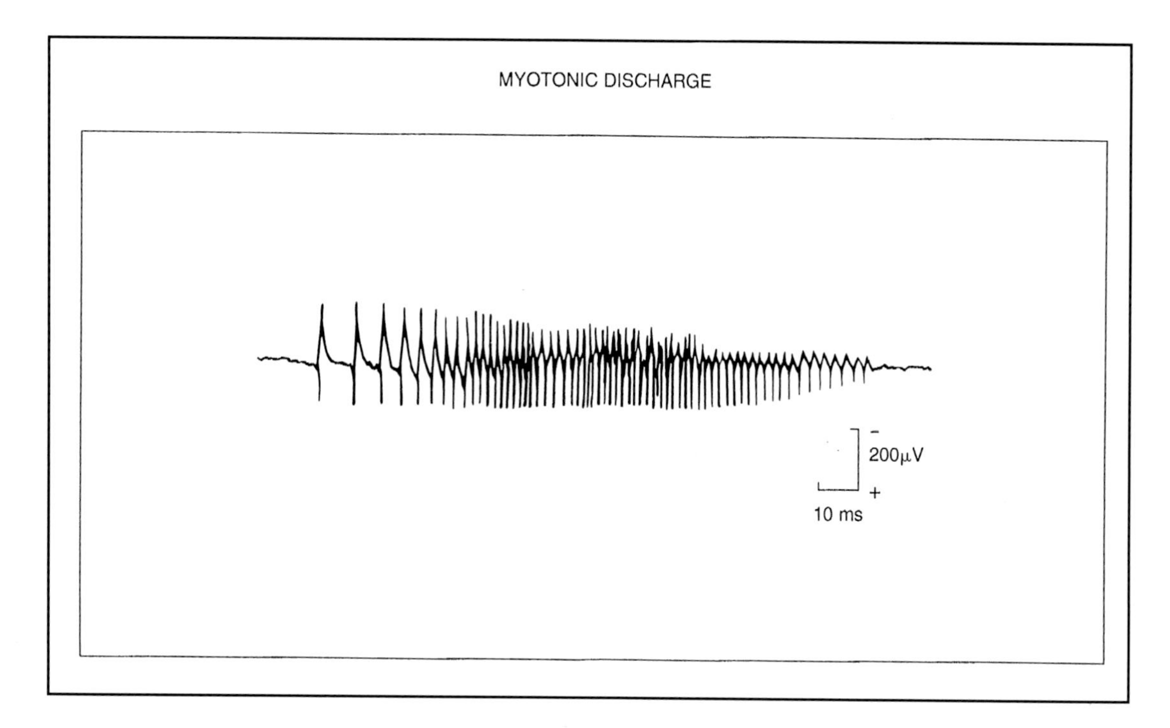

Fig 5–6. Myotonic discharges.

Myotonic potentials (Fig 5–6) are repetitive discharges at rates of 20 Hz to 150 Hz and amplitudes of 20 μV to 1 mV, with the appearance of fibrillation potentials or positive sharp waves. The amplitude and the frequency of the potentials wax and wane, which causes a characteristic "dive bomber" sound in the loudspeaker of the EMG machine. These potentials occur spontaneously, with insertion of the needle, with percussion of the muscle, or with voluntary contractions. They are indicative of muscle membrane instability and are observed most commonly in disorders of clinical myotonia, such as myotonic dystrophy. Rarely, they can be observed in chronic neurogenic and myopathic processes without clinical myotonia.

During minimal voluntary muscle contraction, the morphology of the motor unit potential is evaluated. Abnormalities are characterized by changes in the duration, amplitude, and number of phases (Fig 5–7). In a neuropathic process, the motor unit potential typically has a prolonged duration and increased number (more than 4) of phases (Fig 5–8). During early reinnervation, the amplitude is decreased; when reinnervation is completed, the amplitude is increased. In myopathic processes, the duration of the motor unit potential is short, with an increased number of phases and decreased amplitude. With maximal muscle contraction, the interference pattern and recruitment are

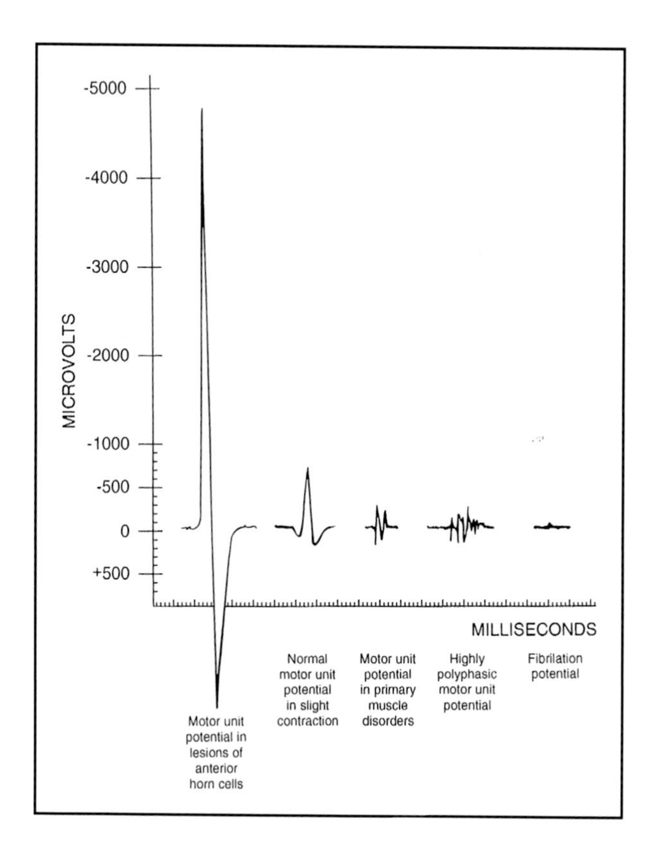

Fig 5–7. Differences in the appearance of the motor unit potential in diseases.

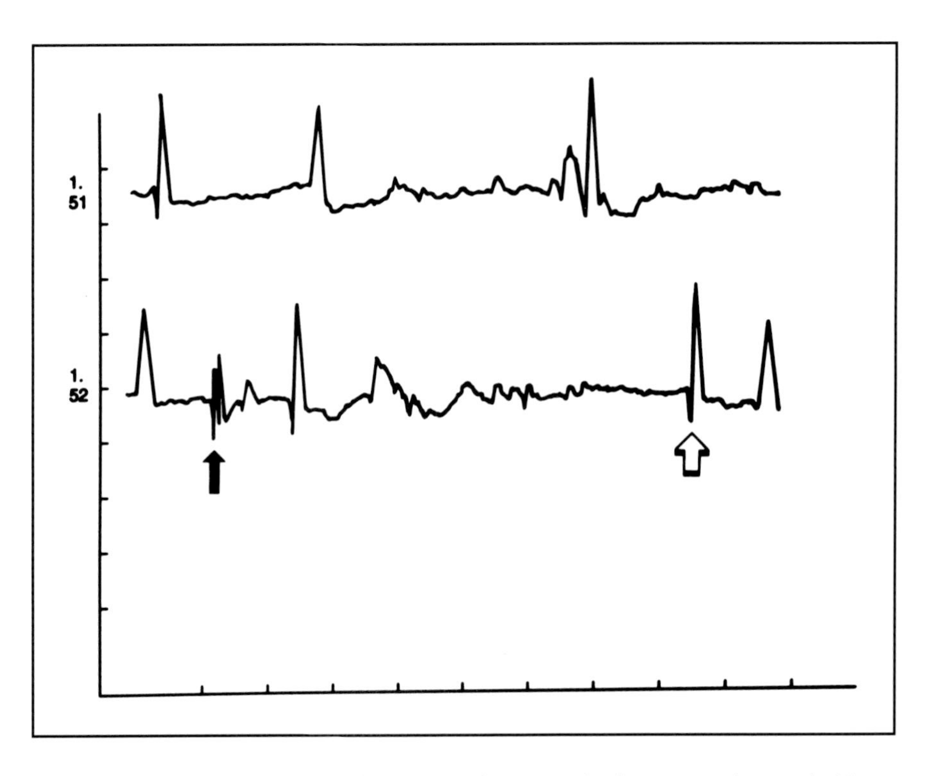

Fig 5–8. Polyphasic (*solid arrow*) and normal motor units *(open arrow)* recorded from the left cricothyroid muscle.

evaluated. In neuropathic processes, there is decreased recruitment, with a few motor units firing at high frequency and a decreased interference pattern (Fig 5–9). In a myopathic process, there is rapid and early recruitment with a low voltage, and a full interference pattern in the context of a weak muscle contraction.

When a nerve impulse arrives at a motor end-plate, muscle fibers depolarize and contract. Because there are numerous fibers in any muscle motor unit, and their distances from the neuromuscular junction vary, not all muscle fibers in a motor unit contract simultaneously. In fact, laryngeal muscles generally exhibit polyphasic contraction.[15,16] In reality, numerous motor units are involved during muscle contraction. As the contraction increases, motor units fire more frequently and, progressively, additional motor units are activated. Consequently, recorded motor units overlap, creating an interference pattern. Potentials that can be identified visually and audibly during very weak contraction overlap during stronger contraction; therefore, some fading can result in a recruitment pattern in which some of the spikes appear to be lost. By looking at, or listening to, the EMG signal, a skilled electromyographer can determine the condition of the muscle. For example, under normal circumstances, the interference pattern described above is present. In complete paralysis, initially there is electrical silence; however, positive sharp waves or fibrillation potentials generally appear within a few weeks. Reinnervation is characterized by larger motor units with polyphasic, high amplitude, and long duration responses. There is usually loss of motor units following paralysis, which results in decreased recruitment (a less dense interference pattern).

Single Fiber EMG

Single fiber EMG evaluates individual muscle fibers. The technique was introduced in 1963 by Ekstedt and Stålberg.[17] It can be helpful in patients with neuromuscular junction abnormalities such as myasthenia gravis[18-21] and those with denervating disorders such as amyotrophic lateral sclerosis (ALS). The needle electrode recording surface is located along the shaft. A wire 25-μm in diameter is embedded in a small resin port 7.5 mm from the tip,[22] with the electrode shaft acting as the reference. Because of the small recording surface, it is possible to record selectively from the isopotential lines generated by a single muscle fiber action potential.[22-24] The electrode must be placed extremely close to the fiber of interest. Visual and

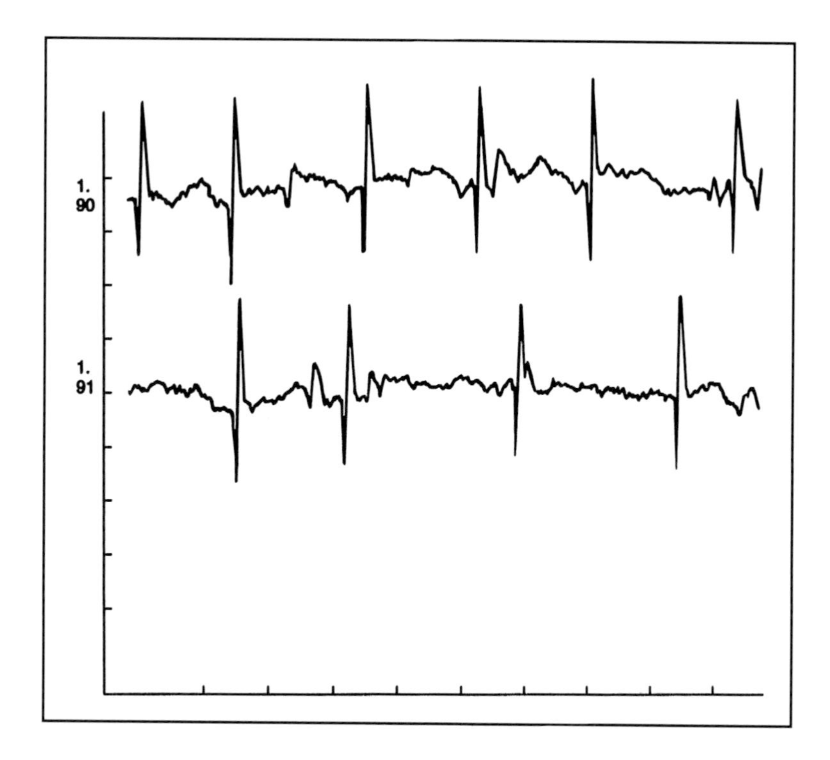

Fig 5–9. Incomplete interference pattern decreased recruitment with rapid discharge rate recorded from the right thyroarytenoid muscle in a patient with recurrent laryngeal neuropathy.

acoustical information is used to adjust placement of the electrode for optimal recording. Movements of as little as 100 μm alter the amplitude of the potential substantially.[24,25] The low-pass filter (high frequency) is set at 8 to 10 KHz, and the high-pass filter (low frequency) is set at about 500 Hz to filter out interference from nearby muscle fibers. A delay line with a threshold trigger is required in order to display single muscle fiber action potentials during successive discharges; and sweep speeds of 2 or 5 msec per division are utilized. Single muscle fiber action potentials are normally only a few milliseconds in duration. Recordings are made generally during uniform voluntary contraction of moderate intensity. Recordings can be made from a single fiber or from two muscle fibers innervated by the same motor unit. Typically, two fibers from the same motor unit (a potential pair) are recorded to allow measurements of jitter and fiber density. The double potential is located by auditory feedback, which has been compared to the sound of castanets.[22] Peak-to-peak amplitude should be greater than 200 μV, and spike rise time should be less than 300 μsec (usually between 67 and 200 μsec, with a median of 112 μsec)[24]; and the waveform should be stable during successive discharges.[26] The spike duration usually ranges from 265 to 800 μsec (with a median for 470 μsec) and voltage ranges from 0.7 to 25.2 mV (with a median of 5.6 mV).[26]

Jitter measures the difference between two time-locked firing potentials of the same motor unit, specifically the variability of their interpotential interval (IPI) during successive discharges.[22,27] Recordings do not have to be made at maximum amplitude but must record at least 50 stable, successive discharges from a potential pair. The IPI is a reflection of the length of the distal axon branch from the motor axon to the end plate, conduction velocity along the distal axon branch, neuromuscular transmission, distance from the recording electrode to the endplate, and muscle fiber conduction velocity.[24] The most important factors are conduction velocity along the distal axon branch, neuromuscular transmission, and muscle fiber conduction velocity. Variation in neuromuscular transmission is dominant if the IPI is 1 msec or less and the firing rate is uniform.[22] Variation of conduction velocity along the distal axon branch and variation of muscle fiber conduction velocity may be dominant factors if the IPI is 10 msec or longer and the discharge rate is not uniform. So, it is preferable to record jitter with IPIs of 4 msec or less.[22] Jitter is expressed as the mean value of consecutive differences (MCD) of the IPIs, measured over short periods of time. In normal subjects, jitter is usually 10 to 50 μsec (MCD), but it is occasionally as low as 5 μsec (MCD).[28] In patients with myasthenia gravis, jitter may exceed 100 μsec (MCD). In myasthenia, impulse blocking may occur. This is a failure of one or more of the time-locked single muscle fiber action potentials to fire in the triggered discharge.[22] Bimodal jitter occurs when variability is distributed around two separate means. This occurs in 1 out of 20 jitter measurements in normal muscles[29] and may be a source of error if it is not recognized and analyzed appropriately. The interested reader is referred to other literature for additional details regarding the complex techniques of jitter measurement and calculation.[22,28-37]

Fiber density provides an index of the number of muscle fibers that comprise a motor unit.[22,38,39] Four or five measurements are made in at least 4 sites within the muscle, and 20 different single muscle fiber action potentials at different sites within the muscle are measured typically. Measurements are made during maximal amplitude. The recording radius of a single fiber electrode is approximately 300 μm.[22] The optimized potential and all of the other time-locked potentials that belong to the same motor unit that can be recorded during the discharge of the motor unit potential are counted. The total number of single fiber muscle action potentials recorded at these 20 different sites are added together, then divided by 20 to determine the mean fiber density.[22,40] Sixty to seventy percent of the time in most muscles, fiber density measurements record only a single muscle fiber action potential,[40] because 76% of all muscle fibers belonging to a motor unit are separated from other muscle fibers from that motor unit.[41] These characteristics have not been studied in specific laryngeal muscles. During fiber density recording, it is also possible to determine the mean of the interspike intervals (MISI). This is determined by dividing the total duration of the potentials that are time-locked to the triggered potential by the number of intervals within the potential complex.[22] The MISI is increased typically in myopathies, such as polio and muscular dystrophies, and in early reinnervation.

Single fiber EMG is more sensitive than conventional repetitive stimulation studies and is felt to be abnormal in 99% of patients with generalized myasthenia gravis. However, studies on patients with focal myasthenia (such as ocular myasthenia and particularly laryngeal myasthenia) are probably less definitive. In individuals with localized myasthenia, the percentage of patients with neuromuscular junction abnormalities in whom the condition is confirmed by single fiber EMG may not be as high as it is when the condition involves forearm muscles; but the technique may still be superior to other conventional EMG techniques and repetitive studies.

Single fiber EMG may be helpful particularly in patients with neuromuscular junction problems such as myasthenia gravis; but it can be influenced by drugs such as Mestinon and can also show abnormalities in any disorder where there may be a failure of neuromuscular junction transmission, including neuropathies and myopathies. Individuals with ALS and those with nerve injury can have similar abnormalities on single fiber EMG. Therefore, the technique cannot be used alone in the absence of clinical data and other EMG studies to establish a definitive diagnosis.

To summarize, in general, jitter measurements can be very helpful in patients with suspected myasthenia; and fiber density can be helpful in individuals with denervation, both recent and longstanding; but there are pitfalls. Single fiber EMG should be interpreted in the context of the clinical presentation and results of other electrodiagnostic procedures.

Laryngeal Electromyography

Laryngeal electromyography (LEMG) is a procedure that evaluates the integrity of the muscular and nervous system of the larynx. LEMG is indicated in patients who have evidence of a movement disorder of the vocal folds. The purposes of the LEMG are to help the physician diagnose and differentiate the causes of these movement disorders and to guide treatment. Several different types of disorders can result in abnormal motions of the vocal fold. These include disorders in movement of the joints that connect the cartilages of the larynx, primary dysfunction within the muscles themselves, and abnormalities in the nerves that supply the muscles of the larynx. Understanding the exact mechanism of the problems is important in helping the physician understand how to treat the patient's voice complaints most effectively.

Laryngeal electromyography was introduced in 1944 by Weddel et al[42] and was advanced substantially by the 1950s by Faaborg-Andersen and others.[43-45] Additional research by various investigators in the 1960s and 1970s began to clarify the potential importance of EMG in laryngology.[46-70]

Throughout the 1980s and 1990s, laryngeal electromyography evolved into an invaluable adjunct to laryngologic assessment, diagnosis, and treatment of voice disorders.[71-74] Laryngeal EMG is easy to perform, well tolerated in the office setting, and presents minimal risks to patients. It is useful in the evaluation of numerous laryngeal disorders, allowing clinicians to differentiate among upper motor neuron, lower motor neuron, peripheral nerve, neuromuscular junction, myopathic, and mechanical disorders. It is also useful in establishing prognosis in laryngeal nerve palsies and for guidance during the injection of botulinum toxin in spasmodic dysphonia. A skilled laryngeal electromyographer is an immeasurable asset to the voice care team.

Laryngeal EMG evaluates the integrity and integrative function of the laryngeal motor system. It is best regarded not as a laboratory test, but rather as an extension of the laryngologic examination. Judgments regarding when to use laryngeal EMG, selection of the muscles to be studied, and the choice of EMG techniques depend on a comprehensive history and physical examination. In addition, laryngeal EMG requires expert interpretation, taking the clinical scenario into account. The procedure is usually performed by a neurologist, physiatrist, electrophysiologist, or laryngologist skilled in electromyography.

There are few contraindications to laryngeal electromyography. It is relatively contraindicated in patients with coagulopathy or those taking anticoagulant medications such as Warfarin (coumadin); but it can be performed even in patients with bleeding tendencies when the clinical value of the electrophysiological information justifies the slightly increased risk. The authors have performed laryngeal EMG, so far without complications, on numerous occasions for patients taking anticoagulants. Repetitive stimulation studies should not be performed on patients who have pacemakers.

The selection of electrode type for laryngeal EMG remains controversial and should be guided by the clinical indications for the study. Surface electrodes placed on the skin or mucosa are not invasive, but they are the least specific and least sensitive. Because the laryngeal muscles are small and in close proximity, surface electrodes are generally not useful for diagnostic EMG. However, they still have some value for the laryngologist. Endotracheal tubes with built-in surface electrodes are utilized to monitor recurrent laryngeal nerve function during thyroid surgery,[75] for example. Surface electrodes have also been used to record posterior cricothyroid muscle activity and other laryngeal muscle function[76,77] and for biofeedback.[78,79]

Invasive concentric or monopolar needle electrodes are used most commonly for clinical testing. A concentric electrode consists of a needle that serves as a reference electrode and a central insulated core. The tip is beveled, and the area of sampling is controlled by the angle of the bevel. Concentric electrodes are used frequently because of their consistent, reproducible results.[80-83] However, slight changes in position or angulation can alter results. Near threshold levels of activity, concentric electrodes may even be capable of recording single motor units.

Monopolar electrodes are needle electrodes that are insulated except for a small distance near their tips; the reference electrode is placed at a remote location and may be a surface electrode. Monopolar electrodes are not as selective as concentric needle electrodes. Thus, concentric electrodes are preferable when one is interested in identifying single motor unit potentials or selectively sampling activity that is very close to the electrode. This can also be accomplished with small bipolar needle electrodes that contain two insulated wires within the needle cannula. However, monopolar needle electrodes may provide a more useful analysis of the overall activity of an intrinsic laryngeal muscle. Although some investigators feel that they are inaccurate because they may detect unwanted signals from adjacent laryngeal muscles, we have not found this to be a problem and use monopolar electrodes for much of our clinical testing. We have used concentric and bipolar electrodes in the past and still do for specific purposes. However, we have found that monopolar electrodes provide better, faster assessment of overall recruitment response of a given intrinsic laryngeal muscle, without artifact from adjacent muscles. Much of the other information sought (eg, presence of fibrillation potentials or sharp waves) can be detected reliably with monopolar electrodes, as well. For more specific information about neuromuscular response, other electrode types are appropriate In addition, monopolar electrodes can be constructed of patent needles that can be used for therapy. Therapeutic needle electrodes are used for EMG-guided injection of substances such as botulinum toxin.

Traditionally, hooked wire electrodes have been used in laryngeal study primarily for research, but they may have clinical value, as well. Hooked wire electrodes are flexible, generally remain in good position despite patient movement, and are tolerated well over time. Therefore, they may be valuable for studying laryngeal function during phonatory tasks and swallowing and in numerous positions of the neck. They also may be placed in children under general anesthesia and then used for laryngeal electromyography during performance of phonatory tasks when the child has awakened. Hooked wire electrodes are fine wires (30 gauge) that are insulated completely except at the tip, which is hooked. A needle is used to insert hooked wire electrodes. When the needle is withdrawn, the hooks on the heads of the wires act as barbs, stabilizing electrode position in the muscle. The electrodes cannot be repositioned, but they can be withdrawn easily because they bend. Their flexibility and small size make them extremely well tolerated. Since Basmajian and Steco reported that concept of hooked wire electrodes in 1962,[84] they have been used for a variety of purposes. Despite early recognition of their advantages for long-term study of a dynamic system, like the larynx,[57] they have not gained widespread popularity for routine clinical use. Nevertheless, some clinicians use hooked wire electrodes to study the posterior cricoarytenoid muscles, using an inserter designed by W. Thumfart and marketed by the Wolf Company (Vernon Hill, Ill); Dr. Peak Woo uses custom-made wire electrode arrays consisting of up to four electrodes in clinical practice (Peak Woo, MD, 2000, personal communication). Hooked wire electrodes may have technical disadvantages. Muscle contraction may alter responses by changing the distance between the two electrodes with regard to the muscle fibers they are intended to measure, and with regard to each other.[64]

The authors use percutaneous monopolar needle electrodes routinely. The patient is placed in the supine position, with the neck extended. Because the procedure is generally not very painful, and because local anesthesia may alter results (especially in the cricothyroid muscle), local anesthesia is not used. A surface electrode is used for the ground electrode, and a reference (also surface) is placed on the cheek. For diagnostic purposes, routinely we test cricothyroid, thyroarytenoid, and posterior cricoarytenoid muscles. In some cases, additional muscles are tested, as well. If there are questions regarding hysteria, malingering, or synkinesis, simultaneous recordings of abductors and adductors are obtained. In cases of laryngeal dystonia, electrical recordings may be coordinated with acoustical data since Blitzer et al observed that the normal delay between the onset of the electrical signal and the onset of the acoustic signal (0–200 milliseconds) can be increased to a delay of from 500 milliseconds to 1 second in patients with spasmodic dysphonia.[81,85]

After cleaning the skin with alcohol, the needle electrode is inserted into the muscle belly. The cricothyroid (CT) notch is the anatomic reference for needle insertion. To locate the CT notch, the patient's neck is extended; and the cricoid cartilage is identified. Immediately above the cricoid cartilage is a small depression, which is the CT notch, also known as the CT space and the CT membrane region. The CT notch may be difficult to find in obese patients or those who have had a tracheotomy. The CT muscles are evaluated by inserting the needle approximately 0.5 cm from the midline and angled laterally 30 to 45 degrees (Figs 5–10 and 5–11). The needle first passes through the sternohyoid muscle. The CT muscle is approximately 1 cm deep. To validate the position of the electrode, the patient is asked to phonate /i/ at a low pitch and then asked to raise the pitch. If the electrode is in a normal CT muscle, the EMG activity will increase sharply.

To evaluate the thyroarytenoid (TA) muscle, the needle is inserted approximately 0.5 cm from the midline of the CT notch and is angled superiorly 30 to 45 degrees. The TA muscle is encountered approximately 1 to 2 cm beneath the skin. If the patient coughs, that generally indicates that the needle has penetrated the airway and is causing irritation of the mucosa. In that case, the needle should be withdrawn and reinserted. The position of the needle is validated by asking the patient to say /i/. During this maneuver, there will be a sharp and sustained increase in EMG activity. If the needle is in the lateral cricoarytenoid (LCA), there will be an increase and rapid drop-off in EMG activity.

The posterior cricoarytenoid muscle (PCA) can be accessed by rotating the larynx and passing the electrode posterior to the thyroid lamina or by passing a needle through the cricothyroid membrane, airway, and cricoid cartilage posteriorly. The latter technique is successful usually only in nonossified larynges such as those of young women. The PCA lies lower in the neck than many physicians realize; inserting the electrode too high is a common reason for difficulty in locating the PCA. Position is confirmed through detection of increased EMG activity during sniffing and with much less EMG activity during swallowing.

The lateral cricoarytenoid muscle (LCA) is slightly lower, more lateral, and more posterior than the TA. Successful insertion can be confirmed electrically because of a difference in the firing pattern between the TA and LCA. When the patient is asked to say /i/ with an electrode in the TA, there is a fairly constant level of activity throughout phonation. In the LCA, a large spike of activity is seen as the LCA brings the vocal process toward the midline; but activity drops promptly to a lower level as it is maintained in the adducted position. Thyroarytenoid, posterior cricoarytenoid, lateral cricoarytenoid, and interarytenoid electrodes can also be positioned indirectly under flexible fiberoptic guidance or directly in the operating room.[86,87]

As with EMG elsewhere in the body, laryngeal EMG examination consists of four parts including insertional activity, spontaneous activity, minimal voluntary contraction, and maximal voluntary contraction. With insertion of the needle into the muscle or with any movement of the needle, bursts of electrical activity are produced by the mechanical stimulation of the muscle membrane. They last no more than several hundred milliseconds (Fig 5–12).

At rest, no electrical activity is recorded, but laryngeal muscles are rarely at physiologic rest. When the electrode is in close proximity to the neuromuscular junction, normal physiological activity, end-plate

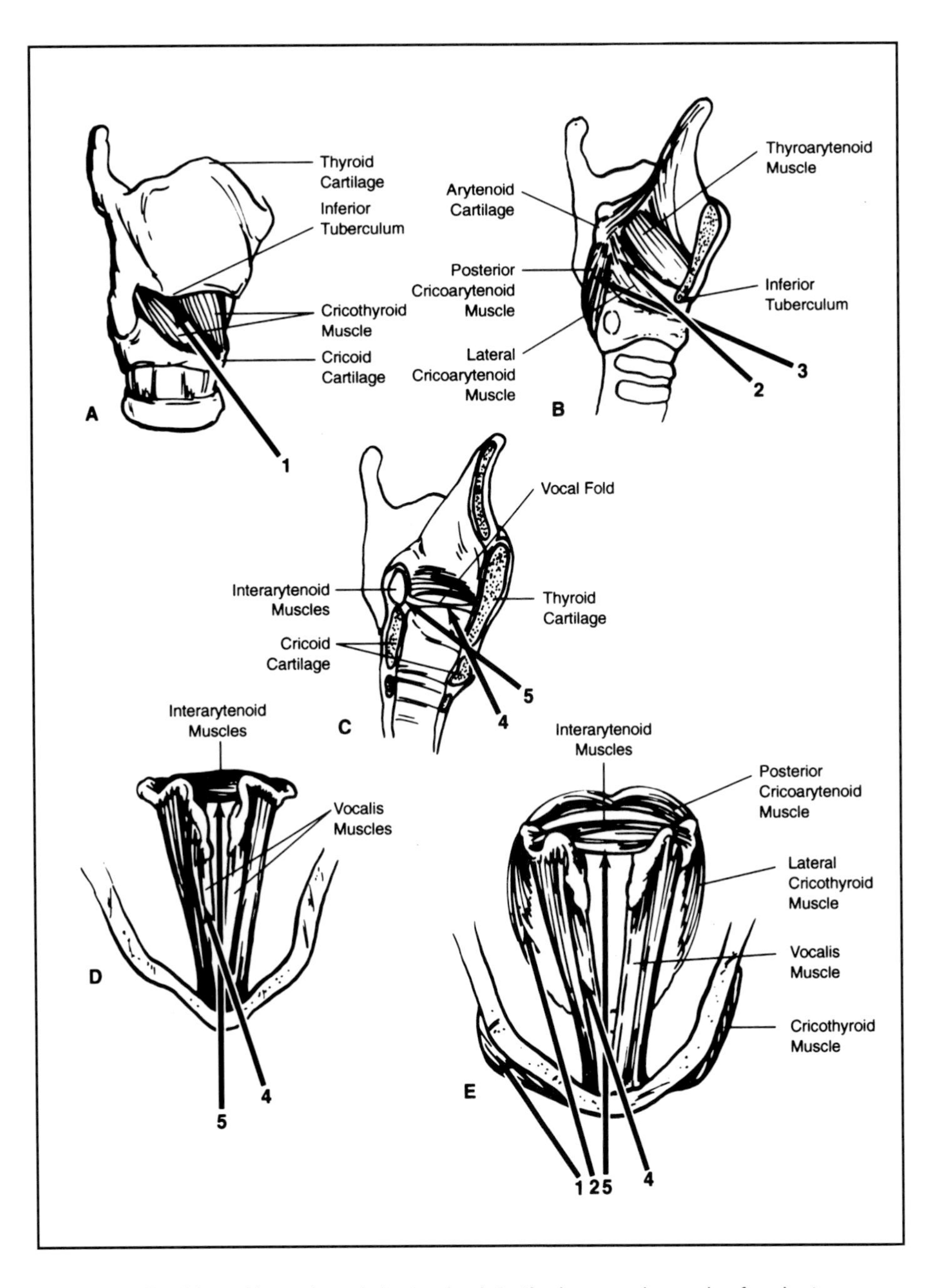

Fig 5–10. Position of insertion of electrodes into the laryngeal muscles for electromyography. Muscles illustrated include the cricothyroid (**A**), lateral and posterior cricoarytenoid muscles (**B**) and the interarytenoid and vocalis muscles (**C**). Also shown are the positions of insertion into five major laryngeal muscles (**D**). **E.** Numbers correspond to the needle position for insertion into the respective muscles (1 = CT, 2 = LCA, 3 = PCA, 4 = TA, 5 = IA). It is possible in some patients to place a needle in the PCA by passing through the IA (E,5) and the cricoid cartilage (usually a few millimeters to the left or right of the midline posteriorly).

spikes, and noise can be recorded. With minimal voluntary contraction, 1 or 2 motor unit potentials can be recorded with a firing rate of 2 to 5 per second (Fig 5–13). The average duration of the motor unit potentials recorded from laryngeal muscles is 3 to 7 milliseconds with an amplitude of 150 to 800 V.[44,51,58,65] Most of the studies used to determine these parameters utilized concentric electrodes. Using monopolar

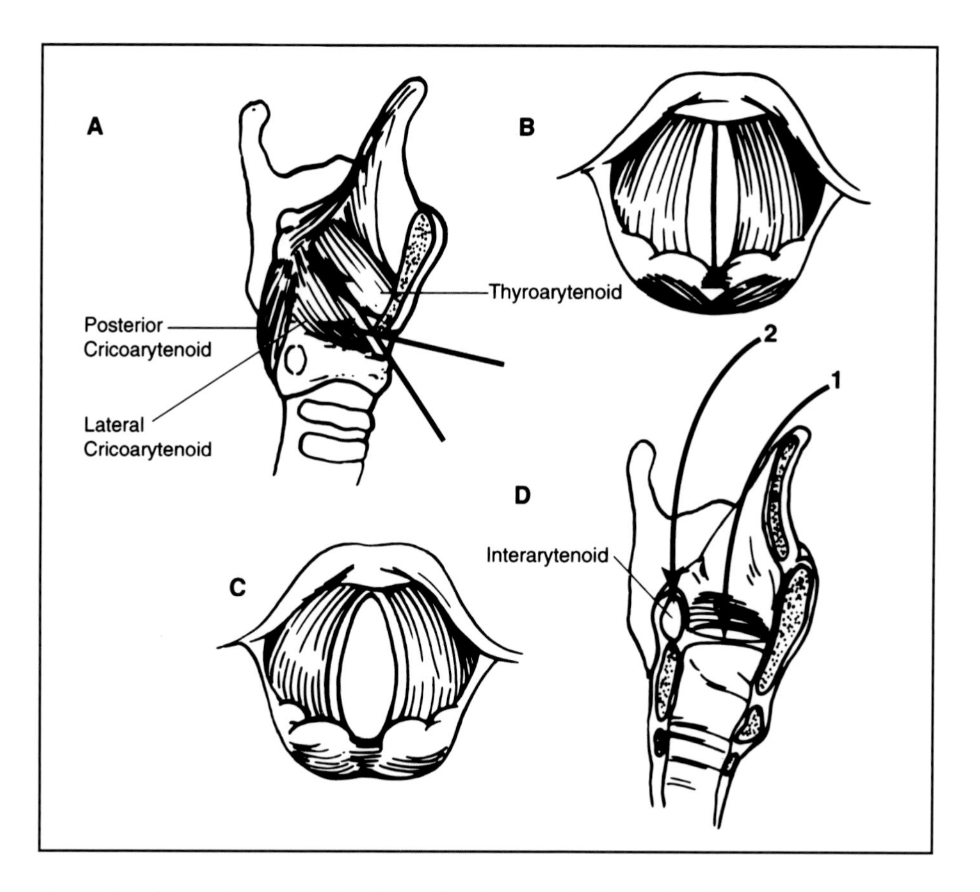

Fig 5–11. Alternative method of inserting laryngeal electrodes for electromyography, including a modified approach to the vocalis (thyroarytenoid) muscles (**A**), peroral point of insertion into the posterior cricoarytenoid muscles (**B**), peroral point of insertion in the interarytenoid muscles (**C**), and peroral point of insertion into the thyroarytenoid ($\mathbf{D_1}$) and interarytenoid muscle ($\mathbf{D_2}$).

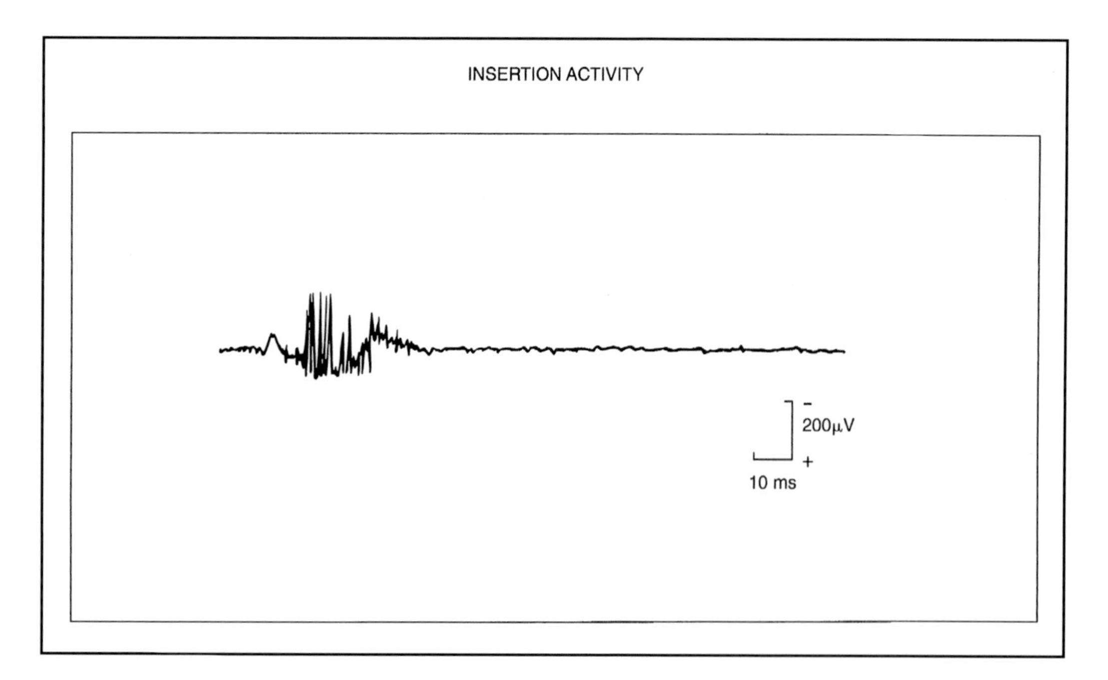

Fig 5–12. Normal insertional activity.

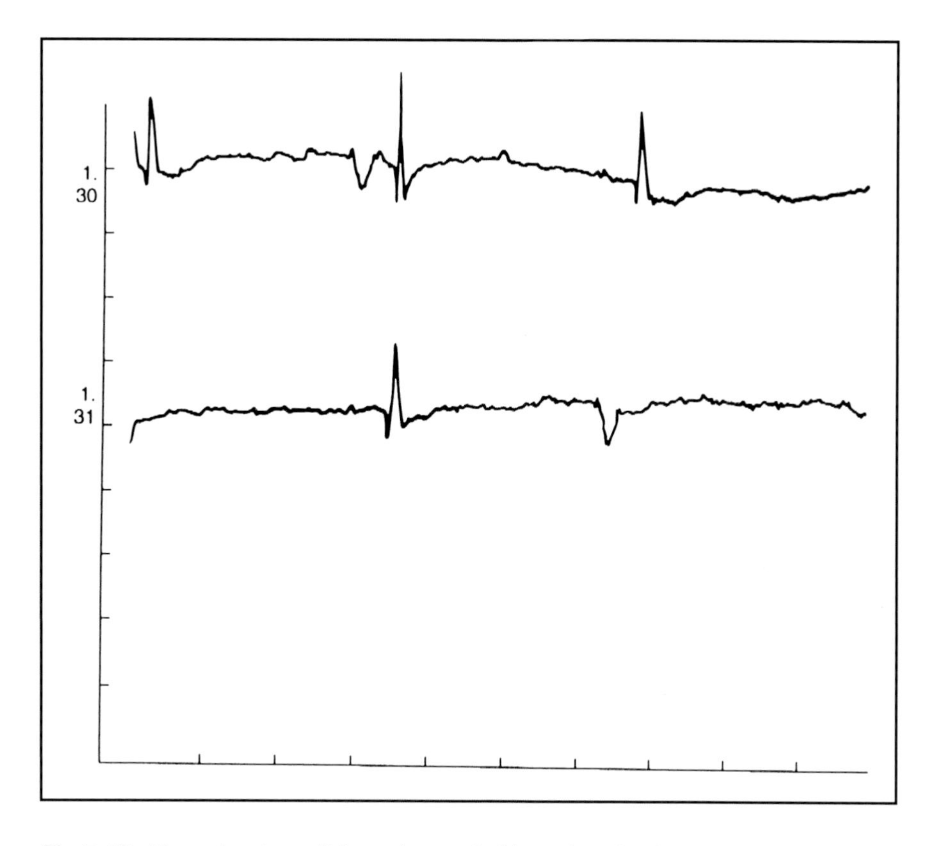

Fig 5–13. Normal motor unit (*arrow*) recorded from the cricothyroid muscle.

electrodes, findings of 5 to 6 milliseconds with an amplitude of 200 to 500 V may be more typical.[88] As the intensity of the contraction increases, the firing rate of the motor unit potentials increases; and new and larger motor units are recruited until the oscilloscope screen is full and single motor unit potentials cannot be distinguished one from the other. This is known as a *full interference pattern*[89] (Fig 5–14), and it is generally achieved at about 30% of maximal isometric contraction.[83] If a concentric electrode is used, only approximately 100 to 150 fibers are within recording distance of the electrode tip; and during full muscle effort, motor units fire asynchronously at frequencies of 30 to 50 motor units per second. So, the potentials generated occur at intervals of about 1 millisecond.[90] Other aspects of laryngeal EMG are similar to EMG elsewhere in the body.

Interpretation of Laryngeal EMG

Laryngeal EMG may be evaluated qualitatively or quantitatively to some extent. The importance of the skill of the electromyographer and the subjective judgments implicit in EMG interpretation must be understood. Qualitative assessment is performed by listening to the amplified signal and viewing the oscilloscope display. A skilled electromyographer can tell much about the condition of the neuromuscular complex. It is important to remember that single motor unit action potentials of laryngeal muscles normally have slight polyphasia (1 to 3 phases); so this should not be interpreted as abnormal.[44,51] However, the presence of more than 4 phases in laryngeal muscles should be considered abnormal. The electrical silence associated with complete denervation is interpreted easily, as long as the electromyographer is certain that the needle is in the appropriate muscle. Other abnormalities such as fibrillation potentials, positive sharp waves, giant motor units, and abnormal amplitudes and durations are also recognized readily. The somewhat thinned interference pattern associated with the loss of motor units following reinnervation may be more difficult to recognize if the electromyographer does not have extensive experience with laryngeal muscles. The electromyographer using auditory and visual data, together with his or her knowledge of anticipated maximal muscle activity, can estimate the percentage of recruitment response in each laryngeal muscle tested with excellent consistency, according to

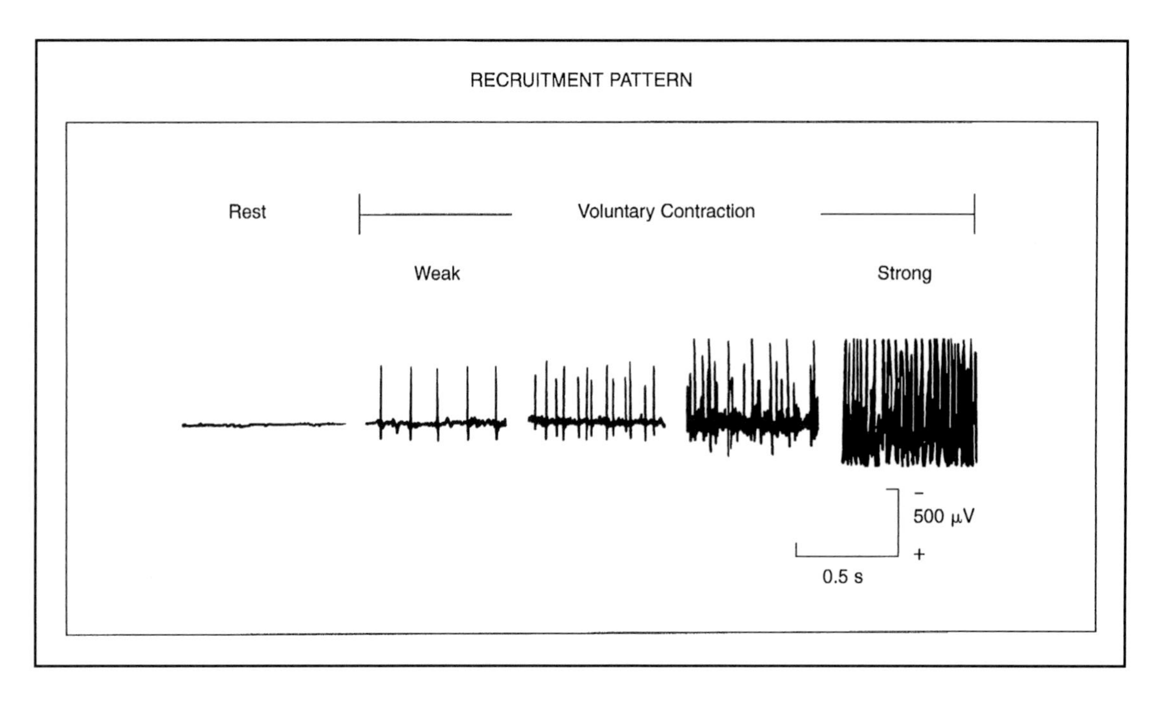

Fig 5–14. Normal recruitment pattern, full interference.

our experience (Fig 5–15). This has proven useful clinically.

More formal quantitative analysis of laryngeal EMG signals has proven challenging. Several investigators have used integrated, digitally smoothed signals.[50,67,91,92] This method utilizes firing frequency and averaged amplitude of the signal. The amplitude of the signal data is reported as a percentage of the estimated maximal electrical activity of the muscle. This is similar to the percentage recruitment method used clinically and discussed above. However, approximation of maximal muscle activity in the larynx may be as challenging in the laboratory as it is in clinical practice and results must be considered approximate, at best. In addition, this method of digitally smoothing and integrating signals loses data with regard to the relationship between firing frequency and amplitude.

Investigators also have attempted to quantify electrical muscle activity by measuring the amplitude of the signal, ignoring its frequency or density.[44,59,70] It should be noted that amplitude can be affected by many factors including age and temperature,[82] as well as distance of the needle electrode from the muscle fibers being tested. The rise time, or distance between the first negative deflection and its subsequent peak, is related to this distance and should be less than 200 microseconds for assessment of a motor unit potential to be meaningful. Because of the basic principles of neurophysiology, direct comparison of EMG muscle recordings from examination to examination is not valid. This is especially true when small areas are sampled through use of concentric bipolar or hooked wire electrodes, but the task appears less problematic clinically when larger areas are sampled using monopolar electrodes. However, concentric electrodes also permit turns/amplitude analysis of the interference pattern, permitting assessment of some of the motor units that "disappear." This technique was introduced in 1964[93] and requires computer analysis. A "turn" is two successive shifts in amplitude of 100 V or more. Mean amplitude between turns over time is measured. Mean amplitude is greatest during maximal muscle contraction effort, but the number of turns is greatest at about 50% of maximal effort[94,95] with increasing force. Small muscles show a greater increase in turns and a smaller increase in amplitude than large muscles[55]; and females have lower values for turns and amplitude than males. Electrical recordings from several positions within a muscle are used to create a "scattergram" for quantitative turns/amplitude analysis. Turns/amplitude analysis has been used in larger skeletal muscles in both normal and pathologic conditions and has been found helpful in discriminating electrical differences comparing normal muscles to those in patients with peripheral nerve lesions[93,96-99] and in neurogenic disorders.[99] Fuglsang-Frederiksen and co-workers have demonstrated that turns/amplitude analysis is most effective when the muscle is contracting at about 30% maximal force.[99-101] Nevertheless, there is very little experience using this technique

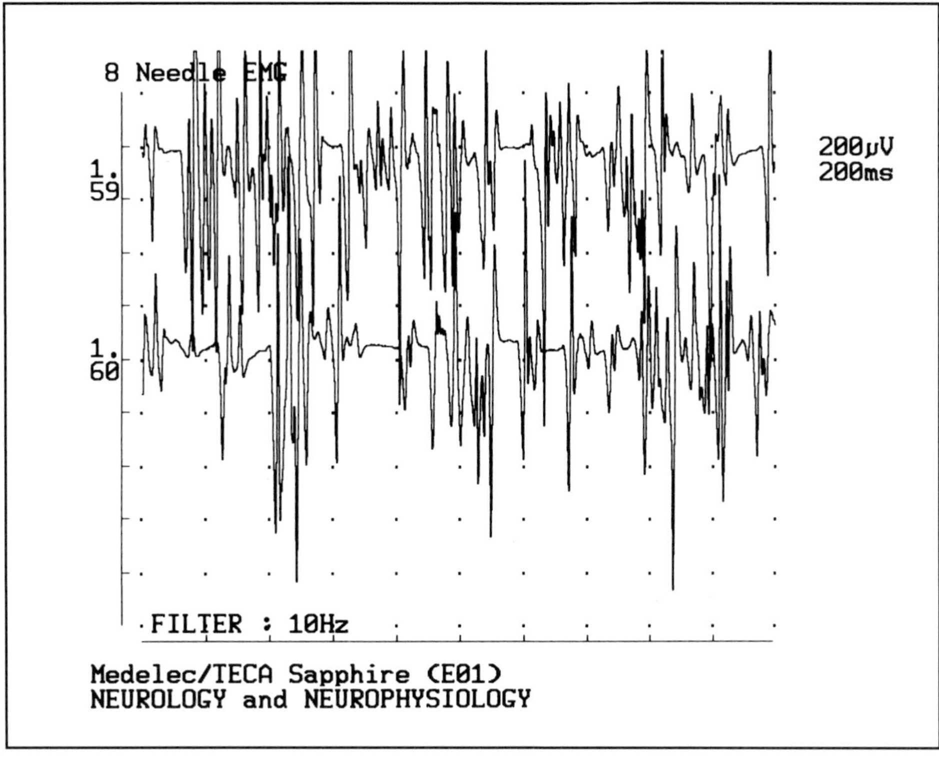

A

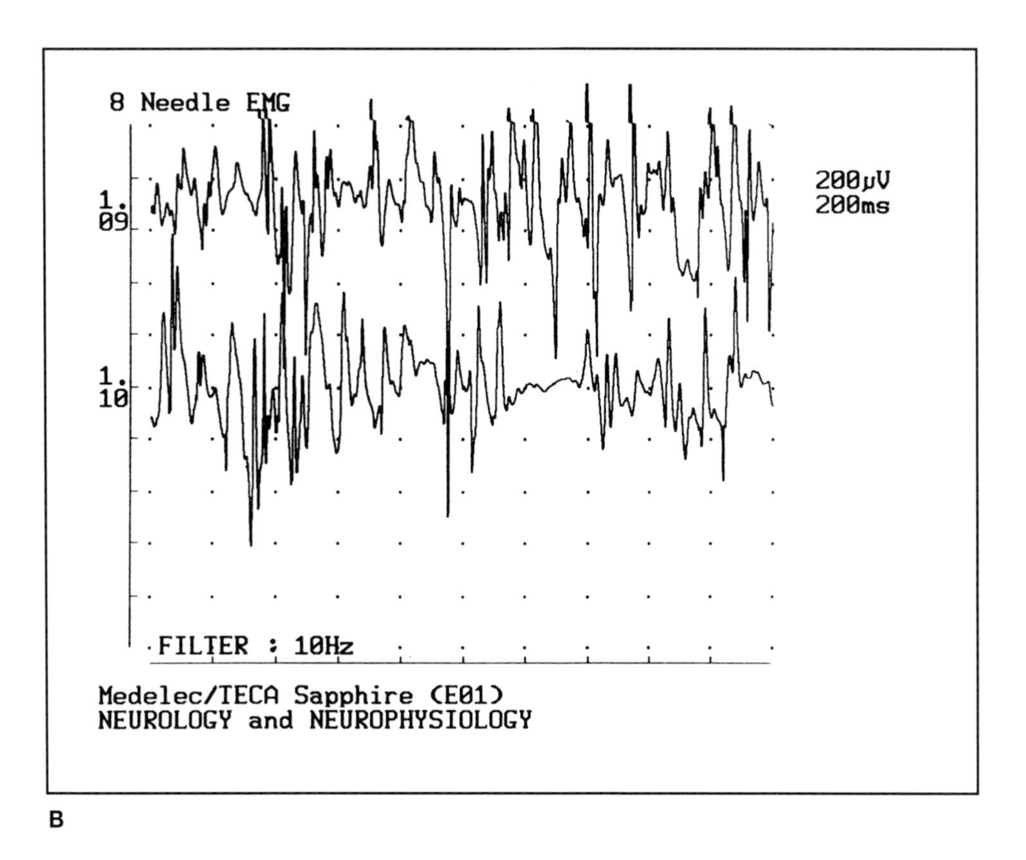

B

Fig 5–15. A. Full recruitment pattern at maximal retraction. **B.** Maximal contraction, motor unit recruitment decreased approximately 30%. *(continues)*

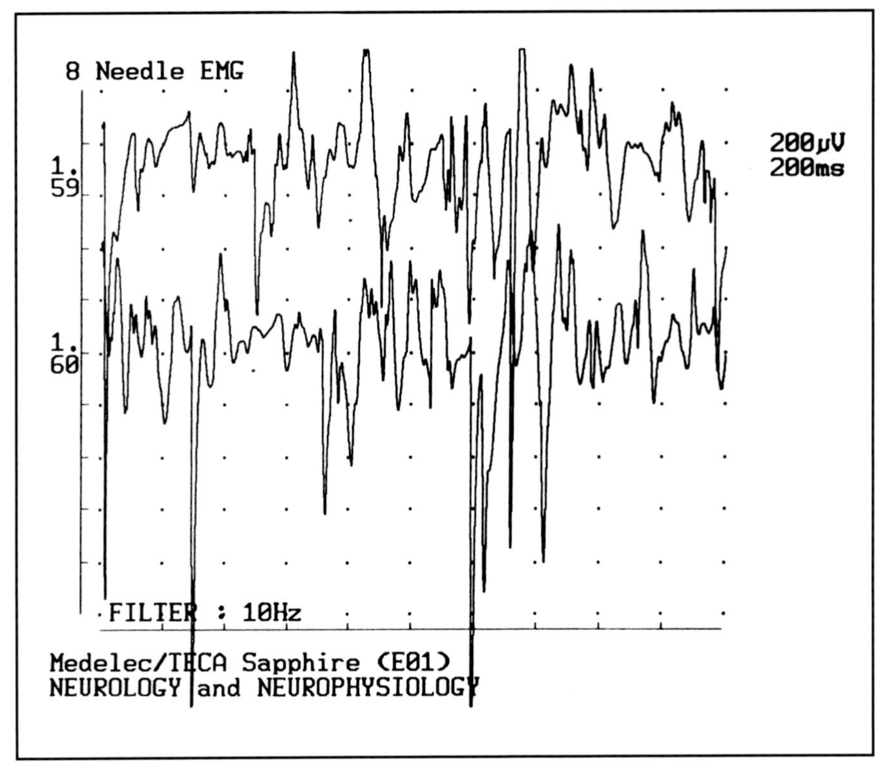

C

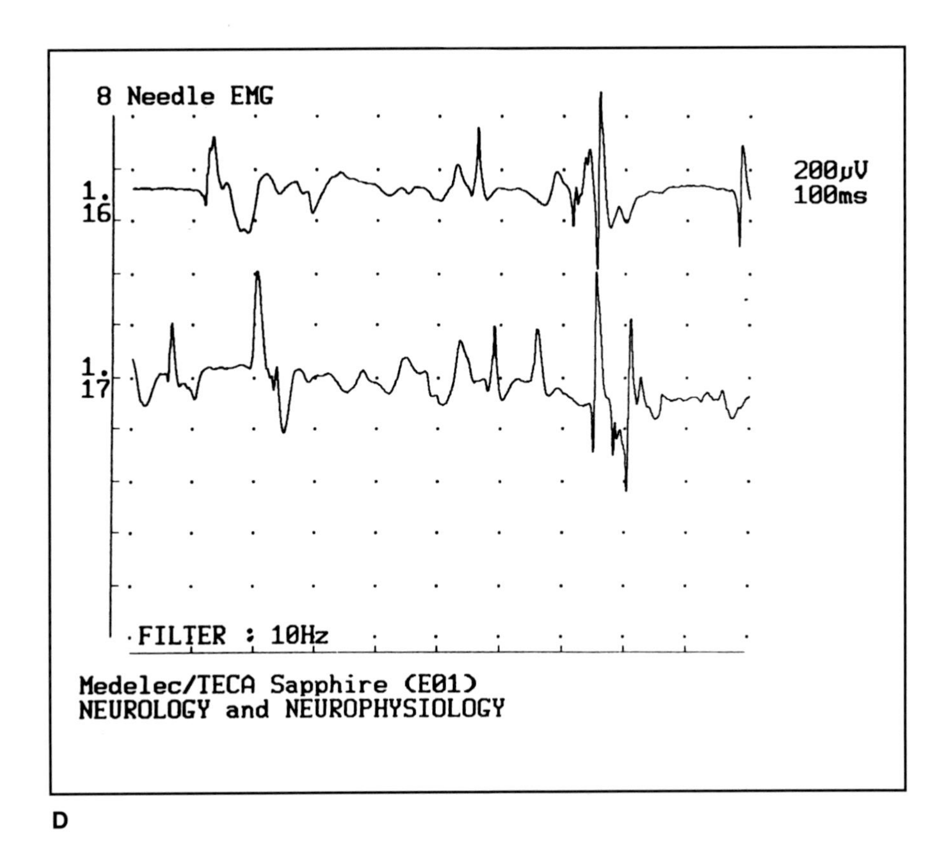

D

Fig 5–15. C. *(continued)* Maximal contraction, motor unit recruitment decreased approximately 50%. **D.** Maximal contraction, motor unit recruitment decreased approximately 70%. *(continues)*

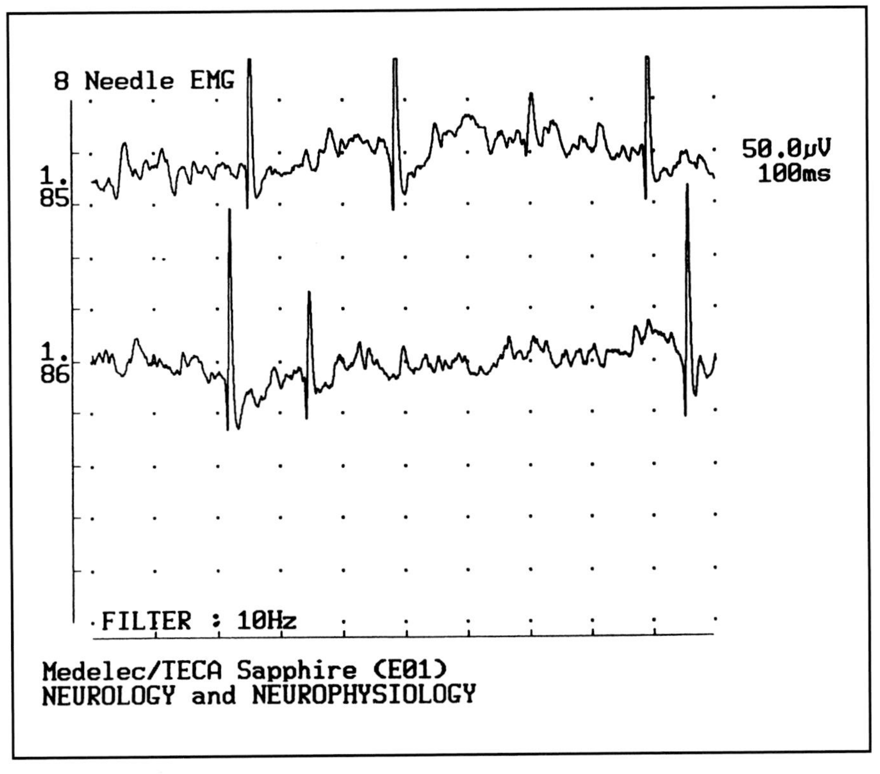

E

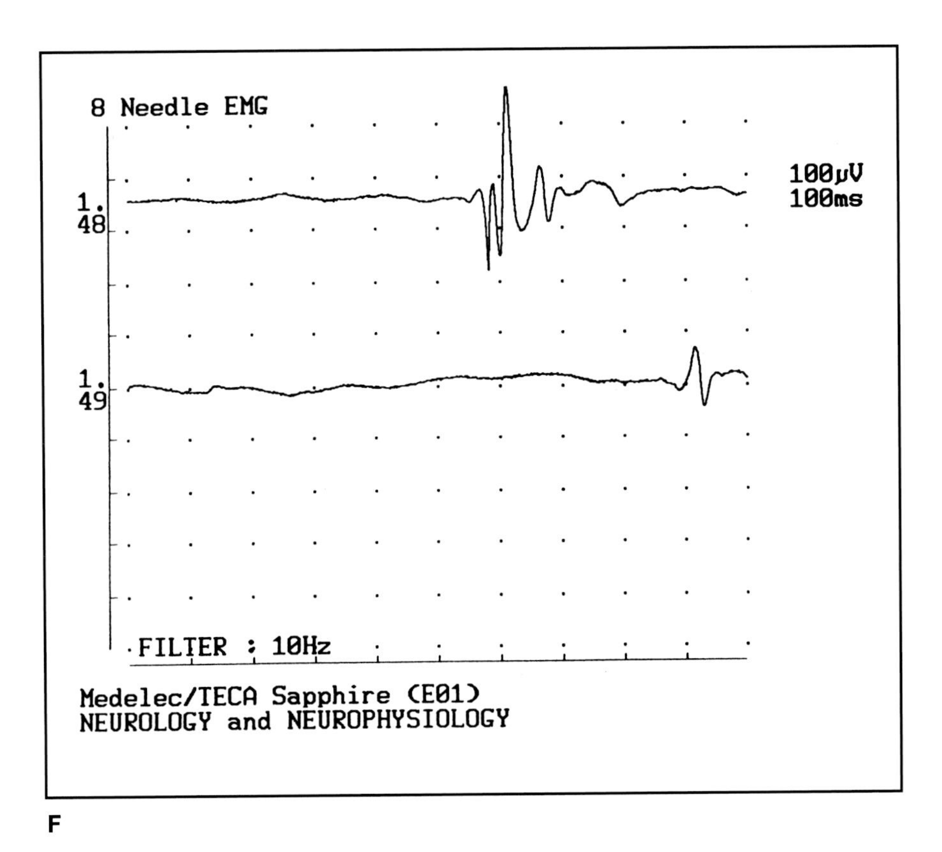

F

Fig 5–15. *(continued)* **E.** Maximal contraction, motor unit recruitment decreased approximately 80 to 90%. **F.** Maximal contraction, revealing a single polyphasic motor unit potential. Approximately 1 year following recurrent laryngeal nerve injury.

for laryngeal muscles; and there is evidence to suggest that turns / amplitude analysis may not be as sensitive as visual analysis or other methods of analyzing motor unit potentials.[102,103] The most definitive investigation of turns/amplitude analysis of laryngeal EMG was carried out by Lindestad, who found that, for diagnostic purposes, it was less valuable than conventional analysis.[90]

Clinical Applications of Laryngeal EMG

Laryngeal EMG can be useful in the diagnosis of a variety of disorders affecting the laryngeal muscles or their innervation. Some of the most common situations in which laryngeal EMG can be helpful include:

1. lower motor neuron disorders
2. evaluation of recurrent or superior laryngeal nerve palsy / paralysis
3. prognosis for recovery of vocal fold paralysis
4. differentiation of paralysis and arytenoid cartilage fixation
5. malingering and psychogenic dysphonia
6. basal ganglia disorder
7. laryngeal dystonias and tremors
8. myopathic disorders
9. neuromuscular junction disorders
10. upper motor neuron disorders

Lower Motor Neuron and Laryngeal Nerve Disorders

In lower motor neuron (LMN) and laryngeal nerve disorders, there is increased insertional activity. Positive wave and fibrillation potentials are frequently observed. Complex repetitive discharges and, rarely, myotonic discharges may also occur. The motor unit potential is prolonged, with an increased number of phases; and the amplitude can be either increased or decreased. There is an incomplete interference pattern with decreased recruitment and rapid firing of the remaining motor units.

Laryngeal EMG can be useful for the evaluation of hoarseness and dysphagia in patients with LMN problems such as amyotrophic lateral sclerosis, Guillain-Barré, polio, post-polio syndrome.[104-106] and multiple system atrophy (Parkinson's Plus syndrome).[107,108] Charcot-Marie-Tooth disease,[109] and other anterior horn cell, nerve root and peripheral nerve degenerative diseases. The laryngeal EMG abnormalities are much the same as those described for laryngeal nerve disorders, because it is a LMN abnormality. Palmer et al[110] found the motor unit action potential recruitment to be the most sensitive (82%) and specific (92%) predictor of lower and upper neuron disorders.

Laryngeal EMG helps in the evaluation of vocal fold palsy.[111] Simpson et al[112] studied 34 patients with idiopathic vocal fold paralysis confirmed by laryngoscopy and laryngeal EMG. In 29 vocal folds, there was evidence of active and chronic denervation in the TA muscle indicating laryngeal neuropathy. In 5 cases, there was denervation of the CT muscle, indicating superior laryngeal neuropathy. In 1 case, there was denervation in both the TA and CT muscle, indicting a proximal laryngeal or vagus nerve neuropathy. Koufman et al[113] reported recently on 50 patients with a diagnosis of vocal fold paresis, with dysphonia as the uniform presenting sign. They found that 40% had a combination recurrent laryngeal nerve (RLN) and superior laryngeal nerve (SLN) paresis, 44% had an isolated RLN paresis, and 16% had isolated SLN neuropathy.

The clinical importance of superior laryngeal nerve paresis is becoming more widely recognized.[107,108,112,114-117] Laryngeal electromyography is particularly helpful in confirming this diagnosis,[116] which may be responsible for vocal fold bowing, loss of projection, and other difficulties with voice control and endurance. Unrecognized superior laryngeal nerve paresis may also lead to compensatory muscular tension dysphonia, which may cause structural pathology such as nodules, pseudocysts, and cysts. In such cases, laryngeal EMG may be invaluable in helping to recognize the underlying primary problem (paresis) and in designing an appropriate therapeutic program.

Laryngeal EMG can assist in predicting the recovery of laryngeal paralysis, and studies show a positive predictive value as high as 90%.[114,118-122] The presence of normal motor unit waveform morphology and recruitment (indicating incomplete nerve injury) predicts good functional recovery. Poor functional recovery may be predicted by the presence of positive sharp waves and fibrillations and by the absence of motor unit potentials (polyphasic or normal).[114,118] However, it should be stressed that the presence of reinnervation does not necessarily guarantee return of function. Synkinesis has been recognized in the larynx at least since 1963.[123] It is possible for opposing muscles to be innervated nearly equally, leaving a reinnervated larynx without appropriate motion. This important problem was studied electromyographically by Blitzer et al.[124] One of the authors (RTS) and Drs. Rontal (Michael Rontal, MD and Eugene Rontal, MD, personal communication, 1997) have utilized botulinum toxin in such situations. Although it may seem counterintuitive to inject botulinum toxin into a "paralyzed" vocal fold, it is possible to use this toxin to eliminate synkinetic reinnervation and improve adduction or abduction (depending on which muscle is injected), as required by the patient's condition. Synkinesis must be distinguished from hysteria and malingering, which also can cause simultaneous firing of abductors and adductors, but in a pattern different from that seen with synkinesis and usually fairly symmetrical bilaterally. Laryngeal EMG also has been found useful in the evaluation of vocal fold paralysis in children, a population somewhat difficult to assess accurately by laryngoscopy and prone to bilateral vocal fold paresis.[125-127]

Laryngeal EMG can be useful in the differentiation of mechanical abnormalities, such as vocal fold fixation or arytenoid subluxation from neurologic etiologies, by demonstrating normal EMG activity in vocal fold fixation and arytenoid subluxation.[128-131] Sataloff et al[131] and Yin et al[132] have noted EMG abnormalities in some patients with arytenoid dislocation. In the author's experience (RTS), this is most common in the thyroarytenoid muscle and may be due to direct trauma and/or hemorrhage associated with the injury that caused the dislocation. However, dislocation and paresis can coexist. More than one muscle innervated by the recurrent laryngeal nerve should be tested (including the PCA); and a quantitative assessment of laryngeal function is helpful. For example, 30% reduced recruitment response in the thyroarytenoid muscle is abnormal, but it is not sufficient to explain an immobile vocal fold. If all of the other muscles innervated by the recurrent nerve are normal and the arytenoid is subluxed or dislocated, the EMG abnormality is probably due to post-traumatic muscle injury and scar; and the patient should not be diagnosed with paresis. If there is decreased function in all of the muscles innervated by the recurrent nerve, then paresis can be diagnosed appropriately even in the presence of an arytenoid dislocation.

Intraoperative laryngeal electrophysiological monitoring during thyroid and laryngotracheal surgery has proven invaluable.[133] The introduction of the Xomed (Jacksonville, Fla) endotracheal tube with RLN sensors provides a convenient method for detecting impending nerve injury during thyroid and other neck surgery and for avoiding permanent injury.[134] It has advantages (eg, ease of placement by a nonlaryngologist) in comparison with needle electrodes, but both techniques may be useful for intraoperative monitoring. It should be noted that thyroid surgery represents the etiology in only 9% of cases of unilateral vocal fold paralysis[135] and that SLN injury not detected currently by intraoperative EMG may be more common in this surgery.[116]

Basal Ganglia Disorders

The insertional activity is normal in basal ganglia disorders. Abnormal spontaneous activity is absent. At rest, there may be excessive motor unit potentials, indicating failure of complete relaxation of the muscle. There may also be poor coordination between agonist and antagonistic muscles or inappropriate activation. In addition, rhythmical and periodic discharges of motor unit potentials can be observed in patients with voice tremor.[136] Stuttering also may be associated with tremorlike EMG activity.[137]

Dystonia

In laryngeal dystonia, there are intermittent sudden increases in muscle activity coinciding with momentary voice rest.[138-140] The EMG can be helpful in differentiating adductor versus abductor dystonia.[141] Rodriguez et al[142] found abnormal activity in 81.3% of spasmodic dysphonia (SD) patients but found no EMG abnormality predictive of severity. Laryngeal EMG is used routinely to guide botulinum injection in patients with laryngeal dystonia and for (controversial) treatment of hyperfunctional dysphonia.[143,144] As noted above, an abnormal delay between the onset of electrical and acoustical activity can help confirm a diagnosis of dystonia. EMG may also help identify the muscle(s) affected most by the dystonia, thereby guiding therapeutic intervention.

Myopathic Disorders

The insertional activity in patients with myopathic disorders is either increased or decreased. Some necrotizing myopathies, such as myositis and some muscular dystrophies, can demonstrate positive waves and fibrillations. Complex repetitive discharges and myotonic potentials can occur. The motor unit potential is short, with an increased number of phases and decreased amplitude. Recruitment is rapid and early with a full interference pattern that is of low amplitude. In myotonic dystrophy, myotonic discharges of TA and CT muscles can produce hoarseness.

Neuromuscular Junction Disorders

In myasthenia gravis (MG) and chemical-induced cholinesterase inhibition such as from exposures to insecticides, the insertional activity is normal. There is no abnormal spontaneous activity. With minimal muscle contraction, the motor unit potential exhibits variation in amplitude and duration, reflecting intermittent failure of conduction across the neuromuscular junction. The recruitment and interference patterns are normal. Repetitive nerve stimulation studies are usually abnormal. Myasthenia gravis can be a cause of intermittent and fluctuating hoarseness and voice fatigue. Laryngeal manifestations can be the first and only sign of myasthenia gravis.[145] Laryngeal MG may occur with systemic MG or as a focal disorder similar to ocular MG.

If there is evidence of fluctuating nerve weakness on laryngeal examination, repetitive stimulation studies and Tensilon testing may be performed. Repetitive stimulation involves stimulating the nerve with electrical shocks and recording the neuromuscular response by EMG. The nerve stimulated is often the spinal accessory nerve, which moves one of the large muscles of the shoulder, the trapezius muscle. This nerve is chosen because it lies just beneath the skin of the neck and is easy to locate for stimulation. Many people describe the sensation experienced during repetitive stimulation studies as being similar to the sensation of an electrical shock going from their shoulder through their arm. Repetitive stimulation gives information regarding the integrity of the neuromuscular junction. With a normal neuromuscular system, recruitment remains normal during repetitive stimulation. If the stimulation causes a progressively decreasing recruitment response, then an abnormality in the neuromuscular junction is suspected. A decrease in the recruitment response implies that motor units that were previously recruited can be actively and continually recruited during repetitive stimulation. The fact that they were unable to be recruited initially and give normal waveform morphology implies that the nerve fibers themselves are intact and that the muscles are able to respond to an impulse signal. The fact that the motor units are unable to keep up with the repetitive stimulation implies that there is an abnormality in the transfer of information across the neuromuscular junction that is apparent only when the system is stressed. If the test is abnormal, or if other abnormalities are seen in the laryngeal EMG, then Tensilon testing may be performed. Repetitive stimulation testing is contraindicated in patients with pacemakers, as noted previously.

Tensilon (edrophonium) is a drug that inhibits the breakdown of acetylcholine in the neuromuscular junction, resulting in increased exposure of the muscle receptors to acetylcholine during neural stimulation. In normal muscles, this has very little effect on muscle activity. In the muscles with decreased numbers of available receptors for acetylcholine (as occurs with myasthenia), in those with increased activity of acetylcholinesterase (the enzyme that normally helps to clear acetylcholine from the neuromuscular junction's preparation for the next nerve signal), or in those with decreased release of acetylcholine from the nerve ending, this results in increased muscle contraction from the prolonged exposure to acetylcholine. When the laryngeal EMG is repeated following administration of Tensilon, the recruitment patterns revert to a more normal pattern with voluntary contraction and with repetitive stimulation. Voice quality may also improve with resolution of breathiness, softness, and fatigue. This positive response to Tensilon further isolates the problem to the neuromuscular junction.

Tensilon testing involves the injection intravenously of edrophonium into a vein and repeating the laryngeal EMG. A syringe containing 10 mg of Tensilon is used for intravenous injection. Initially, 2 mg are injected over 15 to 30 seconds. If there is no reaction after 45 seconds, the remaining 8 mg are injected. If a cholinergic reaction occurs after injection of 2 mg, the test is discontinued and 0.4 to 0.5 mg of atropine sulfate is administered intravenously. Typical signs of cholinergic reaction include skeletal muscle fasciculations, increased muscle weakness, and muscarinic side effects. In patients who have had such reactions, the test may repeated one-half hour after administration of atropine sulfate. In patients with inaccessible veins, Tensilon may be given as an intramuscular injection. Tensilon testing can also be performed in children, with doses adjusted according to the child's weight. The use of Tensilon testing helps to further isolate the problem to the neuromuscular junction.

Tensilon testing is contraindicated in patients with urinary or intestinal obstructions, or in those with known hypersensitivity to anticholinesterase agents. Tensilon is an anticholinesterase drug that inhibits anticholinesterase at sites of cholinergic transmissions within 30 to 60 seconds after injection; and its effect lasts an average of approximately 10 minutes. However, occasionally severe cholinergic reactions occur. Caution must be exercised, particularly in patients with bronchial asthma or cardiac dysrhythmias. The transient bradycardia that sometimes occurs following Tensilon injection can be relieved by atropine sulfate; but isolated incidences of cardiac and respiratory arrest have occurred following administration of Tensilon. A syringe containing 1 mg of atropine sulfate should be available to be given in aliquots intravenously if a severe cholinergic reaction occurs following Tensilon injection. Tensilon also contains sodium sulfite as a preservative. Allergic reactions to sulfites can occur and are more common in asthmatic patients than in other people. The safety of Tensilon for use during pregnancy or lactation has not been established, so use of Tensilon is relatively contraindicated in pregnant woman and nursing mothers.

Upper Motor Neuron Disorders

In upper motor neuron disorders, the insertional activity is normal. There is no abnormal spontaneous activity. The amplitude and duration of the motor unit potential is normal, and there are no excessive polyphasic motor units. There is decreased recruitment and an interference pattern. The firing rate of the motor unit is slow. Most upper motor neuron diseases demonstrate hyperactive reflexes with increased tone and no muscle atrophy. There is a paucity of studies in the literature evaluating laryngeal function with EMG in patients with upper motor neuron disorders.

Other Uses

As the use of laryngeal EMG becomes more common, additional clinical and research applications continue to be developed. Its use in the evaluation and treatment of dysphagia also continues to advance.[146,147] New understanding of the interaction of respiration and TA/CT firing may provide additional information in areas like sudden infant death syndrome (SIDS), obstructive sleep apnea (OSA), and advance the development of laryngeal pacing.[148-153]

Conclusion

Laryngeal EMG is easy to perform, well tolerated in the office setting, and poses minimal risks. It is useful in the evaluation of numerous laryngeal disorders, allowing clinicians to differentiate among upper motor neuron, lower motor neuron, peripheral nerve, neuromuscular junction, myopathic, and mechanical disorders. It is also useful in establishing prognosis in laryngeal nerve palsies and for guidance during the injection of botulinum toxin in spasmodic dysphonia. Our experience is similar to that of Koufman et al who reported 415 laryngeal EMG studies, 83% of which revealed a neuropathic process.[154] They reported unexpected findings in 26% and that LEMG altered clinical management in 40% of cases, highlighting the importance of this simple, quick procedure in the practice of laryngology. We concur and believe that collaboration between the laryngologist and a skilled laryngeal electromyographer is an invaluable and essential asset to the voice care team and can be indispensable to optimal diagnosis and treatment of a variety of voice disorders.[155] However, it should be noted also that there is a striking paucity of evidence-based research to confirm or refute scientifically and incontrovertibly the value of laryngeal EMG for most purposes for which we use and recommend it. Additional prospective, controlled laryngeal EMG research should be encouraged and supported and used to formulate formal practice guidelines for clinical use of laryngeal electromyography.

References

1. Daube JR. *Needle Examination in Clinical Electromyography.* Minimonograph No. 11. Rochester, Minn: American Association of Electromyography and Electrodiagnosis;1991;1–23.
2. Kimura J. *Electrodiagnosis in Diseases of Nerve and Muscles: Principles and Practice.* 2nd ed. Philadelphia, Pa: FA Davis Company; 1989.
3. Lindestad P. *Electromyographic and Laryngoscopic Studies of Normal and Disturbed Voice Function.* Stockholm, Sweden: Departments of Logopedics and Phoniatrics and Clinical Neurophysiology. Huddinge University Hospital; 1994.
4. Kandel ER, Schwartz JH, Hessell TM. Ion channels. In: Kandel ER, Schwartz JH, Jessell TM, eds. *Principles of Neuroscience.* 4th ed. New York, NY: McGraw Hill; 2000; 105–125,
5. Kandel ER. Schwartz JH, Jessell TM. Propagated signaling: the action potential. In: Kandel ER, Schwartz JH, Jessell TM, eds. *Principles of Neuroscience.* 4th ed. New York, NY: McGraw-Hill; 2000:150–175.
6. Burke RE. Physiology of motor unit. In: Engle AG, Franzini-Armstrong C, eds. *Myology.* 2nd ed. New York, NY: McGraw-Hill; 1994:464.
7. Dubowitz V, Pearse AG. A comparative histochemical study of oxidative enzyme and phosphorylase activity in skeletal muscles. *Histochemie.* 1960;2:105–117.
8. Aminoff MJ. Properties and functional organization of motor units. In: Aminoff MJ, ed. *Electromyography in Clinical Practice.* 3rd ed. New York, NY: Churchill Livingston; 1998:33.
9. Gitter AJ, Stolov WC. Instrumentation and measurement in electrodiagnostic medicine. Part I. *Muscle Nerve.* 1995;18:799.
10. Gitter AJ, Stolov WC. Instrumentation and measurement in electrodiagnostic medicine. Part II. *Muscle Nerve.* 1995;18:812.
11. Guld C, Rosenfalck A, Willison RG. Report of the Committee on EMG Instrumentation: technical factors in recording electrical activity of muscles and nerve in men. *Electroencephalog Clin Neurophysiol.* 1970;28:399.
12. Starmer CF, McIntosh HD, Whalen RE. Electrical hazards and cardiovascular function. *N Engl J Med.* 1971;284:181–186.
13. Koufman JA, Walker FO. Laryngeal electromyography in clinical practice: indications, techniques, and interpretation. *Phonoscope.* 1998;1:57–70.
14. Sittel C, Stennert E, Thumfart WF, Dapunt U, Eckel HE. Prognostic value of laryngeal electromyography in vocal fold paralysis. *Arch Otolaryngol Head Neck Surg.* 2001;127:155–160.

15. Faaborg-Andersen K. Electromyographic investigation of intrinsic laryngeal muscles in humans. *Acta Physiol Scand.* 1957;(suppl 140):1–149.
16. Haglund S. The normal electromyogram in human cricothyroid muscle. *Acta Otolaryngol* (Stockh). 1973;75: 478–453.
17. Ekstedt J, Stalberg E. A method of recording extracellular action potentials of single muscle fibres and measuring their propagation velocity in voluntarily activated human muscle. *Bull Am Assoc EMG Electrodiagn.* 1963;10:16.
18. Ekstedt J, Stalberg E. Single muscle fibre electomyography in myasthenia gravis. In: Kunze, K, Desmedt JE, eds. *Studies in Neuromuscular Disease.* Basel, Switzerland: Karger; 1975:157–161.
19. Howard JF, Sanders DB. Serial single-fiber EMG studies in myasthenic patients treated with corticosteroids and plasma exchange therapy. *Muscle Nerve.* 1981;4:254.
20. Schwartz MS, Stalberg E. Myasthenia gravis with features of the myasthenic syndrome. An investigation with electrophysiologic methods including single-fibre electromyography. *Neurology.* 1975;25:80–84.
21. Stålberg E, Ekstedt J, Broman A: The electromyographic jitter in normal human muscles. *Electroencephalogr Clin Neurophysiol.* 1971;31:429–438.
22. Stålberg E, Trontelj JV. *Single Fiber Electromyography in Healthy and Diseased Muscle.* 2nd ed. New York, NY: Raven Press; 1994.
23. Ekstedt J, Stålberg E. How the size of the needle electrode leading-off surface influences the shape of the single muscle fibre action potential in electromyography. *Comput Programs Biomed.* 1973;3:204–212.
24. Ekstedt J, Stålberg E. Single fibre electromyography for the study of the microphysiology of the human muscle. In: Desmedt JE, ed. *New Developments in Electromyography and Clinical Neurophysiology.* Basel, Switzerland: Karger; 1973:89–112.
25. Fuglsang-Frederiksen A, Lo Monaco M, Dahl K. Electrical muscle activity during a gradual increase in force in patients with neuromuscular diseases. *Electroencephalogr Clin Neurophysiol.* 1984;57:320–329.
26. Ekstedt J. Human single muscle fibre action potentials. *Acta Physiol Scand.* 1964;61(suppl 226):1–96.
27. Stålberg E, Ekstedt J, Broman A: The electromyographic jitter in normal human muscles. *Electroencephalogr Clin Neurophysiol.* 1971;31(5):429–438.
28. Ekstedt J, Stålberg E. Abnormal connections between skeletal muscle fibers. *Electroencephalogr Clin Neurophysiol.* 1969;27:607–609.
29. Thiele B, Stålberg E. The bimodal jitter: a single fibre electromyographic finding. *J Neurol Neurosurg Psychiatry.* 1974;37:403–411.
30. Stålberg E. Propagation velocity in human single muscle fibers in situ. *Acta Physiol Scand.* 1966;70(suppl 287): 1–112.
31. Mihelin M, Trontelj JV, Stålberg E. Muscle fiber recovery functions studied in the double pulse stimulation. *Muscle Nerve.* 1991;14:739–747.
32. Sanders DB, Stålberg EV. AAEM Minimonography #36: Single-fiber electromyography. *Muscle Nerve.* 1996;19: 1069–1083.
33. Ekstedt J. Nilsson G, Stålberg E. Calculation of the electromyographic jitter. *J Neurol Neurosurg Psychiatry.* 1974; 37:526–539.
34. Sanders DB, Howard JF. AAEM Minimonograph #25: Single-fiber electromyography in myasthenia gravis. *Muscle Nerve.* 1986;9:809–819.
35. Bromberg MB, Scott DM. Single fiber EMG reference values reformatted in tabular form. Ad Hoc Committee of the AAEM Special Single Fiber Special Interest Group. *Muscle Nerve.* 1994;17(7):820–821.
36. Ad Hoc Committee of the AAEM Special Interest Group on Single Fiber EMG: Single fiber EMG reference values: a collaborative effort. *Muscle Nerve.* 1992;15:151–161.
37. Hilton-Brown P, Stålberg E. The motor unit in muscular dystrophy, a single fibre EMG and scanning EMG study. *J Neurol Neurosurg Psychiatry.* 1983;46:981–995.
38. Gath I, Stålberg E. On the measurement of fibre density in human muscles. *Electroencephalogr Clin Neurophysiol.* 1982;54:699–706.
39. Trontelj JV. H-reflex of single motoneurons in man. *Nature.* 1968;220:1043–1044.
40. Stalberg E, Thiele B: Motor unit fibre density in the extensor digitorum communis muscle. Singe fibre electromyographic study in normal subjects of different ages. *J Neurol Neurosurg Psychiatry.* 1975;38:874–880.
41. Brandstater ME, Lambert EH. Motor unit anatomy: type and spatial arrangement of muscle fibers. In: Desmedt JE, ed. *New Developments in Electromyography and Clinical Neurophysiology.* Basel, Switzerland: Karger; 1973:14–22.
42. Weddel G, Feinstein B, Pattle RE. The electrical activity of voluntary muscle in man under normal and pathological conditions. *Brain.* 1944;67:178–257.
43. Faaborg-Andersen K, Buchtal F. Action potentials from internal laryngeal muscles during phonation. *Nature.* 1956;177:340–341.
44. Faaborg-Andersen K. Electromyographic investigation of intrinsic laryngeal muscles in humans. *Acta Physiol.* 1957;41(suppl 140):1–149.
45. Buchtal F. Electromyography of intrinsic laryngeal muscles. *J Exp Physiol.* 1959;44: 137–148.
46. Dedo HH, Hall WN. Electrodes in laryngeal electromyography. Reliability comparison. *Ann Otol Rhinol Laryngol.* 1969;78:172–180.
47. Dedo HH. The paralyzed larynx: an electromyographic study in dogs and humans. *Laryngoscope.* 1970;80:1445–1517.
48. English ET, Blevins CE. Motor units of laryngeal muscles. *Arch Otolaryngol.* 1969;89:778–784.
49. Fex S. Judging the movements of vocal cords in larynx paralysis. *Acta Otolaryngol* (Stockh). 1970;263:82–83.
50. Gay T, Hirose H, Strome M, Sawashima M. Electromyography of the intrinsic laryngeal muscles during phonation. *Ann Otol Rhinol Laryngol.* 1972;81:401–409.
51. Haglund S. Electromyography in the diagnosis of laryngeal motor disorders. [dissertation]. Departments of Otolaryngology and Clinical Neurophysiology, Karolinska Institute, Stockholm, Sweden; 1973.

52. Haglund S. The normal electromyogram in human cricothyroid muscle. *Acta Otolaryngol* (Stockh). 1973;75: 478–453.
53. Haglund S, Knutsson E, Martensson A. An electromyographic study of the vocal and cricothyroid muscles in functional dysphonia. *Acta Otolaryngol* (Stockh). 1974; 77:140–149.
54. Hast MH. Mechanical properties of the cricothyroid muscle. *Laryngoscope.* 1966;75:537–548.
55. Hast MH. Mechanical properties of the vocal fold muscles. *Practica Oto-Rhino-Laryngologica.* 1967;33:209–214.
56. Hast MH, Golbus S. Physiology of the lateral cricoarytenoid muscles. *Practica Oto-Rhino-Laryngologica.* 1971; 33:209–214.
57. Hirano M. Ohala J. Use of hooked-wire electrodes for electromyography of the intrinsic laryngeal muscles. *J Speech Hear Res.* 1969;12:361–373.
58. Hirano M, Ohala J, Vennard W. The function of laryngeal muscles in regulating fundamental frequency and intensity of phonation. *J Speech Hear Res.* 1969;12: 616–628.
59. Hirano M, Vennard W, Ohala J. Regulation of register, pitch and intensity of voice. *Folia Phoniatr.* 1970;22:1–20.
60. Hirose H, Gay T, Strome M. Electrode insertion techniques for laryngeal electromyography. *J Acoust Soc Am.* 1971;50:1449–1450.
61. Hirose H. Clinical observations on 600 cases of recurrent laryngeal nerve palsy. *Annual Bull RILP (Research Institute of Logopedics and Phoniatrics)*, University of Tokyo, Japan. 1977;11:165–173.
62. Hiroto I, Hirano M, Toyozumi Y, Shin T. A new method of placement of a needle electrode in the intrinsic laryngeal muscles for electromyography. Insertion through the skin. *Pract Otol* (Kyoto). 1962;55:499–504.
63. Hiroto I, Hirano M, Tomita H. Electromyographic investigation of human vocal cord paralysis. *Ann Otol Rhinol Laryngol.* 1968;77:296–304.
64. Jonsson B, Reichmann S. Displacement and deformation of wire electrodes in electromyography. *Electromyography.* 1969;9:210–211.
65. Knutsson E, Martensson A, Martensson B. The normal electromyogram in human vocal fold muscles. *Acta Otolaryngol* (Stockh). 1969;68:526–536.
66. Skoglund CR. Contraction properties of intrinsic laryngeal muscles. *Acta Physiol Scand.* 1964;60:318–336.
67. Shipp T, Doherty ET, Morrissey P. Predicting vocal frequency from selected physiologic measures. *J Acoust Soc Am.* 1979;66:678–684.
68. Sussman HM, Macneilage PF, Powers RK. Recruitment and discharge patterns of single motor units during speech production. *J Speech Hear Res,* 1977;20:613–630.
69. Yanagihara N, von Leden H. The cricothyroid muscle during phonation. Electromyographic, aerodynamic, and acoustic studies. *Ann Otol Rhinol Laryngol.* 1968;75: 987–1006.
70. Arnold GE. Physiology and pathology of the cricothyroid muscle. *Laryngoscope.* 1961;71:687–753.
71. Hirano M. The function of the intrinsic laryngeal muscles in singing. In: Stevens K, Hirano M, eds. *Vocal Fold Physiology.* Tokyo, Japan: University of Tokyo Press; 1981:155–167.
72. Hirano M. Electromyography of laryngeal muscles. In: Hirano M, ed. *Clinical Examination of Voice.* Wien/New York: Springer-Verlag; 1981;11–24.
73. Hirano M. Examination of vocal fold vibration. In: Hirano M, ed. *Clinical Examination of the Voice.* Wien/New York: Springer-Verlag; 1981;43–65.
74. Hirose H, Kobayashi T, Okamura M, et al. Recurrent laryngeal nerve palsy. *J Otolaryngol* (Japan). 1967;70: 1–17.
75. Khan A, Pearlman RC, Bianchi DA, Hauck KW. Experience with two types of electromyography monitoring electrodes during thyroid surgery. *Am J Otolaryngol.* 1997;18:99–102.
76. Guindi GM, Higenbottam TW, Payne JK. A new method for laryngeal electromyography. *Clin Otolaryngol.* 1981; 6:271–278.
77. Fujita M, Ludlow CL, Woodson GE, Naughton RF. A new surface electrode for recording from the posterior cricoarytenoid muscle. *Laryngoscope.* 1989;99:316–320.
78. Andrews S, Warner J, Stewart R. EMG biofeedback in the treatment of hyperfunctional dysphonia. *Br J Disord Commun.* 1986;21:353–369.
79. Hillel AD, Robinson LR, Waugh P. Laryngeal electromyography for the diagnosis and management of swallowing disorders. *Otolaryngol Head Neck Surg.* 1997; 116(3):344–348.
80. Brown WF. *The Physiological and Technical Basis of Electromyography.* Stoneham, Mass: Butterworth Publishers; 1984.
81. Lovelace RE, Blizter A, Ludlow C. Clinical laryngeal electromyography. In: Blitzer A, Brin MF, Sasaki CT. *Neurologic Disorders of the Larynx.* New York, NY: Thieme; 1992:66–82.
82. Aminoff MJ. Clinical electromyography. In: Aminoff MJ, ed. *Electrodiagnosis in Clinical Neurology.* 4th ed. Philadelphia, Pa: Churchill Livingstone; 1999:223–252.
83. Campbell WW. Needle electrode examination. In: Campbell WW, ed. *Essentials of Electrodiagnostic Medicine.* Baltimore, Md: Williams & Wilkins; 1998:93–116.
84. Basmajian JV, Stecko G. A new bipolar electrode for electromyography. *J Applied Physiol.* 1962;17:849.
85. Blitzer A, Lovelace RE, Brin MF, et al. Electromyographic findings in focal laryngeal dystonia (spasmodic dysphonia). *Ann Otol Rhinol Laryngol.* 1985;94:591–594.
86. Thumfart WF. Electromyography of the larynx and related technics. *Acta Otorhinolaryngol Belg.* 1986;40:358–376.
87. Woo P, Arandia H. Intraoperative laryngeal electromyographic assessment of patients with immobile vocal fold. *Ann Otol Rhinol Laryngol.* 1992;101(10): 799–806.
88. Blitzer A, Brin M, Sasaki C. *Neurological Disorders of the Larynx.* New York, NY: Thieme; 1992.
89. Lindestad PA, Persson A. Quantitative analysis of EMG interference pattern in patients with laryngeal paresis. *Acta Otolaryngol.* 1994;114(1):91–97.

90. Lindestad PA. *Electromyographic and Laryngoscopic Studies of Normal and Disturbed Voice Function.* Stockholm, Sweden: Departments of Logopedics and Phoniatrics and Clinical Neurophysiology, Huddinge University Hospital; 1994.
91. Titze IR, Luschei ES, Hirano M. The role of the thyroarytenoid muscles in the regulation of fundamental frequency. *J Voice.* 1989;3:213–324.
92. Ludlow C. Neurophysiological control of vocal fold adduction and abduction for phonation onset and offset during speech. In: Gauffin J, Hammarberg B, eds. *Vocal Fold Physiology: Acoustic, Perceptual, and Physiological Aspects of Voice Mechanisms.* San Diego Calif: Singular Publishing Group; 1991:197–205.
93. Willison R. Analysis of electrical activity in healthy and dystrophic muscles in man. *J Neurol Neurosurg Psychiatry.* 1964;27:386–294.
94. Fuglsang-Frederiksen A, Mansson A. Analysis of electrical activity of normal muscle in man at different degrees of voluntary effort. *J. Neurol Neurosurg Psychiatry.* 1975;38:683–694.
95. Philipson L, Larsson P. The electromyographical signal as a measure of muscular force: a comparison of detection and quantification techniques. *Electromyogr Clin Neurophysiol.* 1988;28:141–150.
96. Stalberg E, Chu J, Bril V, et al. Automatic analysis of the EMG interference pattern. *Electroenceophalogr Clin Neurophysiol.* 1983;56:672–681
97. Rose A, Willison RG. Quantitative electromyography using automatic analysis: studies in healthy subjects and patients with primary muscle disease. *J Neurol Neurosurg Psychiatry.* 1967;30:403–410.
98. Hayward M. Automatic analysis of the electromyogram in healthy subjects of different ages. *J Neurol Sci.* 1977; 33:397–413.
99. Fuglsang-Frederiksen A, Lo Monaco M, Dahl K. Turns analysis (peak ratio) in EMG using mean amplitude as a substitute of force measurement. *Electroencephalogr Clin Neurophysiol.* 1985;60:225–227.
100. Fuglsang-Frederiksen A, Scheel U, Buchthal F. Diagnostic yield of the analysis of the pattern of electrical activity of muscle and of individual motor unit potentials in neurogenic involvement. *J Neurol Neurosurg Psychiatry.* 1977;40:544–554.
101. Fuglsang-Frederiksen A. Quantitative electromyography. II. Modifications of the turns analysis. *Electromyogr Clin Neurophysiol.* 1987;27:335–338.
102. Gilchrist JM, Nandedkar SD, Stewart CS, et al. Automatic analysis of the electromyographic interference pattern using the turns: amplitude ratio. *Electroencephalogr Clin Neurophysiol.* 1988;70:534–540.
103. Fuglsang-Frederiksen A, Ronager J. EMG power spectrum, turns-amplitude analysis and motor unit potential duration in neuromuscular disorders. *J Neurol Sci.* 1990;97:81–91.
104. Driscoll BP, Graeco C, Coelho C, et al. Laryngeal function in postpolio patients. *Laryngoscope.* 1995;105(1): 35–41.
105. Abaza M, Sataloff RT, Hawkshaw MJ, Mandel S. Laryngeal manifestations of post poliomyelitis syndrome. *J Voice.* 2001;14(3):291–294.
106. Robinson LR, Hillel AD, Waugh PF. New laryngeal muscle weakness in post-polio syndrome. *Laryngoscope.* 1988;108(5):732–734.
107. Guindi GM, Bannister R, Gibson WP, Payne JK. Laryngeal electromyography in multiple system atrophy with autonomic failure. *J Neurol Neurosurg Psychiatry.* 1981;44:49–53.
108. Isozaki E, Osanai R, Horiguchi S, et al. Laryngeal electromyography with separated surface electrodes in patients with multiple system atrophy presenting with vocal cord paralysis. *J Neurol.* 1994;241:551–556.
109. Dray TG, Robinson LR, Hillel AD. Laryngeal electromyographic findings in Charcot-Marie-Tooth disease type II. *Arch Neurol.* 1999;56:863–865.
110. Palmer JB, Holloway AM, Tanaka E. Detecting lower motor neuron dysfunction at the pharynx and larynx with electromyography. *Arch Phys Med Rehab*il. 1991; 72(3):214–218.
111. Quiney RE. Laryngeal electromyography: a useful technique for the investigation of vocal cord palsy. *Clin Otolaryngol.* 1989:14(4)305–316.
112. Simpson DM, Sternman D, Graves-Wright J, Sanders I. Vocal cord paralysis: clinical and electrophysiologic features. *Muscle Nerve.* 1993;16(9):952–957.
113. Koufman JA, Postma GN, Cummins MM, Blalock PD. Vocal fold paresis. *Otolaryngol Head Neck Surg.* 2000;122(4)537–541.
114. Parnes SM, Satya-Murti S. Predictive value of laryngeal electromyography in patients with vocal cord paralysis of neurogenic origin. *Laryngoscope.* 1985;95:1323–1326.
115. Tanaka S, Hirano M, Chijiwa K. Some aspects of vocal fold bowing. *Ann Otol Rhinol Laryngol.* 1994;103(5 Pt 1):357–362.
116. Dursun G. Sataloff RT, Spiegel JR, et al. Superior laryngeal nerve paresis and paralysis. *J Voice.* 1996;10(2): 206–211.
117. Dray TG, Robinson LR, Hillel AD. Idiopathic bilateral vocal fold weakness. *Laryngoscope.* 1999;109:995–1002
118. Gupta SR, Bastian RW. Use of laryngeal electromyography in prediction of recovery after vocal fold paralysis. *Muscle Nerve.* 1993;16(9):977–978.
119. Min YB, Finnegan EM, Hoffman HT, et al. A preliminary study of the prognostic role of electromyography in laryngeal paralysis. *Otolaryngol Head Neck Surg.* 1994;111(6):770–775
120. Rodriguez AA, Myers BR, Ford CN. Laryngeal electromyography in the diagnosis of laryngeal nerve injuries. *Arch Phys Med Rehab.* 1990;71(8)587–590.
121. Hirano M, Nosoe I, Shin T, Maeyama T. Electromyography for laryngeal paralysis. In: Hirano M, Kirchner J, Bless D, eds. *Neurolaryngology: Recent Advances.* Boston, Mass: College-Hill Press; 1987:232–248.
122. Thumfart W. Electromyography of the larynx. In: Samii M, Gannetta PJ, eds. *The Cranial Nerves.* Berlin, Germany: Springer-Verlag; 1981:597–606.

123. Siribodhi C, Sundmaker W, Adkins JP, Bonner FJ. Electromyographic studies of laryngeal paralysis and regeneration of laryngeal motor nerves in dogs. *Laryngoscope.* 1963;73:148–163.
124. Blitzer A, Jahn AF, Keidar A. Semon's law revisited: an electromyographic analysis of laryngeal synkinesis. *Ann Otol Rhinol Laryngol.* 1996;105:764–769
125. Gartlan MG, Peterson KL, Luschei ES, et al. Bipolar hooked-wire electromyographic *technique* in the evaluation of pediatric vocal cord paralysis. *Ann Otol Rhinol Laryngol.* 1993;102(9):695–700.
126. Koch BM, Milmoe G, Grundfast KM, Vocal cord paralysis in children studied by monopolar electromyography. *Pediatr Neurol.* 1987;3(5):288–293.
127. Berkowitz RG. Laryngeal electromyographic findings in idiopathic congenital bilateral vocal cord paralysis. *Ann Otol Rhinol Laryngol.* 1996;3:207–212.
128. Hoffman HT, Brunberg JA, Winter P, et al. Arytenoid subluxation: diagnosis and treatment. *Ann Otol Rhinol Laryngol.* 1991;101(1):1–9.
129. Rontal E, Rontal M, Silverman B, Kileny PR. The clinical difference between vocal cord paralysis and vocal cord fixation using electromyography. *Laryngoscope.* 1993;103(2):133–137.
130. Woo P, Arandia H. Intraoperative laryngeal electromyographic assessment of patients with immobile vocal fold. *Ann Otol Rhinol Laryngol.* 1992;101(10): 799–806.
131. Sataloff RT, Bough ID Jr, Spiegel JR. Arytenoid dislocation: diagnosis and treatment. *Laryngoscope.* 1994; 104(10):1353–1361.
132. Yin SS, Qiu WW, Stucker FJ. Value of electromyography in differential diagnosis of laryngeal joint injuries after intubation. *Ann Otol Rhinol Laryngol.* 1996;105: 446–451.
133. Lipton RJ, McCaff4ey TV, Litchy WJ. Intraoperative electrophysiologic monitoring of laryngeal muscle during thyroid surgery. *Laryngoscope.* 1988;98(12): 1292–1296.
134. Khan A, Pearlman RC, Bianchi DA, Hauck KW. Experience with two types of electromyographic monitoring electrodes during thyroid surgery. *Am J Otolaryngol.* 1997;18(2):99–122.
135. Benninger MS, Gillen JB, Altman JS. Changing etiology of vocal fold immobility. *Laryngoscope.* 1998;108(9): 1346–1350.
136. Koda J, Ludlow CL. An evaluation of laryngeal muscle activation in patients with voice tremor. *Otolaryngol Head Neck Surg.* 1992;107(5):684–696.
137. Smith A, Luschei E, Denny M, et al. Spectral analyses of activity of laryngeal and orofacial muscles in stutterers. *J Neurol Neurosurg Psychiatry.* 1993;56(12):1303–1311.
138. Blitzer A, Lovelace RE, Brin MF, et al. Electromyographic findings in focal laryngeal dystonia (spastic dysphonia). *Ann Otol Rhinol Laryngol.* 1985;94:591–594.
139. Shipp T, Izdebski K, Reed C, Morrissey P. Intrinsic laryngeal muscle activity in a spastic dysphonia patient. *J Speech Hear Disord.* 1985;50(1):54–59.
140. Blitzer A, Brin M, Fahn S, Lovelace RE. Clinical and laboratory characteristics of focal laryngeal dystonia: study of 110 cases. *Laryngoscope.* 1988;98:636–640.
141. Watson BC, Schaefer SD, Freeman FJ, et al. Laryngeal electromyographic activity in adductor and abductor spasmodic dysphonia. *J Speech Hear Res.* 1991;34(3): 473–482
142. Rodriquez AA, Ford CN, Bless DM, Harmon RL. Electromyographic assessment of spasmodic dysphonia patients prior to botulinum toxin injection. *Electromyogr Clin Neurophysiol.* 1994;34(7):403–407
143. Andrews S, Warner J, Stewart R. EMG biofeedback and relaxation in the treatment of hyperfunctional dysphonia. *Br J Disord Commun.* 1986;21(3):353–369.
144. Davidson BJ, Ludlow CL. Long-term effects of botulinum toxin injections in spasmodic dysphonia. *Ann Otol Rhinol Laryngol.* 1996;105(1):33–42.
145. Mao VH, Abaza M, Spiegel JR, et al. Laryngeal myasthenia gravis: report of 40 cases. *J Voice.* 2001;15(1): 122–130.
146. Ertekin C, Aydogdu I, Yuceyar N, et al. Effects of bolus volume on oropharyngeal swallowing: an electrophysiologic study in man. *Am J Gastroenterol.* 1997;92(11): 2049–2053.
147. Atkinson SI, Rees J. Botulinum toxin for endopharyngeal dysphagia: case reports of CT-guided injection. *J Otolaryngology.* 1997;26(4):273–276.
148. Chanaud CM, Ludlow CL. Single motor unit activity of human intrinsic laryngeal muscles during respiration. *Ann Otol Rhinol Laryngol.* 1992;101(10):832–840.
149. Brancatisano A, Dodd DS, Engel LA. Posterior cricoarytenoid activity and glottic size during hyperpnea in humans. *J Appl Physiol.* 1991;71(3):977–982.
150. Kuna ST, Insalaco G, Villeponteaux RD. Arytenoideus muscle activity in normal adult humans during wakefulness and sleep. *J Appl Physiol.* 1991;70(4):1655–1664.
151. Eichenwald EC, Howell RG III, Kosch PC, et al. Developmental changes in sequential activation of laryngeal abductor muscle and diaphragm in infants. *J Appl Physiol.* 1992;73(4):1425–1431.
152. Insalaco G, Kuna ST, Catania G, et al. Thyroarytenoid muscle activity in sleep apneas. *J Appl Physiol.* 1993; 74(2):704–709.
153. Broniatowski M, Grundfest-Broniatrowski S, Davies CR, et al. Electronic pacing of incapacitated head and neck structures. *ASAIO Trans.* 1991; 37(4): 553–558.
154. Koufman JA, Postma GN, Whang CH, et al. Diagnostic laryngeal electromyography: The Wake Forest experience 1995–1999. *Otolaryngol Head Neck Surg.* 2001;124(6):603–606.
155. Sataloff RT, Mandel S, Manon-Espaillat R, Heman-Ackah YD, Abaza, M. *Laryngeal Electromyography.* Clifton Park, NY: Thomson Delmar Learning; 2003.

6

Laryngeal Photography and Videography

Eiji Yanagisawa, Brian P. Driscoll, and H. Steven Sims

The Spanish-born singing teacher Manuel García is credited with the first successful visualization of the intact larynx. In 1854, using a dental mirror, with a hand-held mirror for reflecting sunlight, he was able to visualize the movements of his own vocal folds.[1] The first successful photographs of the larynx were taken by Thomas French of New York in 1882. Using a box camera with an attached laryngeal mirror and a device to concentrate sunlight (Figure 6–1A), he was able to produce surprisingly good quality black-and-white photographs (Figure 6–1B).[2,3]

Since the early photographs of the larynx by French, many other methods of laryngeal documentation have been described. These include: (1) indirect laryngoscopic photography,[4,5] (2) direct laryngoscopic photography,[4,6-9] (3) fiberscopic photography,[10-28] (4) telescopic photography,[19,21-24,26-48] and (5) microscopic photography.[5,29,49-58] Although many have contributed to the evolution and refinement of laryngeal documentation, several authors merit special mention.

In 1941, P. Holinger, J. D. Brubaker and J. E. Brubaker introduced the Holinger and Brubaker 35 mm camera.[6,8] This camera, although expensive and bulky, set a new standard for laryngeal photography. Most would agree that the clarity, color, and brilliance of these photographs have not been surpassed even by today's standards. This system is no longer used.

In 1954, Yutaka Tsuiki of Tohoku University, Japan, was the first to "televise" the larynx. He used a "tele-endoscope" attached to a large television camera. He predicted the importance of video recording the larynx as a method of documentation and teaching.[59]

In 1963, Oscar Kleinsasser of Cologne adapted the Zeiss otologic microscope for laryngoscopic use by utilizing a 400 mm objective lens.[51-53] Later with the use of a photoadapter, beam splitter, and single lens reflex (SLR) camera, he produced extremely high-quality pictures of the larynx.[52]

In 1968, Sawashima and Hirose of Tokyo introduced the flexible laryngoscope.[14] This instrument is now standard equipment for the practicing otolaryngologist. The quality of photodocumentation through this instrument, although acceptable, is not of high resolution. The advent of modern telescopes such as the Hopkins rod lens (Karl Storz), the Lumina optic system (Wolf), and the full Lumen system (Nagashima) has made superb endoscopic documentation of the larynx easy. These instruments provide brilliant, magnified images of high resolution and significant depth of field. The use of these instruments by Paul Ward, George Berci, and Bruce Benjamin has brought very high standards to laryngeal photography.[19,32-36,44,46,48] The excellent articles by Benjamin describing his methods of laryngeal photography are highly recommended.[33,60] Videotape recording (VTR), as pioneered by Koichi Yamashita, has become the standard technique of the serious endoscopist who requires high-quality documentation of laryngeal form and function.[18,19,21] Recent advances in video technology produce images of such high quality that Kantor, Berci, Partlow, et al described a technique of *video-microlaryngoscopy* in which the operation is performed while viewing the larynx on a television screen.[39]

There have been essentially three methods of laryngeal documentation: (1) still photography, (2) videography, and (3) cinematography. Cinematography has

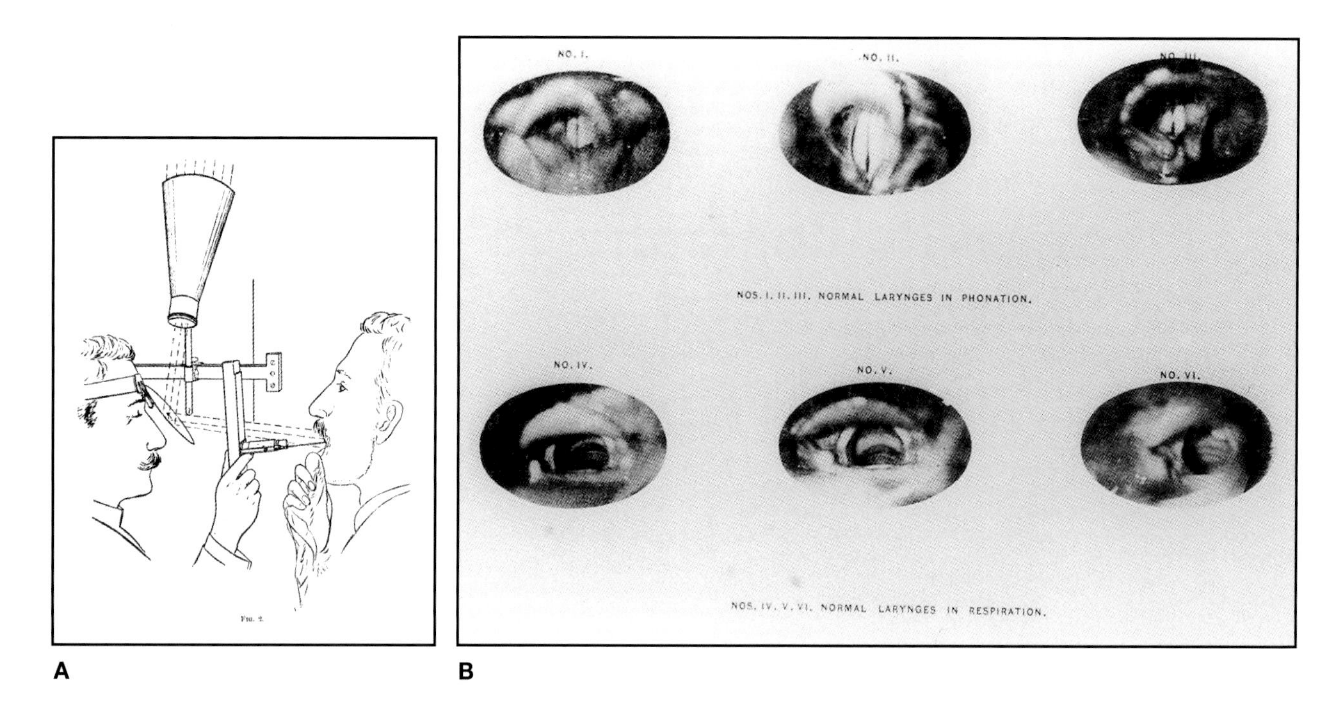

A B

Fig 6–1. A. Dr. French's method of laryngeal documentation used in 1882. He used a sunlight concentrator as a light source. The light was then reflected off a forehead reflector onto a laryngeal mirror. **B.** Sample photographs taken by Dr. French.

been totally replaced by videography because of the time and expense required of the former and the ever-increasing quality of the latter. Still photography retains an important role in laryngeal documentation, although it lacks the dynamics required to study laryngeal function. Digital imaging is the newest technology for permanently recording images using a computer. This technique can also be applied to laryngeal documentation.

A disclaimer: This chapter describes the techniques of still photography and videography of the larynx employed by the senior author (EY). The authors describe equipment that they regularly use. Other brands or makes not described could also be used successfully. Digital imaging is also discussed.

Still Photography of the Larynx

Still photography is the traditional method of laryngeal photography. There are numerous methods in which one can "take a picture" of the larynx. Many of these methods provide high-quality color slides for publication or presentation. The basic equipment is a 35 mm single lens reflex (SLR) camera (Figure 6–2) combined with a light source and a means of visualizing the larynx, such as the laryngeal mirror, laryngoscope, flexible fiberscope, rigid telescope, or operating microscope. Laryngeal photography has recently been made even easier with the use of the newer 35 mm SLR cameras with built-in autowinders combined with the TTL (through the lens) electronic flash system.

Fig 6–2. The single-lens-reflex (SLR) system for still photography. (*Top left*) Olympus OM-2 35 mm SLR camera with an autowinder and 100 mm macrolens. (*Bottom left*) Karl Storz quick-connect adapter. (*Bottom right*) Olympus SMR coupler to which a 2X extender is attached.

Still Photography in the Office

Indirect Still Laryngoscopic Photography

This method is difficult, unpredictable, and requires an experienced photographer. During indirect mirror laryngoscopy (ML) using a fiberoptic headlight as the light source, the laryngeal image appearing in the mirror is photographed. This is accomplished with a 35 mm SLR camera on a tripod to which a 100 mm telephoto lens, such as the Nikon Medical close-up lens, and a ring light are attached. ASA 400 or faster Ektachrome film is recommended. In the authors' experience, satisfactory results are obtained only 20% of the time.

Fiberscopic Still Laryngeal Photography

Although this technique produces a grainy image that is inferior in resolution to that of the telescope, there are distinct advantages to its use. Full functional examination of the larynx can be accomplished with one insertion, even in difficult patients in whom other techniques of laryngeal examination would be difficult or impossible, for example, small children, immobilized adults, and those with a hypersensitive gag or unusual supraglottic anatomy that makes visualization of the anterior larynx difficult with the telescope.

This technique can be accomplished with a number of flexible scopes such as the Olympus ENF-P3 (3.4 mm) or L3 (4.2 mm), Machida 4L (4.0 mm) or 3L (3.3 mm), or Pentax FNL-10S (3.5 mm).[15,16,25]

The senior author's recommended equipment for photodocumentation consists of: (1) the Olympus OM-2 35 mm SLR camera with an autowinder, clear-glass focusing screen 1-9, and 2X teleconverter; (2) Olympus ENF-P2 or P3 fiberscope (the authors' choice); (3) Olympus SMR endoscopic coupler (Fig 6–2); (4) Karl Storz xenon cold light source 487C, 610, or 615; and (5) Ektachrome ASA 400 or 800 daylight film. The camera is set on automatic mode with the appropriate ASA setting. The flexible scope is connected to the 2X teleconverter, which is attached to the SLR camera using either the SMR endoscopic coupler or the 100 mm macrolens with the Karl Storz quick-connect adapter (Fig 6–2). The fiberscope is then advanced to the hypopharynx through an anesthetized (4% lidocaine) and vasoconstricted (3% ephedrine) nose. The images are centered and focused in the viewfinder of the camera, and the larynx is photographed during inspiration and phonation (Fig 6–3A). The clearest pictures are taken immediately after phonating /i/ (Fig 6–3B). It should be noted that the laryngeal image occupies a small portion of the photographic field, and much of what the camera sees is blackened out. This situation will cause the metering system in most automatic cameras to overexpose the photograph, thus washing out the laryngeal image. To prevent this, the compensation dial of the camera should be set at -1 or -2 to underexpose the

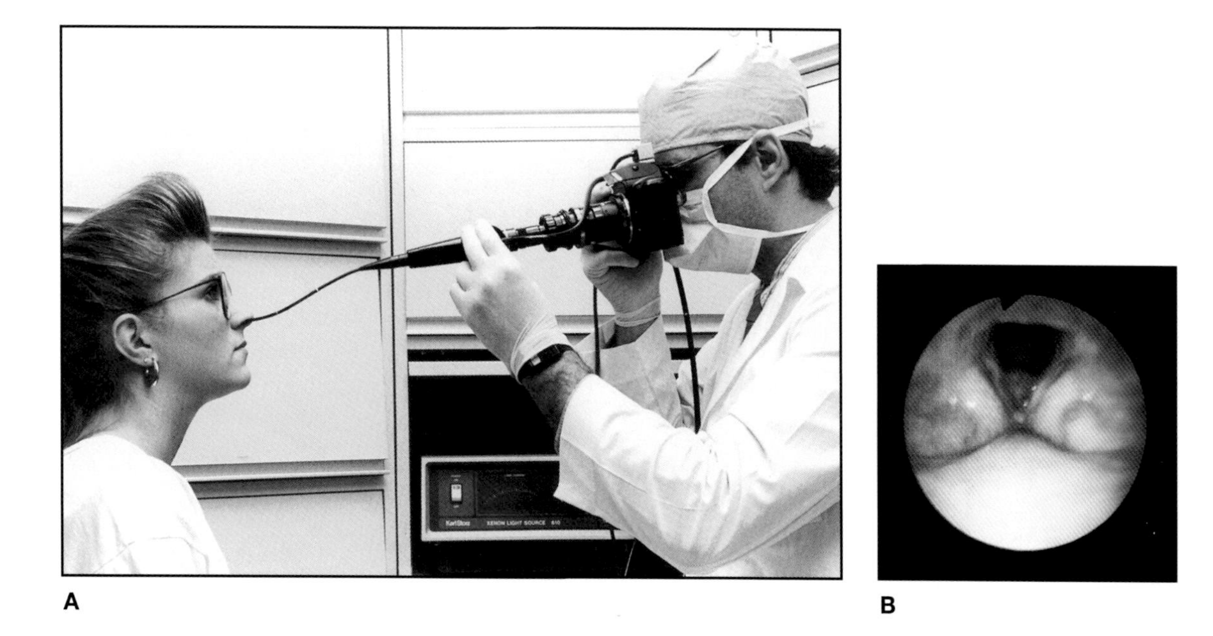

Fig 6–3. A. Method of fiberscopic laryngeal photography in the office. **B.** Photograph taken with the above method showing a laryngeal polyp.

image by 1 or 2 f-stops. A series of photographs should be taken with appropriate bracketing of the shots. When a xenon light source is not available, faster films (ASA 800 or greater) should be used.

More recently the authors have employed the TTL endoscopic flash photography technique as recommended by Karl Storz (Fig 6–4A). This technique uses the Nikon 5005 camera, which is set to manual at a shutter speed of 1/30 of a second, and any aperture setting except S. The Karl Storz 610 light source is set at auto TTL and attached to the camera with a 570MN connection cord (Fig 6–4A and B). The fiberscope is connected to the camera by the Karl Storz 593 T2 lens, and the focal length can be set from 30 mm to 140 mm. The authors routinely use 140 mm as it produces a larger image. Using the TTL system obviates the need to underexpose the image or bracket the photographs. In the authors' hands the success rate of the older method is approximately 50%, which rises to 80% with the TTL system. The readers are advised to consult the Karl Storz company for updated system information.

Telescopic Still Laryngeal Photography

This provides the clearest laryngeal images available in the office. The equipment used by the authors includes: (1) the Olympus 35 mm SLR OM-2 camera system described for fiberscopic laryngoscopy; (2) a telescope, such as the Kay 9105 (70 degree), the Karl Storz rigid telescope 8706 CL (70 degree), the Nagashima SFT-1 (with an "Olympus-type" eyepiece) (70 degree), the Karl Storz right-angled telescope 8702D (90 degree), or the Stuckrad magnifying telescope (Wolf) (90 degree); (3) a xenon light source (Karl Storz 487C, 610 or 615); and (4) ASA 400 or 800 Ektachrome daylight film.

With the soft palate and posterior tongue anesthetized, the patient's tongue is grasped and protruded. The telescope is advanced into the mouth, being careful not to induce gagging by touching the posterior tongue or pharynx (Fig 6–5A). Having the patient vocalize a high-pitched /i/ raises and fully exposes the larynx in most cases. Pictures can be taken during respiration and phonation. The exposures should be bracketed using the automatic compensation dial. Repeated insertions are usually required. The success rate with this method is 70 to 80% (Fig 6–5B).[26,28,47,61] The Karl Storz TTL system as described for the fiberscope can also be used in this setting.

Microscopic Still Laryngeal Photography

The necessary equipment includes: (1) the Zeiss operating microscope with a straightforward eyepiece and the 250 or 300 mm objective lens, (2) a 35 mm SLR camera, (3) a photoadapter, and (4) Ektachrome ASA 320 Tungsten film.

In this technique, the larynx is exposed with a laryngeal mirror and viewed through the microscope. The wall-mounted scope is easier to manipulate and is recommended if available. The microscope is locked dur-

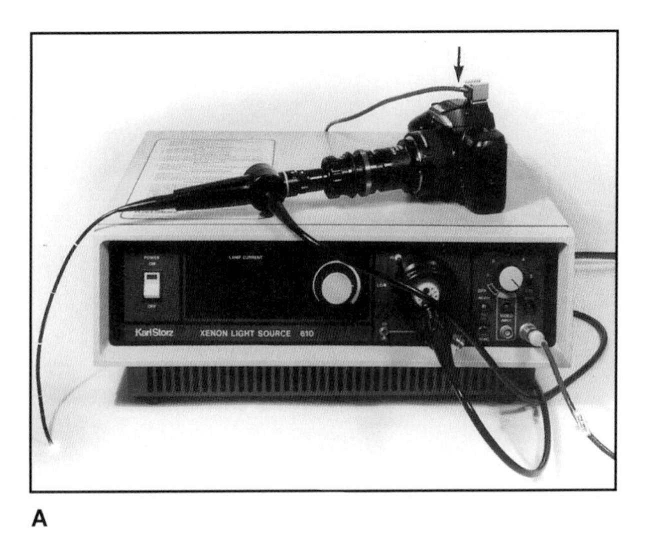

A

B

Fig 6–4. A. Fiberscopic electronic flash still photography system showing Nikon SLR camera, with the Karl Storz 35–140 mm adapter, 570MN TTL light cord (arrow), and the Karl Storz 610 light source. **B.** Enlarged view of the Nikon N5005 with Karl Storz 35–140 mm zoom lens adapter.

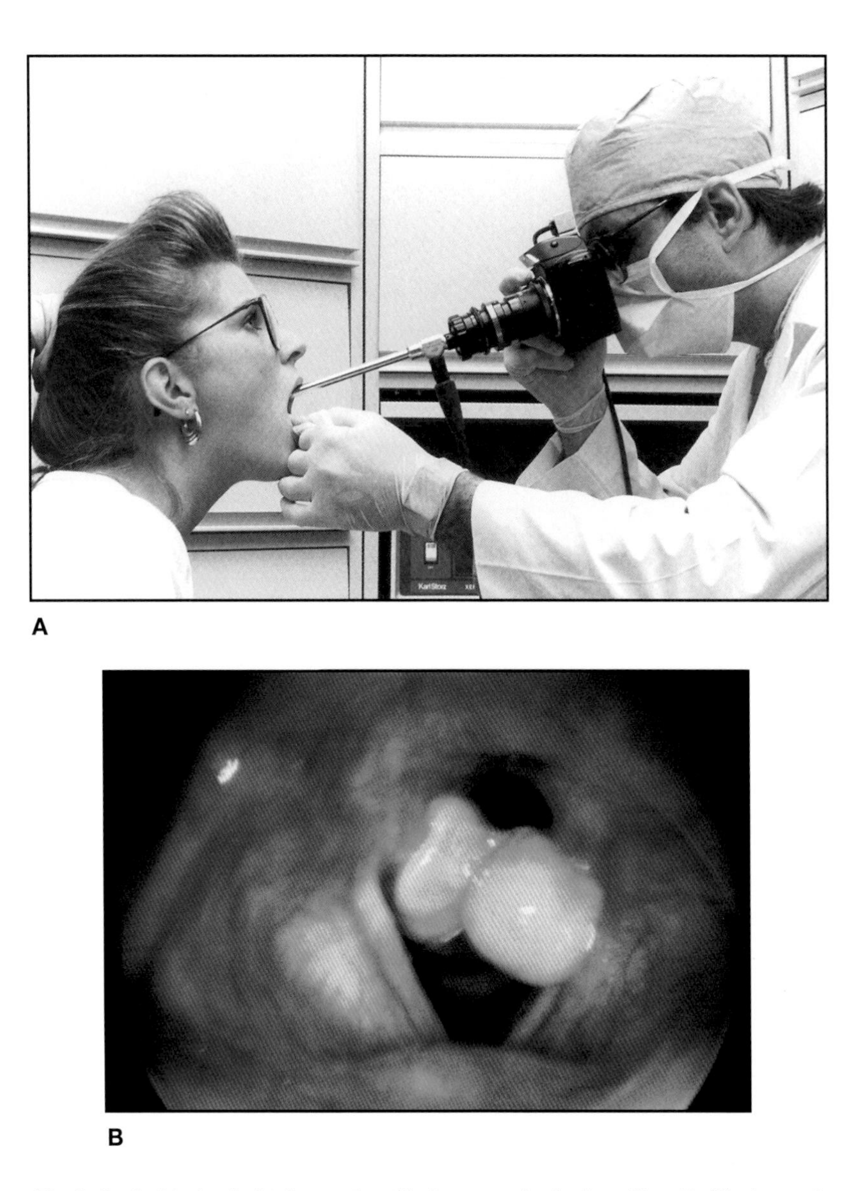

Fig 6–5. **A.** Method of telescopic still photography in the office. **B.** Photograph taken with this method showing post-intubation granulomas.

ing photography to limit camera-shake aberrations. Although some report good results with this method, in the authors' hands the success rate is less than 20%. The difficulty in exposing the larynx while focusing the operating microscope is the disadvantage.

Still Photography in the Operating Room

Direct Laryngoscopic Photography

There are two methods of photographing the larynx directly through the laryngoscope. The first utilizes a 100 mm or 200 mm telephoto lens attached to a 35 mm SLR camera on a tripod (Fig 6–6A and B). Ektachrome Tungsten ASA 320 is used. If the Dedo or Ossoff photographic laryngoscope with two large fiberoptic cables is used, no additional light sources are needed. The major difficulty with this technique is that it is cumbersome. Interruption of the operation and readjustment of the camera and tripod are necessary with each new photograph of the larynx. The success rate is 70 to 80%. The image obtained with this method may be small but quite satisfactory.

The second method requires an aperture-preferred automatic 35 mm SLR camera, such as the Nikon FE or the Olympus OM-2, with a 50 mm macrolens attached.

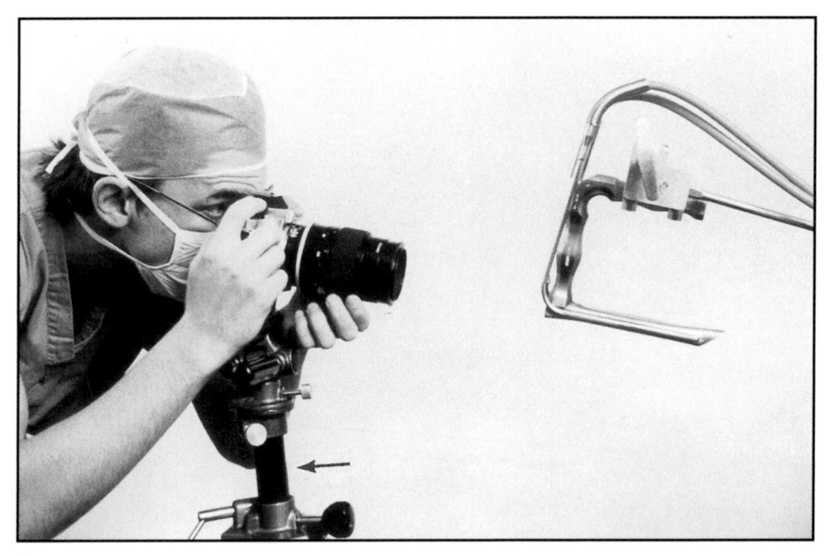

A

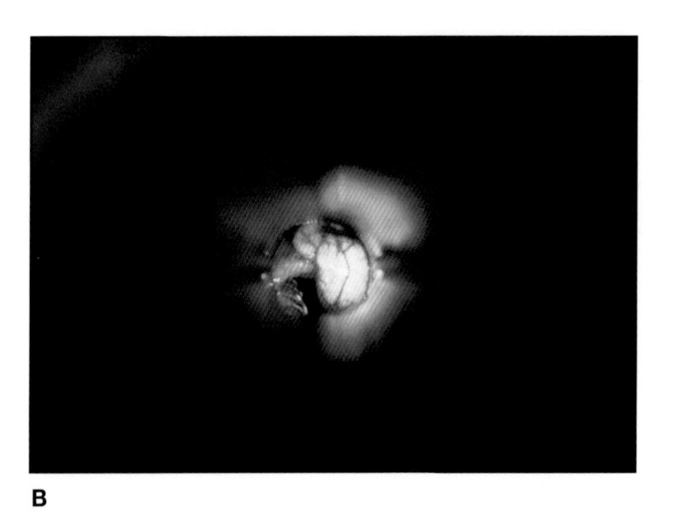

B

Fig 6–6. A. Method of direct laryngeal photography in the operating room with a SLR camera and a 100 mm lens mounted on a tripod (*arrow*). **B.** Photograph taken with this method showing a pedunculated vallecular cyst lying on the top of the epiglottis.

If autofocus cameras such as the Nikon 6006 or 8008 are used, they should be focused manually. This prevents the camera from focusing on the edge of the laryngoscope. Ektachrome Tungsten ASA 320 film is used. For this technique the camera is hand-held, and the larynx is focused through the laryngoscope and photographed (Fig 6–7A). The resulting image, although small, is quite recognizable (Fig 6–7B). The photograph may be cropped and enlarged. The authors feel this is the simplest method of laryngeal photography, and it is recommended for the occasional laryngeal photographer.

Telescopic Laryngeal Photography

In the operating room, telescopic laryngeal photography is accomplished by passing a telescope, attached to a 35 mm SLR camera and light source, through the laryngoscope and then photographing the larynx.[32,33]

The setup the authors use includes the Hopkins 0 degree straightforward telescope 8700A with the Karl Storz 487C or 615 xenon light source. The telescope is attached to the Olympus OM-2 camera with a 100 mm macrolens, a Karl Storz quick-connect adapter, a 1-9 focusing screen, and an autowinder. ASA 400 Ektachrome daylight film is used (Fig 6–8A).

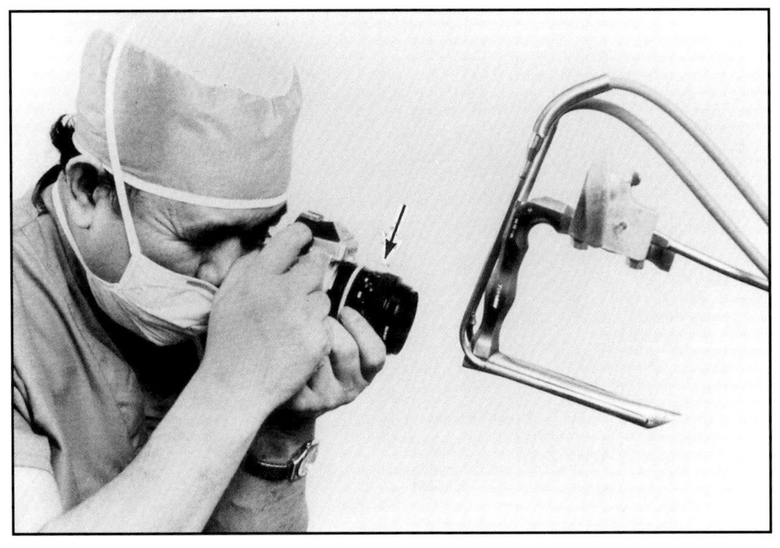

A

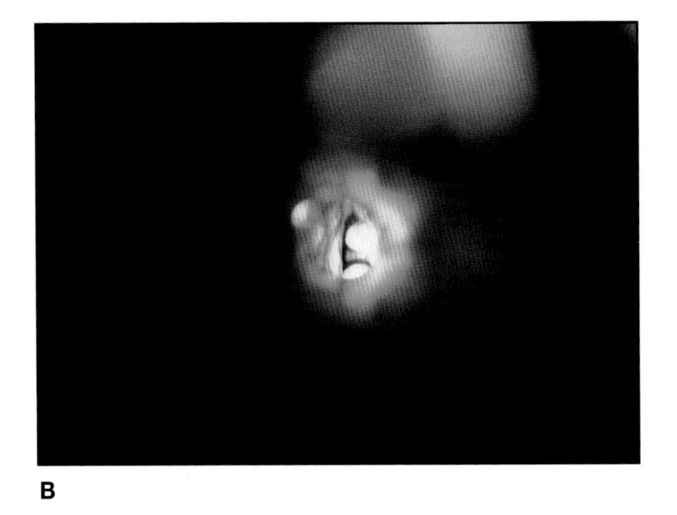

B

Fig 6–7. A. Method of laryngeal photography in the operating room using a hand-held SLR camera with a 50 mm macrolens (*arrow*). **B.** Photograph taken with this technique showing a laryngeal polyp.

This method is highly successful (greater than 90%) and produces excellent pictures of the larynx (Fig 6–8B). The major drawbacks are the expense of the special telescope and adapters and the need to interrupt surgery to photograph the larynx. One can also use a Nikon automatic camera with the Karl Storz TTL flash system.

Microscopic Laryngeal Photography

Laryngeal photography through the operating microscope can be accomplished with or without the use of a photoadapter.[26,50-52,54-58] High-quality images of varying magnification are possible with this technique.

Microscopic Photography With the Use of a Photoadapter. Microscopic photography with the use of a photoadapter requires the following equipment: (1) an operating microscope (the authors prefer Zeiss), (2) a beam splitter, (3) a photoadapter, (4) an automatic 35 mm SLR camera, and (5) a ring adapter for the camera. High-speed Ektachrome Tungsten ASA 320 film is used. After the laryngoscope is suspended, the microscope with the attached beam splitter, photoadapter, and 35 mm SLR camera are positioned for microlaryngoscopy (Fig 6–9A). Photographs can now be taken at any time. Two major advantages of this technique are that the surgeon is the photographer and there is

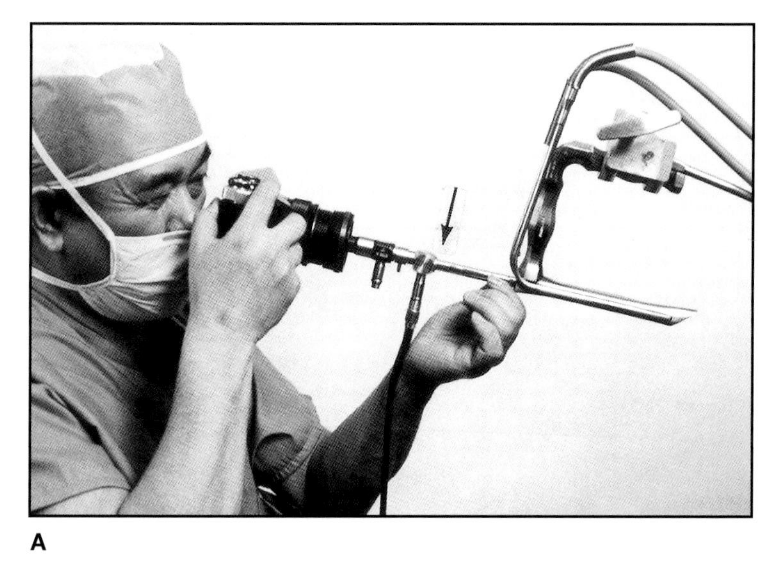

A

B

Fig 6–8. A. Method of telescopic still photography in the operating room with the Hopkins 8700A telescope (arrow). **B.** Photograph of transglottic tumor taken with this method.

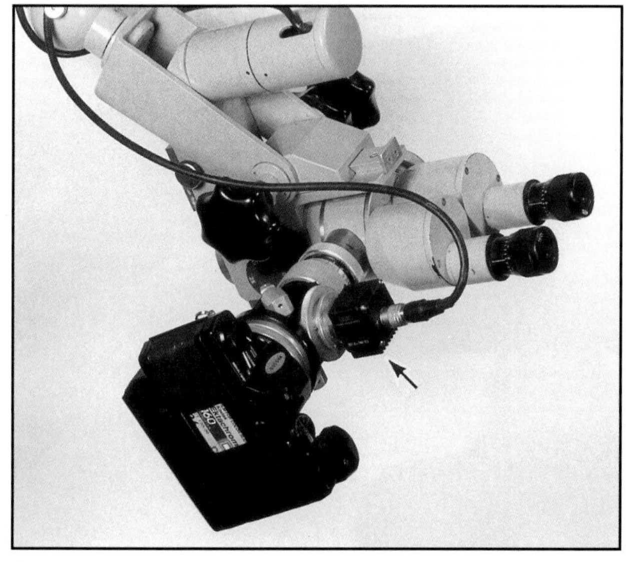

A

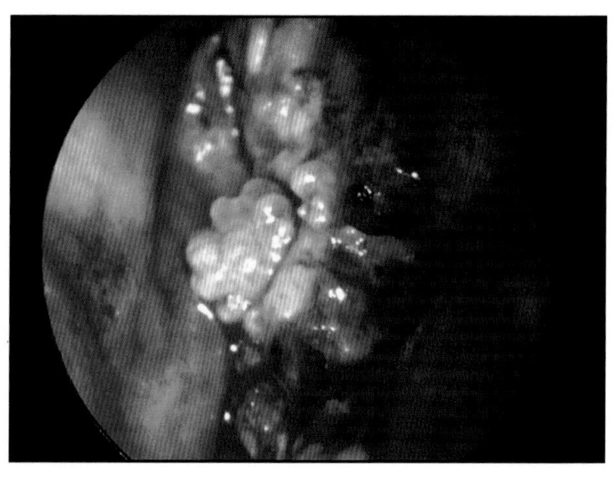

B

Fig 6–9. A. Method for microlaryngoscopic still photography using the SLR camera attached to the Zeiss operating microscope via a photoadapter. Also note a miniature CCD camera on the photoadapter (arrow). **B.** Photograph of extensive squamous cell carcinoma taken with this technique.

minimal disruption of the operation. Other advantages include the following: (1) one can photograph at varying magnifications (6X, 10X, 25X, and 40X), (2) the full-field image of the larynx at higher magnifications obviates the need for copying and enlarging the slides for presentation, and (3) with the use of a Telestill or dual photoadapter, TV and movie documentation are possible.

The disadvantages are: (1) the expense of the beam splitter and the photoadapter, (2) the shallow depth of field, especially at high magnification, and (3) the need for brilliant illumination, such as that provided by the

Dedo or Ossoff (Pilling) photographic laryngoscope. The success rate is approximately 70%.

Microscopic Photography Without the Use of a Photoadapter. This simple, inexpensive means of laryngeal photography known as the *microscopic macrolens technique*[26,58] requires only: (1) the Zeiss operating microscope, (2) an *aperture-preferred* automatic 35 mm SLR camera, such as the Nikon FE, Pentax ME, or Olympus OM-2, (3) a 50 mm macrolens, and (4) the Dedo or Ossoff photographic laryngoscope. Ektachrome Tungsten ASA 320 film is used.

During microscopic laryngoscopy, the larynx is focused through the microscope with the eyepiece set at 0. The microscope is then locked in place. With the camera focused at infinity and the aperture wide open (usually f3.5), the camera is placed on the microscope eyepiece, and the laryngeal image is centered and brought into sharp focus through the camera (Fig 6–10A). The picture is then taken. Surprisingly good quality photographs, with a success rate of 70 to 80%, can be taken with this simple technique (Fig 6–10B). Some disadvantages are that occasionally it may be difficult to hold the camera still on the eyepiece, and it requires interruption of surgery. The ultimate success of this technique depends on illumination, critical focusing, and the stability of the patient, microscope, and camera.

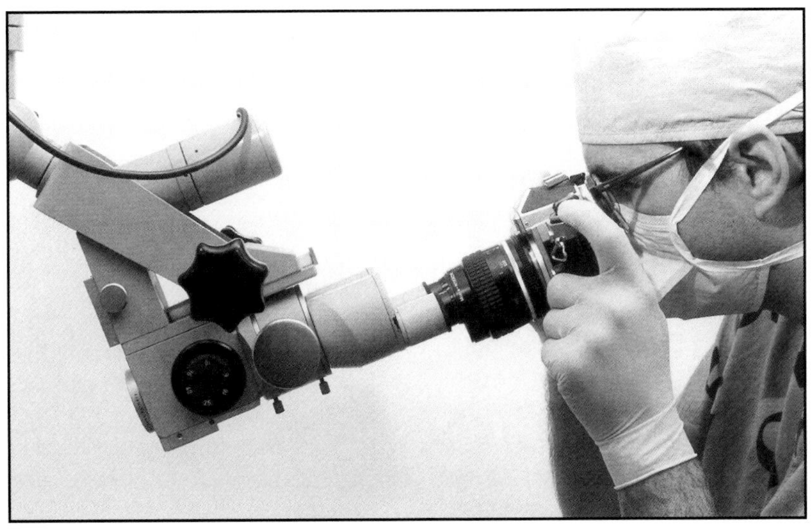

A

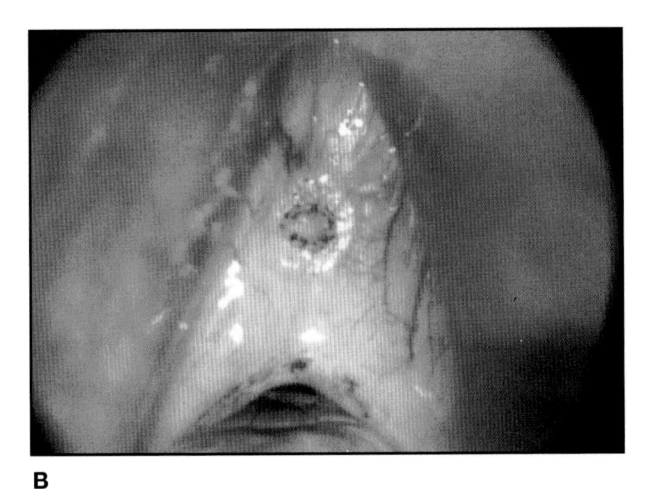

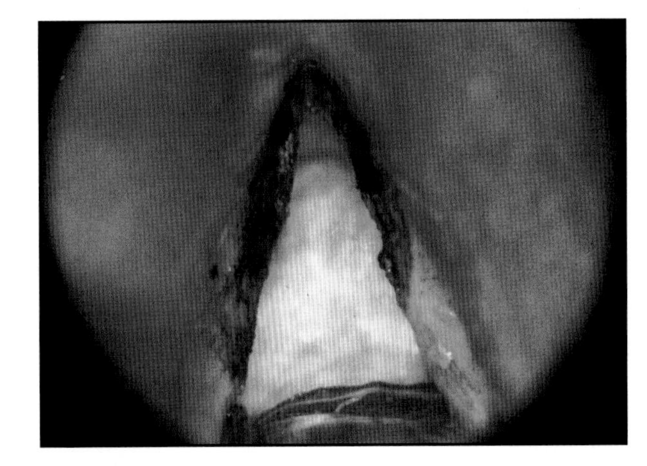

B

Fig 6–10. A. Method of microscopic still photography without photoadapter ("microscopic macrolens technique"). **B.** Photographs of laryngeal web, before (*left*) and after (*right*) CO_2 laser excision, taken with this technique.

Videography of the Larynx

Technologic advances such as the light-sensitive charge-coupled device (CCD) video cameras, xenon light sources, and improved endoscopic equipment have made videographic documentation of the larynx a highly successful and versatile practice. Video images can be obtained through the use of the flexible fiberscope, the rigid telescope, or the operating microscope. Hard copies of excellent quality can be provided instantly by the color video printers.

Videography of the Larynx in the Office

Fiberscopic Videolaryngoscopy

Fiberscopic videolaryngoscopy[23,25,26,28,62-64] is the most widely used technique for video documentation of the larynx. It is the easiest and best tolerated technique and allows a full endoscopic examination of the upper aerodigestive tract with one pass. It allows evaluation of both the form and the function of the larynx, along with simultaneous voice recording. The following equipment is needed: (1) a flexible fiberscope, (2) a color video camera, (3) a video camera adapter, (4) a light source (xenon is preferred), (5) a video recorder (3/4", 1/2", 8 mm), and (6) a color monitor. The fiberscopes available include the Olympus ENF-P3, P4, or L3, Machida ENT 4L or 3L, and Pentax FNL 10S or 15S. There are many fine-quality miniature single-chip CCD video cameras available for fiberscopic videolaryngoscopy. These include: (1) Karl Storz Supercam 9060B (7 lux) and Telecam (3 lux) (Fig 6–11); (2) Olympus OTV-S3 or SC; (3) Toshiba CCD (10 lux) (distributed by Nagashima) (Fig 6–11); (4) Elmo EC-202 CCD (10 lux) and Elmo MN 401X (5 lux) or CN 401E (distributed by Videomedics and Nagashima) (Fig 6–12); (5) Panasonic GP KS 152 (5 lux); (6) Aztec VID 1 (7 lux); and (7) Wolf Endocam CCD (10 lux). Some of these cameras are equipped with C-mount couplers and require special adapters for the endoscopes while others have built-in nondetachable adapters (Fig 6–11). The cost of these single-chip video cameras ranges in price from $2,000 to $5,000 (1999). More recently, three-chip high-resolution cameras have become available. They include the Karl Storz Tricam 9070N and Stryker 780, which cost about $18,000 to $20,000.

Yanagisawa et al advocated the use of home video cameras for videolaryngoscopy in the early 1980s.[22,28,48] They were able to obtain excellent results with reasonably priced ($1,000–$1,500) home video cameras. Some of these cameras include: (1) Olympus Movie 8 VX801-62 (7 lux) (Fig 6–12), (2) Ricoh R620 CCD (4 lux) (Fig 6–12), and (3) Ricoh R66 (4 lux). With the use of the Karl Storz quick-connect adapter, the fiberscope could be attached to the video camera lens. These home video cameras are not used any more because they are obsolete, and much smaller, reasonably priced CCD cameras are now available. Figure 6–11 demonstrates a comparison of the sizes and shapes of the old home video cameras and the newer compact CCD cameras. The examination is performed in the same manner as that described for fiberscopic still photography (Fig 6–13A).

The most significant advantage of fiberscopic videolaryngoscopy is the ease of examination. Other advantages are that (1) it is rapid, (2) it is comfortable for the patient, (3) children and uncooperative adults may be examined, (4) it allows evaluation of form and func-

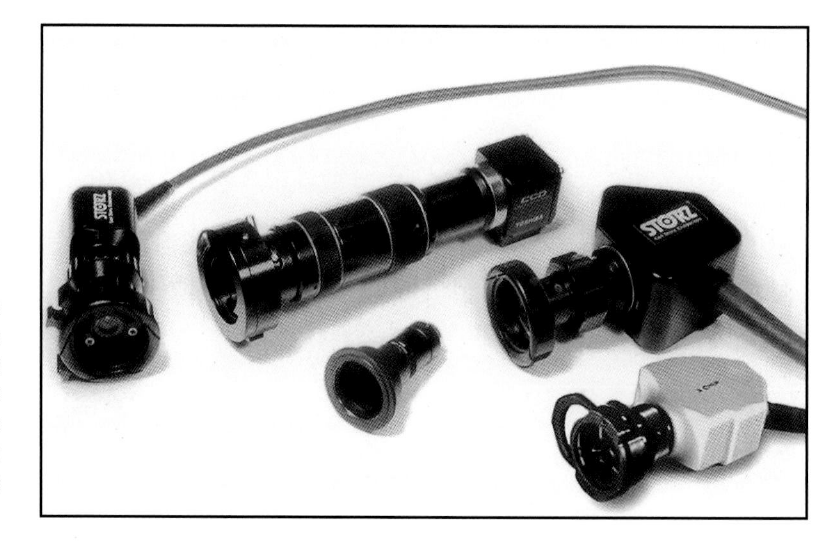

Fig 6–11. Miniature CCD video cameras (*left to right*): 1) Karl Storz supercam camera with a built-in adapter; 2) Toshiba C-mount CCD camera with Nagashima zoom lens videoadapter; 3) Elmo EC-102 miniature CCD camera with a C-mount adapter; 4) Karl Storz Tricam 3-chip CCD camera; 5) Stryker 782 3-chip camera.

Fig 6–12. Hitachi three-tube camera (*left*) and home video cameras (JVC GX-N8U, Olympus VX 801-02, Ricoh R620) compared with the miniature CCD camera, Elmo EC-202 (*far right*).

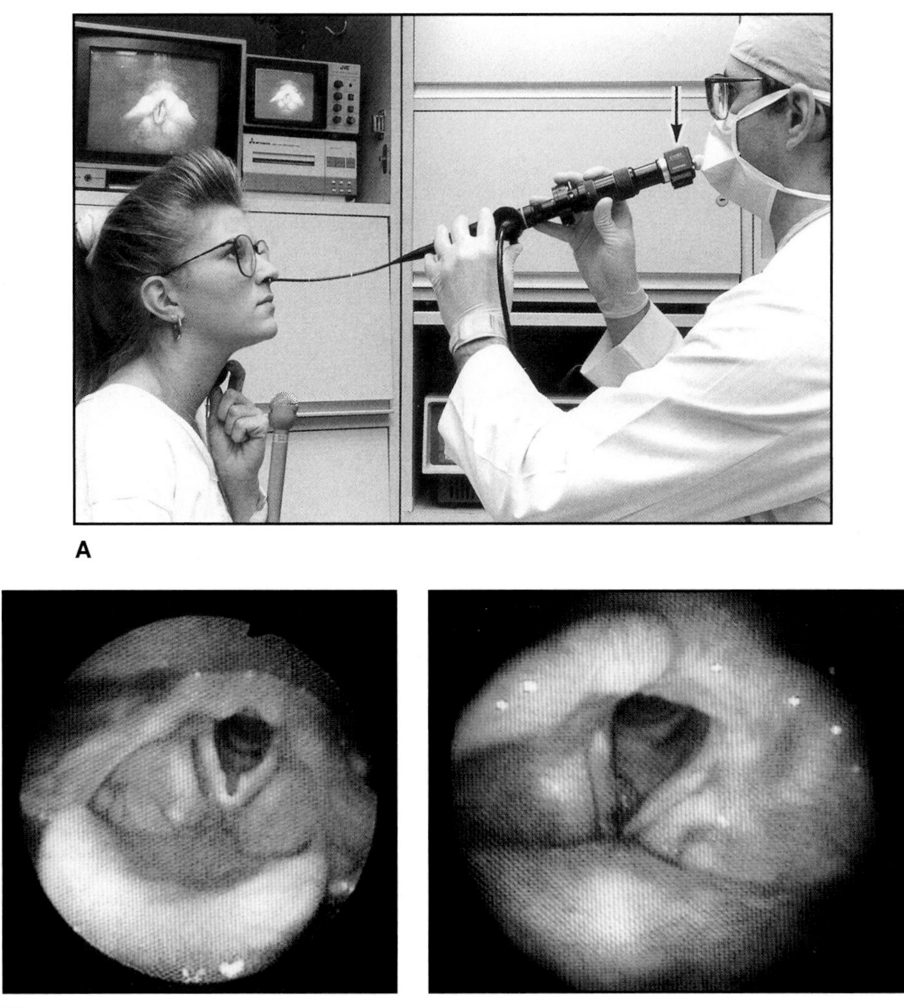

A

B

Fig 6–13. A. Method of flexible fiberscopic videolaryngoscopy in the office using the miniature CCD camera, Elmo EC-202 (*arrow*). **B.** Images of laryngeal nodules taken with Olympus ENF-P3 (3.6 mm) (*left*) and laryngeal polyps taken with Olympus ENF-L3 (4.2 mm) (*right*). Note the difference in size of the images created with these different scopes. The images were produced with a Sony UP-5000 video printer.

tion along with simultaneous voice recording, and (5) it allows limited examination of the subglottis and trachea. Its major disadvantage is that the image produced is smaller, more distorted, and of lower resolution when compared to the telescopes. The use of larger endoscopes such as the Olympus ENF-L3 helps to decrease the impact of edge distortion by providing a larger distortion-free area in the center of the image.

Other disadvantages include: (1) it requires greater illumination because of the small diameter of the scope, (2) it requires a light-sensitive camera (low lux), and (3) it tends to produce the moiré effect (multiple abnormal color strips) on the television screen, interfering with detailed interpretation. The overall success rate approaches 95%, even when used in infants and children (Fig 6–13B).

The senior author currently uses the Olympus ENF-P3 (3.4 mm) and ENF-L3 (4.2 mm) fiberscopes attached to a lightweight three-chip CCD camera with a xenon light source for optimal images. The wider nasal cavity is sprayed with topical anesthetic (4% lidocaine) and decongestant (3% ephedrine). With the patient in an upright sitting position, the fiberscope is passed along the floor of the nose, through the velopharyngeal port, and down to the oropharynx. When one obtains the desired image on the monitor, illumination and focus are optimized and recording begins. A panoramic view of the larynx, the pharynx, and the base of the tongue is obtained. The scope is advanced to the vallecula, then over the epiglottis into the laryngeal vestibule (see Fig 6–3). Close-up views of the glottis, true and false vocal folds, and vestibule (and sometimes even the subglottis) can be obtained as well as views of any lesions. If the moiré effect (unwanted color strips) is seen on the monitor, the camera is turned relative to the endoscope.

When the image is too dark for diagnostic purposes and/or for documentation, the authors recommend the following: (1) use an extra-light-sensitive video camera (low lux), (2) increase the video camera sensitivity by using the gain control switch, (3) advance the tip of the fiberscope very close to the vocal folds, (4) change the image size by using a zoom adapter for a micro CCD camera, or (5) use a fiberscope with a large diameter such as the Olympus ENF-L3 (4.2 mm) (Fig 6–13B). The image and color quality can also be improved during printing using adjustment control of the color video printer.

Telescopic Videolaryngoscopy

Telescopic videolaryngoscopy[23,26,28,62-66] is performed using much the same technique as the fiberscopic method, except that the telescope is passed through the mouth and the camera is connected to a telescope instead of a fiberscope. This method gives a brilliant picture and is particularly well-suited for diagnosing subtle changes in laryngeal structure.

The necessary equipment includes a single- or three-chip CCD miniature camera or a video camera, and a rigid telescope such as the (1) Karl Storz 8706CL, (2) Kay Elemetrics 9105, (3) Nagashima SFT-1, (4) Wolf Stuckrad, or (5) Karl Storz 8702D. These telescopes are attached to the CCD camera via a special adapter if the CCD camera does not have a built-in adapter. The 70 degree telescopes such as the Nagashima SFT-1, Karl Storz 8706CL and Kay Elemetrics 9105 permit excellent visualization of the anterior commissure and posterior portions of the larynx, which makes them especially useful for laryngostroboscopy.

The examination is performed in the following manner: (1) the patient's soft palate and posterior tongue are anesthetized with 4% Xylocaine (lidocaine), (2) the scope is dipped in warm water or sprayed with defogger, (3) the patient's tongue is grasped by the examiner with one hand while the scope is inserted with the other hand, keeping the glossoepiglottic fold in the midline while advancing the scope, ensuring optimal (midline) orientation of the larynx (Fig 6–14A), and (4) video recording is begun when the vocal folds are in clear focus.

The major benefit of this system is the superior optics offered by the telescope. This provides (1) a wide-angle view of the larynx with a large, clear image and (2) a close-up view of the larynx to detect subtle anatomic lesions. The larger diameter of the scope also allows for increased light transmission and a much brighter and clearer stroboscopic image. The disadvantages of this technique include the following: (1) children and some adults with hyperactive gag reflexes may be unable to tolerate the examination, (2) fogging of the scope requires cleaning and reinsertion, and (3) voice and vocal mechanics may be distorted.

The authors prefer the telescopic examination because of the superior image produced (Fig 6–14B): the image is larger, brighter, and sharper than that of the fiberscope. This translates to increased diagnostic capabilities for subtle laryngeal changes. In the authors' hands, this technique has a 90% success rate.

Microscopic Videolaryngoscopy

This technique is similar to that described for microscopic still photography in the office using the Zeiss operating microscope. The only difference is that a video camera hookup is used instead of an SLR camera. This technique (as one might expect) is time-consuming and awkward. The authors have abandoned this technique in favor of the techniques described above.

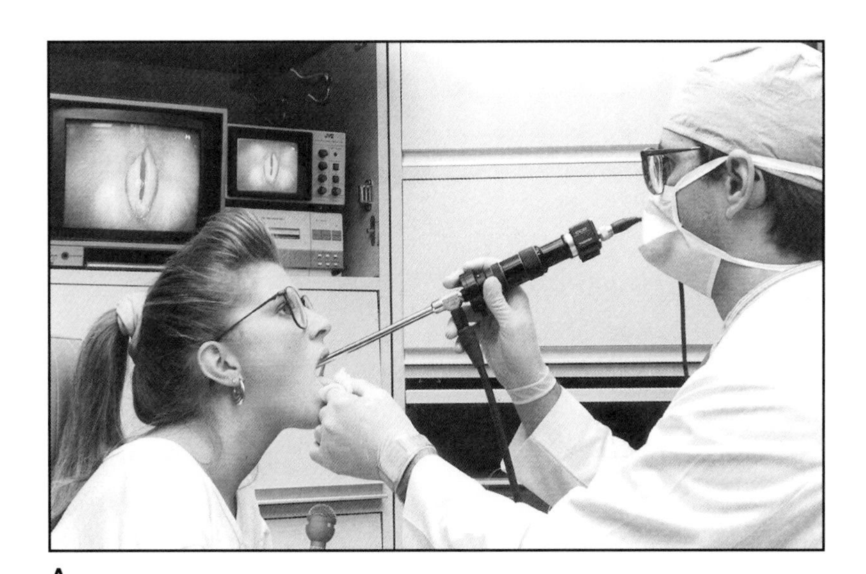

A

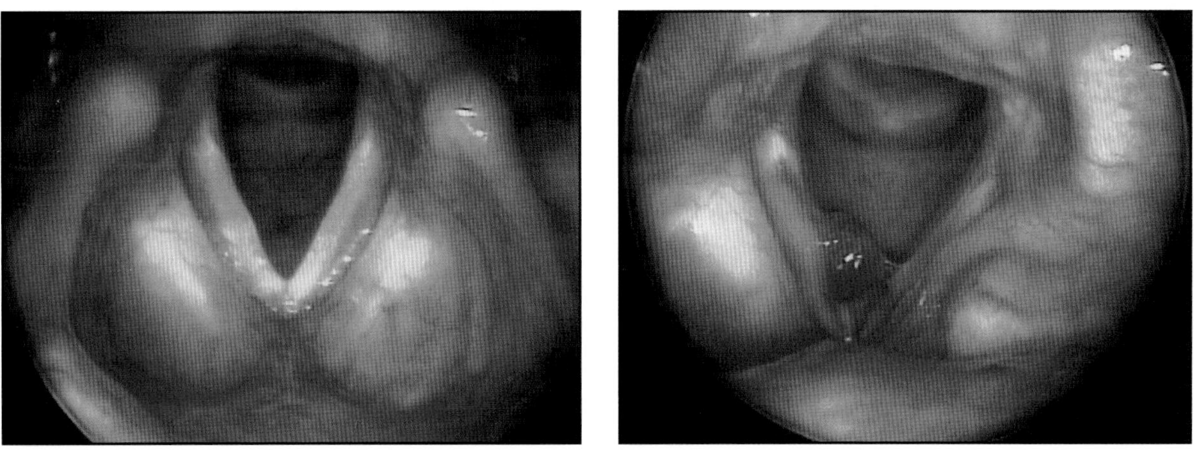

B

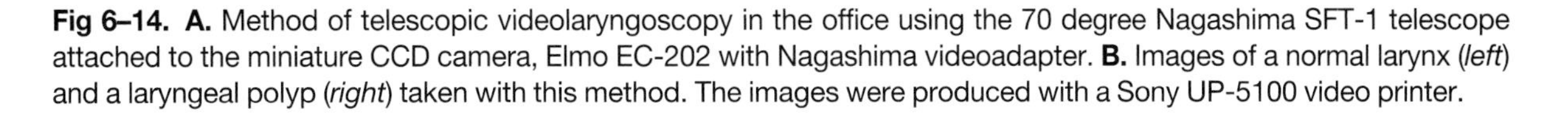

Fig 6–14. A. Method of telescopic videolaryngoscopy in the office using the 70 degree Nagashima SFT-1 telescope attached to the miniature CCD camera, Elmo EC-202 with Nagashima videoadapter. **B.** Images of a normal larynx (*left*) and a laryngeal polyp (*right*) taken with this method. The images were produced with a Sony UP-5100 video printer.

Videography in the Operating Room

Telescopic Videolaryngoscopy

In the operating room, telescopic videolaryngoscopy[62,64-66] is accomplished with the use of the straightforward Hopkins rigid telescope 8700A, a miniature CCD camera (Fig 6–15A), and a xenon light source. In this setting, the miniature CCD camera is more useful and convenient than the home video camera. After the laryngoscope is suspended, the telescope is placed through the laryngoscope and the image is centered. The advantage of this system is the splendid image quality (Fig 6–15B). With the use of a color video printer, still images can be obtained easily during or after the procedure. The major disadvantages are that (1) it requires interruption of the surgical procedure, and (2) it is difficult to document surgical technique.

The senior author always passes the 0° telescope for documentation prior to microlaryngoscopic surgery as he believes telescopic videolaryngoscopy provides the best possible laryngeal images. In selected cases, he uses the other angled telescopes (30°, 70°, 90°, 120°). The 30° and 70° telescopes allow excellent visualization of the anterior commissure. The 70° and 90° telescopes are useful for evaluation and documentation of laryngeal ventricles. The inferior border of the true vocal fold lesion can be readily identified with the 70° or 120° telescopes. The involvement of the anterior commissure by an anterior lesion of the vocal fold can

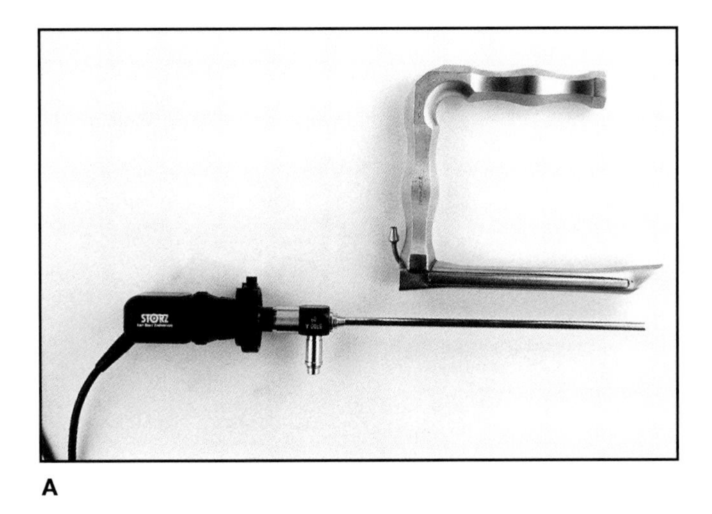

A

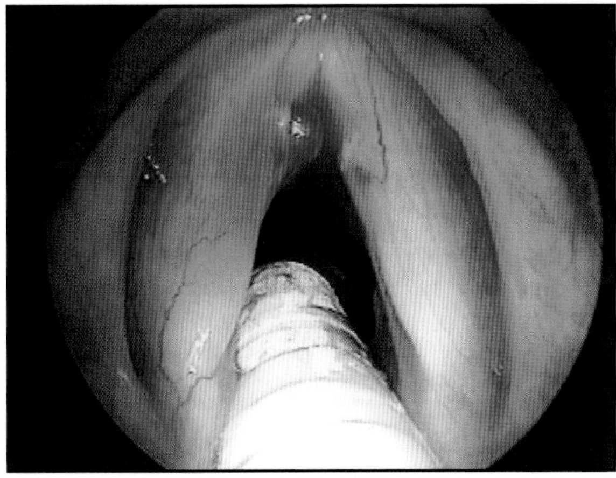

B

Fig 6–15. A. Telescopic videolaryngoscopy in the operating room using the Dedo laryngoscope and the Karl Storz Supercam CCD miniature camera attached to the 8700A 0 degree telescope. **B.** Image of a laryngeal polyp taken with this system. The image was produced with a Sony UP-5100 video printer.

be precisely identified with the 30° and 70° telescopes in most cases.

Telescopic video documentation of subglottic lesions in a tracheotomized patient can be performed through a tracheotomy opening using the Hopkins 4 mm 70° telescope.

Microscopic Videolaryngoscopy

Microscopic videolaryngoscopy[26] remains the single most convenient and effective method to teach and document microsurgery of the larynx. This is the authors' preferred method of operative documentation.[26]

The equipment used includes: (1) a photographic laryngoscope such as the Dedo or Ossoff (these laryngoscopes have two channels that house large-bore fiberoptic cables); (2) a light source, such as the Pilling 2X; (3) the (Zeiss) operating microscope with a straight eyepiece and 400 mm objective lens (Fig 6–16A); (4) a beam splitter; (5) a photoadapter, such as the Zeiss or Telestill photoadapter; (6) a miniature CCD camera or pickup tube camera (Fig 6–16A); (7) a video recorder; and (8) a color TV monitor. With their small size and weight, the miniature CCD cameras interfere minimally with the operative procedure. However, the more expensive and bulkier three-tube cameras, such as the Hitachi DK5050 or Ikegami ITC-350 M, produce video images of excellent quality (Figure 6–16A and B). For those seeking the highest-quality images, the three-tube cameras have been replaced with the newer three-chip cameras, such as the Sony DXC-750 ($16,000) and Hitachi, Ikegami, or Stryker three-chip camera. Sony introduced a moderately priced three-chip CCD camera, Sony DXC 960 MD (approximately $6,000) in 1993.

Some of the multiple advantages of this system are: (1) minimal interference with the operative procedure, (2) live viewing by an unlimited audience, (3) equipment that is readily available in most medical centers, (4) variability of magnification, facilitating precise documentation of small lesions, (5) pediatric and adult use, (6) video documentation for teaching surgical techniques, and (7) the capability of producing instant color prints of publication quality when a color video printer is used. Among the disadvantages are: (1) the depth of field is shallower, (2) instrumentation is more difficult, as the microscope is between the surgeon and the patient, (3) at times surgery must be carried out through one eyepiece because of the small proximal opening of the laryngoscope, and (4) refocusing at various magnifications may be necessary.

Kantor-Berci Telescopic Video Microlaryngoscope

In 1990, Kantor, Berci, Partlow et al introduced a new approach to microlaryngeal surgery and its documentation.[39] Their method is akin to performing endoscopic sinus surgery. Using a specially designed microlaryngoscope that houses a rigid telescope with attached camera, they are able to both video-record and perform the operation while viewing a high-resolution TV screen (Fig 6–17A and B). The required equipment includes: (1) a Kantor-Berci videomicrolaryngoscope (Karl Storz 8590 VJ) (an improved model is now available) and Lewy (or other) laryngoscope holder; (2) a Karl Storz Supercam micro CCD video camera; (3) a xenon light source (Karl Storz 615, or

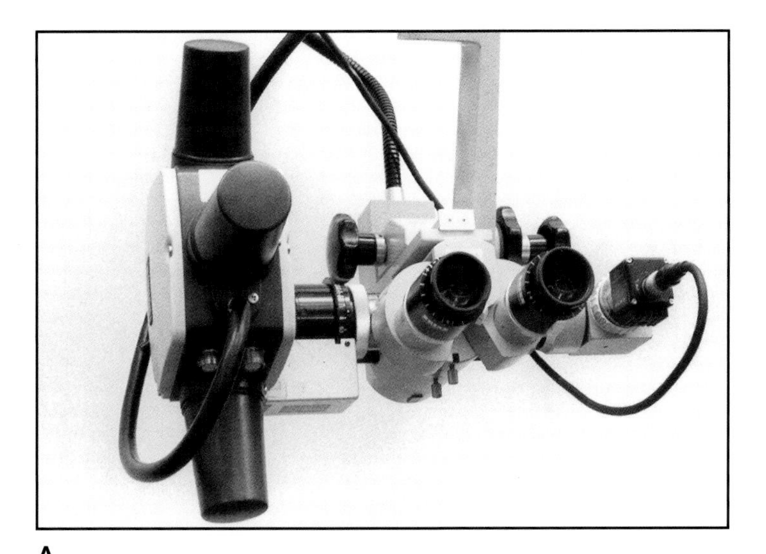

A

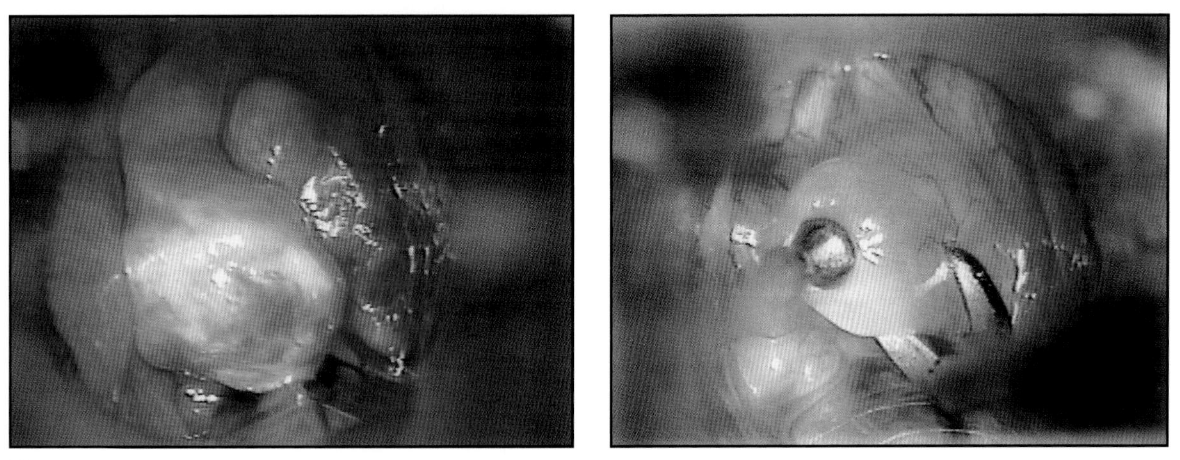

B

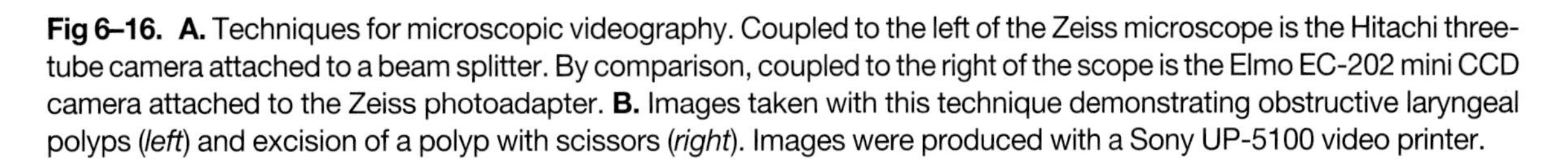

Fig 6–16. A. Techniques for microscopic videography. Coupled to the left of the Zeiss microscope is the Hitachi three-tube camera attached to a beam splitter. By comparison, coupled to the right of the scope is the Elmo EC-202 mini CCD camera attached to the Zeiss photoadapter. **B.** Images taken with this technique demonstrating obstructive laryngeal polyps (*left*) and excision of a polyp with scissors (*right*). Images were produced with a Sony UP-5100 video printer.

487C); (4) a large, high-resolution TV monitor and recorder; and (5) a color video printer (Sony UP-5100).

Some of the advantages of the Kantor-Berci system include the following: (1) it gives a clear, sharp image with excellent depth of field, (2) it facilitates instrumentation of the larynx, as the microscope is not between the surgeon and patient, and (3) it provides superior documentation. Some disadvantages are that: (1) the equipment is costly, (2) specialized equipment such as the angled forceps are needed, (3) it requires a dedicated video camera, (4) refocusing may be necessary (Supercam camera) when the zoom lens is used, (5) there is some image distortion, and (6) depth perception may be impaired because the system creates a monocular image.

In a series of patients, the senior author (EY) has compared this technique with the standard microscope technique at the same setting. While the Kantor-Berci system is an effective means of documenting laryngeal surgery and offers superior visualization of the anterior larynx with an excellent depth of field, the microscopic system has the advantage of variable magnification with a depth of field that is generally better than expected, and permits true binocular vision.

Video Image Transfer to Print and Slide

Video images can be transferred to either prints or slides, in color or black and white. This can be accomplished in several ways.

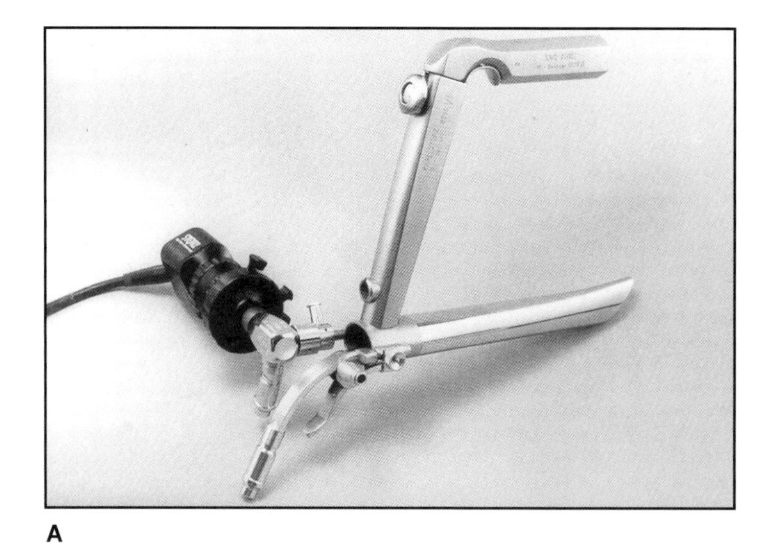

A

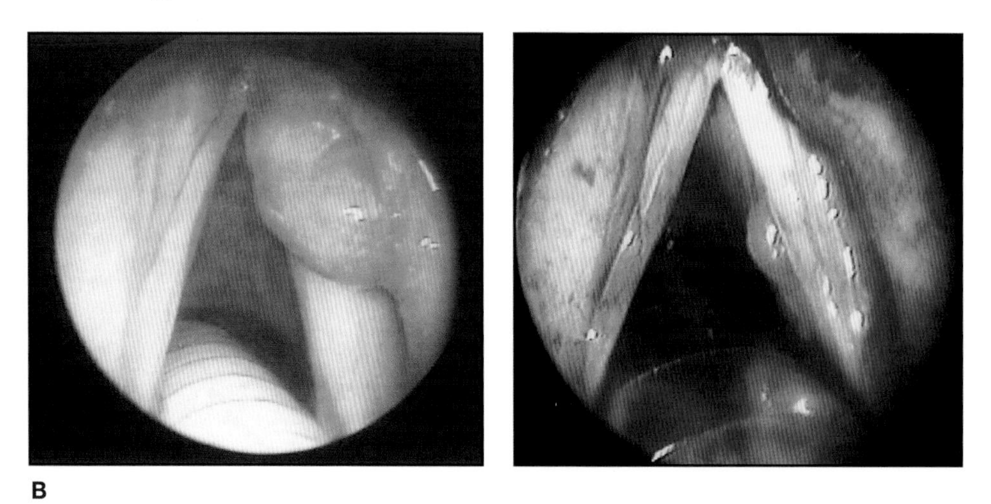

B

Figure 6–17. A. Kantor-Berci's video microlaryngoscopic technique. Karl Storz Supercam CCD miniature camera is attached to the specially designed telescope (Karl Storz 8575A) and inserted into the built-in channel on the left side of the Kantor-Berci video microlaryngoscope (Karl Storz 8590B). **B.** Images taken with this technique showing a false vocal fold polyp (*left*) and laryngeal polyp (*right*). Images were produced with a Sony UP-5100 video printer.

Production of Prints

This can be accomplished instantaneously while videotaping, or at a later viewing through the use of the video printers (Fig 6–18A-C).[26,41] The authors initially used the Sony UP-5000 (Fig 6–18A) but currently prefer the Sony UP-5100 or UP-5500 color video printer, which produces a superior high-resolution image. However, this unit is quite expensive ($7,000 to $8,000). The more affordable Sony CVP G700 ($1,500) or Sony DPM 1000 ($400) (Fig 6–18B), which produces very acceptable images, may be used. However, the time required to produce a print is longer with less expensive printers. Black-and-white prints for publication can also be made by photographing the color video printouts using black-and-white film (such as ASA 400 Tri-X or T-Max). Prints can also be made using a computer, as described in the following digital imaging section.

Production of Slides

There are several methods of producing slides from video images. The first is to photograph the video image on the TV screen (TV screen photography) (Fig 6–18D-F).[26,62-64,67] The equipment necessary is: (1) a

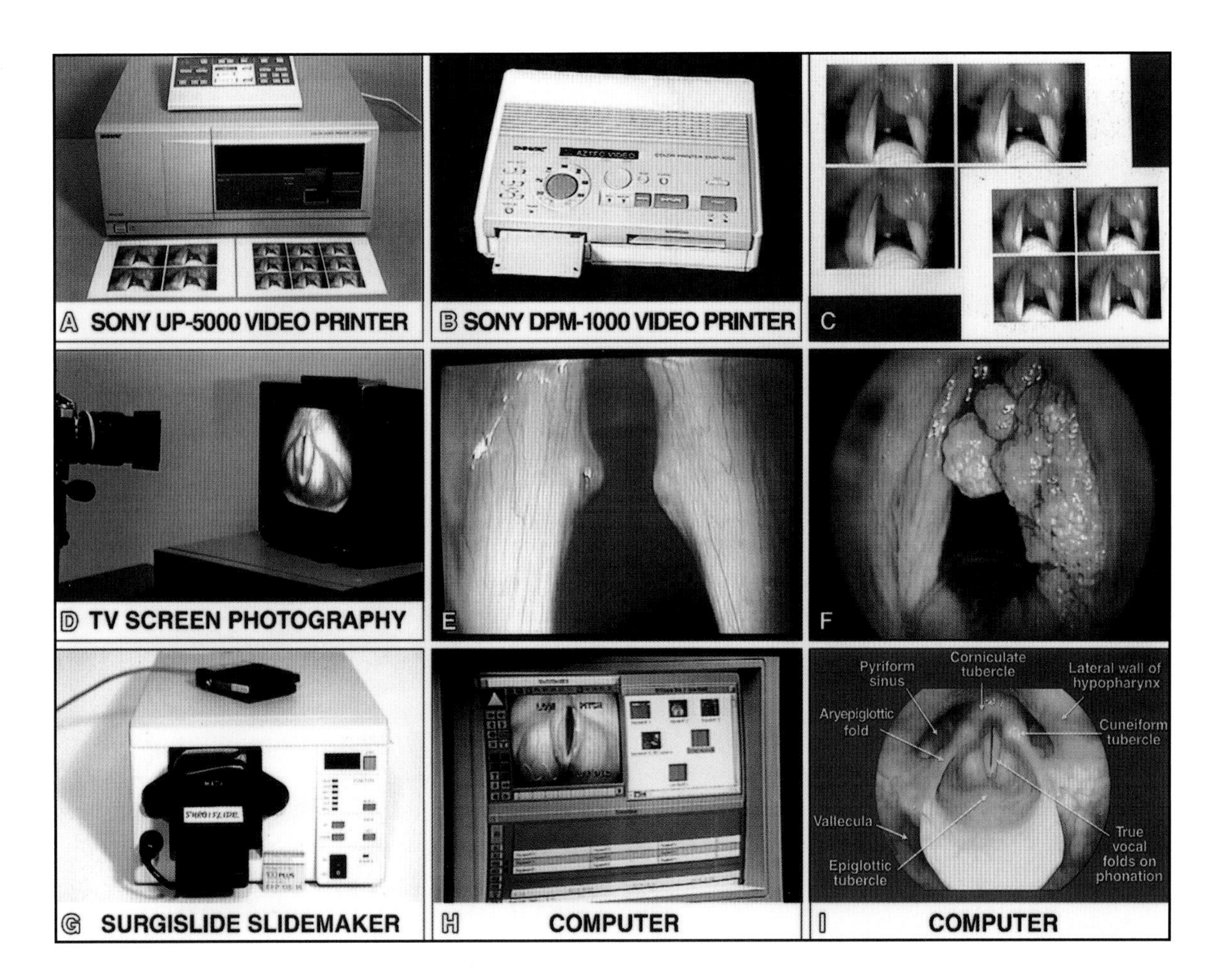

Fig 6–18. Video image transfer to prints and slides. **A.** Sony color video printer UP-5000. **B.** Sony DPM-1000 color video printer. **C.** Color video prints produced by Sony UP-5100 and by Sony CVP-G700. **D.** TV screen photography. **E.** Image of laryngeal nodules produced by TV screen photography. **F.** Image of transglottic laryngeal carcinoma produced by TV screen photography. **G.** Stryker Surgislide slide maker. **H.** Digitized laryngeal image on the computer screen, which can be annotated. Prints are made using a digital color printer. **I.** Annotated image of the normal larynx produced by a digital color printer Sony UP-5500.

35 mm SLR camera, (2) Ektachrome Daylight ASA 400 color film, (3) a 50 mm macrolens, (4) a tripod, and (5) an orange-colored filter (Kodak CC40R or Tiffen CC40) when using color film. The camera is placed on the tripod (Fig 6–18D), and the laryngeal image on the TV screen is brought into focus. The shutter speed should be one-half per second or slower (thus the need for the tripod) to cut out interference (raster) lines. For best results the room should be dark to avoid glare on the TV screen, and the video player should be in the play mode. In the pause mode, unwanted horizontal lines may be seen either at the top or bottom of the screen. Each photograph is usually bracketed (–1, 0, +1) using the exposure compensation dial on the camera. This is the least expensive method of producing quite satisfactory results.

The second method of slide production is to copy the color video printouts using color slide film (Ektachrome ASA 320 Tungsten film).

The third method is to use a video/slide making system such as Sony Slidemaker MD, which receives RGB video signals from a color printer (Sony UP 5100/5500) and allows one to photograph the desired image with its attached 35 mm camera (ISO 100 or Polachrome ISO 40 color slide film).

The fourth method is by the use of the Stryker Surgislide Slidemaker (Fig 6–18G). This is a relatively new analog image capture device for the production of 35 mm slides from either a video camera during videography or a prerecorded video image later. The recommended film is ASA 100 Professional Daylight Ektachrome. A 35 mm automatic SLR camera is attached to the front of the image capture device. This system produces excellent color slides. The advantage of the Stryker Slidemaker is the ability to capture images directly onto 35 mm slide film without the need for additional hardware or software. However, the disadvantage is its high cost (approximately $9,000).

Documentation by Digital Imaging

Digital imaging is the newest technology for permanently recording images. There are a number of advantages to digital imaging: (1) the image is produced immediately and thus can be "re-shot" if needed, (2) the image can be transferred via modem to other computers for immediate consultation, (3) the image does not degrade with time, (4) various types of editing of the image are possible, (5) images taken over time can be displayed on one screen, (6) storage and retrieval of images is much simpler, and (7) photographic quality resolution is possible (though expensive). Disadvantages include the initial start-up expense and the time needed to master the system.[68]

Imaging can be digitized from a video camera, a digital camera (still or video), a videotape, a slide, a print, or a negative.

Laryngeal documentation can be accomplished by digitizing images from prerecorded videotape (Fig 6–18H and I). Video recording has been the senior author's method for many years. Software is available that can capture video images either as still frames or as full-motion video. These digitized images may be made into composite pictures, labeled, and saved as a computer file. The image may be printed with a digital printer. The authors use the Sony UP-5500 digital color video printer, which utilizes a dye sublimation printing process. This printer produces high-quality photo-realistic prints suitable for publication (Fig 6–18I), although the printer is quite expensive (approximately $9,000). Less expensive digital color printers are available. Color slides may be obtained by photographing these computer prints. Alternatively, the computer file may be transferred to photo prints or 35 mm slides by a computer service bureau, usually via high-capacity removable storage devices such as Zip disks, optical drives, or compact disks (CDs).

More recently, still digital image capture devices such as the Sony DKR-700 Digital Still Recorder, the Stryker Digital Capture System SDC, and the Stryker Digital Capture System SDC Pro have become available and can be used for laryngeal imaging. The digital recording systems such as the Kay Digital video recording system (DVRS) and the Pentax Electronics video recording system are useful for digital imaging of the larynx.

Sony Digital Still Recorder

The Sony DKR-700 (Fig 6–19A) is a compact digital still recorder. It captures the images and stores them on convenient high capacity 2.5 inch Sony MD data disks. The images can be easily retrieved, sorted, and annotated. It can store 100 noncompressed images on a MD data disk. The advantages of Sony DKR-700 include its compatibility with popular software programs. A disadvantage of the Sony DKR-700 is its long capture time (approximately 28 seconds). This means that during these 28 seconds, the surgeon cannot take another picture. This is unacceptable for laryngeal documentation unless the capture time is shortened in future versions of this product.

Stryker Digital Capture System SDC

The Stryker SDC (Fig 6–19B) is a device which instantly transports surgical images to a high density computer disk. Software is available which allows for annotation and enhancement of the images. This system is simple to operate. No adjustments are necessary. Images can be saved as a standard bit-map file, which means that they are uncompressed. Image capture time is very fast (about one second) and the system is quite acceptable for laryngeal documentation. The cost of this system is approximately $10,000.

Stryker Digital Capture System SDC Pro

The Stryker SDC Pro (Fig 6–19C-E) capture device is a newer version of the Stryker SDC and can be used to record still images or video segments. Housed within the device are a central processing unit (CPU) and hard drive that can capture digital images or streaming video onto a writeable CD (compact disk). The CD system included within the Stryker SDC Pro digital capture device is the CDWriter Plus 9100 series.

The CD has become the standard for data storage, accessible using either a Macintosh or Windows based operating system. A single CD may hold approximately 650 images captured in bit-map (BMP) format, or approximately 12,000 images in compressed Joint Photographic Expert Group (JPEG) format. Alternatively, a single CD may record up to 20 minutes of continuous video, and a CD may contain a mixture of both still images and video. Capture is nearly immediate without hardware delay.

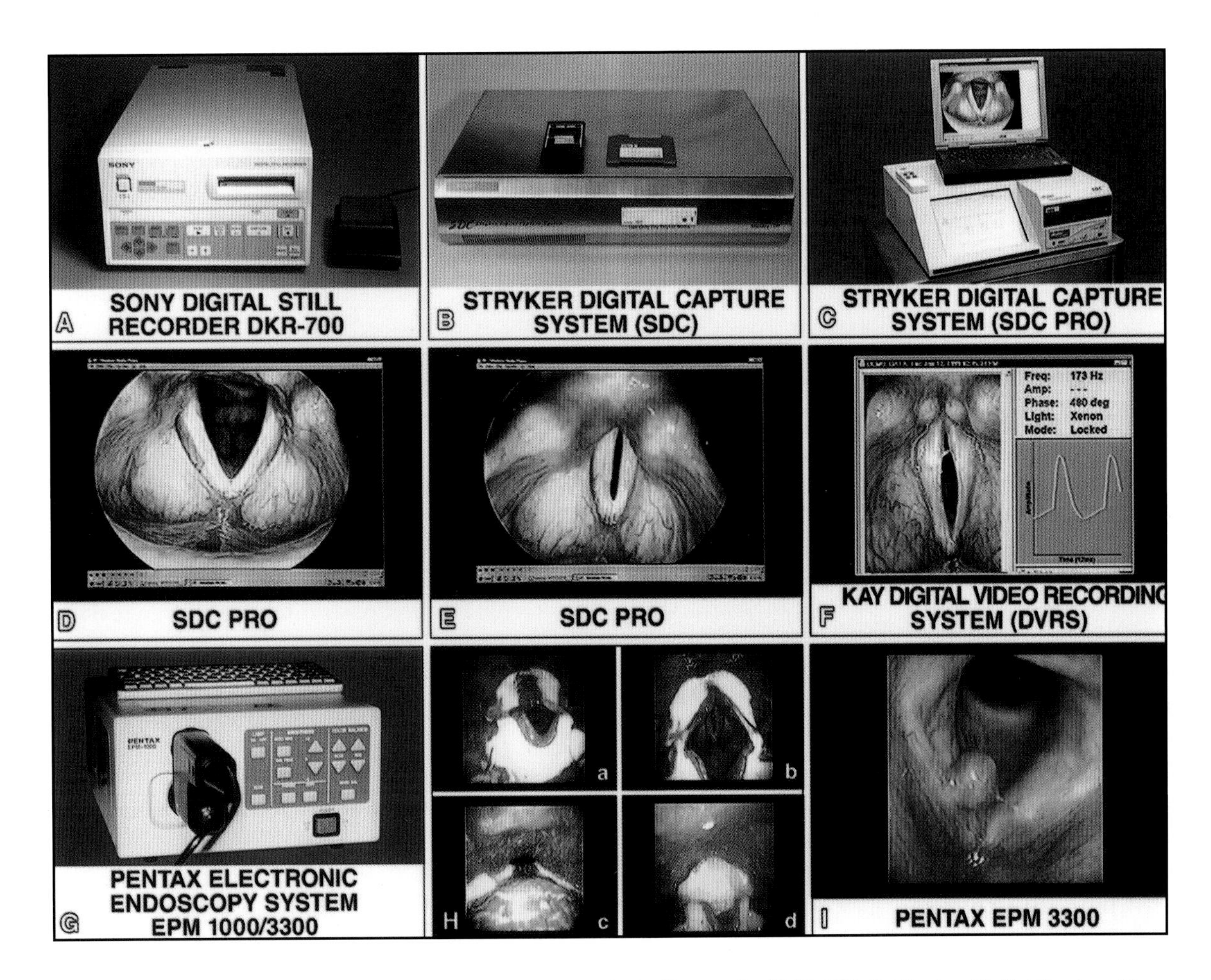

Fig 6–19. Documentation by digital imaging. **A.** Sony digital still recorder DKR-700. **B.** Stryker Digital Capture System SDC. It captures still images only. **C.** Stryker Digital Capture System SDC Pro. It captures both still and motion images. **D.** Computer still image of the larynx on inspiration captured by Stryker SDC Pro. **E.** Computer still image of the larynx on phonation captured by Stryker SDC Pro. **F.** Still computer image of stroboscopic view of the vocal folds on phonation captured by Kay digital video recording system. Note on-screen display of an EGG waveform. **G.** Pentax electronic endoscopy system EPM 1000 (a newer smaller version of EPM 3300). This is an excellent device to capture still images in single and multiple image formats. **H.** Still images of swallowed milk in various stages taken with Pentax EPM 3300. **I.** Computer still image of the laryngeal polyp captured by Pentax EPM 3300.

Advantages to the new Stryker SDC Pro system include the ability to capture not only still images but also streaming video. Although the Zip format used for the Stryker SDC is a popular medium for storage, the CD is a more universally accepted medium for data storage and retrieval. The Stryker SDC Pro allows for the import of images and video into popular software applications for digital annotation, such as Microsoft PowerPoint.

The Stryker SDC Pro system is an excellent technique for documentation of still and motion images of the larynx. The main disadvantages of this system is its high cost (approximately $13,000).

Kay Digital Video Recording System (DVRS)

The Kay digital video recording system (DVRS) (Fig 6–19F) is a newer version of its previous 9100 Stroboscopy Recording System based on VHS or S-VHS videotape recorders. Unlike its predecessor, the DVRS records video images directly to computer storage media. It captures both full-motion video and high-resolution still images. Audio and video are captured together. Image retrieval is easy. It allows instantaneous review of the data, and allows on-screen display of important information such as an EGG waveform (Fig 6–19F).

Pentax Electronic Endoscopy System EPM 1000/3300

The Pentax electronic videoendoscopic system (Fig 6–19G-I) is a highly integrated digital imaging system, utilizing the Pentax EPM 3300 (the EPM 1000 is a smaller unit used for laryngoscopic imaging) and a flexible electronic videolaryngoscope. It was primarily developed for the evaluation of gastrointestinal disorders. However, more recently it has been used for evaluation of the larynx and pharynx. It is useful for the study of swallowing disorders (Fig 6–19H). The Pentax flexible electrolaryngoscope, which has a CCD chip at the tip of the endoscope, provides remarkably clear images of the larynx and hypopharynx (Figure 6–19I). Images of various stages of swallowing of milk taken with the Pentax system are shown in Figure 6–19H.

The Pentax electronic videoendoscopy system has an excellent image capture device. It captures instantaneously. Images can be obtained in single, four, or nine-in-one formats and can be videoprinted right after the examination. The main disadvantage is its cost.

So far, all chip-tip camera flexible endoscopes have had their camera systems combined with their light sources. Therefore, despite their excellent image quality, they cannot be connected to a stroboscope. Recently, Olympus has developed a prototype chip-tip laryngoscope that works with any light source (including a stroboscope) and shows great promise for advancing diagnostic laryngeal imaging (Robert T. Sataloff, MD, personal communication, August 2000).

Conclusion

Laryngeal documentation can be accomplished by videography, still photography, and digital imaging. Various methods of these modalities in the office and in the operating room setting are described.

Still photography remains a valuable method of laryngeal documentation for those who own or are familiar with still photographic equipment. The photographic images obtained through the telescope are clearly superior to those captured through the fiberscope. The main disadvantage of still photography is that one cannot see the results until the films are developed.

At the beginning of this new century (2000), videography is the most versatile and useful means of laryngeal documentation because it permits excellent demonstration of anatomy, pathology, and physiology with simultaneous voice recording. It also serves as an important source for digital imaging. With the use of a color video printer, high-resolution video prints of laryngeal pathology can be obtained instantaneously for medical records and educational purposes. The image can also be replayed immediately after the procedure and shown to the patient.

Videography of the larynx in the office can be accomplished by using a flexible fiberscope or a rigid telescope. Fiberscopic documentation results in images with less resolution but permits examination of laryngeal motion and can be performed in children and adults with hyperactive gag reflexes. Telescopic documentation provides superior structural images with high resolution.

Videography of the larynx in the operating room can be accomplished by means of microscopic, telescopic, and direct laryngoscopic videolaryngoscopy. Microscopic video documentation is currently the preferred method of documenting laryngeal pathology and teaching microlaryngeal surgery. Telescopic videography through the laryngoscope using a (0°, 30°, 70°, 90°, or 120°) telescope produces the clearest images of the larynx.

Digital imaging is the newest technology for permanently recording images. Digital imaging of the larynx can be accomplished by transferring video images from a prerecorded videotape into a computer. High-quality color prints can be produced utilizing a dye sublimation digital color printer. Digital imaging of the larynx can now be accomplished without film or videotape by utilizing a newer digital image capture device such as the Stryker Digital Capture System. This device captures laryngeal still images from a video camera and quickly transports them to a computer disk from which slides and prints can be generated. The newer digital capture systems record both still and motion images.

Advantages of digital imaging include: (1) safe, long-term storage without image degradation, (2) easy computer manipulation and retrieval, and (3) production of superior quality images using a digital printer. Disadvantages are the high cost of the system and the constantly evolving technologic improvements, which make the systems obsolete quickly and make upgrades necessary.

As this new technology improves and the cost of digital imaging decreases, the use of digital imaging of the larynx will likely become widespread.

References

1. García M. Observations on the human voice. *Proc R Soc Lond*. 1855;7:399–420.
2. French TR. On photographing the larynx. *Trans Am Laryngol*. 1882;4:32–35.

3. French TR. On a perfected method of photographing the larynx. *NY Med J*. 1884;4:655–656.
4. Ferguson GB, Crowder WJ. A simple method of laryngeal and other cavity photography. *Arch Otolaryngol*. 1970; 92:201–203.
5. Padovan IF, Christman NT, Hamilton LH, et al. Indirect microlaryngoscopy. *Laryngoscope*. 1973;83:2035–2041.
6. Holinger PH. Photography of the larynx, trachea, bronchi and esophagus. *Trans Am Acad Ophthalmol Otolaryngol*. 1942;46:153–156.
7. Holinger PH, Tardy ME. Photography in otorhinolaryngology and bronchoesophagology. In: English GM, ed. *Otolaryngology*. Vol 5. Philadelphia, Pa: Lippincott; 1986: chap 22.
8. Holinger PH, Brubaker JD, Brubaker JE. Open tube, proximal illumination mirror and direct laryngeal photography. *Can J Otolaryngol*. 1975;4:781–785.
9. Rosnagle R, Smith HW. Hand-held fundus camera for endoscopic photography. *Trans Am Acad Ophthalmol Otolaryngol*. 1972;76:1024–1025.
10. Brewer DW, McCall G. Visible laryngeal changes during voice study. *Ann Otol Rhinol Laryngol*. 1974;83:423–427.
11. Davidson TM, Bone RC, Nahum AM. Flexible fiberoptic laryngo-bronchoscopy. *Laryngoscope*. 1974;84:1876–1882.
12. Hirano M. *Clinical Evaluation of Voice (Disorders of Human Communication, 5)*. New York, NY: Springer-Verlag; 1981.
13. Inoue T. Examination of child larynx by flexible fiberoptic laryngoscope. *Int J Pediatr Otorhinolaryngol*. 1983;5: 317–323.
14. Sawashima M, Hirose H. New laryngoscopic technique by use of fiberoptics. *J Acoust Soc Am*. 1968;43:168–169.
15. Selkin SG. Flexible fiberoptics for laryngeal photography. *Laryngoscope*. 1983;93:657–658.
16. Selkin SG. The otolaryngologist and flexible fiberoptics—photographic considerations. *J Otolaryngol*. 1983;12: 223–227.
17. Silberman HD, Wilf H, Tucker JA. Flexible fiberoptic nasopharyngolaryngoscope. *Ann Otol Rhinol Laryngol*. 1976;85:640–645.
18. Yamashita K. Endonasal flexible fiberoptic endoscopy. *Rhinology*. 1983;21:233–237.
19. Yamashita K. *Diagnostic and Therapeutic ENT Endoscopy*. Tokyo, Japan: Medical View; 1988.
20. Yamashita K, Mertens J, Rudert H. Die flexible Fiberendoskopie in der HNO-Heildunde. *HNO*. 1984;32:378–384.
21. Yamashita K, Oku T, Tanaka H, et al. VTR endoscopy. *J Otolaryngol Jp*. 1977;80:1208–1209.
22. Yanagisawa E. Videolaryngoscopy using a low cost home video system color camera. *J Biol Photogr*. 1984; 52:9–14.
23. Yanagisawa E. Videolaryngoscopy. In: Lee KJ, Stewart CH, eds. *Ambulatory Surgery and Office Procedures in Head and Neck Surgery*. Orlando, Fla: Grune & Stratton; 1986: chap 6.
24. Yanagisawa E, Carlson RD. Physical diagnosis of the hypopharynx and the larynx with and without imaging. In: Lee KJ, ed. *Textbook of Otolaryngology and Head and Neck Surgery*. New York, NY: Elsevier; 1989:chap 37.
25. Yanagisawa E, Yamashita K. Fiberoptic nasopharyngolaryngoscopy. In: Lee KJ, Stewart CH, eds. *Ambulatory Surgery and Office Procedures in Head and Neck Surgery*. Orlando, Fla: Grune & Stratton; 1986:31–40.
26. Yanagisawa E, Yanagisawa R. Laryngeal photography. *Otolaryngol Clin North Am*. 1991;24:999–1022.
27. Yanagisawa E, Carlson RD, Strothers G. Videography of the larynx—fiberscope or telescope? In: Clement PAR, ed. *Recent Advances in ENT—Endoscopy*. Brussels, Belgium: Scientific Society for Medical Information; 1985: 175–183.
28. Yanagisawa E, Owens TW, Strothers G, et al. Videolaryngoscopy—a comparison of fiberscopic and telescopic documentation. *Ann Otol Rhinol Laryngol*. 1983; 92:430–436.
29. Alberti PW. Still photography of the larynx—an overview. *Can J Otolaryngol*. 1975;4:759–765.
30. Albrecht R. Zur *Photographie des Kehlkopfes*. HNO. 1956;5:196–199.
31. Andrew AH. Laryngeal telescope. *Trans Am Acad Ophthalmol Otolaryngol*. 1962;66:268.
32. Benjamin B. Technique of laryngeal photography. *Ann Otol Rhinol Laryngol*. 1984;93(suppl 109).
33. Benjamin B. *Diagnostic Laryngology—Adults and Children*. Philadelphia, Pa: Saunders; 1990.
34. Berci G. *Endoscopy*. New York, NY: Appleton-Century-Crofts; 1976.
35. Berci G, Caldwell FH. A device to facilitate photography during indirect laryngoscopy. *Med Biol Illus*. 1963;13: 169–176.
36. Berci G, Calcaterra T, Ward PH. Advances in endoscopic techniques for examination of the larynx and nasopharynx. *Can J Otolaryngol*. 1975;4:786–792.
37. Gould WJ. The Gould laryngoscope. *Trans Am Acad Ophthalmol Otolaryngol*. 1973;77:139–141.
38. Hahn C, Kitzing P. Indirect endoscopic photography of the larynx—a comparison between two newly constructed laryngoscopes. *J Audiov Media Med*. 1978;1:121–130.
39. Kantor E, Berci G, Partlow E, et al. A completely new approach to microlaryngeal surgery. *Laryngoscope*. 1991; 101:678–679.
40. Konrad HR, Hopla DM, Bussen J, et al. Use of video tape in diagnosis and treatment of cancer of larynx. *Ann Otol Rhinol Laryngol*. 1981;90:398–400.
41. Mambrino L, Yanagisawa E, Yanagisawa K, et al. Endoscopic ENT photography—a comparison of pictures by standard color films and newer color video printers. *Laryngoscope*. 1991;101:1229–1232.
42. Muller-Hermann F, Pedersen P. Modern endoscopic and microscopic photography in otolaryngology. *Ann Otol Rhinol Laryngol*. 1984;93:399.
43. Oeken FW, Brandt RH. Lupenkontrolle endolaryngealer Operationen Modifikation der Schwenklupenhalterung nach Brunings. *HNO*. 1967;15:210–211.
44. Steiner W, Jaumann MP. Moderne otorhinolaryngologische Endoskopie beim Kind. *Padiat Prax*. 1978;20:429–435.
45. Stuckrad H, Lakatos I. Uber ein neues Lupenlaryngoskop (Epipharyngoskop). *Laryngol Rhinol Otol*. 1975; 54:336–340.

46. Ward PH, Berci G, Calcaterra TC. Advances in endoscopic examination of the respiratory system. *Ann Otol Rhinol Laryngol.* 1974;83:754–760.
47. Yanagisawa E. Office telescopic photography of the larynx. *Ann Otol Rhinol Laryngol.* 1982;91:354–358.
48. Yanagisawa E, Casuccio JR, Suzuki M. Video laryngoscopy using a rigid telescope and video home system color camera—a useful office procedure. *Ann Otol Rhinol Laryngol.* 1981;90:346–350.
49. Jako GJ. Laryngoscope for microscopic observations, surgery and photography. *Arch Otolaryngol.* 1970;91:196–199.
50. Jako GJ, Strong S. Laryngeal photography. *Arch Otolaryngol.* 1972;96:268–271.
51. Kleinsasser O. Entwicklung und Methoden der Kehlkopffotografie (Mit Beschreibung eines neuen einfachen Fotolaryngoskopes). *HNO.* 1963;1:171–176.
52. Kleinsasser O. *Microlaryngoscopy and Endolaryngeal Microsurgery.* Philadelphia, Pa: Saunders; 1968.
53. Kleinsasser O. *Tumors of the Larynx and Hypopharynx.* New York, NY: Thieme; 1988:124–130.
54. Olofsson J, Ohlsson T. Techniques in microlaryngoscopic photography. *Can J Otolaryngol.* 1975;4:770–780.
55. Scalo AN, Shipman WF, Tabb HG. Microscopic suspension laryngoscopy. *Ann Otol Rhinol Laryngol.* 1960;69:1134–1138.
56. Strong MS. Laryngeal photography. *Can J Otolaryngol.* 1975;4:766–769.
57. Tardy ME, Tenta LT. Laryngeal photography and television. *Otolaryngol Clin North Am.* 1970;3:483–492.
58. Yanagisawa E, Eibling DE, Suzuki M. A simple method of laryngeal photography through the operating microscope—"Macrolens technique." *Ann Otol Rhinol Laryngol.* 1980;89:547–550.
59. Tsuiki Y. *Laryngeal Examination.* Tokyo, Japan. Kanehara Shuppan; 1956.
60. Benjamin B. Art and science of laryngeal photography. (Eighteenth Daniel C. Baker, Jr, Memorial Lecture). *Ann Otol Rhinol Laryngol.* 1993;102:271–282.
61. Yanagisawa E, Carlson RD. Videophotolaryngography using a new low cost video printer. *Ann Otol Rhinol Laryngol.* 1985;94:584–587.
62. Yanagisawa E. Documentation. In: Ferlito A, ed. *Neoplasms of the Larynx.* Edinburgh, Scotland: Churchill Livingstone; 1993:chap 21.
63. Yanagisawa E, Weaver EM. Videolaryngoscopy: equipment and documentation. In: Blitzer A, et al, eds. *Office-Based Surgery in Otolaryngology.* New York, NY: Thieme; 1998:chap 25.
64. Yanagisawa E. Videography and laryngeal photography. In: Ferlito A, ed. *Diseases of the Larynx.* London, England: Arnold, 2000:chap 7.
65. Yanagisawa E, Horowitz JB, Yanagisawa K, et al. Comparison of new telescopic video microlaryngoscopic and standard microlaryngoscopic techniques. *Ann Otol Rhinol Laryngol.* 1992;101:51–60.
66. Yanagisawa K, Yanagisawa E. Current diagnosis and office practice—technique of endoscopic imaging of the larynx. *Curr Op Otolaryngol Head Neck Surg.* 1996;4:147–153.
67. Yanagisawa K, Shi J, Yanagisawa E. Color photography of video images of otolaryngological structures using a 35 mm SLR camera. *Laryngoscope.* 1987;97:992–993.
68. Stone JL, Peterson RL, Wolf JE. Digital imaging techniques in dermatology. *J Am Acad Dermatol.* 1990;23:913–917.

7

Laryngeal Computed Tomography Virtual endoscopy—Virtual dissection

Jean Abitbol, Albert Castro, Rodolphe Gombergh, and Patrick Abitbol

History

X-ray

Radiology developed as a result of both the understanding of electricity and the ability to create a vacuum lamp. Sir William Crookes, a physician, and a president of the Royal Society of Medicine in London, performed the first experiment to create the cathodic-ray tube in 1856. He found that a few particles of gas remain in the vacuum tube when used as a vehicle of electricity. The molecules of radiation matter in front of the cathode that escape and bombard the surfaces they meet are the cathodic rays.

It was the experiment known as the "Shadow of the Maltese Cross" in which Arthur Willis Goodspeed, from the University of Pennsylvania in Philadelphia, and the English photographer, William Jennings, performed the first "ray photography" with a Crookes tube.[1-3] This experiment took place in 1890 and is considered the embryology of radiology.[4] Wilhelm C. Roentgen, considered the "father of radiology" performed the first x-ray for medical purposes in 1895 when he x-rayed his wife's hand. He gave his name to the process of x-ray of the photonic emission. The medical applications of Roentgen rays (x-rays) began in 1896 and W.C. Roentgen was awarded the Nobel prize in 1901 for his pioneering work.[5-7]

By the end of the 19th century, Otto Glasser reported on the works of 23 pioneers in radiology in the United States alone.[8] For example, in Chicago, in 1896, the surgeon James Burry successfully x-rayed his hands, assisted by an engineer, Charles Ezra Scribner. At the 1896 Medical Society of Philadelphia Meeting, Henry Ware Cattell presented the first communication on radiology. Following this meeting, WW Keen and E.P. Davies published "Medical Applications of X-rays or Roentgen Rays" in the *American Journal of Medical Sciences,* in March of 1896. Thus, the principles and applications of x-rays were established.

Kymography

Kymography was first described by Kaestle, Riedor, and Rosenthal in 1909, in Munich. They used a number of plates running at a speed of 5 cm / sec producing an illusion of a movement: it was also called the radio-cinema. Thus, the Roentgen cinema developed, and allowed the study of the movements of organs inside the body with x-rays.[9] H.P. Mosher, in 1927, studied the movements of the tongue, the epiglottis, and the hyoïd bone during speech and swallowing, which was the first cineradiograph of the vocal tract.[10] In September 1945, G. Henny, and B. Boone, published in the American Journal of Roentgenology, "electrokymography for heart." They studied the parallelism between the electrocardiogram (ECG) and the radiographic movements, while recording their data.[11]

Tomography

The radiograph is a projection of an organ on a film called summation. Tomography is a slice-by-slice image of the organ. Laryngeal radiotomography, developed by André Bocage in 1921, was the first to image "slice the body" with slice-thickness from 1 mm to 10 mm. The principle was to move synchronously the plate and the tube, with the patient being immobile, so the synchronous motion of these parameters would print a specific and precise area of the organ to study.

In 1935, Georges Massiot and his son, Jean, made the first recorded tomography collecting all their data on film.[12-14] Until the early 1960s, the radiograph was merely a view of one plane. Tomography of the lungs or the larynx was interesting and very useful for diagnosis, but it had shortcomings. The density of the tissue was useful in distinguishing a tumor from normal tissue.

Air is used as a differentiating contrast medium within soft tissues when processing radiographs of the vocal tract.[15] However, the overlapping cervical spine disturbs the anterior-posterior views. To try to avoid this disturbance, high-kilovolt (120 kV) filtered radiographs and tomographs have been used with a copper filter placed in front of the x-ray tube to enhance the air-soft tissue interface by obscuring bone shadows.[16,17] There are series of anterior-posterior views at 5 mm intervals from the cervical spine to the thyroid cartilage. The images may be acquired during respiration or sustained phonation on /i/. The radiation exposure will be very high if multiple slices are taken. The most helpful tomography of the larynx is the anterior-posterior view or frontal view avoiding the cervical spine shadow. The lateral plane yields very little additional information. Tomography shows the laryngeal surface and is useful in examination of any soft tissue, benign or malignant mass, laryngocele, or thickening of the mucosa. However, the anterior commissure, the posterior wall of the glottic space, and the cricoarytenoid and cricothyroid joints are poorly visualized. This new technology using multiple and complex movements of the x-ray tube and the receptor improved very satisfactorily the imaging quality.[18]

Conventional and Numerized Radiology

Today, conventional diagnostic x-ray technology utilizes a numerized technique, both direct and indirect.

The direct technique uses an x-ray tube instead of a film as its receptor. This receptor sends the data to a computer, and the result is an image summation. It is then possible to analyze, to magnify, and to distinguish bone from soft tissue, but it is limited to one plane. The indirect technique instead of a receptor uses a support which can be digitalized in a computer and analyzed in the same way as the direct technique.

Computerized Tomography Scanning: CT Scan

In 1967, Hounsfield studied a new concept with the EMI corporation, the analysis of x-ray data with appropriate software.[19] This idea occurred to him when he was asked by EMI to perform research on the shape of blood cells. He studied all angles of these structures, first in two dimensions and later in three dimensions, and found the computer to be crucial in his work. Hounsfield had the idea to take multiple radiographs, with frames being computerized with a specific program. This process was the birth of computerized tomography. Hounsfield published his first manuscript on this subject "Computerized Transverse Axial Scanning" in 1973 in the *British Journal of Radiology* with J. Ambrose, who developed the clinical applications. Cormach and Hounsfield received the Nobel prize in 1979 for this discovery.

Initially, axial transverse tomography was the only possible connection to the computer. Thus, it was named computerized tomography (CT). In 1990, spiral CT was available with one detector; in 1993 it was used with two detectors; and in 1999, it was a technique utilizing multiple detectors. At the same time, important computer advances occurred. In 1995, the first work station with multiplane imaging became available; and in 1999, volume-rendering and transparency techniques became practical.

Magnetic Resonance Imaging: MRI

In 1946, 51 years after Roentgen created the x-ray, Edward Purcell and Felix Bloch developed magnetic resonance imaging (MRI), and in 1952 were awarded the Nobel prize for their work. They analyzed the behavior of the body's own protons on a magnetic field (instead of using x-rays, which bombard the body and the plate), after having been excited by a magnetic system. The protons are oriented with an accurate spin. The first MRI was performed in New York by Demadiour in 1977[20] with the capability of distinguishing tumor mass from normal tissue by analysis of the tissue density. This imaging is often called "protonic imaging" because it uses the variations of the magnetic field or gradient. The x-rays are called "calcic imaging" because they use the photonic transmission of x-rays that are strongly absorbed by the human body because of its high percentage of calcium. MRI is capable of multiplanar, high-resolution imaging and may be superior or more accurate for soft tissue definition compared to the CT scan.[21-23] There is no exposure to irradiation with MRI; however, artifacts are numerous because of the respiratory movements, the pulsatile flow of the carotid and other arteries. These artifacts may be reduced by using fast-spin echo techniques. The sections may be 3 to 5 mm parallel to the vocal folds and perpendicular to the vocal folds. Fatty tissue yields a high signal and gives a very satisfactory anatomic analysis of the paraglottic space. The ossified cartilage will give a bright signal, the non-ossified cartilage, a low signal. MRI must never be used if a patient has surgical clips (after thyroid surgery), pacemakers, or cochlear implants.

Other Techniques

Xeroradiography

Xeroradiography is performed with wider latitude of exposure with edge enhancement; thus, images have a higher resolution with a better contrast.[24] It has provided a large amount of information on laryngeal cartilages, on the soft tissues, and a precise analysis of the ventricles. It has proven accurate when looking for foreign bodies and in distinguishing a subglottic mass not always visible on stroboscopy. It is also a technique that the author (JA) has used to analyze vocal tract behavior during sustained vowels "a," "i," "u." Today, xeroradiography is no longer available because of the high exposure to radiation required, which, compared to numerized radiology and CT scan, is 5 times higher.[24,25]

Fluoroscopy—Laryngography

Fluoroscopy is rarely used to study the larynx, partly because of the high radiation exposure. Pharyngolaryngography with barium contrast was commonly used for the visualization of the posterior wall of the tongue, the vallecula, the piriform sinuses, and the posterior wall of the hypopharynx, in the 1980s.[26]

Positron Emission Tomography: PET Scan

Positron emission tomography or PET scan is a relatively new and interesting imaging technique based on the difference in the uptake and metabolism of glucose, H_2O_3, or fluorine 18-FDG. PET scans should prove very useful in future laryngeal research for voice fatigue and can be compared with the other techniques.[27]

Anatomy Related to Radiography

Phylogenetically, the larynx is an organ which functions as a constrictor-dilator mechanism in the airway. From amphibians to mammals, the larynx develops as a complex structure of cartilages, muscles, and mucosa primarily from branchial arches in utero. At 6 weeks, the epiglottis is seen at the base of the third and fourth pharyngeal arches. At 8 weeks, the thyroid, the cricoid, and the arytenoid cartilages are formed. Around 10 to 12 weeks, the vocal folds are individualized. At 7 months, the larynx is anatomically and functionally a sketch of an adult larynx. An understanding of the skeletal elements and articulations of the vocal tract is necessary to avoid misdiagnosis when interpreting imaging of the larynx.

Cartilages of the Larynx

The cartilages of the larynx, including the thyroid, cricoid, arytenoid, and corniculates consist of three components: non-ossified hyaline cartilage, a cortical bone marrow cavity containing fatty tissue, and scattered bony trabeculae. Enchondral (such as thyroid cartilage) ossification starts around 30 years of age. The ossification process follows specific patterns in each cartilage.[28,29] The epiglottis and the arytenoids are composed of yellow fibrocartilage that does not usually ossify. However, in our series, on helical CT scan at around 70 years of age, the authors have seen numerous ossified arytenoids.[30,31] On CT scan, ossified cartilage shows a high-alternating, outer and inner cortex, and a central, low-alternating medullary space. Nonossified hyaline cartilage and nonossified fibroelastic cartilages have the same attenuation values of soft tissue.[32-38]

The angle of the two laminae of the thyroid or "shield of the folds" is approximately 110° in children, 120° in females, and 90° in males.[39]

The cricoarytenoid joint depends on the articular surface, as described by Lampert in 1926.[40] The facets of the cricoid are cylindrically curved with an axis sharply inclined horizontally. The angles between the horizontal plane and the cricoarytenoid joint axis are primate specific: 25° for the Mycetes, 55° for the *Macacas*, and 55° to 60° for *Homo sapiens*. These facets do not exist in nonprimates.[41,42]

The cricoid cartilage is a complete ring with a height of 2.5 cm at the posterior arch and 0.75 cm at the anterior arch.

The arytenoids measure around 1.2 cm in height and are mobile and symmetric. The corniculate cartilages are at the apices of the arytenoids. The virtual dissection used in helical CT scanning by the authors shows the facet of the arytenoids.

The cricothyroid joint lies between the convex articular facet of the thyroid inferior horn and the flat articular facet of the posterolateral surface of the cricoid cartilage.

The cricoarytenoid joint is a saddle-shaped synovial joint with a strong capsular ligament. The arytenoid joints have complex sliding, rocking, and tilting movements described for decades by the observations gained through indirect and direct laryngoscopy but never by a CT scan "virtual arthroscopy" in vivo. Because of their low mass, they allow abduction-adduction in less than 0.1 second. This joint is critical for understanding not only the function of the laryngeal framework but also the source of most laryngeal pathologies.[43,44]

Soft Tissues of the Larynx

Radiography depends on tissue density in the larynx.

1. The mucosa of the larynx shows no enhancement except with a specific algorithm with the vocal-scan (the technique utilized by the authors to generate the images illustrated in this chapter).
2. Muscular tissue has no relevant enhancement in the conventional CT scan but does with the vocal-scan.
3. Connective tissue is usually not seen except with the vocal-scan, which has a cross-sectional imaging capacity that is ideally suited to differentiate the different compartments of the larynx and hypopharynx. The paraglottic space is symmetric between the mucosa and the laryngeal framework, and extends into the aryepiglottic folds. The supraglottic region (ventricles, false vocal folds) is adjacent to the pre-epiglottic space. The aryepiglottic folds separate the endolarynx (anteromedially) from the piriform sinuses (posteromedially). At the glottic level the medial boundary is the conus elasticus of the vocal ligament to the upper edge of the cricoid cartilage and joins the cricothyroid membrane anteriorly. The cricothyroid membrane posterolaterally forms the lateral boundary of the paraglottic space.[45,46] Also, at the glottic level, the thyroarytenoid muscle forms the bulk and shape of the vocal fold, which also occupies most of the volume of the paraglottic space.[47]

Dynamic Aspects of the Larynx

For the first time, laryngeal movements were observed and analyzed radiographically by the authors using three-dimensional (3D) CT, which allows observations of the movements of cartilages and joints. The anatomy of the soft tissues is well known and does not need any further explanation to understand the "virtual dissection."

The first roentgenologic laryngeal closure study was published in 1940 by Lindsay demonstrating the behavior of a laryngocele during phonation.[48] These tomograms also showed that the laryngeal airway is closed by apposition of both the vocal folds and the vestibular folds. The first observation by the way of laryngeal cineradiography during breathing was published by Ardran, Kemp, and Manen in 1953.[49] They noted that the larynx falls slightly on inspiration and rises on expiration and that the lumen widens on inspiration and narrows during expiration. These findings were confirmed in 1956 by Fink.[50] The first functional tomographies were produced 10 years later in 1966, by Ardran et al. They studied the role of the epiglottis, the cricoid, and the arytenoid cartilages and the ventricles during breathing and phonating.[51,52] R. Fink, in a retrospective on the human larynx, emphasized the role of the cricoarytenoid joint.[53,54] The vocal scan brings us a better understanding of the dynamic and functional aspects of this joint and the cricothyroid joint. It demonstrates the movements of the cricoarytenoid joint laterally, anteriorly and posteriorly.

In the movie *Voice Performers and Voice Fatigue* by the author Jean Abitbol, in 1988, a parallel study between xeroradiography and the flexible laryngoscope gave a satisfactory analysis of the physiology of the larynx during phonation.[55]

Clinical and Multimedia Evaluation of Laryngeal Diseases

Laryngeal diseases usually have a typical clinical history and generally do not require extensive imaging. The laryngologist can assess the laryngeal mass with his or her simple clinical examination, videolaryngoscopy, or videolaryngostroboscopy. The numerous techniques of laryngeal evaluation, developed in the last two decades, have provided an accurate approach of the diagnosis of laryngeal pathologies. The "good morning doctor" from the patient can provide diagnostic guidance by analysis of his or her maximum phonation time and voice characteristics. Listening to the patient's voice is the indispensable first step.

Manuel García developed the first method of indirect laryngoscopy in 1854. This examination is still routinely used, as it provides assessment of the real color of the mucosa and gives information in three dimensions.[56] The stroboscopic light became the second fundamental step in laryngeal examination. To be able to see the vocal folds in slow motion has brought forth a new harvest of unknown diagnoses and misdiagnoses. Video or computerized stroboscopy of the larynx may be stored on tape or DVD and can be compared with other examinations. Photographs of the larynx provide objective data that are helpful when comparing the laryngeal imaging before and after treatment.

Objective acoustic measures such as spectrographic analysis, fundamental F_0 measurements, formants, shimmer, and jitter during speech and singing are also valuable.

Electromyography has become a valuable clinical tool in the evaluation of vocal fold paresis or immobility, and allows for accurate location of the branch of the recurrent nerve or the superior laryngeal nerve that is impaired.[57]

Nowadays, radiology of the larynx is not only used to confirm pathology but also assists in diagnosis as with the 3D CT scan to visualize a "virtual dissection." The data gained from both clinical videolaryngoscopy and imaging provide a better understanding of the disease and lead to a better strategy for therapy.

CT Scan
How does a CT scan work? What was the basis for development of the vocal scan?

Basics of Helical CT Scan

Principles

As previously discussed, x-rays are photons with a wavelength from 10^{-4} nm to 10^{2} nm, are produced by the tube, and require an important power supply.

The x-ray tube moves with a circular movement and x-ray data are gathered by a detector. The table on which the patient lies moves horizontally. This dual movement creates a helical figure in a virtual cylinder.

Projections of data collected are digitized. This revolutionary method was a major radiologic advance in the ability to assess density of the mass. Hounsfield had the ingenious idea to detect x-rays with a crystal, thus producing a visible light spectrum. The CT scan improved resolution dramatically by permitting smaller, more discrete image slices. The detectors are crystals, which increase the sensitivity, and thus, the different densities may be analyzed by the computer. Data analysis was made possible once the computer became available. Algorithms then allowed reconstruction imaging.

Acquisition

- The slice-thickness is defined by the collimation of x-rays (Figures 7–1 through 7–5).
- The flux of photons depends on the power supply of the tube (120 kV usually, at 15 mA). The flux is limited by the heat effect.
- The speed of the table on which the patient lies going in to the gantry is measured in mm/sec. It is related to the collimation.

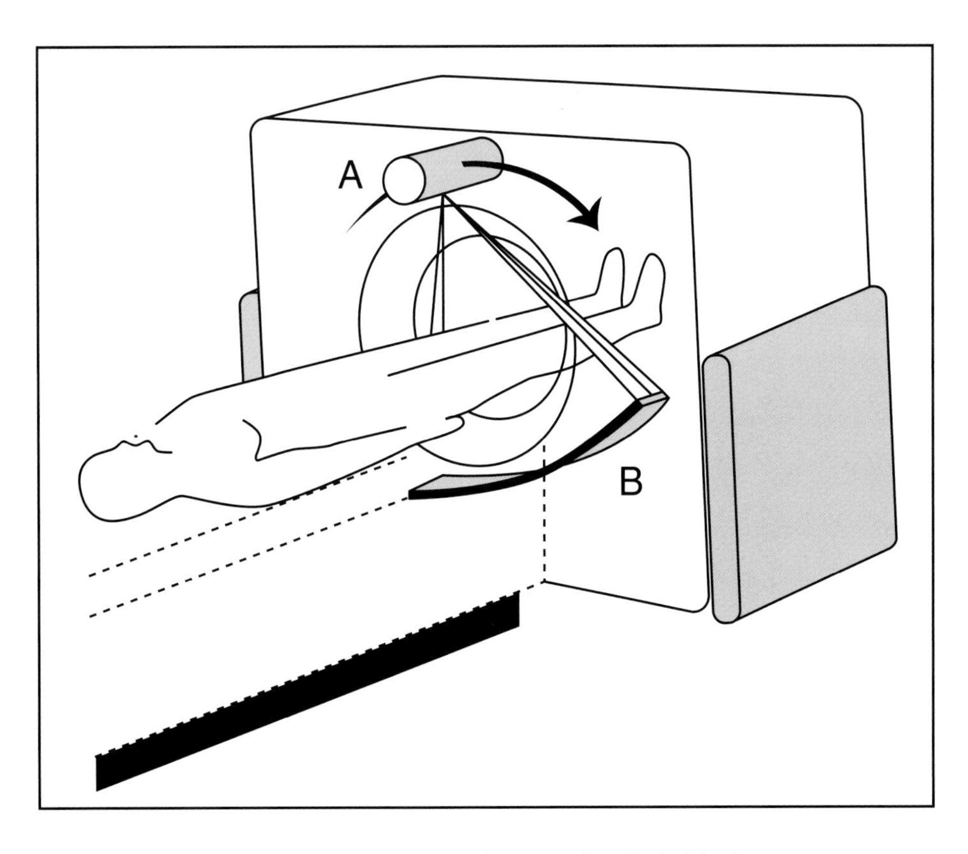

Fig 7–1. X-ray tube with a double detector: **A.** x-ray tube; **B.** double detector.

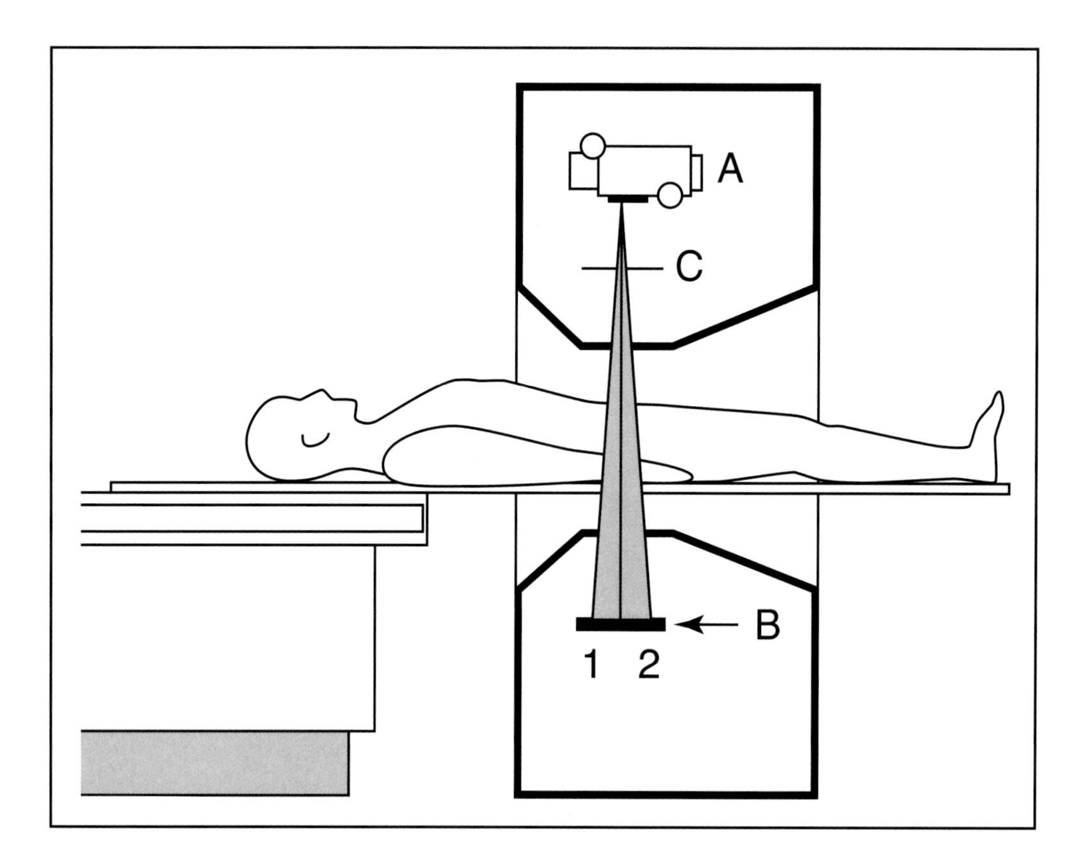

Fig 7–2. A. x-ray tube; **B.** double detector; **C.** collimation.

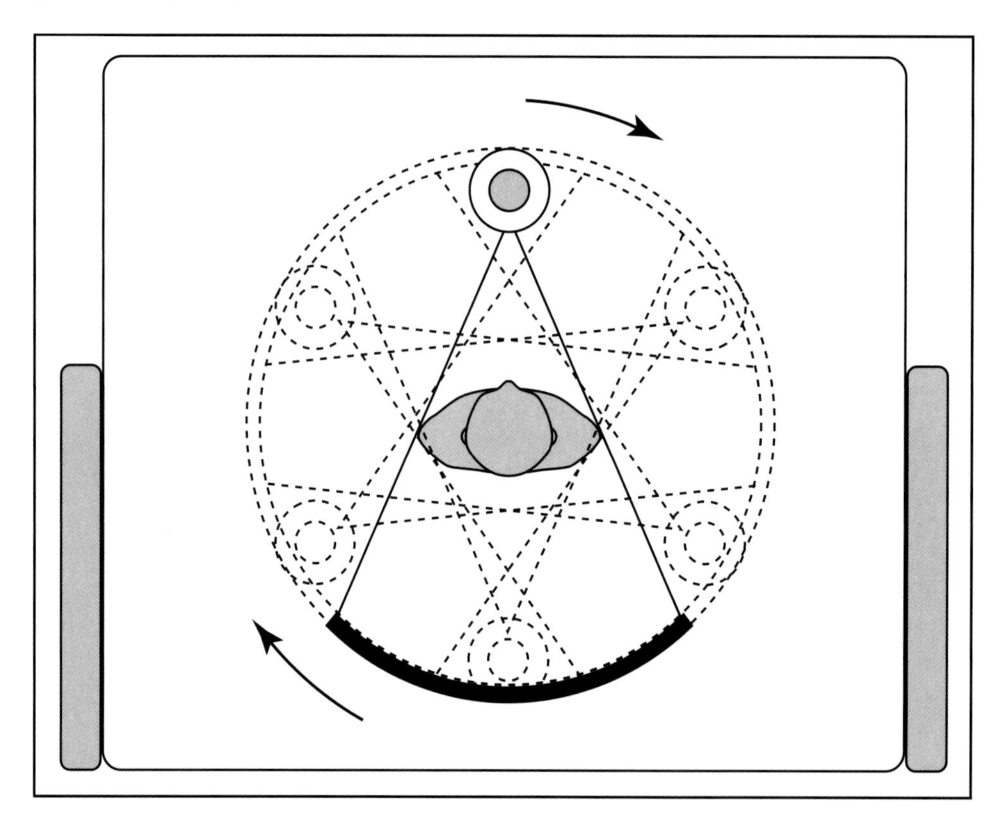

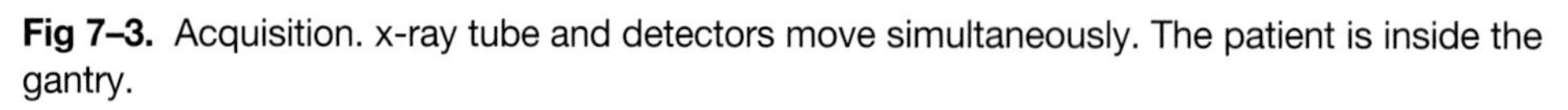

Fig 7–3. Acquisition. x-ray tube and detectors move simultaneously. The patient is inside the gantry.

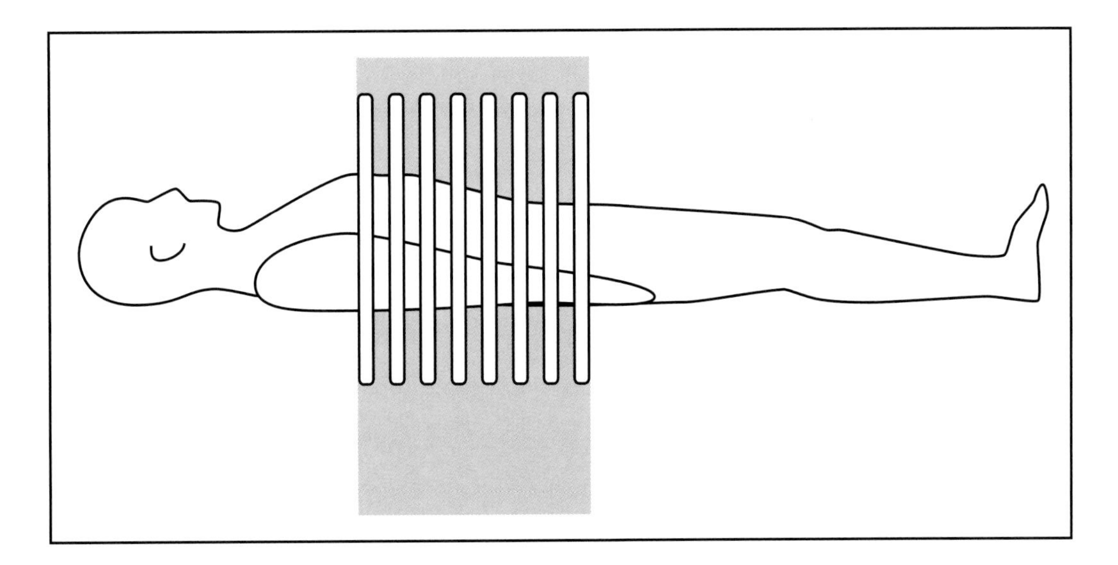

Fig 7–4. Conventional CT scan: slice by slice requiring 30 minutes for acquisition. Each slice needs 6 to10 seconds with a relapse time of 10 to 20 seconds.

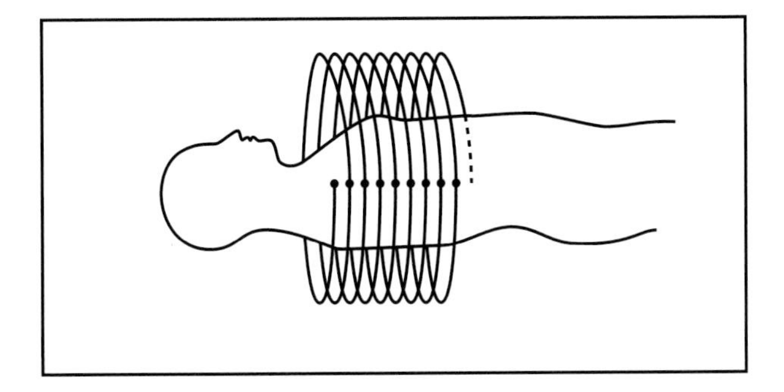

Fig 7–5. Helical CT scan—The spiral technique allows a 20 second acquisition time.

- $\text{Pitch} = \frac{\text{Table incrementation during each gantry rotation}}{\text{Collimation}}$
- The time of the spiral is linked to the volume acquisition and the slice-thickness.

Reconstruction. Algorithms that improve resolution are used. Here a 360° rotation technique is used. There are two rotations of the tube (720°). Then, the image parameters are calculated for a 360° reconstruction essentially doubling the amount of information in the computer from which the image is resolved, thereby enhancing detail. Table speed, related to "pitch" is also important. The more rapidly the table is moving, the more the thickness slices increase.

Applications for Acquisition

The gantry angles used in helical CT scanning are almost the same as those used in conventional CT. For the helical CT scan of the larynx, the gantry angles are parallel to the vocal folds during abduction and adduction.

Inaccurate gantry angle may cause a misdiagnosis with an artificial thickening of the anterior commissure, and the interposed laryngeal ventricle may disturb the evaluation of the paraglottic space.[58,59]

However, misdiagnoses decrease with the practical application of the 3D CT scan with sagittal, coronal, and 120° planes that the authors use, the ability to retrospectively study the images, along with the collaboration of a radiologist and a laryngologist, but a zero risk of misdiagnosis never exists.

Contrast. The rapid acquisition of the helical CT has dramatically decreased the use of intravenous contrast. The contrast dose is reduced by at least one-third for better enhancement of the main vessels and of the soft tissues (thyroarytenoid muscle, cricothyroid membrane).[60]

Approximately 150 ml of intravenous contrast is required if there is an angulation of the gantry and 100 ml if not. Prior to the scan 46 mg of contrast medium at a rate of 1 ml/sec are injected and followed by infusion at a rate of 0.5 ml/sec.

Slice-Thickness/Collimation. The best image quality, as illustrated in this chapter, is obtained when the interval of reconstruction is equal to the slice-thickness with overlapping slices.[61]

For example, an acquisition set obtained with a 3-mm collimation can be reconstructed into images of 3 mm (same slice-thickness) in 1-mm increments only resulting in 2-mm overlap of adjacent images.

Pitch. It is proportional to collimation. Increasing the pitch will decrease the longitudinal resolution; that is why a pitch of 1 seems to be the optimal level for preserving the z-axis resolution. It allows multiplane reconstruction for the arytenoids and the laryngeal joints.

Power Supply. The tube current is a critical factor in helical CT: 200-250 amps and 120 kV are used. If the power supply is not adequate, increased noise, poor contrast enhancement, and grainy images will result.

Applications for Reconstruction

Reconstruction. Accurate and adequate algorithms are necessary for high-quality reconstruction, which depends on slice-thickness, slice overlapping, and contrast resolution.

Slice-thickness is used for a volumetric acquisition and, retrospectively, a reconstruction. Because data acquisition is volumetric, the scanning time of the patient is not increased and the slice-thickness used during the scanning does not have to be equal to the slice-thickness used for reconstruction. To improve the images, the reconstruction can also be obtained with slice overlapping. For laryngeal pathology, we use a 0.6-mm reconstruction interval made with 1-mm collimation through the laryngeal framework. This technique has been performed in the temporal bone.[62] The 3D information displayed is used for diagnosis and aids in planning phonosurgery. To ensure better quality of the images and, thus, more accurate diagnosis, the larynx must be studied with at least two helical acquisitions.[63]

Principles of the CT Scan

Technology with very powerful computers brings us to the third dimension: "virtual endoscopy," and "transparent body."

Evaluation of the tissue density is possible and from this point, the quality of the structures are more precise. To render homage to Hounsfield the units of density in CT were named Hu (Hounsfield unit), the scale is from –1000 to +1000.

Air = –1000 Hu;

Water = 0 Hu; and

Bone = +1000 Hu.

There exist 2000 levels of shades in black and white from –1000 Hu to +1000 Hu. To distinguish the different structures' density and, thus, the different type of tissue, a color is applied on the Hu scale for better definition and imaging.

The color chosen to analyze our frames in 3D CT scan has proven to be indispensable. It should be recalled that the human eye can distinguish only 20 levels of gray but 250,000 colors. It is necessary to adapt the image to the location to be explored. The image is distinguished by two parameters: the width and the density of the window. The more the window is decreased, the more density differentiation is appreciated. Therefore, the threshold of the window must be equal to the average tissue density to be imaged (Fig 7–6). The screen is coupled with a color laser printer to obtain a hard copy and recorded on CD-ROM or a DVD. With this machine, it is possible to do a fly-through, and the CT scan has proven irreplaceable in the diagnosis of deep lesions, which are hard to see. Thus, CT and MR imaging are more useful in these cases.[64-69]

The laryngeal joints are very well observed with the 3D CT scan.

CT is very helpful in cricoarytenoid joint injury when preparing the surgical strategy.

Angiography is helpful in conjunction with 3D CT for providing a better understanding of the laryngeal physiology and pathologies such as angiomas and paragangliomas.[70]

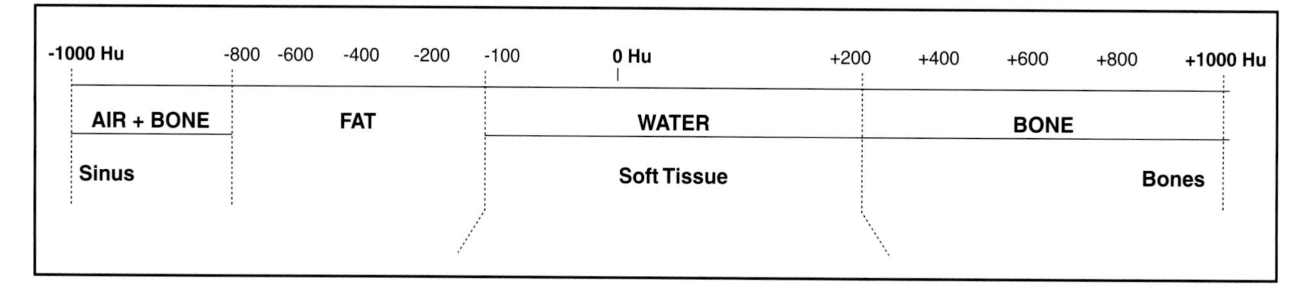

Fig 7–6. Hounsfield units: Density of the tissue in Hu.

Vocal Scan

Helical computer assisted tomography scanning or helical CT scan has been improved by the advances in computer technology. Planes are stored to create the 3D imaging. The program with an accurate workstation can perform reformations/reconstructions. All the planes may be used. For the vocal scan, the authors have determined specific parameters, including orientation of the plane, measurement of tissue density in Hounsfield units (Hu), the time exposure, and the "shadow" work.

Acquisition

Technical advances have not only improved image quality in the last two decades, but also the way in which such images are obtained.

Conventional CT Scanners. Conventional CT scanners need sophisticated cables to couple the x-ray and detector assembly to the reconstruction process. It also needs high voltage. The protocol for individual scans was performed with a 2-second scan time separated by a 6-second interscan delay. This delay allows time to re-orient the source-detector assembly within the gantry, time for table movement, and a short breath for the patient.[71]

The patient lies on a sliding table. The table moves into a gantry, a central circular aperture housing the x-ray source and detectors. The slices are parallel to the vocal folds. The imaging procedure is performed from the inferior maxilla to the sixth cervical vertebra. The more detail needed, the thinner the slices must be and the longer the imaging time required. With the conventional CT scan, most images are 1- to 2-mm thickness-slices, every 3 to 5 mm. The patient moves the prescribed distance through the gantry for each slice; the table moves 3 mm, one image shot, 3 mm, another image is shot with a total imaging time of approximately 20 to 30 minutes.

Vocal Scan. The authors use a spiral CT scanner. The procedure is much faster, requiring only 20 seconds exposure time. The spiral CT scanner moves the subject continuously in a circle and creates a volume acquisition imaging. These data are collected and stored. The first step is a multiplanar study (coronal, sagittal, and axial). Then the analysis begins for three-dimensional imaging. The images are colored regarding the tissue density. We have 2000 levels of gray or 2000 Hu, which are converted to color. The advantages are enormous: rapid acquisition time, few motion artifacts, a color and 3D picture, and animation.[72,73]

Intravenous contrast may be required for some purpose (laryngeal arteries) or presurgical mapping of a hemorrhagic mass (angioma). Data are recorded in the computer with an adequate program capable of analyzing every detail, both from the technical point of view (scale of density rendering) and the anatomic point of view (for example, if the focus of analysis is on the joints or on the vocal ligament), which are intimately linked. The laryngologist must work with and interpret the images with the radiologist at the workstation to change some parameters of contrast if the pathology being evaluated is not visible on the first images. The Hu must be chosen to identify the specific lesion; protocols have been developed accordingly.

One of the successes of the helical CT scan from the very beginning was the ability to analyze the anterior commissure that was previously impossible to see with computed tomography. The anterior commissure was found to have a mean width of 1 to 1.6 mm in normal subjects.[74]

Vocal Scan Reconstruction

The helical CT reconstruction requires multiple angles for the same structures to be analyzed. With the helical CT, there is a 360° view with a complete gantry rotation. During the procedure, the patient moves continuously through the gantry.

Mathematical interpolation with specific parameters allows the reconstruction through the computer. Parameters include collimation, table speed or incrementation, and image reconstruction intervals. Although the slice-thickness of collimation is pre-set before the scan, the computer can generate overlapping images. If a 2-mm collimation is used, slices may be reconstructed every 1 mm. For example, in laryngeal imaging a 1-cm collimation with a 20-sec helical exposure, covering 20 cm of tissue along the z-axis has a pitch of 1.

Advantages of Helical CT Scan

The advantages of helical CT technology are numerous.[75-78]

1. The procedure is fast; in a single 20 second interval an entire vocal tract is helicallly scanned and ready to be reconstructed in 3D.
2. Helical CT is able to eliminate respiratory artifacts and is able to reconstruct overlapping images at arbitrary intervals on the workstation. The 3D CT scan gives a very high quality image with the reconstruction, not only of the image but also of a virtual mobility between two scanning points. For example, aperture and closure of the glottis can be gener-

ated from helical acquisitions; this has dramatically improved the scope of analysis for the vocal tract (and also for the entire body).

3. Helical CT has the ability to shift the location of slice reconstruction and create new images, retrospectively, with the image and the laryngologist in front of the screen of the workstation.
4. In some instances, helical CT scan has replaced the conventional CT in laryngeal imaging as numerized radiology did for conventional radiology. Improved vascular identification allows easier separation of mass lesions from vessels. The contrast enhancement is tremendously improved by the choice of the filter with reconstruction having the same advantages observed in thoracic or color imaging.

Limits of Helical CT Scan

The limits of the helical CT are few as described below:

- The chainsaw artifact: a few slices are missing; this problem is solved by overlapping imaging.
- The lego effect is caused by squared edges of each slice at the convexity. This artifact is corrected by using a smoothing algorithm during the 3D reconstruction or by using a thinner slice-thickness during scanning (1 mm).
- The threshold selection is a crucial factor. 3D images depend both on the algorithm and the threshold chosen during reconstruction.
- Artifacts related to metallic objects (dental crowns, bridges, surgical clips, and prostheses and cochlear implants).
- Volume rendering will create an artificially smooth surface of the endolaryngeal structures.

Image quality also depends on the power source. A high power is needed, especially in large patients, in which the images may be excessively grainy. Refinements in detection technology, higher-heat-capacity of x-rays tubes, and improvements in new workstations will advance the possibilities in achieving optimal images.

Although helical CT allows a rapid acquisition and reduces artifact such as respiratory misregistration, the swallowing artifacts may still cause degradation of images in the vocal tract study. A near perfect acquisition technique is needed.[79]

Virtual Endoscopy and Virtual Dissection

The postprocessing of helical CT data allows creation of a reconstruction from axial slices into a high-quality picture of variable orientation. The virtual endoscopy was described for the first time in 1994 by Vining et al.[80,81] They used an accurate three-dimensional software, the voxel viewer, and a silicon graphics machine. Computer simulations allow creation of virtual endoscopy. A "virtual dissection" from the lumen of the larynx and trachea to the vessels and muscles is performed via the applications of acquisitions and reconstructions. In other words, 3D imaging is accurately created, recorded, and printed.[82-85]

Previously, diagnosis of airway disease was only possible by invasive endoscopy, considered the gold standard for the evaluation of airway obstruction. Virtual endoscopy may prove to be a noninvasive technique to diagnose the nature and the degree of airway obstruction.[86] The anatomy of interest was separated from the surrounding anatomy by a process called image segmentation. A threshold value was determined for each anatomic object to optimally observe its volume elements or voxels. For vocal folds an upper threshold of –100 Hounsfield unit (Hu) and a lower threshold of –700 Hu was used.

The reconstructed anatomy or the "virtual dissection" can be observed from the lumens as in endoscopy, being considered a virtual endoscopy. It is similar to surgical dissection, isolating each soft tissue, muscle, artery, membrane, and ligament; thus, it is a virtual dissection.

The virtual dissection is registered to the helical data set, thus allowing axial, coronal, and sagittal planes.[87-90] Computed tomography virtual endoscopy is a nominative radiologic technique that produces visualization of intraluminal surfaces in 3D reconstruction of air / tissue or fluid / tissue interfaces rarely seen with MRI imaging. Axial helical CT imaging is performed with the patient in the supine position, holding his / her breath or phonating a sustained vowel / "i" / for 20 seconds if possible.

The following parameters are used: collimation thickness of 2 mm, pitch factor of 1 to 1.5, and reconstruction interval of 2 mm. The reconstructed axial CT data images are archived on digital tape and transferred to "a voxel workstation" for review and postprocessing.[91] The 3D virtual dissection or virtual endoscopy are reconstructed from the axial CT data using a navigator software package on the workstation. This results in a surface-shaded display of the lumen from inside.[92-94] A satisfactory evaluation of the surface can also be performed. The images travel via a fly-through path of the lumen from the larynx to the trachea or from the trachea to the larynx.[95,96] Imaging the subglottic space, visible from the trachea, or an inferior perspective is possible. A movie loop of the fly-through path is created and archived. Data are also archived on CD-ROM. The total time to create a fly-through path is less than 10 minutes if studying the ventricles, the vocal folds, the subglottic space, and the trachea. Videolaryngoscopy with a flexible and rigid scope has been performed and compared to the helical 3D CT scan or vocal scan. However, with this technique an inferior view of the vocal fold is impossible.[73,97]

CT scan and MRI enable us to evaluate the deep structures of the larynx, from the vocal ligament to the laryngeal articulators. Although CT scan in 3D and MR imaging is excellent, helical 3D CT scan enables much faster image acquisition and muliplanar or three-dimensional image reconstruction. Videolaryngostroboscopy and vocal scan demand a close, regular, interdisciplinary cooperation in order to have a better understanding of the pathology and to facilitate an accurate therapeutic strategy. This cooperation is of particular importance in pre- and post-therapeutic evaluation of laryngeal neoplasm and carcinoma. CT of the vocal tract may be obtained with dynamic incremental scanning or helical scanning being superior.

For the vocal scan: helical acquisition with 1.2 to 1.5 mm collimation and 1 to 1.5 pitch produces images with excellent details.[98] The acquisition technique requires examination of a patient in supine position, with a hyperextended neck, instructing the patient to resist swallowing or coughing and to hold the breath or to sustain vowel phonation of /"e"/ for 20 seconds. The software is crucial to obtaining three-dimensional volume reconstruction and so-called virtual endoscopy. The surface renderings simulate endoscopic views of the inner surface of the vocal tract by means of computer-generated ray casting.

The practical values of virtual endoscopy are numerous, accomplished by the "virtual dissection," enhancing surgical preparation. Because of the rapid image acquisition, the vocal scan is also performed during phonation on different vowels and different tones in order to analyze the real movements of the vocal tract during singing and speaking. Vocal scans are always reconstructed with a specific standardized soft tissue algorithm.

Cases

Authors' protocols: The examination is accomplished during a period of 20 seconds with a power supply of 120 kV and 150 amps. The machine is a CT gold spiral Elcint-Picker. It works with multiple detectors. Slice-thickness is 1.3 mm every 0.6 mm with a pitch of 2.

First series imaged in this vocal tract protocol: The air is imaged throughout the entire vocal tract. Slice-thickness: 2.7 mm every 1.3 mm with a pitch of 1.5.

The second series is during free breathing (holding one's breath will provide good imaging) and examines soft tissues of the laryngeal muscles and mucosa with the surface-shaded display. Slice-thickness is 1.3 mm every 0.6 mm with a pitch of 2.

The third series is used for evaluating the laryngeal framework, articulations, and cartilages, chiefly the arytenoids. This series has a slice-thickness of 0.6 mm every 0.3 mm with a pitch of 2.

The authors have named this 3D CT scan technique of the vocal tract the "vocal scan," and the protocol is illustrated in Figures 7–7 to 7–30.

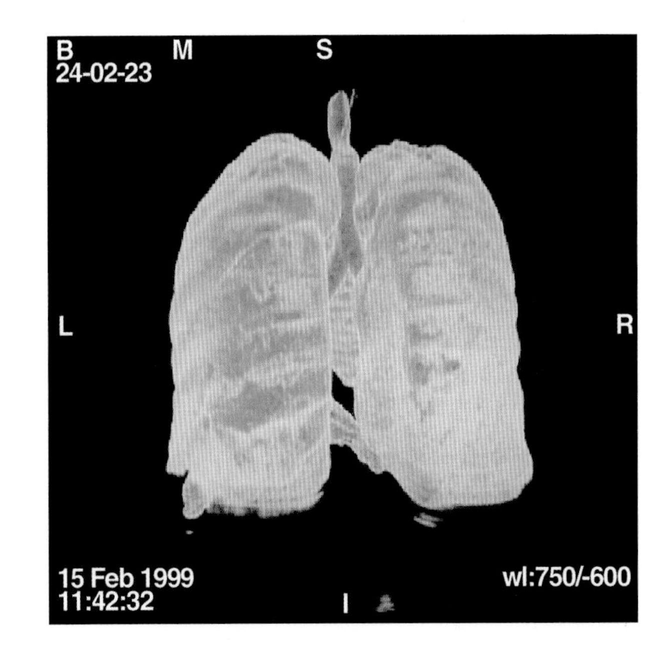

Fig 7–7. The lungs.

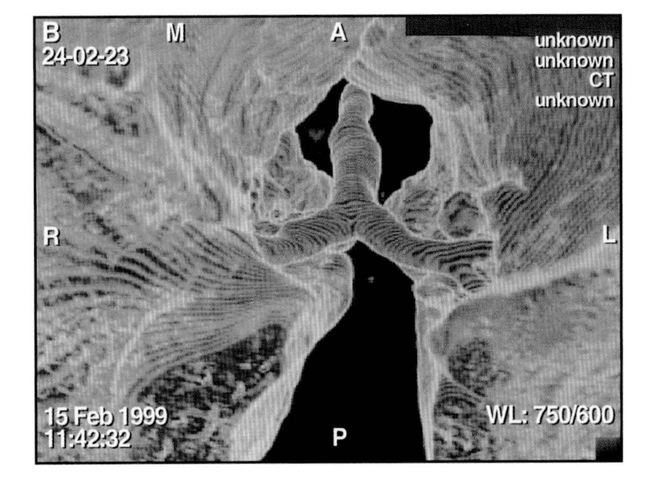

Fig 7–8. Magnified helical CT scan of the carina.

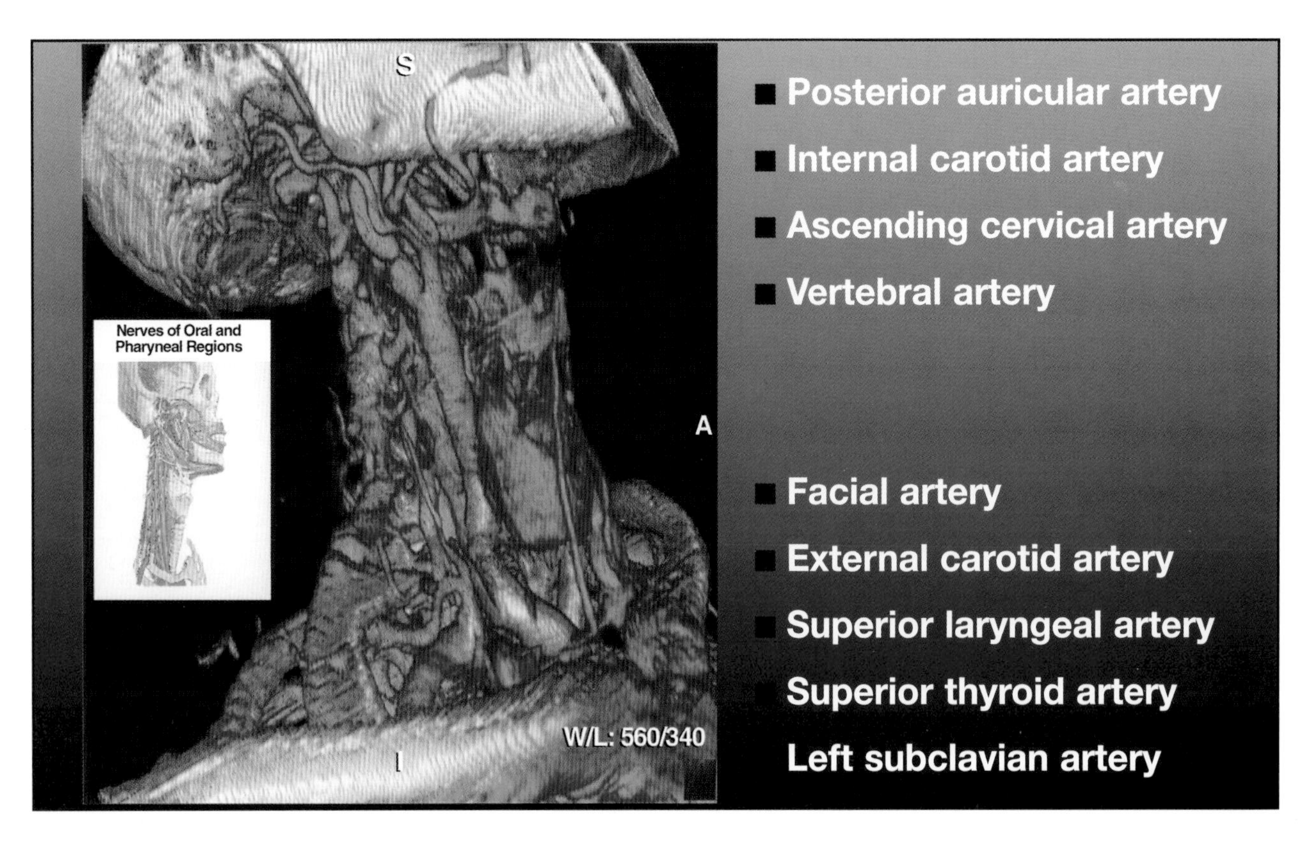

Fig 7–9. Virtual dissection of the neck.

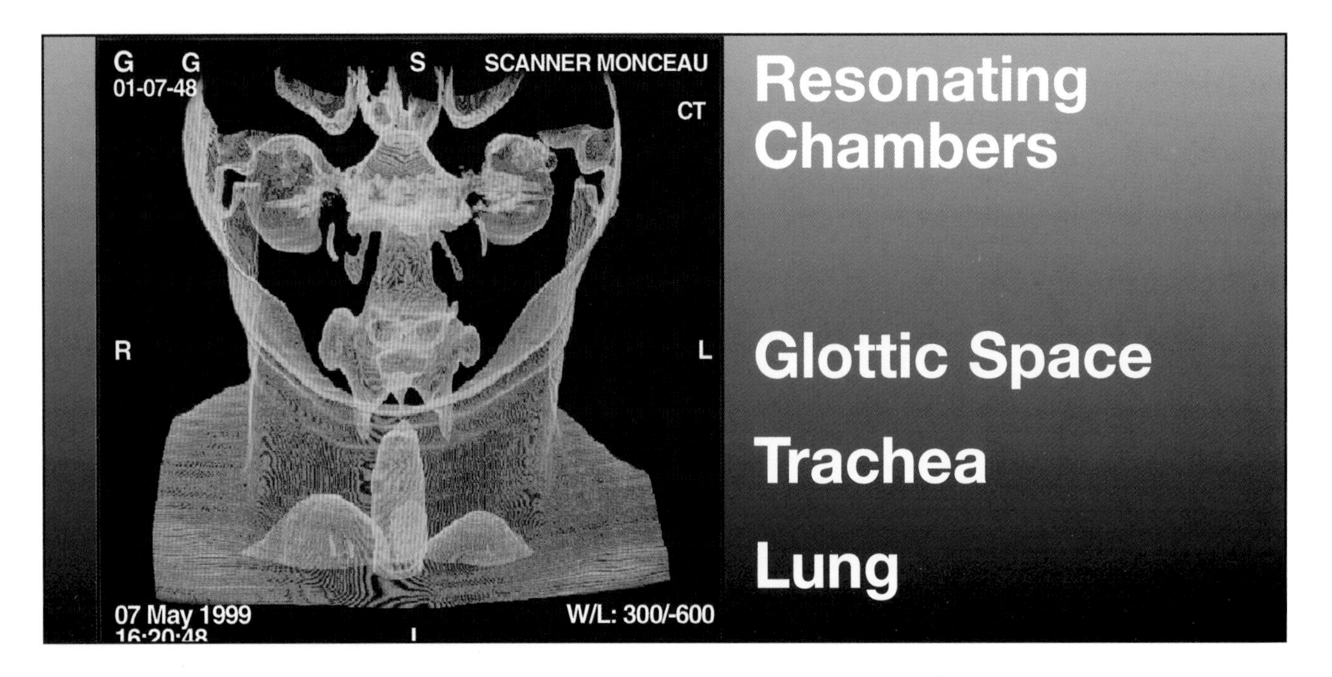

Fig 7–10. Vocal tract transparency: voice production.

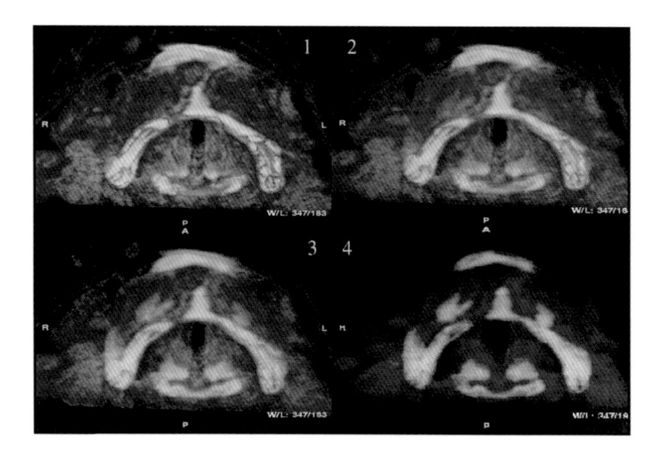

Fig 7–11. Visualization of the glottic area: 4 different transparencies to visualize from the superficial to the deep layer of the cricoarytenoid joint.

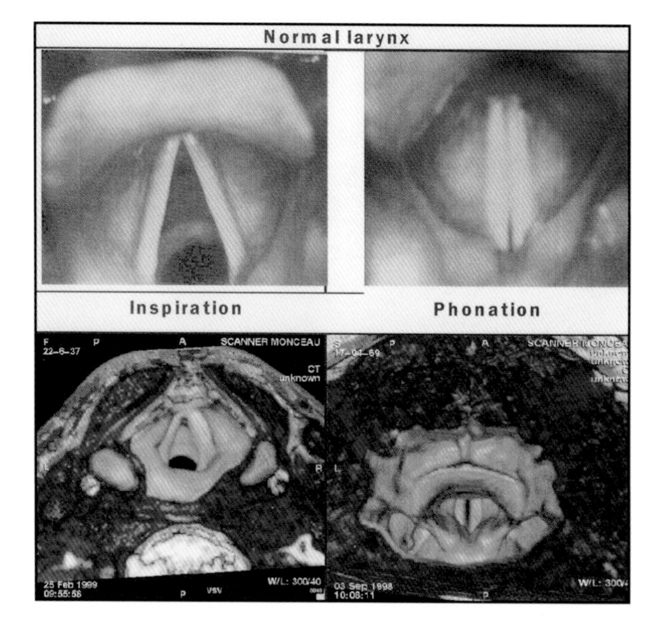

Fig 7–12. Virtual endoscopy provides a superior view in many ways when compared with indirect laryngoscopy in a normal larynx.

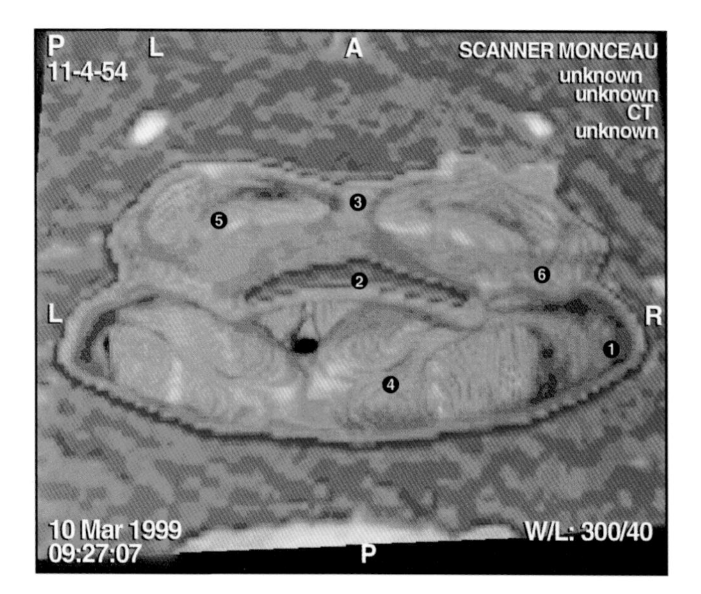

Fig 7–13. Virtual endoscopy of the larynx from a superior view with a Valsalva maneuver. (1. Piriform sinus, 2. Epiglottis, 3. Glossoepiglottic fold, 4. Aryepiglottic fold, 5. Valleculae, 6. Pharyngo-epiglottic fold)

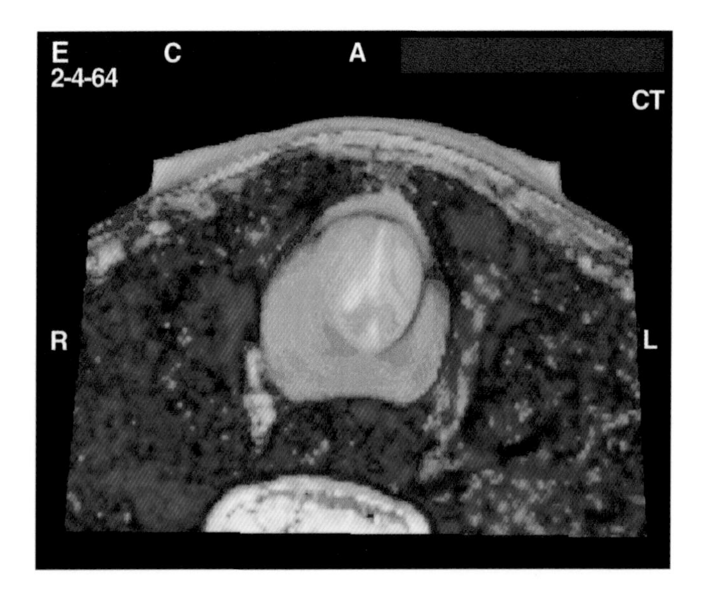

Fig 7–14. Inferior view of the vocal folds: virtual endoscopy. This was not seen during the consultation by scope.

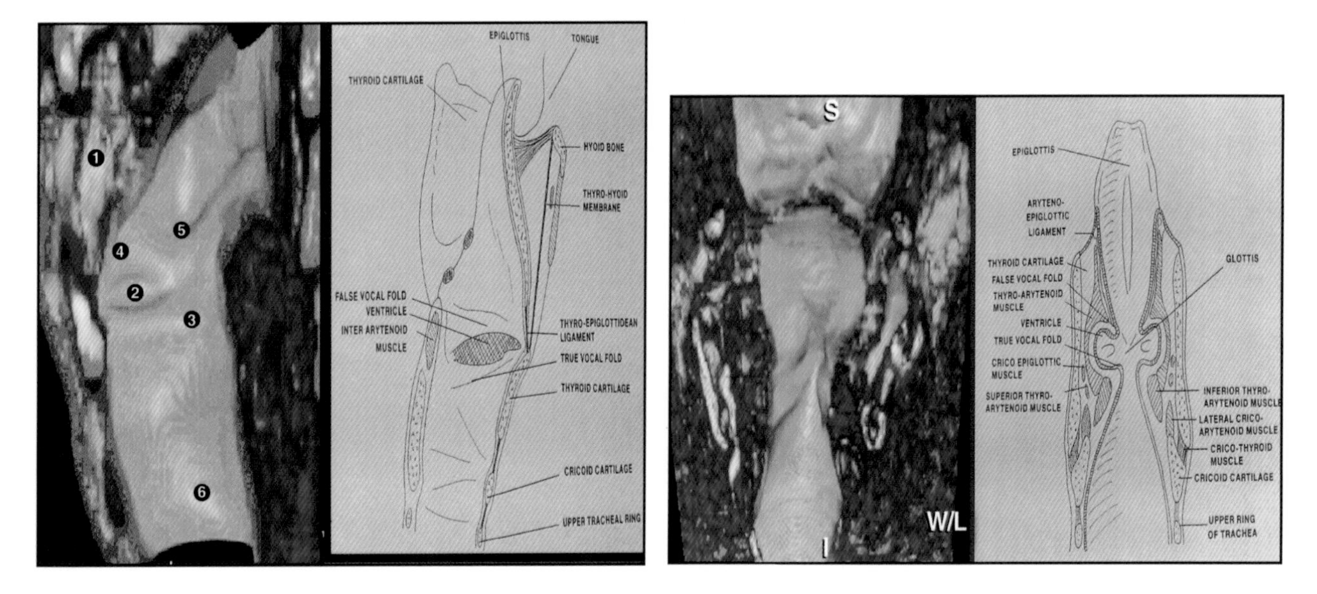

Fig 7–15. Lateral and internal views of the larynx: virtual endoscopy (1. Hyo. Thyro epiglottic space (fat pad), 2. Ventricle, 3. Vocal fold, 4. False vocal fold, 5. Piriform sinus, 6. Trachea)

Fig 7–16. Lateral and internal views of the larynx: virtual endoscopy.

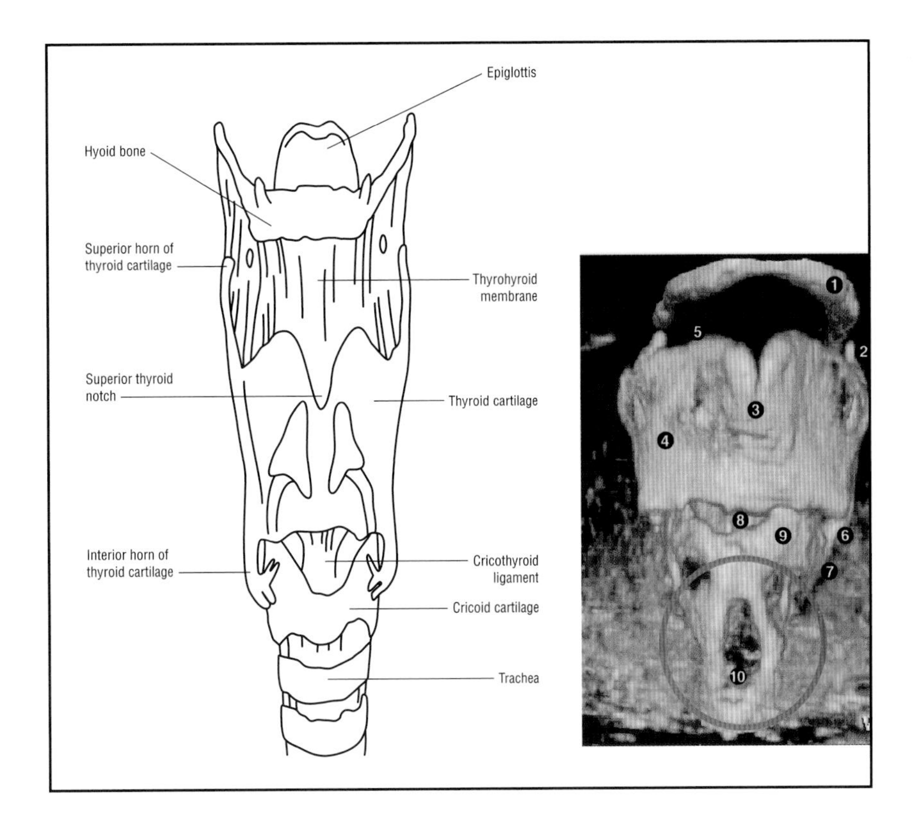

Fig 7–17. Framework of the larynx (can be used to observe a tracheostomy scar): anterior view (post-tracheotomy). (1. Hyoid bone, 2. Superior horn of thyroid cartilage, 3. Laryngeal prominence, 4. Thyroid cartilage, 5. Oblique line, 6. Inferior horn of thyroid cartilage, 7. Cricothyroid joint, 8. C-T ligament, 9. Cricoid cartilage, 10. Old tracheostomy)

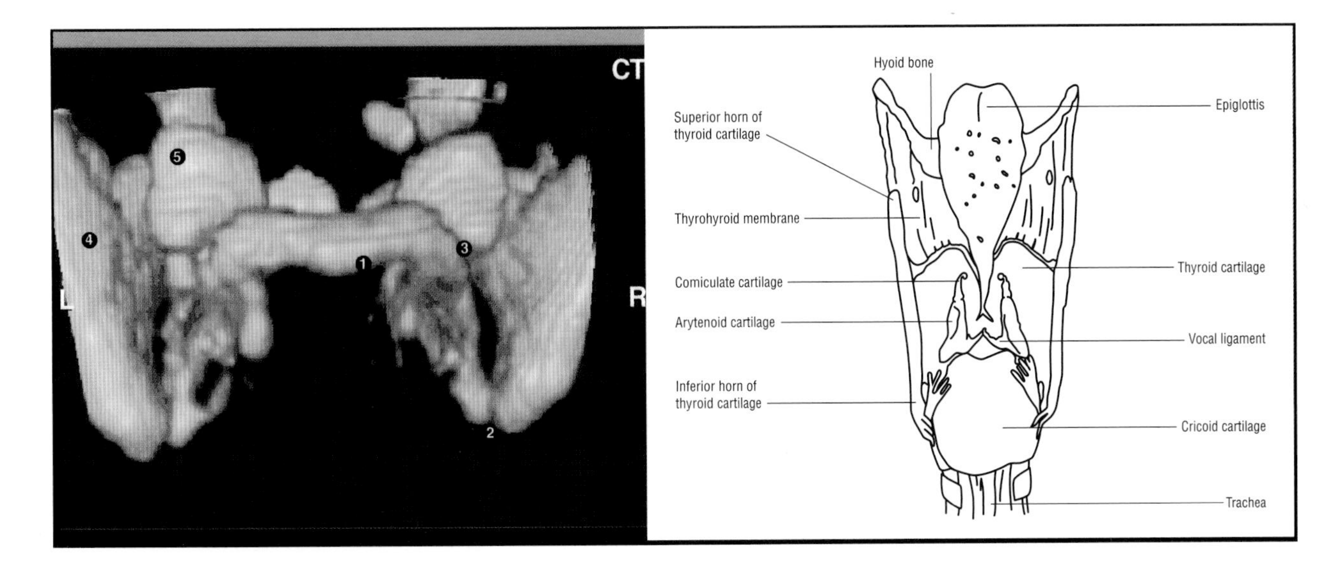

Fig 7–18. Cricoarytenoid joint during slow inspiration: posterior view. (1. Cricoid cartilage, 2. Cricothyroid joint, 3. Cricoarytenoid joint, 4. Thyroid cartilage, 5. Arytenoids)

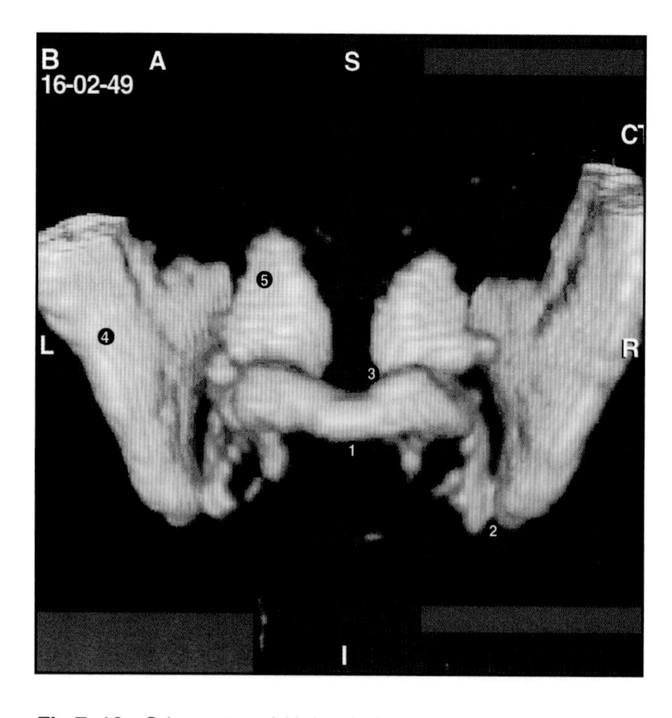

Fig 7–19. Cricoarytenoid joint during phonation with a sustained vowel /i/: posterior view. (1. Cricoid cartilage, 2. Cricothyroid joint, 3. Cricoarytenoid joint, 4. Thyroid cartilage, 5. Arytenoids).

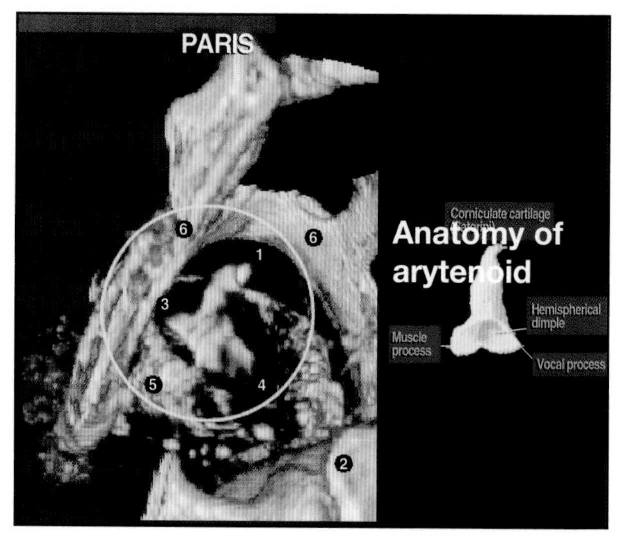

Fig 7–20. Accurate view of the arytenoids: anterosuperior view. (1. Corniculate cartilage, 2. Vertebral body, 3. Muscular process, 4. Vocal process, 5. Cricoid cartilage, 6. Thyroid cartilage)

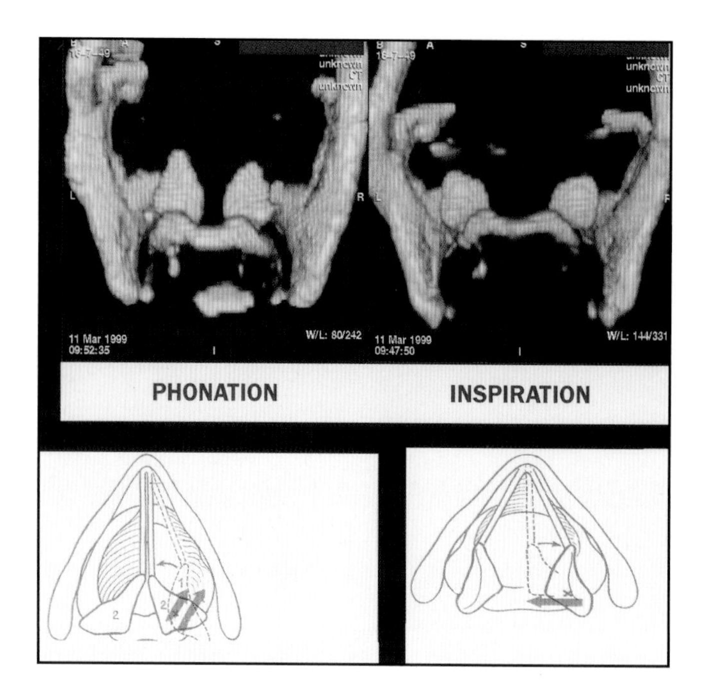

Fig 7–21. Mobility of the arytenoids (1): comparison between phonation and inspiration.

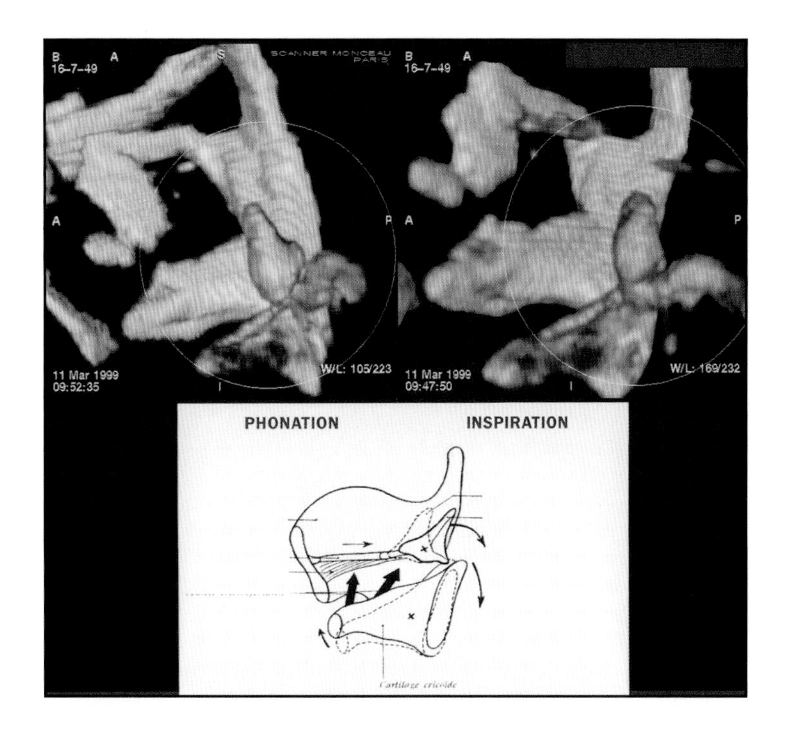

Fig 7–22. Mobility of the arytenoids and the cricothyroid joint (2): comparison between phonation and inspiration.

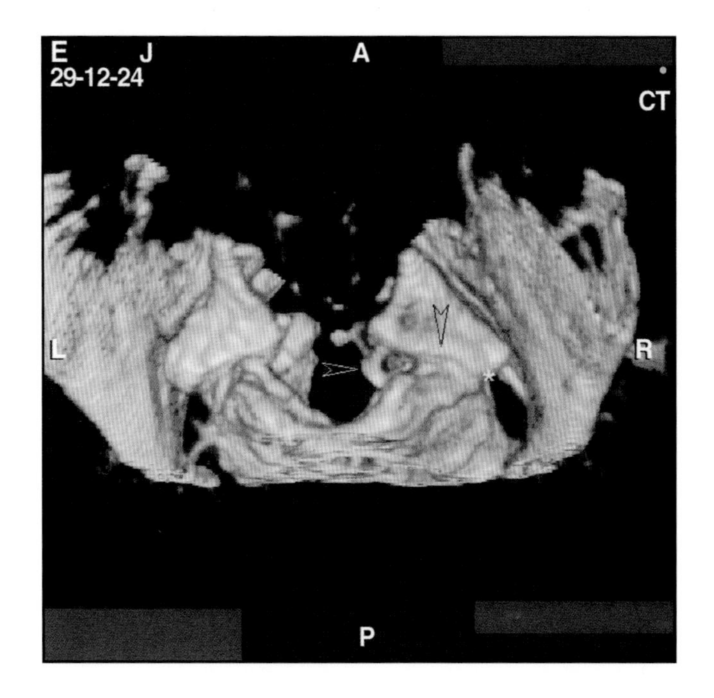

Fig 7–23. Cricoarytenoid arthrosis. Note the 3 signs of arthrosis seen: 1. Narrow joint (*star*) 2. Osteophytic deposit (*yellow arrow*), 3. Calcification of superficial layer of the joint (*black arrow*).

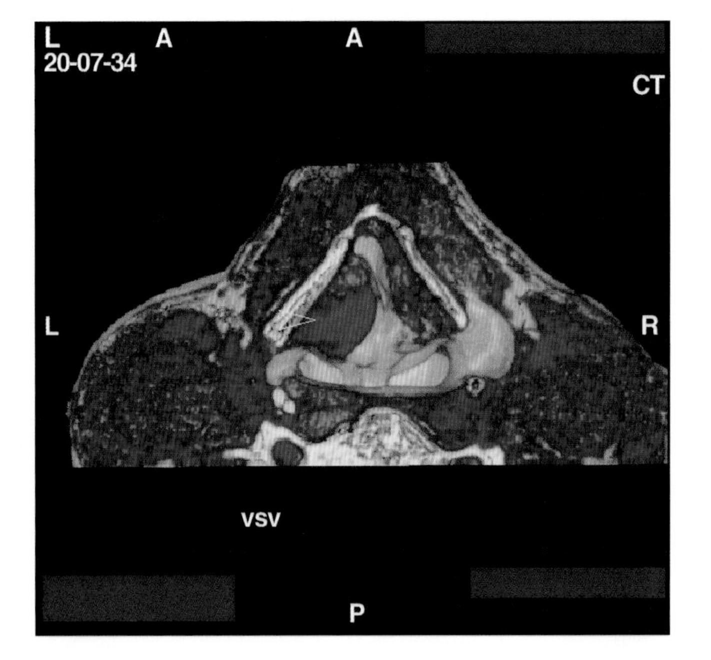

Fig 7–24. Cancer of the left vocal fold.

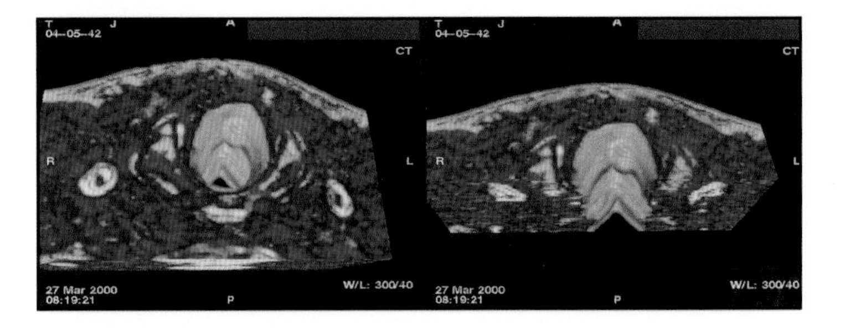

Fig 7–25. Subglottic cancer below the anterior commissure, not visible by fiberoptic laryngoscopy (endotracheal, inferior view).

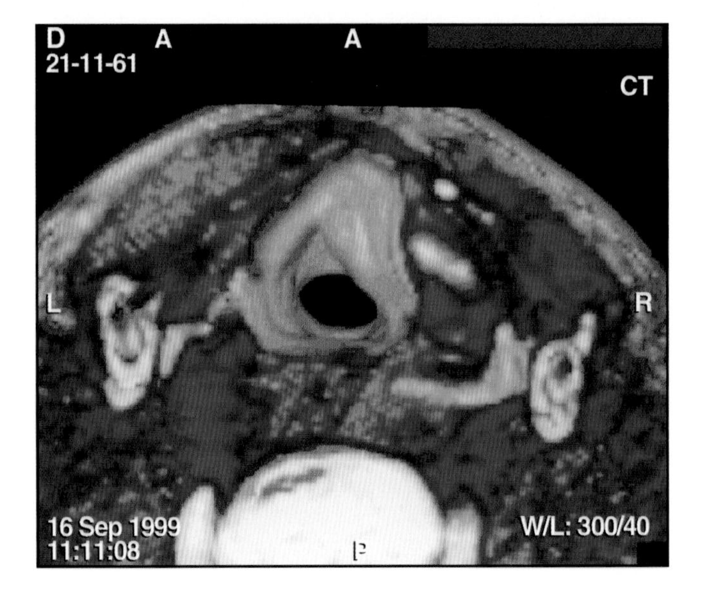

Fig 7–26. Teflon injection (1) in the wrong layer of the right vocal fold (too superficial).

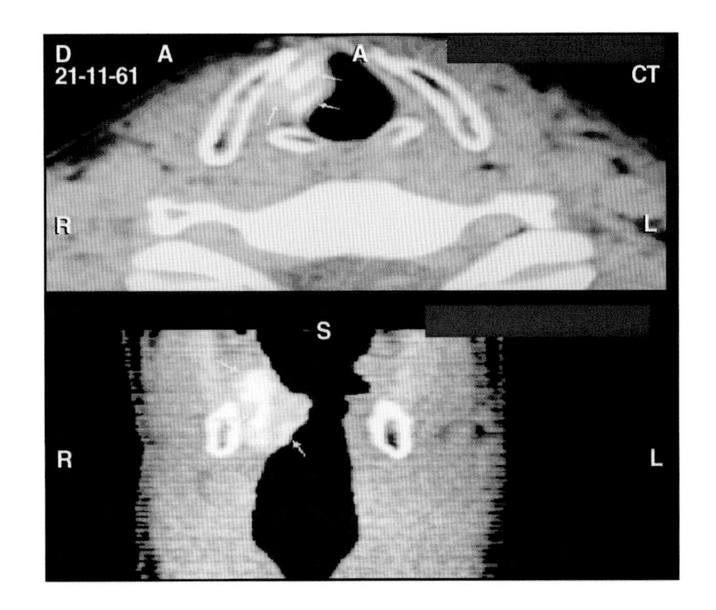

Fig 7–27. Teflon injection (2) in the wrong layer of the right vocal fold (too superficial).

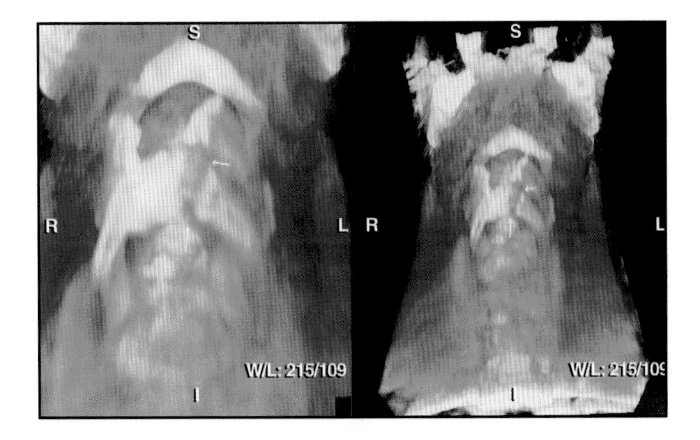

Fig 7–28. Imaging of postsurgical trauma after laryngeal shave (Adam's apple resection) in a transsexual.

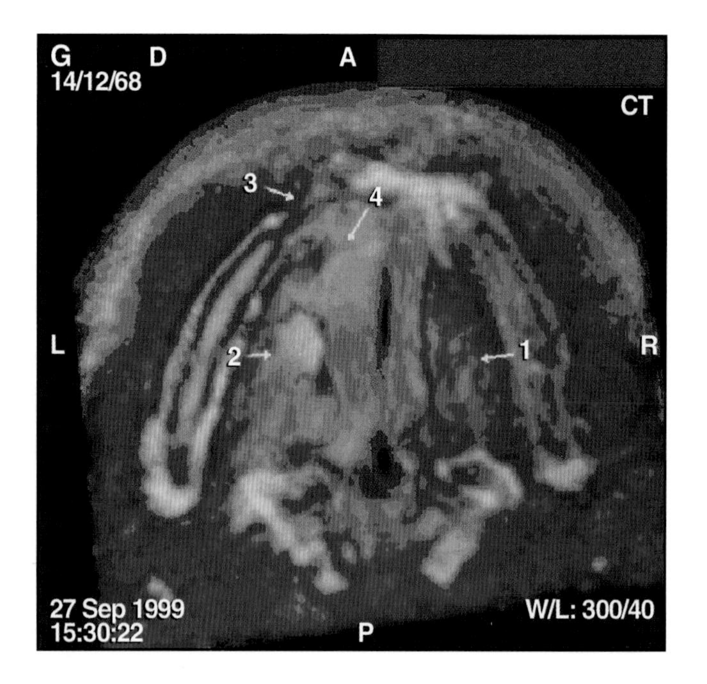

Fig 7–29. Imaging of postsurgical trauma after laryngeal shave (Adam's apple resection) in a transsexual. Analysis of lesion shows: 1. Hypertrophy of arytenoid muscle, 2. Intramuscular calcification (posthematoma), 3. Postsurgical trauma, 4. Tear of vocal ligament

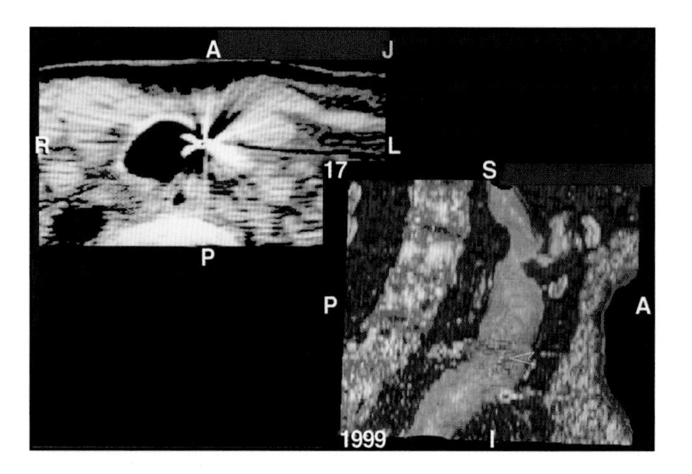

Fig 7–30. Imaging of a postoperative clip and scar in the trachea.

Conclusion

For decades, CT and MR imaging have provided images with satisfactory details of the vocal tract. At the dawn of the third millenium, the dynamic of incremental scanning with helical scanning has already created a new horizon for a better understanding of laryngeal structure and function. Moreover, the vocal scan with volume acquisition, and virtual endoscopy by fly-through (virtual dissection) gives an indispensable adjunct to the new generation of otolaryngologists performing simulation surgery and dynamic anatomic study.

Acknowledgment With special thanks to Jean-Bernard Lenczner, MD, Radiologist; Director du Centre Jean Mermoz (Drancy – France) for his contribution.

References

1. Albers-Schonberg H. *Die Röntgentechnick.* Hambourg: Lucas Gräfe & Sillem; 1903.
2. Beclere A. La radiographie et la radioscopie dans les hôpitaux. *La Presse Médicale.* 21 Octobre 1899; No. 84.
3. Santini EN. *La Photographie à Travers les Corps Opaques par les Rayons Electriques, Cathodiques et de Roentgen.* Paris: Ch. Mendel;1896.
4. Pfahler GE. The early history of roentgenology in Philadelphia 1899–1920. *Am J of Roentgenol.* 1956;75(1): 14–22.
5. Glasser O. The genealogy of the Roentgen rays. *Am J Roentgenol.* 1933;30(2):180–200.
6. Roentgen WC. *Und die Geschichte der Röntgenstrahlen.* Berlin: Springer-Verlag; 1959.
7. Londe A. *Traité Pratique de Radiographie et de Radioscopie.* Paris: Gauthier-Villars; 1898.
8. Glasser O. The genealogy of the Roentgen rays. *Am J Roentgenol.* 1933;30(3):348–367.
9. Lomon, Comandon. La radiocinématographie par la radiographie des écrans renforçateurs. *Bulletins et Mémoires de la Société de Radiologie Médicale de Paris.* 1911:127–135.
10. Mosher HP. X-rays study of movements of the tongue, epiglottis and hyoid bone in swallowing. *Laryngoscope.* 1927;37:235–262.
11. Reynolds RJ. Sixty years of radiology. *Br J Radiol.* 1956; 29(341):238–245.
12. Jaubert de Beaujeu. Les écrans renforçateurs. *Annales d'Electrologie et Radiologie.* 1913:155–168.
13. Morgan RH. Screen intensification. *Am J Roentgenol.* 1956; 75(1):14–31
14. Schinz HR. *60 Jahre Medizinische Radiologie.* Stuttgart: G. Thieme; 1959.
15. Momose KJ, MacMillian AS Jr. Roentgenologic investigation of the larynx and trachea. *Radiol Clin North Am.* 1978;16:321–341.
16. Maguire GH. The larynx: simplified radiological examination using heavy filtration and high voltage radiography. *Radiology.* 1966;87:102–110.
17. Maguire GH, Beigue RA. Selective filtration: a practical approach to high kilovoltage radiography. *Radiology.* 1965;85:345–351.
18. Ardran GM, Ebrys RE. Tomography of the larynx. *Clin Radiol.* 1965;16:369.
19. Hounsfield GN. Computed medical imaging. *Journal de Radiologie.* 1980;61(6–7):459–468.
20. Laugier A. "De Roentgen à Becquerel. La radiologie a 75 ans. *Concours Médical.* 1971;93(17):3174–3202.
21. Castelijns JA, Gerritsen GJ, Kaiser MC, et al. Invasion of laryngeal cartilage by cancer: comparison of CT and MR imaging. *Radiology.* 1988;16:199–206.
22. Lufkin RB, Hanafee WN. Application of surface coil to MR anatomy of the larynx. *Am J Roentgenol.* 1985;145: 483–489.
23. Lufkin RB, Hanafee WN, Wortham D, Hoover L. Larynx and hypopharynx: MR imaging with surface coils. *Radiology.* 1986;158:747–754.
24. Doust BD, Ting YM: *Xeroradiography of the larynx. Radiology.* 1975;110:727–731.
25. Abitbol J. *Atlas of Laser Surgery.* San Diego, Calif: Singular Publishing Group; 1995:101–104.
26. Powers WE, McGee HH, Seaman WB. The contrast examination of larynx and pharynx. *Radiology.* 1957;68: 169–172.
27. Kostakoglu L, Wong JC, Barrington SF, Cronin BF, Dynes AM, Maisey MN. Speech-related visualization of laryngeal muscles with fluorine-18-FDG. *J Nucl Med.* 1996;37:1771–1773.
28. Keem JA, Wainwright J. Ossification of the thyroid, cricoid and arytenoid cartilages. *S Afr J Lab Clin Med.* 1958;4:83–118.
29. Yeager VL, Lawson C, Archer CR. Ossification of laryngeal cartilages as it relates to computed tomography. *Invest Radiol.* 1985;17:11–19.
30. Kahane JC. Connective tissue changes in the larynx and their effects on voice. *J Voice.* 1987;1:27–30.
31. Kahane JC. Histologic structure and properties of the human vocal folds. *Ear Nose Throat J.* 1988;67:322–330.
32. Archer C, Yeager VL: Evaluation of laryngeal cartilages by computed tomography. *J Comput Assist Tomogr.* 1979;3:604–611.
33. Becker M, Hasso AN. Imaging of malignant neoplasms of the pharynx and larynx. In: Taveras JM, Ferrucci JT, eds. *Radiology: Diagnosis-Imaging-Intervention.* Philadelphia, Pa. JB Lippincott; 1996:1–16.
34. Becker M, Zbaren P, Delavelle J, et al. Neoplastic invasion of the laryngeal cartilage: reassessment of criteria for diagnois at CT. *Radiology.* 1997;203:521–532.
35. Becker M, Zbaren P, Laeng H, et al. Neoplastic invasion of the laryngeal cartilage: Comparison of MR imaging and CT with histopathologic correlation. *Radiology.* 1995;194:661–669.
36. Curtin HD. Imaging of the larynx: current concepts. *Radiology.* 1989;173:1–11.
37. Mafee MF, Schild JA, Michael AS, et al. Cartilage involvement in laryngeal carcinoma: correlation of CT and pathologic macrosection studies. *J Comput Assist Tomogr.* 1984;8:969–973.
38. Mancuso AA, Calcaterra TC, Hanafee WN. Computed tomography of the larynx. *Radiol Clin North Am.* 1978; 16:195–208.
39. Fink BR. *The Human Larynx: A Functional Study.* New York, NY: Raven Press; 1975:31–48.
40. Lampert H. Zur Kenntnis des Platyrrhinenkehlkopfes. *Morphol Jb.* 1926;55: 607–654.
41. Napier J. *The Roots of Mankind.* New York, NY: Harper and Row; 1970:29.
42. Napier JR, Walker AC. Vertical clinging and leaping—a newly recognized category of locomotor behavior of primates. *Folia Primatol.* 1967;6:204–219.
43. Von Leden H, Moore P. The larynx and voice: the function of the normal larynx (Motion Picture). *Arch Otolaryngol.* 1957;66:735.
44. Yanagihara N, Von Leden H. The cricothyroid muscle during phonation. Electromyographic, aerodynamic, and acoustic studies. *Ann Otol Rhinol Laryngol.* 1996; 75:987–1006.

45. Curtin HD. The larynx. In: Som PM, Curtin HD, eds. *Head and Neck Imaging*. 3rd ed. St Louis, Mo: Mosby; 1996: 612–707.
46. Mancuso AA. Evaluation and staging of laryngeal and hypopharyngeal cancer by computed tomography and magnetic resonance imaging. In: Silver CE, ed. *Laryngeal Cancer*. New York, NY: Thieme; 1991:46–94.
47. Mafe MF, Schild JA, Valvassori GE, Capek V. Computed tomography of the larynx: correlation with anatomic and pathologic studies in cases of laryngeal carcinoma. *Radiology*. 1983;147:123–128.
48. Lindsay JR. Laryngocele ventricularis. *Ann Otol Rhinol Laryngol*. 1940;49:661–673.
49. Ardran GM, Kemp FH, Manen L. Closure of the larynx. *Br J Radiol*. 1953;26:497–509.
50. Fink BR. The mechanism of closure of the human larynx. *Trans Am Acad Ophthalmol Otolaryngol*. 1956;60:117–127.
51. Ardran GM, Kemp FH, Manen L. The mechanism of the larynx. Part 1: the movement of the arytenoid and cricoid cartilages. *Br J Radiol*. 1966;39:641–654.
52. Ardran GM, Kemp FH, Manen L. The mechanism of the larynx. Part 2: the epiglottis and closure of the larynx. *Br J Radiol*. 1967;40:372–389.
53. Fink BR. *The Human Larynx: A Functional Study*. New York, NY: Raven; 1975:48–52.
54. Maue WM. *Cartilages, Ligaments and Articulations of the Adult Human Larynx* [dissertation] University of Michigan, Ann Arbor, MI: University Microfilms; 1970.
55. Abitbol J. *Voice Performers and Voice Fatigue*. San Diego, Calif: Singular Publishing Group; 1987.
56. García M. Observations on the human voice. *Proc Roy Soc (London)*. 1855;7:399–420.
57. Sataloff RT, Abaza M, Mandel S, Mañon-Espillat R. Laryngeal electromyography. *Curr Opin Otolaryngol Head Neck Surg*. 2000;8:524–529.
58. Metes A, Hoffstein V, Direnfeld V, Chapnick JS. Three-dimensional CT reconstruction and volume measurements of the pharyngeal airway before and after maxillofacial surgery in obstructive sleep apnea. *J Otolaryngol*. 1993;22:20–24.
59. Bushberg JT, Seibert JA, Leidholdt EM, Boone JM. X-ray computed tomography. In: Passano III, WM, ed. *The Essential Physics of Medical Imaging*. Baltimore, Md: Williams & Wilkins; 1994:239–290.
60. Spreer J, Krahe T, Jung G, et al. Spiral versus conventional CT in routine examinations of the neck. *J Comput Assist Tomogr*. 1995;19(6):905–910.
61. Craven CM, Nak KS, Blanshard KS, et al. Multispiral three-dimensional computed tomography in the investigations of craniosynostosis: technique optimization. *Br J Radiol*. 1995;68:724–730.
62. Hermans R, Marchal G, Feenstra L, et al. Spiral CT of the temporal bone: value of image reconstruction at submillimetric table increments. *Neuroradiology*. 1995;37:150–154.
63. Schmalfuss IM, Mancuso AA. Protocols for helical CT of the head and neck. In: *Helical (Spiral) Computed Tomography*. Philadelphia, Pa: Lippincott-Raven; 1998:11–23.
64. Mancuso AA, Hanafee WN. *Computed Tomography and Magnetic Resonance of the Head and Neck*. 2nd ed. Baltimore, Md: Williams & Wilkins; 1985:241–357.
65. Robert Y, Rocourt N, Chevalier D, Duhamel A, Carcasset S, Lemaitre L. Helical CT of the larynx: a comparative study with conventional CT scan. *Clin Radiol*. 1996; 521:882–885.
66. Rodenwaldt J, Niehaus HH, Kopka L, Grabbe E. Spiral CT in arytenoid cartilage dislocation: the optimization of the study parameters with a cadaver phantom and its clinical evaluation. *Rofo Fortschr Geb Rontgenstr Neuen Bildgeb Verfahr*. 1998;168:180–184.
67. Barnes GT, Lakshminarayanan AV. Conventional and spiral computed tomography: physical principles and image quality considerations. In: Lee JKT, Stanley RL, Sagel SS, Heiken JP, eds. *Computed Body Tomography With MRI Correlation*. Philadelphia, Pa: Lippincott-Raven; 1998:1–20.
68. Sataloff RT, Rao VM, Hawkshaw M, Lyons K, Spiegel JR. Cricothyroid joint injury. *J Voice*. 1998;12:112–116.
69. Schaefer SD. Use of CT scanning in the management of the acutely injured larynx. *Otolaryngol Clin North Am*. 1991;24:31–36.
70. Konowitz PM, Lawson W, Som PM, Urchen ML, Breakstone BA, Biller HF. Laryngeal paraganglioma: update on diagnosis and treatment. *Laryngoscope*. 1988;98:40–49.
71. Brink JA. Technical aspects of helical (spiral) CT. *Radiol Clin North Am*. 1995;33:825–841.
72. Silverman PM, Zeiberg AS, Sessions RB, Troost TR, Davros WJ, Zeman RK. Helical CT of the upper airway: normal and abnormal findings on three-dimensional reconstructed images. *Am J Roentgenol*. 1995;165:541–546.
73. Yumoto E, Sanuki T, Hyodo M, Yasuhara Y. Three-dimensional endoscopic mode for observating laryngeal structures by helical computed tomography. *Laryngoscope*. 1997;107:1530–1537.
74. Kallmes DF, Phillips CD. The normal anterior commissure of the glottis. *Am J Roentgenol*. 1997;168:1317–1319.
75. McEnery KW, Wilson AJ, Murphy WA Jr, Marushack MM. Spiral CT imaging of the musculoskeletal system: a phantom study. *Radiology*. 1992;185:118.
76. Ney DR, Fishman EK, Kawashima A, Robertson DD Jr, Scott WW. Comparison of helical and serial CT with regard to three-dimensional imaging of musculoskeletal anatomy. *Radiology*. 1992;185:865–869.
77. Silverman PM, Korobkin M. High resolution computed tomography of the normal larynx. *Am J Roentgenol*. 1983;140:875–880.
78. Silverman PM, Zeiberg AS, Sessions RB, Troost TR, Zeman RK. Three-dimensional (3-D) imaging of the hypopharynx and larynx using helical CT: comparison of radiological and otolaryngological evaluation. *Ann Otol Rhinol Otolaryngol*. 1995;104(6):425–431.
79. Suojanen JN, Mukherji SK, Wippold FJ. Spiral CT of the larynx. *Am J Neuroradiol*. 1994;15:1579–1582.
80. Vining DJ, Shifrin RY, Haponik EF, et al. Virtual bronchoscopy. *Radiology*. 1994;193–261.
81. Frankenthaler R, Moharir VM, Kikinis R, et al. Virtual otoscopy. *Otolaryngol Clin North Am*. 1998;31:183–192.
82. Vining DJ, Liu K, Choplin RH, et al. Virtual bronchoscopy: relationship of virtual reality endobronchial simulations to actual bronchoscopic findings. *Chest*. 1996;109:549–553.

83. Brink JA, Heiken JP, Wang G, et al. Helical CT: principles and technical considerations. *Radiographics*. 1994;14: 887–893.
84. Zeiberg AS, Silverman PM, Sessions RB, et al. Helical (spiral) CT of the upper airway with three dimensional imaging: technique and clinical assessment. *Am J Roentgenol*. 1996;166:293–299.
85. Lacrosse M, Trigauz JP, Vanbeers BE, et al. 3D spiral CT of the tracheobronchial tree. *J Comput Assist Tomogr*. 1995;19:341–347.
86. Burke AJ, et al. Evaluation of airway obstruction using virtual endoscopy. *Laryngoscope*. 2000;110:23–29.
87. Jolesz FA, Lorensen WE, Shinmoto H, et al. Interactive virtual endoscopy. *Am J Roentgenol*. 1997;169:1229–1235.
88. Rodenwaldt J; Kopka L. Roedel R, et al. 3D virtual endoscopy of the upper airway: optimization of the scan parameters in a cadaver phantom and clinical assessment. *J Comput Assist Tomogr*. 1997;21(3):405–411.
89. Fried MV, et al. Virtual laryngoscopy. *Ann Otol Rhinol Laryngol*. 1999;108(3):221–226.
90. Moharir, et al. Computer-assisted three-dimensional reconstruction of head and neck tumors. *Laryngoscope*. 1998;108:1592–1598.
91. Wiegand DA, Channin DS. The surgical workstation: surgical planning using generic software. *Otolaryngol Head Neck Surg*. 1993;109:434–440.
92. Eisele DW, Richtsmeier WJ, Graybeal JC, Koch WM, Zinreich SJ. Three-dimensional models for head and neck tumor treatment planning. *Laryngoscope*. 1994; 104:433–439.
93. Pototschnig C, Veolklein C, Dessl A, Giacomuzzi S, Jaschke W, Thumfart WF. Virtual endoscopy in otorhinolaryngology by postprocessing of helical computed tomography. *Otolaryngol Head Neck Surg*. 1998;119: 536–539.
94. Gallivan RP, Nguyen TH, Armstrong WB. Head and neck computed tomography virtual endoscopy: evaluation of a new imaging technique. *Laryngoscope*. 1999;109: 1570–1579.
95. Vining DJ, Liu K. Choplin RH, Haponik EF. Virtual bronchoscopy: relationships of virtual reality endobronchial simulations to actual bronchoscopic findings. *Chest*. 1996;109:549–553.
96. Vining DJ, Shifrin RY, Grishaw EK. Virtual colonoscopy [abstract]. *Radiology*. 1994;193:446.
97. Gilani S, Norbash AM, Ringl H, Rubin GD, Napel S, Terris DJ. Virtual endoscopy of the paranasal sinuses using perspective volume rendered helical sinus computed tomography. *Laryngoscope*. 1997;107:25–29.
98. Suojanen JN, Mukherji SK, Wippold FJ: Spiral CT of the larynx. *Am J Neuroradiol*. 1993;15:1579–1582.

8

New Dimensions in Measuring Voice Treatment Outcome and Quality of Life

Michael S. Benninger, Glendon M. Gardner, and Barbara H. Jacobson

The voice demands of performing vocalists can lead them to dysfunction and injury. As important as the quality of the human voice is to any individual, the importance of maintaining excellent voice quality in performers is particularly significant. In order to care for performers, it is critical to be able to evaluate not only the sound of their voices but also their perception of their own voice quality. The ability to evaluate objectively both the normal and the disordered human voice has improved dramatically in the last two decades, driven by better understanding of the anatomy and physiology and development of new technologies. With this information, the voice clinician can now make reproducible assessments, recommend treatment, and measure the effects of interventions. Despite the exponential growth in assessment capabilities, there is no agreed-upon gold standard for evaluating voice; and this is particularly true for performers whose voice demands are often exceptional and for whom minute changes in quality can have dramatic effects on the quality of a performance.

Over the past decade, there has also been a movement in the medical community to assess the impact of disease, treatment or non-treatment, on the patient's perception of quality of life. In simplest terms, this quality of life evaluation has been called an assessment of "outcome," and efforts to measure changes in outcome objectively have led to creation of validated outcomes measurement tools or instruments. Although outcomes assessment of voice disorders is in its infancy, there has been great progress. This chapter will describe the outcomes and quality of life movement, review contemporary outcomes assessment as it relates to the abnormal human voice, and address the critical role of outcomes evaluations in the care and prevention of voice disorders in performers.

Quality of Life and Outcomes

Health is a multidimensional concept that, according to the World Health Organization, incorporates physical, mental and social states.[1] Handicap is defined as "a social, economic, or environmental disadvantage resulting from an impairment or disability"; and disability is defined as "restriction or lack of ability manifested in the performance of daily tasks."[2] The degree of change in the parameters of physical, mental, or social status is considered to represent an outcome. These outcomes, however, depend on a number of factors including the baseline level of function, other concomitant medical conditions, a person's perception of quality of life, and cultural or societal influences. In general, medical care strives to prevent and eliminate disease and thereby improve the quality of a patient's life. Traditionally, assessment of only a patient's physical function was used to determine the impact of health or disease. This practice limits the clinician's ability to assess the emotional or social impact of disease or its treatment. An acknowledgment of these limitations led to the development of a whole new way of looking at health and disease, and has been coined the "outcomes" movement.

Traditional assessment of outcomes in medicine has been largely through the perspective of the treating physician or other clinician (eg, as nurses or speech-language pathologists). Therefore, an outcome was identified via changes in the physical examination, an improvement or change in symptoms and functions, or changes in laboratory tests or x-ray examinations. Classically, the simplest two measurements of an outcome of treatment are the presence or absence of disease or the patient living or dying. Despite their simplicity, these gross measures are very important in relationship to medical care. However, although these distinctions are significant, they are often inadequate for assessing general quality of life impact. For example, surgical treatment may be successful for the management of a vocal fold polyp, yielding complete return of normal voice function. However, if the treatment of the polyp resulted in a missed important business appointment, missed audition or performance, or even the ability to cheer at a sports event, its impact on quality of life might be significantly different from the unequivocal success perceived by the surgeon.

The medical profession's early attempts to assess quality of life have revolved around questionnaires, which served to identify key issues that patients may have in relationship to their disease.[3] These questionnaires usually focused on questions that the physician or other person administering the questionnaire felt were important and often did not include factors that the person completing the questionnaire was most concerned about. Over time, following multiple revisions and adaptations, these questionnaires have tended to address, to some degree, both of these perspectives. Furthermore, early questionnaires were not statistically validated; and therefore, one could not be sure that they truly measured what they intended to measure, or whether responses by individuals with disease were different from those without disease. It was also not clear whether the questionnaire maintained its validity over time so that a person who had no change in status would answer questions similarly at different times.

The realization that many critical issues are related both to the presence of a disease or to its treatment and efforts to measure the entire impact of health on individuals and society have driven the outcomes movement. Outcomes research attempts to observe patients in their typical environments and uses patient-centered measures.

Measuring Quality of Life

Quality of life measurement instruments have been developed to attempt to measure the multidimensional nature of health. The questions and items within these tests usually cluster around broad health-related areas that can be measured in direct relationship to disease or response to treatment. Probably the best recognized and most widely utilized quality of life measurement tool is the Medical Outcomes Study 36-Item Short Form General-Health Survey, or "SF-36".[4-6] This instrument is self-administered and assesses eight domains of health that are affected commonly by disease or its treatment: physical functioning, role functioning, social functioning, mental health, bodily pain, general health, vitality, and health transition.[4-6] Each of these subscales provides a score that is reliable and a valid measure of health for that particular dimension. The SF-36 has been used to evaluate a wide range of health issues and to compare quality of life as it relates to different disease processes.[7]

One of the disadvantages of using general health measurement tools to evaluate specific disorders is that they may not assess well the specific impact of the disease on an individual and how it may be affected by other medical conditions. This has led to an effort to develop disease-specific outcomes measurements tools.[8] The creation of these outcomes measurement tools requires a comprehensive, statistically validated assessment of reliability, predictability, reproducibility, responsiveness, and interpretability. In general, they should be easy to use (low burden) and should assist in the evaluation of the specific problems they were designed to assess.

The human voice is unique in all of the animal kingdom and is the fundamental method of human communication. The range of frequency and flexibility of sound production allows the voice to express emotions of the human soul. The voice laughs and cries, yells and whispers, sings and hums, recognizes danger or placidity. For "professional vocalists," both singers and speakers, the voice serves as the primary source of livelihood and income. It allows most others a means to carry out the activities of their occupation or avocation. In general, people take the voice for granted. It is there when you need it, and it usually performs at the level of expectations of the individual. Even for a professional vocalist who has spent years refining the quality and attributes of his or her voice, it is usually dependable and predictable. When the voice fails any person, the impact on general communication for social and occupational needs gains importance. When the voice fails the professional vocalist, the impact is often even more substantial, if not devastating, and potentially career ending.

Developing measures to assess voice quality and health impact has been difficult. Most current measurements deal with objective specifics of voice production; the mechanics of voice production such as posture, support, and resonance; or specific physiologic actions such as vocal fold vibration. Although these measures have great value and are critical for improved understanding and training of the voice, they fail to measure either the importance of voice production and the impact of voice disorders on the overall quality of life of the voice user or the effects from an intervention or treatment. Even with objective tests, there are no generally agreed-on gold standards of measurement. Furthermore, different objective tests have been designed for different measures of function, such as fundamental frequency, frequency range, airflow parameters, perturbation, or vocal fold vibration. Variation in the performance and interpretation of these tests also occurs among clinicians. These limitations have prevented valid comparisons of the impact of an intervention in different environments or comparisons of two different interventions.

Although improvements in objective tests would be expected to correlate with improvements in outcome, severity of disease as measured by these tests does not necessarily measure the impact to an individual. Minimal variations in pitch would likely have a much greater impact for a performing vocalist than for a person who has minimal voice demands. A cured small laryngeal cancer may prevent a singer or other speaker from performing. Its impact on the quality of his or her life would be expected to be greater and likely to be represented poorly by objective tests.

With the development of general quality of life surveys such as the SF-36, the clinician can assess the impact of disease or treatment on quality of life. Furthermore, comparisons can be made between patients and others without the disorder or between patients with two or more different disorders. Our recent study showed significant differences in perception of quality of life between dysphonic (disordered voice) patients and unaffected average people in the United States.[7] When evaluating the specific domains of the SF-36, we found that the domains of "role function emotion" and "role function physical" were both significantly different between dysphonic and nondysphonic people. These two domains deal with the ability to perform work and other daily tasks as a result of the physical or emotional impact of a disorder. Because voice problems might be expected to impact on work and other daily activities, this finding was not unexpected. The "social functioning" score was also worse in dysphonic patients. Because "physical functioning," "vitality," and "mental health" scores were also worse for dysphonic patients than for normals, it can be seen that these voice disorders impact a broader sense of well-being than the specific symptoms. Objective tests of voice function or standard questionnaires would not be expected to measure these quality of life impacts.

The Voice Handicap Index

Traditionally, outcomes for patients with voice disorders have been measured within a clinical or biomedical frame of reference. The variables that are used to indicate a favorable or unfavorable treatment outcome do not rely on attitudinal input from the patients. In an effort to shift the focus from the clinicians' judgments to patients' self-perceptions of their voice disorders, we developed the Voice Handicap Index (VHI)[8] (Fig 8–1). The VHI consists of 30 statements that reflect the variety of experiences that a patient with a voice disorder may encounter. Patients note a frequency of each experience on a 5-point equal-appearing scale (never = 0, almost never = 1, sometimes = 2, almost always = 3, always = 4), with a maximal total score of 120. The VHI is able to measure not only the physical effects of their voice problem but also the functional and emotional aspects, or subscales. The VHI is scored for each of these three individual subscales and a total score. Therefore it can serve as an independent, objective measure of voice dysfunction on quality of life.

Our studies show that the impact of disordered voice on quality of life is substantial even when compared to other chronic diseases such as angina, sciatica, chronic sinusitis, or back pain, particularly in the areas of social functioning and role playing.[7] Overall, however, other chronic diseases tend to produce worse scores than dysphonia.

Because the SF-36 is scaled only relating to the individual domains and not for a total score, direct overall total comparisons to the VHI cannot be made. Nonetheless, by evaluating the individual domains, a comparison of quality of life impact of various disorders can be made between the SF-36 and VHI. For example, when attempting to correlate the VHI with the SF-36, strong correlations were found between the total VHI scores and the individual subscales to the SF-36 domains of social functioning; role functioning, emotional and physical; and mental health. The greatest disability of voice patients is in the functional areas, as was validated by our study in assessing the relationship of the VHI to the SF-36.[7] Because patients with voice disorders generally do not have significant changes in bodily pain, general health, vitality, and general physical functioning, the VHI would not be expected to be very sensitive to changes in these domains of the SF-36.

Patients with vocal fold paralysis had worse scores in many of the domains of the SF-36 than other dysphonic patients, particularly in the domains of role playing physical and physical functioning.[7] This is likely due to the impact of vocal fold paralysis on lift-

3622008629

VOICE HANDICAP INDEX (VHI)

Today's Date [ ][ ] - [ ][ ] - [ ][ ]

First Name

Last Name

MRN

Birth Date (Month - Day - Year)

Age

O Male
O Female

Provider

Date of Operation (Month - Day - Year)

Type of Visit: O New Visit O Return Visit O Pre-Treatment O Post Medical Treatment O Pre-Surgical Treatment O Post Surgical Treatment

Diagnosis:
O Functional Dysphonia
O Spasmodic Dysphonia
O Other Neurogenic Dysphonia
O Bowing/ Presbylarnges
O Benign Masses (polyp/ nodule/ MRC)
O Edidermoid Cyst/ Sulcus
O Vocal Fold Paralysis
O a) unilateral
O b) bilateral
O c) SLN
O Reflux Laryngitis
O Leukoplakia
O Benign Laryngeal Tumor
O Malignant Laryngeal Tumor
O Other (Describe)

Instructions: These are statements that many people have used to describe their voices and the effects of their voices on their lives. Check the response that indicates how frequently you have the same experience.

	Never	Almost Never	Sometimes	Almost Always	Always
F1. My voice makes it difficult for people to hear me.	0	0	0	0	0
P2. I run out of air when I talk.	0	0	0	0	0
F3. People have difficulty understanding me in a noisy room.	0	0	0	0	0
P4. The sound of my voice varies throughout the day.	0	0	0	0	0
F5. My family has difficulty hearing me when I call them throughout the house.	0	0	0	0	0
F6. I use the phone less often than I would like.	0	0	0	0	0
E7. I'm tense when talking with others because of my voice.	0	0	0	0	0
F8. I tend to avoid groups of people because of my voice.	0	0	0	0	0
E9. People seem irritated with my voice.	0	0	0	0	0
P10. People ask "What's wrong with your voice?"	0	0	0	0	0
F11. I speak with friends, neighbors, or relatives less often because of my voice.	0	0	0	0	0
F12. People ask me to repeat myself when speaking face-to-face.	0	0	0	0	0
P13. My voice sounds creaky and dry.	0	0	0	0	0
P14. I feel as though I have to strain to produce voice.	0	0	0	0	0
E15. I find other people don't understand my voice problem.	0	0	0	0	0

Fig 8–1. The figure shows the 30 items included in the Voice Handicap Index with instructions as to how to complete the form. The questions are itemized by letter and number. The letters (P, F, and E) are representative of the three subscales (Physical, Functional, Emotional). The scores for each of the items with the same letter can be added to give the subscale score. The three subscale scores are added to give a total score. A change in 8 points for an individual subscale or 18 points for the total score is considered a significant change.[8] *(continues)*

7177008628

	Never	Almost Never	Sometimes	Almost Always	Always
F16. My voice difficulties restrict my personal and social life.	0	0	0	0	0
P17. The clarity of my voice is unpredictable.	0	0	0	0	0
P18. I try to change my voice to sound different.	0	0	0	0	0
F19. I feel left out of conversations because of my voice.	0	0	0	0	0
P20. I use a great deal of effort to speak.	0	0	0	0	0
P21. My voice is worse in the evening.	0	0	0	0	0
F22. My voice problem causes me to lose income.	0	0	0	0	0
E23. My voice problem upsets me.	0	0	0	0	0
E24. I am less out-going because of my voice problem.	0	0	0	0	0
E25.My voice makes me handicapped.	0	0	0	0	0
P26. My voice "gives out" on me in the middle of speaking.	0	0	0	0	0
E27. I feel annoyed when people ask me to repeat.	0	0	0	0	0
E28. I feel embarrassed when people ask me to repeat.	0	0	0	0	0
E29. My voice makes me feel incompentent.	0	0	0	0	0
E30. I'm ashamed of my voice problem.	0	0	0	0	0

P Scale

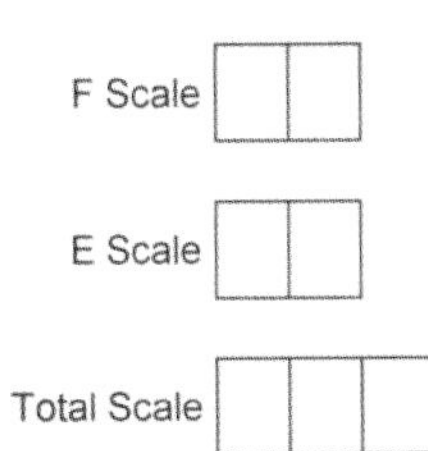

F Scale

E Scale

Total Scale

Please circle the word that matches how you feel your voice is today.

Normal Mild Moderate Severe

Fig 8–1. *(continued)*

ing and straining and other daily activities. In general, paralysis patients appear to be more disabled and have poorer overall quality of life than the other categories of patients with dysphonia as measured by both the SF-36 and VHI. When evaluated with the VHI, the vocal fold edema group had better scores for the total, functional and physical scores than the patients with vocal fold masses (eg, nodules or polyps). In general, individuals with vocal fold paralysis had worse scores than other individuals with voice disorders as measured by the VHI.[7]

In a subsequent study, we attempted to compare the VHI and its three subscales to various objective tests. We were able to show that the functional subscale of the VHI correlated well with both signal-to-noise ratio (SNR) and maximum phonatory time (MPT). Other measures, such as jitter, shimmer, fundamental frequency, semitones, and airflow volume had little correlation with the patients' perception of the impact of their voice disorder on quality of life as measured by the VHI.[9] Although these specific measures did not correlate with the VHI, as the voices of patients worsened as measured by the objective laboratory parameters, a corresponding change in the VHI scores occurred.[9] Objective laboratory measures and the VHI cannot be seen as interchangeable. There are corresponding appropriate changes in both with worsening voice, but strong correlations only in SNR and MPT. This would suggest that the tests likely measure different parameters of voice. It also may suggest that the objective laboratory tests now used may measure specific parameters of voice, but not the global impact of a voice disorder on the patient's emotional, functional, and physical perception of health.

The VHI, therefore, is a statistically validated, objective test that can be used to measure the emotional, physical, functional, and total quality of life impact of a voice disorder. It can be used to measure the response to treatment or nontreatment, perform research related to voice, or evaluate patients in different clinical environments. In the absence of definitive, established gold standards for measuring voice, the VHI may serve as the template for assessing voice outcome. Finally, the VHI can be used along with other objective tools or tests to assess the characteristics of an individual's voice and the impact of those characteristics on quality of voice and quality of life. A few other voice quality of life instruments have been developed. These include the GRBAS,[10] Voice-Related Quality of Life (V-RQOL),[11] the Dysphonia Severity Index,[12] and the Voice Outcome Survey (VOS).[13] All have certain advantages and disadvantages for use in patients with voice disorders, but ultimately all are trying to develop a consistent way of evaluating the vocal quality of patients.

Recently the VHI has been adapted for optical scanning, which allows for immediate interpretation of the three subscales and total score for a voice-disordered patient. In addition, the data are rolled into a database so that the evolution of the disease or response to treatment can be determined for an individual patient or for a group of patients with similar diseases. The forms can be incorporated directly into the database either from fax or digital data (see Fig 8–1).

Outcomes Measurement and Professional Voice

The association among vocal well-being, general health status, and quality of life is probably most evident in the professional voice user with voice pathology. This distinct group of patients would benefit greatly from the application of outcomes research efforts. The impact of specific pathologies on vocal performance and quality of life varies depending on the style and nature of the performer, the severity of the pathology, and the timing of the next rehearsal or performance. For example, a mild amount of Reinke's edema in a soprano auditioning with the Metropolitan Opera may result in a significant decrease in performance quality. Furthermore, subjective and objective analyses of the voice may show few or no abnormalities except when the voice is used at the extremes of pitch and loudness. Conversely, noticeable vocal nodules in a rap musician whose next performance is in 3 months may have little effect on total quality of life, even though subjective and objective analyses show marked abnormalities. Certain musical styles seem to be more tolerant of variability in pitch range and voice quality. A raspy, somewhat sultry voice may be perceived as desirable in certain styles of pop-rock music. If this raspy quality is secondary to chronic vocal nodules, the treatment of choice may not be surgical excision of the lesion. In such a case, information provided by measures like the VHI and the SF-36 Health Survey would contribute to the determination of optimal treatment recommendations for this patient. An assessment of the impact of the voice pathology on the patient's performance and quality of life, from the patient's perspective, is paramount.

Rosen and Murry have used the VHI to evaluate the perception of severity of voice disorders in singers compared with nonsingers.[14] They found that singers had lower scores than nonsingers, suggesting that a lower VHI score may still represent a significant handicap in singers and should not be disregarded. They also noted that singers with vocal fold nodules had lower mean VHI scores than singers with polyps or cysts and classical singers had lower scores than other singers.[14] This information shows us that evaluating outcomes and quality of voice and life in singers is an evolving area requiring ongoing diligence and study. The ultimate goal is to use these newer outcomes tools as part of the objective tools to help maintain good vocal health in performers or to return them to vocal health when they develop a voice disorder.

Conclusion

The future challenges related to outcomes research in voice will revolve around the application of these types of instruments to allow identification of factors important to patients. The first challenge is to determine the severity of a patient's handicap or disability from a particular disorder. This will impact the aggressiveness of treatment, or, in some cases, whether or not to treat. The second challenge is to utilize outcomes research to identify the best treatment. This also may be used to develop new treatments that take into consideration the vocalist's response to treatment. Finally, voice outcomes research should focus on how improvement of a specific disorder will impact the global quality of life for the voice user and for his or her family.

The future in outcomes research in voice is bright. Much effort is being directed at improvement of quality of life and its measurement. These efforts in combination with traditional voice evaluations, basic voice research science and prospective, randomized clinical trials should have a dramatic impact on voice care in the future. The application of objective outcomes tools such as the VHI and the SF-36 to performing vocalists will assure that the global impact of their voice disorders on quality of life is measured. Relationships between demands on the voice and levels of voice training and the magnitude of the impact of a voice disorder will be understood better. The information that results from the outcomes research movement, as it is applied to voice pathologies, should assist otolaryngologists, speech-language pathologists, and voice teachers in providing more realistic prognoses and recommendations to the patient, taking into account the multidimensional, and often idiosyncratic, aspects of the professional voice and its care.

References

1. World Health Organization. The economics of health and disease. *WHO Chronicle.* 1971;25:20–24.
2. World Health Organization. *International Classification of Impairments, Disabilities and Handicaps: A Manual of Classification Relating to the Consequences of Disease.* Geneva, Switzerland: World Health Organization; 1980.
3. Benninger MS, Gardner GM, Jacobson BH, Grywalski C. New dimensions in measuring voice treatment outcomes. In: Sataloff R. *Professional Voice: The Science and Art of Clinical Care.* 2nd ed. San Diego, Calif: Singular Publishing Group, Inc; 1996:789–794.
4. Ware JE Jr, Sherbourne CD. The MOS 36-Item Short Form Health Survey (SF-36). I. Conceptual framework and item selection. *Med Care.* 1993;30:473–483.
5. McHorney CA, Ware JE Jr, Raczek AE. The MOS 36-Item Short Form Health Survey (SF-36). II. Psychometric and clinical tests of validity in measuring physical and mental health constructs. *Med Care.* 1993;31:247–263.
6. McHorney CA, Ware JE Jr, Lu JF, Sherbourne CD. The MOS 36-Item Short Form Health Survey (SF-36). III. Tests of data quality, scaling, assumptions and reliability across diverse patient groups. *Med Care.* 1994;32:40–66.
7. Benninger MS, Ahuja AS, Gardner G, Grywalski C. Assessing outcomes for dysphonic patients. *J Voice.* 1998;12:540–550.
8. Jacobson BH, Johnson A, Grywalski C, et al. The Voice Handicap Index (VHI): development and validation. *Am J Speech-Lang Pathol.* 1997;6:66–70.
9. Ahuja A, Benninger MS, Grywalski C, Gardner G. Correlation between the Voice Handicap Index with objective acoustic and aerodynamic measurements. Presented at the Annual Meeting of the Triologic Society; May 2002; Boca Raton, Fla.
10. Wuyts FL, De Bodt MS, Van de Heyning PH. Is the reliability of a visual analog scale higher than an ordinal scale? An experiment with the GRBAS scale for the perceptual evaluation of dysphonia. *J Voice.* 1999;13:508–517.
11. Hogikyan ND, Sethuraman G. Validation of an instrument to measure Voice-Related Quality of Life (V-RQOL). *J Voice.* 1999;13:557–569.
12. Wuyts F, DeBodt MS, Molenberghs G, et al. The Dysphonia Severity Index: an objective measure of voice quality based on a multiparameter approach. J *Speech Lang Hear Res.* 2000;43:796–808.
13. Gliklich RE, Glovsky RM, Montgomery WW. Validation of a voice outcome survey for unilateral vocal cord paralyis. *Otolaryngol Head Neck Surg.* 1999;120:153–158.
14. Rosen CA, Murry T. Voice Handicap Index in singers. *J Voice.* 2000;14:370–377.

9

Common Medical Diagnoses and Treatments in Patients with Voice Disorders: Introduction and Overview

Robert Thayer Sataloff

Laryngologists specializing in voice devote the majority of their practices to the medical management of benign voice disorders. Indeed, although most of us are active surgeons, the good voice specialist takes pride in avoiding the need for laryngeal surgery through expert medical management. Success depends not only upon an experienced laryngologist, but also on the availability of a voice team including a speech-language pathologist, voice scientist, singing voice specialist, and medical consultants who have acquired special knowledge about voice disorders (neurologists, pulmonologists, endocrinologists, internists, allergists, and others). This chapter provides an overview of many of the benign voice problems encountered by otolaryngologists and current nonsurgical management concepts. It has been included as a convenience suggested by readers of the previous editions. Most topics are covered in greater detail in subsequent chapters.

Numerous medical conditions affect the voice adversely. Many have their origins primarily outside the head and neck. This chapter is not intended to be all-inclusive, but rather to highlight some of the more common and important conditions found in professional voice users seeking medical care.

In the 2286 cases of all forms of voice disorders reported by Brodnitz in 1971,[1] 80% of the disorders were attributed to voice abuse or to psychogenic factors resulting in vocal dysfunction. Of these patients, 20% had organic voice disorders. Of women with organic problems, about 15% had identifiable endocrine causes. A much higher incidence of organic disorders, particularly reflux laryngitis, acute infectious laryngitis, and benign vocal fold masses, is found in this author's practice.

Voice Abuse

When voice abuse is suspected or observed in a patient with vocal complaints, he or she should be referred to a laryngologist who specializes in voice, preferably a physician affiliated with a voice care team.

Common patterns of voice abuse and misuse will not be discussed in detail in this chapter. They are covered elsewhere in this book. Voice abuse and/or misuse should be suspected particularly in patients who complain of voice fatigue associated with voice use, whose voices are worse at the end of a working day or week, and in any patient who is chronically hoarse. Technical errors in voice use may be the primary etiology of a voice complaint or may develop secondarily as a result of a patient's efforts to compensate for voice disturbance from another cause.

Speaking in noisy environments, such as cars and airplanes, is particularly abusive to the voice. So are backstage greetings, postperformance parties, choral conducting, voice teaching, and cheerleading, to name a few. With proper training, all of these vocal activities can be done safely. However, most patients, surprisingly even singers, have little or no training for their speaking voice.

If voice abuse is caused by speaking, treatment should be provided by a licensed, certified speech-language pathologist in the United States or by a phoniatrist in many other countries. In many cases, training the speaking voice benefits singers greatly not only by improving speech, but also by indirectly helping singing technique. Physicians should not hesitate to recommend such training, but it should be performed by an expert speech-language pathologist who specializes in voice. Many speech-language pathologists who are well trained in swallowing rehabilitation, articulation therapy, and other techniques are not trained in voice therapy for the speaking voice; and virtually none are trained through their speech and language degree programs to work with singers with voice disorders.

Conversely, specialized singing training also may be helpful to some voice patients who are not singers, and it is invaluable for patients who are singers. Initial singing training teaches relaxation techniques, develops muscle strength, and should be symbiotic with standard speech therapy. Abuse of the voice during singing is an even more complex problem, as discussed elsewhere in this book.

Infection and Inflammation

Upper Respiratory Tract Infection Without Laryngitis

Although mucosal irritation usually is diffuse, patients sometimes have marked nasal obstruction with little or no sore throat and a "normal" voice. If the laryngeal examination shows no abnormality, a singer or professional speaker with a "head cold" should be permitted to use his or her voice and advised not to try to duplicate his or her usual sound, but rather to accept the insurmountable alterations in self-perception caused by the changes in the supraglottic vocal tract and auditory system. The decision as to whether performing under these circumstances is advisable professionally rests with the voice professional and his or her musical associates. The patient should be cautioned against throat clearing, as this is traumatic and may produce laryngitis. If a cough is present, nonnarcotic medications should be used to suppress it. In addition, the patient should be taught how to "silent cough," which is less traumatic.

Laryngitis With Serious Vocal Fold Injury

Hemorrhage in the vocal folds and mucosal disruption (such as vocal fold tears) associated with acute laryngitis are contraindications to speaking and singing. When these are observed, treatment includes strict voice rest in addition to correction of any underlying disease. Vocal fold hemorrhage in voice professionals is most common in premenstrual women who are using aspirin products or nonsteroidal anti-inflammatory drugs (NSAIDs) for dysmenorrhea. Severe hemorrhage or mucosal scarring may result in permanent alterations in vocal fold vibratory function. In rare instances, surgical intervention may be necessary. The potential gravity of these conditions must be stressed, for singers are generally reluctant to cancel an appearance. As von Leden observed, it is a pleasure to work with "people who are determined that the show must go on when everyone else is determined to goof off."[2] However, patient compliance is essential when serious damage has occurred. At present, acute treatment of vocal fold hemorrhage is controversial, as discussed in chapter 86. Most laryngologists allow the hematoma to resolve spontaneously. Because this sometimes results in an organized hematoma and scar formation requiring surgery, some physicians advocate incision along the superior edge of the vocal fold and drainage of the hematoma in selected cases. Further study is needed to determine optimal therapy guidelines.

Laryngitis Without Serious Damage

Mild to moderate edema and erythema of the vocal folds may result from infectious or from noninfectious causes. In the absence of mucosal disruption or hemorrhage, they are not absolute contraindications to voice use. Noninfectious laryngitis commonly is associated with excessive voice use as in preperformance rehearsals. It may also be caused by other forms of voice abuse and by mucosal irritation (edema and inflammation) produced by allergy, smoke inhalation, and other causes. Mucous stranding between the anterior and middle thirds of the vocal folds is seen commonly in inflammatory laryngitis. Laryngitis sicca is associated with dehydration, dry atmosphere, mouth breathing, and antihistamine therapy. Deficiency of mucosal lubrication causes irritation and coughing and results in mild inflammation. If no pressing professional need for performance exists, inflammatory conditions of the larynx are best treated with relative voice rest in addition to other modalities. Psychologic support is crucial. For example, it is often helpful for the physician to intercede on a singer's behalf and to convey "doctor's orders" directly to agents or theater management. Such mitigation of exogenous stress can be highly therapeutic. However, in some instances, speaking and singing may be permitted. The patient should be instructed to avoid all forms of potential irritation and to rest the voice at all times except during warm-up and performance. Corticosteroids and other medications discussed later may be helpful. If mucosal secretions are copious, low-dose antihistamine therapy may be beneficial, but it must be prescribed with caution and should generally be avoided. Copious, thin secretions are better than scant, thick secretions or excessive dryness. The patient with laryngitis must be kept well hydrated to maintain the desired character of mucosal lubrication. The patient should be instructed to "pee pale," consuming enough water to keep urine diluted.

Infectious laryngitis may be caused by bacteria or viruses. Subglottic involvement, such as tracheitis and bronchitis, frequently indicates a more severe infection, which may be difficult to control in a short period of time. Indiscriminate use of antibiotics must be avoided; however, when the physician is in doubt as to the cause and when a major voice commitment is imminent, vigorous antibiotic treatment is warranted. In this circumstance, the damage caused by allowing progression of a curable condition is greater than the damage that might result from a course of antibiotic therapy for an unproven microorganism while culture results are pending. When a major concert or speech is not imminent, indications for therapy are the same as for the nonsinger or nonprofessional speaker.

Voice rest (absolute or relative) is an important therapeutic consideration in any case of laryngitis and is discussed in greater detail in chapter 69. When no professional commitments are pending, a short course of absolute voice rest may be considered, as it is the safest and most conservative therapeutic intervention. This means absolute silence and communication with a writing pad. The patient must be instructed not to whisper, as this may be an even more traumatic vocal activity than speaking softly. Whistling also involves vocal fold activity and should not be permitted. So does the playing of many musical wind instruments. Absolute voice rest is *necessary* only for serious vocal fold injury such as hemorrhage or mucosal disruption. Even then, it is virtually never indicated for more than 7 to 10 days. Three days are often sufficient. Some excellent laryngologists do not believe voice rest should be used at all. However, absolute voice rest for a few days may be helpful in patients with laryngitis, especially those gregarious, verbal singers who find it difficult to moderate their voice use to comply with relative voice rest instructions. In many instances, considerations of finances and reputation mitigate against a recommendation of voice rest. In advising performers to minimize vocal use, Punt counseled, "Don't say a single word for which you are not being paid."[3] This admonition frequently guides the ailing singer or speaker away from preperformance conversations and backstage greetings and allows a successful series of performances. Patients should also be instructed to speak softly and as infrequently as possible, often at a slightly higher pitch than usual; to avoid excessive telephone use; and to speak with abdominal support as they would in singing. This is relative voice rest, and it is helpful in most cases. An urgent session with a speech-language pathologist is extremely helpful for discussing vocal hygiene and in providing guidelines to prevent voice abuse. Nevertheless, the patient must be aware that some risk is associated with performing with laryngitis even when performance is possible. Inflammation of the vocal folds is associated with increased capillary fragility and increased risk of vocal fold injury or hemorrhage. Many factors must be considered in determining whether a given speech or concert is important enough to justify the potential consequences.

Steam inhalations deliver moisture and heat to the vocal folds and tracheobronchial tree and may be useful. Some people use nasal irrigations, although these have little proven value. Gargling has no proven efficacy, but it is probably harmful only if it involves loud, abusive vocalization as part of the gargling process. Some physicians and patients believe it to be helpful in "moistening the throat," and it may have some relaxing or placebo effect. Ultrasonic treatments, local massage, laryngeal manipulation, psychotherapy, and biofeedback directed at relieving anxiety and decreasing muscle tension may be helpful adjuncts to a broader therapeutic program. However, psychotherapy and biofeedback, in particular, must be expertly supervised if used at all.

Voice lessons given by an expert singing teacher are invaluable. When technical dysfunction is suggested, the singer or actor should be referred to his or her teacher. Even when an obvious organic abnormality is present, referral to a voice teacher is appropriate, especially for younger actors and singers. Numerous "tricks of the trade" permit a voice professional to overcome some of the impairments of a mild illness safely. If a singer plans to proceed with a performance during an illness, he or she should not cancel voice lessons as part of the relative voice rest regimen; rather, a short lesson to ensure optimal technique is extremely useful.

Sinusitis

Chronic inflammation of the mucosa lining the sinus cavities commonly produces thick secretions known as postnasal drip. Postnasal drip can be particularly problematic, because it causes excessive phlegm, which interferes with phonation, and because it leads to frequent throat clearing, which may inflame the vocal folds. Sometimes chronic sinusitis is associated with allergies and can be treated with medications. However, many medications used in the treatment of allergies cause side effects that are unacceptable in professional voice users, particularly mucosal drying. When medication management is not satisfactory in the treatment of chronic sinusitis, functional endoscopic sinus surgery may be appropriate. Acute purulent sinusitis is a different matter. It requires aggressive treatment with antibiotics, sometimes surgical drainage, and treatment of underlying conditions (such as dental abscess).

Allergy

Even mild allergies are more incapacitating to professional voice users than to others. Briefly, patients with mild intermittent allergies can usually be managed with antihistamines, although they should never be tried for the first time immediately prior to a voice performance. Because antihistamines commonly produce unacceptable side effects, trial and error may be needed to find a medication with an acceptable balance between effect and side effect for any individual patient, especially a voice professional. Patients with allergy-related voice disturbances may find hyposensitization a more effective approach than antihistamine use, if they are candidates for such treatment. For voice patients with unexpected allergic symptoms immediately prior to an important voice commitment, corticosteroids should be used rather than antihistamines to minimize the risks of side effects (such as drying and thickening of secretions) that might make voice performance difficult or impossible. Allergies commonly cause voice problems by altering the mucosa and secretions and causing nasal obstruction. Management will not be covered in depth in this brief chapter.

Respiratory Dysfunction

The importance of "the breath" has been well recognized in the field of voice pedagogy. Even a mild degree of obstructive pulmonary disease can result in substantial voice problems. Unrecognized exercise-induced asthma is especially problematic in singers and actors, because bronchospasm may be precipitated by the exercise and airway drying that occurs during voice performance. In such cases, the bronchospastic obstruction on exhalation impairs support. This commonly results in compensatory hyperfunction.

Treatment requires skilled management and collaboration with a pulmonologist and a voice team.[4] Whenever possible, patients should be managed primarily with oral medications; the use of inhalers should minimized. Steroid inhalers should be avoided altogether whenever possible. It is particularly important to recognize that asthma can be induced by the exercise of phonation itself;[5] and in many cases, a high index of suspicion and methacholine challenge test are needed to avoid missing this important diagnosis.

Lower Respiratory Tract Infection

Lower respiratory tract infection may be almost as disruptive to a voice as an upper respiratory infection. Bronchitis, pneumonitis, pneumonia, and especially reactive airway disease impair the power source of the voice and lead to vocal strain, and sometimes injury. Lower respiratory tract infections should be treated aggressively, pulmonary function tests should be considered, and bronchodilators (preferably oral) should be used as necessary. Coughing is also a very traumatic vocal activity, as discussed above.

Tonsillitis

Tonsillitis also impairs the voice through alterations of the resonator system and through technical changes secondary to pain. Although there is a tendency to avoid tonsillectomy, especially in professional voice users, the operation should not be withheld when clear indications for tonsillectomy are present, for example, documented severe bacterial tonsillitis six times per year. However, patients must be warned that tonsillectomy may alter the sound of the voice, even though there is no change at the vocal fold (oscillator) level.

Other Infections

Autoimmune deficiency syndrome (AIDS) is becoming more and more common. This lethal disease may present as hoarseness, and xerostomia. Unexplained oral candidiasis, *Candida* infections of the tracheobronchial tree, and respiratory tract infections with other unusual pathogens should raise a physician's suspicions. However, it should also be remembered that infections with *Haemophilus influenzae, Streptococcus pneumoniae*, and common viruses are the most frequent pathogens in AIDS patients, just as they are in patients without AIDS. This disease should be considered in patients with frequent infections.

The laryngologist must also be alert for numerous other acute and chronic conditions that may cause laryngeal abnormalities or even vocal fold masses that may be mistaken for malignancy and biopsied unnecessarily. Tuberculosis is being seen more often in modern practice. Although laryngeal lesions used to be associated with extensive pulmonary infection, they are now usually associated with much less virulent disease, often only a mild cough. Laryngeal lesions are usually localized.[6,7]

Sarcoidosis, a granulomatous disease, involves laryngeal symptoms in 3 to 5% of cases.[8] Noncaseating granulomas are found in the larynx, and the false vocal folds are involved frequently, producing airway obstruction rather than dysphonia. Less common diseases, including leprosy,[9,10] syphilis,[11] scleroderma,[12] typhoid,[13] typhus,[14] and other conditions, may produce laryngeal lesions that mimic neoplasms and lead the laryngologist to obtain unnecessary biopsy of lesions that can be cured medically.

Confusing lesions may also be caused by a variety of mycotic infections including histoplasmosis,[14-16] coccidioidomycosis,[17] cryptococcosis,[18] blastomycosis,[19,20] actinomycosis,[21,22] candidiasis,[23] aspergillosis,[24-26] mucormycosis,[27] rhinosporidiosis,[28] and sporotrichosis.[29] Parasitic diseases may also produce laryngeal masses. The most prominent example is leishmaniasis.[30] Some viral conditions may also cause laryngeal structural abnormalies, most notably papillomas. However, herpes virus, variola, and other organisms have also been implicated in laryngeal infection.

Systemic Conditions

Aging

Many characteristics associated with vocal aging are actually deficits in conditioning, rather than irreversible aging changes. For example, in singers, such problems as a "wobble," pitch inaccuracies (singing flat), and inability to sing softly, are rarely due to irreversible aging changes; and these problems usually can be managed easily through voice therapy and training.

Hearing Loss

Hearing loss is often overlooked as a source of vocal problems. Auditory feedback is fundamental to speaking and singing. Interference with this control mechanism may result in altered vocal production, particularly if the person is unaware of the hearing loss. Distortion, particularly pitch distortion (diplacusis), may also pose serious problems for the singer. This appears to cause not only aesthetic difficulties in matching pitch, but also vocal strain, which accompanies pitch shifts.[31]

Gastroesophageal Reflux Laryngitis

Gastroesophageal reflux laryngitis is extremely common among voice patients, especially singers.[32] This is a condition in which the sphincter between the stomach and esophagus is inefficient, and acidic stomach secretions reflux, reaching the laryngeal tissues, and thus causing inflammation. The most typical symptoms are hoarseness in the morning, prolonged vocal warm-up time, halitosis and a bitter taste in the morning, a feeling of a "lump in the throat," frequent throat clearing, chronic irritative cough, and frequent tracheitis or tracheobronchitis. Any or all of these symptoms may be present. Heartburn is not common in these patients, so the diagnosis is often missed. Prolonged reflux also is associated with the development of Barrett's esophagus, esophageal carcinoma, and laryngeal carcinoma.[32]

Physical examination usually reveals erythema (redness) and edema of the arytenoid mucosa and interarytenoid pachydermia. A barium swallow radiographic study with water siphonage may provide additional information but is not needed routinely. However, if a patient complies strictly with treatment recommendations and does not show marked improvement within a month, or if there is a reason to suspect more serious pathology, complete evaluation by a gastroenterologist should be carried out. This is often advisable in patients who are over 40 years of age or who have had reflux symptoms for more than 5 years. Twenty-four-hour pH monitoring of the esophagus is often effective in establishing a diagnosis. The results are correlated with a diary of the patient's activities and symptoms. Bulimia should also be considered in the differential diagnosis when symptoms are refractory to treatment and other physical and psychological signs are suggestive.

The mainstays of treatment for reflux laryngitis are elevation of the head of the bed (not just sleeping on pillows), antacids, H2 blockers or proton pump inhibitors, medications that decrease or block acid production, and avoidance of eating for 3 to 4 hours before going to sleep. This is often difficult for singers and actors because of their performance schedule; but if they are counseled about minor changes in eating habits (such as eating larger meals at breakfast and lunch), they usually can comply. Avoidance of alcohol, caffeine, and specific foods is beneficial. It must be recognized that control of acidity is not the same as control of reflux. In many cases, reflux is provoked during singing because of the increased abdominal pressure associated with support. In these instances, it often causes excessive phlegm and throat clearing during the first 10 or 15 minutes of a performance or lesson, as well as other common reflux laryngitis symptoms, even when acidity has been neutralized effectively. Laparoscopic Nissen fundoplication has proven extremely effective and should be considered a reasonable alternative to lifelong treatment with medications in this relatively young patient population.[32]

Endocrine Dysfunction

Endocrine (hormonal) problems warrant special attention. The human voice is extremely sensitive to endocrinologic changes. Many of these are reflected in alterations of fluid content of the lamina propria just beneath the laryngeal mucosa. This causes alterations in the bulk and shape of the vocal folds and results in voice change. Hypothyroidism is a well-recognized cause of such voice disorders, although the mechanism is not fully understood.[33-36] Hoarseness, vocal fatigue, muffling of the voice, loss of range, and a sensation of a lump in the throat may be present even with mild hypothyroidism. Even when thyroid function tests results are within the low-normal range, this diagnosis should be entertained, especially if thyroid-stimulating hormone levels are in the high-normal range or are elevated. Thyrotoxicosis may result in similar voice disturbances.[37]

Voice changes associated with sex hormones are encountered commonly in clinical practice and have been investigated more thoroughly than have other hormonal changes. Although a correlation appears to exist between sex hormone levels and depth of male voices (higher testosterone and lower estradiol levels in basses than in tenors),[38] the most important hormonal considerations in males occur during the maturation process.

When castrato singers were in vogue, castration at about age 7 or 8 resulted in failure of laryngeal growth during puberty and voices that stayed in the soprano or alto range and boasted a unique quality of sound.[39] Failure of a male voice to change at puberty is uncommon today and is often psychogenic in etiology.[40] However, hormonal deficiencies such as those seen in cryptorchidism, delayed sexual development, Klinefelter's syndrome, or Fröhlich's syndrome may be responsible. In these cases, the persistently high voice may be the complaint that causes the patient to seek medical attention.

Voice problems related to sex hormones are most common in female singers. Although vocal changes associated with the normal menstrual cycle may be difficult to quantify with current experimental techniques, unquestionably they occur.[41-44] Premenstrual changes cause significant vocal symptoms in approximately one third of singers. Most of the ill effects are seen in the immediate premenstrual period and are known as laryngopathia premenstrualis. This common condition is caused by physiologic, anatomic, and psychologic alterations secondary to endocrine changes. The vocal dysfunction is characterized by decreased vocal efficiency, loss of the highest notes in the voice, vocal fatigue, slight hoarseness, and some muffling of the voice. It is often more apparent to the singer than to the listener. Submucosal hemorrhages in the larynx are common in the premenstrual period.[42] In many European opera houses, singers used to be excused from singing during the premenstrual and early menstrual days ("grace days"). This practice is not followed in the United States and is no longer in vogue in most European countries. Although ovulation inhibitors have been shown to mitigate some of these premenstrual symptoms,[43] in some women (about 5%),[45] birth control pills may deleteriously alter voice range and character even after only a few months of therapy.[46-49] When oral contraceptives are used, the voice should be monitored closely. Under crucial performance circumstances, oral contraceptives may be used to alter the time of menstruation, but this practice is justified only in unusual situations. Symptoms very similar to laryngopathia premenstrualis occur in some women at the time of ovulation.

Pregnancy frequently results in voice alterations known as laryngopathia gravidarum. The changes may be similar to premenstrual symptoms but may be perceived as desirable changes. In some cases, alterations produced by pregnancy are permanent.[50,51] Although hormonally induced changes in the larynx and respiratory mucosa secondary to menstruation and pregnancy are discussed widely in the literature, the author has found no reference to the coexisting and important alterations in abdominal support. Uterine muscle cramping associated with menstruation causes pain and compromises abdominal support. Abdominal distension during pregnancy also interferes with abdominal muscle function. Any singer whose abdominal support is compromised substantially should be discouraged from singing until the abdominal impairment is resolved.

Estrogens are helpful in postmenopausal singers but generally should not be given alone. Sequential replacement therapy is the most physiologic regimen and should be used under the supervision of a gynecologist. Under no circumstances should androgens be given to female singers, even in small amounts, if any reasonable therapeutic alternative exists. Clinically, these drugs are most commonly used to treat endometriosis or postmenopausal loss of libido. Androgens cause unsteadiness of the voice, rapid changes of timbre, and lowering of the fundamental frequency (masculinization).[52-56] These changes are usually permanent.

Recently, we have seen increasing abuse of anabolic steroids among body builders and other athletes. In addition to their many other hazards, these medications may alter the voice. They are (or are closely related to) male hormones; consequently, they are capable of producing masculinization of the voice. Lowering of the fundamental frequency and coarsening of the voice produced in this fashion are generally irreversible.

Other hormonal disturbances may also produce vocal dysfunction. In addition to the thyroid, ovaries and the gonads, the parathyroid, adrenal, pineal, and pituitary glands are included in hormonally induced dysphonia. Other endocrine disturbances may alter voice as well. For example, pancreatic dysfunction may cause xerophonia (dry voice), as in diabetes mellitus. Thymic abnormalities can lead to feminization of the voice.[57]

Neurological Disorders

Numerous neurologic conditions may adversely affect the voice. Some of them, such as myasthenia gravis, are amenable to medical therapy with drugs such as pyridostigmine (Mestinon). Such therapy frequently restores the voice to normal. An exhaustive neurolaryngological discussion is beyond the scope of this chapter. Nevertheless, when evaluating voice dysfunction, laryngologists must consider numerous neurological problems including Parkinson's disease, various other disorders that produce tremor, drug-induced tremor, multiple sclerosis, dystonias, and many other conditions. Spasmodic dysphonia, a laryngeal dystonia, presents particularly challenging problems. This subject is covered in detail in chapter 13. Stuttering also provides unique challenges. Although still poorly understood, this condition is noted for its tendency to affect speech while sparing singing.

Vocal Fold Hypomobility

Vocal fold hypomobility may be caused by paralysis (no movement), paresis (partial movement), arytenoid cartilage dislocation, cricoarytenoid joint dysfunction, and laryngeal fracture. Differentiating among these conditions is often more complicated than it appears at first glance. A comprehensive discussion is beyond the scope of this chapter, and the reader is referred to other literature. However, in addition to a comprehensive history and physical examination, evaluation commonly includes strobovideolaryngoscopy, objective voice assessment, laryngeal electromyography, and high-resolution computed tomography (CT) of the larynx. Most vocal fold motion disorders are amenable to treatment. Voice therapy should be the first treatment modality in virtually all cases. Even in many patients with recurrent laryngeal nerve paralysis, voice therapy alone is often sufficient in producing a satisfactory voice. When therapy fails to produce adequate voice improvement in the patient's opinion, surgical intervention is appropriate.

General Health

As with any other "athletic" activity, optimal voice use requires reasonably good general health and physical conditioning of the muscles used in phonation. Abdominal and respiratory strength and endurance are particularly important. If a person becomes short of breath from climbing two flights of stairs, he or she certainly does not have the physical stamina necessary for proper respiratory support for a speech, let alone a strenuous musical production. This deficiency usually results in abusive vocal habits used in vain attempts to compensate for the deficiencies.

Systemic illnesses, such as anemia, Lyme disease, mononucleosis, AIDS, chronic fatigue syndrome, or other diseases associated with malaise and weakness may impair the ability of vocal musculature to recover rapidly from heavy use and may also be associated with alterations of mucosal secretions. Other systemic illnesses may be responsible for voice complaints, particularly if they impair the abdominal muscles necessary for breath support. For example, diarrhea and constipation that prohibit sustained abdominal contraction may be reasons for the physician to prohibit a strenuous singing or acting engagement.

Any extremity injury, such as a sprained ankle, affects balance and posture and therefore interferes with customary abdominothoracic support. Voice patients are often unaware of this problem and develop abusive, hyperfunctional compensatory maneuvers in the neck and tongue musculature as a result. These technical flaws may produce voice complaints, such as vocal fatigue and neck pain, that bring the performer to the physician's office for assessment and care.

Anxiety

Voice professionals, especially singers and actors, are frequently sensitive and communicative people. When the principal cause of vocal dysfunction is anxiety, the physician can often accomplish much by assuring the patient that no organic problem is present and by stating the diagnosis of anxiety reaction. The patient should be counseled that anxiety is normal and that recognition of it as the principal problem frequently allows the performer to overcome it. Tranquilizers and sedatives are rarely necessary and are undesirable because they may interfere with fine motor control. For example, beta-adrenergic blocking agents such as propranolol hydrochloride (Inderal) have became popular among performers for the treatment of preperformance anxiety. Beta-blockers are not recommended for regular use; they have significant effects on the cardiovascular and respiratory system and many potential complications, including hypotension, thrombocytopenic purpura, mental depression, agranulocytosis, laryngospasm with respiratory distress, and bronchospasm. In addition, their efficacy is controversial. Although they may have a favorable effect in relieving performance anxiety, beta-blockers may produce a noticeable adverse effect on singing performance.[57] Although these drugs have a place under occasional, extraordinary circumstances, their routine use for this purpose not only is potentially hazardous but also violates an important therapeutic principle. Performers have chosen a career that exposes them to the public. If they are so incapacitated by anxiety that they are unable to perform the routine functions of their chosen profession without chemical help, this should be considered symptomatic of an important underlying psychologic problem. For a performer to depend on drugs to perform is neither routine nor healthy, whether the drug is a benzodiazepine, a barbiturate, a beta-blocker, or alcohol. If such dependence exists, psychologic evaluation by an experienced arts-medicine psychologist or psychiatrist should be considered. Obscuring the symptoms by fostering the dependence is insufficient. However, if the patient is on tour and will only be under a particular otolaryngologist's care for a week or two, the physician should not try to make major changes in his or her customary regimen. Rather, the physician should communicate with the performer's primary otolaryngologist or family physician to coordinate appropriate long-term care.

Because professional voice users constitute a subset of society as a whole, all of the psychiatric disorders encountered among the general public are seen from time to time in voice professionals. In some cases, professionals voice users require modification of the usual psychological treatment, particularly with regard to psychotropic medications. Detailed discussion of this subject can be found elsewhere in the literature.[58]

When voice professionals, especially singers and actors, suffer a significant vocal impairment that results in voice loss (or the prospect of voice loss), they often go through a psychological process very similar to grieving.[58] In some cases, fear of discovering that the voice is lost forever may unconsciously prevent patients from trying to use their voices optimally following injury or treatment. This can dramatically impede or prevent recovery of function following a perfect surgical result, for example. It is essential for otolaryngologists, performers, and their teachers to be familiar with this fairly common scenario; and it is ideal to include an arts-medicine psychologist and/or psychiatrist as part of the voice team.

Other Psychological Problems

Psychogenic voice disorders, incapacitating psychological reactions to organic voice disorders, and other psychological problems are encountered commonly in young voice patients. They are discussed in other literature,[58] as well as elsewhere in this book.

Substance Abuse

The list of substances ingested, smoked, or snorted by many people is disturbingly long. Whenever possible, patients who care about vocal quality and longevity should be educated by their physicians and teachers about the deleterious effects of such habits on their voices and on the longevity of their careers. A few specific substances have already been discussed above.

Structural Abnormalities

Nodules

Vocal nodules are callouslike masses of the vocal folds that are caused by vocally abusive behaviors and are a dreaded malady of singers and actors. Occasionally, laryngoscopy reveals asymptomatic vocal nodules that do not appear to interfere with voice production; in such cases, the nodules should not be treated surgically. Some famous and successful singers have had untreated vocal nodules throughout their careers. However, in most cases, nodules result in hoarseness, breathiness, loss of range, and vocal fatigue. They may be due to abusive speaking rather than improper singing technique. Voice therapy always should be tried as the initial therapeutic modality and will cure the vast majority of patients even if the nodules look firm and have been present for many months or years. Even apparently large, fibrotic nodules often shrink, disappear, or become asymptomatic with 6 to 12 weeks of voice therapy with good patient compliance. Even for those who eventually need surgical excision of the nodules, preoperative voice therapy is essential to prevent recurrence.

It is almost impossible to make the diagnosis accurately and consistently without strobovideolaryngoscopy and good optical magnification. Vocal fold cysts are commonly misdiagnosed as nodules, and treatment strategies are different for the two lesions. Vocal nodules are confined to the superficial layer of the lamina propria and are composed primarily of edematous tissue or collagenous fibers. Basement membrane reduplication is common. They are usually bilateral and fairly symmetrical.

Caution must be exercised in diagnosing small nodules in patients who have been singing or speaking actively. In many singers, for example, bilateral, symmetrical soft swellings at the junction of the anterior and middle thirds of the vocal folds develop after heavy voice use. No evidence suggests that patients with such physiologic swelling are predisposed to the development of vocal nodules. At present, the condition is generally considered to be within normal limits. The physiologic swelling usually disappears with 24 to 48 hours of rest from heavy voice use. The physician must be careful not to frighten the patient by misdiagnosing physiologic swellings as vocal nodules. Nodules carry a great stigma among voice professionals, and the psychological impact of the diagnosis should not be underestimated. When nodules are present, patients should be informed with the same gentle caution used in telling a patient that he or she has a life-threatening illness.

Submucosal Cysts

Submucosal cysts of the vocal folds are probably also traumatic lesions that are the result of a blocked mucous gland duct, in many cases. However, they may also be congenital or occur from other causes. They often cause contact swelling on the contralateral side and can be initially misdiagnosed as nodules. They can usually be differentiated from nodules by strobovideolaryngoscopy when the mass is observed to be obviously fluid-filled. Submucosal cysts may also be suspected when the nodule (contact swelling) on one vocal fold resolves with voice therapy while the mass on the other vocal fold does not resolve. Cysts may also be discovered on one side (occasionally both sides) when surgery is performed for apparent nodules that have not resolved with voice therapy. The surgery should be performed superficially and with minimal trauma. Cysts are ordinarily lined with thin squamous epithelium. Retention cysts contain mucus. Epidermoid cysts contain caseous material. Generally, cysts are located in the superficial layer of the lamina propria. In some cases, they may be attached to the vocal ligament.

Polyps

Vocal polyps, another type of vocal fold mass, usually occur on only one vocal fold. They often have a prominent feeding blood vessel coursing along the superior surface of the vocal fold and entering the base of the polyp. In many cases, the pathogenesis of polyps cannot be proven, but the lesion is thought to be traumatic and sometimes starts as a hemorrhage. Polyps may be sessile or pedunculated. They are typically located in the superficial layer of the lamina propria and do not involve the vocal ligament. In those arising from an area of hemorrhage, the vocal ligament may be involved with posthemorrhagic fibrosis that is contiguous with the polyp. Histological evaluation most commonly reveals collagenous fibers, hyaline degeneration, edema, thrombosis, and often bleeding within the polypoid tissue. Cellular infiltration may also be present. In some cases, even sizable polyps resolve with relative voice rest and a few weeks of low-dose steroid therapy (eg, methylprednisolone 4 mg twice a day). However, most require surgical removal. If polyps are not treated, they may produce contact injury on the contralateral vocal fold. Voice therapy should be used to assure good relative voice rest and prevention of abusive vocal behavior before and after surgery. When surgery is performed, care must be taken not to damage the leading edge of the vocal fold, especially if a laser is used, as discussed later. In all laryngeal surgery, delicate microscopic dissection is now the standard of care. Vocal fold "stripping" is an out-of-date surgical approach formerly used for benign lesions, which often resulted in scar and/or poor unserviceable voice function. It is no longer an acceptable surgical technique in most situations.

Granulomas

Granulomas usually occur in the cartilaginous portion of the vocal fold near the vocal process or on the medial surface of the arytenoid cartilage. They are composed of collagenous fibers, fibroblasts, proliferated capillaries, and leukocytes. They are usually covered with epithelium. Granulomas are associated with gastroesophageal reflux laryngitis and trauma (including trauma from voice abuse and from intubation). Therapy should include reflux control, voice therapy, and surgery if the granuloma continues to enlarge or does not resolve after adequate time and treatment.

Reinke's Edema

Reinke's edema is characterized by an "elephant ear," floppy vocal fold appearance. It is often observed during examination in many nonprofessional and professional voice users and is accompanied by a low, coarse, gruff voice. Reinke's edema is a condition in which the superficial layer of lamina propria (Reinke's space) becomes edematous. The lesion does not usually include hypertrophy, inflammation, or degeneration, although other terms for the condition include polypoid degeneration, chronic polypoid corditis, and chronic edematous hypertrophy. Reinke's edema is often associated with smoking, voice abuse, reflux, and hypothyroidism. Underlying conditions should be treated. However, if voice improvement is desired, the condition may require surgery. The surgery should only be performed if there is a justified high suspicion of serious pathology such as cancer, if there is airway obstruction, or if the patient is unhappy with his or her vocal quality. For some voice professionals, abnormal Reinke's edema is an important component of the vocal signature. Although the condition is usually bilateral, surgery should generally be performed on one side at a time.

Sulcus Vocalis

Sulcus vocalis is a groove along the edge of the membranous vocal fold. The majority are congenital, bilateral, and symmetrical, although posttraumatic acquired lesions occur. When symptomatic (they often are not), sulcus vocalis can be treated surgically if sufficient voice improvement is not obtained through voice therapy.

Scar

Vocal fold scar is a sequela of trauma that results in fibrosis and obliteration of the layered structure of the vocal fold. It may markedly impede vibration, and consequently cause profound dysphonia. Recent surgical advances have made this condition much more treatable than it used to be, but it is still rarely possible to restore voices to normal in the presence of scar.

Hemorrhage

Vocal fold hemorrhage is a potential disaster in singers. Hemorrhages resolve spontaneously in most cases, with restoration of normal voice. However, in some instances, the hematoma organizes and fibroses, resulting in scar. This alters the vibratory pattern of the vocal fold and can result in permanent hoarseness. In specially selected cases, it may be best to avoid this problem through surgical incision and drainage of the hematoma. In all cases, vocal fold hemorrhage should be managed with absolute voice rest until the hemorrhage has resolved (usually about 1 week) and relative voice rest until normal vascular and mucosal integrity have been restored. This often takes 6 weeks, and sometimes longer. Recurrent vocal fold hemorrhages are usually due to weakness in a specific blood vessel, which may require surgical cauterization of the blood vessel using a laser or microscopic resection of the vessel.[59,60]

Papilloma

Laryngeal papillomas are epithelial lesions caused by human papilloma virus. Histology reveals neoplastic epithelial cell proliferation in a papillary pattern and viral particles. At the present time, symptomatic papillomas are treated surgically, although alternatives have been recommended to the usual laser vaporization approach.[60,61] Recently, cidofovir injected into the lesion has shown considerable promise.[62]

Cancer

A detailed discussion of cancer of the larynx is beyond the scope of this chapter. The prognosis for small vocal fold cancers is good, whether they are treated by radiation or surgery. Although it may seem intuitively obvious that radiation therapy provides a better chance of voice conservation than even limited vocal fold surgery, later radiation changes in the vocal fold may produce substantial hoarseness, xerophonia (dry voice), and voice dysfunction. Consequently, from the standpoint of voice preservation, optimal treatments remain uncertain. Prospective studies using objective voice measures and strobovideolaryngoscopy should answer the relevant questions in the near future. Strobovideolaryngoscopy is also valuable for follow-up of patients who have had laryngeal cancers. It permits detection of vibratory changes associated with infiltration by the cancer long before they can be seen with continuous light. Stroboscopy has been used in Europe and Japan for this purpose for many years. In the United States, the popularity of strobovideolaryngoscopy for follow-up of cancer patients has increased greatly in recent years.

The psychological consequences of vocal fold cancer can be devastating, especially in a professional voice user.[58] They may be overwhelming for nonvoice professionals, as well. These reactions are understandable and expected. In many patients, however, psychological reactions may be as severe following medically "less significant" vocal fold problems such as hemorrhages, nodules, and other conditions that do not command the public respect and sympathy afforded to a cancer. In many ways, the management of related psychological problems can be even more difficult in patients with these "lesser" vocal disturbances.

Unusual Vocal Fold Masses

When vocal fold masses are mentioned, laryngologists usually think of nodules, cysts, polyps, and cancer. Although these are certainly the most common problems encountered in clinical practice, many other conditions must be kept in mind. Collagen vascular diseases and other unusual problems may also produce laryngeal masses. Rheumatoid arthritis may produce not only disease of the cricoarytenoid and cricothyroid joints, but also consequent neuropathic muscle atrophy[63] and rheumatoid nodules of the larynx.[64] Rheumatoid arthritis with or without nodules may produce respiratory obstruction. Gout may also cause laryngeal arthritis. In addition, gouty tophi may appear as white submucosal masses of the true vocal fold. They consist of sodium urate crystals in fibrous tissue and have been well documented.[65,66]

Amyloidosis of the larynx is rare but well recognized.[67,68] Amyloidosis is most common in the false vocal folds. Urbach-Wiethe disease (lipoid proteinosis)[69] often involves the mucous membrane of the larynx, usually the vocal folds, aryepiglottic fold, and epiglottis. Other conditions such as Wegener's granulomatosis and relapsing polychondritis may also involve the larynx. They are less likely to produce discrete nodules, but the diffuse edema associated with chondritis and necrotizing granulomas may produce significant laryngeal and voice abnormalities leading to surgical intervention. Granular cell tumors may involve the larynx, and can be misdiagnosed easily as laryngeal granulomas.[70] Unusual laryngeal masses may also be caused by trauma.

A few rare skin lesions may also involve the larynx, producing significant lesions and sometimes airway obstruction. These include pemphigus vulgaris, seen in adults between 40 and 60 years of age. Pemphigus lesions may involve the mucosa, including the epiglottis.[71] Epidermolysis bullosa describes a group of congenital vesicular disorders usually seen at birth or shortly thereafter. This condition may cause laryngeal stenosis.

Other Conditions

Many other conditions could be included in this summary chapter. Most are discussed elsewhere in this text, and more comprehensive information regarding the entities that are reviewed in this chapter can be found also.

Medical Management for Voice Dysfunction

Medical management of many problems affecting the voice involves not only care prescribed by the otolaryngologist, but also voice therapy, which is provided by an interdisciplinary team. The roles and training of the principal members of the team are covered in detail elsewhere in this book and in other literature.[72,73] This chapter provides a brief introduction to their roles in the medical milieu.

Speech-Language Pathologist

An excellent speech-language pathologist is an invaluable asset in caring for professional voice users and other voice patients. However, otolaryngologists and singing teachers should recognize that, like physicians, speech-language pathologists have varied backgrounds and experience in treatment of voice disorders. In fact, most speech-language pathology programs teach relatively little about caring for professional speakers and nothing about professional singers. Moreover, few speech-language pathologists have vast experience in this specialized area; and no fellowships in this subspecialty exist. A speech-language pathologist who subspecializes in the treatment of patients who have had strokes, stutter, have undergone laryngectomy, or have swallowing disorders will not necessarily know how to manage professional voice users optimally or even other less demanding voice patients. The otolaryngologist must learn the strengths and weaknesses of the speech-language pathologist(s) with whom he or she works. After identifying a speech-language pathologist who is interested in treating professional voice users, the otolaryngologist should work closely with the speech-language pathologist in developing the necessary expertise. Assistance may be found through otolaryngologists who treat large numbers of singers or through educational programs such as the Voice Foundation's Symposium on Care of the Professional Voice.

Speech (voice) therapy may be helpful even when a singer has no obvious problem in the speaking voice but has significant technical problems singing. In general, therapy should be directed toward vocal hygiene, relaxation techniques, breath management, and abdominal support.[72] Once a person has been singing for several years, a singing teacher may have difficulty convincing him or her to correct certain technical errors. However, singers are much less protective of their speaking voices. A speech-language pathologist may be able to teach proper support, relaxation, and voice placement in speaking. Once mastered, these techniques can be carried over fairly easily into singing through collaboration between the speech-language pathologist and singing teacher. This "back door" approach has been extremely useful. For the actor, coordinating speech-language pathology sessions with acting voice lessons, and especially with training of the speaking voice provided by the actor's voice teacher or coach, is often helpful. In fact, we have found this combination so helpful that we have added an acting voice trainer to our medical staff. Information from the speech-language pathologist, acting voice trainer, and singing teacher should be symbiotic and should not conflict. If major discrepancies exist, bad training from one of the team members should be suspected; and changes should be made.

Singing Voice Specialist

Singing voice specialists are singing teachers who have acquired extra training to prepare them to work with injured voices, in collaboration with a medical voice team. They are indispensable for singers.

In selected cases, singing lessons may also be extremely helpful to nonsingers with voice problems. The techniques used to develop abdominal and thoracic muscle strength, breath control, laryngeal and neck muscle strength, and relaxation are very similar to those used in speech therapy. Singing lessons often expedite therapy and appear to improve the outcome in some patients.

Otolaryngologists who frequently care for singers are often asked to recommend a voice teacher. This may put them in an uncomfortable position, particularly if the singer is already studying with someone in the community. Most physicians do not have sufficient expertise to criticize a voice teacher, and we must be extremely cautious about recommending that a singer change teachers. However, no certifying agency standardizes or assures the quality of a singing teacher. Although one may be slightly more confident of a teacher associated with a major conservatory or music school or one who is a member of the National Association of Teachers of Singing (NATS), neither of these credentials assures excellence, and many expert teachers have neither affiliation. However, with experience, an otolaryngologist can ordinarily develop valid impressions. The physician should record the name of the voice teacher of every patient and observe whether the same kinds of voice abuse problems occur with disproportionate frequency in the pupils of any given teacher. Technical problems can cause organic abnormalities such as nodules; therefore, any teacher who has a high incidence of nodules among his or her students should be viewed with cautious concern. The physician should be particularly wary of teachers who are reluctant to allow their students to consult a doctor. The best voice teachers usually are quick to refer their students to an otolaryngologist if they hear anything disturbing in a student's voice. Similarly, voice teachers and voice professionals should compare information on the nature and quality of medical care received and its success. No physician cures every voice problem in every patient, just as no singing teacher produces premier stars from every student who walks into his or her studio. Nevertheless, voice professionals must be critical, informed consumers and accept nothing less than the best medical care.

After seeing a voice patient, the otolaryngologist should speak with and/or write a letter to the voice teacher (with the patient's permission) describing the findings and recommendations as he or she would to a physician, speech-language pathologist, or any other referring professional. An otolaryngologist seriously interested in caring for singers should take the trouble to talk with and meet local singing teachers. Taking a lesson or two with each teacher provides enormous insight, as well. Taking voice lessons regularly is even more helpful. In practice, the otolaryngologist will usually identify a few teachers in whom he or she has particular confidence, especially for patients with voice disorders, and should not hesitate to refer singers to these colleagues, especially singers who are not already in training.

Pop singers may be particularly resistant to the suggestion of voice lessons, yet they are in great need of training. The physician should point out that a good voice teacher can teach a pop singer how to protect and expand the voice without changing its quality or making it sound trained or operatic. It is helpful to point out that singing, like other athletic activities, requires exercise, warm-up, and coaching for anyone planning to enter the "big league" and stay there. Just as no major league baseball pitcher would play without a pitching coach and warm-up time in the bullpen, no singer should try to build a career without a singing teacher and appropriate strength and agility exercises. This approach has proved palatable and effective. Physicians should also be aware of the difference between a voice teacher and a voice coach. A voice teacher trains a singer in singing technique and is essential. A voice coach is responsible for teaching songs (repertoire), language, diction, style, operatic roles, and so on but is not responsible for vocal exercises and basic technical development of the voice.

Acting-Voice Trainer

The use of acting-voice trainers (drama voice coaches) as members of the medical team is new.[73] This addition to our team has been extremely valuable to patients and other team members. Like singing voice specialists, professionals with education in theater arts utilize numerous vocal and body movement techniques that not only enhance physical function, but also release tension and break down emotional barriers that may impede optimal voice performance. Tearful revelations shared with the acting-voice trainer are not uncommon; and, like the singing teacher, this individual may identify psychological and emotional problems interfering with professional success that have been skillfully hidden from other professionals on the voice team and in the patient's life.

Others

A nurse, physician assistant, medical assistant, psychologist, psychiatrist, neurologist, pulmonologist, and others with special interest and expertise in arts-medicine (especially voice performance) are also invaluable to the voice team. Every comprehensive center should seek out such people and collaborate with them, even if some of them are not full-time members of the voice team.

Surgery

A detailed discussion of laryngeal surgery is beyond the scope of this chapter. However, a few points are worthy of special emphasis. Surgery for vocal nodules should be avoided whenever possible and should almost never be performed without an adequate trial of expert voice therapy, including patient compliance with therapeutic suggestions. A minimum of 6 to 12 weeks of observation should be allowed while the patient is using therapeutically modified voice techniques under the supervision of a speech-language pathologist and ideally a singing voice specialist. Proper voice use rather than voice rest (silence) is correct therapy. The surgeon should not perform surgery prematurely for vocal nodules under pressure from the patient for a "quick cure" and early return to performance. Permanent destruction of voice quality is a very real complication.

Even after expert surgery, voice quality may be diminished by submucosal scarring, resulting in an adynamic segment along the vibratory margin of the vocal fold. This situation produces a hoarse voice with vocal folds that appear normal on indirect examination under routine light, although under stroboscopic light the adynamic segment is obvious. No reliable cure exists for this complication. Even large, apparently fibrotic nodules of long standing should be given a chance to resolve without surgery. In some cases, the nodules remain but become asymptomatic; and voice quality is normal. In these cases, stroboscopy usually reveals that the nodules are on the superior surface rather than the leading edge of the vocal folds during proper, relaxed phonation (although they may be on the contact surface and symptomatic when hyperfunctional voice technique is used and the larynx is forced down).

When surgery is indicated for vocal fold lesions, it should be limited as strictly as possible to the area of abnormality. Virtually no place exists for "vocal fold stripping" in patients with benign disease. Submucosal resection through a laryngeal microflap used to be advocated. In fact, the technique was introduced and first published by this author. Microflap technique involved an incision on the superior surface of the vocal fold, submucosal resection, and preservation of the mucosa along the leading edge of the vocal fold. The concept that led to this innovation was based on the idea that the intermediate layer of the lamina propria should be protected to prevent fibroblast proliferation. Consequently, it seemed reasonable to preserve the mucosa as a biological dressing. This technique certainly produced better results than vocal fold stripping. However, close scrutiny of outcomes revealed a small number of cases with poor results and stiffness beyond the limits of the original pathology. Consequently, the technique was abandoned in favor of a mini-microflap, or local resection strictly limited to the region of pathology.[74] Lesions such as vocal nodules should be removed to a level even with the vibratory margin rather than deeply into the submucosal layer. This minimizes scarring and optimizes return to good vocal function. Naturally, if concern about a serious neoplasm exists, curing of cancer always takes precedence over voice preservation. Surgery should be performed under microscopic control. Preoperative and postoperative objective voice measures are essential for outcome assessment and self-critique. Only through such analysis can we improve surgical techniques. Outcome studies are especially important in voice surgery since all of our technical pronouncements are anecdotal because there is no experimental model for vocal fold surgery. The human adult is the only species with a layered lamina propria.

Lasers are an invaluable adjunct in the laryngologists' armamentarium, but they must be used knowledgeably and with care. Considerable evidence suggests that healing time is prolonged and the incidence of adynamic segment formation is higher with the laser on the vibratory margin than with traditional instruments. Two early studies raised serious concerns about dysphonia after laser surgery.[75,76] Such complications may result from using a laser wattage that is too low, causing dissipation of heat deeply into the vocal fold; thus high power density for short duration has been recommended. Small spot size is also helpful. Nevertheless, pending further study, many laryngologists caring for voice professionals avoid laser surgery in most cases. When biopsy specimens are needed, they should be taken before destroying the lesion with a laser. If a lesion is to be removed from the leading edge, the laser beam should be centered in the lesion, rather than on the vibratory margin, so that the beam does not create a divot in the vocal fold. The CO_2 laser is particularly valuable for cauterizing isolated blood vessels responsible for recurrent hemorrhage. Such vessels are often found at the base of a hemorrhagic polyp. However, a nonlaser technique has proven even better for managing these vessels.[77]

Voice rest after vocal fold surgery is controversial. Although some laryngologists do not acknowledge its necessity at all, many physicians recommend voice rest for approximately 1 week or until the mucosal surface has healed. Even after surgery, silence for more than 7 to 10 days is nearly never necessary and represents a real hardship for many patients.

Too often, the laryngologist is confronted with a desperate patient whose voice has been "ruined" by vocal fold surgery, recurrent or superior laryngeal nerve paralysis, trauma, or some other tragedy. Occasionally, the cause is as straightforward as a dislocated arytenoid cartilage that can be reduced.[78,79] However, if the problem is an adynamic segment, decreased bulk of one vocal fold after "stripping," bowing caused by superior laryngeal nerve paralysis, or some other complication in a mobile vocal fold, great conservatism should be exercised. None of the available surgical procedures for these conditions is consistently effective. If surgery is considered at all, the procedure and prognosis should be explained to the patient realistically and pessimistically. The patient must understand that the chances of returning the voice to professional quality are very slim and that it may be made worse. Zyderm collagen (Xomed) injection has been studied and is helpful in some of these difficult cases.[80] Zyderm collagen presently is not approved by the FDA for use in the vocal fold. If used at all, the material should be used under protocol with an Institutional Review Board's approval. However, human collagen can be used and does not have the same shortcomings. Collagen may be particularly helpful for small adynamic segments. In the author's opinion, the best technique for extensive vocal fold scarring is the recently introduced method of autologous fat implantation into the vibratory margin.[81]

Occasionally, voice professionals inquire about surgery for pitch alteration. Such procedures have been successful in specially selected patients (such as those undergoing sex-change surgery), but they do not consistently provide good enough voice quality and range to be performed on a professional voice user.

Discretion

The excitement and glamour associated with caring for voice patients, particularly a famous performer, naturally tempt the physician to talk about a distinguished patient. However, this tendency must be tempered. Having it known that he or she has consulted a laryngologist, particularly for treatment of a significant vocal problem, is not always in a voice professional's best interest. Famous singers, actors, politicians, and other professional voice users are ethically and legally entitled to the same confidentiality we assure for our other patients; and they are among those most likely to be harmed by breaches of confidentiality. Physicians must not only be careful themselves but also must train their office staff not to divulge information about patients to anyone (even their spouses), including the names of patients (especially famous ones). Laryngologists should also discuss these concerns with colleagues to whom they refer voice patients so that collaborating doctors and their staff will be careful about confidentiality issues, as well.

Voice Maintenance

Prevention of vocal dysfunction should be the goal of all professionals involved in the care of professional voice users. Good vocal health habits should be encouraged in childhood. Screaming, particularly outdoors at athletic events, should be discouraged. Promising young singers who join choirs should be educated to compensate for the Lombard effect. Youngsters interested in singing, acting, debating, or other vocal activities should receive enough training to prevent voice abuse and should receive enthusiastic support for performing works and activities suitable for their ages and voices. Training should be continued during or after puberty, and the voice should be allowed to develop naturally without pressure to perform operatic roles prematurely.

Excellent regular training and practice are essential; and avoidance of irritants, particularly smoke, should be stressed early. Educating voice professionals about hormonal and anatomic alterations that may influence the voice allows him or her to recognize and analyze vocal dysfunction, compensating for it intelligently when it occurs. The body is dynamic, changing over a lifetime; and the voice is no exception. Continued vocal education, training, and monitoring are necessary throughout a lifetime, even in the most successful and well-established voice professionals. Even in premier singers, vocal problems are commonly caused by cessation of lessons, excessive schedule demands, and other correctable problems rather than by irreversible alterations of aging. Anatomical, physiological, and serious medical problems may affect the voices of patients of any age. Cooperation among the laryngologist, speech-language pathologist, acting teacher, and singing teacher provides an optimal environment for cultivation and protection of the vocal artist.

References

1. Brodnitz F. Hormones and the human voice. *Bull NY Acad Med*. 1971;47:183–191.
2. von Leden H. Presentation at the Seventh Symposium on Care of the Professional Voice; June 16, 1978; The Juilliard School, New York.
3. Punt NA. Applied laryngology—singers and actors. *Proc R Soc Med*. 1968; 61:1152–1156.
4. Spiegel JR, Sataloff RT, Cohn JR, et al. Respiratory function in singers. Medical assessment, diagnoses and treatments. *J Voice*. 1988;2(1):40–50.
5. Cohn JR, Sataloff RT, Spiegel JR, et al. Airway reactivity-induced asthma in singers (ARIAS). *J Voice*. 1991;5(4): 332–337.
6. Bull TR. Tuberculosis of the larynx. *Br Med* J. 1966;2: 991–992.
7. Hunter AM, Millar JW, Wightman AJ, et al. The changing pattern of laryngeal tuberculosis. *J Laryngol Otol*. 1981;95:393–398.
8. Devine KD. Sarcoidosis and sarcoidosis of the larynx. *Laryngoscope*. 1965;75:533–569.
9. Munor MacCormic CE. The larynx in leprosy. *Arch Otolaryngol*. 1957;66:138–149.
10. Binford CH, Meyers WM. Leprosy. In: Binford CH. Connor DH, eds. *Pathology of Tropical and Extraordinary Disease*. Vol 1. Washington DC: Armed Forces Institute of Pathology; 1976:205–225.
11. MacKenzie M. *A Manual of Diseases of the Throat and Nose. Vol 1. Diseases of the Pharynx, Larynx and Trachea*. London, England: J & A Churchill; 1884.
12. Astacio JN, Goday GA, Espinosa FJ. *Excleroma. Experiences en El Salvador. Seconda Mongrafia de Dermatologia Iberolatino-Americana*. Suplemento AO 1. Lisboa, Portugal: 1971.
13. Hajek M. *Pathologie und Therapie der Erkrankungen des Kehlkopfes, der Luftrohre und der Bronchien*. Leipzig, Germany: Curt Kabitzsch; 1932.
14. Withers BT, Pappas JJ, Erickson EE. Histoplasmosis primary in the larynx. Report of a case. *Arch Otolaryngol*. 1963; 77:25–28.
15. Calcaterra TC. Otolaryngeal histoplasmosis. *Laryngoscope*. 1970;81:111–120.
16. Gould WJ, Sataloff RT, Spiegel JR. *Voice Surgery*. St. Louis, Mo: Mosby Year Book; 1993:1–359.
17. Friedmann I. Diseases of the larynx. Disorders of laryngeal function. In: Paparella MM, Shumrick DA, eds. *Otolaryngology*. 2nd ed. Philadelphia, Pa: Saunders; 1980: 2449–2469.
18. Reese MC, Conllasure JB. Cryptococcosis of the larynx. *Arch Otolaryngol*. 1975;101:698–701.
19. Bennett M. Laryngeal blastomycosis. *Laryngoscope*.1964;74:498–512.
20. Hoffarth GA, Joseph DL, Shumrick DA. Deep mycoses. *Arch Otolaryngol*. 1975;97:475–479.
21. Brandenburg JH, Finch WW, Kirkham WR. Actinomycosis of the larynx and pharynx. *Otolaryngology*. 1978;86:739–742.
22. Shaheen SO, Ellis FG. Actinomycosis of the larynx. *J R Soc Med*. 1983;76:226–228.
23. Tedeschi LG, Cheren RV. Laryngeal hyperkeratosis due to primary monilial infection. *Arch Otolaryngol*. 1968;87: 82–84.
24. Rao PB. Aspergillosis of the larynx. *J Laryngol Otol*. 1968; 83:377–379.
25. Ferlito A. Clinical records: primary aspergillosis of the larynx. *J Laryngol Otol*. 1974;88:1257–1263.
26. Kheir SM, Flint A, Moss JA. Primary aspergillosis of the larynx simulating carcinoma. *Hum Pathol*. 1983;14:184–186.
27. Anand CS, Gupta MC, Kothari MG, et al. Laryngeal mucormycosis. *Indian J Otolaryngol*. 1978;30:90–92.
28. Pillai OS. Rhinosporidiosis of the larynx. *J Laryngol Otol*. 1974;88:277–280.
29. Lyons GD. Mycotic disease of the larynx. *Ann Otol Rhinol Laryngol*. 1966;75:162–175.
30. Zinneman HH, Hall WH, Wallace FG. Leishmaniasis of the larynx. Report of a case and its confusion with histoplasmosis. *Am J Med*. 1961. 31:654–658
31. Sundberg J, Prame E, Iwarsson J. Replicability and accuracy of pitch patterns in professional singers. In: *Vocal Fold Physiology: Controlling Chaos and Complexity*. San Diego, Calif: Singular Publishing Group, Inc; 1996:291–306.
32. Sataloff RT, Castell DO, Katz PO, Sataloff DM. *Reflux Laryngitis and Related Disorders*. San Diego, Calif: Singular Publishing Group, Inc; 1999:1–112.
33. Ritter FN. The effect of hypothyroidism on the larynx of the rat. *Ann Otol Rhinol Laryngol*. 1964;67:404–416.
34. Ritter FN. Endocrinology. In: Paparella M, Shumrick D, eds. *Otolaryngology*. Vol 1. Philadelphia, Pa: WB Saunders; 1973:727–734.
35. Michelsson K, Sirvio P. Cry analysis in congenital hypothyroidism. *Folia Phoniatr* (Basel). 1976;28:40–47.
36. Gupta OP, Bhatia PL, Agarwal MK, et al. Nasal pharyngeal and laryngeal manifestations of hypothyroidism. *Ear Nose Throat J*. 1977;56(9):349–356.
37. Malinsky M, Chevrie-Muller, Cerceau N. Etude clinique et electrophysiologique des alterations de la voix au cours des thyrotoxioses. *Ann Endocrinol* (Paris). 1977;38: 171–172.
38. Meuser W, Nieschlag E. Sexual hormone und Stimmlage des Mannes. *Dtsch Med Wochenschr*. 1977;102: 261–264.
39. Brodnitz F. The age of the castrato voice. *J Speech Hear Disord*. 1975;40:291–295.
40. Brodnitz F. Medical care preventive therapy (panel). In: Lawrence V, ed. *Transcripts of the Seventh Annual Sympo-*

sium: Care of the Professional Voice. New York, NY: The Voice Foundation; 1978:86.
41. Schiff M. The influence of estrogens on connective tissue. In: Asboe-Hansen G, ed. *Hormones and Connective Tissue*. Copenhagen, Denmark: Munksgaard Press; 1967: 282–341.
42. Lacina O. Der Einfluss der Menstruation auf die Stimme der Sangerinnen. *Folia Phoniatr* (Basel). 1968;20:13–24.
43. Wendler J. [Cyclicly dependent variations in efficiency of the voice and its influencing by ovulation inhibitors.] *Folia Phoniatr* (Basel). 1972;24(4):259–277.
44. van Gelder L. Psychosomatic aspects of endocrine disorders of the voice. *J Commun Disord*. 1974;7:257–262.
45. Christine Carroll, M.D. Arizona State University at Tempe: Personal communication with Dr. Hans von Leden.
46. Dordain M. Etude Statistique de l'influence des contraceptifs hormonaux sur la voix. *Folia. Phoniatr* (Basel). 1972;24:86–96.
47. Pahn V, Goretzlehner G. Stimmstorungen durch hormonale Kontrazeptiva. *Zentralbl Gynakol*. 1978;100:341–346.
48. Schiff M. "The pill" in otolaryngology. *Trans Am Acad Ophthalmol Otolaryngol*. 1968;72:76–84.
49. Flach M, Schwickardi H, Simon R. Welchen Einfluss haben Menstruation and Schwangerschaft auf die augsgebildete Gesangsstimme? *Folia Phonatr* (Basel). 1968;21: 199–210.
50. von Deuster CV. Irreversible Stimmstorung in der Schwangerscheft. *HNO*. 1977;25:430–432.
51. Damsté PH. Virilization of the voice due to anabolic steroids. *Folia Phoniatr* (Basel). 1964;16:10–18.
52. Damsté PH. Voice change in adult women caused by virilizing agents. *J Speech Hear Disord*. 1967;32:126–132.
53. Saez S, Sakai F. Recepteurs d'androgenes: mise en evidence dans la fraction cytosolique de muqueuse normale et d'epitheliomas pharyngolarynges humains. *C R Acad Sci* (Paris). 1975:280:935–938.
54. Vuorenkoski V, Lenko HL, Tjernlund P, et al. Fundamental voice frequency during normal and abnormal growth, and after androgen treatment. *Arch Dis Child*. 1978;53:201–209.
55. Bourdial J. Les troubles de la voix provoques par la therapeutique hormonale androgene. *Ann Otolaryngol Chir Cervicofac*. 1970;87:725–734.
56. Imre V. Hormonell bedingte Stimmstorungen. *Folia Phoniatr* (Basel). 1968;20:394–404.
57. Gates GA, Saegert J, Wilson N, et al. Effects of betablockade on singing performance. *Ann Otol Rhinol Laryngol*. 1985;94:570–574.
58. Rosen DC, Sataloff RT. *Psychology of Voice Disorders*. San Diego, Calif: Singular Publishing Group, Inc; 1997:1–261.
59. Hochman I, Sataloff RT, Hillman R, Zeitels S. Ectasias and varicies of the vocal fold: clearing the striking zone. *Ann Otol Rhinol Laryngol*. 1999;108(1):10–16.
60. Zeitels SM. Phonomicrosurgical techniques. In: Sataloff RT. *Professional Voice: Science and Art of Clinical Care*. 2nd ed. San Diego, Calif: Singular Publishing Group, Inc; 1997: 647–658.
61. Zeitels SM, Sataloff RT. Phonomicrosurgical resection of glottal papillomatosis. *J Voice*. 1999;13(1):123–127.
62. Wellens W, Snoeck R, Desloovere C, et al. Treatment of severe laryngeal papillomatosis with intralesional injections of Cidofovir [(S)-1-(3-Hydroxy-Phosphonylmethoxypropyl) Cytosine, HPMPC, Vistide®]. In: McCafferty G, Coman W, Carroll R. eds. *Proceedings of the XVI World Congress of Otolaryngology Head and Neck Surgery* (March 2–7, 1997; Sydney, Australia). Bologna, Italy: Monduzzi Editore; 1997:455–549.
63. Wolman L, Darke CS, Young A. The larynx in rheumatoid arthritis. *J Laryngol Otol*. 1965;79:403–434.
64. Bridger MW, Jahn AF, van Nostrand AW. Laryngeal rheumatoid arthritis. *Laryngoscope*. 1980;90:296–303.
65. Virchow R. Seltene Gichtablagerungen. *Virchows Arch Pathol*. 1868;44:137–138.
66. Marion RB, Alperin JE, Maloney WH. Gouty tophus of the true vocal cord. *Arch Otolaryngol*. 1972;96:161–162.
67. Stark DB, New GB. Amyloid tumors of the larynx, trachea or bronchi; report of 15 cases. *Ann Otol Rhinol Laryngol*. 1949;58:117–134.
68. Michaels L, Hyams VJ. Amyloid in localized deposits and plasmacytomas of the respiratory tract. *J Pathol*. 1979;128:29–38.
69. Urbach E, Wiethe C. Lipoidosis cutis et mucosae. *Virchows Arch Pathol Anat*. 1929;273:285–319.
70. Sataloff RT, Hawkshaw M, Ressue J. Granular cell tumor of the larynx. *Ear Nose Throat J*. 1998;77(8):582–584.
71. Charow A, Pass F, Ruben R. Pemphigus of the upper respiratory tract. *Arch Otolaryngol*. 1971;93:209–210.
72. Rulnick RK, Heuer RJ, Perez KS, Emerich KA, Sataloff RT. Voice therapy. In: Sataloff RT. *Professional Voice: The Science and Art of Clinical Care*. 2nd ed. San Diego, Calif: Singular Publishing Group, Inc; 1997: 699–720.
73. Freed SL, Raphael BN, Sataloff RT. The role of the acting voice trainer in medical care of professional voice users. In: Sataloff RT. *Professional Voice: The Science and Art of Clinical Care*. 2nd ed. San Diego, Calif: Singular Publishing Group, Inc; 1997:765–774.
74. Sataloff RT, Spiegel JR, Heuer RJ, et al. Laryngeal minimicroflap: a new technique and reassessment of the microflap saga. *J Voice*. 1995;9(2):198–204.
75. Abitbol J. Limitations of the laser in microsurgery of the larynx. In: Lawrence VL, ed. *Transactions of the Twelfth Symposium: Care of the Professional Voice*. New York, NY: The Voice Foundation; 1984:297–301.
76. Tapia RG, Pardo J, Marigil M, Pacio A. Effects of the laser upon Reinke's space and the neural system of the vocalis muscle. In: Lawrence VL, ed. *Transactions of the Twelfth Symposium: Care of the Professional Voice*. New York, NY: The Voice Foundation; 1984:289–291.
77. Hochman I, Sataloff RT, Hillman RE, Zeitels SM. Ectasias and varices of the vocal fold: clearing the striking zone. *Trans Am Laryngol Assoc*. 1998;119:10–16
78. Sataloff RT, Feldman M, Darby KS, et al. Arytenoid dislocation. *J Voice*. 1988;1(4):368–377.
79. Sataloff RT, Bough ID, Spiegel JR. Arytenoid dislocation: diagnosis and treatment. *Laryngoscope*. 1994;104(10): 1353–1361.
80. Ford CN, Bless DM. Collagen injected in the scarred vocal fold. *J Voice*. 1988;1(1):116–118.
81. Sataloff RT, Spiegel JR, Hawkshaw M, Rosen DC, Heuer RJ. Autologous fat implantation for vocal fold scar. *J Voice*. 1997;11(2):238–246.

10

Psychological Aspects of Voice Disorders

Deborah Caputo Rosen, Reinhardt J. Heuer, Steven H. Levy, and Robert Thayer Sataloff

Professional performers are not only demanding, but also remarkably self-analytical. Like athletes, performers have forced health care providers to refine our definition of normalcy. Ordinarily, physicians, psychotherapists and other professionals are granted great latitude in the definition of "normal." Arts-medicine practitioners have learned to recognize, often quantify, and sometimes restore very high levels of human performance, approaching perfection. The process has required advances in scientific knowledge, clinical management, technology for voice assessment, voice therapy, and surgical technique. The drive to expand our knowledge also has led to unprecedented teamwork and interdisciplinary collaboration. As a result, voice care professionals have come to recognize important psychological problems found commonly in patients with voice disorders. Such problems were ignored routinely in past years. Now they are searched for diligently throughout evaluation and treatment. When identified, they often require intervention by a psychological professional with special knowledge about voice disorders, as well as by a speech-language pathologist (SLP) and other voice team members.

Arts-medicine psychologists specializing in the management of performance anxiety are becoming more common, but there are still very few psychological professionals with extensive experience in diagnosing and treating other psychologic concomitants of voice disorders. It is important for physicians and all other members of the voice care team to recognize the importance of psychological factors in patients with voice disorders and to be familiar with mental health professionals in various disciplines in order to build a multidisciplinary team, generate appropriate referrals, and coordinate optimal patient care.

Psychiatrists are licensed physicians who have completed medical training, residency in psychiatry, and often additional training. They are qualified not only to establish medical and psychiatric diagnoses and provide therapy but also to prescribe medications. Psychologists make mental health diagnoses, administer psychological tests, and provide therapy. In most locations, they do not prescribe medications but often work closely with a physician (usually a psychiatrist) who may prescribe and help manage psychotropic medications during the course of psychotherapy. Clinical psychologists have a master's or doctoral degree in psychology and may have subspecialty training. Other clinical disciplines (ie, social work, nursing, counseling) license graduate-level practitioners to provide psychotherapy. Laryngologists, phoniatrists, and speech-language pathologists are not mental health professionals, although all have at least limited training in psychological diagnosis. Specialty definitions vary from country to country. In the United States, laryngologists are responsible for medical diagnosis and treatment and voice surgery. They also prescribe any medications needed to treat organic voice problems and occasionally take responsibility for prescribing psychoactive medications. Speech-language pathologists are responsible for behavorial therapy for speech, language, and swallowing disorders. In many other countries, phoniatrists perform behavioral therapy in addition to making diagnoses. Phoniatrists are physicians. Traditionally, in some countries, they have been members of an independent specialty that does not include laryngeal surgery. In other countries, they have been subspecialists of otolaryngology. The European Union recently determined that, in the future, phoniatry will be a subspecialty of otolaryngology in member countries. Both speech-language pathologists and phoniatrists include at least some psychological assessment and support in their therapeutic paradigms. However, they are not formally trained mental health professionals and must be constantly vigilant to recognize significant psychopathology and recommend appropriate referral for treatment by a mental health practitioner. Finding a mental health professional familiar with the special needs and problems of voice patients, especially singers and actors, is not easy. Arts-medicine psychology is a relatively new field, as voice was in otolaryngology in the early 1980s. Nevertheless, it is usually possible to find a psychological professional who is either knowledgeable about arts-medicine or the principles of mind-body medicine with whom to collaborate. Resources are available in the literature to assist the interested mental health professional,[1] and incorporating such a colleague into the voice care team is extremely beneficial.

Psychology and Voice Disorders: An Overview

Patients seeking medical care for voice disorders come from the general population. Consequently, a normal distribution of comorbid psychopathology can be expected in a laryngology practice. Psychological factors can be causally related to a voice disorder and/or consequences of vocal dysfunction. In practice, they are usually interwoven. The first task of the otolaryngologist treating any patient with a voice complaint is to establish an accurate diagnosis and its etiology. Only as a result of a thorough, comprehensive history and physical examination (including state-of-the-art technology) can the organic and psychologic components of the voice complaint be elucidated. All treatment planning and subsequent intervention depend on this process. However, even minor voice injuries or health problems can be disturbing for many patients and devastating to some professional voice users. In some cases, they even trigger responses that delay the return of normal voice. Stress and fear of the evaluation procedures often heighten the problem and may cloud diagnostic assessment. Some voice disorders are predominantly psychogenic, and psychological assessment may be required to complete a thorough evaluation. The essential role of the voice in communication of the "self" creates special potential for psychologic impact. Severe psychological consequences of voice dysfunction are especially common in individuals in whom the voice is pathologically perceived to be the self, such as professional voice users. However, the sensitive clinician will recognize varying degrees of similar reactions among most voice patients who are confronted with voice change or loss.

Our work with professional voice users has provided insight into the special intensification of psychological distress they experience in association with lapses in vocal health. This has proved helpful in treating all patients with voice disorders and has led to recognition of psychological problems that may delay recovery following vocal injury or surgery.

In all human beings, self-esteem comprises not only who we believe we are, but also what we have chosen to do as our life's work. A psychological double-exposure exists for performers who experience difficulty separating the two elements. The voice is in, is therefore of, indeed is, the self. Aronson's extensive review of the literature provides an opportunity to examine research that supports the maxim that the "voice is the mirror of the personality"—both normal and abnormal. Parameters such as voice quality, pitch, loudness, stress pattern, rate, pauses, articulation, vocabulary, syntax, and content are described as they reflect life stressors, psychopathology. and discrete emotions.[2] Sundberg describes Fonagy's research on the effects of various states of emotion on phonation. These studies revealed specific alterations in articulatory and laryngeal structures and in respiratory muscular activity patterns related to 10 different emotional states.[3]

Vogel and Carter include descriptive summaries of the features, symptoms, and signs of communication impairment in their text on neurologic and psychiatric disorders.[4] The mind and body are inextricably linked. Thoughts and feelings generate neurochemical transmissions that affect all organ systems. Therefore, disturbances of physical function can have profound emotional effects, and disturbances of emotion can also have profound bodily and artistic effects.

Professional Voice Users: A Special Case

It is useful to understand in greater depth the problems experienced by professional voice users who suffer vocal injuries. Most of our observations in this population occur among singers and actors. However, although they are the most obvious and demanding professional voice users, many other professionals are classified as professional voice users. These include politicians, attorneys, clergy, teachers, salespeople, broadcasters, shop foremen (who speak over noise), football quarterbacks, secretaries, telephone operators, and others. Although we are likely to expect profound emotional reactions to voice problems among singers and actors, many other patients may also demonstrate similar reactions. If we do not recognize these reactions as such, they may be misinterpreted as anger, malingering, or other "difficult patient" behavior. Some patients are unconsciously afraid that their voices are lost forever and are psychologically unable to make a full effort at vocal recovery after injury or surgery. This blocking of the frightening possibilities by rationalization (eg, "I haven't made a maximum attempt so I don't know yet if my voice will be satisfactory") can result in prolonged or incomplete recovery after technically flawless surgery. It is incumbent on the laryngologist and other members of the voice team to understand the psychological consequences of voice disturbance and to recognize them not only in extreme cases, but even in their subtler manifestations.[1]

Typically, successful professional voice users (especially actors, singers, and politicians) may fall into a personality subtype that is ambitious, driven, perfectionistic, and tightly controlled. Externally, they present themselves as confident, competitive, and self-assured. Internally, self-esteem, the product of personality development, is often far more fragile. Children and adolescents do the best they can to survive and integrate their life experiences. All psychological defense mechanisms are means to that end. Most of these defenses are not under conscious control. They are a habitual element of the fabric of one's response to life, especially in stressful or psychologically threatening situations.

All psychological adjustment expresses itself through the personality of the patient, and it is essential to focus on the personality style of every performer who seeks psychological help. This can best be done during psychological assessment and evaluation by exploring daily activities, especially those pertaining to the performer's involvement with his or her art, the patient's growth and personality development as an artist, and relationships with people both within and outside his or her performing environment. Each developmental phase carries inherent coping tasks and responsibilities, which can play an important part in the patient's emotional response to vocal dysfunction. Learning about, cherishing, and managing our unique, individual psychological vulnerabilities are critical to adaptive psychological function throughout life.

Research into body image theory also provides a theoretical basis for understanding the special impact of stress or injuries to the voice in vocal performers.[5] The body is essential to perception, learning, and memory; and it serves as a sensory register and processor of sensory information. Body experience is deeply personal and constitutes a private world typically shared with others only under conditions of closest intimacy. Moreover, the body is an expressive instrument, the medium through which individuality is communicated verbally and nonverbally. It is therefore possible to anticipate direct correspondence between certain physical illnesses or injuries and body and self-image. Among these are psychosomatic conditions and/or body states with high levels of involvement of personality factors. In these cases, body illness or injury may reactivate psychopathologic processes that began in early childhood or induce an emotional disorder such as denial or inappropriately prolonged depression. Psychological reactions to a physical injury are not uniformly disturbing or distressing and do not necessarily result in maladjustment. However, Shontz notes that reactions to body injury are more a function of how much anxiety is generated by the experience than by the actual location, severity, or type of injury. [5]

Patients are notoriously adaptive and capable of living with most types of difficulties, injuries, or disabilities if they feel there is a good reason for doing so. If one's life has broad meaning and purpose, any given disorder takes on less significance. When a physical disability or any given body part becomes the main focus of concern or has been the main source of self-esteem in a person's life, that life becomes narrowed and constricted. Patients adapt satisfactorily to a personal medical condition when the problems of living related to the injury cease to be the dominant element in their total psychological life.

A unique closeness exists between one's body and ones' identity; this body-self is a central part of self-concept. The interdependence of body image and self-esteem means that distortion of one will affect the other. The cognitive-behavioral model for understanding body image includes the perceptual and affective components, as well as attitudinal ones. From the cognitive perspective, any body image producing dysphoria results from irrational thoughts, unrealistic expectations, and faulty explanations.[6] Body-image constructs and their affective and cognitive outcomes relate to personality types and cognitive styles. For example, depressive personality types chronically interpret events in terms of deficiencies and are trapped by habitual self-defeating thoughts. Anxious personality types chronically overestimate risks and become hypervigilant. These types of cognitive errors generate automatic thoughts that intensify body-image-related psychopathology.[1]

It is the task of personality theorists to explain the process of the genesis of the self. There are numerous coherent personality theories, all substantially interrelated. The framework of Karen Horney (1885–1952) is particularly useful in attempting to understand the creative personality and its vulnerabilities. In simplification, she formulated a "holistic notion of the personality as an individual unit functioning within a social framework and continually interacting with its environment."[7] In Horney's model, there are three selves. The *actual self* is the sum total of the individual's experience; the *real self* is responsible for harmonious integration; and the *idealized self* sets up unrealistically high expectations, which, in the face of disappointment, result in self-hatred and self-alienation.[7] We have chosen Horney's theory as a working model in evolving therapeutic approaches to the special patient population of professional voice users. They are the laryngologist's most demanding consumers of voice care and cling to their physician's explanations with dependency.[1,8]

For theoretical clarity, it is useful to divide the experience of vocal injury into several phases. In practice, however, these often overlap or recur; and the emotional responses are not entirely linear.

- *Problem recognition.* The patient feels that something is wrong but may not be able to clearly define the problem, especially if the onset has been gradual or masked by a coexisting illness. Usually, personal first-aid measures will be tried; and when they fail, the performer will manifest some level of panic. This is often followed by feeling of guilt when the distress is turned inward against the self, or rage or blame when externalized.
- *Diagnosis.* This may be a protracted period if an injured performer does not have immediate access to a laryngologist experienced in the assessment of vocal injury. He or she may have already consulted with voice teachers, family physicians, allergists, nutritionists, peers, or otolaryngologists and speech-language pathologists without specialized training in caring for professional voice users. There may have been several, possibly contradictory, diagnoses and treatment protocols. The voice dysfunction persists, and the patient grows more fearful and discouraged. If attempts to perform are continued, they may exacerbate the injury and/or produce embarrassing performances. The fear is of the unknown, but it is intuitively perceived as significant.
- *Treatment: acute/rehabilitative.* Now, fear of the unknown becomes fear of the known, and of its outcome. The performer, now in the sick role, initially feels overwhelmed and powerless. There is frequently a strong component of blame that may be turned inward. "Why me? Why now?" is the operant, recurrent thought. Vocal rehabilitation is an exquisitely slow, carefully monitored, often frustrating process; and many patients become fearful and impatient. Some will meet the criteria for major depression, which will be discussed in additional detail, as will the impact of vocal fold surgery.
- *Acceptance.* When the acute and rehabilitative treatment protocol is complete, the final prognosis is clearer. When there are significant lasting changes in the voice, the patient will experience mourning. Even when there is full return of vocal function, a sense of vulnerability lingers. These individuals are likely to adhere strictly, even ritualistically, to preventive vocal hygiene habits and may be anxious enough to become hypochondriacal.[1,8,9]

The psychological professional providing care to this special population must be well versed in developmental psychology, experience the world of the performer, and retain an unshakable empathy for the extraordinary psychologically disorganizing impact of potential vocal injury. It is critical to harken back to one of the earliest lessons taught to all psychotherapists-in-training. That is, the therapist must, through accurate empathy, earn the right to make interpretations and interventions. When this type of insightful and accurate support is available to the professional voice user, the psychotherapist may well be the patient's rudder in the rough seas of diagnosis, treatment, and rehabilitation.

Psychogenic Voice Disorders

Voice disorders are divided into organic and nonorganic etiologies. Various terms have been used interchangeably (but imprecisely) to label observable vocal dysfunction in the presence of emotional factors that cause or perpetuate the symptoms. Aronson argues convincingly for the term psychogenic, which is "broadly synonymous with functional, but has the advantage of stating positively, based on an exploration of its causes, that the voice disorder is a manifestation of one or more types of psychological disequilibrium, such as anxiety, depression, conversion reaction, or personality disorder, that interfere with normal volitional control over phonation.[2]

Psychogenic disorders include a variety of discrete presentations. There is disagreement over classification among speech-language pathologists, with some excluding musculoskeletal tension disorders from this heading. Aronson and Butcher et al conclude that the hypercontraction of extrinsic and intrinsic laryngeal muscles, in response to emotional stress, is the common denominator behind the dysphonia or aphonia in these disorders. In addition, the extent of pathology visible on laryngeal examination is inconsistent with the severity of the abnormal voice. They cite four categories:

- musculoskeletal tension disorders, including vocal abuse, vocal nodules, contact ulcers, and ventricular phonation;
- conversion voice disorders, including conversion muteness and aphonia, conversion dysphonia, and psychogenic adductor "spasmodic dysphonia";
- mutational falsetto (puberphonia);
- childlike speech in adults.[2,10]

Psychogenic dysphonia often presents as total inability to speak, whispered speech, extremely strained or strangled speech, interrupted speech rhythm, or speech in an abnormal register (such as falsetto in a male). Usually, involuntary vocalizations during laughing and coughing are normal. The vocal folds are often difficult to examine because of supraglottic hyperfunction. There may be apparent bowing of both vocal folds consistent with severe muscular tension dysphonia, creating anterior-posterior squeeze during phonation. Longstanding attempts to produce voice in the presence of this pattern may even result in traumatic lesions associated with vocal abuse patterns, such as vocal fold nodules. Normal abduction and adduction of the vocal folds may be visualized during flexible fiberoptic laryngoscopy by instructing the patient to perform maneuvers that decrease supraglottic load, such as whistling or sniffing. In addition, the singing voice is often more easily produced than the speaking voice in these patients. Tongue protrusion and stabilization during the rigid telescopic portion of the examination will often result in clear voice. The severe muscular tension dysphonia associated with psychogenic dysphonia can often be eliminated by behavioral interventions by the speech-language pathologist, sometimes in one session. In many instances, moments of successful voice have been restored during stroboscopic examination.

Electromyography may be helpful in confirming the diagnosis by revealing simultaneous firing of abductors and adductors. Psychogenic dysphonia has been frequently misdiagnosed as spasmodic dysphonia, partially explaining the excellent "spasmodic dysphonia" cure rates in some series.

Psychogenic voice disorders are not merely the absence of observable neurolaryngeal abnormalities. This psychiatric diagnosis cannot be made with accuracy without the presence of a psychodynamic formulation based on "understanding of the personality, motivations, conflicts, and primary as well as; secondary gain" associated with the symptoms.[1,11]

Conversion disorders are a special classification of psychogenic symptomatology and reflect loss of voluntary control over striated muscle or the sensory systems as a reflection of stress or psychological conflict. They may occur in any organ system, but the target organ is often symbolically related to the specifics of the unconsciously perceived threat. The term was first used by Freud to describe a defense mechanism that rendered an intolerable wish or drive innocuous by translating its energy into a physical symptom. The presence of an ego-syntonic physical illness offers *primary gain*: relief from the anxiety, depression, or rage by maintaining the emotional conflict in the unconscious. *Secondary gain* often occurs by virtue of the sick role.

Classic descriptions of findings in these patients include indifference to the symptoms, chronic stress, suppressed anger, immaturity and dependency, moderate depression and poor sex role-identification.[11,12] Conversion voice disorders also reflect a breakdown in communication with someone of emotional significance in the patient's life—wanting but blocking the verbal expression of anger, fear, or remorse, and significant feelings of shame.[1,2]

Confirmed neurologic disease and psychogenic voice disorders do coexist and are known as somatic compliance.[13,14] Of course, potential organic causes of psychiatric disorders must always be thoroughly ruled out. Insidious onset of depression, personality changes, anxiety, or presumed conversion symptoms may be the first presentation of central nervous system (CNS) disease.[15]

General Psychopathologic Presentations

Otolaryngologists and all other health care providers involved with patients with voice disorders should be able to recognize significant comorbid psychopathology and should be prepared to consult an appropriate mental health care professional. Psychologists and psychiatrists are responsible for psychologic diagnosis and treatment, but it is important to select a mental health professional with advanced understanding of the special problems associated with voice disorders (especially, but not exclusively, in professional voice users). Patterns of voice use may provide clues to the presence of psychopathology, although voice disturbance is certainly not the principal feature of a major psychiatric illness. Nevertheless, failure to recognize serious psychopathology in voice patients may result not only in errors in voice diagnosis and failures of therapy but, more importantly, in serious injury to the patient, sometimes even death.

Although a full depressive syndrome, including melancholia, can occur as a result of loss, it fulfills the criteria for a major depressive episode when the individual becomes preoccupied with feelings of worthlessness and guilt, demonstrates marked psychomotor retardation and other biologic markers, and becomes impaired in both social, and occupational functioning.[16] Careful listening during the taking of a history will reveal a flat affect, including slowed rate of speech, decreased length of utterance, lengthy pauses, decreased pitch variability, monoloudness, and frequent use of vocal fry.[1,4,17] William Styron described his speech during his depressive illness as "slowed to the vocal equivalent of a shuffle."[18] Major depression may be part of the patient's past medical history, may be a comorbid illness, or may be a result of the presenting problem. The essential feature is a prominent, persistent dysphoric mood characterized by a loss of pleasure in nearly all activities. Appetite and sleep are disturbed; and there may be marked weight gain or loss, hypersomnia, or one of three insomnia patterns. Psychomotor agitation or retardation may be present. Patients may demonstrate distractibility, memory disturbances, and difficulty concentrating. Feelings of worthlessness, helplessness and hopelessness are a classic triad. Suicidal ideation, with or without a plan, and / or concomitant psychotic features, may necessitate emergency intervention.

Major affective disorders are classified as unipolar or bipolar. In bipolar disorder, the patient will also experience periods of mania, a recurrent elated state first occurring in young adulthood. (Manic episodes occurring for the first time in patients over 50 should alert the clinician to medical or CNS illness or to the effects of drugs.) The presentation of the illness includes the following major characteristics on a continuum of severity: elevated mood, irritability / hostility, distractibility, inflated self-concept, grandiosity, physical and sexual overactivity, flight of ideas, decreased need for sleep, social intrusiveness, buying sprees, and inappropriate collections of possessions. Manic patients demonstrate impaired social and familial behavior patterns. They are manipulative, alienate family members, and tend to have a very high divorce rate.[16,19] Vocal presentation will manifest flight of ideas (content), rapid-paced pressured speech, and often increased pitch and volume. There may be dysfluency related to the rate of speech, breathlessness, and difficulty interrupting the language stream. Three major theories, based on neuroanatomy, neuroendocrinology, and neuropharmacology, are the most currently promulgated explanations for these disease states, but they are beyond the scope of this chapter.[19-21]

Treatment of affective disorders includes psychotherapy. Diagnosis and short-term treatment of reactive depressive states may be performed by the psychologist on the voice team, utilizing individual or group therapy modalities. Longer term treatment necessitates referral to a community-based psychotherapist, ideally one whose skills, training, and understanding of the medical and artistic components of the illness are well known to the referring laryngologist. The use of psychopharmacologic agents is a risk / benefit decision. When the patient's symptom severity meets the criteria for major affective disorder, the physiological effects of the disease, as well as the potential for self-destructive behavior, must be carefully considered.

Anxiety is an expected reaction to any medical diagnosis and the required treatment. However, anxiety disorders are seen with increasing incidence. Vocal presentations of anxiety vary with the continuum of psychiatric symptoms, ranging from depression to agitation and including impairment of concentration. Psychotherapy, including desensitization, cognitive / behavioral techniques, stress management, hypnosis, and insight-oriented approaches are helpful. Patients must learn to tolerate their distress and identify factors that precipitate or intensify their symptoms (see the stress management discussion that follows). Medications may be used to treat underlying depression and decrease the frequency of episodes. However, it leaves the underlying conflict unresolved and negatively affects artistic quality.[1,8,22] Some medical conditions are commonly associated with the presenting symptom of anxiety. These include CNS disease, Cushing's syndrome, hyperthyroidism, hypoglycemia, the consequences of minor head trauma, premenstrual syndrome, and cardiac disease such as mitral valve prolapse and various arrhythmias. Medications prescribed for other conditions may have anxiety as a side effect. These include such drugs as amphetamines, corticosteroids, caffeine, decongestants, cocaine, and the asthma armamentarium.[4]

Although psychotic behavior may be observed with major affective disorders, organic CNS disease or drug toxicity, schizophrenia occurs in only 1 to 2% of the general population.[23] Its onset is most prominent in mid- to late adolescence through the late 20s. Incidence is approximately equal for males and females, and schizophrenia has been described in all cultures and socioeconomic classes. This is a group of mental disorders in which massive disruptions in cognition or perception, such as delusions, hallucinations, or thought disorders, are present. The fundamental causes of schizophrenia are not known; but the disease involves excessive amounts of neurotransmitters, chiefly dopamine. There is a genetic predisposition. Somatic delusions may present as voice complaints.

However, flattening or inappropriateness of affect, a diagnostic characteristic of schizophrenia, will produce voice changes similar to those described for depression and mania. Where the hallucinatory material creates fear, characteristics of anxiety and agitation will be audible. Perseveration, repetition, and neologisms may be present. The signs and symptoms also include clear indications of deterioration in social or occupational functional personal hygiene, changes in behavior, changes in behavior and movement, an altered sense of self, and the presence of blunted or inappropriate affect.[16,23] The disease is chronic and control requires consistent use of antipsychotic medications for symptom management. Social support and regulating activities of daily living are crucial in maintaining emotional control. Family counseling and support groups offer the opportunity to share experiences and resources in the care of individuals with this difficult disease.

Psychoactive Medications

All psychoactive agents have effects that can interfere with vocal tract physiology. Treatment requires frequent, open collaboration between the laryngologist and the biologic psychiatrist. The patient and physicians need to carefully weigh the benefits and side effects of available medications. Patients must be informed of the relative probability of experiencing any known side effect. This is especially critical to the professional voice user and plays an important role in developing a treatment plan when there is no imminent serious psychiatric risk.

Antidepressant medications include compounds from several different classes. Tri- and tetracyclic antidepressants (TCAs) block the reuptake of norepinephrine and serotonin and have secondary effects on pre-and postsynaptic receptors. An H1-H2-receptor blockade has also been demonstrated.[24]

Schatzberg and Cole summarize the side effects of TCAs as:

- anticholinergic (dry mouth and nasal mucosa, constipation, urinary hesitancy, gastroesophageal reflux);
- autonomic (orthostatic hypotension, palpitations, increased cardiac conduction intervals, diaphoresis, hypertension, tremor);
- CNS (stimulation, sedation, delirium, twitching, nausea, speech delay, seizures, extrapyramidal symptoms); and
- other (weight gain, impotence).[24,25]

These may be dose-related and agent-specific.

Monoamine oxidase inhibitors (MAOIs) are useful in treating depression that is refractory to tricyclics. The mode of action involves inhibiting monoamine oxidase (MAO) in various organs, especially MAO-A, for which norepinephrine and serotonin are primarily substrates. The full restoration of enzyme activity may take 2 weeks after the drug has discontinued.

The side effects of MAOIs may be extremely serious and troublesome. The most commonly reported is dizziness secondary to orthostatic hypotension. When MAOIs are taken, hypertensive crisis with violent headache and potential cerebrovascular accident, or hyperpyrexic crisis with monoclonus and coma, may be produced by ingesting foods rich in tyramine or by many medications, including meperidine (Demerol), epinephrine, local anesthetics containing sympathomimetics, decongestants, selective serotonin reuptake inhibitors (SSRIs), and surgical anesthetics. Other side effects include sexual dysfunction, sedation, insomnia, overstimulation, myositislike reactions, myoclonic twitches, and a small incidence of dry mouth, constipation, and urinary hesitancy.[24,25]

A few antidepressants has been developed with different chemical structures and side effect profiles. Trazodone (Desyrel, Geneva) is pharmacologically complex. It weakly inhibits serotonin reuptake and acts post-synaptically as a 5-HT_2 antagonist.[26] It has proved helpful in depression associated with initial insomnia. Three side effects are particularly noteworthy: sedation, acute dizziness with fainting (especially when taken on an empty stomach), and priapism.[1,27,28]

Nefazodone hydrochloride (Serzone, Bristol-Myers Squibb) is another antidepressant with a complex mechanism. It weakly inhibits serotonin and norepinephrine uptake, but mostly blocks the post-synaptic 5-HT_2 serotonin receptors.[26] Its chemical structure is different from the SSRIs, tri/tetracyclics, and MAOIs. It appears to inhibit neuronal reuptake of serotonin and norepinephrine. It has been advertised as useful in depressions characterized by anxiety. Side effects include significant orthostasis, potential activation of mania, and a questionable potential for priapism. Decreased cognitive and motor performance, dry mouth, nausea, and dizziness are also noted as well as other frequently recurring side effects. This drug has notable medication interactions with Hismanal, Halcion, Xanax, and Propulsid. It is not recommended for patients with unstable heart disease.[29] Life-threatening hepatic failure has been reported in patients treated with Serzone. Patients should be alerted to the signs and symptoms of liver disease (jaundice, anoxia, malaise, and gastrointestinal complaints).

Bupropion (Wellbutrin, Glaxo Smith Kline) was released in 1989. Its biochemical mode of action is not well understood. It is not anticholinergic. The most commonly reported side effect is nausea. However, a potential risk of seizures exists; and the drug is not recommended in patients with a history of seizures, head trauma, or anorexia or bulimia.[25,25]

A group of antidepressant drugs that selectively inhibit the reuptake of serotonin are most likely to be selected as first pharmacological agents. These include fluoxetine (Prozac, Lilly), sertraline (Zoloft, Pfizer), and paroxetine (Paxil, Glaxo Smith Kline). They appear to be effective in typical episodic depression and for some chronic refractory presentations.[24,26] Major side effects are significant degrees of nausea, sweating, headache, mouth dryness, tremor, nervousness, dizziness, insomnia, somnolence, constipation, and sexual dysfunction. There are drug interactions with the concomitant administration of tryptophan, MAOIs, warfarin, cimetidine, phenobarbital, and phenytoin.[27-36] Citalopram (Celexa, Forest) and S-citalopram (Lexapro, Forest) are the latest addition to this group of antidepressants that selectively inhibit the re-uptake of serotonin.[26]

Venlafaxin (Effexor, Wyeth-Ayerst) inhibits the uptake of both serotonin and norepinephrine at higher doses. Its side effect profile is similar to the SSRIs. At higher doses, some patients may develop hypertension. Duloxetine (Cymbala, Lilly) also inhibits the uptake of both serotonin and norepinephrine. Mirtazapine (Remeron, Organon) does not inhibit serotonin or norepinephrine reuptake. It is an antagonist of 5-HT_2A, 5-HT_2C, and alpha-2-adrenergic autoregulators, therapy affecting the serotonergic and noradrenergic systems. It can be very sedating and is associated with increased appetite and weight gain.[26]

A small percentage of adolescents and adults will experience agitation and suicidal ideation when started on antidepressants or when the dose is increased. Patients should be warned of this adverse reaction.

Mood-stabilizing drugs are those that are effective in manic episodes and prevent manic and depressive recurrences in patients with bipolar disorder. These include lithium salts and several anticonvulsants. Lithium is available in multiple formulations, and prescribing is guided by both symptom index and blood levels. Lithium side effects are apparent in diverse organ systems. The most commonly noted is fine tremor, especially noticeable in the fingers. With toxic lithium levels, gross tremulousness, ataxia, dysarthria, and confusion or delirium may develop. Some patients describe slowed mentation, measurable memory deficit, and impaired creativity. Chronic nausea and diarrhea are usually related to gastrointestinal tract mucosal irritation but may be signs of toxicity. Some patients gain weight progressively and may demonstrate edema or increased appetite. Lithium therapy affects thyroid function. In some cases it is transitory; but there may be goiter with normal T_3 and T_4 but elevated TSH levels.[24]

Polyuria and secondary polydipsia are complications of lithium and may progress to diabetes insipidus. In most cases, discontinuing the medication reverses the renal effects. Prescribed thiazide diuretics can double the lithium level and lead to sudden lithium excretion. Cardiovascular effects include the rare induction of sick sinus syndrome. The aggravation of psoriasis, allergic skin rashes, and reversible alopecia are associated with lithium therapy, as are teratogenic effects.[24]

Three anticonvulsant compounds appear to act preferentially on the temporal lobe and the limbic system. Carbamazepine (Tegretol, Novartis) carries a risk of agranulocytosis or aplastic anemia and is monitored by complete blood counts and symptoms of bone marrow depression. Care must be taken to avoid the numerous drug interactions that accelerate the metabolism of some drugs or raise carbamazepine levels.[24]

Valproic acid (Depakote, Depakene, Abbott) is especially useful when there is a rapid-cycling pattern. The major side effect is hepatocellular toxicity. Thrombocytopenia and platelet dysfunction have been reported. Sedation is common; and tremor, ataxia, weight gain, alopecia, and fetal neural tube defects are all side effects that patients must comprehend.[24,30]

Anxiolytics are the psychotropic drugs most commonly prescribed, usually by nonpsychiatric specialists, for somatic disorders. It behooves the laryngologist to probe for a history of past or current drug therapy in markedly anxious or somatically focused patients with vocal complaints. Benzodiazepines produce effective relief of anxiety but have a high addictive potential that includes physical symptoms of withdrawal, including potential seizures, if the drug is stopped abruptly. It is well to remember that this class of drugs is commonly available on the streets and from colleagues. The most common benzodiazepine side effect is dose-related sedation, followed by dizziness, weakness, ataxia, decreased motor performance, and mild hypotension. Clonazepam (Klonopin, Roche Laboratories) is a benzodiazepine and may produce sedation, ataxia, and malcoordination, as well as (rarely) disinhibition, agitation or asituational anger.[24] Alterations of sensory input, either by CNS stimulants (cocaine, amphetamines, and over-the-counter vasoconstrictors) or depressants, are potentially dangerous in a voice professional. The patient who is unaware of these effects should be apprised of them promptly by the laryngologist.[1,31]

Phenobarbital and meprobamate are no longer commonly used as anxiolytics in the United States. Clomipramine (Anafranil, Novartis) is useful in the anxiety evident in obsessive-compulsive disorder. Side effects are similar to those of the tricyclic antidepressants: dry mouth, hypotension, constipation, tachycardia, sweating, tremor, and anorgasmia.[24] Fluoxetine has also proven effective for some patients with obsessive-compulsive disorder and appears better tolerated.[24] Fluvoxamine maleate (Luvox, Solvay) is also particularly useful for the treatment for obsessive-compulsive disorder.

Hydroxyzine, (Vistaril, Pfizer), an antihistamine, is occasionally prescribed for mild anxiety and/or pruritus. It does not produce physical dependence but does potentiate the CNS effects of alcohol, narcotics, CNS depressants, and tricyclic antidepressants. Side effects include notable mucous membrane dryness and drowsiness.[26]

Buspirone (Buspar, Bristol-Myers Squibb) is nonsedating at its usual dosage levels, and it has little addictive potential. Side effects include mild degrees of headache, nausea, and dizziness. However, it is poorly tolerated in patients accustomed to the more immediate relief of benzodiazepines.[24]

Beta-blockers are used by some clinicians to mask physiologic symptoms of sympathetic arousal in performance anxiety. Although the problem of upper respiratory tract secretion dryness may be diminished and other symptoms of performance anxiety may be lessened by beta-blockers, their side effects are serious and may include bradycardia, hypotension, weakness, fatigue, clouded sensorium, impotence, and bronchospasm.[31] In addition, they may induce depression. Moreover, they leave the underlying conflict unresolved and affect negatively artistic quality.[22] Some authors still prefer them, especially in those patients who may be at risk for drug dependency.

Various antipsychotic drugs (haloperidol (Haldol, Ortho McNeil), chlorpromazine hydrochloride (Thorazine, Glaxo Smith Kline), perphenazine (Trilafon, Schering), molindone (Moban, Endo Labs), loxapine HCl (Loxitane, Watson) have a mode of action that involves dopamine antagonism, probably in the mesolimbic or mesocortical areas. They also have endocrine effects through dopamine receptors in the hypothalamic-pituitary axis.[24] These potent agents have very significant side effects. Sedation, accompanied by fatigue during early dosing and akinesia with chronic administration, is frequently described. Anticholinergic effects include postural hypotension, dry mouth, nasal congestion, and constipation. The endocrine system is also affected, with a direct increase in blood prolactin levels. Breast enlargement and galactorrhea are seen in men and women and correlate with impotence and amenorrhea. Weight gain is often excessive and frequently leads to noncompliance. Skin complications, such as rash, retinal pigmentation, and photosensitivity, occur. Rare but serious complications include agranulocytosis, allergic obstructive hepatitis, seizures, and sudden death secondary to ventricular fibrillation.[24]

Risperidone (Risperdal, Janssen), olazapine (Zyprexa, Lilly), ziprasidone (Geodon, Pfizer), quetiapine (Seroquel, Astrazeneca), and clozapine (Clozaril, Novartis) are atypical antipsychotic medications. They have the ability to block serotonin 5-HT$_2$A receptors and they have weak affinity for dopamine receptors.[26] Aripiprazole (Abillify, Bristol-Myers Squibb) is the newest of the antipsychotic medicines.

Approximately 14% of patients receiving long-term (more than 7 years) treatment with antipsychotic agents develop tardive dyskinesia ranging from minimal tongue restlessness to incapacitating, disfiguring choreiform and/or athetoid movements, especially of the head, neck, and hands. Unfortunately, there is no cure for the condition once it develops, nor are there accurate predictors for which patients will be affected.[24] The atypical antipsychotics have a much lower risk of causing tardive dyskinesia.

The mode of action in neurologic side effects of the neuroleptics is primarily cholinergic-dopaminergic blockade. Dystonia usually involves tonic spasm of the tongue, jaw, and neck but may range from mild tongue stiffness to opisthotonos.[24] Pseudoparkinsonism may occur very early in treatment and is evidenced by muscle stiffness, cogwheel rigidity, stooped posture, and masklike facies with loss of salivary control. Pill-rolling tremor is rare. Akathisia, an inner-driven muscular restlessness with rhythmic leg jiggling, hand wringing, and pacing, is extremely unpleasant. Multiple drug regimens are employed to diminish these symptoms.[24]

Neuroleptic malignant syndrome is a potentially fatal complication of these drugs. Patients manifest hyperthermia, severe extrapyramidal signs and autonomic hyperarousal. Neuroleptics also affect temperature regulation generally and can predispose users to heat stroke.[24]

Ongoing psychiatric treatment of patients with voice disorders mandates a careful evaluation of current and prior psychoactive drug therapy. In addition, numerous psychoactive substances are used in the medical management of neurologic conditions such as Tourette's syndrome (haloperidol), chronic pain syndromes (carbamazepine), and vertigo (diazepam, clonazepam).

The laryngologist must thus identify symptoms that may be causally related to drug side effects and avoid drug interactions. It is appropriate (with the patient's consent) to consult with the prescribing physician directly to advocate the use of the psychoactive drug least likely to produce adverse effects on the voice while adequately controlling the psychiatric illness.[24]

Additional Psychological Etiologies and Treatments

Eating Disorders and Substance Abuse

Rapport with the laryngologist and voice team members may also allow patients to reveal other self-defeating disorders. Among the most common in arts-medicine are body dysmorphic (eating) disorders and substance-abuse problems. Comprehensive discussion of these subjects is beyond the scope of this chapter; but it is important for the laryngologist to recognize such conditions, not only because of their effects on the voice, but also because of their potentially serious general medical and psychiatric implications. In addition to posterior laryngitis and pharyngitis, laryngeal findings associated with bulimia include subepithelial vocal fold hemorrhages, superficial telangiectasia of the vocal fold mucosa, and vocal fold scarring.[23]

Bulimia is a disorder associated with self-induced vomiting, laxative or diuretic abuse, or exercise excess following episodes of binge eating. It may occur sporadically, or it may be a chronic problem. Vomiting produces signs and symptoms similar to severe chronic reflux as well as thinning of tooth enamel. Bulimia nervosa can be a serous disorder and may be associated with anorexia nervosa. Bulimia may be more prevalent than is commonly realized. It has been estimated to occur in as many as 2 to 4% of female adolescents and female young adults. Laryngologists must be attentive to the potential for anorexia and exercise addiction in the maintenance of a desirable body appearance in performers.

Appetite Suppressants

There is enormous popular interest in the use of appetite suppressants in weight management. Many myths persist about proper weight management approaches in singers and the value and/or risk of weight loss. The availability and popularity of appetite suppressant drugs, and mass marketing approaches, which include making them available in franchised weight loss centers, led many Americans to explore the use of Fen-Phen [phentermine (Ionamine and others) and fenfluramine (Pondomin)]. Another drug that gained popularity is dexfenfluramine hydrochloride (Redux). These medications have limited efficacy in changing metabolism and limiting craving. Many patients took these drugs in combinations that were never approved for concomitant use. Laryngologists and psychologic professionals caring for singers and other performers should be certain to investigate the potential use of these medications, which were voluntarily withdrawn from the market by their manufacturer in 1997 because of a significant correlation with cardiac valve damage and with pulmonary hypertension.

Alcohol, benzodiazepines, stimulants, cocaine, and narcotics are notoriously readily available in the performing community and on the streets. In patients who demonstrate signs and symptoms, or who admit that these areas of their lives are out of control, these problems should be acknowledged while efficiently arranging treatment for them. The window of opportunity is often remarkably narrow. The physician should establish close ties to excellent treatment facilities where specialized clinicians can offer confidential outpatient management, with inpatient care available when required for safety.[1]

Neurogenic Dysphonia

Patients with neurological disease are likely to experience psychiatric symptoms, especially depression and anxiety. These disorders cause physiological changes that may exacerbate or mask the underlying neurological presentation. Metcalfe and colleagues cite the incidence of severe depression and/or anxiety in neurological patients at one third.[32] Site of lesion affects the incidence, with lesions of the left cerebral hemisphere, basal ganglia, limbic system, thalamus, and anterior frontal lobe more likely to produce depression and anxiety.[33] The same structures are important in voice, speech and language production; so depression and anxiety logically coexist with voice and language disorders resulting from CNS pathology.[33,34] Dystonias and stuttering are also associated with both neurological and psychogenic etiologies and must be carefully distinguished by the laryngologist before instituting interdisciplinary treatment.[35]

Stress Management

Stress pervades virtually all professions in today's fast-moving society. A singer preparing for a series of concerts, a teacher preparing for presentation of lectures, a lawyer anticipating a major trial, a businessperson negotiating an important contract, or a member of any other goal-oriented profession, each must deal with a myriad of demands on his or her time and talents. In 1971, Brodnitz reported on 2286 cases of all forms of voice disorders and classified 80% of the disorders as attributable to voice abuse or psychogenic factors resulting in vocal dysfunction.[17] However, regardless of the incidence, it is clear that stress-related problems are important and common in professional voice users. Stress may be physical or psychological, and it often involves a combination of both. Either may interfere with performance. Stress represents a special problem for singers, because its physiologic manifestations may interfere with the delicate mechanisms of voice production.[1]

Stress is recognized as a factor in illness and disease and is probably implicated in almost every type of human problem. It is estimated that 50 to 70% of all physicians' visits involve complaints of stress-related illness.[36] Stress is a psychological experience that has physiological consequences. A brief review of some terminology may be useful. *Stress* is a term that is used broadly. Our working definition is emotional, cognitive, and physiological reactions to psychological demands and challenges. The term *stress level* reflects the degree of stress experienced. Stress is not an all-or-none phenomenon. The psychological effects of stress range from mild to severely incapacitating. The term stress response refers to the physiologic reaction of an organism to stress. A *stressor* is an external stimulus or internal thought, perception, image, or emotion that creates stress.[37] Two other concepts are important in a contemporary discussion of stress: *coping* and *adaptation*. Lazarus has defined coping as "the process of managing demands (external or internal) that are appraised as taxing or exceeding the resources of the person."[38] In the early 1930s, Hans Selye, an endocrinologist, discovered a generalized response to stressors in research animals. He described their responses using the term *general adaptation syndrome*. Selye (cited in Green and Snellenberger[37]) postulated that the physiology of the test animals was trying to adapt to the challenges of noxious stimuli. The process of adaptation to chronic and severe stressors was harmful over time. There were three phases to the observed response: *alarm*, *adaptation*, and *exhaustion*. These phases were named for physiologic responses during a sequence of events. The alarm phase is the characteristic fight-or-flight response. If the stressor continued, the animal appeared to adapt. In the adaptation phase, the physiologic responses were less extreme; but the animal eventually became more exhausted. In the exhaustion phase, the animal's adaptation energy was spent, physical symptoms occurred, and some animals died.[20]

Stress responses occur in part through the autonomic nervous system. A stressor triggers particular brain centers, which in turn affect target organs through nerve connections. The brain has two primary pathways for the stress response, neuronal and hormonal; and these pathways overlap. The body initiates a stress response through one of three pathways: through sympathetic nervous system efferents that terminate on target organs such as the heart and blood vessels; via the release of epinephrine and norepinephrine from the adrenal medulla; and through the release of various other catecholamines.[37] A full description of the various processes involved is beyond the scope of this chapter. However, stress has numerous physical consequences. Through the autonomic nervous system, it may alter oral and vocal fold secretions, heart rate, and gastric acid production. Under acute, anxiety-producing circumstances, such changes are to be expected. When frightened, a normal person's palms become cold and sweaty, the mouth becomes dry, heart rate increases, his or her pupils change size, and stomach acid secretions may increase. These phenomena are objective signs that may be observed by a physician; and their symptoms may be recognized by the performer as dry mouth and voice fatigue, heart palpitations, and "heartburn." More severe, prolonged stress is also commonly associated with increased muscle tension throughout the body (but particularly in the head and neck), headaches, decreased ability to concentrate, and insomnia. Chronic fatigue is also a common symptom. These physiologic alterations may lead not only to altered vocal quality, but also to physical pathology. Increased gastric acid secretion is associated with ulcers, as well as reflux laryngitis and arytenoid irritation. Other gastrointestinal manifestations, such as colitis, irritable bowel syndrome, and dysphagia, are also described. Chronic stress and tension may cause numerous pain syndromes, although headaches, particularly migraines in vulnerable individuals, are most common. Stress is also associated with more serious physical problems such as myocardial infarction, asthma, and depression of the immune system.[22,37,39] Thus, the constant pressure under which many performers live may be more than an inconvenience. Stress factors should be recognized, and appropriate modifications should be made to ameliorate them.

Stressors may be physical or psychological and often involve a combination of both. Either may interfere with performance. There are several situations in which physical stress is common and important. Generalized fatigue is seen frequently in hard-working singers, especially in the frantic few weeks preceding major performances. To maintain normal mucosal secretions, a strong immune system to fight infection, and the ability of muscles to recover from heavy use, rest, proper nutrition, and hydration are required. When the body is stressed through deprivation of these essentials, illness (such as upper respiratory infection), voice fatigue, hoarseness, and other vocal dysfunctions may supervene.

Lack of physical conditioning undermines the power source of the voice. A person who becomes short of breath while climbing a flight of stairs hardly has the abdominal and respiratory endurance needed to sustain him or her optimally through the rigors of performance. The stress of attempting to perform under such circumstances often results in voice dysfunction.

Oversinging is another common physical stress. As with running, swimming, or any other athletic activity that depends on sustained, coordinated muscle activity, singing requires conditioning to build up strength and endurance. Rest periods are also essential for muscle recovery. Singers who are accustomed to singing for 1 or 2 hours a day stress their physical voice-producing mechanism severely when they suddenly begin rehearsing for 14 hours daily immediately prior to performance.

Medical treatment of stress depends on the specific circumstances. When the diagnosis is appropriate but poorly controlled anxiety rather than a physical problem, the physician's evaluation itself may reassure the patient. Under ordinary circumstances, once the singer's mind is put to rest regarding the questions of nodules, vocal fold injury, or other serious problems, his or her training usually allows compensation for vocal manifestations of anxiety, especially when the vocal complaint is minor. Slight alterations in quality or increased vocal fatigue are seen most frequently. These are often associated with lack of sleep, oversinging, and dehydration associated with the stress-producing commitment. The singer or actor should be advised to modify these and to consult his or her voice teacher. The voice teacher should ensure that good vocal technique is being used under performance and rehearsal circumstances. Frequently, young singers are not trained sufficiently in how and when to "mark." For example, many singers whistle to rest their voices, not realizing that active vocalization and potentially fatiguing vocal fold contact occur when whistling. Technical proficiency and a plan for voice conservation during rehearsal and performances are essential under these circumstances. A manageable stressful situation may become unmanageable if real physical vocal problems develop.

Several additional modalities may be helpful in selected circumstances. Relative voice rest (using the voice only when necessary) may be important not only to voice conservation but also to psychological relaxation. Under stressful circumstances, a singer needs as much peace and quiet as possible, not hectic socializing, parties with heavy voice use in noisy environments, and press appearances. The importance of adequate sleep and fluid intake cannot be overemphasized. Local therapy, such as steam inhalation and neck muscle massage, may be helpful in some people and certainly does no harm. The doctor may be very helpful in alleviating the singer's exogenous stress by conveying "doctor's orders" directly to theater management. This will save the singer the discomfort of having to personally confront an authority and violate his or her "show must go on" ethic. A short phone call by the physician can be highly therapeutic.

When stress is chronic and incapacitating, more comprehensive measures are required. If psychological stress manifestations become so severe that they impair performance or necessitate the use of drugs to allow performance, psychotherapy is indicated. The goal of psychotherapeutic approaches to stress-management includes changing:

- external and internal stressors;
- affective and cognitive reactions to stressors;
- physiologic reactions to stress; and
- stress behaviors.

A psychoeducational model is customarily used. Initially, the psychotherapist will assist the patient in identifying and evaluating stressor characteristics. A variety of assessment tools are available for this purpose. Interventions designed to increase a sense of efficacy and personal control are designed. Perceived control over the stressor directly affects stress level, and it changes one's experience of the stressor. Laboratory and human research has determined that a sense of control is one of the most potent elements in the modulation of stress responses. Concrete exercises that impose time management are taught and practiced. Patients are urged to identify and expand their network of support as well. Psychological intervention requires evaluation of the patient's cognitive model. Cognitive restructuring exercises are used, as well as classical conditioning tools that patients easily learn and utilize effectively with practice. Cognitive skills include the use of monitored perception, thought, and internal dialogue to regulate emotional and physiological responses. A variety of relaxation techniques are available and are ordinarily taught in the course of stress-management treatment. These include progressive relaxation, hypnosis, autogenic training and imagery, and biofeedback training. Underlying all of these approaches is the premise that making conscious normally unconscious processes leads to control and self-efficacy.[1]

As with all medical conditions, the best treatment for stress in singers is prevention. Awareness of the conditions that lead to stress and its potential adverse effect on voice production often allows the singer to anticipate and avoid these problems. Stress is inevitable in performance and in life. Performers must learn to recognize it, compensate for it when necessary, and incorporate it into their singing as emotion and excitement. Stress should be controlled, not pharmacologically eliminated. Used well, stress should be just one more tool of the singer's trade.

Reactive Responses

Reaction to illness is the major source of psychiatric disturbance in patients with significant voice dysfunction. Loss of communicative function is an experience of alienation that threatens human self-definition and independence. Catastrophic fears of loss of productivity, economic and social status, and, in professional voice users, creative artistry contribute to rising anxiety. Anxiety is known to worsen existing communication disorders, and the disturbances in memory, concentration and synaptic transmission secondary to depression may intensify other voice symptoms and interfere with rehabilitation.

The self-concept is an essential construct of Carl Rodger's theories of counseling. Rodgers described self-concept as composed of perceptions of the characteristics of the self and the relationships of the self to various aspects of life, as well as the values attached to the perceptions. Rodgers suggested that equilibrium requires that patients' self-concepts be congruent with their life experiences. It follows, then, that it is not the disability per se that psychologically influences the person, but rather the subjective meaning and feelings attached to the disability. According to Rodgers, the two major psychologic defenses that operate to maintain consistent self-concept are denial and distortion.[9]

Families of patients are affected as well. They are often confused about the diagnosis and poorly prepared to support the patient's coping responses. The resulting stress may negatively influence family dynamics and intensify the patient's depressive illness.[40] As the voice-injured patient experiences the process of grieving, the psychologist may assume a more prominent role in his or her care. Essentially, the voice-injured patient goes through a grieving process similar to patients who mourn other losses, such as the death of a loved one. In some cases, especially among voice professionals, the patients actually mourn the loss of their self as they perceive it. The psychologist is responsible for facilitating the tasks of mourning and monitoring the individual's formal mental status for clinically significant changes.[1,8,41] There are a number of models for tracking this process. The most easily understood is that of Worden,[42] as adapted by the author (DCR). Initially, the task is to accept the reality of the loss. The need for and distress of this is vestigial during the phase of diagnosis, is held consciously in abeyance during the acute and rehabilitative phases of treatment, but is reinforced with accumulating data measuring vocal function. As the reality becomes undeniable, the mourner must be helped to express the full range of grieving affect. The rate of accomplishing this is variable and individual. Generally, it will occur in the style with which the person usually copes with crisis and may be florid or tightly constricted. All responses must be invited and normalized. The psychologist facilitates the process and stays particularly attuned to unacceptable, split-off responses or the failure to move through any particular response.

As attempts to deny the loss take place and fail, the mourner gradually encounters the next task: beginning to live and cope in a world in which the lost object is absent. This is the psychoanalytic process of *decathexis,* which requires the withdrawal of life energies from the other and the reinvesting of them in the self. For some professional voice users, this may be a temporary state as they make adjustments required by their rehabilitation demands. In other cases, the need for change will be lasting; change in fach, change in repertoire, need for amplification, altered performance schedule, or, occasionally, change in career.[1,8,41]

As the patient so injured seeks to heal his or her life, another task looms. Known as *recathexis,* it involves reinvesting life energies in other relationships, interests, talents, and life goals. The individual is assisted in redefining and revaluing the self as apart from the voice. The voice is then seen as the *product* of the self, rather than an equivalent to the self. For many performers, this is painfully difficult.[1,8,41,42] Rosen and Sataloff have described in detail research applying the various theoretical models of grief resolution to the perception of vocal injury in professional voice users.[8]

The Surgical Experience

When vocal fold surgery is indicated, many individuals will demonstrate hospital-related phobias or self-destructive responses to pain. Adamson et al describe the importance of understanding how the patient's occupational identity will be affected by surgical intervention.[43] Vocal fold surgery impacts on the major mode of communication that all human beings utilize; the impact is extraordinarily anxiety-producing in professional voice users. Even temporary periods of absolute voice restriction may induce feelings of insecurity, helplessness, and dissociation from the verbal world. Carpenter details the value of an early therapy session to focus on the fears, fantasies, misconceptions, and regression that frequently accompany a decision to undergo surgery.[44]

A proper surgical discussion highlights vocal fold surgery as *elective*. The patient chooses surgery as the only remaining means to regaining the previously normal voice or to attain a different but desirable voice. Responsible care includes a thorough preoperative and written discussion of the limits and complications of surgery, with recognition by the surgeon that anxiety affects both understanding and retention of information about undesirable outcomes. Personality psychopathology or unrealistic expectations of the impact of surgery on their lives are elements for which surgical candidates can be screened.[12,45,46] Recognizing such problems preoperatively allows preoperative counseling and obviates many postoperative difficulties.

Although a thorough discussion is outside the scope of this chapter, surgically treated voice patients include those undergoing laryngectomy, with or without a voice prosthesis. The laryngectomized individual must make major psychological and social adjustments. These include not only those adjustments related to a diagnosis of cancer but also to those of a sudden disability: loss of voice. With the improvement in prognosis, research has begun to focus on the individual's quality of life after the laryngectomy. There is wide variability in the quality of preoperative and postoperative psychological support reported by patients during each phase of care. Special psychological issues in professional voice users diagnosed with laryngeal cancer are discussed in detail in other works.[1] Providing this support is a crucial role for the voice team's psychologist.[47,48,49]

Role of the Psychological Professional

Both psychology and psychiatry specialize in attending to emotional needs and problems. Psychiatrists, as physicians, focus on the neurological and biological causes and treatment of psychopathology. Psychologists have advanced graduate training in psychological function and therapy. They concern themselves with cognitive processes such as thinking, behavior, and memory; the experiencing and expression of emotions; significant inner conflict; characteristic modes of defense in coping with stress; and personality style and perception of self and others, including their expression in interpersonal behavior. Other mental health professionals also provide psychotherapy to performers. In the authors' practice, clinical psychologists serve as members of the voice team. They work directly with some patients and offer consultation to the physician and other professionals.[1]

In our center, assessment of patients is done throughout the physicians' history-taking and physical examinations, as well as in a formal psychiatric interview when appropriate. Personality assessment, screening for or evaluating known psychopathology, and assessment of potential surgical candidates are performed. Occasionally, psychometric instruments are added to the diagnostic interview. Confidentiality of content is extended to the treatment team to maximize interdisciplinary care. Because of their special interest in voicing parameters, the voice team psychologists are especially attuned to the therapeutic use of their own voices for intensifying rapport and pacing/leading the patient's emotional state during interventions.[30,50-53]

Psychotherapeutic treatment is offered on a short-term, diagnosis-related basis. Treatment is designed to identify and alleviate emotional distress and to increase the individual's resources for adaptive functioning. Individual psychotherapeutic approaches include brief insight-oriented therapies, cognitive/behavioral techniques, Gestalt interventions, stress-management skill building, and clinical hypnosis.

After any indicated acute intervention is provided, and in patients whose coping repertoire is clearly adequate to the stressors, a psychoeducational model is used. The therapy session focuses on a prospective discussion of personal, inherent life stressors and predictable illnesses. Stress management skills are taught, and audiotapes are provided. The tapes offer portable skill building, and supplemental sessions may be scheduled by mutual decision during appointments at the center for medical examinations and speech or singing voice therapy. A group therapy model, facilitated by the psychologist, has also been used to provide a forum for discussion of patient responses during the various phases of treatment. Participants benefit from the perspective and progress of other patients, the opportunity to decrease their experience of isolation, and the sharing of resources.

Long-term psychodynamic psychotherapy, chronic psychiatric conditions, and patients requiring psychopharmacologic management are referred to consultant mental health professionals with special interest and insight in voice-related psychological problems. The voice team's psychologists also serve in a liaison role when patients already in treatment come to our center for voice care. In addition, the psychologist participates in professional education activities in the medical practice. These include writing, lecturing, and serving as a preceptor for visiting professionals. Specially trained psychologists have proven to be an invaluable addition to the voice team, and close collaboration with team members has proven to be valuable and stimulating for psychologists interested in the care of professional voice users.

The Speech-Language Pathologist's Role in Treating Psychological Disturbances in Patients with Voice Disorders

Speech-language pathology is a relatively new profession in the United States. Its roots are in psychology. The original members of the field came primarily from psychology backgrounds. Early interest in the psychological aspects of voicing are evidenced in texts such as *The Voice of Neurosis*.[54] Luchsinger and Arnold present an excellent review of the early literature in their text, *Voice-Speech-Language*.[55] At the present time, speech-language pathologists need to be familiar with models of treatment from the psychological tradition, the medical tradition, and the educational tradition. When discussing the speech-language pathologist's role in managing functional voice problems, it must be made clear at the outset that the speech-language pathologist does not work in isolation but as a part of a team, including, at a minimum, a laryngologist and speech-language pathologist. Singing instructors, acting instructors, stress specialists, psychologists, neurologists, and psychiatrists must be readily available and cognizant of the special needs to voice patients.

Psychology is defined as the study of human behavior, and the speech-language pathologist's role in treating voice-disordered patients is normalizing the patient's speaking and communication behavior. In this sense, all of the activities of speech-language pathologists with voice-disordered patients are "psychological." The purpose of this chapter is not to present a full description of the role of the speech-language pathologist but to describe areas in which the speech-language pathologist must deal with issues not directly related to the physical vocal mechanism. However, a brief overview of the activities engaged in by the speech-language pathologist and the voice patient helps set the groundwork for a discussion of psychological issues. A more detailed description has been published elsewhere.[56]

Preparation for Treatment

The speech-language pathologist must be aware of, and be able to interpret, the findings of the laryngologist, including strobovideolaryngoscopy. Particular attention should be paid to findings demonstrating muscle tension or lack of glottic closure not associated with organic or physical changes. The perceptions of the laryngologist regarding organic and functional aspects of the patient need to be known.

A case history is taken, reviewing and amplifying the case history reported by the laryngologist. The case history should include but not be limited to the following:

1. Circumstances surrounding the onset, development, and progress of the voice disorders, including:
   - illnesses of the patient
   - recent changes in employment
   - speaking responsibilities associated with the patient's employment
   - employment environment
   - speaking activities outside of employment
   - environment in which social speaking activities occur
   - effects of the voice disorder on social exchange and social activities
   - activities the patient has had to give up because of the voice disorder
   - illness or difficulty among family members or friends
   - stress factors at work and at home
   - methods of dealing with stress.
2. Exploration of the social structure of the patient and environment, including:
   - family and living arrangements
   - friends and social gathering places
   - relationships with coworkers and superiors.
3. The patient's response to the voice disorder needs to be explored, including:
   - what bothers the patient most about the voice disorder?
   - what has the patient done to change voicing and how effective have these attempts been?
   - estimates of the speaking times at work and socially, now and before the voice disorder
   - how does the patient feel about speaking at the present time—stressed, indifferent, depressed, challenged?
4. General health issues should be explored, including:
   - chronic illness, including asthma, allergies, gastroesophageal reflux disease (GERD), diabetes, thyroid dysfunction, chronic fatigue
   - head and neck trauma, including whiplash, concussion, spinal degeneration, temporomandibular joint disease, facial injury
   - surgery
   - high fevers

- nonvocal symptoms, including swallowing difficulty, pain on speaking or swallowing, numbness, neck stiffness or reduced range of motion, voice quality, speaking rate, movement limitations of the articulators, nasal regurgitation, tremor or shakiness.

5. Medications:
   - prescription medications
   - over-the-counter drugs, including NSAIDs, cough drops, decongestants, antihistamines, mouthwash, vitamins, alcohol, tobacco and caffeine products, and water intake.

Subjective and objective measures of the patient's vocal mechanism and communication skills need to be obtained including the following:

1. Average fundamental frequency and loudness of the patient's conversational voice.
2. Average fundamental frequency, loudness and speaking rate during a selected reading passage, both in normal reading and in his or her professional voice (if a professional speaker).
3. Acoustic and aerodynamic measures of sustained vowels, including measure of:
   - perturbation
   - breathiness and noise
   - vocal breaks and quality change
   - airflow
   - glottic pressure
4. Preferred breathing patterns for speech:
   - shallow, deep, appropriate for phrase length
   - clavicular, thoracic, abdominal, or mixed
   - coordination with voicing: exhalation initiated before voicing, glottic
   - closure prior to initiation of exhalation, coordinated breath/voicing.
5. Neck and laryngeal use, including:
   - positioning of the larynx during speech: high, low, inflexible
   - tension in the extralaryngeal muscles, particularly the omohyoid
   - laryngeal/hyoid space: present, reduced
   - positioning of the hyoid: tipped, tense, discomfort on palpation of the cornu
6. Use of the articulators, including:
   - oroperipheral examination including lip movements and symmetry, tongue movements and symmetry, palatal sufficiency in nonspeech contexts, diadochokinetic rates
   - ability to separate jaw and anterior tongue activity during the production of /l/, /t/, /d/, /n/
   - tongue tension during speech
   - jaw tension and jaw jutting during speech
   - looseness of temporomandibular joint during speech movements.

The speech-language pathologist should be able to develop a plan of behavioral changes. The case history provides an ample sample of the patient's voice use in an interview situation. It is important to note how the patient's voice changes when talking about certain topics and to note evidence of improvement or fatigue as the interview proceeds. It provides data on what speaking activities are most important to the patient and which may need to be addressed initially in therapy. It provides information on the patient's willingness to talk about stressful issues or needs beyond direct focus on voicing and speech skills, which may be important regarding referral to other specialists dealing with stress and emotional or physical health. It establishes an initial rapport, or lack of it, with the clinician that may predict success, or failure, in therapeutic intervention. It also provides the speech-language pathologist with a sample of the patient's communication style and verbosity.

The physical assessment provides the speech-language clinician with objective support for what the clinician has heard and information about how the patient is producing the voice. Because behavioral change instituted during therapy is based on eradication of symptoms of maladaptive voice or communication, to list and evaluate confirmed symptoms at this stage leads to the development of an overall therapeutic plan. The focus should be on identification of the underlying behavior or behaviors responsible for maintaining the current voice in order to address these underlying behaviors first, which reduces the length of therapy and should predict improvement of voicing.

Therapeutic Stage

Information giving is essential at the beginning of therapy and throughout the course of therapy. Patients need to know the reason for the activities in which they are engaging and why these activities are important in changing their current voice problem. Without a thorough understanding of the reasons for changing behavior, the probabilities of behavioral change are poor.

The patient needs to know that a voice disorder is not usually caused by a single factor, but is maintained by a combination of physical changes, if present; communication demands on the voice; the patient's skills in producing speech; and the patient's attempts to compensate for vocal changes. Initially, the goal in therapy is to manage communicative demands and improve the patient's ability to produce more normal voice. Reassessment of the need for medical and/or surgical interventions for physical changes is planned with the patient. The patient is reassured that the goal of therapy is not to change personality or limit communication opportunities, but to return them at least to the level of communication enjoyed prior to the onset of the voice problem.

Patients need information regarding their current breathing pattern. It may be insufficient for the demands placed on the patient's voice or contribute to increased tension in the vocal mechanism. Abdominal breathing is the natural and preferred method of breathing by the body. Abdominal breathing is not a new skill. Patients engage in abdominal breathing when they are relaxed and when they are sleeping.

Patients can be asked to observe or recall the breathing patterns of their pets. They can be asked to observe or recall the breathing patterns of babies engaging in comfort sounds versus painful or paroxysmal crying. They can be asked to observe or recall the breathing of significant others in repose. Their observations can be discussed and used as confirmation of the above information.

Patients need to be informed that predominantly clavicular or thoracic breathing is usually the product of stress, a societal preference toward tight clothing, and/or demands by parents, teachers, and society in maintaining a tight tucked-in stomach. All of these factors lead to a reduction of abdominal release during inhalation that leads to restriction in diaphragmatic downward motion and maximal inflation of the lungs.

Patients are taught that taking a deep, high-chest breath increases air pressures in the lungs greatly, triggering a Valsalva response with closure of the glottis and laryngeal and chest muscle tension. The kind of breath the patient takes may influence tension in other parts of the vocal mechanism. High-chest breathing can contribute to a feeling of breathlessness and tightness in the chest. Abdominal breathing produces lesser increases in lung air pressure and removes the tension from the neck and larynx. The patient needs to know what he or she is about to say before he or she inhales the breath to say it, and this concept is discussed and practiced. This simple construct eliminates respiratory/laryngeal incoordination, reduces revisions and struggle during speaking and allows the patient to focus on how he or she is saying something rather than on the content of what is being said. Speech should be a continuous breath event, beginning with inhalation of the appropriate amount of air and continuing through easy transition to exhalation and voicing to the end of the utterance. Instruction and discussion of these matters prior to the initiation of a program of breath-support exercises increases the patient's willingness to change and turns the reluctant patient into an active participant in the process of change. Specific breathing exercises to incorporate abdominal breathing are available in many other publications.

Similarly, the patient needs to know that modification of articulation postures and open, relaxed jaw positioning improve loudness and acuity in noisy environments and can be invaluable in improving communication without effort and fatigue in most speaking circumstances. Tongue tension or pulling the tongue back in the mouth leads to tension in the hyoid and larynx region. These effects can be demonstrated and discussed by having the patient tense the tongue or retract the tongue while digitally monitoring tension under the chin and at the sides of the larynx. The same effects can be demonstrated during talking activities. Patients need to learn to explore the feelings associated with tension and extra effort speaking.

Instruction in phonatory behavior is provided so that the patient understands that the vocal folds are opened by the flow of air from the lungs and closed due to their own elasticity and Bernoulli's principle. The vocal folds are vibrating much too rapidly to be manipulated by laryngeal effort, and patients need to comprehend that the emotional system and the conscious speech system share control of voicing, which varies with emotional context. The patient needs to know that laryngeal control is primarily automatic and that efforts to produce voice are counterproductive. The quality of the patient's voice during physiologic sound-making, such as laughter, and a gentle cough, can predict the quality of sound when extra effort is removed. Humming and sighing are also effective means of demonstrating the effect of reduced effort. Modeling by the clinician of easy, well-supported, well-resonated voice during these conversations can be a highly effective means of modifying the patient's vocal production in the therapy setting.

Closed, tense jaw articulation and substitution of jaw movement for tongue and lip movements increase tension and fatigue in the face and increase the amount of pulling on the temporomandibular joint capsule. The same methods of speaking reduce loudness in noisy speaking situations and impede the ability of listeners to read the speaker's lips. Patients learn that in American English only six sounds, /s/, /z/, /ch/, /dz/, and /z/, require closure of the jaw. All other consonants and all vowels can be produced by modifying the position of the lips and tongue with no, or minor, jaw adjustment. Most of speech can be produced with the jaw in a relaxed, partially open, neutral position. This can be demonstrated by monitoring tension in the masseter muscle (placing the fingers of both hands in front of the ears and alternately clenching and opening the jaw). The patient will be able to feel the bulking of the masseter muscle fibers when the jaw is wide open. The neutral speaking position is identifiable by the absence of muscle bulk or stretched fibers. The patient needs to experience the feeling of relaxation associated with this speaking position. The patient can then be instructed in producing the syllable /la/ by simply lifting the tongue and touching the roof of the mouth behind the upper front teeth and then dropping the tongue to a relaxed position behind, but touching, the lower front teeth. This is extended to other consonants (/ta/, /da/, /na/, and /ga/).

When the patient is proficient in eliminating jaw tension in these contexts, the effect of lip movement in addition to relaxed jaw and tongue is practiced by producing words such as, too, due, coo, load, coat, and so on. Lip consonants without tensing the jaw are then added. The sounds /f/, /v/, /th/, and voiced /th/ need to be monitored for jaw jutting. An open relaxed jaw with improved oral resonance and a relaxed tongue can then be practiced in words, phrases, and finally in sentences. Initially, practice should be done while monitoring jaw position and movement with fingers between the posterior molars and with a mirror. As the patient begins to feel comfortable with a relaxed jaw, the tactile monitoring and then the visual monitoring can be eliminated. At this point, the patient should identify phrases and sentences that he or she uses frequently, such as, "Hello," "Put them away," "I don't like that behavior," and so on, which can be used as frequent daily reminders in his or her normal speech of more normal oral resonance and speech production. This assists in carryover. Practice continues with sentences including jaw closure sounds and open vowels, such as, "He is going," "Let me have a piece of pie," "I chose two friends to go with me," and so on. The open relaxed jaw can then be extended into question-and-answer activities, monologue, and dialogue.

A pattern of frequent tension checks needs to be established with the cooperation of the patient. These need not be elaborate warm-up exercises or cooldown practices. The patient may decide to practice abdominal breathing in the shower, blowing the water away from his or her face or humming with a relaxed jaw while inhaling the warm steamy air. The patient may be able to stroke the face, jaw, or neck at each stoplight while driving to or from work or take an easy belly breath followed by a relaxed sigh. The patient may check his or her jaw tension before picking up the telephone to say "hello." A brief reminder note can be taped to the inside of the telephone receiver. Abdominal breathing can be practiced leaning over the desk while reading memos or correcting examination papers. A sip of water between tasks can help the patient focus on relaxation of the jaw and throat and can be preceded by a deep abdominal inhalation. Patients can be very creative and very helpful in identifying times when correct vocal behavior can be practiced. Multiple reminders during the busy day can be more effective, and are more likely to be done, than a half-hour practice in the isolation of the patient's home.

All of these exercises are helpful in aiding the patient to become aware of the subtle nature of tension in the speaking mechanism but may be overwhelmed by overriding tension not associated directly with speaking behavior in the face and neck. A decision must be made as to whether the speech-language pathologist has the skill to develop a more stringent relaxation regimen or if the patient needs, and is amenable to, a referral to an expert in stress management.

If the patient talks excessively, a discussion of relevant and irrelevant talking is necessary. The patient needs to know that total vocal rest, if extended past a week, can lead to muscle atrophy and an additional voice problem. The concept of vocal "naps" during the day and the possibility of reducing talking or, more positively, becoming a better listener in noisy environments, should be introduced. The patient is more knowledgeable than the therapist in when and how long these quiet times can be inserted into his or her daily schedule.

Patients under stress will bring their "job-voice" home with them. The patient will often complain that family members nag about his or her use of too loud a voice, being too demanding, or giving too many directions. A vocal nap during the ride home with an added cooldown protocol can be helpful in providing a positive transition. The patient should be reminded that singing in the car over the noise of traffic and radio and engine noises can be abusive.

The patient needs to know that everyone lip-reads in noisy environments. If the patient has been successful in developing open oral resonance and articulation patterns, the ability of the patient's listeners to understand in noisy situations is enhanced. A slower rate of talking is also helpful in improving comprehension. The patient should be instructed in the effective use of light to highlight his or her face during such conversations.

Voice patients under stress often violate the rules of conversation, including rules of relevance, brevity, and turn-taking. A discussion of these rules may lead to an awareness of inappropriate communication patterns or the revelation of an underlying personality difficulty that may lead to a referral to a psychologic professional. Often persons with difficulty in personal relationships and/or coping with their circumstances can admit to a voice disorder but not the underlying personal difficulties. The experience of voice therapy, especially supportive rather than prescriptive voice therapy, may lead to the acceptance of a referral to a professional trained in dealing with these underlying difficulties that might have been rejected at initial interview. The combination of an inability to relax following focal voice exercises, an inability to modify communication behaviors, a tendency for the patient to revert to discussions of personal problems rather than focus on the process of communication, all assist the therapist in reinforcing the idea that the patient's problem lies outside the realm of traditional voice therapy. A statement by the therapist such as, "You have very real problems, but I am not trained to deal with them. I know someone who can help you" can be the beginning of a successful referral.

Finally, the patient needs to know that voice therapy is short term and finite. The goal of therapy is to identify underlying behavioral, emotional, and physical factors; modify current vocal behaviors; and develop better communication skills. The therapist must be aware that the stressed patient can develop inappropriate dependence on the therapist. If therapy sessions begin to focus more on the patient's day-to-day personal problems than on voice, the time for referral is long past. Patients need to know that voice therapy usually is successful in only a few sessions unless there are other problems that maintain the maladaptive vocal behavior. This is a difficult concept for some patients, particularly singers, who are used to taking singing lessons most of their lives. The therapeutic goal in these cases is to identify the underlying problems and make the appropriate referrals.

Examples of Psychological Aspects of Voice Disorders

Patients often respond to a voice change by struggling to continue to use their voices in their daily jobs. Teachers will continue to teach, preachers continue to preach, and sales personnel continue to sell. The fear of losing their livelihood drives them to modify their speaking techniques, usually applying extra effort, which results in fatigue, pain, and progressive voice loss. They will stop doing enjoyable leisure activities that involve talking and begin to feel impoverished both personally and socially. Feelings of self-worth are also diminished. They feel as though they are not doing their job as well as possible and often consider job changes that do not suit their training or skills.

The speech-language pathologist (SLP) can be very helpful in reducing these feelings by focusing on a plan to return the patient to comfortable functioning in his or her current occupation. If the patient is successful in modifying the effortful and compromised voice, using the techniques described above, these reactions subside. It behooves the SLP to develop a therapeutic program that will provide the most rapid return of better voicing. The patient needs to be evaluated for the key elements producing vocal fatigue and vocal quality changes. A program of vocal hygiene that can alleviate environmental and behavioral stresses in the workplace; a program of reasonable vocal rest during the work day; and the initiation of a program that will reinstate the balance between respiratory, voicing, and resonance effort in vocal technique are very important. A timetable of when the patient can resume specific activities or when the treatment options will be reviewed to assess alternative treatment options gives the patient something to work toward.

Case 1

Case 1 had been a fifth-grade school teacher for 20 years. She denied having any previous voice problems, other than vocal fatigue by the end of the week at the end of the school year. She also assisted her husband, a pediatrician, as his receptionist during evening office hours. However, she now presented with progressive hoarseness. She was diagnosed with vocal fold swelling, gastroesophageal reflux laryngitis, and pinpoint vocal nodules by a laryngologist. She was seen by a speech-language pathologist 1 month prior to the end of the school year.

Her case history revealed important life differences. The previous summer the regular receptionist at her husband's office had taken a maternity leave, and she had volunteered her services over the summer months. It was a busy office, and she spent many hours on the telephone and talking with patients. Her voice did not feel rested at the beginning of the school year.

Because of her excellent teaching record she had been assigned a student teacher who required a great deal of counseling, typically after school hours. She found herself rushing from school to her husband's office without time to eat. She began eating after office hours, experiencing heartburn and disrupted sleep. Her voice was worse in the morning and even more fatigued after the school day. She was physically tired before the day began. She had been given a prescription for ranitidine (Zantac, Glaxo Smith Kline) but did not believe it was helping her.

She noted that her students, her husband, and the patients at her husband's office complained that she was "yelling at them." She was very worried about her ability to continue teaching with no voice. She was worried about the status of her marriage. She was frustrated by the fact that she was at least a month behind in school lesson plans and correction of homework papers and tests. She had tried correcting papers at her desk in her husband's office but found the situation intolerable and interfering with her receptionist tasks. She said: "Now I have to carry three bags of work home, and somehow it never gets done." She was seriously considering quitting teaching but was ambivalent because she really enjoyed teaching and felt she had a great deal to give both to her students and student teachers. Her principal was urging her to make a decision about teaching the next year and also about taking on another student teacher. She felt that engaging in voice therapy would only complicate her already busy schedule. She stated: "The harder I try, the worse things seem to get." She then cried.

Evaluation of her voice revealed a shallow thoracic breathing pattern. She had developed a pattern of taking a quick breath and holding it prior to initiation of voicing, resulting in glottal attack rates of 54% (normal = 15%). Her voice was loud, low-pitched, and rough. She was using a tense jaw, jutting it forward during speech. These characteristics were even worse when demonstrating her current teaching voice. She felt her voice was very different in the classroom now than before her voice problems began.

The following therapeutic plan was developed. Direct voice therapy was deferred until July following the end of school and a brief vacation. In the meantime, she was urged to continue using the ranitidine and to institute a more rigorous program to control her reflux. The program included the use of liquid antacids following each meal and at bedtime to neutralize the contents of her stomach should she reflux, elevation of the head of her bed to reduce nighttime reflux and to promote better sleep, and to try to find time to eat a light meal prior to the onset of office hours. The matter of paper work was discussed. She felt she might be able to combine her counseling sessions with her student teacher with grading activities and also decided she would allow the student teacher to help her with the paper grading. This left her with lesson plans, which she felt she could accomplish by coming in to work 20 minutes early. She decided not to take a new student teacher in the fall, but to try to teach. Because of this decision, she committed herself to six sessions of voice therapy over the summer. A plan was developed to provide those sessions followed by reevaluation by the laryngologist. If the therapy was unsuccessful, she could apply for a 3-month leave of absence from teaching.

She returned for therapy in July. She was feeling better physically and was sleeping better. Therapy focused on reducing vocal effort, reestablishing abdominal breathing, reducing glottal stopping, jaw relaxation, and open oral resonance for loudness. Classroom teaching materials were used for exercises. She was able to modify her vocal behaviors easily, although she continued to voice concern about her ability to use them in the classroom. A probable set of voice rests during the school day was discussed, and cooldown procedures to implement on the trip to the office were planned. At the end of the therapy, evaluation by the laryngologist demonstrated a reduction in the size of the vocal nodules, resolution of vocal swelling, and reduced reflux findings. She decided to try teaching but was still worried. A plan was developed to see her for therapeutic review 2 weeks into the school year and then, if needed, in mid-fall, at winter break, at spring break, and at the end of the school year. If she felt she did not need to come in, she would call and report how her voice was progressing.

At the meeting 2 weeks into the school year, she reported that she was surviving. She was still concerned about whether she was using her voice correctly. Through discussion, she decided she would enlist her students as monitors, particularly for loudness. During the fall, she called to say she was doing well. Her voice was strong, and she was much less tired. She reported that her class had taken their role in monitoring her voice very enthusiastically and seriously. Her admission of voice problems and the need for help had become an advantage for noise control in her classroom and in student-teacher interactions. She was planning to develop a vocal hygiene section in her curriculum.

At winter break, she attended one session for review. Her glottal attacks were reduced to 8%. She reported her voice was not as fatigued, and she was eagerly looking forward to return to teaching after the break. Breath support and oral resonance had improved.

At spring break, she reported her voice was different. She no longer experienced vocal fatigue. She was using a lighter voice in the classroom. Glottal attacks remained under 10%. She was sleeping all night. Her reflux appeared to be under control. She stated: "I now realized that I don't have to take all responsibility for communicating in the classroom. The kids have been very responsive." She was dismissed from therapy but reminded to contact the therapist if she experienced any problems.

Some patients appear to react to life stresses by overuse of their voices and excessive tension focused in the speaking mechanism. They may consider themselves talkative and congenial persons; but actually they talk constantly, rapidly, or in an excessively loud voice. They appear to be afraid of silence or afraid that if they give up their turn to talk they will not be able to talk again. They often complain of pain and tension in the neck and jaw or of a feeling of breathlessness. They may seek treatment when their inappropriate speaking patterns lead to benign lesions of the larynx or when some other organic change in the vocal mechanism causes their voice to break down. Modeling lower, softer voicing and turn-taking during therapeutic sessions can be very helpful in reducing these vocal faults and providing a more reasonable speaking pattern. The development of relaxation programs for the face and neck to be used frequently during the day is useful. Discussions of the rules of discourse may be helpful.

Some patients bring with them a severe overall body reaction to the stresses of their lives. They complain of fatigue, sleeplessness, tension, and pain. They are unable to turn off their "work voice" at home. They complain of lack of time to complete all the activities in which they are engaged. Standard therapeutic procedures often are ineffective, because they are unable to distinguish the subtle changes in support, voicing, or resonation due to the overriding levels of general tension. These patients appear to be out of harmony with their bodies. Focal relaxation of the vocal mechanism is unsuccessful. They usually deny having emotional problems and have difficulty dealing with the daily stress, but continue to return to nonvocal issues during the course of therapy. The SLP can be helpful in allowing these patients to experience a supportive one-on-one relationship as a prelude to referral to a psychologic professional. Often after several sessions with the SLP protesting that, "We are talking about issues I am not able to help you with, but Dr X can," the patient is receptive to referral. Often referral to a stress manager professionally trained in Feldenkrais or Alexander technique or some other relaxation/body awareness method can be useful. The patient may return to the SLP following resolution of some of these issues. The SLP needs to be careful not to continue the therapeutic relationship so long that the patient becomes dependent on an ineffectual but sympathetic ear.

Case 2

Case 2 presented with a large hemorrhagic cyst on one vocal fold and a reactive lesion directly opposite the cyst on the other vocal fold. She was married and had an adopted son. She was a grade school teacher. She had been forced to take a sabbatical because her voice had deteriorated. On evaluation, she presented with a loud, hoarse voice with frequent glottal attacks and frequent aphonic breaks. She was extremely verbal with frequent run-on sentences and sentence revisions. She demonstrated a pattern of taking a rapid, large chest breath followed by holding the breath with her larynx at the end of inhalation. She demonstrated excessive tension in the speech musculature. Her conversational style was repetitious. Interestingly, her teacher's voice was better controlled. She admitted that yelling at a sporting event probably caused the cyst. She was seen by the speech-language pathologist prior to surgery. Therapy consisted in promoting a softer, more breathy voice. The combination of being relieved from teaching duties and modifying voicing behaviors was successful in eliminating the reactive lesion. Surgery for the hemorrhagic cyst was planned and carried out successfully. She was able to complete a week of voice rest following the surgery. The following weeks of gradual increase in voice use were difficult for her. Therapy focused on reducing glottal attacks, improving breath support, and monitoring loudness. Materials included readings and repeated sentences and phrases. Materials from her classroom texts were used in preparation for her return to the classroom. She made excellent progress. However, when therapy moved to monitoring her new skills in general conversation, it became clear that she was unable to recognize her loudness level, control her excessive talking, or identify hard glottal attacks.

She returned to school and was seen on a limited schedule similar to that used with the previously described patient. She complained of continued vocal fatigue and hoarseness. She developed a pattern of bringing small gifts. She had limited success in developing self-monitoring skills outside of controlled materials or classroom activities. She successfully completed the school year with no return of vocal fold masses. However, her monitoring skills and general levels of tension remained unchanged. The termination of therapy was discussed. She was very anxious about the termination, citing the continued fatigue and difficulties in monitoring her speech outside of the classroom. It was suggested that emotional factors might play a role in her lack of success in changing behaviors and that she might wish to begin seeing the psychologist associated with practice. At this point, she admitted to a long history of both physical and verbal abuse, first from her father and then from her husband. It became clear that her failures in therapy led to criticism by the therapist that satisfied her unconscious need for abuse.

Patients with Aphonia

There appear to be three categories of patients who have little voicing capability in the absence of structural or neurological etiology. Some patients present with a whispered voice without vocal paralysis, vocal injury, or other pathology. Usually, the vocal folds appear to be normal. The initial case history may or may not reveal psychological trauma associated with the onset. Nonspeech sounds such as cough, laugh, cry, and throat clearing are present and normal. These sounds can be extended gradually into speech. If the patient is ready to give up the aphonic behavior, therapy is relatively brief, usually within one session.

Case 3

Case 3 presented with a loud, strained, whispered voice. The laryngologist had found no laryngeal pathology. Case history revealed no changes in lifestyle or environment at the time of onset. However, the voice problem began about 1 year after her husband's retirement as owner and manager of a large grocery store. The family lived in a small town some distance from any cultural area. She felt the voice loss was related to a bad cold and allergy she had experienced at the time of onset. Normal voice was observed during throat clearing, coughing, and laughter. When asked what bothered her about her voice loss, she answered, "I can't talk to my friends"!

Therapy consisted of extending the throat clear from "ah? hum" to longer and longer hum-m-m-m sounds. She was then able to produce the hum word without the throat clear. The hum was extended into single "m" words and phrases beginning with "m" words. At this point, she reverted to whisper. The process was repeated with additional focus on relaxed production. This time she was able to extend to days of the week, counting, short phrases, sentences, and, finally, conversation. It is not unusual to have to start at the beginning several times with these patients. She was very relieved and thankful to be able to talk again. During the ensuing conversation, she said: "Now, maybe he will let me rejoin my bridge club." When asked again about changes in her lifestyle, she admitted that since her husband's retirement her life had changed extensively. She had thought, however, that it was only part of what to expect when one's spouse retired. He had begun to criticize her housekeeping in the same managerial style he used with his employees at the store. He had always done this; but now that he was retired and at home, it became almost constant. She was resentful because he did not volunteer to help. After about a year, he became more and more concerned with expenses and living on a fixed income. He complained about her extravagance in entertaining her bridge club every other month, even though he continued to golf regularly and attend his bowling team matches. He finally forbade her to entertain her bridge club and essentially took away her only source of pleasure and enjoyment. It was at this point her voice deteriorated.

Some patients achieve secondary gain from a voice disorder. Often these patients come to the laryngologist on the insistence of others. There frequently is a lack of affect surrounding the patient's feeling about his or her voice problem.

Case 4

Case 4 was a very wealthy widowed woman. She was brought to the voice center at the insistence of her unmarried sister who had come to live with her after the death of her husband. Onset of the aphonic voice problem had been gradual, beginning with speech within the home. The laryngologist reported normal vocal folds with no evidence of structural or neurologic pathology. The patient demonstrated little concern about her voice problem other than as an inconvenience. When asked how her voice interfered with her life, she stated, with a little smile: "Well, when I am at parties, everyone has to come up to me to converse; and of course, I cannot reprimand or manage the servants; and I can't do the grocery shopping, my sister has to do that." Although physiologic sounds were present in normal voice, she was unable to extend them into any semblance of speech voicing. She took umbrage at the suggestion of counseling or any emotional etiology for her voice problem and terminated contact. She refused to have her case discussed with her sister. It was clear that her voice problem would not improve until her sister and friends stopped reinforcing the positive impact of her voice problem.

A second group of aphonic patients present with tense aphonic speech with intermittent squeaky, high-pitched syllables or words. They are often misdiagnosed with spasmodic dysphonia, which is currently thought to be a neurological disorder. Careful differential diagnosis is important. However, regardless of the initial diagnosis, initial evaluation and treatment are similar.

These patients may present with a history of emotional disorder or severe stress, reflux, asthma, and/or chemical sensitivity resulting in laryngospasm. Strobovideolaryngoscopy usually reveals severe muscle tension with anterior-posterior constriction; elevated laryngeal position; reduced abduction and adduction; and, in many cases, evidence of reflux laryngitis. Evaluation of the vocal mechanism finds the larynx held high in the neck. There is tension in the jaw, tongue, and extralaryngeal muscles. Breathing is high in the chest with excessive inspiratory effort. Therapy includes Aronson's digital manipulation[2] and yawn-sigh, swallow, and gargling activities to lower and relax the larynx. The tongue and jaw must be relaxed, using techniques described previously. Good abdominal breathing must be developed. Therapy needs to be intensive, on a daily basis. Appointments on a weekly basis allow too much time for the tension reactions to re-establish themselves, reducing the effectiveness or therapeutic intervention. Referral to a stress management clinician or psychologist is sometimes necessary. If voice therapy is successful in establishing normally pitched voice with little evidence of tension, but spasmodic aphonic breaks persist, the patient should be re-evaluated for the presence of spasmodic dysphonia.

Case 5

Case 5 presented with a high-pitched squeaky voice with frequent aphonic breaks. He felt his voice problem was directly related to his work situation. He was a middle manager in a utility company. He felt his company was in the process of downsizing; but instead of firing of employees, the company designated some employees as eligible for upgrade training. The training consisted of "EST-like" sessions with no bathroom or food breaks and constant berating of the employee. Several of his fellow employees quit. He vowed to fight the system. However, at this point, he lost his voice. He was transferred within the company from sales to a computer-intensive position. His voice returned to the presenting squeaky quality. He felt the stress of his treatment at work and resulting stress at home were directly related to his problem. Evaluation revealed high, tense laryngeal position, pain on palpation of the hyoid bone supporting the tongue, and "chest heave" breathing pattern. He was seen for a period of 3 days. Initially, he was unable to maintain a relaxed lowered laryngeal position. He was able to monitor his larynx position digitally and was aware of the mechanism. When his larynx was lowered, he produced normally pitched but breathy voice. Cues to make his voice louder improved voice quality but tended to introduce laryngeal tension and lifting of the larynx. Continued therapy to relax the tongue and jaw and to develop abdominal breathing was effective in producing normal voice. He refused suggestions for referral to the voice team psychologist. He contacts the therapist on occasion and continues to be symptom-free.

Case 6

Case 6 was a teacher's assistant in a preschool program. She came to school early one day and found the janitor cleaning the floors with a strong disinfectant liquid cleaner. Excessive cleaning fluid had spilled from the container and had spread across the floor. She was unable to breathe and was sent to emergency care, requiring muscle relaxants and oxygen to restore breathing. Her breathing improved but her voice became high-pitched and squeaky. She experienced two other incidents of breathing difficulties associated with the smells in a new store and when buying carpet. She was unable to use commercial cleaning products in her home without experiencing shortness of breath. She was diagnosed with laryngospasm. Strobovideolaryngoscopy revealed severe muscle tension and elevated larynx, but normal laryngeal positioning; extreme tension in the neck and extralaryngeal muscles; and a rapid, shallow, thoracic breathing pattern. The patient was convinced that her voice problem was related to "damage while hospitalized" and was considering suing the hospital.

Gentle digital massage and head and neck relaxation exercises restored her voice to normal. Therapy then focused on reducing fears of breathing and voicing. She was given strategies, including slow, deep, abdominal breathing and jaw and throat relaxation patterns, to counteract the return of the laryngeal spasms. She consented to referral to stress management/psychology. Therapy with the psychologist focused on deep relaxation and hypnotic suggestion to reduce fears and anxiety. She was able to return to work. She still avoided areas with strong smells but was able to utilize her compensation techniques. She has not required hospitalization for breathing difficulties since.

A third group of aphonic patients present with aphonia accompanied with a low-pitched, rough, strangled voice quality. Strobovideolaryngoscopy reveals extreme supralaryngeal tension with both anterior/posterior and medial compression of supralaryngeal structures. Often laryngeal examination is discontinued, and voice therapy is pursued because of the difficulty in viewing the vocal folds beneath the extreme supralaryngeal closure. Emotional trauma is usually present in these cases. Again, these patients are often misdiagnosed as having spasmodic dysphonia. Frequently, the same techniques utilized with whispering patients are helpful in modifying their vocal behavior towards normal. In addition, inhalation speech can be helpful in breaking the supraglottic tension.

Case 7

Case 7 lost her voice following the death of her grandson. Her voice was low, rough, strangled, and intermittently aphonic. Voice evaluation demonstrated generalized reduction of movement in the respiratory and articulatory systems with excessive tension in the extralaryngeal musculature. During the history, she described the death of her grandson. Her daughter and son-in-law went out to dinner, leaving their son with her and her husband. During the evening, the child suffered a severe asthma attack and died in her arms despite cardiopulmonary resuscitation. During the telling of this story, her voice became more and more strangled. The therapist commented that she sounded like she wanted to cry and offered a tissue. At this, she burst into tears and great sobbing. She began to cry in a normal voice: "I am so angry." The therapist asked if she was angry because of the death of her grandson. She replied: "No, I am angry because I have not had a chance to grieve." Continuing in a normal voice, she related that her husband, daughter and son-in-law were devastated by the death, which left her to make all arrangements for the autopsy, funeral, and burial. Her anger was especially directed toward her husband, who did not help or give her any expression of sympathy or sensitivity to the depth of her feelings about her grandson's death and its aftermath. At the end of this revelation, the therapist gently brought her attention to the fact that her voice had become quite normal. She said: "Yes, but that's not the problem." She agreed to and was immediately referred to the voice team psychologist. She was followed periodically by speech therapy. Her voice remained stable. The psychologist reported that her problems with her family were much more extensive than those she had related to the speech-language pathologist.

Case 8

Case 8 was referred from his local speech-language pathologist to be evaluated for possible spasmodic dysphonia. He had been unable to obtain any normal speech after several months of therapy. His therapy had focused on relaxation techniques and breathing.

The patient presented with severe muscle tension dysphonia and low-pitched rough voice with a predominating whisper. Laryngoscopy could not be completed due to the severe supraglottic constriction. He denied any emotional trauma associated with the onset of his voice problem. His wife, however, felt it might be related to the death of his mother, followed within a month by the death of his father. He was also in the process of beginning retirement. All direct attempts at relaxing his voice, including inhalation speech, were ineffective or caused his voice to become worse. During instructional episodes and general conversation, he produced an occasional normal word or phrase. The therapist decided that direct therapy was not effective and began modeling normal easy voicing in conversation. Normal words and phrases were pointed out, and he was asked to reproduce the same voice feeling and style in further conversation. Conversation focused on positive experiences and pleasurable activities. Over the course of four sessions, the frequency of normal voice continued to increase. His wife reported episodes of normal voice at home. By the fifth session, his voice was consistently normal except for a reduction in vocal loudness. There was no evidence of spasm. At this point, strobovideolaryngoscopy was completed and was within normal limits. At the next session, the subject of his parent's deaths was broached. He denied that this was a problem, saying, "a good man should not let it bother him. A man should be strong enough to deal with such an inevitable occurrence." He felt it had been inappropriate of his previous female therapist to focus on that problem and found it difficult to cooperate with her in relaxation and breathing tasks. He was not ready to discuss his reaction. At the next session, he maintained his voicing. He also was able to begin to modify his breathing pattern to increase support and loudness. At the next session, he announced that he felt his voice had returned to normal and terminated therapy. He was seen at 6 months follow-up with the laryngologist and continued to maintain relatively normal voice.

A fourth form of aphonia is voluntary muteness. Voluntary muteness in the absence of severe laryngeal pathology, developmental language delay, or severe hearing loss is very rare. Physicians and speech-language pathologists should be alert for serious underlying psychological problems in any patient with psychogenic dysphonia, especially if the patient reacts with excessive emotion (fear, crying, panic) to routine visualization of the larynx. The author (RTS) has seen a few such patients whose aphonia was causally related to deeply repressed memories of sexual abuse, for example. Such patients require referral for formal intervention by a licensed psychological professional.

Case 9

Case 9 was a 12-year-old boy. His mother, a loquacious and verbal woman, brought him to the voice center. She was concerned about his preparation for bar mitzvah. She was planning a large ceremony and big party, which she thought he would enjoy. However, he would not talk to her about the event or talk to the cantor or rabbi during training lessons. She had taken him to a psychologist, but he would not talk to her either. He was doing well in school, although she did not know how much talking he did there. She reported that his father was a soft-spoken man of few words. She felt that voice therapy might be helpful in increasing her son's loudness and ability to perform at his bar mitzvah.

Strobovideolaryngoscopy demonstrated a normal larynx. However, the laryngologist was unable to get him to vocalize with any strength. The therapist agreed to attempt short-term therapy, but felt that he had found a powerful tool to control his mother.

He reluctantly participated in breathing exercises and gained better oral resonance. He would practice portions of the readings required at the bar mitzvah service, but only in exchange for a turn at a computer game.

He arrived at the third session more animated than he had ever been before. His teacher had given the class a book report assignment. Each student was to read a book and then report orally to the class about the story from the point of view of one of the characters in the book. The report could only be 5 minutes long. He had chosen *Tom Sawyer* and wanted to report in the guise of that character. He discussed in detail his plans for a costume and asked for help in presenting an already prepared presentation. We worked on appropriate breath support and phrasing, projection and open oral resonance and editing for length. He asked for an additional session to give us more time prior to his presentation. It was hoped that a breakthrough had occurred. He was working as hard as any aspiring actor, reporting that he received an A+ on his presentation. However, when the work resumed on his bar mitzvah readings, the old reluctance returned. He was able to demonstrate his skills if rewarded, but continued to be silent at home. His mother reported that he would at least mumble his readings to the cantor. Plans for a large bar mitzvah were canceled. His mother was reluctant to re-engage in psychotherapy, and the patient discontinued voice therapy.

Voice Problems Associated with Psychosis

Rarely does the voice of the psychotic patient present as the most relevant symptom. Several studies have been published characterizing the speech of the schizophrenic. These characteristics are considered to be the byproduct of affect, aura, and relational disturbances. Speech therapy for those voice characteristics is rarely considered. However, occasionally such a patient will be seen in a voice center.

Case 10

Case 10 had a successful career in a medical subspecialty. However, she aspired to a career in opera. She had taken many lessons but had been discouraged by her family and teachers from pursuing this professionally. She had been highly unsuccessful while auditioning for roles. She came to the voice center to have her singing/speaking voice evaluated.

Strobovideolaryngoscopy revealed normal laryngeal structures. During history-taking, she revealed that her voice was fine at work, because of the lead shielding at the hospital." However, at home, her voice was disrupted and changed in quality, particularly when she was practicing singing and acting and at auditions. When asked why, she reported that "'they' were shooting laser beams at her" and shocking her, which disrupted her voice and made her voicing very tense. When asked, "who they were?' She replied, "Certain others who are jealous of my talents and want to thwart my career in singing." She also reported that the beams "they" were using burned her and produced changes in her skin color around her neck and shoulders.

When reading a passage, she winced, dodged, and several times cried out in pain. When this behavior was questioned, she reported calmly that "they" had followed her to the voice center and were shooting laser beams and using electric shock on her. She was reluctant to work on her speaking voice, because the problems of tension that she had were caused by an external force and not by her.

Her evaluation by our singing specialist was similar. She was urged by the entire team to submit to evaluation by a psychiatrist, but would not do so.

Voice Problems Associated with Adolescence

Mutational falsetto is high-falsetto voicing, often with frequent pitch breaks. The voice is thin and high pitched. Falsetto voice requires a different shaping of the glottis and different breath support than typical voicing. The larynx must ride high in the neck to produce falsetto. It is a normal phenomenon; most males can produce it. It is used frequently in singing by rock and roll singers and developed extensively by classical countertenors, but it is not a preferred means of speech communication. It occurs in some young men following the onset of laryngeal growth associated with adolescence. The techniques described above for use with patients with "squeaky" voices are useful in this group. Usually, normal voicing is easily achieved during the evaluation and trial therapy sessions. Often the patient has both falsetto and normal voice, but prefers the falsetto for various personal reasons. Most of these patients are nonmuscular young men with little self-confidence. This speech disturbance has often been misdiagnosed as spasmodic dysphonia because of the pitch breaks.

Case 11

Case 11 was a 23-year-old auto body repairman. He was concerned about laryngeal cancer. His girlfriend and parents accompanied him to the voice clinic. Strobovideolaryngoscopy revealed a normal larynx and the presence of falsetto voicing. During the voice evaluation, he was asked if he had any other voices. In a normal deep baritone he answered, "Yes." He used the deep voice around his colleagues at the auto body shop. He used the falsetto voice with his girlfriend, his family, and his high school friends. His life was organized around the premise that the two groups of people were never present at the same time. When asked why he needed the dichotomy of voice, he answered that he was afraid his girlfriend and family wouldn't like his other voice. He was asked if he would be willing to try. His girlfriend was brought into the room and he used his deep voice. She, of course, was thrilled. He was relieved, and his voice problem was solved.

Case 12

Case 12 was a 19-year-old college student who had just completed his freshman year at a religious college. He had attended a choir school during his primary school years and had sung many soprano solos. His best singing occurred just prior to adolescent voice change. He continued to sing soprano although his voice became thin and he had difficulty keeping his voice from cracking following vocal mutation. His speaking voice continued to be high, breathy, and characterized by pitch breaks.

When he arrived at college, he enrolled in the religious music department, hoping to continue a career in choral singing. His singing teacher, instead of being impressed by his high voice, referred him to a local speech-language pathologist. He was diagnosed with spasmodic dysphonia, presumably because of the numerous pitch breaks. He was referred for neurological workup and Botox injection. His singing teacher was not convinced of this diagnosis and referred him to our voice center.

Strobovideolaryngoscopy revealed a normal larynx with falsetto voice patterning. He was convinced that, "spasmodic dysphonia had destroyed his singing voice." He was counseled on the effects of adolescent voice change. We explored the large size and angular shape of his larynx, comparing it to the much smaller, rounded larynx of a child. The symptoms of spasmodic dysphonia were described and tapes of spasmodic dysphonic voices were played for him.

Attempts at producing low-pitched normal voice extending from cough and throat-clearing sounds were successful but transition into speech sounds was difficult. He was asked to put his finger across his Adam's apple and tuck his chin down toward his chest. This maneuver made falsetto voicing impossible. Normal low-pitched voicing was achieved and transferred to syllables, words, phrases, questions and answers, and monologue. The positioning cues were faded to gentle downward tactile cues. He was engaged in conversation using the "new" voice for at least 30 minutes. He was asked to use his new voice with other personnel, his family (who had accompanied him to the center), and on the telephone to his singing teacher. His family was relieved that Botox injections would not be necessary. Breath support was practiced in context of his speech. By the end of the evaluation and trial therapy session, he was convinced that he was a baritone and could continue singing in that role. He no longer felt he had spasmodic dysphonia. The singing specialist at the voice center saw him and reported that he was able to maintain his speaking voice and begin some singing exercises focusing on lower range extension and breath support. He was asked to call the center the following day to report on continued use of the "new" voice. During that call, the patient reported that he had retained his lower voice. He was looking forward to returning to college and working with his singing teacher on developing his baritone voice.

Occasionally, males with mutational falsetto demonstrate personal conflicts with their fathers, attachment problems with their mothers, or gender confusion. These patients tend to produce normal voice reluctantly and fail to maintain it, often complaining that such a voice is not appropriate for them. Counseling and referral to a psychological professional to focus on these difficulties is necessary.

Young women do not present with mutational falsetto. Rarely, a young postpubescent girl will present with immature voice. This is characterized by high pitch and melody, inflection, articulation, and word choice more reminiscent of a preschool child than a postpubertal young adult. Usually, strong dependent behaviors are described in the history.

Case 13

Case 13 was a 17-year-old high school student who aspired to a career in musical theater. She had been highly successful in obtaining roles as a child in productions of *Annie*. She had been thwarted lately in winning any role because of her voice. She was close to tears and appeared to be very depressed. Laryngeal examination demonstrated normal structures but muscle tension associated with high pitch. Her voice was very high pitched and immature with a mild lisp and "r" sound distortions. She was seen in therapy and made progress in controlled contexts. However, she was unable to transfer her more mature voice to home and school environments. She was very unhappy about this and felt that something was blocking her ability to use her more mature voice outside the SLP's office. She and her family readily accepted her referral for psychologic services. However, because of travel distance, she was seen by someone closer to her home.

Conclusions

Psychophysiological research informs our treatment and maximizes the benefits of medical interactions in every specialty. The rightful role of the arts-medicine psychological professional is to possess mastery of the knowledge bases of psychology and medicine and also an experiential understanding of the performing arts, so that he or she may stand in alliance with the injured performer on the journey to explore, understand, and modify the psychological impact of performance-related injuries. The speech-language pathologist must understand the psychological factors that may cause, or be caused by, voice disorders. The speech-language pathologist must be able to modify disordered voices into functional voices with sufficient stamina to endure the demands of their lifestyle and environment. The speech-language pathologist provides a caring and supportive environment that allows patients to explore possible underlying causes. The SLP must also recognize his or her limits as a psychotherapist and know when to refer to and collaborate with a mental health professional while maintaining responsibility for voice modification and some degree of psychological support. The laryngologist must recognize the need for therapy in individual patients, accurately diagnose the presence of organic and functional disorders, select and coordinate the therapy team, and retain overall responsibility for the therapeutic process and the patient's outcome. Those who are privileged to care for that uniquely human capability—the voice—quickly come to understand the essential role of psychologic awareness in our treatment failures and successes.

References

1. Rosen DC, Sataloff RT. *Psychology of Voice Disorders.* San Diego, Calif: Singular Publishing Group; 1997.
2. Aronson A. *Clinical Voice Disorders.* 3rd ed. New York, NY: Thieme Medical Publishers; 1900:117–145, 314–315.
3. Sundberg J. *The Science of the Singing Voice.* DeKalb, Ill: Northern Illinois University Press; 1985:146–156.
4. Vogel D, Carter J. *The Effects of Drugs on Communication Disorders.* San Diego, Calif: Singular Publishing Group; 1995:31–143.
5. Shontz F. Body image and physical disability. In: Cash T, Pruzinsky T, eds. *Body Images: Development, Deviance and Change.* New York, NY: The Guilford Press; 1990: 149–169.
6. Freedman R. Cognitive behavioral perspectives on body image change. In: Cash TF, Pruzinsky T, eds. *Body Images: Development Deviance and Change.* New York, NY: Guilford Press; 1990:273–295.
7. Horney K. Cited by: Meissner W. Theories of personality. In: Nicholi A, ed. *The New Harvard Guide to Psychiatry.* Cambridge, Mass. Harvard University Press; 1988: 177–199.
8. Rosen DC, Sataloff RT. Psychological aspects of voice disorders. In: Gould WJ, Rubin J, Korovin G, Sataloff RT, eds. *Diagnosis and Treatment of Voice Disorders.* New York, NY: Igaku-Shoin Medical Publishers; 1993:491–501.
9. Rodgers CA. A theory of personality and interpersonal relationships as developed in a client centered framework. In: Koch S. ed. *Psychology: a Study of a Science.* New York, NY: McGraw-Hill; 1959:184–256.
10. Butcher P, Elias A, Raven R. *Psychogenic Voice Disorders and Cognitive-Behavior Therapy.* San Diego, Calif: Singular Publishing Group; 1993:3–22.
11. Nemiah J. Psychoneurotic disorders. In: Nicholi A, ed. *The New Harvard Guide to Psychiatry.* Cambridge, Mass: Harvard University Press; 1988:234–258.
12. Ziegler FJ, Imboden JB. Contemporary conversion reactions: II conceptual model. *Arch Gen Psychiatry.* 1962;6:279–287.
13. Hartman DE, Daily WW, Morin KN. A case of superior laryngeal nerve paresis and psychogenic dysphonia. *J Speech Hear Disord.* 1989;54:526–529.
14. Sapir S, Aronson AE. Coexisting psychogenic and neurogenic dysphonia: a source of diagnostic confusion. Br *J Disord Commun.* 1987;22:73–80.
15. Cummings JL, Benson DF, Houlihan JP, Gosenfield LF. Mutism: loss of neocortical and limbic vocalization. *J Nerv Ment Dis.* 1983;171:255–259.
16. American Psychiatric Association. *Diagnostic and Statistical Manual of Mental Disorders.* 3rd ed. rev. Washington, DC: American Psychiatric Association; 1987:206–210.
17. Brodnitz FS. Hormones and the human voice. *Bull NY Acad Med.* 1971;47:183–191.
18. Styron W. *Darkness Visible: A Memoir of Madness.* New York, NY: Random House; 1990.
19. Klerman G. Depression and related disorders of mood. In: Nicholi A, ed. *The New Harvard Guide to Psychiatry.* Cambridge, Mass: Harvard University Press; 1988: 309–336.
20. Ross E, Rush A. Diagnosis and neuroanatomical correlates of depression in brain-damaged patients: implications for a neurology of depression. *Arch Gen Psychiatry.* 1981;38:1344–1354.
21. Weissman MM. The psychological treatment of depression. Evidence for the efficacy of psychotherapy alone, in comparison with, and in combination with pharmacotherapy. *Arch Gen Psychiatry.* 1979;38:1261–1269.

22. Sataloff RT. Stress, anxiety and psychogenic dysphonia. In: Sataloff RT. *Professional Voice: The Science and Art of Clinical Care.* New York, NY: Raven Press; 1991:195–200.
23. Tsuang M, Faraone S, Day M. Schizophrenic disorders. In: Nicholi A, ed. *The New Harvard Guide to Psychiatry.* Cambridge, Mass: Harvard University Press; 1988: 259–295.
24. Schatzberg A, Cole J. *Manual of Clinical Psychopharmacology.* 2nd ed. Washington, DC: American Psychiatric Association Press; 1991:40, 50, 55, 58, 66, 68, 69, 72–77, 110–125, 158–165, 169–177, 185–227, 313–348.
25. Cole JO, Bodkin JA. Antidepressant drug side effects. *J Clin Psychiatry.* 1990;51:S21–S26.
26. Arana GW, Rosenbaum JR. *Handbook of Psychiatric Drug Therapy.* 4th ed. Philadelphia, Pa: Lippincott, Williams and Wilkins; 2000:85–90.
27. *Physician's Desk Reference.* Oradell, NJ: Medical Economics Data; 1994:200–203, 2267–2270.
28. *Physician's Desk Reference.* Oradell, NJ: Medical Economics Data; 1996:B20.
29. *Physician's Desk Reference.* Oradell, NJ: Medical Economics Data; 1997:1615, 1878, 2239.
30. King M, Novick L, Citrenbaum C. *Irresistible Communication: Creative Skills for the Health Professional.* Philadelphia, Pa: Saunders; 1983:21, 22, 115–127.
31. Sataloff RT, Lawrence VL, Hawkshaw M, Rosen DC. Medications and their effects on the voice. In: Benninger MS, Jacobson BH, Johnson AF, eds. *Vocal Arts Medicine: The Care and Prevention of Professional Voice Disorders.* New York, NY: Thieme Medical Publishers; 1994: 216–225.
32. Metcalfe R, Firth D, Pollock S, Creed F. Psychiatric morbidity and illness behaviour in female neurological inpatients. *J Neurol Neurosurg Psychiatry.* 1988;51:1387–1390.
33. Gainotti G. Emotional behavior and hemispheric side of lesion. *Cortex.* 1972;8:41–55.
34. Alexander MP, LoVerne SR Jr. Aphasia after left hemispheric intracerebral hemorrhage. *Neurology.* 1980;30: 1193–1202.
35. Mahr G, Leith W. Psychogenic stuttering of adult onset. *J Speech Hear Res.* 1992;35:283–286.
36. Everly GS Jr. *A Clinical Guide to the Treatment of the Human Stress Response.* New York, NY: Plenum Press; 1989:40–43.
37. Green J, Snellenberger R. *The Dynamics of Health and Wellness. A Biopsychosocial Approach.* Fort Worth, Tex: Holt Reinhardt and Winston; 1991:61–64, 92, 98, 101–136.
38. Lazarus RS, Folkman S. *Stress Appraisal and Coping.* New York, NY: Springer-Verlag; 1984:283.
39. Stroudemire AG. *Psychological Factors Affecting Medical Conditions.* Washington, DC: American Psychiatric Press; 1995:187–192.
40. Zraick RI, Boone DR. Spouse attitudes toward the person with aphasia. *J Speech Hear Res.* 1991;34:123–128.
41. Rosen DC, Sataloff RT, Evans H, Hawkshaw M. Self-esteem and singing: singing healthy, singing hurt. *NATS J.* 1993;49:32–35.
42. Worden JW. *Grief Counseling and Grief Therapy.* New York, NY: Springer-Verlag; 1982:7–18.
43. Adamson JD, Hersuberg D, Shane F. The psychic significance of parts of the body in surgery. In: Howells JG, ed. *Modern Perspectives in the Psychiatric Aspects of Surgery.* New York, NY; Brunner/Mazel; 1976:20–45.
44. Carpenter B. Psychological aspects of vocal fold surgery. In: Gould WJ. Sataloff RT, Spiegel JR, eds. *Voice Surgery.* St. Louis, Mo: Mosby; 1993:339–343.
45. Macgregor FC. Patient dissatisfaction with results of technically satisfactory surgery. *Aesthetic Plast Surg.* 1981;5:27–32.
46. Ray CJ. Fitzgibbon G. The socially mediated reduction of stress in surgical patients. In: Oborne DJ, Grunberg M, Eisner JR, eds. *Research and Psychology in Medicine.* vol 2. Oxford, England: Pergamon Press; 1979:521–527.
47. Berkowitz JF, Lucente FE. Counseling before laryngectomy. *Laryngoscope.* 1985;95:1332–1336.
48. Gardner WH. Adjustment problems of laryngectomized women. *Arch Otolaryngol.* 1966;83:31–42.
49. Starm H, Koopmans J, Mathieson C. The psychological impact of a laryngectomy: a comprehensive assessment. *J Psychosoc Oncol.* 1991;9:37–58
50. Bady SL. The voice as curative factor in psychotherapy. *Psychoanal Rev.* 1985;72:479–490.
51. Crasilneck HB, Hall J. *Clinical Hypnosis: Principles and Applications.* 2nd ed. Orlando, Fla: Grune and Stratton; 1985:60–61.
52. Lankton S. *Practical Magic: A Translation of Basic Neurolinguistic Programming into Clinical Psychotherapy.* Cupertino, Calif: Meta Publications; 1980:174.
53. Watkins JG. *Hypnotherapeutic Techniques.* New York, NY: Irvington Publishers; 1987:114.
54. Moses PJ. *The Voice of Neurosis.* New York, NY: Grune and Stratton; 1954.
55. Luchsinger R, Arnold GE. *Voice, Speech, Language; Clinical Communicology: Its Physiology and Pathology.* Belmont. Calif: Wadsworth; 1965.
56. Rulnick RK, Heuer RJ, Perez KS, et al. Voice therapy. In: Sataloff RT. *Professional Voice: the Science and Art of Clinical Care.* 2nd ed. San Diego, Calif: Singular Publishing Group; 1997:699–720.

11

Neurologic Disorders Affecting the Voice in Performance

Robert Thayer Sataloff, Steven Mandel, Reena Gupta, and Heidi Mandel

The complex activities necessary for normal voice function require coordinated interactions among multiple body systems. Neurological dysfunction that impairs control of these interactions commonly causes vocal dysfunction. In fact, it is not unusual for voice disorders to be the presenting complaint in patients with neurologic disease. There have been substantial advances in our knowledge of neuroanatomy related to phonation, neurological diagnosis, and treatment of neurologically based voice disorders. It is essential for laryngologists to be familiar with current concepts in neurolaryngology.

Neurolaryngology

Neurolaryngology has emerged as a new subspecialty. The first book in this field was published in 1992.[1] Although still in its infancy, further development of neurolaryngology is inevitable. In many ways, the field is analogous to neurotology. In 1960, there was no such field as neurotology. A few years later, Dr. William House perfected the translabyrinthine approach for excision of acoustic neuromas. From this humble beginning, neurotology developed as one of the most sophisticated subspecialties in otolaryngology. It came to incorporate not merely elegant and complex surgical procedures, but also diagnostic and therapeutic advances in the management of inner ear, ear-brain interface, and central auditory system abnormalities. These developments were made possible through the efforts of courageous and creative clinicians and close collaboration with colleagues in other fields such as neurology, neurosurgery, and basic science. Many of the scientists were trained in disciplines that seemed relatively far afield, at first. Biochemists, physicists, physiologists, engineers, and others grouped together at places like the House Ear Institute and the Kresge Hearing Research Institute. Their collaboration produced a vastly expanded understanding of the ear and its related structures, development of a new interdisciplinary subspecialty of physicians dedicated to neurotological problems, and dramatic advances in patient care. Neurolaryngology today stands where neurotology stood in the 1970s.

Just as the ear and hearing were fairly well understood 30 years ago, current knowledge of the human voice includes reasonable notions of how the voice works and of the central pathways involved in volitional voice and speech functions. Yet, there are great gaps in both knowledge and application. The neuroanatomy and physiology of voice and speech are not appreciated fully, and the interactions that constitute control mechanisms are largely undefined. Consequently, many neurogenic problems of voice and speech remain obscure. Even in conditions known to have possible neurological or neuromuscular etiologies, treatment approaches seem every bit as unsophisticated as the acoustic neuroma surgery of the 1950s. For example, until the 1990s, spasmodic dysphonia commonly was treated by surgical division of the recurrent laryngeal nerve. Injection with botulinum toxin appears to be an improvement. However, 10 years from now, if the true nature of the disease process has been discovered, poisoning muscles with botulinum may appear as barbaric as cutting recurrent laryngeal nerves. In fact, there are no universally accepted, standardized surgical procedures for even the most clear-cut neurolaryngologic injury: traumatic recurrent laryngeal nerve paralysis. Reanastamosis or grafting of an injured facial nerve generally results in acceptable function. Why are the results so frequently unsatisfactory after similar procedures with laryngeal nerves? What can be done to restore function? These are fairly basic neurolaryngologic questions. They do not even begin to address issues such as restoration of voice control in people with more complex neurogenic dysfunction or major surgical challenges such as laryngeal transplantation after laryngectomy or neurological concomitants of professional voice training.

At this point, neurolaryngology presents many exciting questions but not enough credible answers. However, given the kind of interdisciplinary interest and collaboration that nurtured neurotology, neurolaryngology promises to continue developing into an even more exciting, challenging, and enlightening subspecialty. This maturing field undoubtedly will answer many compelling clinical questions, raise as many exciting new questions, and augment the practice of laryngology as richly as neurotology has altered the practice of otology.

Neuroanatomy and Neurophysiology of Phonation

A comprehensive discussion of the neuroanatomy and neurophysiology of phonation is beyond the scope of this book, and knowledge is being added so quickly that this section would surely be out of date before publication if an all-inclusive discussion were attempted. For example, research has revealed clinically important information about periaqueductal gray matter control of respiration and phonation, premotor cortical control of voluntary respiration, unusual differences in afferent and efferent conduction speed for intercostal and abdominal muscles, effects of auditory feedback on phonation (particularly with regard to singing), and many other subjects.[2]

Interest in laryngeal evoked brainstem responses (LBR) has emphasized the importance of laryngeal brainstem reflex pathways. For example, the superior laryngeal nerve has neural connections with the nucleus tractus solitarius, nucleus ambiguus, the retrofacial nucleus, the tenth nerve nucleus, and the nucleus of the reticular formation. Numerous subcortical and cortical regions also are involved in laryngeal motor regulation and possibly in laryngeal reflexes. Involved structures appear to include the amygdala, thalamus, hypothalamus, and basal ganglia. This anatomy suggests the possibility of potentially useful, measurable, middle and late latency LBR waves.

In addition, new research methods are resulting in many more discoveries about phonation, including neurological functions. Foremost among these new methodologies is the application of chaos, or nonlinear dynamic theory, to voice research and analysis. This new methodology has already provided clinically important insights, and it has enormous potential to improve our understanding of voice control, function, and dysfunction.[3,4] It is essential for laryngologists to maintain familiarity with the latest literature in neuroanatomy and neurophysiology so that new scientific insights can be applied clinically as soon as possible. They already have changed the approach to and treatment of some neurolaryngologic disorders, and many future refinements are anticipated in the near future.

Laryngeal EMG

Laryngeal electromyography (LEMG) can be useful in the diagnosis and management of many disorders, including neurolaryngeal diseases, swallowing disorders, laryngeal joint injury, and spasmodic dysphonia. It can also be therapeutic, as in localization for botulinum toxin injection, or prognostic, as in helping determine the need for surgery in patients with vocal fold paresis. Laryngeal EMG is discussed in chapter 5.

Neurological Dysfunction and Voice

This chapter focuses on specific neurolaryngologic problems and their effects on voice. It is not intended to be all-inclusive. Many of the more common and important topics have been selected for inclusion, but the reader is encouraged to consult other otolaryngologic, neurologic, and research literature for additional information.

Dysphonia and Dysarthria

Dysphonia is voice disturbance that usually involves a problem at the level of the larynx. *Dysarthria* means imperfect articulation in speech and is symptomatic of a group of disorders related to strength, speed, and coordination involving the brain and the nerves and musculature of the mouth, larynx, and respiratory system as they relate to speech. Because of the importance of articulation in professional voice users and their awareness of voice and speech function, neurological problems that cause dysarthria may present initially (and early in the course of the disease) as subtle speech or voice complaints.

The cause of dysarthria can be vascular, metabolic, motor, traumatic, or infectious. It is never rooted in a language deficit. The time course of presentation and duration of dysarthria varies. It can be acute, as in stroke, and permanent or temporary; transient, as with a single episode of unknown cause or following head trauma; slowly progressive, as in neurologic diseases, such as Parkinson's; or rapidly progressive, due to metabolic causes or infection.

Physicians should be familiar with the characteristics of neurogenic voice disorders, dysarthrias, and dysphonias and should understand the diagnostic significance of each of the six types of dysarthria.[5,6] *Flaccid dysarthria* occurs in lower motor neuron disease, commonly in primary muscle disorders such as myasthenia gravis, and with tumors or strokes involving the brainstem nuclei. *Spastic dysarthria* is found in upper motor neuron disorders (pseudobulbar palsy) such as multiple strokes and cerebral palsy. *Ataxic dysarthria* is seen with cerebellar disease, alcohol intoxication, and multiple sclerosis. *Hypokinetic dysarthria* accompanies Parkinson's disease. *Hyperkinetic dysarthria* may be spasmodic, as in Gilles de la Tourette syndrome, or dystonic, as in chorea and cerebral palsy. *Mixed dysarthria* is seen in amyotrophic lateral sclerosis. Dysarthria may affect the tongue, lips, or mandible, and phonation or respiration. When dysarthria involves the larynx, it affects phonation; when it involves the velopharynx, it affects resonance; and when it involves the tongue, lip, mandible area, it affects articulation. The classification above actually combines *dysphonic* and *dysarthric* characteristics but is very useful clinically.

In addition to the articulation dysfunctions described above, clinicians should be familiar with specific voice characteristics associated with various neurologic deficits. They can be elicited through careful examination that includes a variety of voice tasks (running speech, rapidly varying speech, sustained phonation, and other maneuvers). The type of voice associated with lesions producing flaccid dysfunction depends on the site of the lesion. Flaccid paralysis from a problem located high in the vagus nerve typically produces a very breathy, whispered voice with hypernasal resonance. A lower vagus nerve lesion (recurrent laryngeal nerve, below the nodose ganglion) produces no resonance defect, but a hoarse, breathy voice often associated with diplophonia. Spastic conditions due to lesions in the corticobulbar region of the brain bilaterally produce hypernasal resonance and a hoarse, strained voice. Combined spastic and flaccid signs occur when bilateral corticobulbar lesions are present in addition to tenth nerve paralysis. This combination results in hypernasal resonance, vocal flutter, and a strained voice with hoarseness and crackling from poorly controlled secretions on the vocal folds. Cerebellar lesions associated with ataxia usually do not affect resonance, but they cause vocal tremor and irregularities. Hoarseness and breathiness typically are not present. Parkinson's disease provides the classic example of hypokinetic dysfunction. It is associated with lesions in the basal ganglia and causes a soft, breathy voice with little pitch variability but fairly normal resonance. Basal ganglia lesions also are responsible for dystonias and choreas. Dystonic disorders frequently are accompanied by a hoarse, strained voice with vocal arrests, similar to those seen in adductor spastic dysphonia; and resonance may be hypernasal or normal. In chorea, vocal arrests are the most prominent vocal feature.

Brainstem lesions produce two typical voice abnormalities. One is *essential (organic) tremor.* This condition involves a regular voice tremor occurring at a rate of approximately 7 to 10 times per second (although rates as slow as 4 per second may occur) with interruptions that sometimes are mistaken for abductor or adductor spastic dysphonia. Visible tremor in the head or neck and elsewhere is common. The other is *action myoclonus*, in which rapid, machine-gun-like voice arrests can be heard on sustained vocalization. In contrast, *palatopharyngeal myoclonus* produces regular voice arrests so slow that they may be missed in running speech without careful examination. They occur at a rate of about 1 to 4 times per second and are associated with obvious myoclonic contractions of the palate, pharynx, larynx, and related structures. This condition is believed to be due most commonly to lesions in the region of the dentate, red, and inferior olivary nuclei. Recognition of these disordered voice characteristics may lead the astute clinician to an early diagnosis of important and treatable neurological disease. The value of a comprehensive neurolaryngological evaluation cannot be overstated.[7,8]

Cranial nerve involvement with dysarthria is characterized by impairment in movement, referred to as *hypokinetic* (decreased movement), *kinetic* (altered movement), or *hyperkinetic* (increased movement). Hyperkinetic dysarthria causes increased tone or flow with lack of inhibition, known as dystonia or dyskinesia (ie, involuntary movements). The hypokinetic type is exhibited as monotone and slowed speech.

Ataxic dysarthria, an irregular, articulatory breakdown in speech, is exhibited as excess stress in the voice. Multiple sclerosis can have ataxic dysarthria as one of the earliest signs and presents often in young adults. Ataxic dysarthria can affect the tongue, causing it to appear to have decreased control, and affecting sounds heavily dependent on the tongue. Spinal nerves also can cause problems in phonation if, for example, cervical nerves or muscles are affected or weakened. Flaccid dysarthria will present as an inability to move the mandible or as a drooping mouth. The unilateral type will involve drooping on one side; bilateral conditions will affect both sides.

Many conditions contribute to dysarthria. Some causal conditions are serious. Others are minor. Many are amenable to treatment. The observant voice care professional may be the first to recognize such a problem by observing the person's smile, tongue movements, swallowing patterns, breathing patterns, and facial expressions. Can the person whistle? Move the tongue over a wide range of motion? Puff out and suck in his or her cheeks? Abnormalities in movement and/or inability to articulate may lead to early diagnosis of numerous serious problems.

Diagnosing neurological problems responsible for dysarthria can be complex. The physician must consider the age of onset, type of speech abnormality, constancy versus intermittency, progression (slow, rapid, or none), and other factors. When indicated, various tests are helpful in determining the cause of the problem. In many cases, medications improve the condition and even may eliminate the dysarthria. In others, the physician's ability to determine the site of lesion permits guidance for the development of compensatory strategies that permit improved speaking and singing. The patient's response to medication and other treatments also may be helpful in confirming the diagnosis.

Spasmodic Dysphonia and Respiratory Dystonia

These conditions are covered in chapter 13.

Stuttering

Multiple areas of the nervous system, alone or in combination, can cause stuttering; and stuttering can be due to many causes, including developmental, psychogenic, and neurogenic. Persistent developmental stuttering (PDS) appears to be the most frequent, with onset usually early in life. It is estimated that developmental stutterers comprise over 1% of the adult population. Cerebral processes that regulate speech are disrupted in stutterers. When stuttering occurs in later life, it may be the presenting sign of a brain lesion and requires neurological evaluation before it can be ascribed to developmental or psychogenic causes. Acquired stuttering can accompany a number of neurologic syndromes, including cerebrovascular accident. Although stress worsens stuttering, it is not a cause, as demonstrated by the lack of efficacy of psychiatric-oriented therapy. Similarly, psychiatric theory cannot explain the occurrence of dysfluency at the beginning of sentences, the strong male prevalence, monozygotic twin concordance, or the fluency that is seen with singing.[9] Studies conflict regarding laryngeal muscle activation during dysfluencies. One study performed spectral analysis of electromyographic (EMG) activity in laryngeal and orofacial muscles and found tremorlike oscillations in both muscle groups during stuttered speech. Further, these oscillations appeared to be entrained in some subjects, suggesting the possibility that autonomic systems may provide some mechanism through which oscillations in different muscle groups may be entrained.[10] However, Smith et al examined laryngeal muscles via EMG in normal and stuttering adults and found no difference in activation of laryngeal muscles during periods of dysfluency.[11]

Few studies have examined the potential for anomalous anatomy as a basis for the development of PDS. A study by Heuer et al attempted to localize and define abnormalities in three patients with recent onset of stuttering using MRI, CT, and SPECT imaging. Their findings suggested that neurogenic stuttering may be a sequelae of diffuse bilateral lesions of multiple hemispheres or damage to the region of the thalamus. This study suggested further the usefulness of SPECT imaging in confirming and supporting CT and MRI findings, noting that one patient's abnormalities would have been missed had SPECT imaging not been used.[12]

In another recent study by Foundas et al, the planum temporale, a part of the classic Wernicke's area responsible for higher order processing of linguistic information, was found to be larger and planar asymmetry reduced in adults with PDS.[13] Although most controls and adults with PDS had a leftward planar asymmetry, the difference in PDS refers to the magnitude of this asymmetry. Further findings include gyrification pattern differences between people in the PDS and control groups, specifically in the quantity, variability of patterns, and frequency of occurrence of gyral variants in the areas of the sylvian fossa and frontal operculum. A hypothesis of two functional speech control loops, one mediated by perisylvian speech-language cortex, suggests that the altered anatomy in this area affects processing efficiency and thus produces dysynchrony and stuttering.[13]

Stuttering is discussed widely in speech-language pathology and neurology literature but is not a common problem among professional voice users. It is interesting to note, however, that stuttering rarely affects the singing voice. Consequently, even people with severe stuttering in speech have had successful professional singing careers. Botulinum toxin has been tried as a treatment for some stutterers without consistent success.

Vocal Tremor

Voice tremors require comprehensive neurologic evaluation. One of the most common causes is essential tremor, also known as *benign heredofamilial tremor*. A positive family history is found in more than 60% of patients with essential tremor. It has been suggested that the etiology of essential tremor lies in a functional disturbance involving the olivocerebellar circuit. It is thought that the cells of the inferior olive are synchronized, and that this synchronous activity is transferred to the motor neurons through the cerebellum and reticulospinal projections.[14] Before making a diagnosis of essential tremor, it is important to rule out serious conditions such as cerebellar disease (as in symptomatic palatal tremor), Parkinson's disease, psychogenic tremor, thyrotoxicosis, and drug-induced tremor. In contrast to Parkinson's disease, essential tremor (ET) is characterized by postural and kinetic tremor, not primarily resting tremor. "Pill rolling" tremor involving fingers is typical. In addition, the bradykinesia and rigidity that typify Parkinson's disease are not seen in ET.

Vocal tremor has been defined as rhythmic alternations of the loudness and pitch of vowels. In some cases, tremor can be associated with voice arrests when the timing of the tremor and speech are not coordinated well. In a study conducted at Baylor College of Medicine, 350 tremor patients were analyzed to further define clinical features and correlates of essential tremor. Sixty-two of the 350 subjects (17.7%) had voice tremor. However, only one of these patients had simple voice tremor. Sites of tremor in the remaining subjects included hand, legs, jaw, face, trunk, and tongue. Attempts to identify clinical correlates based on characteristics such as familial tendency or early-onset were unsuccessful.[15] A case has been reported of a 67-year-old female with voice and orthostatic tremor. The orthostatic tremor was observable primarily in her lower extremities at a frequency of 4.4 to 4.8 Hz between antagonist muscle groups. The frequency of her voice tremor ranged from 4.8 to 8.8 Hz. The fact that her orthostatic and voice tremors were of the same frequency suggests a common origin.[16]

Evaluation of patients with vocal tremor has attempted to elucidate the etiology of this condition. Tomoda et al, in a study of three patients with voice tremor, found it to be an action tremor of the muscles involved in voluntary expiration, resulting from an impaired regulation of the central nervous system innervation of these muscles.[17] Further study provided some confirmation of this expiratory component, in that the incidence of tremor in eight patients studied was greater during exhalation than inhalation. However, additional components clearly play a role in that phonation and whisper, which require comparable degrees of expiratory-respiratory drive, produced differences in incidence of tremor. It was found that tremor resulted from oscillation in vocal fold tension and length, and not subglottic pressure. It follows, therefore, that partial paralysis of these oscillations using botulinum toxin, specifically in the thyroarytenoid muscles, may improve voice tremor by reducing oscillations in these variables.[18] However, practical experience has shown that botulinum toxin injection usually is not effective enough in controlling tremor to be of practical value to patients. There are exceptions, so therapeutic trials are reasonable.

A small number of patients will improve somewhat with medication, although concurrently occurring tremors (ie, hand tremors) are more responsive to treatment.[19] Primidone (Mysoline, Elan) and propranolol (Inderal, Wyeth-Ayerst) have been studied and found to reduce essential tremor by 50 to 60%, thus allowing resumption of activities of daily living.[20] Emerging therapeutic agents include antiepileptic drugs [ie, gabapentin (Neurontin, Parke-Davis), topiramate (Topamax, Ortho-McNeil)], carbonic anhydrase inhibitors [ie, methazolamide (Methazolamide, Lederle Standard)], acetazolamide], antidepressants [ie, mirtazapine (Remeron, Organon)], alcohol, and botulinum toxin (Botox, Allergan)]. Surgery (deep brain stimulators) has also been reported as effective in controlling vocal tremor.[21,22]

Parkinson's Disease

Parkinson's disease is one of the most common movement disorders affecting persons over age 55, with a prevalence of up to 1 in 1000. Parkinson's disease is a progressive movement disorder caused by degeneration of the substantia nigra, resulting in decreased dopamine availability. The primary etiology of Parkinson's disease has not been determined. Depression and dementia may occur coincident with Parkinson's disease. As the disease progresses, patients experience increasing difficulty with verbal, speech, and motor skills. It causes rigidity, characteristic tremor, and movement disorders, including bradykinesia (slowed movement), hypokinesia (reduced movement), akinesia (difficulty initiating movement), gait difficulty, and postural instability.

The signs and symptoms are subtle in the early stages. Because Parkinson's disease does not progress quickly and is highly variable in its progression and staging, it may take up to 10 years to reach a stage in which the person is unable to function for normal daily activities. Performance impairment may come much sooner.

Prosody, the melody of language, as it relates to pitch, loudness, and duration, is affected eventually by Parkinson's disease, with the development of aprosody, characterized by monopitch, monoloudness, diminished stress contrasts, and rate abnormalities. The person will often exhibit increased or prolonged silent hesitation during speech. Control of sentence duration can become impaired. The disorder can cause jaw problems that, in turn, may affect speech. In fact, jaw functioning is often within normal range, but the speed with which the jaw moves is greatly reduced. Additionally, reduced lip movements will factor into voice performance. Strobovideolaryngoscopy and laryngoendoscopy have revealed significant laryngeal abnormalities in patients with Parkinson's disease, such as abnormal abduction and adduction, bilateral vocal fold atrophy, and phase asymmetries, which, interestingly, show a high degree of gender differences.[23] This gender difference may be derived from the commonly observed sexual dimorphism of laryngeal size.[24] Videofluoroscopic swallowing studies have demonstrated abnormalities of laryngeal movement during deglutition, with slowed vertical laryngeal excursion and true vocal fold closure or altered opening of the true vocal folds.[25] Parkinson's disease also may have an impact on lung function, causing irregular chest wall movements while the individual performs vowel prolongation and syllable repetition tasks. Nasal airflow may be affected, changing the individual's ability to produce nasal consonants.

It has been estimated that voice and speech disorders are present in more than 70% of Parkinson's patients. Parkinson's disease has a multitude of effects on voice production and perception, including weak and breathy phonation and dysarthria. Patients often overestimate the volume of their speech[26]; and it has been observed that patients with Parkinson's disease must produce a significantly higher level of subglottal pressure to attain the same intensity of phonation as a normal subject. This indicates a higher mean laryngeal resistance and thus correlates with the perception of increased work of phonation.[27] Holmes et al[28] characterized the voices of Parkinson's patients, both in early and later stages, as limited in pitch and loudness variability, harsh, breathy, and reduced in loudness. There was also a reduced maximum phonational frequency range and mean intensity level, compared to non-Parkinson's subjects. Of these characteristics, breathiness, monopitch and monoloudness, low volume, and reduced maximum frequency range worsened as disease progressed.[28] Reduced loudness variability has been characterized further as a decreased responsiveness to implicit cues necessary for volumetric scaling. Parkinson's patients are less capable of increasing volume to compensate for background noise and decreasing volume as instantaneous auditory feedback increases. However, low volume of speech has been described as being possibly related to inattention. Parkinson's patients have demonstrated an ability to produce normal volume speech when consciously attending to loud speech, suggesting a reduced cortical motor set in the articulatory system.[29] Bilateral vocal fold paralysis has been observed in patients with Parkinson's disease and may represent advanced disease. This may become more common as advances in therapy allow these patients to survive longer.[30]

Time-tested, new, and experimental medications and treatments are available not to cure but to arrest the progression of this disease. Parkinson's disease is treated primarily by pharmacotherapy, including anticholinergic medications, preparations of L-dopa (a dopamine agonist), and amantadine hydrochloride (Symmetrel, EndoLabs), which stimulates the release of dopamine from the remaining intact dopaminergic neurons. L-dopa has been shown to increase sound pressure level, decrease tremor, and reduce laryngeal rigidity, as assessed by acoustic and electroglottographic recordings.[31] Dopamine receptor agonists such as bromocriptine hydrochloride (Parlodel, Novartis), MAO inhibitors, and, occasionally, neuroleptic drugs are prescribed. These drugs have potential effects on mood, cognition, and perception.

Surgical treatments have been used in some settings to decrease the symptoms of Parkinson's disease. These include creating lesions in specific areas of the brain (pallidotomy, thalatomy) and tissue implantation into the striatum. Hariz et al[32] reported a patient with advanced Parkinson's disease who underwent bilateral subthalamic nucleus stimulation. Although speech and cognition continued to decline, there was a marked improvement in generalized motor symptoms. Thus, this surgery can be offered to patients to alleviate akinetic motor symptoms before speech and cognitive disturbances are exhibited.[32] Collagen augmentation of the vocal folds has produced significant patient satisfaction with improvement of dysphonia.[33] Although the improvement is temporary in most cases, more permanent medialization procedures may be more appropriate. Other neurologic diseases may mimic the symptoms of Parkinson's disease, but their descriptions are beyond the scope of this chapter. Specialized voice therapy, such as Lee Silverman Voice Treatment, has proven effective in overcoming many of the voice and speech problems associated with later stages of the disease, as reported by Dr. Lorraine Ramig.[34-38] Voice rehabilitation has been shown to improve glottic efficiency, produce increased maximal phonation times and vocal intensity, decreased complaints of strained voice and monotonous and unintelligible speech, and has eliminated complaints of altered swallowing.[27]

Vocal Fold Paralysis/Paresis

This topic is addressed in chapter 12.

Myasthenia Gravis

Myasthenia gravis is an autoimmune disease of the myoneural junction caused by autoantibodies against the acetylcholine receptor (Ach-R). These autoantibodies are detectable in the serum of up to 90% of patients with generalized myasthenia but in a minority of patients with laryngeal myasthenia gravis. Ordinarily, nerve endings release acetylcholine, which depolarizes the endplate of the muscle fiber, causing excitation and muscle contraction. In myasthenia gravis, the muscle fails to depolarize, either because of insensitivity of the muscle endplate, a defect in acetylcholine release from the nerve ending, or both.

Myasthenia gravis occurs most commonly in women in their 20s and 30s and in men in their 50s and 60s. The prognosis is better in young women. Ocular symptoms (ie, ptosis, diplopia) are often the presenting complaints, although virtually all areas of the body can be affected by myasthenia. Otolaryngologic manifestations include dysphonia, dysphagia, weakness of mastication, and weakness of facial musculature. Alterations in voice quality consist of hypernasality, difficulty sustaining pitch, vocal fatigue, intermittent aphonia, and stridor. Localized disease is well recognized and may involve only one eye, for example. Myasthenia gravis also may be isolated to the larynx. This results in rapid voice fatigue, breathiness, moderate hoarseness, and loss of range. In professional voice users, voice dysfunction may be the first symptom the patient notices of more widely disseminated myasthenia.

Myasthenia gravis should be in the physician's differential diagnosis whenever the complaint of voice fatigue is present. Dysphonia is the presenting symptom in 6% of cases of myasthenia gravis, with 60% of patients developing dysphonia at some point in the course of their disease.[39] In a study by Mao et al, 40 patients who presented with dysphonia as their initial and primary complaint were examined.[40] Strobovideolaryngoscopic examination of these patients most commonly revealed a deficit in vocal fold mobility, either unilateral (most commonly mimicking superior laryngeal nerve paralysis) or bilateral (mostly fluctuating asymmetries). Fluctuating asymmetries (one vocal fold appears sluggish, then moves briskly while the other vocal fold appears sluggish), a sign reported initially by the author (RTS) in the first edition of this book, should be regarded as particularly suggestive, although not diagnostic, of myasthenia gravis. Other common findings included muscle tension dysphonia and incomplete glottic closure. In addition, a positive response to edrophonium (Tensilon, Valeant Pharmaceuticals) documented on laryngeal EMG was the most consistent finding in the studied population, with all but one patient testing positive. However, a confounding variable is the lower titer of anti-Ach-R antibodies in patients with myasthenia confined to the larynx, compared to those with generalized myasthenia gravis. This phenomenon is seen in patients with ocular myasthenia as well.

Imaging studies to rule out thymoma are required if the diagnosis is confirmed. The disease usually can be treated well with pyridostigmine bromide (Mestinon, Valeant Pharmaceuticals) to avoid long-term steroid therapy. Common medications for autoimmune disorders, including cytotoxic drugs, may have a role.. Careful training in speech and singing is essential; because before the diagnosis is made, nearly all professional voice users with this problem develop undesirable vocal habits in vain attempts to compensate for vocal impairment. Good technique must be established in conjunction with disease control. In some instances, thymectomy is appropriate. Because of the risk of injury to the recurrent laryngeal nerves, it is best to avoid this procedure in professional voice users when possible and to monitor nerve function intraoperatively when surgery is required.

Postpolio Syndrome

Postpolio syndrome may cause neuromuscular abnormalities beginning years after recovery from acute poliomyelitis.[41-43] Caused by a member of the picornovirus family, only 1 to 5% of infected patients develop the paralytic form of the disease, which is characterized by gradually declining muscle strength. Muscle biopsies and electromyography generally reveal signs of new and chronic denervation. The polio virus infects neurons, with a particular affinity for anterior horn cell motor neurons, and either damages or destroys them. The muscle fibers that remain are then reinnervated by the terminal axonal sprouting of unaffected motor neurons. If all denervated fibers receive such reinnervation, the motor unit stabilizes and previously evident fibrillation potentials disappear. However, this denervation-reinnervation pattern is evident by electromyography (EMG) as motor unit potentials of increased amplitude and duration, reflecting the new, larger size of the motor unit. Another characteristic finding is a decreased recruitment pattern, reflecting the decreased number of motor units available for recruitment.

In the 1970s, reports began surfacing of 20- and 30-year polio survivors with new onset fatigue, pain, and progressive weakness in muscle groups not involved originally with the disorder. Predisposing factors to the development of postpoliomyelitis syndrome (PPS) include residual deficit and female sex, with more severe residual deficits increasing the risk most significantly.[44] Cerebrospinal fluid analysis may show oligoclonal bands, but there is no evidence of *in situ* antibody production to polio virus at the time of diagnosis of PPS.[41] Estimates of the likelihood that poliomyelitis survivors will contract this disorder have ranged from 25 to 80%.

The etiology of PPS is unclear. Dalakas performed several studies to elucidate the possible pathophysiology of this disease.[41] He concluded that PPS was related to an ongoing innervation-denervation pattern seen first at the axonal branch points. Symptoms appeared to be related to oversprouting of the motor neurons, which can no longer support additional axonal support. He also found ongoing immune activation and the presence of defective viral particles in some patients, but their role is unclear.

Multiple studies have continued to describe postpoliomyelitis patients. In 1995, Driscoll et al performed laryngeal evaluations on nine PPS patients, all of whom demonstrated some abnormality on videostrobosocopic examination. Of these nine, three underwent laryngeal electromyography, which universally showed electromyographic evidence of neuronal dropout.[45] In 1998, Robinson et al reviewed three cases of laryngeal weakness in PPS with similar findings.[46] In 2000, Abaza et al reviewed three cases of the laryngeal manifestations of PPS.[44] All three cases revealed reflux laryngitis, compensatory muscle tension dysphonia, and significant other videostroboscopic and electromyographic abnormalities in addition to movement abnormalities and weakness typical of PPS.[44] Knobil et al[47] presented the case of a 50-year-old woman with a history of childhood poliomyelitis requiring tracheotomy and ventilation, with new onset breathlessness in the setting of normal spirometry. Flow volume loop analysis demonstrated fixed upper airway obstruction or neuromuscular weakness, and exercise testing confirmed flow limitation. Left vocal fold paralysis and tracheomalacia were diagnosed eventually, highlighting the multifaceted nature of laryngeal abnormalities in PPS.[47]

Treatment for PPS has spanned the spectrum from voice therapy to tracheotomy. Rehabilitation exercises for the extremities have been shown to increase strength and elevate maximal oxygen uptake. Similarly, patients who complied with treatment recommendations for exercise in the form of voice therapy improved.

Multiple Sclerosis

Multiple sclerosis (MS) is a disease of the central nervous system that involves loss of myelin and lesions in the cerebral cortex, brainstem, cerebellum, or spinal tracts. The diagnosis of MS is based on history and the diagnostic appearance of the brain on magnetic resonance imaging. Cerebrospinal fluid may demonstrate abnormal immunoglobulin production (oligoclonal bands) or myelin breakdown products. The disease is characterized by exacerbations and remissions. Five to 10% of patients develop a more chronic progressive illness. The cause of multiple sclerosis is unknown, but it is clearly an autoimmune disease in which the helper T-cells attack and destroy myelin. Unfortunately, early in the disease when neurologic abnormalities are minimal, many of these patients are misdiagnosed as anxious, depressed, hypochondriacal, or somatosizing. Both sensory and motor abnormalities appear as the disease progresses. Speech may eventually manifest as a mixed flaccid, spastic, and/or ataxic dysarthria, depending on the regions of the nervous system that are affected.

There is currently no known cure for multiple sclerosis, and drug therapy focuses on reducing the number of attacks of demyelination or reducing the damage caused by each attack. Corticosteroids are utilized often for immune modulation, although interferon beta (Avonex, Biogen), intravenous immunoglobulin, and other newer therapies are promising. Psychotherapy to address the associated depression, emotional lability, and occasional psychosis that may be the result of the disease or the drug therapy can be an important part of patients' treatments. Speech-language pathologists treat MS patients to enhance intelligibility, and some patients also undergo swallowing therapy and/or physical therapy for ataxia, tremor, and muscle weakness. Rontal et al described botulinum toxin injection in the treatment of MS-related vocal fold paralysis.[48] A patient with an 18-year history of MS was diagnosed with vocal fold paralysis with partial motor unit recruitment during EMG recording. The abductor musculature was injected to allow the weak adductors to return the vocal fold to the midline. One month post-injection, rather than the anticipated results, the entire fold was found to be mobile, with resumption and maintenance of normal speech 1 year later. This is a case in which clinically paralyzed vocal folds with partial voluntary motor activity were manipulated to restore vocal function.

Diphtheria

Diphtheria, due to its effects on myelin, has been postulated to cause vocal fold paralysis. Caused by *Corynebacterium diphtheriae*, diphtheria is transmitted by aerosol, causing a severe throat infection, which proceeds to soft palate paralysis in 1 to 4 weeks; pharyngeal, laryngeal, or diaphragmatic paralysis in 5 weeks; and generalized peripheral neuropathy in 8 to 12 weeks. Its toxin interferes with myelin synthesis, with demyelinating neuropathy seen in approximately 21% of cases. Generally, complete recovery is seen within weeks to months. Although various studies have attempted to assess larygneal involvement during the acute illness, with incidence ranging from 0 to 32% of diphtheria patients, no cases of residual, post-infectious vocal fold dysfunction of the sort seen in polio patients have been found. Thus, the onset of progressive muscular atrophy with sensory loss after resolution of the acute infection should prompt further investigation of the possibility of a neuromuscular disorder.[49]

Cerebrovascular Accident

Cerebrovascular accident (CVA or stroke) is a sudden, rapid onset of a focal neurologic deficit caused by cerebrovascular disease. Blood supply to the brain is disrupted, resulting in damage that affects the function of the part of the brain nourished by the damaged blood vessel. There are two primary mechanisms for a CVA: cerebral ischemia from cerebral thrombosis or cerebral embolism, or intracranial hemorrhage. Some patients experience strokelike symptoms that last for minutes or hours and then resolve. This is referred to as transient ischemic attack (TIA). Strokes can produce sudden loss of neurologic function, including motor control, sensory perception, vision, language, visuo-spatial function, and memory. CVAs cause a wide variety of communication difficulties including aphasia, dysarthria, and cognitive impairment.

The features and extent of communication impairment depend on the site of lesion. For example, Wallenberg's syndrome, due to brainstem infarct, commonly includes dysphonia and dysphagia. Clinical symptoms correlate highly with neuroimaging findings.[50] Infarction of choroidal arteries produces areas of infarction near the junction of the internal capsule and corona radiata. Such lesions produce pure, acute, pseudobulbar palsy.[51] Dysphagia and aspiration are two other possible sequelae of stroke, often resulting in aspiration pneumonia and death. Presumably, laryngeal and pharyngeal motor deficits play a large role, although recent studies indicate the possible contribution of laryngopharyngeal sensory deficits to the development of aspiration pneumonia.[52]

A case has been studied of supranuclear hypoglossal nerve palsy with Avellis syndrome due to a medullary infarct.[53] Avellis syndrome is a brainstem lesion that limits vagal innervation unilaterally, resulting in ipsilateral vocal fold and soft palate paralysis and contralateral loss of sensitivity to pain and temperature in the leg, trunk, arm, neck, and skin over the scalp. On examination, there was slight disturbance of consciousness, ocular lateropulsion to the right, rotary nystagmus, dysarthria, absent right gag reflex, deviation of the uvula to the left side, right vocal fold paralysis, and tongue deviation to the left side. MRI revealed a small medullary lesion, solely in the lateral medulla and part of the reticular formation medial to the nucleus ambiguus.[53]

Treatment of CVAs may include use of thrombolytic agents to degrade clots, anticoagulants to prevent further clot formation, and rehabilitative services including physical and occupational therapy and speech-language therapy. A case has been reported of right posterior brainstem infarction with resulting severe dysphagia and ataxia. Subsequent evaluation revealed that cranial nerves IX and X were dysfunctional, specifically the pharyngeal and laryngeal branches. This resulted in a paralyzed right vocal fold, as well. Extensive dysphagia rehabilitation facilitated improvement in pharyngeal and laryngeal function with restoration of swallowing capabilities and prevention of aspiration.[54] Patients who have experienced CVA and their families require psychological support and care. This is provided ordinarily during the acute and rehabilitative phases of treatment. Neuropsychologists may perform formal testing batteries, prescribe and implement cognitive rehabilitation, and offer psychotherapy for treatment of the affective consequences associated with such significant changes in level of communication ability and other functions.

Other vascular abnormalities may produce vocal dysfunction. For example, a cervical carotid aneurysm has presented as hoarseness due to recurrent laryngeal nerve compression locally as well as syncopal attacks due to embolic or flow-related phenomena. Clearly, patients with cardiovascular disease may present to an otolaryngologist due to such symptoms, and the physician should not fail to include this among possible diagnoses.[55]

Amyotrophic Lateral Sclerosis

Amyotrophic lateral sclerosis (ALS) is a degenerative, progressive, and fatal disease involving motor neurons of the cortex, brainstem, and spinal cord. The etiology is unknown. Mean onset age is 56 years, and the disease is twice as common in men as in women. Vogel and Carter report that, in 50% of all cases, death occurs within 3 years after identification of the symptoms; approximately 10% of the patients survive up to 10 years; and some patients live as long as 20 years after diagnosis.[23] The entire body is involved eventually, and communication is impaired by a mixed spastic-flaccid dysarthria with severe compromise of speech intelligibility.[56]

More than one quarter of patients with ALS have complaints related to the head and neck (bulbar palsy). Patients with early bulbar symptoms often present to otolaryngologists with complaints of change in voice, such as hypernasality, slowed or increased efforts with speech, breathiness, articulation defects (often misinterpreted as alcohol intoxication), or swallowing changes. The authors cared for a patient misdiagnosed with adductor spasmodic dysphonia and referred for botulinum toxin injection (which was not given) who was subsequently found to have ALS. This highlights the need to delay botulinum injection or other treatment in any patient with recent onset of symptoms pending a full speech/voice, otolaryngologic, and neurologic evaluation.[57] The combined presence of speech and swallowing difficulties may be a key clue to the diagnosis of ALS. Adult onset of hypernasality, articulation defects, and harsh voice should also alert the clinician to the possible presence of ALS.[58] Objective testing of frequency range and phonatory stability in early ALS may be significantly abnormal before the occurrence of perceptually abnormal voice characteristics.[59] Often, 12 to 14 months elapse before patients finally present to the otolaryngologist. Occasionally, patients present with such advanced swallowing disorders that they are failing to thrive already. Characteristic salivary manifestations include drooling and/or gurgling with speech. Physical examination will reveal thick saliva, a sign of chronic dehydration. Poor secretion clearance and concentrated urine also are common.

Diagnostic assessment may reveal imprecise speech, slowness with repetitive sounds, and low volume. Swallowing should be evaluated for difficulty in swallow initiation on dry swallow and incomplete pharyngeal clearance of swallowed water, heard as a "moist phonation." Tongue fasciculations may be visible at rest. Vocal fold examination is remarkable for complete adduction but limited abduction. Paradoxical adduction may be seen during rapid inspiration because weakened abductor muscles cannot resist the Venturi effect. Strobovideolaryngoscopy may reveal aperiodicity, with signs of both weakness and spasticity. Speech tends to have a short phonation time so that only a few words can be spoken on one breath. This results from reduced vital capacity, poor vocal fold adduction with air leakage causing poor voice efficiency, and air loss from ineffective valving of the supralaryngeal structures, such as the tongue and palate.[60] There may be a rapid voice tremor or flutter in patients with ALS.[61,62] One study showed that patients with ALS had vocal frequency and amplitude modulations of varied magnitude and frequency.[62] Frequency and amplitude modulations are more prominent in patients with ALS than in normal subjects. The cause of the aberrant frequency and amplitude modulations in ALS remains unknown; but they may be peripheral, rather than central, nervous system anomalies.[62]

Speech-language pathologists treat these patients with interventions designed to improve communication and instruction in the use of augmentative communication devices as the disease progresses. Prostheses for palatal lift and surgical interventions using pharyngeal flaps have also been used. A number of drugs have been tried for the treatment of ALS, but all have been disappointing. The initial therapeutic effects of the drugs are eventually overcome by the progression of the disease. The need for percutaneous gastrostomy can be determined by a combined evaluation of a swallowing score (based on the ALS Severity Scale) and remaining vital capacity (threshold is 2 liters). Guaifenesin (Mucinex, Adams) can help thin secretions to make them more manageable. The primary indication for surgical procedures such as tracheotomy and laryngeal diversion procedures is continued aspiration pneumonia in a patient with no oral intake who has failed medical management and submaxillary gland resection. Laryngeal diversion procedures may produce complete relief of signs and symptoms of aspiration. The primary disadvantage is complete loss of phonation. Hillel et al found no need for these procedures in 211 ALS patients.[60] However, Carter et al report a case of a 67-year-old man with severe aspiration in whom laryngeal diversion produced complete relief of aspiration symptoms.[63] An additional cited benefit of this procedure, over a tracheotomy, was the elimination of possible future aspiration. Otolaryngologists may also offer such treatment as medialization procedures, obturator fitting, cricopharyngeal myotomy, or cervical esophagostomy for speech, swallowing, and aspiration problems, although these are more for patient quality of life.[58]

Primary Progressive Aphasia

Primary progressive aphasia (PPA) is essentially a speech disorder rather than a voice disorder. It is diagnosed in patients who have experienced progressive deterioration in speech (language) for 2 or more years without substantial deterioration in cognitive functions or in the ability to perform activities of daily living. Commonly, the condition is associated with abnormalities on imaging studies. Patients may be either fluent or nonfluent, and anosmia is usually the earliest and most prominent symptom.[64] For example, Sinnatamby et al found focal atrophy affecting primarily the left temporal lobe in 4 of 10 patients with PPA on CT scan and 10 of 12 patients on MRI scan.[65] The atrophy was concentrated in the superior and middle temporal gyri on MRI. All of the 12 patients who underwent SPECT scan had unilateral temporal lobe perfusion defects, although 2 of them had normal MRIs. Other authors also agree that dynamic imaging studies such as SPECT and PET are useful in assessing PPA.[66-70] The usefulness of these studies is not surprising because their value has also been established in the evaluation of dementia,[71-82] a condition that may be similar or related to PPA. Most authors who have studied patients with PPA have identified perfusion defects predominantly in the left temporal and frontal regions, although other areas or hypoperfusion have been identified. Janicek et al reported the results of brain perfusion in patients with acute aphasia (not PPA) and reported findings that may have localizing value in patients with aphasia with various causes.[67] They found nonfluent aphasia in only 6 of 10 patients with perfusions defects in Broca's area, and fluent aphasia in only 5 of 10 patients with lesions in Wernicke's area. Perfusion defects in the inferior parietal region were associated with auditory comprehension defects in 9 of 12 patients; 8 of 11 patients with perfusion defects involving the inferior parietal cortex, supramarginal and angular gyri, and the ipsilateral thalamus had repetition defects; and reading and writing abnormalities correlated with hypoperfusion in the posterior frontal cortex, superior and inferior parietal cortex, and superior temporal gyri. Molina reported histopathology on a patient with a 3-year history of PPA.[70] Neuropathologic examination of a temporal lobe biopsy demonstrated Gallyas-positive intracytoplasmic inclusions looking like fibrillary tangles and of Gallyas-positive cell processes, probably from glial cells. Glial intracytoplasmic inclusions immunolabeled with antibodies to ubiquitin and with phosphorylation-dependent antitau antibodies indicated the presence of hyperphosphorylated tau in the inclusions. There was only mild pathology of cortical neurons consisting of rare perikarya diffusely stained with antitau antibodies. There were no senile plaques, neurofibrillary tangles, "achromatic" neurons, ballooned cell, Pick or Lewy bodies, nor microvacuoles or spongiform changes of the neuropil.[70] Although voice changes have not been discussed prominently in patients with progressive aphasia, they may be present. There is not enough experience to be certain if such changes are coincidental or related as primary or compensatory abnormalities. We have observed soft (hypotonic) voice associated with primary progressive aphasia, as well as strained, hyperfunctional dysphonia that appeared to be secondary to the patient's compensatory efforts as she struggled to be understood. We suspect that various conditions may be classified together under the category "primary progressive aphasia," and additional research is clearly needed to elucidate the nature of this condition. At present, there is no accepted treatment for PPA. However, anecdotally, the author (RTS) is aware of patients who have been treated with medications usually used for Alzheimer's disease, and it appears that such medications may have efficacy in some patients with PPA. However, additional experience and evidence-based studies are needed to confirm or refute this very preliminary impression.

Huntington's Chorea

Huntington's disease (Huntington's chorea) is an inherited disorder characterized by degeneration in the striatum (the caudate and putamen). The defective gene is carried on chromosome four. Onset is usually between the ages of 25 and 45 years, and duration averages 15 years. Symptoms include involuntary tics and twitching, usually in the extremities. Choreic movements can be suppressed partially and hidden in semipurposeful movements. The condition is often accompanied by "motor impersistence," or the inability to sustain contraction. This is often manifested as the dropping of objects. In the later stages, the movements become grotesque contortions, and dementia develops and progresses. The natural history of Huntingon's disease involves development of dysphagia and aspiration, with death usually occurring about 15 years after onset. Gag and cough reflexes are impaired, and the airway often is compromised during swallowing due to neck hyperextension. The disease is diagnosed by history, genetic findings, and characteristic abnormalities on CT and MRI of the brain. There is no cure, and drug therapy is offered for the suppression of involuntary movement. The drugs themselves commonly cause extrapyramidal symptoms and also may produce tardive dyskinesia.

Shy-Drager Syndrome

Shy-Drager syndrome is a result of degeneration of the central nervous system, resulting in a depletion of CNS neurotransmitters. The autonomic nervous system is not spared, resulting in presenting symptoms that may include orthostatic hypotension, laryngeal stridor, and Parkinsonlike symptoms. Laryngeal symptoms are due to neurogenic paralysis of both posterior cricoarytenoid muscles. Hanson et al studied 12 patients with Shy-Drager syndrome and evaluated them for laryngeal movement disorders and speech impairment.[83] Eleven patients were found to have vocal fold abductor paresis, 10 of whom were affected bilaterally. Speech evaluation described the voice as breathy and strained, lower in volume, and characterized by monopitch, monoloudness, imprecise consonants, rate alterations, and rate-slowing. These seem to suggest a flaccid dysarthria. In contrast to patients with Parkinson's disease, patients with Shy-Drager had excess hoarseness and a slow and deliberate speaking rate. Key distinguishing factors between the two conditions, aside from the aforementioned voice quality, include the orthostatic hypotension and laryngeal stridor that characterize patients with Shy-Drager.[83]

To date, treatment of this poorly studied disorder is symptomatic. Specifically, laryngeal stridor can be treated with tracheotomy and eventually a cricoarytenoidopexy or other procedures to open the laryngeal airway.[84]

Multiple-System Atrophy

Multiple-system atrophy (MSA) is a neurodegenerative disorder that overlaps with three syndromes (Shy-Drager, olivopontocerebellar atrophy, striatonigral degeneration) and also shares features with Parkinson's disease. However, unlike Parkinson's disease, it does not respond well to therapy with levodopa. In MSA, myelinated nerve fibers are affected. Often, small fibers such as those innervating the vocal folds are affected first; and no signs are apparent. However, with the progressive loss of large myelinated fibers, mostly alpha motor axons innervating intrinsic laryngeal muscles, vocal fold palsy develops. Neuronopathy of the recurrent laryngeal nerve may be responsible for this palsy. Specifically, it has been observed that the number of small myelinated fibers, with a diameter less than 7 microns, decreases first, and without vocal fold abnormalities. Large myelinated fibers were observed to be affected only in patients with vocal fold palsy, suggesting that vocal fold palsy develops only after loss of large myelinated fibers, which comprise the alpha motor axons that innervate the intrinsic laryngeal muscles.[85] Occasionally, bilateral vocal fold abductor paralysis is observed. This is a life-threatening complication of MSA and may cause nocturnal sudden death. Early symptoms of this condition include nocturnal inspiratory stridor. This stridor contrasts with other causes of nocturnal stridor, such as that which results from sleep apnea syndrome, in that the stridor associated with MSA is due to narrowing of the larynx (vocal folds) and not the soft palate or pharynx (as in sleep apnea).[86] Laryngoscopy has revealed paradoxical movement of vocal folds during sleep, with high-pitched inspiratory stridor.[87] This abnormal adduction during inspiration has been confirmed by thyroarytenoid electromyographical study.[88] Traditionally, this problem has been ascribed to abductor vocal fold paralysis; but in 2002, Merlo et al presented data (including laryngeal electromyography) suggesting that the laryngeal adduction in these patients is due to dystonia, rather than abductor paralysis.[89] Tracheotomy may be necessary as vocal fold abductor paralysis progresses to the stage at which paradoxical movement occurs during sleep and abduction restriction occurs during wakefulness.[87] The cause of the dysphagia commonly experienced by these patients remains uncertain.

Gilles de la Tourette Syndrome

Gilles de la Tourette syndrome (GTS) is a dual neurological and psychiatric diagnosis. It is often familial, and onset may be as early as the first year of life. An autosomal dominant mode of inheritance is supported currently. The median age at onset is 7 years. Tourette syndrome is characterized by multiple motor and one or more vocal tics that worsen intermittently during the life of the affected individual. The term "tic" refers to brief, repetitive, usually purposeless movements involving multiple muscle groups. These movements, vocalizations in the case of GTS, can be suppressed voluntarily for a period of time; but suppressed movements are followed often by a flurry of movements. GTS is considered one of the most severe forms of tic disorder. The involuntary vocalizations characteristic of this condition tend to become more intense in periods of stress. Vocal tics include voluntary sound such as grunts, clicks, yelps, barks, sniffs, coughs, screams, snorts, and coprolalia (the uttering of obscenities), which is present in up to 50% of cases.[23,56,90] These vocalizations typically occur during speech, most commonly replacing the hesitation phenomena that characterize normal speech. Obsessive-compulsive behaviors may coexist. Patients with Tourette syndrome sometimes have dysphagia with incoordination of swallowing. Drug therapy utilized in the treatment of Tourette syndrome includes neuroleptics, clonidine (Catapres, Boehringer Ingleheim), and pimozide (Orap, Gate). However, the waxing and waning nature of this disorder makes efficacy assessment difficult. Patients with Tourette syndrome usually benefit from stress management techniques, because emotional overload often increases the frequency and intensity of the tics.

Odynophonia

Odynophonia, or pain caused by phonation, can be a disturbing symptom. It is not uncommon, but relatively little has been written or presented on the subject. A detailed review of odynophonia is beyond the scope of this publication. However, laryngologists at least should be familiar with the diagnosis and treatment of a few of the most common causes.

Muscle tension dysphonia (hyperfunctional voice use) is by far the most common cause of discomfort associated with phonation. This cause is easily recognized and managed. Technical errors in breathing and support, and associated tension in the tongue, jaw, and neck musculature, are usually obvious. In professional voice users, more subtle manifestations of hyperfunction may be responsible for voice discomfort and fatigue. Usually, odynophonia from this cause resolves through voice therapy and singing training when appropriate.

It must be remembered that structural abnormalities may also present with odynophonia. Peptic laryngitis caused by reflux can cause painful phonation and may even be responsible for referred otalgia. Granulomas with ulceration and other neoplasms, including malignancies, may also present with odynophonia. These conditions are also usually obvious, following visualization of the larynx.

Patients with no structural abnormalities, and those whose odynophonia does not resolve after voice therapy, represent greater challenges to laryngologists. The two most important causes are musculoskeletal and neurological.

Musculoskeletal odynophonia is analogous to tendonitis. It often follows an episode of trauma (external or phonotrauma); but in many cases a specific traumatic event cannot be identified. Patients with this condition generally can point to a specific area of maximal tenderness in the laryngeal framework. It is most commonly on the superior lateral edges of the thyroid cartilage, superior posterior edge of thyroid cartilage, or hyoid bone. As with tennis elbow, anti-inflammatory medicines may be helpful occasionally; but usually they are not. If nonsteroidal anti-inflammatory medications are utilized, voice use must be restricted; and great care must be exercised to avoid activities that might precipitate vocal fold hemorrhage. Treatment involves voice therapy to eliminate aggravating hyperfunction; and corticosteroid injection is often required. The steroid may be mixed with Xylocaine. This is helpful, because the anesthetic injected numbs the area of soft tissue inflammation. Consequently, immediately after the injection the laryngeal pain is gone. This confirms that the steroid has been deposited in the correct location. Patients should be warned that their discomfort will be worse for a few days following injection and then will subside gradually. It is essential that hyperfunction be avoided following treatment. Neuropathy also may produce extremely disturbing odynophonia. It may be caused by a virus (such as herpes). It may involve one nerve or multiple cranial nerves. Glossopharyngeal neuralgia and related disorders cause pain that is deeper and more difficult for the patient to localize. Other cranial nerves should be checked carefully, and special attention should be paid to the superior laryngeal nerves. Often, subtle sensory deficits are present, in particular, a slightly reduced gag reflex on the side of the pain. When the complaint is pain, the physician should always look for hypesthesia. Other sensory nerves should also be examined, including, for example, all divisions of the fifth nerve.. Patients with odynophonia caused by neuralgia often respond to medications such as gabapentin or carbamazepine. In some cases, additional medications such as amitriptyline might also be given. However, it is usually possible to at least control, if not eliminate, neurogenic odynophonia.

Other Neurological Conditions Affecting Voice Performance

Many conditions that do not involve the larynx or even the vocal tract directly may adversely affect performance. Physicians must be familiar with the consequences of neurological dysfunction. Important conditions include not only major neurological problems such as quadriplegia, but also more common disorders such a headache, facial paralysis, dizziness, and other disorders that impair memory, concentration, and optimal athletic function.

Quadriplegia

Abdominal muscle support is essential for singing and acting. Therefore, it would seem that quadriplegia following a cervical fracture would end a professional singing career and possibly an acting career. Sataloff et al described the rehabilitation of a quadriplegic professional singer in 1984.[91] Since that report, the singer has been able to continue a limited recording career and occasionally public and television appearances; and he is now able to do so without the device that was designed for him. In this patient and other quadriplegic people deprived of voice support, frequent problems with voice fatigue and decreased volume, range, and projection are encountered. The degree of dysfunction and potential for rehabilitation are dependent particularly on the level of the lesion. Additional activity in therapy and research should provide greater insights into the best methods to help the voices of quadriplegic patients in general and to restore performance ability to quadriplegic professional voice users. In addition, quadriplegic patients provide scientists with an opportunity to observe the consequences of consistent, drastic reduction in the support mechanism.

Facial Paralysis in Singers and Actors

Facial paralysis is a relatively common affliction, and it can be devastating for a singer or actor. Facial paralysis creates cosmetic and functional deficits that may be extremely troublesome. Usually, the condition involves one side of the face. If the muscles cease working altogether, the condition is *facial paralysis*. If the muscles are merely weak, the condition is *facial paresis*. In this chapter, we will use the word paralysis to refer to complete paralysis or severe paresis. This condition results in drooping of one side of the face, inability to close the eye (which exposes it to dryness and injury), and incompetence of the corner of the mouth, which may cause drooling of liquids and difficulty articulating some sounds.

One of the principal problems of facial paralysis is the widespread tendency in many sectors of the medical community to underevaluate the problem and to misdiagnose it. In 1821, Sir Charles Bell studied the innervation of the facial musculature and named the motor nerve of the face the facial nerve. Soon, all conditions of facial paralysis came to be known as Bell's palsy. As time passed, the true cause of many cases of facial paralysis was discovered. Bell's palsy is now the name that should be used to describe only cases of facial paralysis in which the cause cannot be determined. Unfortunately, many physicians still diagnose "Bell's palsy" without going through the comprehensive evaluation necessary to diagnose and treat important causes of facial paralysis. A proper evaluation includes a complete history; careful physical examination of the ears, nose, throat, neck, and parotid gland; at least a partial neurological examination; imaging studies (usually CT scan and MRI); audiogram; facial nerve electromyography and/or electroneuronography; and blood tests. These tests are designed to detect the cause of the problem. If none is found, the condition properly may be called Bell's palsy. Patients with Bell's palsy always recover, at least partially, although recovery may take as long as a year. If the face remains paralyzed without recovery of facial function, the diagnosis of Bell's palsy generally is wrong; and the true cause should be sought again.

There are many etiologies of facial paralysis, and this chapter will provide a brief overview of only a few of them. Facial paralysis can be *congenital*; that is, some people are born with paralysis of one side or both sides of the face. This problem may result from various causes ranging from syndromes to brain dysfunction to delivery forceps trauma.[92] *Acquired* facial paralysis is much more common. Infection and inflammation are well-established causes. The infection may be viral, particularly herpetic, and is often associated with a herpetic cold sore or fever blister. This problem also may involve the hearing nerve, which runs in close proximity to the facial nerve. Viral or bacterial infections of the ear (otitis media) or brain (meningitis) also cause facial paralysis, as do Lyme disease and AIDS. Facial paralysis also has been associated with toxic effects from exposure to heavy metals, such as lead, and to an immunologic response after injections for tetanus, rabies, and polio. Metabolic conditions, including diabetes, hypothyroidism, and pregnancy, may precipitate facial paralysis, as well. So may blood vessel problems associated with vasculitis, some of which may accompany arthritis syndromes. Trauma is also an important cause of facial paralysis, particularly temporal bone fracture associated with motor vehicle accidents or falls, and surgical trauma (facial paralysis is a potential complication of ear, brain, or parotid gland surgery). Paralysis of any cranial nerve can be a presenting sign of a generalized neurological disorder. This must be suspected, especially if more than one cranial nerve is involved.

In addition, facial paralysis may be the first presenting sign of a tumor. The tumor may be benign or malignant. It may occur anywhere along the course of the facial nerve, which starts in the brainstem, courses circuitously through the ear encased in a tight bony canal, exits the mastoid bone at the skull base, and spreads out along the face. Tumors of the facial nerve itself (facial neuromas, more properly called schwannomas) commonly present with facial paralysis, as do cancerous tumors of the middle ear, parotid gland, and upper neck. For this reason alone, if for no other, a thorough, systematic evaluation is required in any patient with facial paralysis until a diagnosis has been established with the greatest possible degree of certainty. Tumors, and many of the other conditions discussed above, are potentially treatable if they are discovered soon enough.

Treatment for facial paralysis depends on the cause. If a specific disease or tumor is identified, it is treated appropriately; and in many cases, facial function can be restored. If no cause is found, and the condition is truly Bell's palsy, various treatments are available. The medical specialists most involved in caring for facial paralysis are neurotologists. Most of us specializing in facial nerve disorders base our treatment recommendations for Bell's palsy on electrical testing of the facial nerve called *electroneuronography*. Treatment may involve observation, use of high-dose steroids, or surgery. Surgery is always a last resort. However, it should be considered if electrical excitability decreases by 90% or more; if facial paralysis is sudden, total, and associated with severe pain; and in selected other situations. In general, if recovery from facial paralysis begins within 3 weeks, it is excellent and total. If recovery does not start until after 3 months, it is usually imperfect. In these cases, the nerve usually develops some degree of synkinesis, that is, inappropriate neuromuscular function caused by aberrant reinnervation. This results, for example, in a slight smiling of the lips when the person closes his or her eyes. "Crocodile tears" and "gustatory sweating" result similarly from misdirected nerve fibers that should have gone to salivary glands. Hence, when the person eats, tears fall from the eye, and the side of the face perspires. These problems often can be minimized with early, accurate diagnosis and appropriate treatment.

Headache

Headache is one of the most common complaints in American medicine. An estimated 10 to 20% of people have suffered from severe headaches at one time, and approximately 8 to 12 million Americans have suffered from migraine headaches. An even larger number have a variety of additional headache complaints, including muscular tension headaches and headaches from more serious sources. Even an occasional headache can be annoying, as most of us know. However, chronic, recurring headaches may be more than annoying. Headaches may interfere with concentration, impair a person's ability to memorize scores, distract the singer or actor enough to impair performance, and create many other impediments to a performing career or any other occupation. They can undermine the effectiveness of voice lessons or therapy, and headaches are a common cause of absenteeism, a problem that is not tolerated in the performance world.

Although many headaches are secondary to stress, many serious causes also exist. Consequently, it is important for the voice professional with frequent and/or severe headaches to seek expert evaluation (usually a neurologist) and to pursue the tests necessary to achieve an accurate diagnosis. Fortunately, many headaches can be treated, usually with medications that do not impair performance. An overview of the most common, and most important headache causes is helpful in understanding the complexity and diversity of this problem.

The first step in the evaluation of a headache sufferer is to obtain the history. Physicians must ascertain whether the headaches are of recent onset or of long duration. If they are of recent onset, patients should be asked about associated symptoms, such as blurring of vision, dizziness, numbness and tingling, and the localization of the headache. Is the headache associated with any nasal discharge? Does it occur as an explosion, suggesting a subarachnoid hemorrhage? Is fever associated with the headache, which would indicate a meningitis? Is there a history of recent dental infections, ear infections, or recent viral illness? Has there been contact with other individuals who may have had headaches?

When headaches have been present for a long period of time, several questions need to be asked. Are they recurrent? Are they getting worse? Have there been any changes of personality? What brings on the headaches? Can they be associated with changes in body position or allergies?

One should question what brings on the headache, what provides relief, associated symptoms, what treatment the patient has received, and special implications regarding the headache. Are there problems with work? Does it interfere with concentration or bring on anxiety? Is the medication used to treat the headaches intolerable because of tiredness, nausea, stomach upset, or difficulty concentrating?

What are the different types of headaches and the symptoms that may accompany them? Migraine headaches are episodic. They usually affect one side of the head, but the affected side can vary. They are pounding, frequently accompanied by nausea; and there can be visual changes. Patients may experience diarrhea, palpitations, or feelings of coldness. The pain may last for 48 hours, and the scalp may be tender to the touch.

Classic migraines present with an aura preceding the headache by up to 30 minutes. This may be accompanied by scintillating scotoma where visual fields may be obscured, or there may be spots before the eyes. There can also be diplopia or problems with speech, such as the inability to say words, or transient paresis. The aura provides warning time during which medicines may be taken to ward off the headache.

In common migraines, the aura is not present. The implication for patients with common migraine is that there is no warning time during which one can take medication to abort the headache. Complicated migraine can be associated with attacks of blindness, hemiplegia, and aphasia. Migraine can lead to stroke with permanent neurological deficit. This can occur as part of a migraine attack or be precipitated by the use of ergotamine drugs.

Chronic daily headaches can be associated with prolonged tension or migraine headaches. Many of these headaches are precipitated by over-the-counter analgesics as part of a withdrawal syndrome. Opioids can be used inappropriately, and this also can lead to withdrawal symptoms and ongoing headache complaints as a "drug withdrawal headache syndrome" leading to a chronic daily headaches.

Cluster attacks generally occur at night, but can also occur during the day either at a regular time interval or randomly. The pain is usually around the eye on one side; but it then can spread to the jaw, shoulder, face, and neck. Patients have a tendency to walk around banging their heads and squeezing their scalps, as compared to migraine patients who cannot tolerate even the stimulation of a dimly lit room. These headaches can last up to 2 hours, can occur once or twice a day, or 10 times per day. They last for weeks to months, and then there is a remission for months or years. The patients' eyes may water, and they may feel as if their nose is blocked. This condition is eight times more common in males than in females. Some patients with cluster headaches can also have migraine headaches in combination. Other individuals can have episodic attacks of vertigo, tinnitus, and even deafness as associated manifestations of a cluster or a migraine headache. Some individuals can have speech disturbances or difficulty expressing themselves as part of a migraine. They may have dysarthria or slurring of words, difficulty reading, confusion, or experience transient paresis not followed by headache. This is called migraine aura without headaches and is thought also to be a migraine equivalent.

Headaches can be related to exertion, sports, and even sexual intercourse. Many patients have either a history of migraine or a family history of migraine. Some exertion headaches can be benign, with the etiology obscure; or they may be seen in patients with brain tumors, subdural hematomas, and vascular malformations. Patients can have a cough headache. Once again, these can be benign or indicative of underlying masses or vascular malformations. Joggers or football players can have severe headaches, generally associated with the start of a fitness program. Coital cephalalgia has been described related to sexual activity. It can develop suddenly, occurring before and after intercourse, and is most commonly benign, although subarachnoid hemorrhage following orgasm has been reported.

Of great relevance for the singer and actor are allergic headaches. Migraine headaches can occur occasionally after eating or exposure to various drugs or allergens. In most patients who have allergies as well as migraine, the allergies do not cause the migraine, although occasionally the allergic rhinitis, thickening of the nasal membrane, and pressure within the sinuses can precipitate a migraine attack. Certain foods and beverages, such as coffee, tea, chocolate, alcoholic beverages, hot dogs, Chinese foods, cheese, or liver, can bring about a migraine attack. Migraine headaches can also be precipitated by hypoglycemia, by not eating, and by withdrawal from caffeine.

Muscle contraction headaches, or tension headaches, are described as pressure in the head or a vise-like attack. They can be unilateral or bilateral. Patients may be under a great deal of stress and tend to abuse over-the-counter medication.

Headaches can occur from underlying cerebral problems, such as cerebrovascular disease. In subarachnoid hemorrhage, pain is described as very severe, generally the worst headache of their lives. The headache comes on suddenly and only rarely evolves over hours. There may be problems with vision, including blurring of vision, or dull vision, confusion, or changes in the level of consciousness. On examination, there may be significant neck rigidity. This kind of headache requires immediate neurologic attention including CT scan studies and lumbar puncture.

Cerebral hemorrhages are frequently associated with hypertension. This headache may not be severe, but it is generally present in addition to more localized neurologic findings such as weakness, numbness, visual changes, unsteadiness, vertigo, and speech difficulties out of proportion to the extent of the headache itself.

Headaches of infectious origin, including meningitis, usually proceed rapidly and develop over hours. They may be in the front or back portion of the scalp radiating to the neck, and they are increased with activity. They may also be associated with fever, nausea, vomiting, and confusion. Lumbar puncture, as well as CT scan, is usually required.

Patients with AIDS and other HIV-related conditions can present with headaches, changes in mental status, or focal neurologic findings. This headache or a focal neurologic complaint can be the presenting symptoms of an opportunistic central nervous system infection or malignancy that requires urgent neurologic evaluation. The headache or the focal neurological complaint can be the presenting symptom.

Brain tumors have accompanying headache in 60 to 90% of individuals. The pain associated with this is dull, deep, aching, intermittent, and generally worse in the morning. Vomiting may also be associated. The pain is generally not as severe as the migraine headache. There might not be localization to the site of the underlying tumor. Postural changes may increase the episodic nature of the headache in some cases.

Intracranial pressure has been associated with increased headache in young individuals. The entity to be most considered is benign intracranial hypertension, or pseudotumor cerebrii. Patients may have headaches with visual disturbances such as blurring of vision or double vision; and the headache may be present for several weeks, with more severe pain in the early morning. Diagnosis is made by CT scan and lumbar puncture.

Following trauma, various types of headache syndromes can occur. For example, a patient can have postconcussion syndrome with headache, dizziness, cognitive difficulties, hypersensitivity to light and sound, anxiety, nervousness, and changes in libido. Trauma can induce migraine or even clusterlike headaches. Patients can have similar headaches with cervical whiplash (with or without underlying cervical disc disease), producing headaches that can begin in the occiput and radiate to the front portion of the scalp. One also has to be aware that even minor trauma can precipitate the development of a subdural hematoma. Subdural hematomas especially occur in patients who are alcoholic or epileptic or who are taking anticoagulants, including aspirin.

Several neuralgias should be considered when diagnosing headache. Patients with post-herpetic neuraligia (following herpes zoster infection) can develop facial pain that mimics tic doloureux or occipital neuralgia (pain in the back of the scalp), superior laryngeal neuralgia, or glossopharyngeal neuralgia (associated with syncope and cardiac arrhythmias). These patients (Fig 11–1) develop symptoms such as pain in the throat or ear with trigger zones within the tonsillar

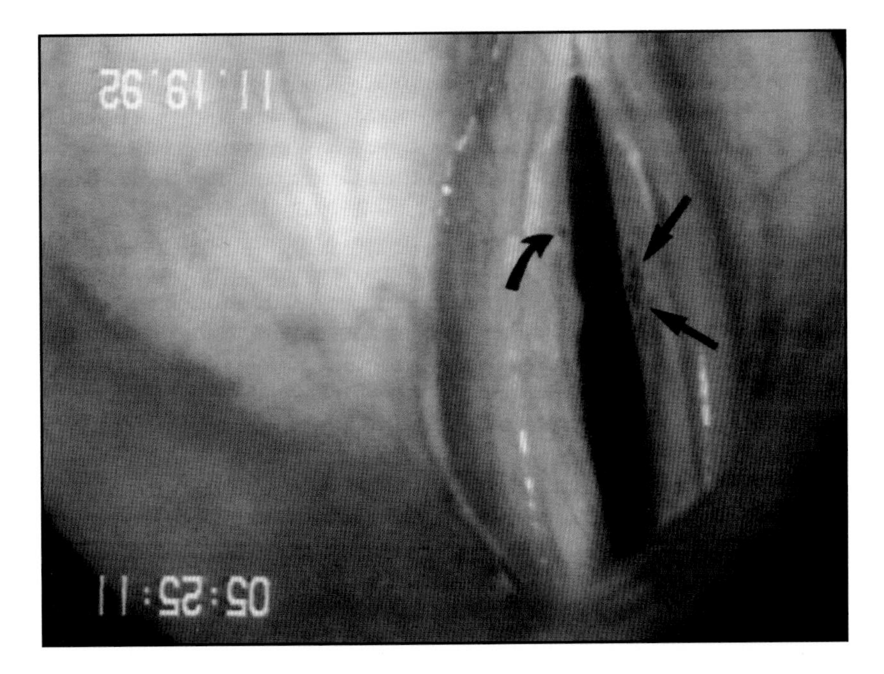

Fig 11–1. This videoprint came from a 35-year-old college professor who developed severe pain when speaking. The pain was localized in the larynx, and was severe enough to interfere with her ability to function as a college professor. It had started following an upper respiratory infection accompanied by laryngitis. The hoarseness resolved but the pain persisted. Vocal fold varicosities had been diagnosed elsewhere. Laser surgery had been recommended as a treatment for her pain. She came to us for a second opinion. Our examination revealed a small varicosity on her left vocal fold (*curved arrow*) and a cluster of varicosities with a surrounding blush on her right vocal fold (*straight arrows*). However, vocal fold vibration was normal, and her voice was normal. We considered the varicosities asymptomatic. A diagnosis of atypical pain (probably postviral neuralgia) was established, and the patient was treated with Tegretol. No surgery was performed. Her pain disappeared promptly, returned when she stopped the medication because of planned pregnancy, and resolved again when Tegretol was resumed after delivery.

area or pharyngeal region. Pain may also be triggered by swallowing, speaking or singing. In some instances, patients with post-herpetic neuralgias have no recollection of ever having had a skin lesion. If symptoms are constant rather than intermittent, a structural cause must be sought diligently.

Headaches can occur secondary to ear infection. They can also be caused by tumors within the ear, acoustic neuromas, and even barotraumas from an air flight. Toxins and metabolic causes can occur secondary to acute mountain sickness, This has been estimated to occur in 50% of mountain hikers. Patients on a variety of medications can suffer from headaches, and headaches may also be associated with consumption of various foods. Headaches also can occur secondary to substance withdrawal, alcohol withdrawal or consumption, dental pain, or endocrine conditions related to hypoglycemia, menses and menopause, birth control pills, or pituitary tumors. Headaches can be accompanied by seizurelike activity and anemia, as well as more serious problems in some instances.

In summary, we need to recognize subtleties in the history of headaches and their implications for either benign or serious origins. The headache itself, the underlying neurologic or other medical condition, and the treatment can lead to problems in daily performance, including voice performance. Headaches can also produce anxiety, which can interfere with a person's ability to function in competitive employment. Severe recurrent or persistent headache deserves thorough, expert evaluation and should never be minimized or neglected.

Dizziness

Dizziness can affect anyone. Sometimes imbalance develops gradually. Sometimes, it can strike suddenly--even on stage. Loss of equilibrium is not only extremely frightening, but it can also impair a performer's ability to walk and move effectively for an indefinite period of time. Dizziness is often associated with ear problems. However, the ear is only one part of the balance system. Evaluation of disequilibrium disorders is extremely complex and often not managed well.

The terms *dizziness* and *vertigo* are used by patients to describe a variety of sensations, many of which are not related to the vestibular system. It is convenient to think of the balance system as a complex conglomerate of senses that each sends the brain information about one's position in space. Components of the balance system include the vestibular labyrinth, the eyes, neck muscles, proprioceptive nerve endings, cerebellum, and other structures. If all sources provide information in agreement, equilibrium is not a problem. However, if most of the sources tell the brain that the body is standing still, for example, but one component says that the body is turning left, the brain becomes confused; and we experience dizziness. It is the physician's responsibility to systematically analyze each component of the balance system to determine which component or components are providing incorrect information, or whether the correct information is being provided and analyzed in an aberrant fashion by the brain.

Typically, *labyrinthine dysfunction* is associated with a sense of motion. It may be true spinning, a sensation of being on a ship or of falling, or simply a vague sense of imbalance when moving. In many cases, it is episodic. Fainting, lightheadedness, body weakness, spots before the eyes, tightness in the head, and loss of consciousness are generally not of vestibular origin. However, such descriptions are of only limited diagnostic help. Even some severe peripheral (vestibular or eighth nerve) lesions may produce only mild unsteadiness or no dizziness at all, such as seen in many patients with acoustic neuroma. Similarly, lesions outside the vestibular system may produce true rotary vertigo, as seen with trauma or microvascular occlusion in the brainstem, and with cervical vertigo.

Dizziness is a relatively uncommon problem in healthy individuals. In contrast to a 24% incidence of tinnitus, Sataloff et al found only a 5% incidence of dizziness in their study of 267 normal senior citizens.[93] However, the general population is not as healthy as this selected sample. Five to 10% of initial physician visits involve a complaint of dizziness or imbalance, accounting for over 11 million physician visits annually.[94] Dizziness is the most common reason for a visit to a physician in patients over 65 years of age. Approximately one third to one half of people age 65 and older fall each year, and the consequences can be serious.[95] Falls result in approximately 200,000 hip fractures per year, and this injury carries a 10% mortality rate. Falls are the leading cause of death by injury in persons over 75 years old. Dizziness is also a common consequence of head injury. Over 450,000 Americans suffer serious head injuries annually.[96] Many of these persons complain of dizziness for up to 5 years following the injury, and many are disabled by this symptom. Dizziness may also persist for even longer periods of time following minor head injury.[97]

However, the causes of dizziness are almost as numerous as causes of hearing loss; and some of them are medically serious (multiple sclerosis, acoustic neuroma, diabetes, cardiac arrhythmias, etc). Consequently, any patient with an equilibrium complaint needs a thorough examination. For example, although dizziness may be caused by head trauma, the fact that it is reported for the first time following an injury is insufficient to establish causation without investigating other possible causes.

It is important to pursue a systematic inquiry in all cases of disequilibrium, not only because the condition is caused by serious problems in some patients, but also because many patients with balance disorders can be helped. Many people believe incorrectly that sensorineural hearing loss, tinnitus, and dizziness are incurable; but many conditions that cause any or all of these symptoms may be treated successfully. It is especially important to separate peripheral causes (which are almost always treatable) from central causes, such as brainstem contusion, in which the prognosis is often worse.

Vestibular disturbance may be suspected with a history of vertigo described as motion, particularly if associated with tinnitus, hearing loss, or fullness in the ear. However, even severe peripheral disease of the eighth nerve or labyrinth may produce vague unsteadiness rather than vertigo, especially when caused by a slowly progressive condition such as acoustic neuroma. Similarly, central disorders such as brainstem vascular occlusions may produce true rotary vertigo typically associated with the ear. Therefore, clinical impressions must be substantiated by thorough evaluation and testing.

One of the most common causes of periperhal vertigo is Ménière's disease. The vertigo is classically of sudden onset, comparatively brief in duration, and recurs in paroxysmal attacks. During the attack, it generally is accompanied by an ocean-roaring tinnitus, fullness in the ear, and hearing loss. Pitch distortion (diplacusis) is common and may cause significant problems for singers. Occasionally, there may be some residual imbalance between attacks, but this does not happen often. Similar symptoms may accompany inner-ear syphilis and certain cases of diabetes mellitus, hyperlipoproteinemia, or hypothyroidism.

Another type of vertigo associated with an abnormality in the inner ear is being recognized more frequently. In benign positional paroxysmal vertigo (BPPV), the attack often occurs briefly with sudden movements of the head. Classically, there is a slight delay in onset; and if the maneuver is repeated immediately after the vertigo subsides, subsequent vertiginous responses are less severe. BPPV generally is not associated with deafness or tinnitus. The posterior semicircular canal is most often the source of the difficulty.

Therapy for this condition is symptomatic. Vestibular exercise helps more than medications. When the condition is disabling, it may be cured surgically by dividing all or part of the vestibular nerve. In most cases, hearing can be preserved. If the problem can be localized with certainty to one posterior semicircular canal, an alternative surgical procedure called *singular neurectomy* may be considered. Benign positional paroxysmal vertigo must be distinguished from *cervical vertigo*. Cervical vertigo is another common cause of disequilibrium, especially following head or neck trauma, including whiplash. This condition is usually associated with neck discomfort, spasm in the posterior neck musculature, limitation of motion, and dizziness when turning or extending the head. Cervical vertigo is often misdiagnosed as BPPV. Although the symptoms may be similar, the treatments are different, and prescribing vestibular exercises for cervical vertigo patients may actually make symptoms worse. Certain viruses such as herpes classically produce vertigo by involving the peripheral end-organ. The attack usually is of sudden onset, associated with tinnitus and hearing loss, and subsides spontaneously. In the absence of tinnitus and hearing loss, the virus is assumed to have attacked the nerve itself; this condition is called *vestibular neuritis*. Certain toxins also readily produce vertigo.

Whenever a patient complains of vertigo and there is evidence of chronic otitis media, it is essential to determine whether a cholesteatoma is present that is eroding into the semicircular canal and causing the vertigo. Vertigo can also be present with certain types of otosclerosis that involve the inner ear. In all such cases, the specific cause of the vertigo should be determined; and whenever possible, proper therapy based on the specific cause should be instituted. Perilymph fistula as cause of vertigo is particularly amenable to surgical treatment.

In cases in which the labyrinth has been completely destroyed on both sides, some patients develop oscillopsia, that is, the horizon bounces when they walk. This is a particularly disturbing symptom and is very difficult to treat. Fortunately, it is uncommon.

Disequilibrium involving the central nervous system is an urgent problem and must be ruled out in every case, especially when it is associated with other symptoms outside the ear. Certain symptoms strongly suggest that the cause of the vertigo must be sought in the central nervous system. If spontaneous nystagmus (flickering eye movement) is present and persists, the physicians should look for associated neurological signs such as falling. This is especially true if the condition has persisted for a long time. If the rotary vertigo is associated with a loss of consciousness, physicians also should suspect that the vertigo originates in the central nervous system or cardiovascular system. The association of intense vertigo with localized headache makes it mandatory to rule out a central brain lesion.

Among the common central nervous system causes of vertigo are vascular crisis, tumors of the posterior fossa, multiple sclerosis, epilepsy, encephalitis, and concussion.

The dizziness in a vascular crisis is of sudden onset and generally is accompanied by nausea and vomiting as well as tinnitus and deafness. This is a form of stroke. In many instances, other cranial nerves are involved.

It is also possible to have a much more discrete vascular defect in the vestibular labyrinth without involvement of the cochlea. This usually results in an acute onset of severe vertigo. Recovery is rather slow, and the vertigo may persist as postural imbalance. The nystagmus may subside, but unsteadiness and difficulty walking may continue much longer.

A still milder form of vascular problem related to dizziness occurs in hypotension and vasomotor instability. People with these problems have recurrent brief episodes of imbalance and instability, particularly after a sudden change of position, such as suddenly arising from tying their shoelaces or turning quickly. Many such maneuvers are required during opera and theater performance. This condition requires evaluation and management by an internist and is potentially treatable by increased salt intake, sodium retention medications, and beta-blockers.

In multiple sclerosis, vertigo is commonly a symptom; but it is rarely severe enough to confuse the picture with other involvement of the vestibular pathways. In epilepsy, vertigo occasionally may be a premonitory sensation before an epileptic attack and helps to distinguish the condition.

A complaint of vertigo in postconcussion syndrome is extremely common. The vertigo usually is associated with movement of the head or the body, severe headache, and marked hypersensitivity to noise and vibration. Patients usually are jittery, tense, and very irritable.

Basilar artery compression syndrome is another condition associated with head motion, particularly neck extension. It is due to compression of the basilar artery with resultant interference with blood flow to the brainstem. This diagnosis cannot be made with certainty without objective confirmation through arteriography or other tests.

Carotid sinus syndrome and psychic disturbances frequently produce vertigo that may be confused with vertigo of vestibular origin. Taking a careful history and testing the carotid sinus make it possible to distinguish these conditions.

Of special interest to the otologist is the dizziness that sometimes is associated with a lesion of the posterior cranial fossa and particularly with an acoustic neuroma. It is a standing rule in otology that, when a patient complains of true vertigo, an acoustic neuroma must be ruled out. This is especially true when the vertigo is accompanied by a hearing loss or tinnitus in one ear. Vertigo is not always a symptom in all posterior fossa lesions; but when it occurs, a number of simple tests help to establish the possibility that a tumor is present.

Other occasional causes of dizziness include encephalitis, meningitis, direct head injuries, and toxic reactions to alcohol, tobacco, or other drugs such as streptomycin.

Evaluation of the dizzy patient is extremely involved and will not be reviewed in this chapter. It includes taking a complete history; a thorough physical examination including neurological assessment, blood tests, radiologic tests (such as CT, MRI, and SPECT); hearing tests; and balance tests. Otolaryngologists subspecializing in neurotology are particularly expert in the evaluation and treatment of balance disorders, although other specialists, particularly neurologists, are often involved too. Many patients with disequilibrium can now be helped. In some cases, the problem can be cured. This treatment may involve medicine, surgery, physical therapy, or other modalities, depending on the cause of the problem.

When disequilibrium occurs in professional voice users, especially singers or actors, every effort must be made to determine its cause and cure or minimize the symptoms to avoid disturbing interference with performance and prevent potentially serious safety hazards during maneuvers on stage.

Conclusion

Many other neurologic disorders may affect voice performance. Familiarity with the latest concepts in neurolaryngology, clinical voice disorders, and a close working relationship between laryngologists and neurologists optimize treatment for the many patients with these troublesome problems.

References

1. Blitzer A, Brin M, Sasaki CT, Fahn S, Harris K, eds. *Neurologic Disorders of the Larynx*. New York, NY: Thieme Medical Publishers, Inc; 1992.
2. Davis P, Fletcher N, eds. *Vocal Fold Physiology: Controlling Chaos and Complexity*. San Diego, Calif: Singular Publishing Group; 1996.
3. Sataloff RT, Hawkshaw M, Bhatia R. Medical applications of chaos theory. In: Davis P, Fletcher N, eds. *Vocal Fold Physiology: Controlling Chaos and Complexity*. San Diego, Calif: Singluar Publishing Group; 1996: 369–387.

4. Sataloff RT, Hawkshaw MJ, eds. *Chaos in Medicine: Source Readings*. San Diego, Calif: Singular Publishing Group; 2001.
5. Darley FL, Aronson AE, Brown JR. Differential diagnostic in patterns of dysarthria. *J Speech Hearing Res*. 1969;12: 246–249.
6. Darley F, Aronson AE, Brown JR. Clusters of deviant speech dimensions in the dysarthrias. *J Speech Hearing Res*. 1969;12:462–496.
7. Rosenfield DB. Neurolaryngology. *Ear Nose Throat J*. 1987;66(8):323–326.
8. Aronson AE. *Clinical Voice Disorders*. 2nd ed. New York: Thieme Medical Publishers; 1985:77–126.
9. Rosenfield DB. Do stutterers have different brains? *Neurology*. 2001;57:171–172.
10. Smith A, Luschei E, Denny M, et al. Spectral analyses of activity of laryngeal and orofacial muscles in stutterers. *J Neurol Neurosurg Psychiatry*. 1993;56(12):1303–1311.
11. Smith A, Denny M, Shaffer LA, et al. Activity of intrinsic laryngeal muscles in fluent and dysfluent speech. *J Speech Hear Res*. 1996;39(2):329–348.
12. Heuer RJ, Sataloff RT, Mandel S, Travers N. Neurogenic stuttering: further corroboration of site of lesion. *Ear Nose Throat J*. 1996;75(3):161–168.
13 Foundas AL, Bollich AM, Corey DM, et al. Anomalous anatomy of speech-language areas in adults with persistent developmental stuttering. *Neurology*. 2001;57(2): 207–215.
14. Deuschl G, Raethjen J, Lindemann M, Krack P. The pathophysiology of tremor. *Muscle Nerve*. 2001;24(6): 716–735.
15. Connor GS, Ondo WG, Stacy MA, Jankovic J, eds. Essential tremor: a practical guide to evaluation, diagnosis, and treatment. *Clinician*. 2001;19(2):1–15. [Available from: Baylor College of Medicine, Office of Continuing Education.]
16. Yokota J, Imai H, Seki K, Ninomiya C, Mizuno Y. Orthostatic tremor associated with voice tremor. *Eur Neurol*.1992;32(6):354–358.
17. Tomoda H, Shibasaki H, Kuroda Y, Shin T. Voice tremor: dysregulation of voluntary expiratory muscles. *Neurology*. 1987;37:117–122.
18. Koda J, Ludlow CL. An evaluation of laryngeal muscle activation in patients with voice tremor. *Otolaryngol Head Neck Surg*. 1992;107(5):684–696.
19. Wasielewski PG, Burns JM, Koller WC. Pharmacologic treatment of tremor. *Mov Disord*. 1998;13(suppl 3):90–100.
20. Koller WC, Vetere-Overfield B. Acute and chronic effects of propranolol and primidone in essential tremor. *Neurology*. 1989;39(12):1587–1588.
21. Sataloff RT, Heuer RJ, Munz MS, et al. Vocal tremor reduction with deep brain stimulation: a preliminary report. *J Voice*. 2002;16(1):132–135.
22. Yoon MS, Munz M, Sataloff RT, et al. Vocal fold tremor with deep brain stimulation. *Stereotact Func Neurosurg*. 1999;72:241–244.
23. Stelzig Y, Hochhaus W, Gall V, Henneberg A. Laryngeal manifestations in patients with Parkinson's disease. *Laryngorhinootologie*. 1999;78(10):544–551.
24. Hertrich I, Ackermann H. Gender-specific vocal dysfunctions in Parkinson's disease: electroglottographic and acoustic analyses. *Ann Otol Rhinol Laryngol*. 1995; 104(3):197–202.
25. Leopold NA, Kagel MC. Laryngeal deglutition movement in Parkinson's disease. *Neurology*. 1997;48(2):373–376.
26. Ho AK, Bradshaw JL, Iansek T. Volume perception in parkinsonian speech. *Mov Disord*. 2000;15(6):1125–1131.
27. de Angelis EC, Mourao LF, Ferraz HB, et al. Effect of voice rehabilitation on oral communication of Parkinson's disease patients. *Acta Neurol Scand*. 1997;96(4):199–205.
28. Holmes RJ, Oates JM, Phyland DJ, Hughes AJ. Voice characteristic in the progression of Parkinson's disease. *Int J Lang Commun Disord*. 2000;35(3):407–418.
29. Ho AK, Bradshaw JL, Iansek R, Alfredson R. Speech volume regulation in Parkinson's disease: effects of implicit cues and explicit instructions. *Neuropsychologia*. 1999; 37(13):1453–1460.
30. Plasse HM, Lieberman AN. Bilateral vocal cord paralysis in Parkinson's disease. *Arch Otolaryngol*. 1981;107(4): 252–253.
31. Jiang J, Lin E, Wang J, Hanson DG. Glottographic measures before and after levodopa treatment in Parkinson's disease. *Laryngoscope*. 1999;109(8):1287–1294.
32. Hariz MI, Johansson F, Shamsgovara P, et al. Bilateral subthalamic nucleus stimulation in a parkinsonian patient with preoperative deficits in speech and cognition: persistent improvement in mobility but increased dependency: a case study. *Mov Disord*. 2000;15(1):136–139.
33. Berke GS, Gerratt B, Kreiman J, Jackson K. Treatment of Parkinson hypophonia with percutaneous collagen augmentation. *Laryngoscope*. 1999;109(8):1295–1299.
34. Ramig LO, Scherer RC. Speech therapy for neurologic disorders of the larynx. In: Blitzer A, Brin MF, Sasaki CT, Fahn S, Harris KS, eds. *Neurologic Disorders of the Larynx*. New York, NY: Thieme Medical Publishers; 1992:163–181.
35. Ramig LO. The role of phonation in speech intelligibility: a review and preliminary data from patients with Parkinson's disease. In: Kent RD, ed. *Intelligibility in Speech Disorders: Theory, Measurement, and Management*. Philadelphia, Pa: John Benjamins Publishing Co; 1992: 119–156.
36. Ramig LO, Scherer RC, Titze IR, Ringel SP. Acoustic analysis of voices of patients with neurologic disease: rationale and preliminary data. *Ann Otol Rhinol Laryngol*. 1988;97:164–172.
37. Ramig LO. Speech therapy for patients with Parkinson's disease. In: Koller W, Paulson G, eds. *Therapy of Parkinson's Disease*. New York, NY: Marcel Dekker; 1995.
38. Ramig LO, Sapir S, Fox C, Countryman S. Changes in vocal loudness following intensive voice treatment (LVST) in individuals with Parkinson's disease: a comparison with untreated patients and normal age-matched controls. *Mov Disord*. 2001;16(1):79–83.
39. Neal GD, Clarke LR. Neuromuscular disorders. *Otolaryngol Clin N Am*. 1987;20(1):195–201.

40. Mao VH, Abaza M, Spiegel JR, et al. Laryngeal myasthenia gravis: report 40 cases. *J Voice*. 2001;15(1):122–130.
41. Dalakas MC, Elder G, Hallett M, et al. A long-term follow-up study of patients with post-poliomyelitis neuromuscular symptoms. *N Engl J Med*. 1986;314(15):959–963.
42. Agre JC, Rodriquez JA, Taffel JA. Late effects of polio: critical review of the literature on neuromuscular function. *Arch Phys Med Rehabil*. 1991;72:923–931.
43. Rodriquez AA, Agre JC, Harmon RL, et al. Electromyographic and neuromuscular variables in post-polio subjects. *Arch Phys Med Rehabil*. 1995;76(11):989–993.
44. Abaza M, Sataloff RT, Hawkshaw MJ, Mandel S. Laryngeal manifestations of postpoliomyelitis syndrome. *J Voice*. 2001;15(2):291–294.
45. Driscoll BP, Gracco C, Coelho C, et al. Laryngeal function in postpolio patients. *Laryngoscope*. 1995;105:35–41.
46. Robinson LR, Hillel AD, Waugh PF. New laryngeal muscle weakness in post-polio syndrome. *Laryngoscope*. 1998;108:732–734.
47. Knobil K, Becker FS, Harper P, Graf LB, Wolf GT, Martinez FJ. Dyspnea in a patient years after severe poliomyelitis. The role of cardiopulmonary exercise testing. *Chest*. 1994;105(3):777–781.
48. Rontal E, Rontal M, Wald J, Rontal D. Botulinum toxin injection in the treatment of vocal fold paralysis associated with multiple sclerosis: a case report. *J Voice*. 1999;13(2):274–279.
49. Reichler BD, Scelsa SN, Simpson DM. Hereditary neuropathy and vocal cord paralysis in a man with childhood diphtheria. *Muscle Nerve*. 2000; 23(1):132–137.
50. Rigueiro-Veloso MT, Pego-Reigosa R, Branas-Fernandez F, Martinez-Vasquez F, Cortes-Laino JA. [Wallenberg syndrome: a review of 25 cases.] Spanish. *Rev Neurol*. 1997;25(146):1561–1564.
51. Leys D, Lejeune JP, Bourgeois P, Blond S, Petit H. [Acute pseudobulbar syndrome. Bilateral infarction of the junction of the internal capsule with the corona radiata.] *Rev Neurol* (Paris). 1985;141(12):814–818.
52. Aviv JE, Martin JH, Sacco RL, Zagar D, Diamond B, Keen MS, Blitzer A. Supraglottic and pharyngeal sensory abnormalities in stroke patients with dysphagia. *Ann Otol Rhinol Laryngol*. 1996;105(2):92–97.
53. Nakaso K, Awaki E, Isoe K. [A case of supranuclear hypoglossal nerve palsy with Avellis' syndrome due to a medullary infarction.] *Rinsho Shinkeigaku*. 1996;36(5): 692–695.
54. Saltzman LS, Rosenberg CH, Wolf RH. Brainstem infarct with pharyngeal dysmotility and paralyzed vocal cord: management with a multidisciplinary approach. *Arch Phys Med Rehabil*. 1993;74(2):214–216.
55. Ito M, Nitta T, Sato K, Ishii S. Cervical carotid aneurysm presenting as transient ischemia and recurrent laryngeal nerve palsy. *Surg Neurol*. 1986;25(4);346–350.
56. Andrews M. *Manual of Voice Treatment: Pediatrics through Geriatrics*. San Diego, Calif: Singular Publishing Group Inc; 1995:268–270.
57. Roth CR, Glaze LE, Goding GS Jr., David WS. Spasmodic dysphonia symptoms as initial presentation of amyotrophic lateral sclerosis. *J Voice*. 1996;10(4):362–367.
58. McGuirt WF, Blalock D. The otolaryngologist's role in the diagnosis and treatment of amyotrophic lateral sclerosis. *Laryngoscope*. 1980;90(9):1496–1501.
59. Silbergleit AK, Johnson AF, Jacobson BH. Acoustic analysis of voice in individuals with amyotrophic lateral sclerosis and perceptually normal vocal quality. *J Voice*. 1997;11(2):222–231.
60. Hillel A, Dray T, Miller R, Yorkston K, et al. Presentation of ALS to the otolaryngologist/head and neck surgeon: getting to the neurologist. *Neurology*. 1999;53(8 suppl 5):S22–S25.
61. Carrow E, Rivera V, Mauldin M, Shamblin L, Deviant speech characteristics in motor neuron disease. *Arch Otolaryngol*. 1974;100:212–218.
62 Aronson AE, Ramig LO, Winholtz WS, Silber SR. Rapid voice tremor, or "flutter," in amyotrophic lateral sclerosis. *Ann Otol Rhinol Laryngol*. 1992;101(6):511–518.
63. Carter GT, Johnson ER, Bonekat HW, Lieberman JS. Laryngeal diversion in the treatment of intractable aspiration in motor neuron disease. *Arch Phys Med Rehabil*. 1992;73(7):680–682.
64. Radanovic M, Senaha ML, Mansur LL, et al. Primary progressive aphasia: analysis of 16 cases. *Arq Neuropsiquiatr*. 2002;59(3-A):512–520.
65. Sinnatamby R, Antoun NA, Freer CE, Miles KA, Hodges JR. Neuroradiological findings in primary progressive aphasia: CT, MRI, and cerebral perfusion SPECT. *Neuroradiology*. 1996;38(3):232–238.
66. San Pedro EC, Deutsch G, Liu HG, Mountz JM. Frontotemporal decrease in rCBF correlate with degree of dysnomia in primary progressive aphasia. *J Nucl Med*. 2000;41(2):228–233.
67. Janicek MJ, Schwartz RB, Carvalho PA, et al. Tc-99m HMPAO brain perfusion SPECT in acute aphasia. Correlation with clinical and structural findings. *Clin Nucl Med*. 1993;18(12):1032–1038.
68. Turner RS, Kenyon LC, Trojanowski JQ, et al. Clinical, neuroimaging, and pathologic features of progressive nonfluent aphasia. *Ann Neurol*. 1996;39(2):166–173.
69. Calmon G, Roberts N. Automatic measurement of changes in brain volume on consecutive 3D MR images by segmentation progpagation. *Magn Reson Imaging*. 2000; 18(4):439–453.
70. Molina JA, Probst A, Villanueva C, et al. Primary progressive aphasia with glial cytoplasmic inclusion. *Eur Neurol*. 1998;40(2):71–77.
71. Gonzalez RG, Fischman AJ, Guimaraes AR, et al. Functional MR in the evaluation of dementia: correlation of abnormal dynamic cerebral blood volume measurements with changes in cerebral metabolism on positron emission tomography with fludeoxyglucose F 18. *Am J Neuroradiol*. 1995;16(9):1763–1770.
72. Jagust WJ, Johnson KA, Holman BL. SPECT perfusion imaging in the diagnosis of dementia. *J Neuroimaging*. 1995;5 (suppl 1):S45–S52.
73. Buchpiguel CA, Mathias SC, Itaya KY, et al. Brain SPECT in dementia. A clinical scintigraphic correlation. *Arq Neuropsiquiatri*. 1996;54(3):374–383.

74. Pasquier F, Lavenu I, Lebert F, et al. The use of SPECT in a multidisciplinary memory clinic. *Dement Geriatr Cogn Disord*. 1997;8(2):85–91.
75. Holman BL, Johnson KA, Gerada B, et al. The scintigraphic appearance of Alzheimer's disease: prospective study using technetium-99m-HMPAO SPECT. *J Nucl Med*. 1992;33(2):181–185.
76. Villa G, Cappa A, Tavolozza M, et al. Neuropsychological tests and (99mTc)-HM PAO SPECT in the diagnosis of Alzheimer's dementia. *J Neurol*. 1995;242(6):359–366.
77. Defebvre LJ, Leduc V, Duhamel A, et al . Technetium HMPAO SPECT study in dementia with Lewy bodies, Alzheimer's disease and idiopathic Parkinson's disease. *J Nucl Med*. 1999;40(6):956–962.
78. Zimmer R, Leucht S, Radler T, et al. Variability of cerebral blood flow deficits in 99mTc-HMPAO SPECT in patients with Alzheimer's disease. *J Neural Transm*. 1997;104(6–7):689–701.
79. Masterman DL, Mendez MF, Fairbanks LA, Cummings JL. Sensitivity, specificity, and positive predictive value of technetium 99-HMPAO SPECT in discriminating Alzheimer's disease from other dementias. *J Geriatr Psychiatry Neurol*. 1997;10(1):15–21.
80. Charpentier P, Lavenu I, Defebvre L, et al. Alzheimer's disease and frontotemporal dementia are differentiated by discriminant analysis applied to (99m) Tc HmPAO SPECT data. *J Neurol Neurosurg Psychiatry*. 2000;69(5): 661–663.
81. Mitchener A, Wyper DJ, Patterson J, et al. SPECT, CT, and MRI in head injury: acute abnormalities followed up at six months. *J Neurol Neurosurg Psychiatry*. 1997; 62(6):633–636.
82. Steinling M, Defebvre L, et al. Is there a typical pattern of brain SPECT imaging in Alzheimer's disease? *Dement Geriatr Cogn Disord*. 2001;12(6):371–378.
83. Hanson DG, Ludlow CL, Bassich CJ. Vocal fold paresis in Shy-Drager syndrome. *Ann Otol Rhinol Laryngol*. 1983; 92(1 pt 1):85–90.
84. Segers JM. [An unusual case of laryngeal stridor: the Shy-Drager syndrome.] *Acta Otorhinolaryngol Belg*. 1990; 44(1):43–45.
85. Hayashi M, Isozaki E, Oda M, et al. Loss of large myelinated nerve fibres of the recurrent laryngeal nerve in patients with multiple system atrophy and vocal cord palsy. *J Neurol Neurosurg Psychiatry*. 1997; 62(3):234–238.
86. Isozaki E, Hayashi M, Hayashida T, et al. [Vocal cord abductor paralysis in multiple system atrophy—paradoxical movement of vocal cords during sleep.] *Rinsho Shinkeigaku*. 1996;36(4):529–533.
87. Isozaki E, Naito A, Horiguchi S, et al. Early diagnosis and stage classification of vocal cord abductor paralysis in patients with multiple system atrophy. *J Neurol Neurosurg Psychiatry*. 1996;60(4):399–402.
88. Isozaki E, Osanai R, Horiguchi S, et al. Laryngeal electromyography with separated surface electrodes in patients with multiple system atrophy presenting with vocal fold paralysis. *J Neurol*. 1994;241(9):551–556.
89. Merlo DM, Occhini A, Pacchetti C, Alfonsi E. Not paralysis, but dystonia causes stridor in multiple system atrophy. *Neurology*. 2002;58:649–662.
90. American Psychiatric Association. *Diagnostic Statistical Manual of Mental Disorders-IV*. Washington, DC: American Psychiatric Association; 1994:71–73.
91. Sataloff RT, Heuer RJ, O'Connor MJ. Rehabilitation of a quadriplegic professional singer. *Arch Otolaryngol*. 1984; 110(10): 682–685.
92. Sataloff RT. *Embryology and Anomalies of the Facial Nerve*. New York, NY: Raven Press; 1991.
93. Sataloff J, Sataloff RT, Lueneberg W. Tinnitus and vertigo in healthy senior citizens with no history of noise exposure. *Am J Otol*. 1987;8(2):87–89.
94. US Dept of Health and Human Services, Public Health Services. *National Health Care Survey*. Washington, DC: 1978. National Center for Health Statistics; 1978: Series 13, No. 56.
95. Jenkins HA, Furman JM, Gulya AJ, et al. Dysequilibrium of aging. *Otolaryngol Head Neck Surg*. 1989;100:272–282.
96. Head injury: hope through research. Washington, DC: National Institute of Neurological Disorders and Stroke; 1984. Publication NIH 84-2478. Available at: http//: www.bgsm.edu/bgsm/surgi-sci/ns/NIH84-278html
97. Mandel S, Sataloff RT, Schapiro S. *Minor Head Trauma: Assessment, Management and Rehabilitation*. New York, NY: Springer-Verlag; 1993.

12

Vocal Fold Paresis and Paralysis

Adam D. Rubin and Robert Thayer Sataloff

Diagnosis and treatment of the immobile or hypomobile vocal fold are challenging for the otolaryngologist. An immobile vocal fold is not synonymous with a paralyzed vocal fold. True paralysis and paresis result from vocal fold denervation secondary to injury to the laryngeal or vagus nerve. Immobility of the vocal fold may be the result of paralysis or mechanical abnormalities. Vocal fold paralysis may be unilateral or bilateral, central or peripheral; and it may involve the recurrent laryngeal nerve, superior laryngeal nerve, or both (Figs 12–1 through 12–4). The physician's first responsibility in any case of vocal fold paralysis is to confirm the diagnosis and be certain that the laryngeal movement impairment is not caused by arytenoid cartilage dislocation or subluxation, cricoarytenoid arthritis or ankylosis, neoplasm, or other mechanical causes. Efforts should be made to determine the etiology. Strobovideolaryngoscopy, endoscopy, radiologic and laboratory studies, and electromyography are all useful diagnostic tools.

Anatomy

Recurrent Laryngeal Nerve

Anatomy of the larynx and related structures is discussed in detail elsewhere. This chapter reviews only a few of the relationships that are most important when evaluating vocal fold mobility disorders.

The nuclei of the recurrent laryngeal nerve (RLN) axons lie within the nucleus ambiguus in the medulla of the brainstem. The RLN axons travel with the vagus nerve down the neck until they branch off at the level of the aortic arch on the left and the subclavian artery on the right. On the left, the nerve passes inferior and posterior to the aortic arch and reverses its course to continue superiorly into the visceral compartment of the neck. The right RLN loops behind the right subclavian artery and ascends superomedially toward the tracheoesophageal groove. Both RLNs travel just lateral to or within the tracheoesophageal groove and enter the larynx posterior to the cricothyroid joint. The positions of the nerves in the neck make them susceptible to iatrogenic injury during surgery. Low in the neck, the course of the right recurrent nerve is more oblique, lateral, and probably more prone to injury than the left RLN.[1]

Approximately 5 out of 1000 people have a nonrecurrent laryngeal nerve on the right. A nonrecurrent laryngeal nerve occurs only on the right, except in the rare case of situs inversus. It branches from the vagus nerve at the level of the cricoid cartilage and enters the larynx directly, without looping around the subclavian artery. This anomaly occurs in conjunction with a retroesophageal right subclavian artery.[1]

Superior Laryngeal Nerve

The superior laryngeal nerve (SLN) branches from the vagus nerve just inferior to the nodose ganglion, which contains the sensory cell bodies of the SLN. The nerve travels inferiorly along the side of the pharynx, medial to the carotid artery, and splits into two branches about the level of the hyoid bone. The internal division of the SLN penetrates the thyrohyoid membrane with the superior laryngeal artery and supplies sensory innervation to the larynx. The external division of the SLN provides motor innervation to the cricothyroid (CT) muscle. The CT muscle changes vocal fold tension by elongating the fold. It is responsible for increasing the fundamental frequency of the voice. The external division of the SLN lies close to the supe-

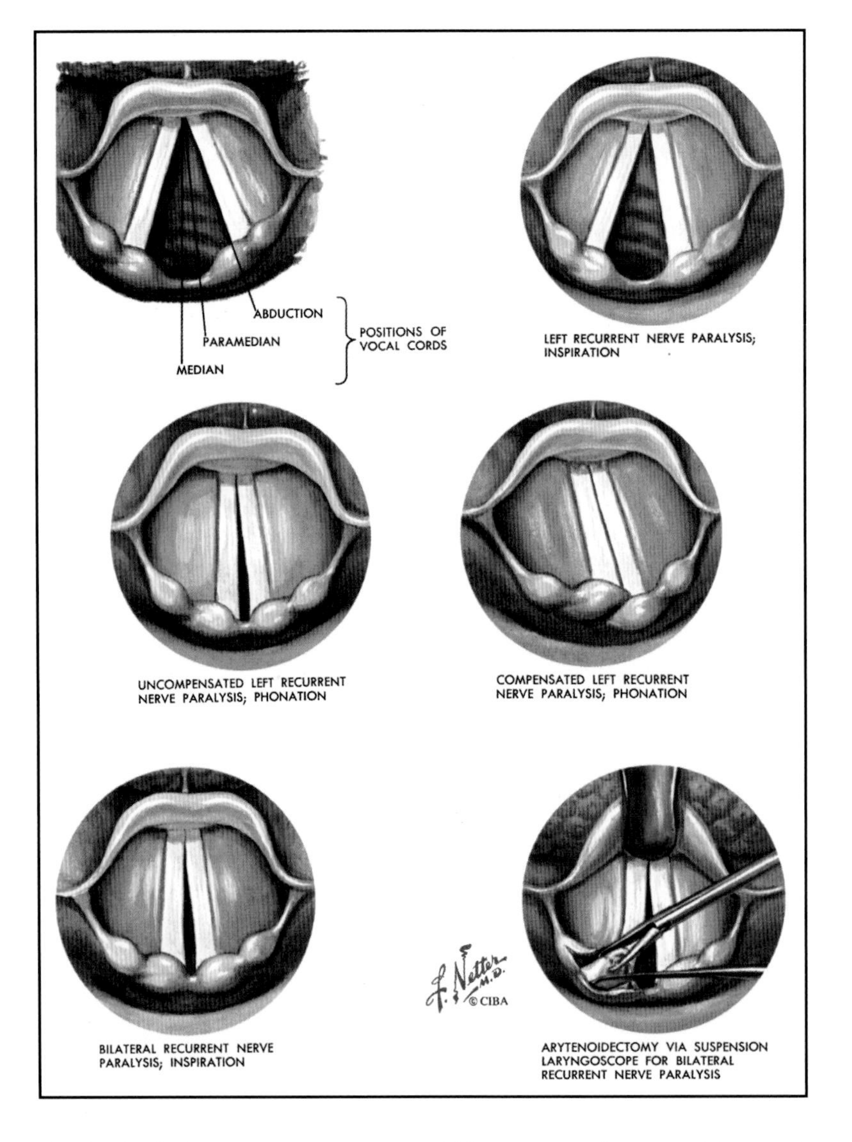

Fig 12–1. Typical appearances of vocal fold in cases of recurrent laryngeal nerve paralysis. The illustration in the lower right-hand corner depicts endoscopic arytenoidectomy. This is one procedure to help reestablish an adequate airway for patients with bilateral vocal fold paralysis. However, it does so at the expense of vocal quality. (From The larynx. *Clinical Symposia*. Summit, NJ: CIBA Pharmaceutical Company; 1964: 16(3):Plate VII. Copyright 1964. Icon Learning Systems, LLC, a subsidiary of Medi Media USA, Inc. Reprinted with permission from ICON Learning Systems, LLC, illustrated by Frank Netter, MD. All rights reserved.

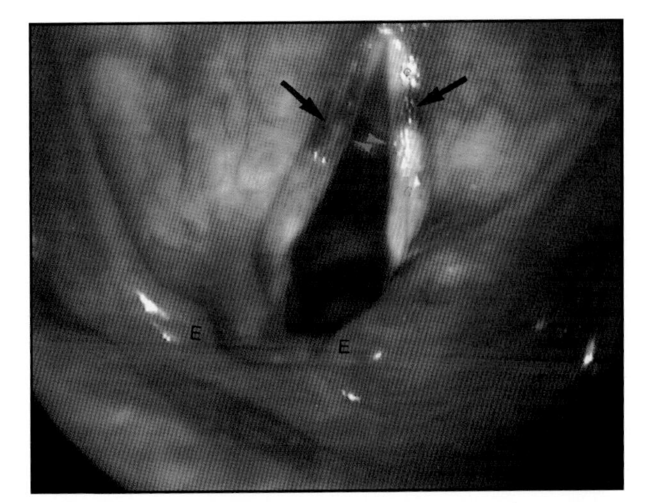

Fig 12–2. Forty-year-old woman with a 2-month history of sudden hoarseness. Right recurrent laryngeal nerve paralysis had been diagnosed. The position of the right vocal fold during abduction in this videoprint is typical. The vocal fold is in the paramedian position, and the height of the vocal process and vibratory margin is normal and the same as the mobile left side. However, this patient had other findings of interest. She had been struggling vocally to compensate for her paralyzed vocal fold. At the time of examination, there were small nodular swellings on both vocal folds *(white arrows)*. Most interestingly, she had bilateral, acute submucosal vocal fold hemorrhages *(black arrows)*. This is not the only case in which the authors have seen this problem, and it serves to illustrate the fact that voice disorders traditionally classified as "hypofunctional" (such as vocal paralysis) do not necessarily protect patients from severe injury from voice abuse. The authors have seen similar findings that occurred during therapy with forced adduction exercises (pushing) at other facilities. Incidental note was also made of arytenoid erythema *(E)*. In this case, it was due to voice abuse rather than reflux. Reflux rarely causes erythema this severe along the aryepiglottic folds and petiolus (not shown); but erythema in these regions is common with severe hyperfunction.

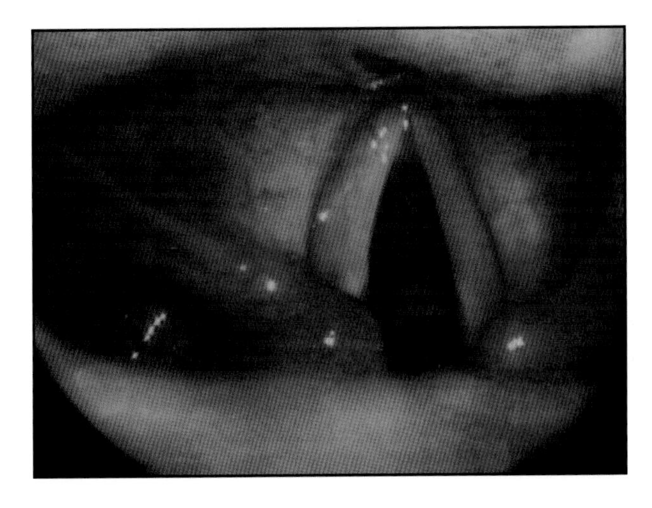

A

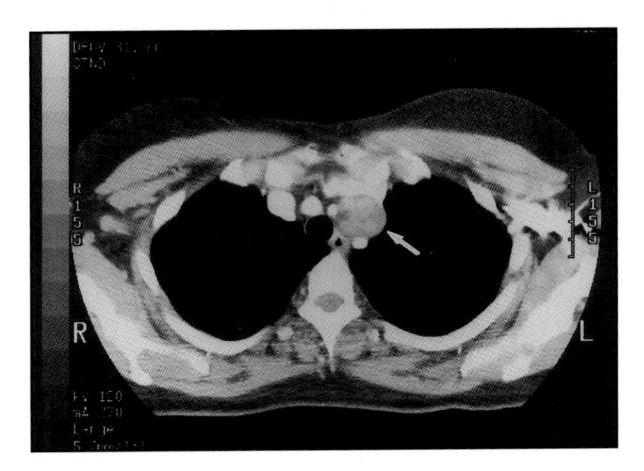

B

Fig 12–3. Videoprint from a 42-year-old teacher who had developed gradually progressive hoarseness and breathiness. **A.** The left vocal fold is abducted, bowed, and flaccid. It appeared short and its longitudinal tension did not increase normally with changes in pitch. A jostle sign was present (the left arytenoid moved passively when contacted by the right arytenoid). Laryngeal electromyography confirmed left recurrent laryngeal nerve paralysis with marked weakness of the superior laryngeal nerve. **B.** A CT scan revealed a left mediastinal mass *(white arrow)*, which proved to be a vagus nerve schwannoma.

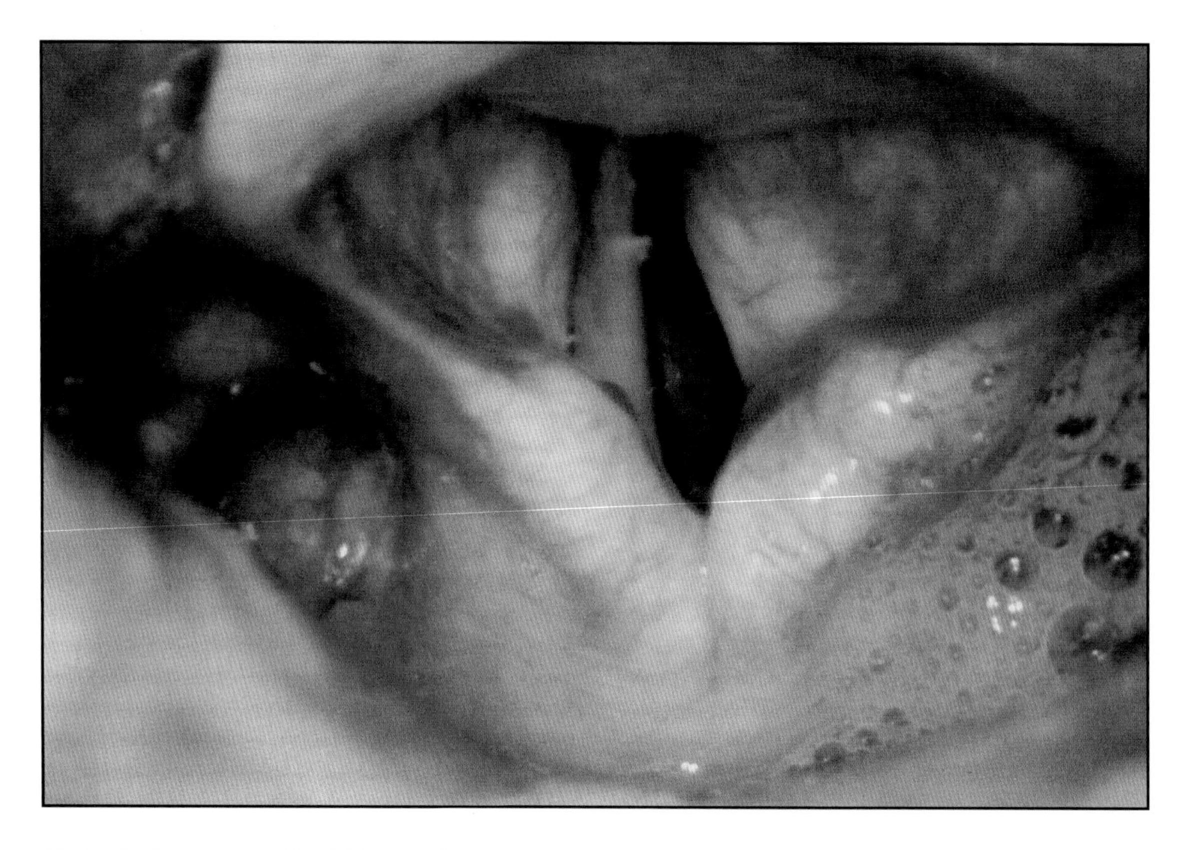

Fig 12–4. Appearance of total right superior and recurrent nerve paralysis, with prolapse of supraglottic tissues partially obscuring the abducted vocal fold, lower vertical position of the paralyzed vocal fold, and pooling of saliva in the right piriform sinus. This is another interesting case of vocal fold hemorrhage occurring in the presence of vocal fold paralysis. The submucosal hemorrhage extends throughout the superior surface of the right vocal fold.

rior thyroid artery, although its exact relationship to the artery is variable.[2,3]

The RLN innervates four of the intrinsic muscles of the larynx: the thyroarytenoid (TA), posterior cricoarytenoid (PCA), lateral cricoarytenoid (LCA), and interarytenoid (IA) muscles. Muscle innervation is unilateral except for the interarytenoid (IA) muscle, which receives contributions from both RLNs.[4] The TA and LCA muscles are both vocal fold adductors. Unilateral denervation of these muscles results in an inability to close the glottis with resulting breathy voice and possible aspiration.

The PCA is the main vocal fold abductor. Paralysis of this muscle results in an inability to abduct during inspiration. Denervation of the PCA usually causes the arytenoid cartilage to subluxate anteromedially in unilateral vocal fold paralysis. The denervated PCA no longer counters the anterior pull on the arytenoid cartilage by the vocal ligament.[4] If both PCA muscles are denervated, as in the case of bilateral RLN paralysis, airway obstruction may occur.

The IA muscle is actually made up of three muscles, including the transverse arytenoideus muscle and two oblique arytenoideus muscles. The function of the IA muscle is not completely understood; however, it may assist in vocal fold adduction[4] and provide medial compression to close the posterior glottis.

Vocal Fold Paresis and Paralysis

Vocal fold paralysis implies complete denervation, with lack of muscle fiber recruitment during voluntary attempts at motion. This situation occurs after nerve transection and is less common than vocal fold paresis. Vocal fold paresis may be the result of weakness of the RLN, SLN, or both, or previous paralysis with regeneration. Nerve injury may be unilateral or bilateral. Vocal fold paresis may present as dysphonia, loss of the upper register of the voice, hoarseness, breathiness, throat pain, choking episodes, and decreased vocal stamina. Laryngeal findings may be subtle and include asymmetrical vocal fold movement, bowing, and rotation of the larynx. Vocal fold paresis may also present as muscle tension dysphonia or as benign vocal fold lesions such as vocal nodules or cysts resulting from compensatory hyperadduction.

Recurrent Laryngeal Nerve Paresis/Paralysis

The RLN may be injured by a number of means, including iatrogenic or non-iatrogenic trauma, neurologic disease, tumor infiltration or compression, infection, collagen-vascular disease, or by unknown etiology (idiopathic). This may occur with or without concomitant SLN injury depending on the etiology and site of the lesion. The RLN is at risk for injury during many surgical procedures, such as thyroid, anterior cervical spine, and thoracic surgery. The true incidence of vocal fold paralysis remains unknown. The incidence of injury to the recurrent laryngeal nerve from thyroid surgery has been reported as between 0.3 and 13.2%,[5] and from anterior cervical spine surgery as between 2 and 21.6%.[6] Mechanisms of iatrogenic injury include intubation, transection, crush, traction, inadvertent ligature placement, and burns.

The laryngologist must always consider unusual causes. A number of neurologic diseases may affect vocal fold movement, including multiple sclerosis,[7] amyotrophic lateral sclerosis,[8,9] syringomyelia,[10] myasthenia gravis,[11,12] Guillain-Barré,[13] and Parkinson's disease.[14] Cerebrovascular accidents may result in injury to RLN neurons,[15] but typically other neurons are affected, as well. CNS tumors such as gliomas can cause RLN paralysis[16]; and diabetics may develop RLN neuropathy.[17,18] More unusual cases include disorders such as Gerhard's syndrome, laryngeal abductor paralysis that may be familial (autosomal dominant, autosomal recessive or X-linked inheritance and with adult onset) or acquired secondary to bulbar lesions or neurodegenerative disease.[19]

Aggressive thyroid malignancies may invade and injure the RLN. Compression by large thyroid goiters, benign neoplasms,[20] and nonthyroid malignancies, such as the classic "pancoast tumor" of the left upper lung, may also injure the nerve.

Idiopathic vocal fold paralysis is not well understood. Some suspect a viral etiology, as many patients report an upper respiratory infection prior to the onset of vocal symptoms. A number of infectious etiologies have been reported to cause RLN paralysis, such as Lyme disease,[21] syphilis,[22] Epstein-Barr[23] virus, and herpes.[24] Other etiologies of RLN injury reported include systemic lupus erythematosus,[25] patent ductus arteriosus,[26] mediastinal radiation,[27] I-131 therapy,[28] amyloidosis,[29] Charcot-Marie-Tooth disease,[30] mitochondrial disorders,[31] porphyria,[32] polyarteritis nodosa,[33] silicosis,[34] and familial hypokalemic periodic paralysis.[35]

The natural history of vocal fold paralysis will depend on the mechanism and degree of injury to the nerve. The Sunderland classification system describes different degrees of nerve injury. First-degree injury means neuropraxia. Nerve function should recover completely. Second-degree injury means that Wallerian degeneration has occurred distal to an injured site (axonotmesis). Second-degree injury usually occurs after a crush injury and also results in complete recovery. Because the endoneural sheaths remain intact in a second-degree injury, synkinesis does not occur. Third-degree injury includes endoneural scarring, which can cause misdirected regeneration. Fourth- degree injury involves scarring that may block regenerating axons. Fifth-degree injury signifies complete transection of the nerve.[36,37]

Clinically, unilateral RLN injury presents as a breathy voice. Diplophonia and aspiration symptoms may occur. After a few weeks, the contralateral vocal fold may compensate by adducting further to improve vocal quality and aspiration. Should reinnervation occur, typically it will not be detectable for about 4 months.[38,39] The clinical course after 4 months will be determined by the degree of reinnervation and synkinesis.

Synkinesis

Reinnervation prevents muscle atrophy. Shindo et al demonstrated in a canine model that during the first 3 months after transection of the RLN there is atrophy of both the TA and PCA muscles.[39] After 3 months, however, the muscle fiber diameters of the denervated muscle begin to increase. By 9 months, the fiber diameters of the denervated muscles approach those of normal muscle. Spontaneous reinnervation may occur after nerve transection and prevent muscle atrophy. The source of the reinnervation is not known, but may include regenerating fibers from the transected RLN, the SLN, cervical autonomic nerves, and nerve branches innervating pharyngeal constrictors.[39]

Although reinnervation after a complete RLN transection will prevent muscle wasting, typically it does not restore useful movement to the vocal fold because of synkinesis. Synkinesis results from nonselective innervation of adductor and abductor muscles. As a result, muscles that perform opposite functions contract simultaneously, resulting in immobility or hypomobility of the vocal fold.[40] The clinical picture will depend on the proportion of adductor and abductor fibers reinnervated.

Crumley describes a classification system for laryngeal synkinesis.[38] In Type I sykinesis, or "favorable synkinesis," there is little or no vocal fold movement. However, the patient's airway and voice are fairly normal. Types II, III, and IV are considered "unfavorable sykinesis." A spastic vocal fold that may twitch without control characterizes type II. Voice quality is poor. In type III sykinesis, there is tonic adduction of the vocal fold. This results in a reasonable voice, but the airway may be compromised. Finally, type IV synkinesis involves tonic abduction of the vocal fold, resulting in a breathy voice and greater risk of aspiration. Type III sykinesis probably results from greater reinnervation of the LCA in comparison to the PCA fibers; whereas in Type IV, the opposite likely occurs.

Superior Laryngeal Nerve Paresis/Paralysis

SLN paresis or paralysis may be caused by a variety of conditions. Historically, iatrogenic trauma during thyroidectomy has been accepted as the most frequent cause of SLN paralysis.[41,42] In 1980, Adour et al[43] reported that SLN "palsy" was part of a combined cranial polyneuropathy due to viral infections. Similarly, Dursun, Sataloff, Spiegel, et al suggested that viral infections, such as herpetic cold sores and upper respiratory infections, are commonly associated with this condition.[44] A likely explanation is that infections lead to viral neuritis, resulting in SLN damage. To the best of our knowledge, this retrospective review included the largest population of confirmed SLN paresis and paralysis in the medical literature. Out of the total sample ($n = 126$), 118 patients (93.6%) reported a viral infection immediately prior to the sudden onset of vocal impairment. Some of the patients used aspirin to relieve pain or fever accompanying acute infection. In some patients, aspirin ingestion probably contributed to vocal fold hemorrhage, which resulted in further voice dysfunction. Often, several months elapsed after the causative infection before the patients sought medical attention. Prior to the diagnostic examination, these patients attributed the symptoms of SLN damage to upper respiratory infections. The development of compensatory mechanisms, such as muscle tension dysphonia (MTD), which subjectively improved voice quality, sometimes resulted in further delays in seeking treatment. As expected, singers were more aware of their symptoms than nonsingers, and delay in seeking attention tended to be shorter in this population. This observation was confirmed in a study by Eckley, Sataloff, Hawkshaw, et al that demonstrated that voice range measurement is a useful parameter for analyzing the effects of SLN paresis or paralysis on voice and may also be used for measuring outcome following voice therapy.[45] The effects of SLN paresis on vocal range help explain the sensitivity of professional voice users (especially singers) to the effects of the condition. Laboratory investigations performed during selected patient evaluations often demonstrated increased serum titers, indicative of herpes virus types I and II, as well as antibodies to influenza type A and other common viruses. This evidence suggested infection at some undetermined time in the past.

There were only eight patients in Dursun's study with iatrogenic etiologies such as thyroid surgery or external trauma. Such findings suggest that iatrogenic trauma is not as frequent a cause of isolated SLN paralysis as previously believed. However, extreme care must be taken, particularly during thyroid surgery, to protect the external branch of the SLN in the superior pole of the thyroid where it descends very close to the superior thyroid vessels. Jannson et al performed pre- and postoperative electromyography (EMG) on 20 patients undergoing thyroid surgery. Nine patients had postoperative SLN paresis by EMG.[46] Additionally, three patients with goiters had preoperative SLN paresis, which worsened postoperatively. Fifty-eight percent of the SLN pareses were present at 1-year follow-up, although most cases had some nerve recovery. To avoid harming the SLN during thyroid surgery, some authors recommend ligating distal branches of the superior thyroid artery as close to the thyroid capsule as possible; others suggest identification of the external branch of the SLN to prevent injury.[47] Less common etiologic factors have also been reported, including neurological disorders, anterior approach to the cervical vertebrae during surgery, carotid endarterectomy, nonsurgical trauma, and Reye's syndrome.[41,48,49]

The clinical manifestations of SLN paresis and paralysis are variable. The variability relates to different degrees of impairment, other associated pathologies, and the voice needs and awareness of each patient. Normally, the CT muscle contracts briskly in falsetto or modal phonation to increase tension in the vocal fold.[50] In SLN paresis and paralysis, the loss of this function may lead to lowered pitch and poor vocal performance, especially at higher pitches.[41,44] SLN paresis and paralysis may cause vocal fatigue, hoarseness, impairment of volume, loss of upper range, loss of projection, and breathiness. Vocal fatigue may be caused by the additional effort required to raise vocal pitch and to project, by hyperfunctional compensatory gestures, and/or by pathologic neuromuscular fatigue in cases of marked paresis. The clinical manifestations of SLN paresis or paralysis, particularly loss of upper range, are more troublesome in singers and professional speakers. These patients often develop MTD to generate a "stronger"voice. In Dursun's series, 23.8% of the patients had MTD that appeared to be compensatory.[44] Thus, it must be remembered that

SLN paresis may be the underlying cause of voice misuse and consequent structural lesions.

Although not a commonly described finding, choking with or without regurgitation and throat clearing may also occur especially if there is associated neuralgia, hypoesthesia, or paresthesia.[51] Anesthesia of the upper laryngeal space suggests injury to the internal branch of the SLN. However, the absence of anesthesia does not always rule out SLN paresis or paralysis; because the external branch may be the only affected portion. Although anesthesia usually is not seen even with complete paralysis of the SLN, subtle decreased ispilateral gag (hypoesthesia) is fairly common.

Indirect laryngoscopy or mirror examination may or may not reveal vocal fold abnormalities. A strong activation of normal CT muscle must occur to cause laryngeal tilt toward the weak side, another sign of unilateral SLN paresis.[51] Flaccidity of the affected vocal fold may cause irregular vertical movements during respiration, which in turn cause various configurations of the glottis. A bowed vocal fold (only three significant cases in our study) may be evident in SLN paresis or paralysis. These vocal folds are slightly concave, and glottic closure is usually incomplete. However, this finding may be associated with other coexisting conditions, such as recurrent laryngeal nerve paresis or paralysis, advanced age, or other neurological disorders. Tanaka et al[52] state that bowing of the vocal folds is not related to CT activity, but rather to atrophy of the TA muscle. This condition occurs in recurrent nerve dysfunction, not SLN paresis or paralysis. Our observations support this opinion.

Several authors have discussed the position of the vocal folds and glottic configuration in SLN paresis and paralysis. The studies reflect different opinions.[51,53-55] Contraction of a normal CT muscle rotates the posterior commissure toward the inactive side, which causes the paralyzed vocal fold to shorten and form an obliquely shaped glottis.[48,50,51,56] A thinned, shortened, and bowed vocal fold and an oblique glottis deviating to the paralyzed side are most consistent signs described in previous reports.[41,42,56,57] However, these signs are evident only in some cases of unilateral paralysis; and in our experience, the lack of these signs does not rule out paralysis or paresis. Moreover, these findings may be observed if CT contractions are weak or if the patients have MTD, which involves not only the hyperadduction of the normal vocal fold but also anterior-posterior compression of the glottis.[55,58] In the senior author's experience (RTS), vocal fold lag (sluggish motion) during phonation requiring rapidly repeated adduction is the most consistent and easily observed sign of SLN paresis or paralysis.

Evaluation

Evaluation of vocal fold paralysis or paresis begins with a history and physical examination. The history should define the main complaints and symptoms of the patient and likely etiology of the hypomobility. One should inquire about previous surgeries, prolonged intubations, and trauma. A complete medical history should be taken, including a thorough neurologic review of systems, smoking and alcohol history, and other questions to evaluate for possible malignancy. Questions pertaining to possible infectious etiologies should be asked; and a thorough vocal history should be taken to define the patient's vocal habits and needs, as reviewed elsewhere in this book.

The physical examination should include a complete head and neck examination with particular attention to examination of the cranial nerves. The laryngologist should assess the patient's gag reflex and palatal movement to evaluate vagus nerve function. If the patient has a unilateral high lesion of the vagus nerve, the palate will deviate to the intact side. The physician should listen carefully to the patient's voice, and the larynx should be visualized. A mirror examination should be performed first, followed by laryngoscopy with either a rigid or flexible endoscope, or both. The voice should be evaluated during a variety of phonatory tasks at several frequencies and intensities, as discussed in chapter 4. The laryngologist should look for asymmetrical movement, vocal fold bowing, horizontal and vertical position of the vocal folds, and tilting of the posterior larynx. The presence of structural lesions and signs of laryngopharyngeal reflux disease can be observed, as well. Video documentation is important. However, even thorough, routine otolaryngologic examination generally is not sufficient for establishing a diagnosis in these patients.

Patients with vocal fold paralysis deserve comprehensive evaluation. Strobovideolaryngoscopy and various objective evaluations are extremely helpful in diagnosis, treatment planning, and assessment of treatment efficacy. They are reviewed in previous chapters of this book and in other publications.[59] Laryngeal electromyography (EMG) is especially helpful in distinguishing paralysis from paresis, in confirming clinical impressions, and in detecting abnormalities in other laryngeal nerve-muscle complexes that may be missed because of distortion related to the most severe injury. For example, in a total right recurrent nerve paralysis, a left superior laryngeal nerve paresis will be considerably less obvious than usual. However, such information is important in designing optimal therapy. Laryngeal EMG is discussed in detail in chapter 5. We have found it a practical and invaluable component of voice evaluation, as have other authors.[60]

Each vocal fold is moved by many intrinsic laryngeal muscles. These muscles permit adduction, abduction, and longitudinal tension of the vocal folds. The superior laryngeal nerves supply the cricothyroid muscle, which is the primary structure responsible for increasing longitudinal tension. Maintaining stretch of the vocal fold is extremely important for pitch control, volume, and stability during soft singing, especially from the upper mid-range and higher. The recurrent laryngeal nerves innervate all of the other intrinsic muscles of the larynx. Paralysis or paresis may involve one or both vocal folds, although only one vocal fold is involved in the vast majority of cases. When the recurrent laryngeal nerve is paralyzed, the vocal fold appears to stand still, except for slight respiratory motion. However, the ability to alter longitudinal tension is maintained. The vocal processes are, therefore, usually at the same level; and even the paralyzed side lengthens as pitch is increased. Consequently, if the normal vocal fold can cross the midline far enough to reach the paralyzed vocal fold, compensation is possible; and glottic closure and reasonably good phonation can be achieved. However, the normal vocal fold can only compensate in the horizontal plane. It cannot move superiorly or inferiorly to meet the injured side if superior laryngeal nerve paralysis is present and has resulted in differences in vocal fold height. Over time, atrophy of the thyroarytenoid may occur making even horizontal compensation more difficult.

When the superior laryngeal nerve is involved, longitudinal tension is impaired and the vocal fold is bowed, or sagging. Consequently, it typically lies in a lower plane; and compensation is difficult. This is especially true if both recurrent and superior laryngeal nerves are paralyzed, but problems occur even with isolated superior laryngeal nerve paralysis in the presence of abduction and adduction. Superior laryngeal nerve paralysis is relatively common, especially following viral illnesses, particularly those accompanied by a cold sore or "fever blister." Often, paresis, or even paralysis, of the superior or recurrent laryngeal nerve can resolve spontaneously. Resolution may occur in a matter of days or may take as long as 12 to 14 months; and medical treatment may help prevent prolonged or permanent dysfunction.

Briefly, if vocal fold paralysis appears to occur below the level of the nodose ganglion, complete evaluation from the skull base through the chest (including the thyroid) is essential. This localization can usually be made reliably in isolated unilateral recurrent laryngeal nerve paralysis. If the paralysis is complete (recurrent and superior) or if there are other neurological findings, intracranial studies should be performed, as well. Occasionally, central disease (especially multiple sclerosis) can produce unexpected neurologic signs. If no etiology is found after a recurrent laryngeal nerve has been worked up, addition of a magnetic resonance image (MRI) of the brain and other studies should be considered. Because of the seriousness of missing intracranial lesions, many physicians obtain MRI of the brain and tenth cranial nerve (with enhancement) in all cases; and this practice certainly is not unreasonable. Superior laryngeal nerve paralysis is suspected when one vocal fold lags in adduction and when the larynx is tilted (usually toward the side of the lesion, and more prominently at high pitches). When it is complete, superior laryngeal nerve paralysis usually impairs volume and projection and causes "threadiness" and crackling in the singer's mid-range and loss of the highest notes and stability in the upper range.

Paresis produces the same symptoms as paralysis, but to a lesser degree. In addition to confirmation by electromyography, the authors have found a few clinical maneuvers particularly useful for making paresis more apparent. Repeated maneuvers alternating a sniff with the sound /i/ are particularly helpful in unmasking mild PCA paresis. Repeated rapid phonation on /i/ with a complete stop between each phonation frequently causes increased vocal fold lag, because the pathologic side fatigues more rapidly than the normal side. Other rapidly alternating tasks also are helpful, including /i/-/hi/-/i/-/hi/-/i/-/hi/ . . . and /pɑ/-/tɑ/-/kɑ/-/pɑ/-/tɑ/kɑ/-/pɑ/tɑ/kɑ/ .... The vocal fold lag is sometimes easier to see during whistling. Laryngeal posture during this maneuver provides particularly good visibility of rapid vocal fold motions. A glissando maneuver, asking the patient to slide slowly from his or her lowest to highest note and then slide back down is invaluable for assessing SLN function. The vocal process should be observed under continuous and stroboscopic light. If a superior laryngeal nerve is injured, longitudinal tension will not increase as effectively on the abnormal side, disparities in vocal fold length will be apparent at higher pitches, and the vocal folds may actually scissor slightly with the normal fold being higher.

Bilateral superior laryngeal nerve paralysis is often more difficult to diagnose and is probably missed frequently. Patients with this condition have a "floppy" epiglottis, rendering their larynges difficult to see. Their vocal quality, volume, and pitch range are impaired. It is often particularly helpful to confirm a clinical impression of bilateral superior laryngeal nerve paralysis through electromyography.

Appropriate laboratory studies should be considered to rule out specific causes of vocal fold paresis and paralysis. In addition to imaging studies such as MRI and CT, these may include tests for syphilis, Lyme disease, diabetes, thyroid dysfunction, collagen vascular disease, myasthenia gravis, thyroid neoplasm, and other conditions. In addition to testing gag reflex, more quantitative sensory testing may be helpful, using functional endoscopic evaluation of sensory threshold (FEEST).

Treatment

Treatment for unilateral vocal fold paralysis is designed to eliminate aspiration and improve voice. When there is no aspiration, treatment depends on the patient's need and desire for improved voice quality. Recovery of laryngeal nerve function is common if the injury was not caused by transection of the nerve. Even when the nerve is transected, some innervation may occur. Consequently, it is best to delay surgical intervention for approximately 1 year, if possible, unless the nerve is known to have been divided or resected. However, this does not mean that therapy should be delayed, only irreversible surgery! The collaboration of an excellent speech-language pathologist is invaluable.

Voice Therapy

Objective voice analysis, assessment, and therapy by speech-language pathologists specializing in voice are helpful in virtually all patients with dysphonia. Voice therapy is invaluable in the management of vocal fold paralysis. In all cases, the speech-language pathologist can provide detailed pre- and postoperative assessment. Such assessment is often of diagnostic value. It is also of great help to the surgeon in objectively evaluating the efficacy of treatments. In addition, voice therapy sometimes avoids the need for surgery, saving the patient from exposure to unnecessary surgical risks. Heuer, Sataloff, Rulnick, et al studied 19 female patients and 22 male patients with unilateral recurrent nerve paralysis and found that, after excellent voice therapy, 68% of the female patients and 64% of the male patients considered their voices satisfactory and elected not to have surgery. Final outcome satisfaction data were similar for surgical and nonsurgical patients.[61] Even when surgery is eventually required, preoperative voice therapy helps the patient while surgical decisions are pending, provides training for optimal postoperative phonation, and prepares the patient psychologically for surgery with the knowledge that everything possible has been done to avoid unnecessary operative intervention. This results in superior patient cooperation, motivation, and understanding through educated participation in the voice restoration process. The importance of this factor should not be overlooked in terms of both the art of medicine and medical legal prudence.

In people with unilateral vocal fold paralysis, initial assessment not only quantitates and documents vocal dysfunction but also explores a wide range of potentially useful compensatory strategies. In addition, the speech-language pathologist identifies spontaneous compensatory behaviors that may be counterproductive. For example, although speech pathology textbooks generally classify and treat vocal fold paralysis as a "hypofunctional" disorder,[62,63] undesirable compensatory hyperfunctional behavior is common in these patients. This is responsible for most of the voice strain, neck discomfort, and fatigue that may accompany unilateral vocal fold paralysis. Such gestures often can be eliminated even during the first assessment and trial therapy session, increasing vocal ease and endurance. Moreover, if the assessment reveals improved voice with a different pitch, training in safe pitch modification in combination with other techniques may also provide rapid improvement. Indeed, under good guidance, therapy sometimes produces astonishingly rapid improvements in voice quality despite persistence of the neurologic deficit. In any case, initial assessment is worthwhile to document vocal condition before surgery is considered and to get an estimate of how much the patient's voice can be improved without surgery.

Most often, initial assessment results in modest but noticeable improvement in voice quality and subjectively important improvement in ease and endurance. Generally, several therapy sessions are needed to optimize vocal function. The speech-language pathologist provides patients with educational information about the workings of phonation, about their specific abnormality, and about vocal hygiene. The importance of and rationale for therapy are also explained. Therapy is directed toward avoidance of hyperfunctional compensation and progressive development of optimal breathing, abdominal support, and intrinsic laryngeal muscle strength and agility. Training includes head and neck muscle relaxation exercises, aerobic conditioning, abdominal and thoracic muscle strength and control exercises, attention to respiration, and various exercises that build limb strength through multiple repetitions with light weights. Forced adduction exercises, often recommended in speech pathology texts, such as pushing or pulling on chairs, must be avoided or monitored closely and used with extreme caution.

Although such exercises are still in fairly common use, other techniques may be more effective and have less potential for harm. When available, traditional voice therapy combined with a few expert singing lessons may expedite improvement. This is analogous to including jogging or running in a rehabilitation program aimed at improving limb strength for walking.

Like surgery, therapy is least successful in combined paralysis. In the majority of patients with unilateral vocal fold paralysis, therapy results in improvement. In many cases, the improvement is sufficient for the patients' needs. When the patient has complied with voice therapy, improvements have reached a plateau and he or she feels that his or her voice quality is not satisfactory, surgery may be indicated.

If preoperative voice therapy was optimal and the surgery was successful, the course of postoperative voice therapy should be short. Nevertheless, the patient is working with a "new voice." At least a few sessions with a speech-language pathologist generally will help the patient to apply the principles learned in preoperative therapy effectively. It is particularly important for the voice therapist and speech-language pathologist to monitor the patient, avoiding development of abusive habits and stressing the importance of vocal hygiene measures. At the conclusion of therapy, objective voice measures should be repeated.

If the patient is interested in optimizing voice quality, it is reasonable to continue therapy as long as it continues to produce voice improvement. This judgment usually is made jointly by the patient, speech-language pathologist, and laryngologist. In most patients who have had good preoperative voice therapy, this juncture or goal is reached within 1 to 3 months after surgery.

Bilateral vocal fold paralysis creates much greater problems; this is true for bilateral recurrent, bilateral superior, or bilateral combined nerve paralysis, or combinations thereof. There is still no satisfactory treatment for bilateral recurrent nerve paralysis. Frequently, this condition leaves the patient in the uncomfortable position of choosing between good voice and tracheotomy or a good airway and bad voice. Therapy may provide some help to these patients, but it is rarely definitive. Hopefully, laryngeal pacing will provide a solution to these problems, as discussed later in this chapter. If so, there will be an important role of the voice therapist following pacemaker implantation.

Surgical Therapy

The two main surgical options for patients with unilateral vocal fold paralysis are medialization and reinnervation. The most common and important techniques for surgical management of patients with vocal fold paresis and paralysis are discussed in chapter 82. In this chapter, we have included only a brief overview of some of these procedures and have highlighted discussions of techniques of reinnervation, gene therapy, and laryngeal pacing that are not discussed comprehensively elsewhere in this book. Medialization procedures include injection laryngoplasty and laryngeal framework surgery. A number of materials have been injected to medialize the vocal fold and improve glottic competence. These include Teflon, Gelfoam, fat, collagen, Alloderm, and others. Teflon used to be the most popular choice; however, it has few (if any) indications today. The senior author (RTS) has not used Teflon since 1988. Teflon is permanent and leads to a chronic granulomatous inflammatory response.[64] Teflon can also migrate and may even spread to other parts of the body.[65] Teflon granulomas are difficult to remove and often result in a poor vocal outcome.[59]

Gelfoam is used as a temporary measure, typically when future return of vocal fold function is possible, but the patient needs or wants immediate symptomatic improvement. Gelfoam is absorbed within 3 months. If vocal fold function has not returned by then, the surgeon must decide whether reinjection or a more permanent procedure is warranted.

Fat is resorbed partially within 3 to 4 months,[65] but improvement may be permanent. Autologous fat is harvested easily using liposuction or by direct excision and generally allows the vocal fold to maintain normal vibratory qualities.

Allogeneic, autologous, and bovine collagen have been used to medialize paralyzed vocal folds.[64,66] Collagen incorporates into host tissue.[64] Some report collagen lasting as long as 3 years. Collagen may be injected into the vocal ligament. It softens scar tissue and can improve the vibratory qualities of the vocal fold.

Medialization

Type I thyroplasty was popularized by Isshiki.[67] Arytenoid adduction surgery was designed by Isshiki as well to improve closure of the posterior glottis.[68]

Some laryngologists believe that, after a long duration of vocal fold paralysis, the cricoartyenoid joint scars and becomes fixed. In this case, the ankylosis must be addressed for a medialization procedure to be effective.[69] However, several animal and cadaver studies suggest that the cricoarytenoid joint remains normal for as long as 17 years after RLN injury.[70,71]

Reinnervation

A number of reinnervation procedures for the paralyzed vocal fold have been described using the ansa cervicalis,[69] phrenic nerve,[72,73] preganglionic sympathetic neurons,[74] hypoglossal nerve,[75] and nerve-muscle pedicles.[76,77] The main purpose of reinnervation procedures is to prevent denervation atrophy of laryngeal muscles. Crumley reports improved vocal quality, as well as restoration of the mucosal wave after reinnervation using the ansa cervicalis.[69] The ansa cervicalis provides weak tonic innervation to the intrinsic laryngeal muscles. Reinnervation of the TA muscle restores tension resulting in a more normal mucosal wave. Reinnervation of the PCA and LA muscles stabilizes the arytenoids and prevents inferior displacement of the vocal process, which may occur in some patients. Crumley reports additionally that the ansa cervicalis—RLN anastamosis is particularly useful in cases of synkinesis after nerve injury resulting in "jerky" movements of the vocal folds. Although there will still be synkinesis after ansa-RLN anastamosis, the weak tonic innervation supplied by the ansa produces a vocal fold that is less spastic.[69]

Attempts to design reinnervation techniques that might avoid sykinesis and restore movement to the paralyzed vocal fold have been reported.[78,79] Hogikyan et al examined muscle-nerve-muscle neurotization in the cat.[80] In this technique, the paralyzed thyroarytenoid muscle is reinnervated via axons that sprout from the contralateral, innervated TA muscle through an interposed nerve graft. The authors demonstrated histologic and EMG evidence of this specific reinnervation pathway in over half of the cats used. Actual return of vocal fold adduction was demonstrated in one cat. This technique of motion-specific reinnervation is promising for restoration of physiologic movement after vocal fold paralysis.

Tucker has reported improvement in voice quality and restoration of adduction of the unilateral paralyzed vocal fold after nerve-muscle pedicle transfer.[76] This technique involves implanting a piece of strap muscle innervated by nerve terminals from the ansa cervicalis into one of the denervated laryngeal muscles, usually the LCA or TA.[77,81] Tucker also reports better vocal quality in patients with unilateral vocal fold paralysis when they are treated with nerve-muscle pedicle and medialization than when treated with medialization alone.[81]

Bilateral Vocal Fold Paralysis

Although voice quality is typically good in the presence of bilateral vocal fold paralysis (BVFP), airway patency is jeopardized by the paramedian position of the vocal folds. Tracheotomy may be required acutely, followed by surgery to improve the size of the glottic airway. Surgical techniques are designed to lateralize one or both vocal folds in order to improve airway patency and assist with decannulation. Voice quality is impaired when the paralyzed vocal fold is lateralized. The most important of these techniques are reviewed in *Professional Voice*.[82]

Cordectomy and arytenoidectomy are the most commonly performed lateralization procedures to treat bilateral vocal fold paralysis. These procedures are typically performed endoscopically with use of the CO_2 laser. The advantages of using the CO_2 laser include, arguably, increased precision through the narrow endoscope and improved hemostasis requiring less need for tissue manipulation.[83] Potential complications include granuloma formation, scar, perichondritis, and endotracheal tube fire. Patients should be put on antireflux medication postoperatively to reduce the risk of scar and granuloma formation.[83,84]

Good results have been reported using the above techniques. However, efforts continue to improve lateralization techniques. Cummings et al have developed a polyethylene device with a double-helix screw that engages and lateralizes the vocal fold. The authors have reported in animals, promising potential advantages of this new device including more control of the lateralization process and adjustability to fine-tune voice and airway results.[85]

A number of reinnervation procedures to the PCA muscle have been described.[72,74,76] Given its inspiratory activity, the phrenic nerve is an obvious candidate for anastamosis. However, despite animal models, there has been no reported clinical success with such a technique.[86] Tucker has reported airway improvement and return of abductor function after nerve-muscle pedicle transfer. However, such success has not been universal.[87]

The use of botulinum toxin injection in the treatment of bilateral paralysis has been explored in animal models.[88,89] Injection of toxin into the cricothyroid muscle results in decreased tension in the vocal fold and subsequent lateralization with airway improvement. The author (RTS) has also used botulinum toxin injections in the adductor muscles (TA and LCA) for bilateral severe paresis to eliminate synkinesis and permit unopposed action of the PCA to abduct the vocal folds.

When both vocal folds are paralyzed in the cadaveric position, as from a high vagal lesion, the airway may be fine; however, voice and swallowing may be impaired. In this setting, unilateral or bilateral medialization procedures may be useful.

Laryngeal Pacing

Functional electrical stimulation (FES) of the larynx or laryngeal pacing continues to be explored as a potential therapeutic option for both unilateral and bilateral paralysis.[86,90-97] FES systems have been used to restore motor function to patients with spinal cord injury, to control heart rhythms in cardiac disease, and to restore sensory function (cochlear implant, for example).[86]

Unlike cardiac pacemakers, laryngeal pacers require both an efferent and an afferent limb. An afferent limb is needed to provide information to enable effective timing of muscle contracture.[90] For example, in the setting of unilateral vocal fold paralysis (UVFP), if the paralyzed side is stimulated to adduct when the innervated side is abducted, this will not result in improvement of glottic competence or voice. In the setting of BVFP, firing of the phrenic nerve, a change in intrathoracic pressure, or chest wall expansion can provide the afferent input signaling inspiration.[86,91] This would result in stimulation of the PCA muscles to abduct the vocal folds. In the setting of UVFP, the contralateral TA or LCA muscles would be the best candidates for afferent input.[92]

The efferent limb of the system may be connected to a nerve, either the vagus or RLN if it is still intact,[86] to the nerve of a nerve-muscle pedicle,[90] or to the denervated muscles themselves.[86,93,94] After a RLN transection, axons may fail to regrow through a neurorraphy or other reinnervation procedure. By placing the electrodes in the denervated muscles, themselves, the system would bypass this potential pitfall. In addition, one would not have to wait for axons to regenerate in order for the system to function.

Several animal studies have been performed to explore the ideal parameter settings for laryngeal pacemakers. These parameters will differ depending on where electrodes are placed and what muscles are being stimulated.[86,95] In the canine PCA muscle, the optimal stimulation frequency is between 60 and 90 Hz; whereas the optimal pulse duration is 2.0 milliseconds (ms). Stimulation intensities up to 6V are tolerated without tissue damage. In a model of canine UVFP, maximal adduction was achieved with stimulation intensities from 3 to 7 V, pulse duration of 0.5 ms, and frequencies from 84 to 100 Hz.[92] In human patients with vagal nerve stimulators placed for intractable seizures, abduction was noted at 20 Hz; whereas 40 Hz was required for adduction. Pulse duration of 3 ms and stimulation intensities of 3 mA were used for all patients.[96] There have been some implantations of laryngeal pacers done around the world in patients with bilateral vocal fold paralysis. Over half of the patients have been decannulated. Patients must turn on the device manually and train themselves to breathe synchronously with the device. In the future, pressure-sensing devices may be added to stimulate abduction with inspiration.[97]

Gene Therapy

Gene therapy may offer future treatment options for recurrent laryngeal nerve injury. A number of growth factors that promote neuronal survival and sprouting have been identified. Delivery of genes encoding such growth factors into host tissue may protect against neuronal degeneration and stimulate regeneration after nerve injury. Shiotani et al delivered the gene for IGF-I in a nonviral vector to the rat thyroarytenoid muscle after RLN transection. Rats that received the gene demonstrated greater reinnervation and less muscle atrophy than rats that did not receive the treatment.[97]

Viral vectors carrying gene products can be delivered to the central nervous system by retrograde transport after peripheral injection into nerve or muscle. Rubin et al demonstrated that delivery of viral vectors to the central nervous system (CNS) is possible through the recurrent laryngeal nerve.[99] This technique could be useful in the treatment of neurodegenerative diseases, such as amyotrophic lateral sclerosis, or for RLN injury with a partially intact nerve.

Vocal Fold Paralysis in Children

Vocal fold paralysis (VFP) represents 10% of congenital anomalies of the larynx, second only to laryngomalacia.[100,101] It is also the second most common cause of neonatal stridor.[100,102] The most common cause of pediatric vocal fold paralysis is controversial. CNS anomalies are the most common causes of bilateral vocal fold paralysis.[100] Of these, Arnold-Chiari malformation is the most common.[100,103] This anomaly involves herniation of the cerebellum and brainstem due to an abnormally small posterior fossa and results in either unilateral or bilateral paralysis. Some controversy exists as to whether the reason for paralysis is increased intracranial pressure secondary to hydrocephalus or pressure on the vagus nerve exerted by the herniating central nervous system tissue.[100,104] Other etiologies of VFP in children include birth trauma, iatrogenic injury, blunt trauma, mediastinal masses, cardiac anomalies, and other neoplasms.[100,103,105]

Stridor is the most common sign of vocal fold paralysis in children, unilateral or bilateral. UVFP also may present as a breathy cry, feeding difficulties, and aspiration. Bilateral vocal fold paralysis typically presents with airway obstruction and aspiration. Evaluation for VFP includes a complete history, careful listening to the airway and child's cry, full head and neck examination with particular attention to the neurologic exam, fiberoptic examination of the airway, direct laryngoscopy and bronchoscopy to assess cricoarytenoid joint function, and to look for other anomalies, and radiographic imaging (MRI) from the brain and skull base through the mediastinum. EMG is used at some centers.[106]

Recovery rates from 16 to 64% have been reported for pediatric VFP. Function may return after 6 weeks to 5 years.[99] Children with UVFP can be observed in most cases, although occasionally a tracheostomy may be warranted. Positioning maneuvers can be performed to try to prevent aspiration. Type I thyroplasty has been performed in some cases.[107] Bilateral vocal fold paralysis typically requires urgent airway management and tracheotomy. Lateralization procedures, such as arytenoidectomy or cordotomy,[100,102] may be performed if bilateral paralysis does not recover. Many otolaryngologists recommend waiting at least 12 months before surgery. However, this too is controversial.[100] EMG may provide prognostic information.[102]

Conclusion

Vocal fold paralysis and paresis remain incompletely understood phenomena. Although evaluation techniques continue to improve, we still diagnose too many cases as "idiopathic." Although current surgical techniques enable us to improve voice, swallowing, and airway, we have not been able to restore useful movement consistently to the paralyzed vocal fold. With the development of new diagnostic and surgical techniques, we will continue to improve our understanding and treatment of the paralyzed or paretic vocal fold.

References

1. Hollinshead WH. *Anatomy for Surgeons: The Head and Neck*. 3rd ed. Philadelphia, Pa: Harper & Row, Publishers; 1982.
2. Kierner AC, Aigner M, Burian M. The external branch of the superior laryngeal nerve: its topographical anatomy as related to surgery of the neck. *Arch Otolaryngol Head Neck Surg*. 1998;124(3):301–303.
3. Loré, JM Jr, Kokocharov SI, Kaufman S, et al. Thirty-eight-year evaluation of a surgical technique to protect the external branch of the superior laryngeal nerve during thyroidectomy. *Ann Otol Rhinol Laryngol*. 1998;107:1015–1022.
4. Crumley RL. Unilateral recurrent laryngeal nerve paralysis. *J Voice*. 1994;8(1):79–83.
5. Crumley R. Repair of the recurrent laryngeal nerve. *Otolaryngol Clin North Am*. 1990;23(3):553–563.
6. Jellish WS, Jensen RL, Anderson DE, Shea JF. Intraoperative electromyographic assessment of recurrent laryngeal nerve stress and pharyngeal injury during anterior cervical spine surgery with Caspar instrumentation. *J Neurosurg Spine*.1999;91:170–174.
7. Rontal E, Rontal M, Wald J, Rontal D. Botulinum toxin injection in the treatment of vocal fold paralysis associated with multiple sclerosis: a case report. *J Voice*. 1999; 13(2):264–269.
8. Tyler HR. Neurology of the larynx. *Otolaryngol Clin North Am*. 1984;17(1):75–79.
9. Isozaki E. Osanai R. Horiguchi S, et al. Laryngeal electromyography with separated surface electrodes in patients with multiple system atrophy presenting with vocal cord paralysis. *J Neurol*. 1994;241(9):551–556.
10. Willis WH. Weaver DF. Syringomyelia with bilateral vocal cord paralysis. report of a case. *Arch Otolaryngol*. 1968;87(5):468–470.
11. Cridge PB, Allegra J, Gerhard H. Myasthenic crisis presenting as isolated vocal cord paralysis. *Am J Emerg Med*. 2000;18(2):232–233.
12. Mao V, Abaza M, Spiegel JR, et al. Laryngeal myasthenia gravis: report of 40 cases. *J Voice*. 2001;15(1):122–130.
13. Yoskovitch A, Enepekides DJ, Hier MP, Black MJ. Guillain-Barre syndrome presenting as bilateral vocal cord paralysis. *Otolaryngol Head Neck Surg*. 2000;122(2):269–270.
14. Plasse HM, Lieberman AN. Bilateral vocal cord paralysis in Parkinson's disease. *Arch Otolaryngol*. 1981;107(4): 252–253.
15. Venketasubramanian N, Seshadri R. Chee N. Vocal cord paresis in acute ischemic stroke. *Cerebrovasc Dis*. 1999;9(3):157–162.
16. Ross DA, Ward PH. Central vocal cord paralysis and paresis presenting as laryngeal stridor in children. *Laryngoscope*. 1990;100(1):10–13.
17. Sommer DD, Freeman JL. Bilateral vocal cord paralysis associated with diabetes mellitus: case reports. *J Otolaryngol*. 1994;23(3):169–171.
18. Kabadi UM. Unilateral vocal cord palsy in a diabetic patient. *Postgrad Med*. 1988;84(4):53–56.
19. Barbieri F, Pellecchia MT, Esposito E, et al. Adult-onset familial laryngeal abductor paralysis, cerebellar, ataxia, and pure motor neurophathy. *Neurology*. 2001;56:1412–1414.
20. Slomka WS, Abedi E, Sismanis A, Barlascini CO Jr. Paralysis of the recurrent laryngeal nerve by an extracapsular thyroid adenoma. *Ear Nose Throat J*. 1989;68(11): 855–856, 858–860, 863.
21. Schroeter V, Belz GG, Blenk H. Paralysis of recurrent laryngeal nerve in Lyme disease. *Lancet*. 988;2(8622):1245.
22. Maccioni A, Olcese A. [Laryngeal paralysis caused by congenital neurosyphilis.] *Pediatria*.1965;8(1):71–75.
23. Feleppa AE Vocal cord paralysis secondary to infectious mononucleosis. *Trans Pa Acad Ophthalmol Otolaryngol*. 1981;34(1):56–59.
24. Magnussen R, Patanella H. Herpes simplex virus and recurrent laryngeal nerve paralysis: report of a case and

review of the literature. *Arch Intern Med.* 1979;139: 1423–1424.
25. Imauchi Y, Urata Y, Abe K. Left vocal cord paralysis in cases of systemic lupus erythematosus. *J Otorhinolaryngol Relat Spec.* 2001;63(1):53–55.
26. Nakahira M, Nakatani H, Takeda T. Left vocal cord paralysis associated with long-standing patent ductus arteriosus. *Am J Neuroradiol.* 2001;22(4):759–761.
27. Johansson S, Lofroth PO, Denekamp J. Left sided vocal cord paralysis: a newly recognized late complication of mediastinal irradiation. *Radiother Oncol.* 2001;58(3):287–294.
28. Coover LR. Permanent iatrogenic vocal cord paralysis after I-131 therapy: a case report and literature review. *Clin Nucl Med.* 2000;25(7):508–510.
29. Conaghan P. Chung D, Vaughan R. Recurrent laryngeal nerve palsy associated with mediastinal amyloidosis. *Thorax.* 2000;55(5):436–437.
30. Lacy PD, Hartley BE, Rutter MJ, Cotton RT. Familial bilateral vocal cord paralysis and Charcot-Marie-Tooth disease type II-C. *Arch Otolaryngol Head Neck Surg.* 2001;127(3):322–324.
31. Lin YC, Lee WT, Wang PJ, Shen YZ. Vocal cord paralysis and hypoventilation in a patient with suspected Leigh disease. *Pediatr Neurol.* 1999;20(3):223–225.
32. Ratnavalli E, Veerendrakumar M, Christopher R, et al. Vocal cord palsy in porphyric neuropathy. *J Assoc Physicians India.* 1999;47(3):344–345.
33. Fujiki N, Nakamura H, Nonomura, M, et al. Bilateral vocal fold paralysis caused by polyarteritis nodosa. *Am J Otolaryngol.* 1999;20(6):412–414.
34. Lardinois D, Gugger M, Balmer MC, Ris HB. Left recurrent laryngeal nerve palsy associated with silicosis. *Eur Respiratory J.* 1999;14(3):720–722.
35. Rosen, CA, Thomas, JP, Anderson, D. Bilateral vocal fold paralysis caused by familial hypokalemic periodic paralysis. *Otolaryngol Head Neck Surg.* 1999;120(5):785–786.
36. Bridge PM, Ball DJ, Mackinnon SE, et al. Nerve crush injuries—a model for axonotmesis. *Exp Neurol.* 1994;127: 284–290.
37. Horn KL, Crumley RL. The physiology of nerve injury and repair. *Otolaryngol Clin North Am.* 1984;17(2):321–333.
38. Crumley RL. Laryngeal synkinesis revisited. *Ann Otol Rhinol Laryngol.* 2000;109:365–371.
39. Shindo ML, Herzon GD, Hanson DG, et al. Effects of denervation on laryngeal muscles: a canine model. *Laryngoscope.* 1992;102:663–669.
40. Flint PW, Downs DH, Coltrera MM. Laryngeal synkinesis following reinnervation in the rat. *Ann Otol Rhinol Laryngol.* 1991;100:797–806.
41. Ward PH, Berci G, Calcaterra TC. Superior laryngeal nerve paralysis: an often overlooked entity. *Trans Sect Am Acad Ophthalmol Otolaryngol.* 1977;84:78–89.
42. Bevan K, Griffiths MF, Morgan MH. Cricothyroid muscle paralysis: its recognition and diagnosis. *J Laryngol Otol.* 1989;103:191–195.
43. Adour KK, Schneider GD, Hilsinger RL Jr. Acute superior laryngeal nerve palsy: analysis of 78 cases. *Otolaryngol Head Neck Surg.* 1980;88:418–424.
44. Dursun G, Sataloff, RT, Spiegel, JR., et al. Superior laryngeal nerve paresis and paralysis. *J Voice.* 1996;10(2):206–211.
45. Eckley CA, Sataloff RT, Hawkshaw M, et al. Voice range in superior laryngeal nerve paresis and paralysis. *J Voice.* 1998.12(3):340–348.
46. Jansson S, Tisell LE, Hagne I, et al. Partial superior laryngeal nerve (SLN) lesions before and after thyroid surgery. *World J Surg.* 1988;12:522–527.
47. Droulias C, Tzinas S, Harlaftis N, et al. The superior laryngeal nerve. *Am Surg.* 1976;42(9):635–638.
48. Beyer TE. Traumatic paralysis of the cricothyroid muscle. *Laryngoscope.* 1941;51:296.
49. Thompson JW, Rosenthal P, Camilon FS Jr. Vocal cord paralysis and superior laryngeal nerve dysfunction in Reye's syndrome. *Arch Otolaryngol Head Neck Surg.* 1990;116:46–48.
50. Tanaka S, Hirano M, Umeno H. Laryngeal behavior in unilateral superior laryngeal nerve paralysis. *Ann Otol Rhinol Laryngol.* 1994;103:93–97.
51. Arnold GE. Physiology and pathology of the cricothyroid muscle. *Laryngoscope.* 1961;71:687–753.
52. Tanaka S, Hirano M, Chijiwa K. Some aspects of vocal fold bowing. *Ann Otol Rhinol Laryngol.* 1994;103:357–362.
53. Dedo HH. The paralyzed larynx: an electromyographic study in dogs and humans. *Laryngoscope.* 1970;80:1455–1517.
54. Faaborg-Anderson K, Jensen AM. Unilateral paralysis of the superior laryngeal nerve. *Acta Otolaryngol.* 1964; 57:155–159.
55. Woodson GE. Configuration of the glottis in laryngeal paralysis I. Clinical study. *Laryngoscope.* 1993;103:1227–1234.
56. Mygind H. Die paralyse des m. cricothyreoideus. *Arch Laryngol.* 1906;18:403.
57. Sanders I, Wu BL, Mu L, et al. The innervation of the human larynx. *Arch Otolaryngol Head Neck Surg.* 1993; 119:934–939.
58. Woodson GE. Configuration of the glottis in laryngeal paralysis. II. Animal experiments. *Laryngoscope.* 1993; 103:1235–1241.
59. Benninger MS, Crumley RL, Ford CN, et al. Evaluation and treatment of the unilateral paralyzed vocal fold. *Otolaryngol Head Neck Surg.* 1994;111(4):497–508.
60. Woo P. Laryngeal electromyography is a cost-effective clinically useful took in the evaluation of vocal fold function. *Arch Otolaryngol Head Neck Surg.* 1998;124(4):472–475.
61. Heuer R, Sataloff RT, Rulnick R, et al. Unilateral recurrent laryngeal nerve paralysis: the importance of "preoperative" voice therapy. *J Voice.* 1997;11(1):88–94.
62. Aronson AE. *Clinical Voice Disorders.* 3rd ed. New York. NY: Thieme Medical Publishers, Inc; 1990:339–345.
63. Greene MCL, Mathieson L. *The Voice and Its Disorders.* 5th ed. London, England: Whurr Publishers; 1989:305–306.
64. Harries ML. Unilateral vocal fold paralysis: a review of the current methods of surgical rehabilitation. *J Laryngol Otol.* 1996;110:111–116.

65. Shindo ML, Zaretsky LS, Rice DH. Autologous fat injection for unilateral vocal fold paralysis. *Ann Otol Rhinol Laryngol.* 1996;105(8):602–606.
66. Remacle M, Lawson G, Keghian J, Jamart J. Use of injectable autologous collagen for correcting glottic gaps: initial results. *J Voice.* 1999;13(2):280–288.
67. Isshiki N, Morita H, Okamura H. Thyroplasty as a new phonosurgical technique. *Acta Otolaryngol.* 1974;78:451–457.
68. Isshiki N, Tanabe M, Sawada M. Arytenoid adduction for unilateral vocal cord paralysis. *Arch Otolaryngol.* 1978;104:555–558.
69. Crumley, R. Update: ansa cervicalis to recurrent laryngeal nerve anastomosis for unilateral laryngeal paralysis. *Laryngoscope.* 1991;101:384–387.
70. Gacek M, Gacek RR. Cricoarytenoid joint mobility after chronic vocal cord paralysis. *Laryngoscope.* 1996;106(12 Pt 1):1528–1530.
71. Colman, MF, Schwartz I. The effect of vocal cord paralysis on the cricoarytenoid joint. *Otolaryngol Head Neck Surg.* 1981;89(3 Pt 1):419–422.
72. Baldissera F, Tredeci G, Marini G, et al. Innervation of the paralyzed laryngeal muscles by phrenic motoneurons. A quantitative study by light and electron microscopy. *Laryngoscope.* 1992;102:907–916.
73. Baldissera F, Cantarella G, Marini G, et al. Recovery of inspiratory abduction of the paralyzed vocal cords after bilateral reinnervation of the cricoarytenoid muscles by one single branch of the phrenic nerve. *Laryngoscope.* 1989;99:1286–1292.
74. Jacobs IN, Sanders I, Wu BL, Biller HF. Reinnervation of the canine posterior cricoarytenoid muscle with sympathetic preganglionic neurons. *Ann Otol Rhinol Laryngol.* 1990;99:167–174.
75. Paniello RC, Lee P, Dahm JD. Hyposglossal nerve transfer for laryngeal reinnervation: a preliminary study. *Ann Otol Rhinol Laryngol.* 1999;108:239–244.
76. Tucker HM. Long-term results of nerve-muscle pedicle reinnervation for laryngeal paralysis. *Ann Otol Rhinol Laryngol.* 1989;98:674–676.
77. Goding, GS Jr. Nerve-muscle pedicle reinnervation of the paralyzed vocal cord. *Otolaryngol Clin North Am.* 1991;24(5):1239–1252.
78. Sercarz J, Nguyen L, Nasri S, et al. Physiologic motion after laryngeal nerve reinnervation: a new method. *Otolaryngol Head Neck Surg.* 1997;116(4):466–474.
79. Van Lith-Bijl JT, Stolk RJ, Tonnaer JA, et al. Selective laryngeal reinnervation with separate phrenic and ansa cervicalis nerve transfers. *Arch Otolaryngol Head Neck Surg.* 1997;123:406–411.
80. Hogikyan ND, Johns MM, Kileny PR, et al. Motion-specific laryngeal reinnervation using muscle-nerve-muscle neurotization. *Ann Otol Rhinol Laryngol.* 2001;110(9): 801–810.
81. Tucker, H. Long-term preservation of voice improvement following surgic medialization and reinnervation for unilateral vocal fold paralysis. *J Voice.* 1999;13(2): 251–256.
82. Sataloff RT. Vocal fold surgery. In: Sataloff RT. *Professional Voice: The Art and Science of Clinical Care.* San Diego, Calif: Plural Publishing; 2005:
83. Ossoff RH, Duncavage JA, Shapshay SM, et al. Endoscopic laser arytenoidectomy revisited. *Ann Otol Rhinol Laryngol.* 1990;99(10 Pt 1):764–771.
84. Segas J, Stavroulakis P, Manolopoulos L, et al. Management of bilateral vocal fold paralysis: experience at the University of Athens. *Otolaryngol Head Neck Surg.* 2001;124(1):68–71.
85. Cummings CW, Redd EE, Westra WH, Flint PW. Minimally invasive device to effect vocal fold lateralization. *Ann Otol Rhinol Laryngol.* 1999;108(9):833–836.
86. Sanders I. Electrical stimulation of laryngeal muscle. *Otolaryngol Clin North Am.* 1991;24(5):1253–1274.
87. Netterville JL, Aly A, Ossoff RH. Evaluation and treatment of complications of thyroid and parathyroid surgery. *Otolaryngol Clin North Am.* 1990;23(3):529–552.
88. Cohen SR, Thompson JW, Camilon FS. Botulinum toxin for relief of bilateral abductor paralysis of the larynx: histologic study in an animal model. *Ann Otol Rhinol Laryngol.* 1989;98(3):213–216.
89. Cohen S, Thompson, JW. Use of botulinum toxin to lateralize true vocal cords: a biochemical method to relieve bilateral abductor vocal cord paralysis. *Ann Otol Rhinol Laryngol.* 1987;96(5):534–541.
90. Broniatowski M, Tucker HM, Nose Y. The future of electronic pacing in laryngeal rehabilitation. *Am J Otolaryngol.* 1990;11(1):51–62.
91. Bergmann K, Warzel H, Eckhardt HU, et al. Long-term implantation of a system of electrical stimulation of paralyzed laryngeal muscles in dogs. *Laryngoscope.* 1988; 98(4):455–459.
92. Goldfarb D, Keane WM, Lowry LD. Laryngeal pacing as a treatment for vocal fold paralysis. *J Voice.* 1994;8(2): 179–185.
93. Kano S, Sasaki CT. Pacing parameters of the canine posterior cricoarytenoid muscle. *Ann Otol Rhinol Laryngol.* 1991;100:584–588.
94. Kojima H, Omori K, Nonomura M, et al. Electrical pacing for dynamic treatment of unilateral vocal cord paralyis. *Ann Otol Rhinol Laryngol.* 1991;100:15–18.
95. Broniatowski M, Vito KJ, Shah B, et al. Contraction patterns of intrinsic laryngeal muscles induced by orderly recruitment in the canine. *Laryngoscope.* 1996;106:1510–1515.
96. Lundy DS, Casiano RR, Landy HJ, et al. Effects of vagal nerve stimulation on laryngeal function. *J Voice.* 1993; 7(4):359–364.
97. Hillel AD, Benninger M, Blitzer A, et al. Evaluation and management of bilateral vocal cord immobility. *Otolaryngol Head Neck Surg.* 1999;121(6):760–765.
98. Shiotani A, O'Malley BW Jr, Coleman ME, Flint PW. Human insulinlike growth factor 1 gene transfer into paralyzed rat larynx: single vs multiple injection. *Arch Otolaryngol Head Neck Surg.* 1999;125:555–560.
99. Rubin AD, Hogikyan ND, Sullivan K, et al. Remote delivery of rAAV-GFP to the rat brainstem via the recurrent laryngeal nerve. *Laryngoscope.* 2001;111:2041–2045.

100. de Jong AL, Kuppersmith RB, Sulek M, Friedman EM. Vocal cord paralysis in infants and children. *Otolaryngol Clin North Am.* 2000;33(1):131–149.
101. Cotton RT, Richardson MA. Congenital laryngeal anomalies. *Otolaryngol Clin North Am.* 1981;14(1):203–218.
102. Bower CM, Choi SS, Cotton RT. Arytenoidectomy in children. *Ann Otol Rhinol Laryngol.* 1994;103:271–278.
103. Rosin DF, Handler SD, Potsic WP, et al. Vocal cord paralysis in children. *Laryngoscope.* 1990;100:1174–1179.
104. Miller R, Nemechek A. Hoarseness and vocal cord paralysis. In: Bailey BJ, ed. *Head and Neck Surgery—Otolaryngology.* 2nd ed. Philadelphia, Pa: Lippincott-Raven Publishing; 1998:741–751.
105. Holinger LD, Holinger PC, Holinger PH. Etiology of bilateral abductor vocal cord paralysis. *Ann Otol Rhinol Laryngol.* 1976;85:428–436.
106. Berkowitz R. Laryngeal electromyography findings in idiopathic congenital bilateral vocal cord paralysis. *Ann Otol Rhinol Laryngol.* 1996;105:207–212.
107. Link DT, Rutter MJ, Liu JH, et al. Pediatric type I thyroplasty: an evolving procedure. *Ann Otol Rhinol Laryngol.* 1999;108:1105–1110.

13

Spasmodic Dysphonia

Robert Thayer Sataloff and Daniel A. Deems

Introduction: An Overview Of Dystonia

Dystonias are neurological syndromes characterized by involuntary contractions of a muscle or groups of muscles. These involuntary muscle activities often cause pain, distort movement, and interfere with function. They may be spasmodic (clonic or rapid patterns), or tonic (sustained), or a combination of these two types; and they may be repetitive or patterned. Dystonias may involve any voluntary muscle and may be generalized, segmental, or focal.

Generalized dystonias involve voluntary muscles throughout the body. Segmental dystonias involve contiguous groups of muscles. Focal dystonias affect an isolated small group of muscles, such as torticollis and oromandibular dystonia, writer's cramp, blepharospasm, and spasmodic dysphonia.[1-9] Regardless of location, primary dystonias usually are aggravated when the involved muscles are used (action-induced dystonia); the affected muscles may appear normal at rest.

Dystonias may be primary or secondary. Patients with primary dystonias have no history of developmental abnormality, neurological disease, or exposure to drugs associated with acquired dystonia. However, patients with genetic disorders associated with dystonias are considered to have primary dystonias. In addition, diagnostic studies to rule out conditions that may cause dystonia must be normal. Neurological examination must be normal apart from the dystonia, as well, with particular attention paid to sensory, cerebellar, pyramidal, and intellectual assessment. Secondary dystonias are caused by a variety of conditions, many of which are reviewed below.

In all dystonic states, various abnormal muscle movement patterns may occur. For example, torticollis involves twisting; writer's cramp, retrocollis, and anterocollis involve flexion or extension; blepharospasm involves contraction and relaxation; and spasmodic dysphonia affects abduction or adduction. The prevalence of idiopathic dystonia in the United States is unknown but has been estimated to be at least 200,000 cases (Mitchell Brin, MD, personal communication, 1997).

The pathophysiology of primary idiopathic dystonia remains uncertain. Laboratory tests and imaging studies generally are normal, although lesions have been described on magnetic resonance imaging (MRI) of the basal ganglia, upper brainstem, putamen, and head of the caudate nucleus. Abnormalities in the sensory or motor cortex have been observed on positron emission tomography (PET) scan in some cases of primary dystonia. In chromosomal x-linked dystonia/parkinsonism, motor cortex abnormalities may be found on PET scan as well. However, causal association between brain abnormalities and dystonia has not been established; thus the significance of these findings remains uncertain. In addition, the mechanism of action and biochemical events of dystonia are unknown. Electrophysiologic studies have revealed evidence of central disinhibition in patients with oromandibular dystonia and those with blepharospasm, but patients with spasmodic dysphonia have not been studied yet.[10] Electroencephalographic (EEG) studies have revealed no cortical trigger, suggesting a problem either in the basal ganglia or pyramidal tract.[11] Autopsy studies of patients with dystonia have demonstrated altered levels of serotonin, norepinephrine, and dopamine in the putamen, caudate, globus pallidus, and dentate nuclei, suggesting that the pathologic defect is probably in the basal ganglia.[12] Although none of these studies involved laryngeal dystonia patients specifically, it is postulated that the mechanisms of laryngeal dystonia are similar to those of dystonias involving other muscle groups.

Familial dystonias also occur and may involve focal, segmental, or generalized dystonia. Severity often varies among family members. Laryngeal dystonia (spasmodic dysphonia) may be associated with a family history of dystonia (not necessarily laryngeal) and with chromosomal abnormalities, particularly involving chromosomes 8[13] and 9.[14] Brin et al reported that 11 to 31% of patients with laryngeal dystonia had other family members with dystonic symptoms and that those with a family history of dystonia had the onset of symptoms at a younger age.[15,16] Brin et al have also noted that family history often is negative, but examination of family members may reveal previously unrecognized dystonia.[16] They also reported 744 patients with primary dystonia involving the larynx, 90 of whom had a family history of dystonia. Of those, the onset of dystonia involved the larynx in 64 patients, and 26 had symptoms initially in other body systems. The age of onset was earlier in those in whom dystonia first affected other body systems than it was in those in whom the larynx was involved initially. However, in both groups of genetic cases, the age of onset was earlier than in patients with no family history of dystonia.

Particularly strong evidence has been put forward for the association of a gene in the 9q region with increased susceptibility to torsion dystonia.[14]

Treatment of dystonias remains imperfect. Some secondary dystonias respond well to treatment of the underlying disorder. One such condition is Wilson's disease, which is managed with medications that interfere with copper absorption or deplete copper from the body. Drug-induced dystonias can be caused by a variety of substances including quinine-related medications, anticonvulsants, dopamine receptor blocking agents, including antipsychotic medications,[17-28] and other medications. They often improve or resolve when the medication is discontinued. A small number of dystonias are responsive to levodopa;[29-30] but for the majority of dystonic patients, the various medications that are tried produce limited benefit at best. Patients with generalized and segmental dystonia are usually treated with baclofen (Lioresol, Watson) or a benzodiazepine or anticholinergic medication. Receptor blocking agents, dopamine-depleting medications, and other pharmacotherapies are used in selected, challenging cases. In generalized or intersegmental dystonia, pharmacotherapy may be augmented with botulinum toxin injections into particularly symptomatic muscle groups. There may also be a place for other invasive therapy, including intrathecal baclofen, deep brain stimulation, and surgery. Bidus et al reported the effects of electrical stimulation in 10 patients with abductor spasmodic dysphonia.[31] They stimulated the thyroarytenoid muscle and cricothyroid muscles and compared voiceless consonant duration with and without adductor laryngeal muscle stimulation during syllable repetitions and sentences. They found significant improvements, and the improvement was greatest in the most severely affected patients. However, for patients with focal dystonia including spasmodic dysphonia, botulinum toxin (Botox, Allergan) injection has been the mainstay of therapy since the 1980s. In general, botulinum toxin injection fails to produce sufficient therapeutic benefit in at least 5% of patients, and in some focal dystonias (eg, abductor spasmodic dysphonia), the failure rate is much higher.

Laryngeal Dystonia

Spasmodic dysphonia is a term applied to patients with specific voice characteristics and difficulties. Importantly, there are many types of interruptions in vocal fluency that are incorrectly diagnosed as spasmodic dysphonia. It is important to avoid this error, because each type of dysphonia requires distinct evaluation and treatment and has its own prognostic implications.

Spasmodic dysphonia is encountered only occasionally in professional voice users. However, because the disorder is so disabling and public interest in the subject is so great, this chapter has been included to provide an introductory review of the topic.

In 1871, Traube first reported the disorder, which he described as a nervous hoarseness.[32] Unfortunately, he believed that the disorder was entirely psychogenic in origin, and that fallacy persisted in the literature for approximately 100 years until Aronson (1968) demonstrated in his population of spasmodic dysphonics that few, if any, of the patients had causally related psychiatric disorders or psychological maladjustment.[33] Schnitzler (1875) coined the term *spastic dysphonia*.[34] Over the last decade, the term spastic has been replaced with the term spasmodic, because the phonatory characteristics are more consistent with speech spasm than with spasticity or rigidity. The literature still remains replete with authors using the terms spastic and spasmodic interchangeably, just as authors are still using the words "vocal cords" instead of its modern day terminology "vocal folds." However, in the latter example, "cords" and "folds" do mean more or less the same thing. Spasmodic and spastic do not have the same meaning and should not be used interchangeably.

The mean age of the patients with spasmodic dysphonia is about 62 years. Approximately two thirds of afflicted patients are female. Onset often occurs slowly over a period of months to years. In cases with sudden onset and rapid progression, a diagnosis of secondary, rather than idiopathic spasmodic dysphonia should be presumed until proven otherwise.

Spasmodic dysphonia is divided into two main classifications: adductor spasmodic dysphonia and abductor spasmodic dysphonia. The adductor subdivision is much more common, whereas abductor spasmodic dysphonia occurs in 10% or less of patients.[35] Adductor spasmodic dysphonia (hyperadduction of the vocal folds) produces an irregularly interrupted, effortful, strangled, strained, staccato voice. Abductor spasmodic dysphonia is characterized by cocontraction of the posterior cricoarytenoid muscles and produces breathy interruptions. The former is produced by hyperadduction, whereas the latter is characterized by hyperabduction, closed versus open vocal folds during spasm. Mixed adductor/abductor spasmodic dysphonia occurs occasionally.

As previously stated, spasmodic dysphonia must be differentiated from numerous other conditions. For example, spasmodic dysphonia, a neurological disorder of muscle tonicity, is a true dystonia. Essential or familial tremor, which can present solely as a vocal tremor at approximately 7 to 10 Hz, can be confused with spasmodic dysphonia.[36] Spasmodic dysphonia and tremor may coexist; and patients with both conditions are often harder to treat successfully.

Other disorders of speech, such as hyperkinetic and hypokinetic dysarthria, also are commonly mistaken for spasmodic dysphonia. Severe muscular tension dysphonia and psychogenic dysphonia are the two conditions most likely to be misdiagnosed as spasmodic dysphonia. It is especially important to differentiate spasmodic dysphonia from other neurologic disorders that may have similar speech disturbances. The list of neurologic diseases associated with voice disorders is extensive (Table 13–1).

Spasmodic dysphonia has been considered neurologic, psychogenic, or idiopathic in etiology; but psychogenic origins are now considered less common. In fact, when the cause is psychological, the voice disorder should be classified as psychogenic dysphonia, rather than spasmodic dysphonia. Differentiating psychogenic and spasmodic dysphonia can be difficult, especially because patients with spasmodic dyspho-

Table 13–1. Neurological Diseases Associated with Voice Dysfunction.

Alzheimer's disease	Hyperparathyroidism	Olivopontocerebellar degeneration
Amyotrophic lateral sclerosis	Hypothyroidism with myxedema	Orofacial dyskinesia
Arnold-Chiari malformation	Hypoxia	Paraneoplastic syndrome
Autoimmune deficiency syndrome (AIDS)	Jugular foramen syndrome	Parkinson's disease
Cerebrovascular accident (stroke)	Creutzfeldt-Jakob disease	Peripheral neuropathy
Cerebral palsy	Lesch-Nyhan disease	Peripheral vascular disease
Cerebrovascular disease	Lingual neuralgia	Progressive supranuclear palsy
Charcot-Marie-Tooth disease	Locked-in syndrome	Pseudobulbar palsy
Collagen diseases	Meige syndrome	Sarcoidosis
Drug toxicity	Möbius syndrome	Shy-Drager syndrome
Dystonia musculorum deformans	Multiple sclerosis	Spasmodic torticollis
Eaton-Lambert syndrome	Muscular dystrophy	Sturge-Weber syndrome
Essential (familial) tremor	Myasthenia gravis	Sydenham's chorea
Friedreich's ataxia	Myasthenia syndrome	Syringobulbia
Glossopharyngeal neuralgia	Myoclonic epilepsy	Tardive dyskinesia
Guillain-Barré syndrome	Myoclonus of vagal innervation	Tourette's syndrome
Head trauma	Myoclonus intention	Vascular malformations
Hepatolenticular disease (Wilson's)	Neoplasm	Wallenberg's syndrome
Huntington's chorea		

nia also commonly have some psychological response to their condition. As one clinical guideline, it should be noted that patients with spasmodic dysphonia rarely have intervals during which they are completely free of symptoms, although symptoms may fluctuate in severity in association with stress, voice use, and voice or generalized fatigue. However, patients who report intervals during which their voices are normal are more likely to have psychogenic or functional dysphonia than laryngeal dystonia. The severity of spasmodic dysphonia varies substantially among patients and over time. It is generally considered a focal laryngeal dystonia. In many cases, the voice may be normal or more normal during laughing, coughing, crying, or other involuntary vocal activities or during singing. Adduction may involve the true vocal folds alone, or it may include the false vocal folds and supraglottis also squeezing shut. Often, neck and facial muscle hyperfunction is prominent. Because of the possibility of serious underlying neurologic dysfunction or association with other neurologic problems, as seen in Meige syndrome (blepharospasm, medial facial spasm, and spasmodic dysphonia), a complete neurologic and neurolaryngologic evaluation is required. Adductor spastic dysphonia may also be associated with spastic torticollis and extrapyramidal dystonia.

Abductor spasmodic dysphonia is similar to adductor spasmodic dysphonia except that the voice is interrupted by breathy, unphonated bursts, rather than constricted and shut off, as with the adductor subdivision. Caused by forceful contraction of the posterior cricoarytenoid muscles, (classically) cricothyroid muscles, or both, it is less common than the adductor form, occurring in only about 10% of cases.[35] Like adductor spasmodic dysphonia, various causes may be responsible. Abductor spasms tend to be most severe during unvoiced consonants, better during voiced consonants, and absent or least troublesome during vowel production. Both abductor and adductor spasmodic dysphonia characteristically progress gradually, and both are aggravated by psychological stress.

The existence of precipitating or predisposing factors remains somewhat controversial. Brin et al report a family history of dystonia in more than 10% of patients with laryngeal dystonia,[16] although the dystonia in the other family members does not necessarily involve the larynx, as noted above.[13,14] Spasmodic dysphonia is associated commonly with antecedent stress, upper respiratory infection, long-term medication use, and trauma, including phonotrauma (voice abuse or misuse). Post-traumatic dystonia is particularly controversial. Articles have been published suggesting that trauma may lead to dystonia.[37,38] However, review of available literature shows no proof, and no compelling evidence, that injuries in patients who develop dystonia are causally related to the dystonia, although there is commonly some antecedent event that might be blamed. This is a classic flaw in logic called "post hoc, ergo propter hoc" reasoning; that is, the fact that event B (SD) occurs after event A (trauma) does not mean that event B was caused by event A. For example, people who develop spasmodic dysphonia also may have had a recent cold, just ridden in a city bus, just lost a loved one, or just eaten a hamburger with a piece of toothpick in it. In an effort to explain a new and disturbing dystonia, it is easy for patients and their doctors to blame it on the cold, bus ride, grief, or hamburger. In fact, it is somewhat surprising that the mistake of associating the cause of a dystonia with some antecedent event is made only in about 10% of patients with focal dystonia. However, the causes and mechanisms of most dystonias in general, and of laryngeal dystonia (spasmodic dysphonia) in particular, remain mysterious. No physician or research scientist has ever been able to cause dystonia through peripheral stimulation or injury in scientific experiments involving animals or humans. Moreover, millions of people suffer throat traumas annually, including sore throats, canker sores, foreign body ingestion, blunt or penetrating injuries, cancer, tonsillectomy, and other surgery. If these conditions caused spasmodic dysphonia, it would probably not be such a rare condition. However, it is not surprising that a patient who develops spasmodic dysphonia has also experienced one of these throat traumas or other traumas (ie, a significant psychological or personal problem) coincidentally in the recent past. Although all historical details should be sought diligently, interpretation of their clinical importance requires considerable analysis and expertise, particularly with regard to establishing causation.

Diagnostic Evaluation

Every patient with spasmodic dysphonia warrants a comprehensive medical evaluation. This should include a thorough laryngologic (including strobovideolaryngoscopy and objective voice measures), neurolaryngologic, and neurologic evaluation including laryngeal electromyography (EMG), metabolic and radiologic assessment, and evaluation by a speech-language pathologist. Most patients with spasmodic dysphonia demonstrate at least some level of superimposed compensatory muscular tension dysphonia. This must be recognized and resolved for the nature and severity of the spasmodic dysphonia to be assessed adequately. Moreover, because patients with severe muscular tension dysphonia or psychogenic dysphonia are commonly misdiagnosed as having spasmodic dysphonia, it is essential to eliminate any contribution made by these conditions to guarantee accurate diagnosis and optimal treatment planning. Patients with these conditions usually respond to voice therapy alone or in combination with psychotherapy. Patients with true laryngeal dystonias often do not improve significantly with voice therapy alone, although voice therapy should always be attempted. Spasmodic dysphonia also must be differentiated from the numerous other conditions listed in Table 13–1 and discussed elsewhere in this book. Therefore, when a diagnosis of spasmodic dysphonia is considered on the basis of history, physical examination, speech-language assessment, and objective voice analysis, workup should also include an MRI of the brain, a laryngeal EMG, and laboratory tests appropriate to dystonia patients (Table 13–2).

Strobovideolaryngoscopy should be performed using a protocol that includes continuous and stroboscopic light, flexible transnasal fiberoptic endoscopy, and examination with a laryngeal telescope. The recommended protocol is described in chapter 4. Careful endoscopic evaluation during various phonatory maneuvers is often helpful in recognizing tremor, neuromuscular asymmetries, dystonia, and other relevant abnormalities. Flexible fiberoptic laryngoscopy frequently reveals supraglottic hyperfunction, with decrease in anterior/posterior and lateral dimensions. Such compensatory hyperfunction must be recognized and eliminated so that the dystonia can be heard and seen well in order to establish an accurate diagnosis. As hyperfunction is diminished through therapy, abductor, adductor, and mixed dystonias become more apparent, as do concomitant conditions such as vocal tremor. Dysdiadochokinesis, indicative of neurologic dysfunction such as cerebellar disease, may be particularly easy to identify during strobovideolaryngoscopy. Repetitive phonatory maneuvers often help distinguish abductor from adductor spasms. For example, abductor spasms may be elicited by repeated phonation of /I/-/hi/, /I/-/hi/, and so on. Patients with abductor spasmodic dysphonia have difficulty with voice onset after voiceless sounds such as /f/, /sh/, /ch/, /h/, /k/, /p/, /s/, and /t/. Symptoms are elicited by sentences such as "she sells seashells by the seashore," and by counting from 60 to 69. The dystonia symptoms are worse typically when singing Happy Birthday. Adductor spasms are more apparent with repeated phonation of /pɑ/-/tɑ/-/kɑ/, and they are apparent typically during voiced reading segments such as the all-voiced passage "Albert Eats Eggs Every Easter Early in the A.M." They may also be heard during the Rainbow Passage, which is a mix of voiceless and voiced material. Symptoms are prominent when counting from 80 to 89 and much less troublesome when counting from 60 to 69. Patients with adductor spasmodic dysphonia tend to have trouble with voiced consonants, such as /b/,/d/, /g/, /v/, /z/, /zh/, and /dz/; and they tend to improve when whispering or singing Happy Birthday. Detailed complex voice analysis including strobovideolaryngoscopy with flexible and rigid endoscopes is also helpful in detecting other neurologic problems, such as superior or recurrent laryngeal nerve paresis, myasthenia gravis, and other neurologic deficits, that sometimes lead to compensatory muscular tension dysphonia mimicking spasmodic dysphonia.

Voice tremor is common and may be associated with spasmodic dysphonia. Essential tremor is one common form and may be familial. Essential tremor is more common in women than men and usually appears during middle age, although it can occur in women (occasionally men) in their 20s. Essential tremor can be generalized or focal, and sometimes involves only (or primarily) muscles involved in phonation. Also it may be apparent only during specific tasks such as phonation. In such cases, botulinum toxin injections have improved symptoms in up to 60% of patients.[39] When there is associated head tremor, laryngeal injections of botulinum toxin have not proven helpful in most cases. Beta blockers and baclofen are helpful occasionally; and preliminary reports of deep brain stimulation for control of vocal tremor are encouraging.[40-42] Essential tremor is usually most obvious during sustained vowels. The characteristics of the tremor can be analyzed objectively, and the tremor is most commonly found to have a frequency of about 5 Hz.[43] The patient should be warned that treatment of spasmodic dysphonia/tremor with botulinum toxin sometimes improves fluency by eliminating spasmodic breaks; but in some cases, it may make the tremor more apparent.[44] Tremor usually is adductory in nature, although abductor tremor (breathy phonatory breaks) can occur. It is heard most commonly in isolation, but it may occur in combination with adductor, abductor, or mixed spasmodic dysphonia. The tremor-related component of the voice disturbance sometimes improves in response to use of beta-blocker medication such as propranolol (Inderal, Wyeth-Ayerst), usually under the guidance of a neurologist.

Traditional objective voice measures for patients with spasmodic dysphonia may not always be helpful in the differential diagnosis of spasmodic dysphonia due to the wide variation of findings across subjects. For example, in a sample of 24 female patients diag-

Table 13–2. Dystonia Metabolic Evaluation.

Diagnostic Test	*Comments*
Serum ceruloplasmin 27-37 mg/100 ml	Absent with Wilson's disease Increased with chronic inflammation Increased with pregnancy, oral contraceptive use Decreased with severe liver disease Apoceruloplasmin deficiency
Serum uric acid 3.0-7.0 mg/100 ml	Increased serum levels Gout Cytolytic treatment of malignancies Polycythemia Myeloid metaplasia Psoriasis Sickle cell Alcohol ingestion Thiazide diuretics Lactic acidosis Ketoacidosis Renal failure Lesch-Nyhan disease Decreased serum levels from drugs Probenecid Sulfinpyrazone Aspirin <4 g/day Corticosteroids ACTH Coumadin anticoagulants Estrogens Allopurinol
Urine uric acid	Increase in Lesch-Nyhan Disease and selected conditions listed above
Lysosomal enzymes in peripheral white blood cells	GM_1 and GM_2 (Tay-Sachs disease) gangliosidosis Metachromatic leukodystrophy Sialidosis
Alpha-fetoprotein	Malignancies Increased serum levels occur in conditions of abnormal cell multiplication
Alpha-fetoprotein Serum immunoglobins	Ataxia-Telangiectasia
Serum lactate Moderate elevation (3-5 times normal)	Increased in any disease state in which there is cell damage or destruction. Muscular dystrophy Myocardial infarction Pulmonary infarction Delirium tremens
Acanthocytosis (irregularly spiculated surface)	Seen in liver disease, abeta-lipoproteinemia

(continues)

Table 13–2. *(continued).*

Diagnostic Test	*Comments*
Serum LDH Acanthocytes Serum CPK Urine amino acids Urine organic acids	Mitochondrial disease
CK (creatinine kinase) Female 10-79 U/L Male 10-148 U/L	Pronounced increase (5 or more times normal): Duchenne's muscular dystrophy Polymyositis Dermatomyositis Myocardial infarction

nosed with spasmodic dysphonia in our facility (RTS), mean fundamental frequency obtained from a conversational sample ranged from 129 Hz to 412 Hz, with a group average of 182 Hz; whereas conversational loudness estimates ranged from 62 dB to 83 dB. However, such findings are extremely useful in identifying each patient's compensatory strategy for managing his or her vocal spasms, in providing a pretreatment baseline, and for demonstrating the effectiveness of treatment. For example, the patient with a very high average conversational speech frequency (412 Hz) also had a very soft voice (69 dB) and was compensating with extreme muscle tension. This produced a high-pitched, low-intensity squeaky voice. Therapy was tailored accordingly. J.A. Koufman (personal communication) has suggested that voice spectrograms of patients with muscle tension dysphonia demonstrate blurred formants; whereas patients with spasmodic dysphonia have sharper formant boundaries but demonstrate "vertical lines" at points of spasm captured on the spectrogram.

Several objective measures were consistently abnormal in our population of 24 females with spasmodic dysphonia. Physiologic range for all subjects was between 5 semitones and 32 semitones, with a mean of 20.78 semitones (SD = 9.19). Relative average perturbation as measured by the Kay DSP Sona-Graph 5500 (Pinebrook, New Jersey) also tended to be very high (9.145). Because the Kay program measures perturbation derived glottographic signals, it is unclear whether these high perturbation values are related to actual glottic perturbation or to the difficulty in obtaining clear glottographic signals from spasmodic dysphonic patients. Bough et al[45] have discussed these interpretation difficulties in detail.

Objective measures also assist in identification and quantification of tremors, which may coexist in some patients with spasmodic dysphonia. Occasionally these tremors are mistaken for spasmodic dysphonia in patients who actually have another neurogenic dysphonia in the absence of laryngeal dystonia. Tremors obtained from our sample tended to cluster around 6 cycles per second.

Electromyography (EMG) is particularly useful in the evaluation of spasmodic dysphonia. First, it is helpful in detecting other neurologic disorders including paresis, tremor, myasthenia gravis, muscular tension dysphonia, and psychogenic dysphonia, as discussed elsewhere in this book. Second, it has specific value in spasmodic dysphonia patients. EMG can be time-locked with a voice spectrogram to measure delay from the onset of the electrical signal to the onset of audible phonation. Normally, the delay is 0 to 200 milliseconds. In spasmodic dysphonia, the delay may range from 500 milliseconds to 1 second.[48] EMG is also helpful in localizing the most active areas of thyroarytenoid, posterior cricoarytenoid, or cricothyroid muscle activity, important information for guiding therapeutic injections of botulinum toxin. For example, treatment failure rate for abductor spasmodic dysphonia is notoriously high. In some patients, we have detected abductor spasms in the cricothyroid muscle instead of, or in addition to, the posterior cricoarytenoid muscle. Injection sites are selected accordingly. Patients who have abductor spasms related primarily to cricothyroid muscle abnormalities also typically show marked pretreatment voice improvement when speaking near the bottom of their frequency range where the cricothyroid muscles are least involved in phonation; whereas this vocal maneuver is less helpful for patients with abductor spasms caused primarily by posterior cricoarytenoid muscle activity.

Interestingly, some laryngeal EMG studies have not shown the anticipated abnormalities consistently in the thyroarytenoid and posterior cricoarytenoid muscles. Schaefer et al could not demonstrate a consistent pattern of abnormal activity in these muscles, although muscle activity variation was greater in adductor spasmodic dysphonia patients than it was in controls,[47] particularly when patients were asked to repeat words and sentences (complex speech tasks). Watson et al found increased activation in the thyroarytenoid muscles of some patients with SD compared with controls but found normal activity in other patients.[48] Van Pelt et al examined intrinsic and extrinsic laryngeal muscles during tests that were difficult for the patients with abductor and adductor spasmodic dysphonia included in their series. They found normal muscle activation patterns with spasmodic voice breaks overlaid on normal activation patterns.[49] Nash and Ludlow reported an increase of thyroarytenoid (TA) muscle activity during voice breaks in patients with abductor spasmodic dysphonia, and a trend toward increased activity in the cricothyroid (CT) muscle during speech breaks, as well. Again, the overall level of muscle activity was essentially normal with superimposed bursts of spasmodic activity.[50] In a particularly interesting study, Bielamowicz et al confirmed that the number of spasmodic bursts in adductor spasmodic dysphonia decreased after botulinum toxin injection in not only the thyroarytenoid muscle, but also in untreated laryngeal muscles.[51] This is consistent with typical clinical observations. Studies by Ludlow and her coworkers have examined the possible mechanisms involved in generation of spasmodic muscle bursts. They stimulated the superior laryngeal nerves of humans electrically and demonstrated an ipsilateral thyroarytenoid muscle response (R1) followed by a later, bilateral response (R2).[52] When the reflex is elicited by pairs of stimuli in rapid succession (rather than a single stimulus) the responses to the second stimulus are reduced. This conditioning effect indicates normal inhibitory mechanisms.[53] They found that the conditioning effects are absent or reduced in most patients with adductor spasmodic dysphonia[53] and less consistently in those with abductor spasmodic dysphonia.[54]

A few additional studies on patients with abductor spasmodic dysphonia have also demonstrated interesting findings. Ludlow et al found spasmodic bursts more commonly in the cricothyroid muscle than in the posterior cricoarytenoid muscle of six patients (albeit a small sample size) with abductor SD; and some of their subjects had simultaneous spasms in the cricothyroid, thyroarytenoid, and posterior cricoarytenoid muscle. One patient demonstrated lack of muscle activity rather than spasmodic bursts.[55] Watson et al reported one patient with abductor SD who had thyroarytenoid muscle activation levels higher than even the adductor SD patients.[48] In a particularly interesting report, Cyrus et al[56] showed bilateral asymmetries in abductor SD patients, with increased levels on the right and apparent reduced movement on the left during phonatory tasks. This suggests the possibility of vocal instability due to tension differences between the two sides. In preliminary data, the senior author (RTS) has studied laryngeal sensory responses in patients with adductor SD using functional endoscopic evaluation of sensory threshold testing (FEEST). The data suggest that there may be higher than normal sensory differences between the two sides, suggesting another neurological asymmetry that may affect control of vocalization. However, this observation must be considered preliminary.

When spasmodic dysphonia is idiopathic in origin, associated neurologic deficits are common. For instance, Finitzo and Freeman[57] demonstrated that approximately 80% of their patients had associated central lesions, with 50% of the patients having cortical lesions, primarily left perisylvian lacunar infarcts. Schaefer et al demonstrated that approximately 32% of patients with spasmodic dysphonia had basal ganglia infarcts,[58] and Aminoff et al showed that approximately 75% of their patients had other coexisting neurological disorders.[59] Although no specific locus in the brain has been identified as the consistent origin of spasmodic dysphonia, it is likely that this heterogeneous group of dystonic voice disorders originates from disruption of complex neural control mechanisms of speech—afferent, efferent, or both.

Treatment

Once spasmodic dysphonia has been diagnosed, three basic treatment strategies have been used: speech therapy, nerve destruction, and neuromuscular blockade. Speech therapy is important; because it reduces the struggle, effort, and fatigue associated with the disease. It also eliminates compensatory hyperfunction, allowing the severity and nature of the dystonia to be assessed accurately. In some cases, especially in milder conditions, speech therapy alone may provide adequate control. Unfortunately, traditional voice therapy is often not successful, although speaking on inhalation has worked well in some cases. Patients who are able to sing without spasms but are unable to speak may benefit from singing lessons. We have used singing training as a basic approach to voice control and then bridged the singing voice into the speaking voice. In a few patients, medications such as baclofen or phenytoin (Dilantin) have also been helpful, but these patients are in the minority. When all other treatment modalities fail, invasive techniques have been used. Combining speech therapy with medical and/or invasive therapy yields greater success than a single treatment modality alone. Attention should also be paid to psychological factors. Although spasmodic dysphonia is not psychogenic in etiology, it is always stressful; and the stress may aggravate symptoms and impede therapeutic progress. It is ideal to have a psychological professional collaborating with the voice team.[60]

Recurrent laryngeal nerve destruction as described by Dedo[61] was considered by many to be the invasive therapy of choice from approximately the mid-1970s to mid-1980s. Because the recurrent laryngeal nerve innervates all of the intrinsic muscles of the larynx, except the cricothyroid, its destruction, by either crush injury or transection was theorized to reduce or eliminate the hyperadduction characteristic of the disease. Although initial data were very encouraging, this procedure was found to have up to an 85% failure rate at 3 years.[62] Aronson and DeSanto also reported that 48% of patients had worse vocal function than before nerve section.[63] Selective section of the branch to the thyroarytenoid muscle has been used,[64-66] and this technique has proven valuable in the author's (RTS) hands in certain patients. To be successful consistently, the operation must involve more than simply cutting the thyroarytenoid nerve. Special considerations with regard to the technique of thyroarytenoid neurectomy are discussed in *Professional Voice*.[67] Other surgical techniques that alter vocal fold length and modify the thyroid cartilage may also be efficacious.[68]

The most recent treatment and research have focused on neuromuscular blockade using a number of toxins originating from bacterial or other biologic sources. For example, alpha-Bungaro toxin (venom from the banded krait, of the *Bungarus* genus of snakes), a noncompetitive inhibitor of the neuromuscular junction, has been used to study laryngeal acetylcholine receptors; and (botulinum) toxin has been used to provide long-term (not usually permanent) neuromuscular blockade for the relief of muscle spasms including laryngeal dystonia.[35,69,70] At present, the most encouraging treatment for patients disabled with severe spasmodic dysphonia is botulinum toxin injection because of its exceptional potency, specificity, and low antigenicity.

Botulinum neurotoxin is classified into seven serotypes, labeled A, B, C, D, E, F, and G. They are structurally similar, but immunologically different. Only botulinum neurotoxin A is approved for clinical use, but research with other serotypes (and other toxins) is in progress. Botulinum neurotoxin type A is a single-chain polypeptide with a molecular weight of about 150,000 Da.[71] The toxin inhibits release of acetylcholine from cholinergic terminals. Its complex mechanism of action has not yet been fully defined. Clinically, the effect is delayed in onset, often 48 hours or more. Botulinum toxin has been used for numerous muscular dystonias, including strabismus,[72] for which it was first reported; hemifacial spasm; blepharospasm; and writer's cramp.[73] It is important to note that it has not yet been approved by the FDA for the treatment of spasmodic dysphonia. Thus, treatment of spasmodic dysphonia with botulinum toxin remains an off-label use, even though safety and efficacy are well established,[74] and well over 1,000 patients have received botulinum toxin for this indication. Its use has been supported strongly and is described in a National Institutes of Health Consensus Conference Statement on the use of botulinum toxin.[75]

The procedure for botulinum toxin laryngeal injection most commonly entails EMG guidance of a hypodermic needle electrode. Typically, a 27-gauge × 1.5 inch needle, Teflon-coated (except at the tip) for EMG recording, is used. In adductor spasmodic dysphonia, botulinum toxin is injected into the vocalis muscle through an anterior approach traversing the cricothyroid membrane. In abductor spasmodic dysphonia, the injection is placed into the posterior cricoarytenoid muscle with an approach posterior to the thyroid lamina[67] or through the larynx from the midline. Peroral routes have also been used successfully in abductor and adductor spasmodic dysphonia, usually under indirect or flexible fiberoptic laryngoscopic guidance. When the cricothyroid muscle is injected (as in selected cases of abductor SD), the injection is performed using an external approach, usually with EMG guidance as described in chapter 5.

The dosing of Botox is based on the mouse LD-50, which is considered one mouse unit (MU). The monkey LD-50 is approximately 40 MU/kg; and therefore, the estimated human LD-50 is approximately 2800 MU. Human dosing of Botox for laryngeal dystonia can range anywhere from 2.5 MU to 30 MU, diluted in saline to yield approximately 0.1 mL. Onset is more rapid with higher doses, but side effects such as dysphagia, aspiration, and breathy dysphonia are greater. It is important to note that the American and British commercial forms of botulinum toxin have substantial differences in unit definition. The British preparation of botulinum toxin is called Dysport. Estimates of the potency comparison between Botox and Dysport range from 1:2.41 to 1:5.[76] Typically, the authors use 2.5 to 5 MU of Botox in each thyroarytenoid muscle for adductor spasmodic dysphonia patients, although some respond to doses as low as 1.25 units, and some require 7.5 units or more. For patients with abductor spasmodic dysphonia, usually we inject 5 to 10 mouse units of Botox in one posterior cricoarytenoid muscle and 2.5 to 5 units in one or both cricothyroid muscles if indicated by laryngeal EMG findings. Results seem to be best when the posterior cricoarytenoid muscles are reinjected about every 3 months, alternating sides.

Onset of botulinum effect usually ranges from 2 to 7 days, although it may be more rapid with higher dosing. The duration of botulinum toxin varies from about 2 months to about 1 year, with an average of 85 days.[69] Higher doses result in longer duration of action but also a longer period of dysphonia immediately following injection. This may be disabling temporarily to professional voice users who may prefer more frequent injections of lower doses.

Until 2001, botulinum toxin type A was the only botulinum neurotoxin that had been used in the larynx. Sataloff et al introduced the use of botulinum toxin type B for spasmodic dysphonia.[77,78] More information about botulinum toxin type B may be found in *Professional Voice*.[79]

The side effects from botulinum toxin are discussed thoroughly with patients and are usually transient. Patients often experience hoarseness, breathy hypophonia, and mild aspiration. Also, occasionally a patient may report brief symptoms simulating an upper respiratory infection immediately following injection. Breathy hypophonia lasts an average of 1 to 2 weeks. Aspiration usually lasts approximately 2 days and is virtually never significant enough to produce clinical pneumonia in the absence of underlying neurologic or pulmonary disease. More than 90% of patients will have improved vocal function. Hence, injections may be repeated periodically in most patients, as needed. Tsui et al[80] have noted that antibodies to botulinum toxin may develop. This generally does not occur with fewer than 300 units of the toxin and has not proven clinically significant in the voice patient population. In other words, it has not been necessary to gradually increase the dosing of the Botox, as more and more procedures are performed, and patients rarely if ever receive a total dose even approaching 300 U. However, our observations indicate that antibodies may occur following much lower cumulative doses, such as occurred in the first spasmodic dysphonia patient who was treated with botulinum toxin type B.[77,78] Long-term optimal treatment requires concurrent speech therapy to optimize vocal rehabilitation and prolong the interval between injections (anecdotal and convincing but unproven).

Contraindications to botulinum toxin injection include previous allergic reaction to the drug, development of antibodies that render the drug ineffective, and concurrent aminoglycoside therapy, because this class of drug interferes with neuromuscular transmission and thus may potentiate the effect of botulinum therapy. Pregnancy and lactation are contraindications, based primarily on a small patient population in which one patient of nine receiving Botox injections delivered several weeks prematurely.[81] It is recommended that Botox generally not be used in patients with other pre-existing neuromuscular diseases such as Eaton-Lambert syndrome or myasthenia gravis. However, the existence of concurrent neurologic diseases producing deficits such as weakness and aspiration should be considered a relative contraindication requiring careful individualized judgment. Although only about 0.1 mL of Botox is injected, it is certainly conceivable that some of this may be delivered systemically and exacerbate a concurrent neurologic condition. Finally, because few data on the use of botulinum toxin in the pediatric population are available, it has not generally been used in children.

There are several reasons why botulinum toxin injections may fail to cause improvement. Misdiagnosis must be considered as one explanation. The diagnosis of laryngeal dystonia can be challenging at times; and patients with other conditions such as psychogenic dysphonia and severe muscular tension dysphonia typically do not respond as well as adductor spasmodic dysphonia patients. Occasionally, patients who respond to treatment initially and have a decreasing response to subsequent treatment may have developed antibodies, even following injection of relatively low doses (sometimes less than 50 MU of Botox, total cumulative dose in the author's [RTS] experience). Failure is also high in patients with abductor spasmodic dysphonia, with accepted failure rates generally around 40%.[82] These findings are consistent with the author's (RTS) experience. Botox injections may also fail when patients develop an upper respiratory infection within a few days following injection. The reason for this phenomenon has not been proven; but reinjection after resolution of the upper respiratory infection usually results in improvement, typical for the individual, as established during prior injections. Failure to inject the desired muscle is also a possibility, although this should happen rarely.

Recently, chemomyectomy has been proposed as a possible alternative to botulinum toxin injection. Goding and Pernell tested doxorubicin-hydrochloride (3 mg) and verapamil hydrochloride (0.5 mg) in the vocal folds of 16 dogs.[83] Doxorubicin hydrochloride (3 mg) and verapamil hydrochloride (3.5 mg) were injected unilaterally into the thyroarytenoid muscle of half of the subjects. They were evaluated 2 months following injection. The average evoked vocal fold tension on the injected side was decreased by 74.7% compared with average side-to-side difference of 12.7% in the control group. Injection did not appear to change the vocal fold appearance or mucosal wave amplitude. The authors suggest that chemomyectomy may have potential as an alternative treatment for laryngeal dystonia. Considering the effects of surgical myectomy, the author (RTS) considers this a promising treatment that deserves further investigation. Recurrent laryngeal nerve stimulation has also been proposed as a treatment for spasmodic dysphonia.[84,85] Friedman et al implanted a stimulator with a cuffed electrode around an EMG needle. Adduction occurred at rates between 10 and 25 Hertz and was associated with improvement in voice quality in the patient tested initially; no respiratory or cardiac abnormalities occurred.[84] Friedman et al reported later on their initial five patients, observing improvement in all cases.[85] It ranged from minimal to marked, but no patient achieved a near-normal voice. Permanent recurrent nerve paralysis occurred in one patient. Cough, throat pain, and hoarseness occurred, as well. In the same paper, the authors also reviewed their experience with vagus nerve stimulation for control of epilepsy in 113 patients. A spiral electrode had been placed around the vagus nerve of each patient. An additional patient in that group developed recurrent nerve paralysis due to a system malfunction that resulted in sustained stimulation. The most common side effects were hoarseness, cough, and throat pain. The authors found the techniques sufficiently safe and effective to warrant further investigation.

Information about spasmodic dysphonia is increasing rapidly. The reader is encouraged to consult other sources for the latest concepts in diagnosing and treating this troublesome disorder. Of particular interest is a special issue of the *Journal of Voice* (Vol. 6, No. 4, 1992). This issue contains 17 classic articles on spasmodic dysphonia, including the National Institutes of Health Consensus Conference Statement on the use of botulinum toxin. It is a particularly valuable resource for those who wish to understand this disease. It should also be recognized that ongoing research is changing our concepts of laryngeal dystonia. For example, Baken has pointed out that nonlinear dynamic analysis of spasmodic dysphonia voices reveals bifurcations.[86] Specifically, voice breaks and interruptions that we have always considered random actually may have an underlying hidden order that can be described using chaos theory, specifically fractal analysis. This strongly supports the notion that spasmodic dysphonia is actually a neurologic control system disorder, a belief that many of us have long held. Careful attention to the latest research is essential for anyone involved in the care of patients with spasmodic dysphonia.

Respiratory Dystonia and Paradoxical Vocal Fold Motion

Paradoxical vocal fold motion (PVFM) is an uncommon disorder that manifests as episodic glottic obstruction in which the vocal folds adduct on inspiration. It was reviewed recently by Altman et al [87] but was described originally by Patterson et al[88] in 1974 as a "Munchausen's stridor," suggesting a psychiatric (nonorganic) etiology, and was subsequently documented with indirect laryngoscopy by Rogers and Stell.[9] PVFM also may be caused by central neurologic etiologies or respiratory dystonia and may have an association with asthma. It has a female preponderance. Most patients are diagnosed initially with episodic asthma, but they also may be misdiagnosed as having asthma that is found to be unresponsive to bronchodilator and steroid treatment.[90,91] However, PVFM may also present as an acute emergency, prompting airway intervention such as tracheotomy.[92-94] More commonly, the airway distress resolves with supportive medical care and relaxation.

A variety of etiologies may cause paradoxical vocal fold motion, and the condition may be multifactorial. Psychogenic paradoxical vocal fold motion and respiratory dystonia are the most common causes. Vocal fold hypermobility secondary to a Bernoulli effect may mimic paradoxical adduction and be seen in patients with Reinke's edema and/or bilateral vocal fold immobility with a narrow glottis. The preponderance of psychiatric disorders even in some recent reports suggests that the supposition of a psychogenic or "conversion" disorder may still be valid in some patients,[87] although these represent the minority of the author's (RTS) cases.[85] The clinical presentation in a number of case reports from the literature supports this concept. Medical treatment of the psychiatric disorder (and comorbid conditions such as gastroesophageal reflux and asthma) is generally thought to be effective in these patients, and hypnotherapy was reported to be partially effective in one patient whose laryngeal symptoms were considered to have a psychosomatic basis. Visual laryngoscopic biofeedback in association with speech therapy was effective as definitive treatment in one of our patients and was partially effective in another; this treatment modality may represent an emerging treatment option in selected patients. Laryngeal image biofeedback, introduced by Bastian and Nagorsky,[95] has been shown to be an effective learning tool for patients to mimic target tasks.

Vocal fold hypermobility secondary to a Bernoulli effect is not well documented in the literature; however, collapse of the upper airway at the vocal fold level has been observed during increased respiratory effort. McFadden and Zawadski[96] reported seven patients who developed acute dyspnea during athletic activities that was ultimately determined not to be exercise-induced asthma, but rather vocal fold dysfunction. Acute respiratory distress due to vocal fold dysfunction also has been reported in cystic fibrosis, a disorder with a variable baseline of increased respiratory effort. It is also recognized that the Bernoulli effect during inspiration may "imitate" vocal fold adduction. This condition has also been observed by the author (RTS) in patients with bilateral vocal fold immobility near the midline caused by bilateral paralysis, amyotrophic lateral sclerosis, cricoarytenoid joint dysfunction, and Reinke's edema (despite abduction). This pseudo-paradoxical abduction must be distinguished from true paradoxical abduction in which there is neuromuscular closure of the glottis. Laryngeal electromyography (EMG) may be helpful in confirming or differentiating this diagnosis in some of the previously mentioned conditions.

However, there is also substantial evidence that PVFM may be a manifestation of a true respiratory dystonia. The use of botulinum toxin (Botox) for respiratory and obstructive laryngeal dystonia was introduced by Brin et al.[97] In their series of seven patients with PVFM, four were offered vocalis muscle Botox injections with an "outstanding" relief of laryngeal symptoms (5 of the 7 patients had additional dystonias). Five of the ten patients reported by Altman et al[85] responded at least partially to botulinum toxin injection into the thyroarytenoid muscle, and two of them had other dystonias. There is also a body of literature that describes peripheral dystonias (including spasmodic dysphonia) resulting from central neurologic etiologies. Kellman and Leopold[98] reported a patient with a brainstem abnormality causing PVFM and suggested that the proximity of adductor and abductor neurons to each other in the nucleus ambiguus may permit inappropriate stimulation from the respiratory centers. The series by Maschka et al[99] also documented two patients with known central neurologic etiologies to their laryngeal movement disorders.

We also report a strong association of PVFM with a history of gastroesophageal reflux (GER), 80% in our series.[87] This observation was also recognized by Newman et al.[100] Treatment of GER without also addressing psychiatric and pulmonary conditions was not shown to be effective. It is possible that increased laryngeal irritability due to GER laryngitis is a contributing factor to the multifactorial process. This laryngeal irritability is a different entity than GER-induced laryngospasm, which tends to cause a sudden, prolonged, forceful apposition of the vocal folds and is frequently related to eating or awakens a patient from sound sleep.

PVFM is best diagnosed with the use of laryngoscopy documenting inappropriate adduction of the vocal folds on inspiration and either a passive or active abduction on expiration. Airway fluoroscopy may also be used in the diagnostic evaluation and has the ability to confirm diaphragmatic dyssynergism with the vocal folds. Flow-volume spirometry may be used to support the diagnosis of PVFM by observing a "flattening" of the inspiratory limb, demonstrating an extrathoracic airway obstruction. This diagnostic modality may also be used in association with a methacholine challenge or bronchodilator medication to rule out concomitant asthma. Laryngeal EMG is especially dramatic, revealing obvious thyroarytenoid activity during inspiration (which may be monitored with contraction of the diaphragm).

Respiratory dystonia is a particularly important cause of PVFM. It is a condition related to spasmodic dysphonia, affecting respiration rather than voice. It is characterized by stridor, with paradoxical vocal fold adduction during inspiration; but phonation is usually normal. Interestingly, these patients usually respond extremely well to low doses of botulinum toxin (1.25-3.75 MU) injected into the thyroarytenoid muscles, although associated respiratory dysrhythmia may persist.[101] A variety of other therapeutic approaches have been used as noted above and by the author (RTS) with varying success including respiratory retraining, psychological educational approaches, biofeedback using a flexible laryngoscope, and other techniques to help restore sensory and motor function and control. Behavioral management may be partially effective in some cases. For example, many patients have less prominent paradoxical adduction during nasal breathing than during oral breathing; and some find it helpful to concentrate on nasal breathing especially during "crisis" situations. Botulinum toxin injection remains the treatment of choice. Interested readers are encouraged to consult the growing body of literature on this subject.[102-115]

Respiratory dystonia should be differentiated from psychogenic stridor and reflux-induced laryngeal spasm. Patients with true respiratory dystonia tend to demonstrate fairly consistent patterns of paradoxical vocal fold movement (adduction during inspiration) during respiratory and speech tasks, although the severity may vary. Many patients have worsening of their symptoms during stress and exertion. Patients with symptoms of a psychogenic etiology are often less consistent when examined videostroboscopically and may be less symptomatic when they are not aware that they are being observed. Patients with reflux-induced laryngospasm have acute episodes of sudden airway obstruction due to forceful vocal fold adduction, rather than chronic adduction associated with inspiration. Laryngeal EMG in patients with respiratory dystonia typically shows increased recruitment in adductor muscles during sniffing, a task during which increased recruitment normally occurs in the posterior cricoarytenoid muscle, not the thyroarytenoid muscle. In the experience of the author (RTS), the vast majority of patients who present with paradoxical vocal fold adduction during respiration have a dystonic, not psychogenic, etiology.

Conclusion

Spasmodic dysphonia is a dystonia characterized by bursts of irregular neuromuscular activity that interrupt phonation. It can be divided into adductor, abductor, and mixed types with adductor spasmodic dysphonia being the most common. A family history of dystonia is common. There are frequently associated neurologic deficits; however, no one site of injury has been credited solely with the production of spasmodic dysphonia. Voice therapy reduces the effort and counterproductive muscular compensation and should be utilized. Psychotherapy should be used, when indicated, to manage the stress associated with spasmodic dysphonia and to treat any concomitant psychopathology. After treatable underlying etiologies have been ruled out, medications used to treat dystonias may be tried therapeutically; but the likelihood of success is low. The present treatment of choice is the botulinum toxin type A injection, which can be repeated as frequently as is symptomatically necessary. New toxins and related treatments are currently under investigation, and human use of botulinum toxin type B has been reported. Selective section of the thyroarytenoid branch of the recurrent laryngeal nerve is an option for some patients. However, the real key to this disease lies in elucidating its neurolaryngological mechanism. Undoubtedly, the future will bring a clearer understanding of the etiology of laryngeal and other dystonias along with more precise, efficient, and lasting therapy.

References

1. Golper LA, Nutt JG, Rau MT, Coleman RO. Focal cranial dystonia. *J Speech Hear Disord.* 1983;48:128–134.
2. Blitzer A, Lovelace RE, Brin MF, et al. Electromyographic findings in focal laryngeal dystonia (spastic dysphonia). *Ann Otol Rhinol Laryngol.* 1985;94;591–594.
3. Jankovic J. Etiology and differential diagnosis of blepharospasm and oromandibular dystonia. *Adv Neurol.* 1988;49:103–117.
4. Jankovic J, Nutt JG. Blepharospasm cranial-cervical dystonia (Meige's syndrome): familial occurrence. *Adv Neurol.* 1988;49:117–123.
5. Sheehy MP, Rothwell JC, Marsden CD. Writer's cramp. *Adv Neurol.* 1988;50:457–472.
6. Blitzer A, Brin MF, Fahn S, Lovelace RE. Clinical and laboratory characteristics of focal laryngeal dystonia: study of 110 cases. *Laryngoscope.* 1988;98:636–640.
7. Fahn S. Concept and classification of dystonia. *Adv Neurol.* 1988;50:1–8.
8. Lagueny A, Deliac MM, Julien J, et al. Jaw closing spasms—a form of focal dystonia? An electrophysiological study. *J Neurol Neurosurg Psychiatry.* 1989;52:652–655.
9. Blitzer A, Brin MF. Laryngeal dystonia: a series with botulinum toxin therapy. *Ann Otol Rhinol Laryngol.* 1991; 100:85–89.
10. Tolosa E, Montserrat L, Bayes A. Blink reflex studies in patients with focal dystonias. *Adv Neurol.* 1988;50:517–524.
11. Beradelli A, Rothwell JC, Day BL, Marsden CD. Pathophysiology of blepharospasm and oromandibular dystonia. *Brain.* 1985;108(Pt 3):593–609.
12. Hornykiewicz O, Kish SJ, Becker LE, et al. Brain neurotransmitters in dystonia musculorum deformans. *N Engl J Med.* 1986;315:347–353.
13. Almasy L, Bressman SB, Raymond D, et al. Idiopathic torsion dystonia linked to chromosome 8 in two Mennonite families. *Ann Neurol.* 1997;42(4):670–673.
14. Ozelius L, Kramer PI, Moskowitz CB, et al. Human gene for torsion dystonia located on chromosome 9q32-q34. *Neuron.* 1989;2:1427–1434.
15. Brin MF, Fahn S, Blitzer A, et al. Movement disorders of the larynx. In: Blitzer A, Brin M, Sasaki CT, et al, eds. *Neurological Disorders of the Larynx.* New York, NY: Thieme Medical Publishers; 1992:256.
16. Brin MF, Blitzer A, Stewart C. Laryngeal dystonia (spasmodic dysphonia): observations of 901 patients and treatment with botulinum toxin. *Adv Neurol.* 1998; 25:237–252.
17. Hassin GB. Quinine and dystonia musculorum deformans. *JAMA.* 1939;113:12–14.
18. Akindele MO, Odejide AO. Amodiaquine-induced involuntary movements. *Br Med J.* 1976;2:214–215.
19. Umez-Eronini EM, Eronini EA. Chloroquine induced involuntary movements. *Br Med J.* 1977;1:945–946.
20. Crosley CJ, Swender PT. Dystonia associated with carbamazepine administration: experience in brain-damaged children. *Pediatrics.* 1979;63:612–615.
21. Soman P, Jain S, Rajsekhar V, et al. Dystonia—a rare manifestation of carbamazepine toxicity. [letter.] *Postgrad Med J.* 1994;70:54–55.

22. Marsden CD, Jenner P. The pathophysiology of extrapyramidal side-effects of neuroleptic drugs. *Psychol Med.* 1980;10:55–72.
23. Keepers GA, Casey DE. Clinical management of acute neuroleptic-induced extrapyramidal syndromes. *Curr Psychiatr Ther.* 1986;23:139–157.
24. Grohmann R, Koch R, Schmidt LG. Extrapyramidal symptoms in neuroleptic recipients. *Agents Actions Suppl.* 1990;29:71–82.
25. Malhotra AK, Litman RE, Pickar D. Adverse effects of antipsychotic drugs. *Drug Saf.* 1993;9:429–436.
26. Kastrup O, Gastpar M, Schwarz M. Acute dystonia due to clozapine. [letter.] *J Neurol Neurosurg Psychiatry.* 1994; 57:119.
27. Aguilar EJ, Keshavan MS, Martinez-Quiles MD, et al. Predictors of acute dystonia in first-episode psychotic patients. *Am J Psychiatry.* 1994;151:1819–1821.
28. Rupniak NM, Jenner P, Marsden CD. Acute dystonia induced by neuroleptic drugs. *Psychopharmacology* (Berlin). 1986;88:403–419.
29. Fletcher NA, Holt IJ, Harding AE, et al. Tyrosine hydroxylase and levodopa responsive dystonia. *J Neurol Neurosurg Psychiatry.* 1989;52:112–114.
30. Nygaard TG, Trugman JM, de Yebenes JG, Fahn S. Dopa-responsive dystonia: the spectrum of clinical manifestations in a large North American family. *Neurology.* 1990;40:66–69.
31. Bidus KA, Thomas GR, Ludlow CL. Effects of adductor muscle stimulation on speech in abductor spasmodic dysphonia. *Laryngoscope.* 2000;110:1943–1949.
32. Traube L. Spastisch Form der nervosen Heiserkeit. In: Traube L, ed. *Gesammelte Betragen zur Pathologie und Physiologie.* Vol 2. Berlin, Germany: Hirschwald; 1871: 674–678.
33. Aronson AE, Brown JR, Litin EM, Pearson JS. Spastic dysphonia. II. Comparison with essential (voice) tremor and other neurologic dysphonias. *J Speech Hear Disord.* 1968;33:219–231.
34. Schnitzler J. Aphonia spastica. *Wiener Medizinische Presse.* 1875;16:429–432, 477–479.
35. Blitzer A, Brin MF. Laryngeal dystonia: a series with botulinum toxin therapy. *Ann Otol Rhinol Laryngol.* 1991; 100:85–89.
36. Case JL, ed. *Clinical Management of Voice Disorders.* Austin, Tex: Pro-Ed; 1995:149–185.
37. Marsden CD. Peripheral movement disorders. In: Marsden CD, Fahn S, eds. *Movement Disorders 3.* Oxford, England: Butterworth-Heinemann; 1994:406–417.
38. Jankovic J. Post-traumatic movement disorders: central and peripheral mechanisms. *Neurology.* 1994;44:2006–2014.
39. Hertegard S, Granqvist S, Lindestad PA. Botulinum toxin injections for essential voice tremor. *Ann Otol Rhinol Laryngol.* 2000;109:204–209.
40. Yoon MS, Munz M, Sataloff RT, et al. Vocal tremor education with deep brain stimulation. *Stereotact Funct Neurosurg.* 1999;72:241–244.
41. Carpenter MA, Pahwa R, Miyawaki KL, et al. Reduction in voice tremor under thalamic stimulation. *Neurology.* 1998;50:796–798.
42. Sataloff RT, Heuer RJ, Munz M, et al. Vocal tremor reduction with deep brain stimulation: a preliminary report. *J Voice.* 2002;16:132–135.
43. Koda J, Ludlow CL. An evaluation of laryngeal muscle activation in patients with voice tremor. *Otolaryngol Head Neck Surg.* 1992;107:684–696.
44. Izdebski K, Shipp T, Dedo HH. Predicting postoperative voice characteristics of spastic dysphonia patients. *Otolaryngol Head Neck Surg.* 1979;87:428–434.
45. Bough ID Jr, Heuer RJ, Sataloff RT, et al. Intrasubject variability of objective voice measures. *J Voice.* 1996; 10(2):166–174.
46. Blitzer A. Laryngeal electromyography. In: Rubin JS, Sataloff RT, Korovin GS, Gould WJ, eds. *Diagnosis and Treatment of Voice Disorders.* New York, NY: Igaku-Shoin; 1995:316–326.
47. Schaefer SD, Roark RM, Watson BC, et al. Multichannel electromyographic observations in spasmodic dysphonia patients and normal control subjects. *Ann Otol Rhinol Laryngol.* 1992;101:67–75.
48. Watson BC, Schaefer SD, Freeman FJ, et al. Laryngeal electromyographic activity in adductor and abductor spasmodic dysphonia. *J Speech Hear Res.* 1991;34:473–482.
49. Van Pelt F, Ludlow CL, Smith PJ. Comparison of muscle activation patterns in adductor and abductor spasmodic dysphonia. *Ann Otol Rhinol Laryngol.* 1994;103(3):192–200.
50. Nash EA, Ludlow CL. Laryngeal muscle activity during speech breaks in adductor spasmodic dysphonia. *Laryngoscope.* 1996;106:484–489.
51. Bielamowicz S, Ludlow CL. Effects of botulinum toxin on pathophysiology in spasmodic dysphonia. *Ann Otol Rhinol Laryngol.* 2000;109:194–203.
52. Ludlow CL, Van Pelt F, Koda J. Characteristics of late responses to superior laryngeal nerve stimulation in humans. *Ann Otol Rhinol Laryngol.* 1992;101:127–134.
53. Ludlow CL, Schulz GM, Yamashita T, Deleyiannis FW. Abnormalities in long latency responses to superior laryngeal nerve stimulation in adductor spasmodic dysphonia. *Ann Otol Rhinol Laryngol.* 1995;104:928–935.
54. Deleyiannis F, Gillespie M, Bielamowicz S, et al. Laryngeal long latency response conditioning in abductor spasmodic dysphonia. *Ann Otol Rhinol Laryngol.* 1999; 108:612–619.
55. Ludlow CL, Naunton RF, Terada S, Anderson BJ. Successful treatment of selected cases of abductor spasmodic dysphonia using botulinum toxin injection. *Otolaryngol Head Neck Surg.* 1991;104:849–855.
56. Cyrus CB, Bielamowicz S, Evans FJ, Ludlow CL. Adductor muscle activity abnormalities in abductor spasmodic dysphonia. *Otolaryngol Head Neck Surg.* 2001;124(1): 23–30.
57. Finitzo T, Freeman F. Spasmodic dysphonia, whether and where: results of seven years of research. *J Speech Hear Res.* 1989;32:541–555.
58. Schaefer SD, Freeman F, Finitzo T, et al. Magnetic resonance imaging findings and correlations in spasmodic dysphonia patients. *Ann Otol Rhinol Laryngol.* 1985;94: 595–601.

59. Aminoff MJ, Dedo HH, Izdebski K. Clinical aspects of spasmodic dysphonia. *J Neurol Neurosurg Psychiatry.* 1978;41:361–365.
60. Rosen DC, Sataloff RT. *Psychology of Voice Disorders.* San Diego, Calif: Singular Publishing Group; 1997:1–284.
61. Dedo HH, Behlau MS. Recurrent laryngeal nerve section for spastic dysphonia: 5- to 14-year preliminary results in the first 300 patients. *Ann Otol Rhinol Laryngol.* 1991; 100:274–279.
62. Dedo HH. Recurrent laryngeal nerve section for spastic dysphonia. *Ann Otol Rhinol Laryngol.* 1976;85:451–459.
63. Aronson AE, De Santo LW, Adductor spastic dysphonia: three years after recurrent laryngeal nerve section. *Laryngoscope.* 1983;93:1–8.
64. Iwamura S. Selective intralaryngeal excision of the thyroarytenoid branch of the recurrent laryngeal nerve for treatment of adductor spasmodic dysphonia and its long-term results. Presented at the Voice Foundation's 21st Annual Symposium: Care of the Professional Voice; June 20, 1992; Philadelphia, Pa.
65. Carpenter RJ III, Henley-Cohn JL, Snyder GG III. Spastic dysphonia: treatment by selective section of the recurrent laryngeal nerve. *Laryngoscope.* 1979;89:2000–2003.
66. Berke GS, Blackwell KE, Gerratt BR, et al. Selective laryngeal adductor denervation-reinnervation: a new surgical treatment for adductor spasmodic dysphonia. *Ann Otol Rhinol Laryngol.* 1999;108:227–231.
67. Sataloff RT. Structural abnormalities of the larynx. In: Sataloff RT. *Professional Voice: The Science and Art of Clinical Care.* San Diego, Calif: Plural Publishing, Inc. 2005:1255–1290.
68. Tucker HM. Laryngeal framework surgery in the management of spasmodic dysphonia: preliminary report. *Ann Otol Rhinol Laryngol.* 1989;98:52–54.
69. Brin MF, Blitzer A, Stewart C, Fahn S. Treatment of spasmodic dysphonia (laryngeal dystonia) with local injection of botulinum toxin: review and technical aspects. In: Blitzer A, Brin MF, Sasaki, et al, eds. *Neurologic Disorders of the Larynx.* New York, NY: Thieme Medical Publishers; 1992:214–228.
70. Ludlow CL, Naunton RF, Sedory SE, et al. Effects of botulinum toxin injections on speech in adductor spasmodic dysphonia. *Neurology.* 1988;38:1220–1225.
71. DasGupta BR, Foley J Jr. C. botulinum neurotoxin types A and E: isolated light chain break down into two fragments. Comparison of their amino acid sequence with tetanus neurotoxin. *Biochimie.* 1989;71:1193–2000.
72. Scott AB. Botulinum toxin injection of eye muscles to correct strabimus. *Trans Am Ophthalmol Soc.* 1981;79:734–770.
73. American Academy of Neurology. Assessment. The clinical usefulness of botulinum toxin-A in treating neurologic disorders. Report of the Therapeutics and Technology Assessment Subcommittee. *Neurology.* 1990;40: 1332–1336.
74. Blitzer A, Brin MF, Stewart CF. Botulinum toxin management of spasmodic dysphonia (laryngeal dystonia): a 12-year experience in more than 900 patients. *Laryngoscope.* 1998;108:1435–1441.
75. NIH Consensus Development Conference. Clinical use of botulinum toxin. National Institutes of Health Consensus Development Conference Statement, Nov 12–14, 1990. *Arch Neurol.* 1991;48:1294–1298.
76. Dressler D, Rothwell JC, Marsden CD. Comparing biological potencies of Botox and Dysport with a mouse diaphragm model may mislead. *J Neurol.* 1998;245:332.
77. Sataloff RT, Heman-Ackah YD, Simpson LL, et al. Botulinum toxin type B for treatment of spasmodic dysphonia: a preliminary case report. Poster Presentation. The Voice Foundation Symposium; June 13–17, 2001; Philadelphia, Pa.
78. Sataloff RT, Heman-Ackah YD, Simpson LL, et al. Botulinum toxin type B for treatment of spasmodic dysphonia: a case report. *J Voice.* 2002;16-422–424.
79. Neuenschwander MC, Pribitkin, EA, Sataloff RT. Botulinum toxin in otolaryngology. In: Sataloff RT. *Professional Voice: The Science and Art of Clinical Care.* San Diego, Calif: Plural Publishing, Inc. 2005:933–944.
80. Tsui JK, Wong NLM, Wong E, Calne DB. Production of circulating antibodies to botulinum-A toxin in patients receiving repeated injections for dystonia. [Abstract]. *Ann Neurol.* 1988;23:181.
81. Scott AB. Clostridial toxins as therapeutic agents. In: Simpson LL, ed. *Botulinum Neurotoxin and Tetanus Toxin.* San Diego, Calif: Academic Press; 1989:399–412.
82. Blitzer A, Brin M, Stewart C, et al. Abductor laryngeal dystonia: a series treated with botulinum toxin. *Laryngoscope.* 1992;102:163–167.
83. Goding GS Jr, Pernell KJ. Doxorubicin chemomyectomy: effects of evoked vocal fold tension in mucosal wave. *Ann Otol Rhinol Laryngol.* 2000;108:294–300.
84. Friedman M, Toriumi DM, Grybauskas VT, Applebaum EL. Implantation of a recurrent laryngeal nerve stimulator for the treatment of spastic dysphonia. *Ann Otol Rhinol Laryngol.* 1989;98:130–134.
85. Friedman M, Wernicke JF, Caldarelli DD. Safety and tolerability of the implantable recurrent laryngeal nerve stimulator. *Laryngoscope.* 1994;104:1240–1244.
86. Baken RJ. Fundamental cencepts of nonlinear dynamics (Chaos) theory with applications to physiologic function in and—just maybe—to the physiology of the larynx. Presented at the Voice Foundation's 22nd Annual Symposium: Care of the Professional Voice; June 10, 1993; Philadelphia, Pa.
87. Altman KW, Mirza N, Ruiz C, Sataloff RT. Paradoxical vocal fold motion: presentation and treatment options. *J Voice.* 2000;14:99–103.
88. Patterson R, Schatz M, Horton M. Munchausen's stridor: non-organic laryngeal obstruction. *Clin Allergy.* 1974; 4:307–310.
89. Rogers JH, Stell PM. Paradoxical movement of the vocal cords as a cause of stridor. *J Laryngol Otol.* 1978;92: 157–158.
90. Newman KB, Mason UG III, Schmaling KB. Clinical features of vocal cord dysfunction. *Am J Respir Crit Care Med.* 1995;152:1382–1836.
91. O'Connell MA, Sklarew PR, Goodman DL. Spectrum of presentation of paradoxical vocal cord motion in ambu-

latory patients. *Ann Allergy Asthma Immunol.* 1995;74: 341–344.

92. Hayes JP, Nolan MT, Brennan N, FitzGerald MX. Three cases of paradoxical vocal cord adduction followed up over a 10-year period. *Chest.* 1993;104:678–680.
93. Lloyd RV, Jones NS. Paradoxical vocal fold movement: a case report. *J Laryngol Otol.* 1995;109:1105–1106.
94. Kellman RM, Leopold DA. Paradoxical vocal cord motion: an important cause of stridor. *Laryngoscope.* 1982;92:58–60.
95. Bastian RW, Nagorsky MJ. Laryngeal image biofeedback. *Laryngoscope.* 1987;97:1346–1349.
96. McFadden ER Jr, Zawadski DK. Vocal cord dysfunction masquerading as exercise-induced asthma. A physiologic cause for "choking" during athletic activities. *Am J Respir Crit Care Med.* 1996;153;942–947.
97. Brin MF, Blitzer A, Stewart C, Fahn S. Treatment of spasmodic dysphonia (laryngeal dystonia) with local injections of botulinum toxin: review and technical aspects. In: Blitzer A, et al, eds. *Neurologic Disorders of the Larynx.* New York, NY: Thieme; 1992:225.
98. Kellman RM, Leopold DA. Paradoxical vocal cord motion: an important course of stridor. *Laryngoscope.* 1982;92:58–60.
99. Maschka DA, Bauman NM, McCray PB Jr, et al. A classification scheme for paradoxical vocal cord motion. *Laryngoscope.* 1997;107:1429–1435.
100. Newman KB, Mason UG III, Schmaling KB. Clinical features of vocal cord dysfunction. *Am J Respir Crit Care Med.* 1995;152:1382–1386.
101. Blitzer A, Brin MF, Sasaki CT, Fahn S, Harris KS. *Neurologic Disorders of the Larynx.* New York, NY: Thieme Medical Publishers; 1992:225
102. Martin RJ, Blager FB, Gay, ML, Wood RP. Paradoxic vocal cord motion in presumed asthmatics. *Semin Respir Med.* 1987;8(4):332–338.
103. Aronson, A. *Clinical Voice Disorders.* New York, NY. Thieme; 1990.
104. Austin J H, Ausubel P. Enhanced respiratory muscular function in normal adults after lessons in proprioceptive musculoskeletal education without exercises. *Chest.* 1992;102:486–490.
105. Garibaldi E, LeBlance G, Hibbett A, et al. Exercise-induced paradoxical vocal cord dysfunction: diagnosis with videostroboscopic endoscopy and treatment with clostridium toxin. *Allergy Clin Immunol.* 1993;91–200.
106. Blager FB. Treatment of paradoxical vocal cord dysfunction. *Voice and Voice Disorders, SID3 Newsletter* 1995;5:8–11.
107. Reisner C, Borish L. Heliox therapy for acute vocal cord dysfunction. *Chest.* 1995;108:1477.
108. Gallivan GJ, Hoffman L, Gallivan KH. Episodic paroxysmal laryngospasm: voice and pulmonary assessment and management. *J Voice.* 1996;10:93–105.
109. Brugman SM, Howell JH, Mahler JL, et al. A prospective study of the diagnostic features of adolescent vocal cord dysfunction. *Amer J Respir Crit Care Med.* 1997; 155:A973.
110. Pinho SMR, Tsuji DH, Sennes L, Menezes M. Paradoxical vocal fold movement: a case report. *J Voice.* 1997; 11:368–372.
111. Brugman SM, Simons SM. Vocal cord dysfunction: don't mistake it for asthma. *Physician Sports Med.* 1998; 26:1–14.
112. Christopher KL, Wood RP Jr, Eckert RC, et al. Vocal cord dysfunction presenting as asthma. *New Engl J Med.* 1998;308:1566–1570.
113. Andrianopoulos MV, Gallivan GJ, Gallivan KH. PVCM, PVCD, EPL, and irritable larynx syndrome: what are we talking about and how do we treat it? *J Voice.* 2000;14:607–618.
114. Morrison M, Rammage L, Emami AJ. The irritable larynx syndrome. *J Voice.* 1999;13:612–617.
115. Altman KW, Mirza N, Ruiz C, Sataloff RT. Paradoxical vocal fold motion: presentation and treatment options. *J Voice.* 2000;14(1):99–103.

14

Structural Abnormalities of the Larynx

Robert Thayer Sataloff

This chapter discusses selected common and/or important structural abnormalities of the larynx that may affect the voice. There are many others, of course; but those discussed in this chapter have been selected for their relevance to professional singers and actors or because of their incidence, unusual presentation, or special rehabilitation problems. A few selected structural abnormalities and their surgical treatment are discussed in subsequent chapters. This chapter briefly addresses principles and selected details of nonsurgical treatments.

Vocal Nodules

Vocal fold nodules are ordinarily caused by voice abuse. Normally, they are bilateral, fairly symmetrical, solid benign masses at the junctions of the anterior and middle thirds of the vocal folds (Figs 14–1, 14–2, 14–3). Functionally, this is the midpoint of the musculomembranous portion of the vocal fold, the area known as the "striking zone." It is the area of maximal excursion and most forceful contact during phonation. Typically, these whitish masses increase the mass and stiffness of the vocal fold cover, interfering with the vibration and causing hoarseness and breathiness. They may be fibrotic, and thickening or reduplication of the basement membrane is common (Dr. Steven Gray, personal communication, June 1995). These and other consequences of vocal fold trauma are discussed more fully in chapter 10. Occasionally, laryngoscopy reveals asymptomatic vocal fold nodules that do not appear to interfere with voice production. In such cases, the nodules should not be treated surgically. Some famous and successful singers have had untreated vocal nodules. However, in most cases, nodules are associated with hoarseness, breathiness, loss of range, and vocal fatigue. They may be due to abuse of the voice during speaking or singing. Caution must be exercised in diagnosing small nodules in patients who have been singing actively. Many singers develop bilateral, symmetrical, soft swellings in the striking zone following heavy voice use. There is no evidence to suggest that singers with such "physiologic swellings" are predisposed toward development of vocal nodules. At present, the condition is generally considered to be within normal limits. The physiologic swelling usually disappears during 24 to 48 hours of rest from heavy voice use. Care must be taken not to frighten the patient or embarrass the physician by misdiagnosing physiologic swelling as vocal nodules. Strobovideolaryngoscopy is essential for accurate diagnosis of vocal nodules.[1-5] Without strobovideolaryngoscopy, vocal fold cysts and other lesions will be misdiagnosed routinely as vocal nodules. Because the conditions respond differently to treatment, accurate differentiation is essential.

Nodules carry a great stigma among singers and actors, and the psychological impact of the diagnosis should not be underestimated. When nodules are present, the patient should be informed with the same gentle caution used in telling a patient that he or she has cancer. Voice therapy always should be tried as the initial therapeutic modality and will cure the vast majority of patients, even if the nodules look firm and have been present for many months or years. Even for those who eventually need surgical excision of their nodules, preoperative voice therapy is essential to help prevent recurrence of the nodules.

Surgery for vocal fold nodules should be avoided whenever possible and should virtually never be performed without an adequate trial of expert voice therapy including patient compliance with therapeutic suggestions. A minimum of 6 to 12 weeks of observa-

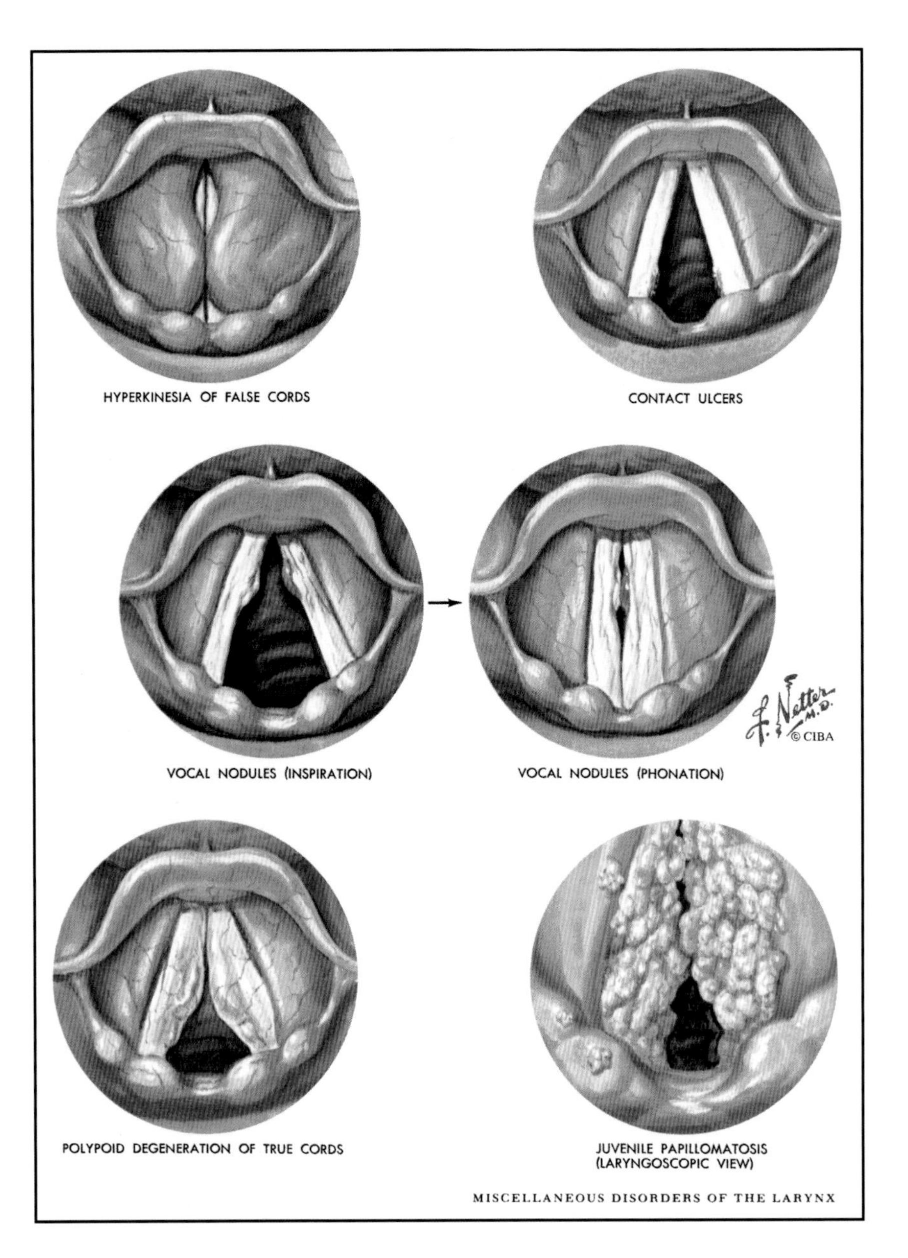

Fig 14–1. Miscellaneous disorders of the larynx. Hyperkinesia of the false vocal folds is seen in hyperfunctional voice abuse. In its more severe form, phonation may actually occur primarily with the false vocal folds. This condition is known as *dysphonia plica ventricularis. Contact ulcers* occur in the posterior portion of the vocal folds, generally in the cartilaginous portion. *Vocal fold nodules* are smooth, reasonably symmetrical benign masses at the junction of the anterior and middle thirds of the vocal folds. Although Netter's classic drawing is labeled "vocal nodules," the mass on the right appears hemorrhagic in origin. It may be a hemorrhagic cyst or fibrotic hematoma from hemorrhage of one of the prominent blood vessels on the superior surface. The mass on the left has the typical appearance of a reactive vocal nodule. The illustration of vocal nodules during phonation shows failure of glottic closure anterior and posterior to the masses. This is responsible for the breathiness heard in the voices of patients with nodules. Polypoid degeneration, *Reinke's edema,* has a typical floppy "elephant ear" appearance. *Juvenile papillomatosis* is a viral disease. This disease and its treatment frequently result in permanent disturbance of the voice. (From The larynx. In: *Clinical Symposia*. Summit, NJ: CIBA Pharmaceutical Company; 1964:16[3]: Plate VIII. Copyright 1964 Icon Learning Systems, LLC, a subsidiary of MediMedia USA, Inc. Reprinted with permission from ICON Learning Systems, LLC, illustrated by Frank Netter, MD. All rights reserved.)

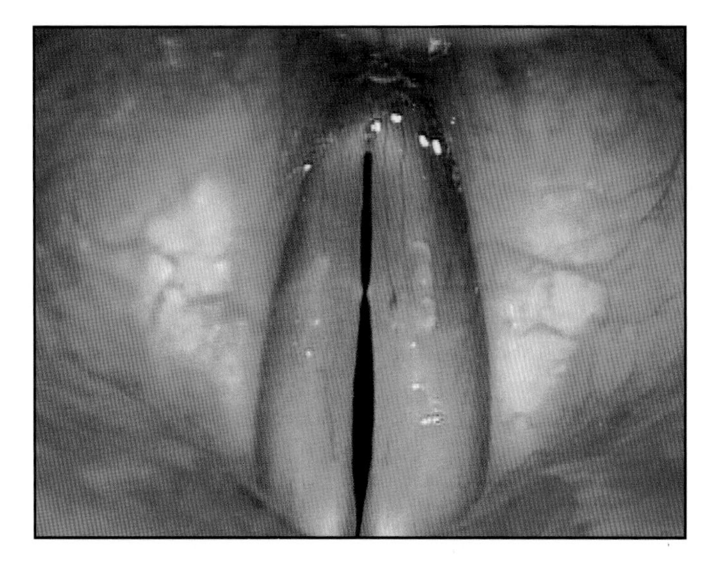

Fig 14–2. Typical appearance of vocal nodules.

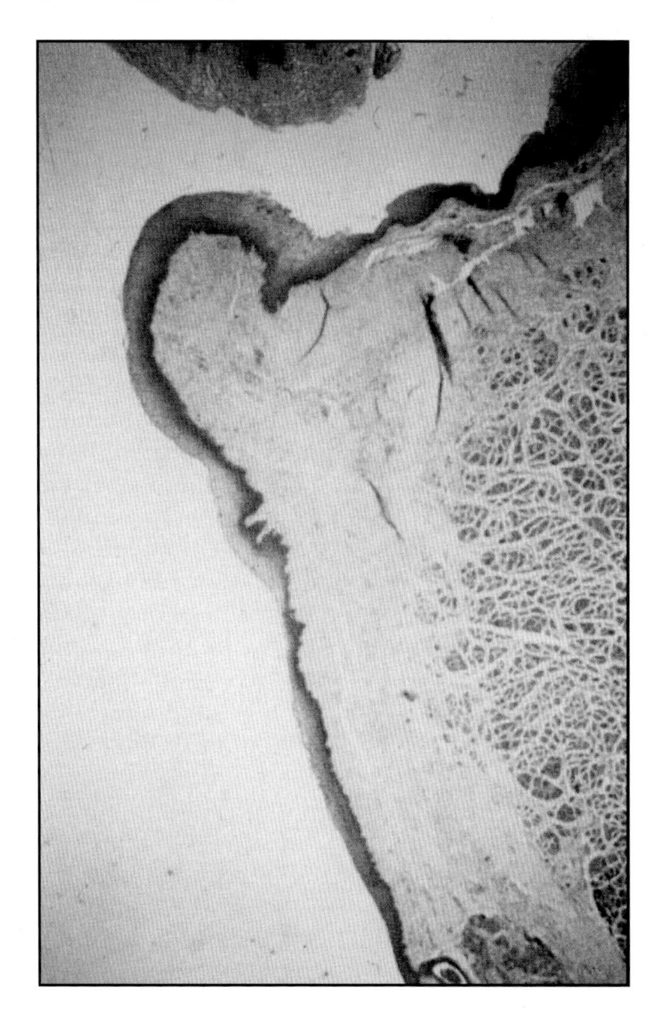

Fig 14–3. Typical histologic appearance of a vocal fold nodule. The lesion is sessile and involves the epithelium and superficial layer of the lamina propria. The lesion contains collagenous fibers and edema. Intermediate and deep layers of the lamina propria are not involved. (Courtesy of Minoru Hirano, MD.)

tion should be allowed while the patient is using therapeutically modified voice techniques under the supervision of a speech-language pathologist and ideally a singing voice specialist. Proper voice use rather than voice rest (silence) is correct therapy. It has been recognized for many years and is effective in curing vocal nodules.[1,2,4,6-19] In our hands, nodules are cured by therapy alone in more than 90% of cases. However, this success rate depends on accurate diagnosis (eg, differentiating nodules from cysts), which cannot be accomplished without strobovideolaryngoscopy.[20,21]

Vocal nodules in children represent a special case. There are differing opinions on management, and especially on the efficacy of voice therapy. In the United States, the consensus has been that nodules should generally not be operated on until after puberty. In the author's opinion, children with vocal nodules should be treated, especially if they are bothered by their dysphonia. Dysphonia commonly results in teasing by other children, exclusion from activities such as plays and choirs, and other hardships that should not be allowed to mar childhood. Treatment begins with accurate diagnosis. Stroboscopy can be performed easily on most children over the age of 6, and we have used this diagnostic technique successfully on children as young as 6 months. Once it is clear that the masses are nodules rather than cysts, treatment should start with voice therapy. Successful therapy generally requires treating the whole family, not just the child. Frequently, voice abuses are learned behavior. The patient should be instructed to monitor the vocal behavior of other family members (gold stars for mom when she doesn't yell) just as other family members help monitor his or her vocalization and remind the child about proper voice use and avoidance of abuse. If the voice therapy results in behavioral modification and proper voice use is carried over into daily life but the nodules persist and symptoms remain disturbing, surgical excision is reasonable. If the child is close to puberty and not terribly disturbed by the phonatory quality, waiting until after voice mutation is also reasonable and often results in spontaneous voice improvement. It should be noted that there may be at least a theoretical advantage to operating on younger children, although it has not been tested or even explored clinically. Hirano has shown that the layered structure of the vocal ligament (layered structure of the lamina propria)[22] does not begin to develop until approximately 6 to 8 years of age. One might suspect, then, that the risk if scarring and permanent dysphonia might be lower if surgery were performed prior to that time. However, this notion must be considered purely speculative. Permanent destruction of voice quality is not a rare complication of surgery on the vocal fold. Even after expert surgery, this may be caused by submucosal scarring, resulting in an adynamic segment along the vibratory margin of the vocal fold. This situation results in a hoarse voice with vocal folds that appear normal with regular light, although under stroboscopic light the adynamic segment is obvious. There is no reliable cure for this complication. Consequently, even large, apparently fibrotic nodules of long standing should be given a chance to resolve without surgery. In some cases, the nodules remain but become asymptomatic, with voice quality returning to normal. Stroboscopy in these patients usually reveals that the nodules are on the superior surface rather than the leading edge of the vocal folds during proper, relaxed phonation (although they may be on the contact surface and symptomatic when hyperfunctional voice technique is used and the larynx is forced down).

Vocal Fold Cysts

Vocal fold cysts are generally unilateral, although they can cause contact swelling on the contralateral side (Fig 14–4). They may also be bilateral (Fig 14–5). They are frequently misdiagnosed as vocal nodules initially. Cysts commonly protrude onto the vibratory margin (Fig 14–6), increase the mass of the cover, and sometimes increase stiffness (particularly when they were associated with hemorrhage initially; Fig 14–7). Whether they are unilateral or bilateral, they may cause bilateral vibratory interference. Usually, they involve the superficial layer of the lamina propria, but in uncommon cases they may be attached to the vocal ligament. Cysts are often caused by trauma that blocks a mucous gland duct. However, other etiologies are possible. Cysts may be congenital or acquired. Acquired cysts may have epithelial linings and can be glandular, ciliary, or oncolytic. Most are probably retention cysts and are filled with mucoid fluid. Congenital cysts are generally epidermoid, lined with squamous or respiratory epithelium (Fig 14–8). They may contain caseous material. Cysts are generally easy to differentiate from nodules by strobovideolaryngoscopy. This examination reveals the mass to be fluid-filled. A cyst should also be suspected when "nodules" are diagnosed and only one side resolves after voice therapy. The persistent lesion frequently turns out to be a fluid-filled cyst. Cysts generally require surgery, although the patient should undergo a trial of voice therapy first. The author generally tentatively schedules surgery to be performed 4 to 6 weeks after the time of diagnosis, with a preoperative examination following the trial of voice therapy. Occasion-

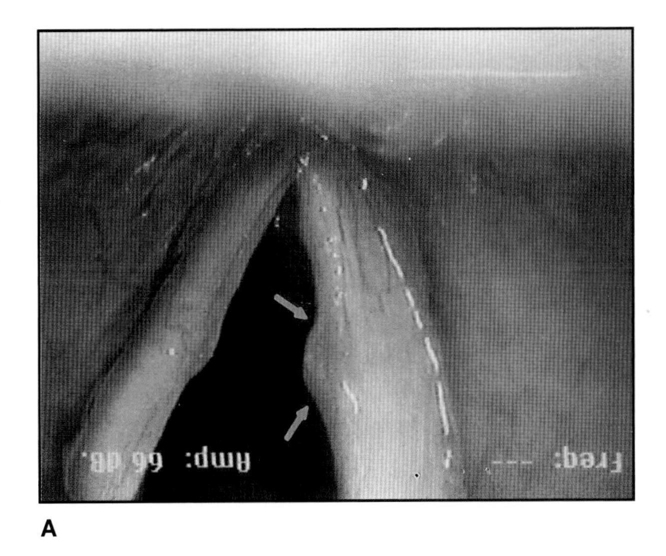

A

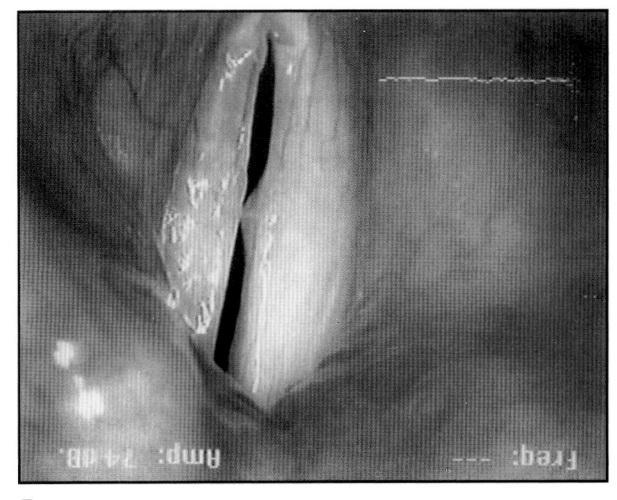

B

Fig 14–4. Videoprint showing right vocal fold fluid-filled cyst (*white arrows*) and a left reactive nodule in abduction (**A**) and adduction (**B**), in a 52-year-old singing teacher and former Metropolitan Opera lead singer. In adduction, the shape of the mass is slightly different from that in abduction, due to shifting the fluid within the mass. Both masses required microsurgical removal, although in some cases the reactive mass will resolve following voice therapy and excision of the cyst.

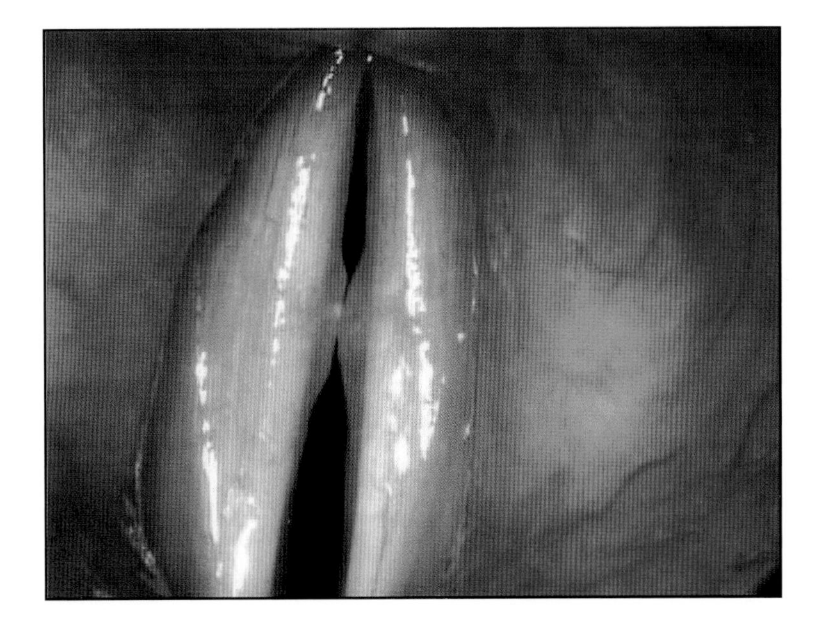

Fig 14–5. This 29-year-old female is a high school mathematics teacher, aerobics instructor, sales representative, cheerleader, and cheerleading coach. She has a 5-year history of hoarseness. Her voice worsened following extensive use. She had previously been told that she had vocal nodules. Strobovideolaryngoscopy revealed bilateral, slightly asymmetric, fluid-filled masses that deformed with contact. However, they were large enough to interfere with vibration and prevent glottic closure. The left mass was clearly a cyst or a soft reactive nodule. Voice therapy resulted in no significant improvement. The above videoprint was taken at the time of microlaryngoscopy. At the time of surgery, both masses were found to be fluid-filled cysts. She healed well after resection of both masses, and her voice is within normal limits.

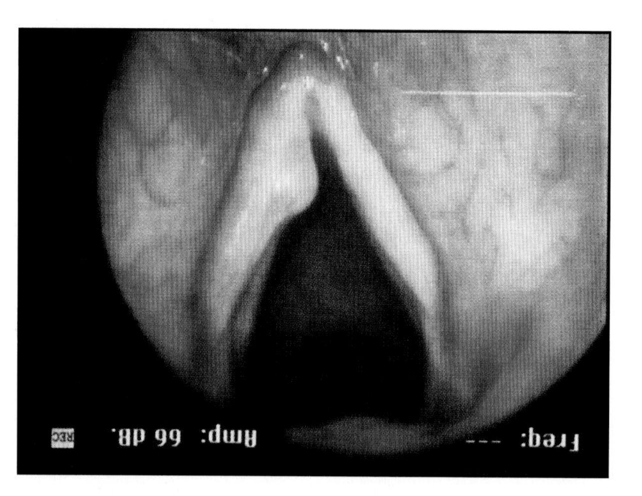

Fig 14–6. This 47-year-old professional popular singer has a 17-year history of hoarseness. In January 1994, he developed gradually worsening hoarseness, raspiness, and inability to sing. His vocal deterioration plateaued several months before our examination in August 1995. The videoprint reveals a left vocal cyst, which did not respond to voice therapy. The patient underwent excision of the left vocal fold cyst, which contained milky fluid. The cyst was removed with overlaying mucosa, but without disturbing any normal surrounding tissues. He recovered well and was able to resume his professional career.

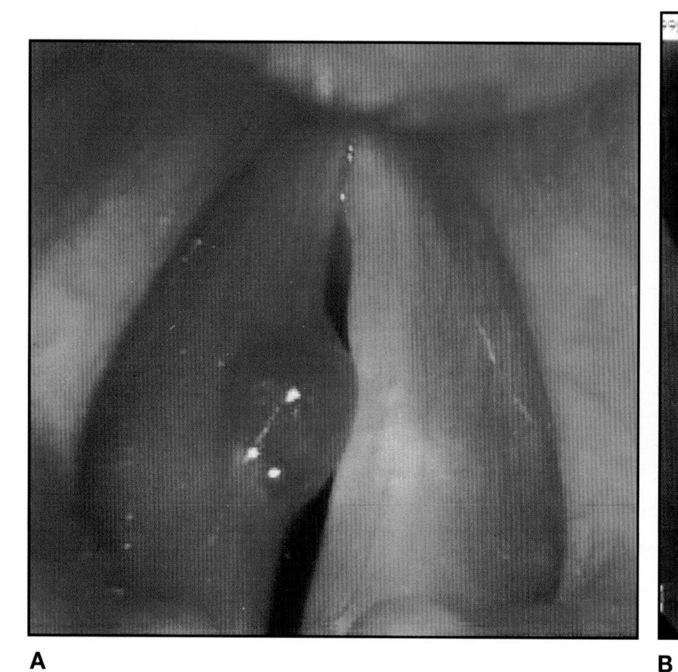

A

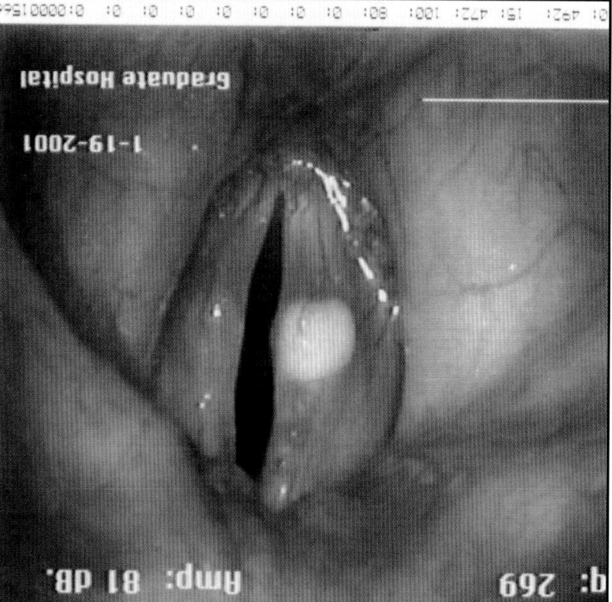

B

Fig 14–7. A. Videoprint showing left post-hemorrhagic vocal fold cyst and resolving hemorrhage with minimal contact-induced swelling of the right vocal fold. Following complete resolution of the hemorrhage, mild stiffness remained persistent anterior and posterior to the mass, but severe at the base of the mass. However, phonation improved to normal for this patient's purpose as a university professor and a lecturer. **B.** This figure shows the typical appearance of a right epithelial cyst involving the superior surface and vibratory margin.

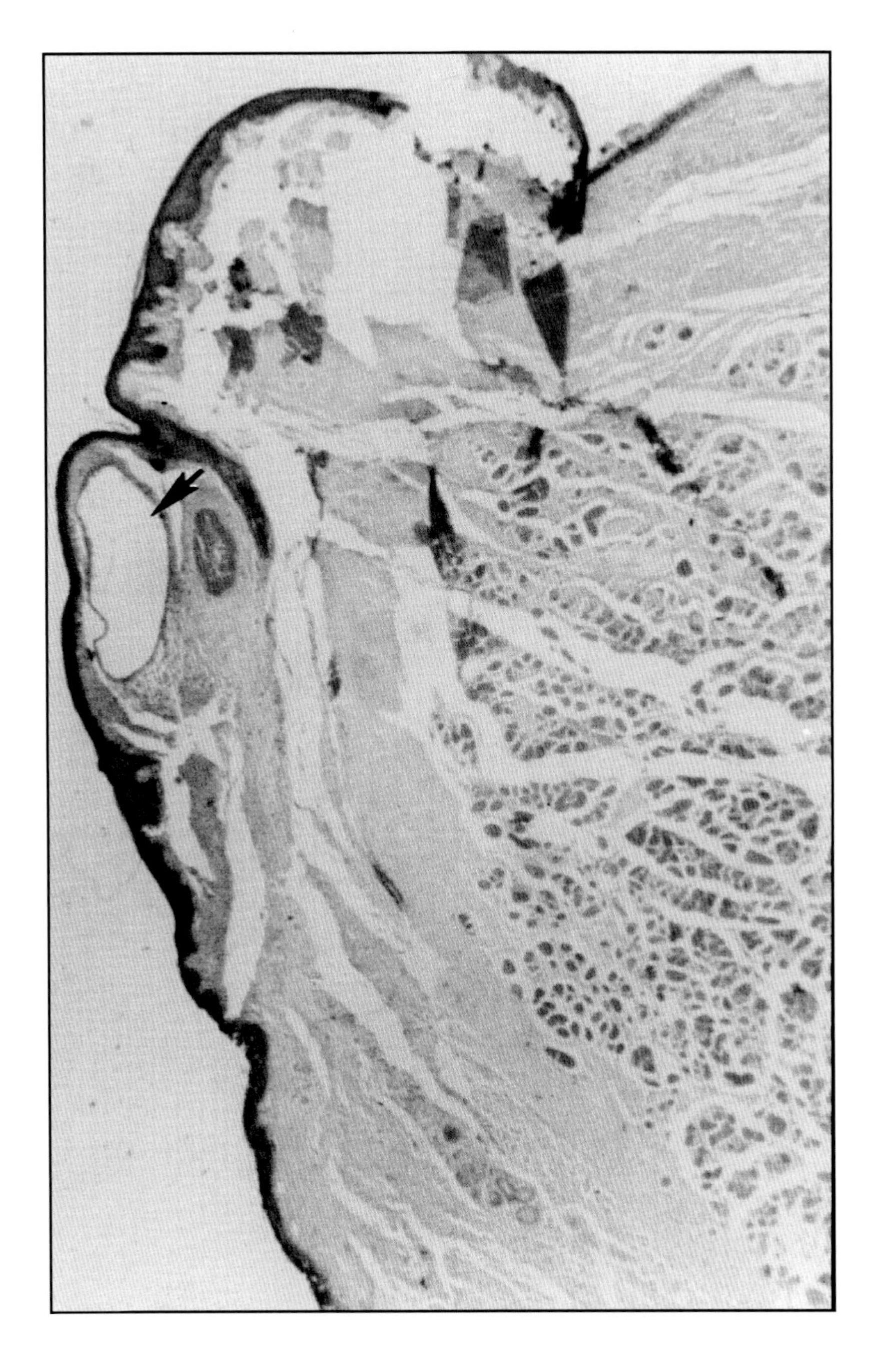

Fig 14–8. Typical histological appearance of a vocal fold cyst (*arrow*). It involves the superficial layer of the lamina propria and epithelium, probably extended into deeper layers. They generally have a squamous epithelial cyst wall. Cysts of epidermoid origin have caseous contents. Retention cysts are filled with mucoid material; and posthemorrhagic cysts contain evidence of blood products. (Courtesy of Minoru Hirano, MD.)

ally, the cyst disappears and does not recur or becomes asymptomatic. Although most diagnosed cysts occur on the vocal fold, it should also be recognized that cysts occur commonly on the ventricular fold and epiglottis, as well. Cysts in these areas are probably more common than appreciated, but they often go unrecognized because they are asymptomatic. Histologically, they are generally similar to acquired vocal fold cysts, although epiglottic cysts may also contain lymphoid stroma.

Vocal Fold Polyps

Many other structural lesions may appear on the vocal folds, of course, and not all respond to nonsurgical therapy. Polyps are usually unilateral, and they often have a prominent feeding blood vessel coursing along the superior surface of the vocal fold and entering the base of the polyps (Figs 14–1, 14–9, 14–10, 14–11, 14–12, 14–13, 14–14, 14–15). The etiology of vocal fold polyps often remains unknown. Some appear to be traumatic. Some are clearly preceded by localized vocal fold hemorrhage.

Polyps may be loose, gelatinous masses, fibrinoid, or hyaline. Polyps have also been classified as angiomatous, mucoid, and myxomatous. They are generally unilateral and may be extremely small, or in-

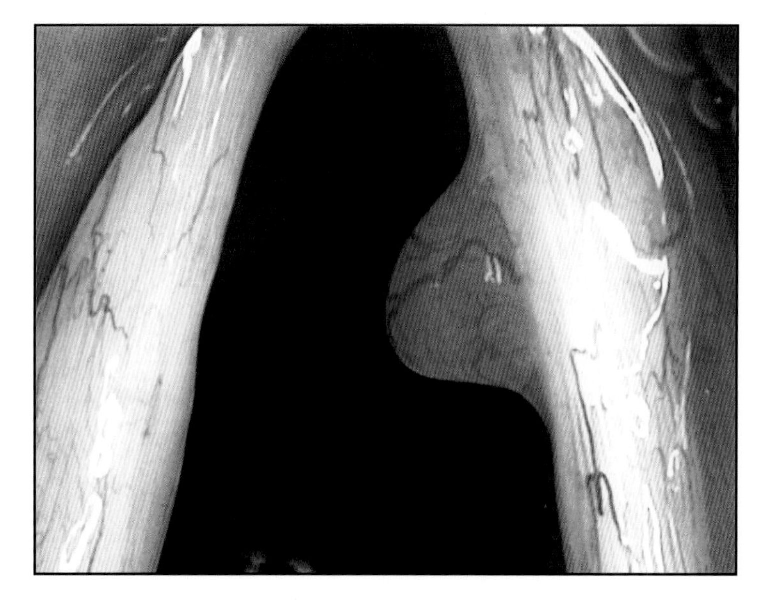

Fig 14–9. Intraoperative videoprint showing typical appearance of a sessile, unilateral polyp of the right vocal fold.

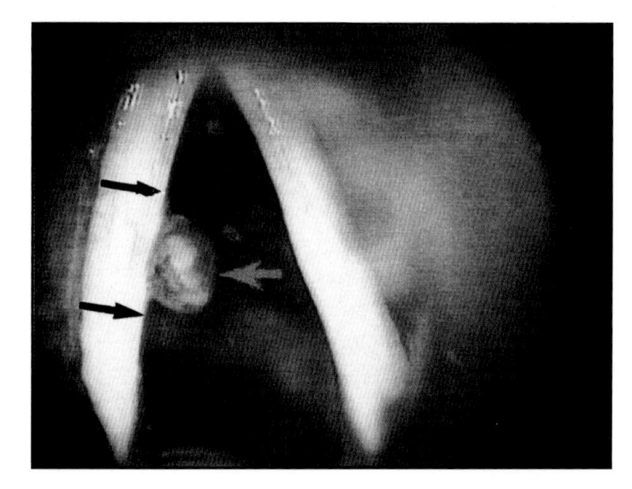

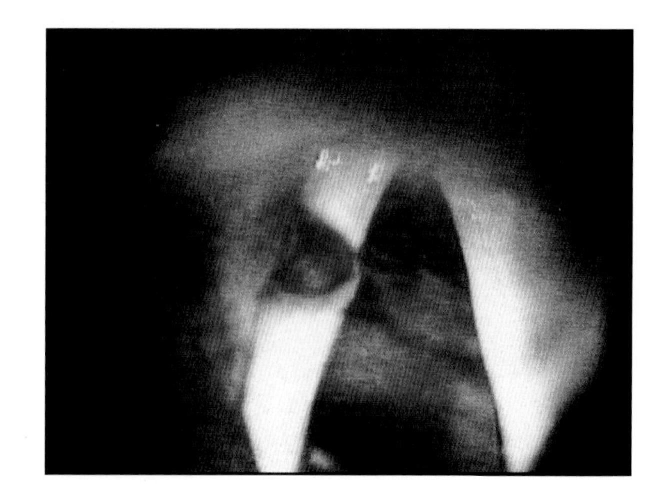

Fig 14–10. This figure was taken intraoperatively and shows (*left*) a pedunculated hemorrhagic polyp (*white arrow*), with prominent feeding vessel on the vibratory margin of the vocal fold (*straight black arrows*). The pedunculated nature of the lesion can be seen (*right*) as the lesion is displaced onto the superior surface of the vocal fold. (From *ENT J* 1993:72[7] with permission.)

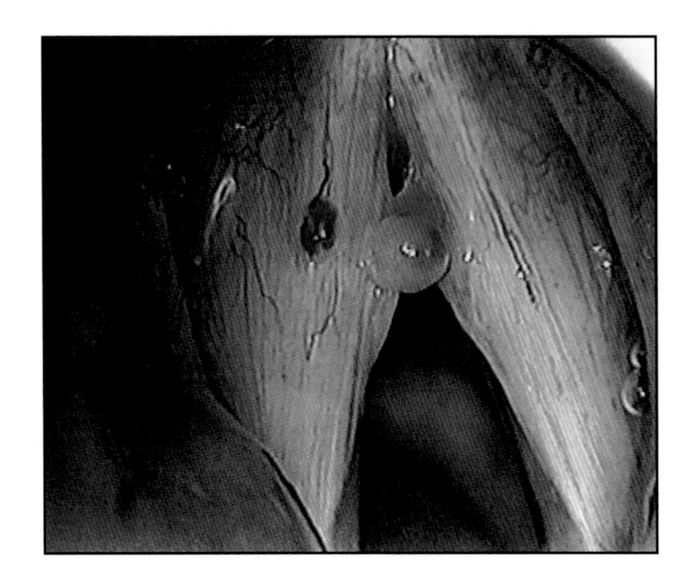

Fig 14–11. Intraoperative videoprint showing right post-hemorrhagic vocal fold polyp with a vascular blush in its base anteriorly and with jagged vessels feeding it from anterior. There are also varicosities on the superior surface of the right vocal fold. The left vocal fold shows a varicosity and large ectasia on the superior surface, and a cyst on the left vibratory margin (partially obscured by the right polyp).

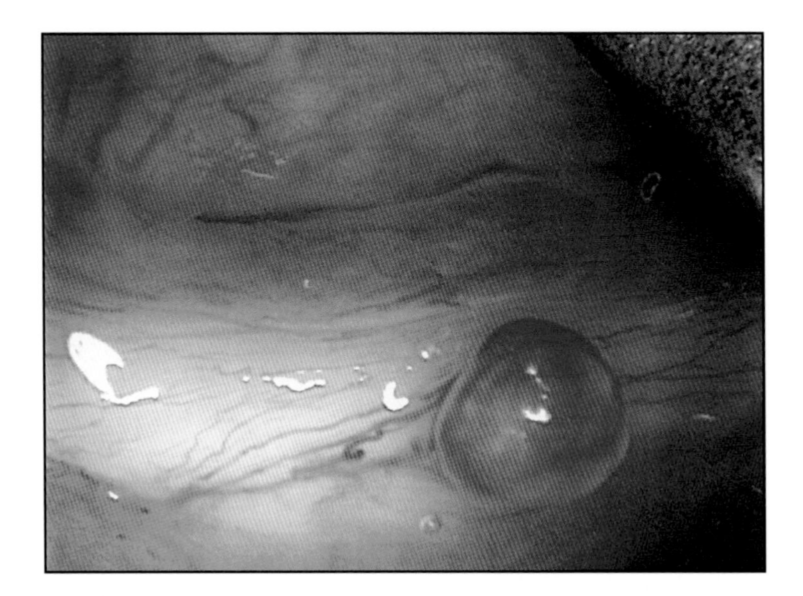

Fig 14–12. Left post-hemorrhagic vocal fold polyp as seen intraoperatively through a 70° telescope. The polyp is located on the vibratory margin. The metal laryngoscope can be seen anteriorly, and the laryngeal ventricle is visualized well above the vocal fold.

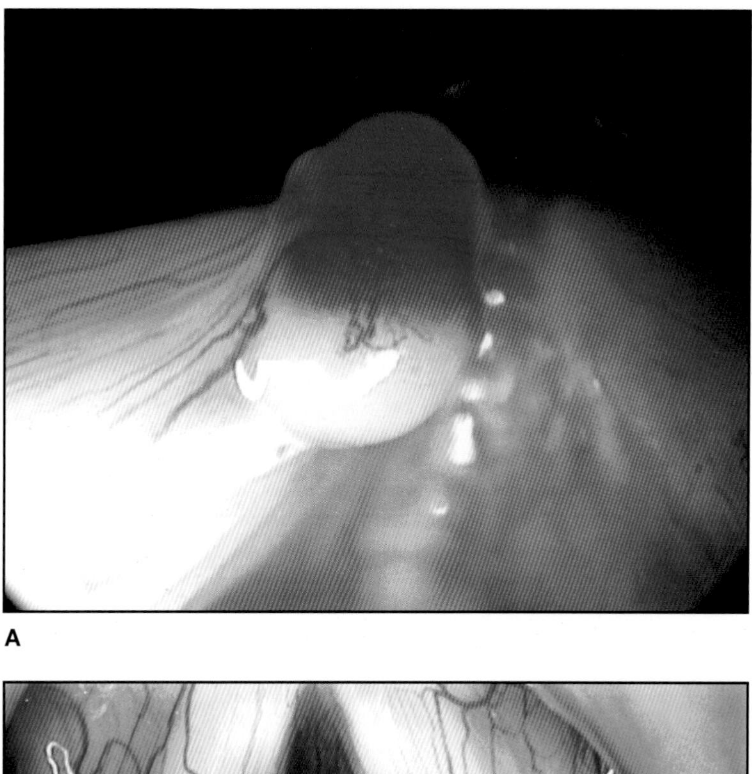

A

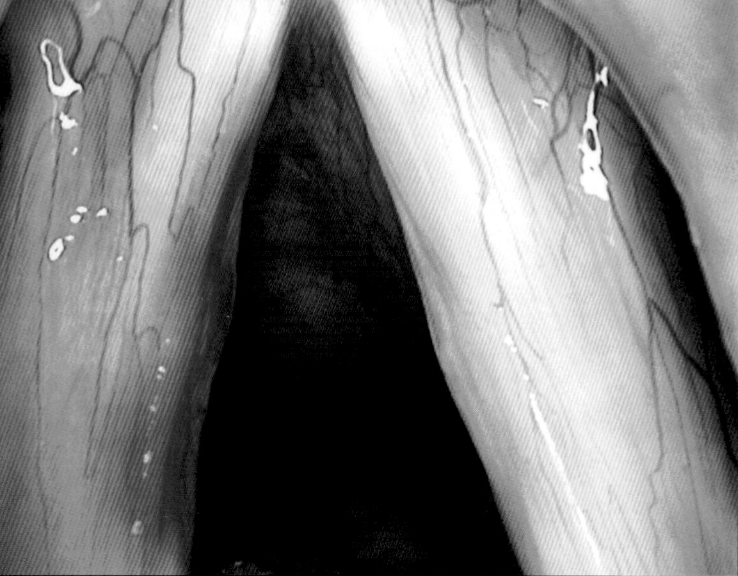

B

Fig 14–13. A. Some polyps are clearly associated with hemorrhage. Residual blood can be seen within the left vocal fold polyp, in a videoprint taken through a 70 degree laryngeal telescope. A feeding vessel along the vibratory also is seen clearly. Such vessels are often difficult to visualize from above, or using a 0 degree telescope. **B.** Even a broad-based sessile polyp that is inseparable from overlying epithelium can be excised without extensive mucosal resection. This intraoperative photograph shows that the mucosal edges meet spontaneously almost completely, forming a fairly linear epithelial deficit. The indentation in the area of resection reflects dissection along the medial aspect of the lesion in an area that was adynamic preoperatively. No uninvolved tissue was disturbed. This approach is useful in many cases, although in some instances it is better to transect fibrotic tissue and leave a straight vocal fold edge.

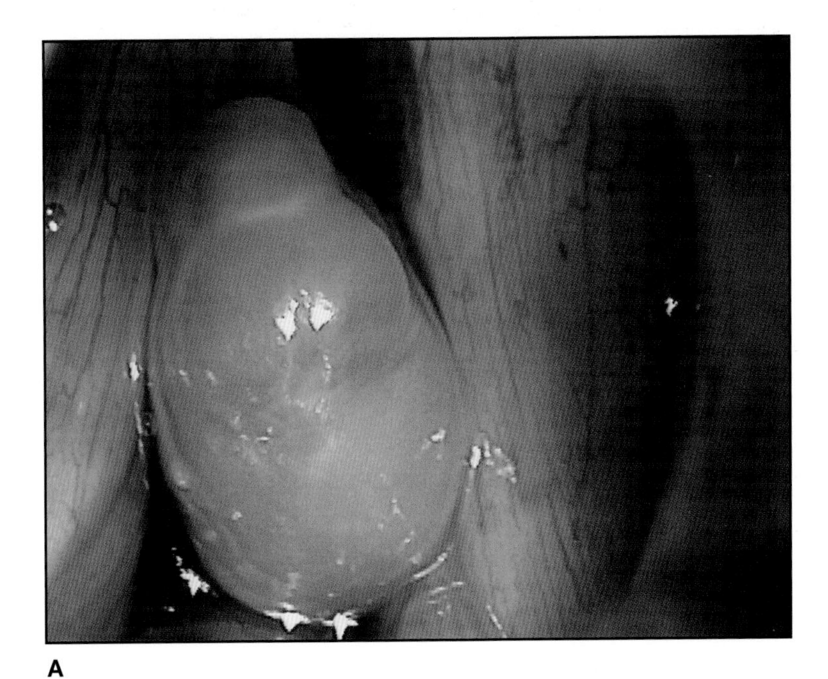

A

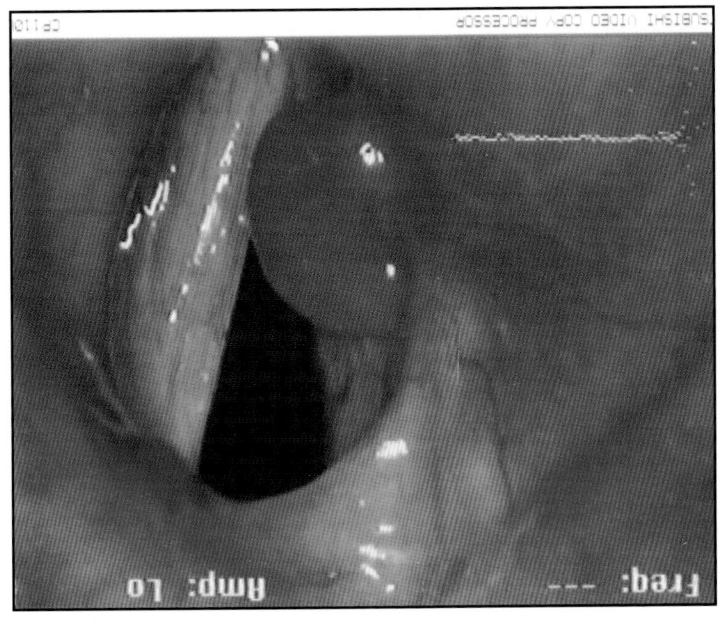

B

Fig 14–14. A. Although this is a large polyp, it is based on a relatively small area along the vocal fold. Consequently, excision involves a risk of scarring to only a small area of the vibratory margin. This risk is reduced further because of the amount of redundant mucosa seen anterior to the mass and the relatively enlarged Reinke's space. **B.** Polyp located on the right false vocal fold. When the mass was not in contact with the vocal folds, the voice was normal. As the mass enlarged slightly, it touched the superior surfaces of the vocal folds intermittently causing irregular dysphonia. Resecting a polyp from this region of the false vocal fold generally is not associated with a substantial risk of hoarseness.

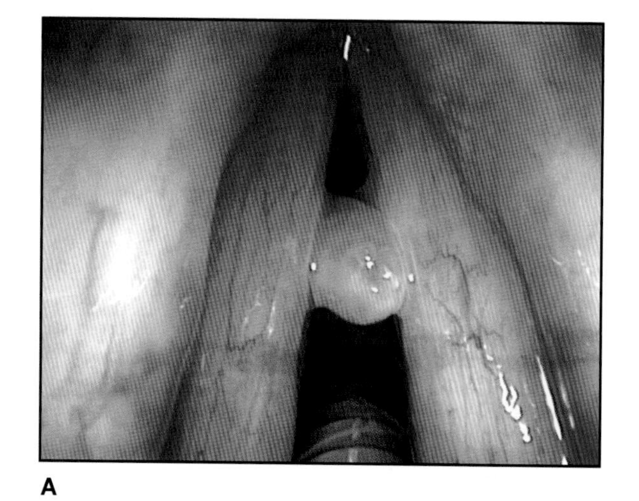

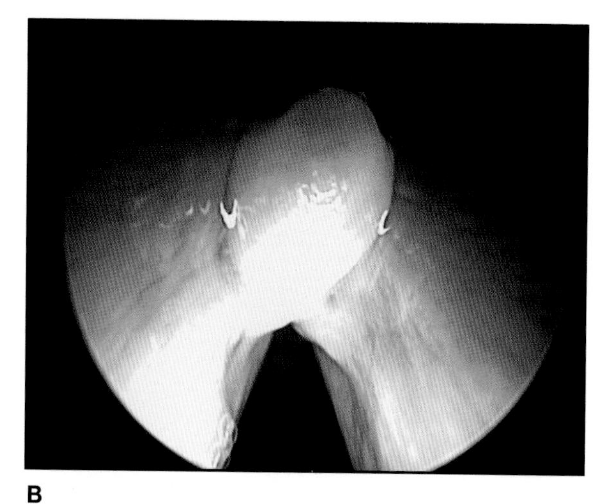

Fig 14–15. From above, this intraoperative videoprint shows a broad-based left vocal fold polyp partially obscuring a right vocal fold mass in a 42-year-old rabbi with a 1½- year history of gradually progressive dysphonia (**A**). A 70° laryngeal telescope (**B**) clarifies the relation between the right mass and the overlying left polyp. The right contact lesion was much more firm and fibrotic than the larger left polyp. Both lesions were removed, and the voice improved substantially.

volve an entire vocal fold. Larger polyps frequently extend into the subglottic area. The functional effect of polyps depends on whether they are unilateral or bilateral, sessile or pedunculated, symmetrical or asymmetrical, and situated on the margin or elsewhere. Functional effect depends also on the pathology. With edematous polyps, the mass of the cover layer may function as if it were decreased. If polyps contain blood and/or fibrosis, the mass is increased. Polyps may interfere with vibration unilaterally or bilaterally; or, in some cases, they may not interfere with vibration at all (if they are not located on the vibratory margin; Figs 14–15 and 14–16). Historical characteristics generally allow for the differentiation of polyps from nodules and cysts (Fig 14–16). However, it must be recognized that not all lesions that look clinically like polyps are simple, benign polyps. Some may be neoplastic (Figs 14–17, 14–18, 14–19).

In some cases, even sizable polyps resolve with relative voice rest and a few weeks of low-dose steroid therapy such as methylprednisolone 4 mg twice a day. However, most of them require surgical removal. If polyps are not treated, they may produce contact injury on contralateral vocal fold. Voice therapy should be used to ensure good relative voice rest and to avoid voice abusive behaviors before and after surgery.

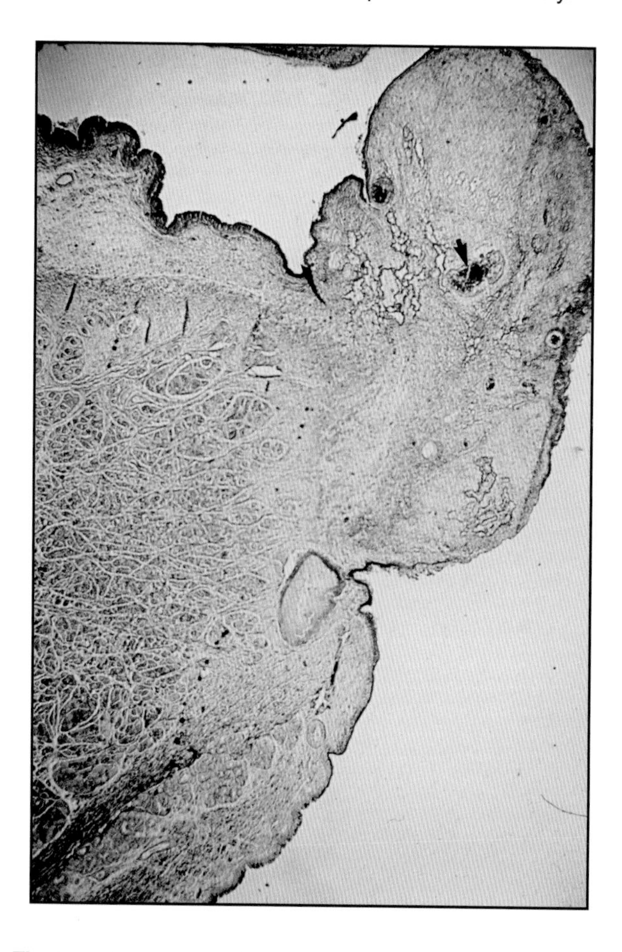

Fig 14–16. Typical histologic appearance of a polyp. It involves the epithelium and superficial layers of the lamina propria. Evidence of bleeding into the tissue is apparent (*arrow*), and hyaline degeneration, thrombosis, edema, collagen fibrous proliferation, and cellular infiltration are common. (Courtesy of Minoru Hirano, MD.)

"Contact" Granulomas and Vocal Process Ulcers

Granulomas usually occur on the posterior aspect of the vocal folds, often in or above the cartilaginous por-

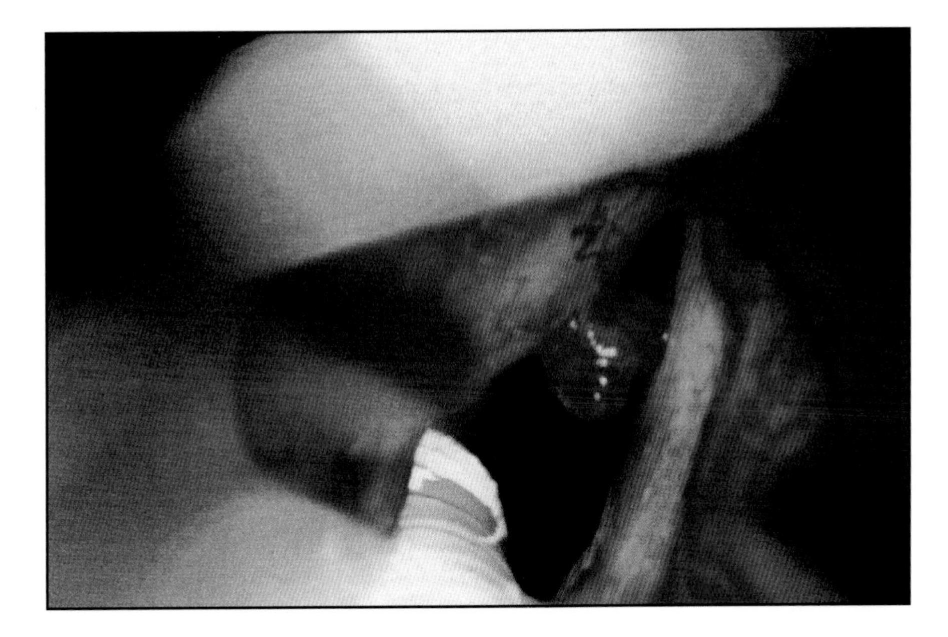

Fig 14–17. Intraoperative photograph from a 35-year-old male with a 6-month history of hoarseness. Although the lesion looks like a hemorrhagic polyp, histologic assessment revealed it to be a hemangioma. This was suspected intraoperatively, because of unusually profuse hemorrhage. The possibility of neoplasm should always be kept in mind, and biopsy should not be unduly delayed when a lesion fails to respond promptly to noninvasive therapy.

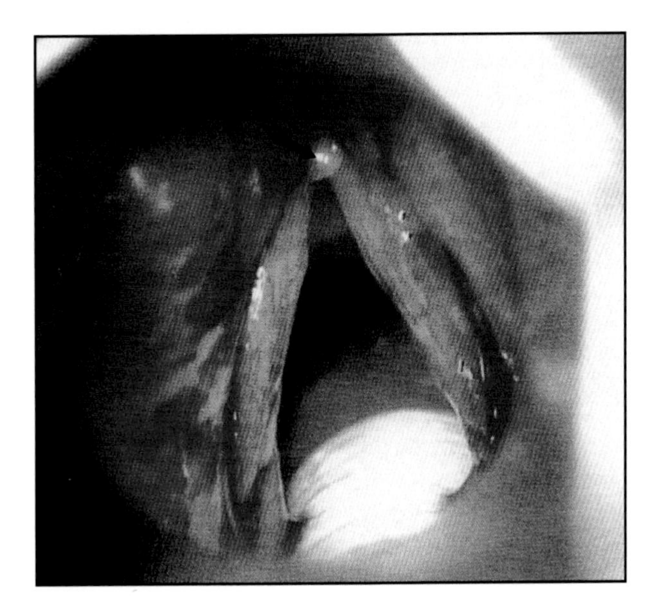

Fig 14–18. This 79-year-old female had a 3-month history of hoarseness. She has smoked at least one pack of cigarettes daily for 70 years. She has no history of throat pain or otalgia, and she denied dysphagia. The intraoperative videoprint above reveals a mass that might have been mistaken for a benign polyp (*arrow*). Erythema and fullness are present anteriorly. Actually, this "polyp" is the tip of a squamous cell carcinoma extending into the supraglottic and infraglottic regions, with cartilage invasion. It involves the true and false vocal folds bilaterally. The tumor was stage $T_4N_0M_0$.

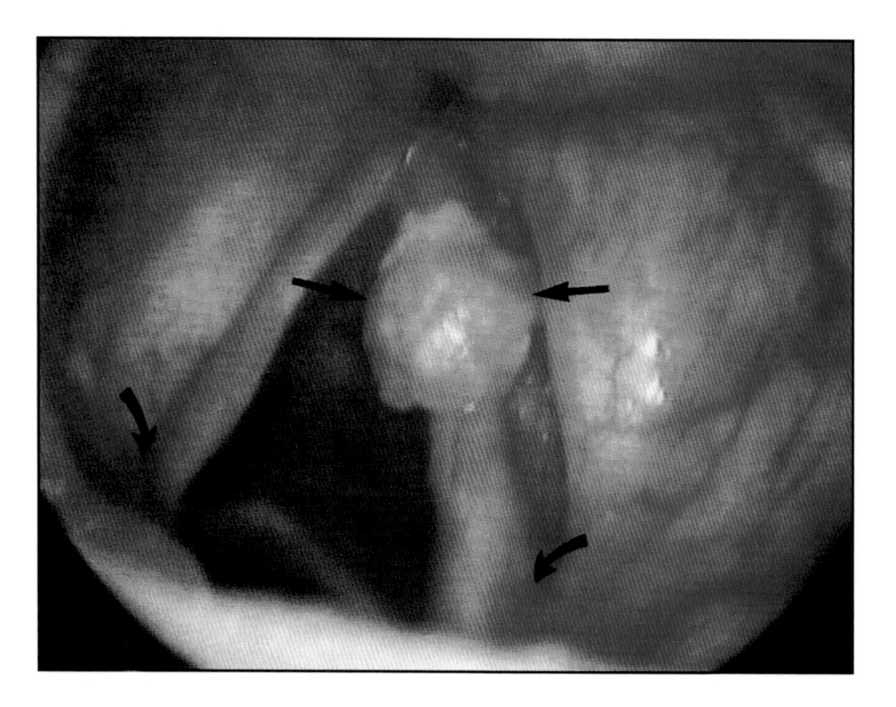

Fig 14–19. This videoprint shows an irregular, polypoid, right vocal fold mass (*arrows*). There is also arytenoid erythema associated with reflux. The arytenoids are not visible in this picture, but acid-induced erythema extending into the cartilaginous portion of the vocal folds can be seen (*curved arrows*). This patient had not smoked for more than 10 years. This pedunculated mass was $T_1N_0M_0$ well differentiated squamous cell carcinoma, which was excised with adequate margins. The patient is being monitored closely, and no further treatment is planned unless the tumor recurs (From *ENT J* 1994;73[8], with permission.).

tion (Figs 14–20, 14–21, 14–22, 14–23, 14–24, 14–25, 14–26, 14–27). Granulomas may be unilateral. They occur commonly on the medial surface of the arytenoids. Histopathologic evaluation reveals fibroblasts, collagenous fibers, proliferated capillaries, leukocysts, and sometimes ulceration. Thus, they are actually chronic inflammatory tissue, not true granulomas such as those seen in tuberculosis or sarcoidosis. Granulomas and ulcers in the region of the vocal process traditionally have been associated with trauma, especially intubation injury. However, they are also seen in young, apparently healthy professional voice users with no history of intubation or obvious laryngeal injury. Previous teachings have held that the lesion should be treated surgically but that the incidence of recurrence is high. In fact, the vast majority of granulomas and ulcerations (probably even those from intubation) are aggravated or caused by acid reflux; and voice abuse and misuse are associated commonly. Ylitalo has published an extensive review of granuloma, including its relationship to reflux.[23] In our experience, when the reflux is controlled and voice therapy is begun, the lesions usually resolve within a few weeks. If they do not, they should be removed for biopsy to rule out other possible causes. So long as a good specimen is obtained, the laser may be used in this surgery, because the lesions usually are not on the vibratory margin, and they are often friable. However, this author usually uses traditional instruments, wishing to avoid the third-degree burn caused by the laser in the treatment of this condition.

Occasionally, patients present with multiply recurrent granulomas, which may present even after excellent reflux control (including fundoplication), surgical removal including steroid injection into the base of the granuloma, and voice therapy. Medical causes other than reflux and muscle tension dysphonia must be ruled out, particularly granulomatous diseases including sarcoidosis and tuberculosis. When it has been established that the recurrent lesions are typical granulomas occurring in the absence of laryngopharyngeal reflux, the cause is almost always phonatory trauma. When voice therapy is insufficient to permit adequate healing, some of these uncommon and diffi-

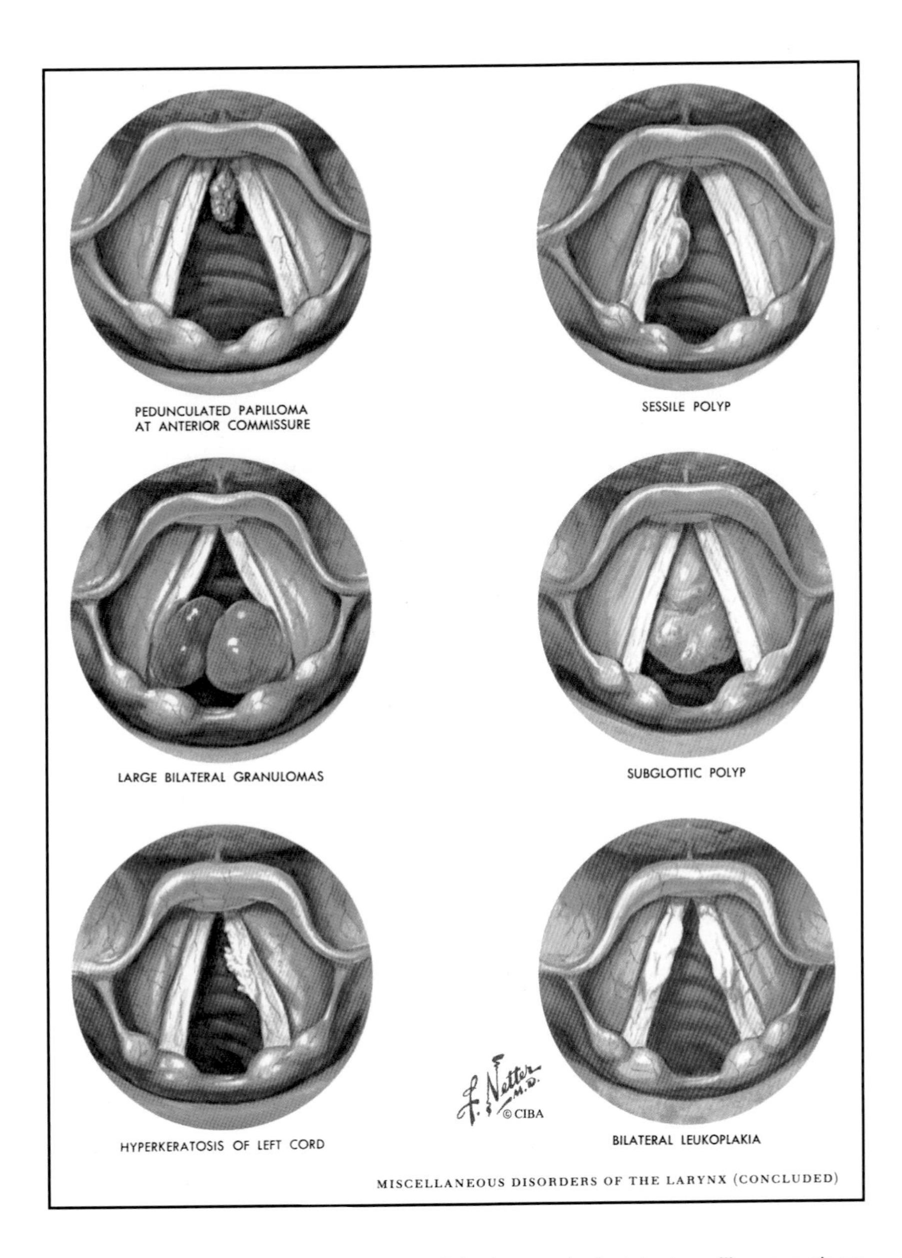

Fig 14–20. Miscellaneous disorders of the larynx. An isolated papilloma such as that illustrated in the top left usually has less grave implications than the papillomatosis illustrated in Figure 14–1. Nevertheless, careful removal with a laser is appropriate. The broad-based sessile polyp illustrated has typically prominent vascularity at its base and along the superior surface of the vocal fold. The contact granulomas illustrated are considerably large than those shown in Figure 14–1. Even granulomas of this size sometimes resolve with antireflux therapy and low-dose steroids, although more often excision is required. Subglottic lesions such as the polyp illustrated usually can be removed safely without adverse effect on the voice. Potentially malignant or premalignant lesions are discussed elsewhere in this book. (From The larynx. In: *Clinical Symposia.* Summit, NJ: CIBA Pharmaceutical Company; 1964:16[3]: Plate IX. Copyright 1964 Icon Learning Systems, LLC, a subsidiary of MediMedia USA, Inc. Reprinted with permission from ICON Learning Systems, LLC, illustrated by Frank Netter, MD. All rights reserved.)

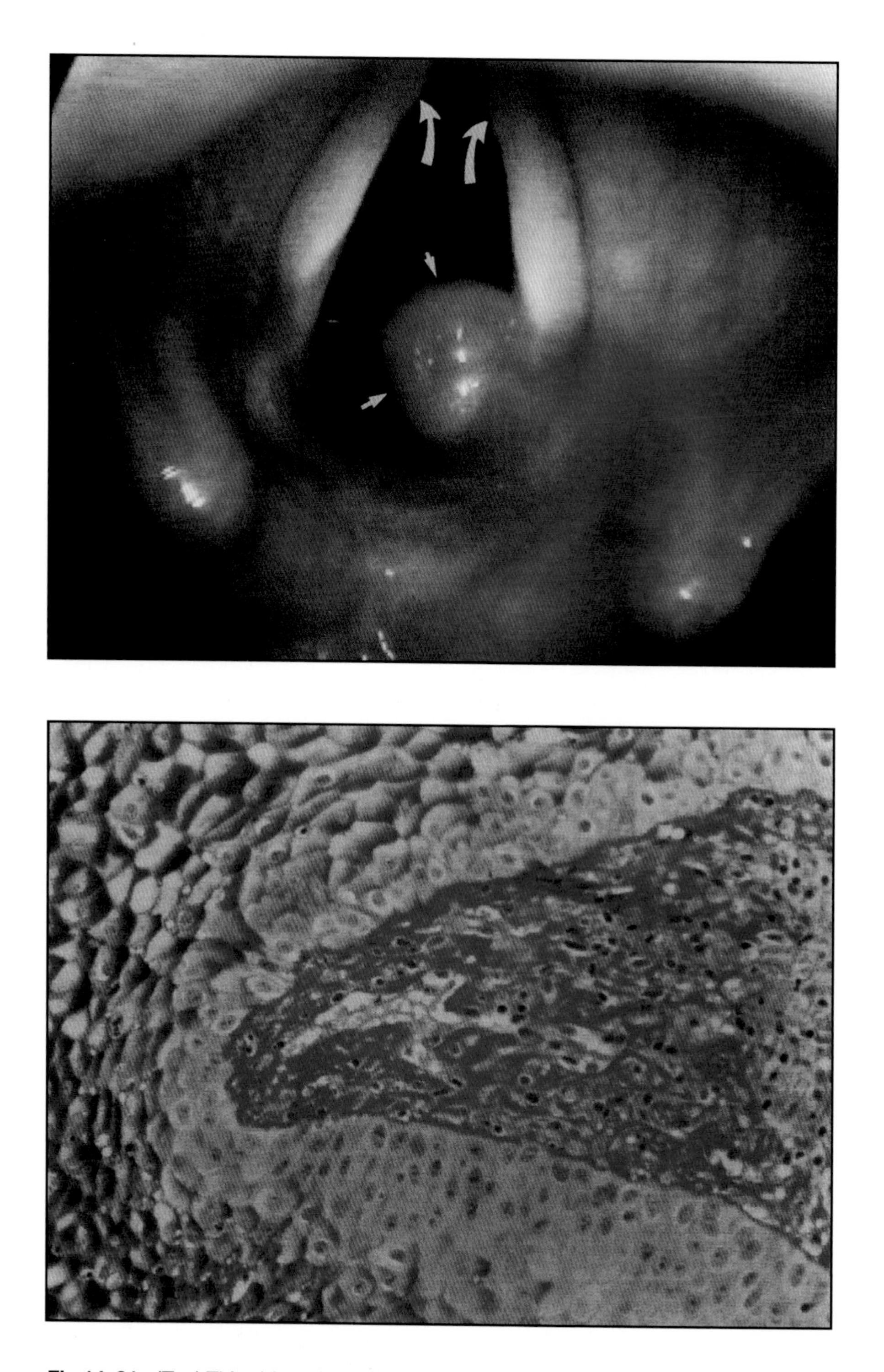

Fig 14–21. (*Top*) This videoprint shows a large right vocal process granuloma *(straight arrows)*, bilateral prenodular swellings (*curved arrows*), and marked diffuse erythema of both regions consistent with gastroesophageal reflux laryngitis. (From *ENT J.* 1994;73[7], with permission.) (*Bottom*) Typical appearance of a laryngeal granuloma composed primarily of fibroblasts, proliferated capillaries, collagenous fibers, and leukocysts. An epithelial covering may or may not be present.

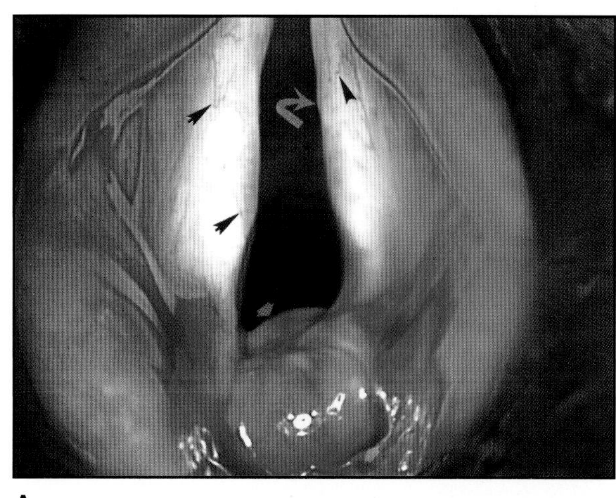

A

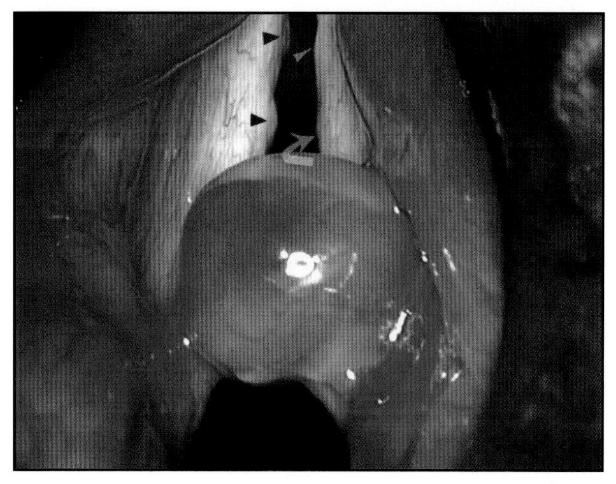

B

Fig 14–22. A. During gentle inspiration, a large right pyogenic granuloma fills the posterior glottis (*solid white arrow*) of this 42-year-old executive. The mass is based on a stalk attached to the base of the right vocal process. There are varicosities on the superior surfaces of both folds (*black arrows*), including a vessel that crosses toward the vibratory margin into a small cyst (*curved white arrow*) on the right. **B.** On expiration, the small cyst (*curved white arrow*) and its associated vessels are seen more easily. There are also contact swellings more anteriorly on the right (*white arrowhead*) and two left vocal fold cysts (*black arrowheads*). During exhalation, the large pyogenic granuloma is displaced superiorly out of the posterior glottis. The severe erythema of the posterior portion of the larynx is due to reflux. The pyogenic granuloma and cysts were excised. The granuloma recurred despite voice therapy and reflux control. Botulinum toxin was injected at the time of repeat excision, and he had no recurrence in the subsequent 4 years.

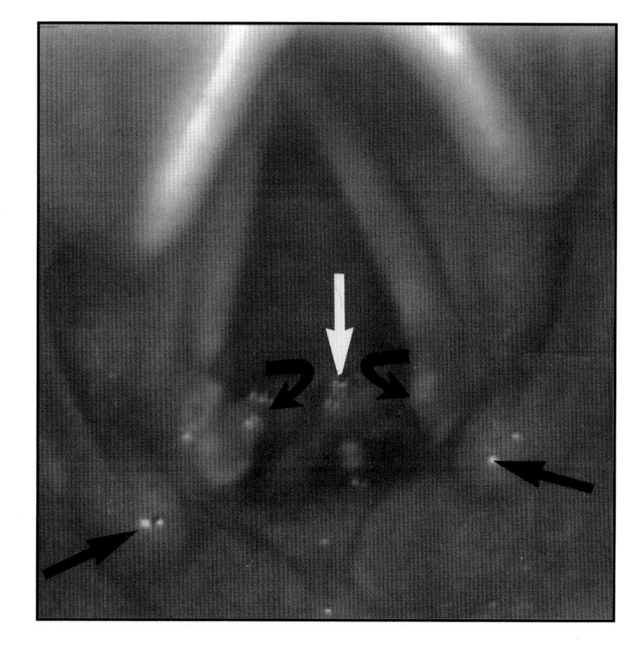

Fig 14–23. Videoprint from a 45-year-old male with recurrent laryngospasm. He had undergone tracheotomy prior to referral to the author (RTS). Strobovideolaryngoscopy revealed bilateral laryngeal granulomas (*curved arrows*). A Montgomery T tube (*white arrow*) was visible in the subglottic area. He also had marked erythema of his arytenoids (*straight arrows*) and posterior laryngeal mucosa consistent with reflux laryngitis. The reflux was confirmed by 24-hour pH monitor. Vigorous therapy was instituted. The laryngospasm, cough, and other reflux symptoms stopped. The granulomas resolved spontaneously, and the patient was decannulated. He has had no difficulty in the subsequent 7 years. (From *ENT J.* 1995;74[10], with permission.)

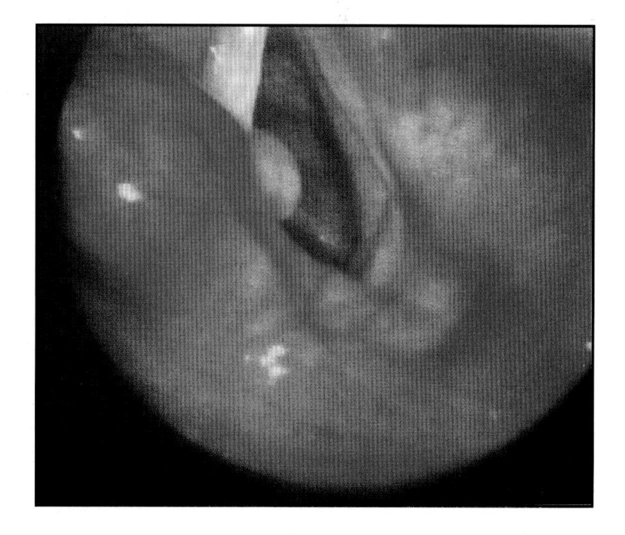

Fig 14–24. Typical appearance of a laryngeal granuloma occurring near the region of the medial surface of the arytenoids above the level of the glottis.

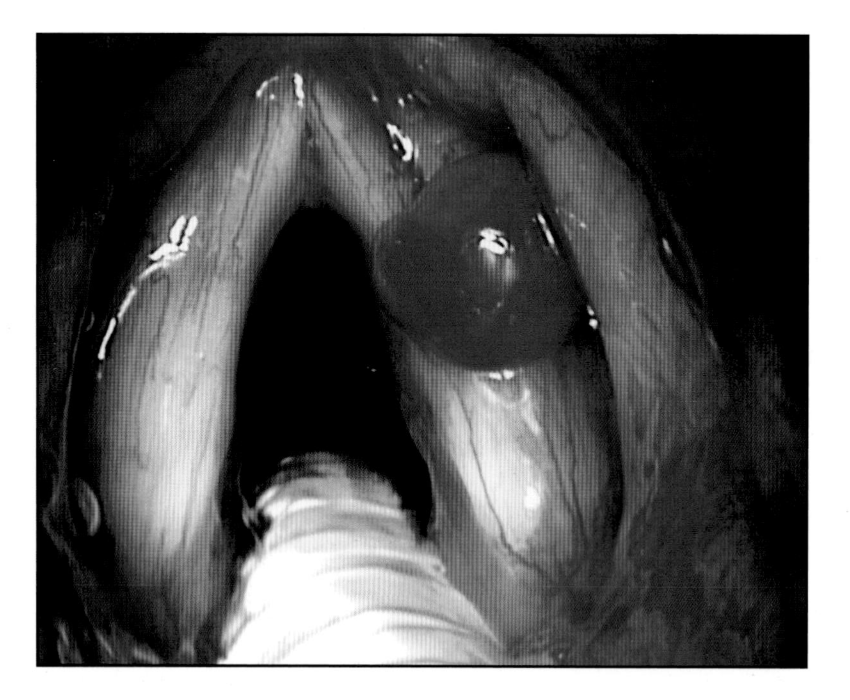

Fig 14–25. Although granulomas typically occur near the vocal process and medial surface of the arytenoid, they may be seen elsewhere. This videoprint reveals a granuloma arising from the right vocal false vocal fold and ventricle in an area of previous trauma. There is also varicosity anteriorly along the right vocal fold, as well as a small anterior web.

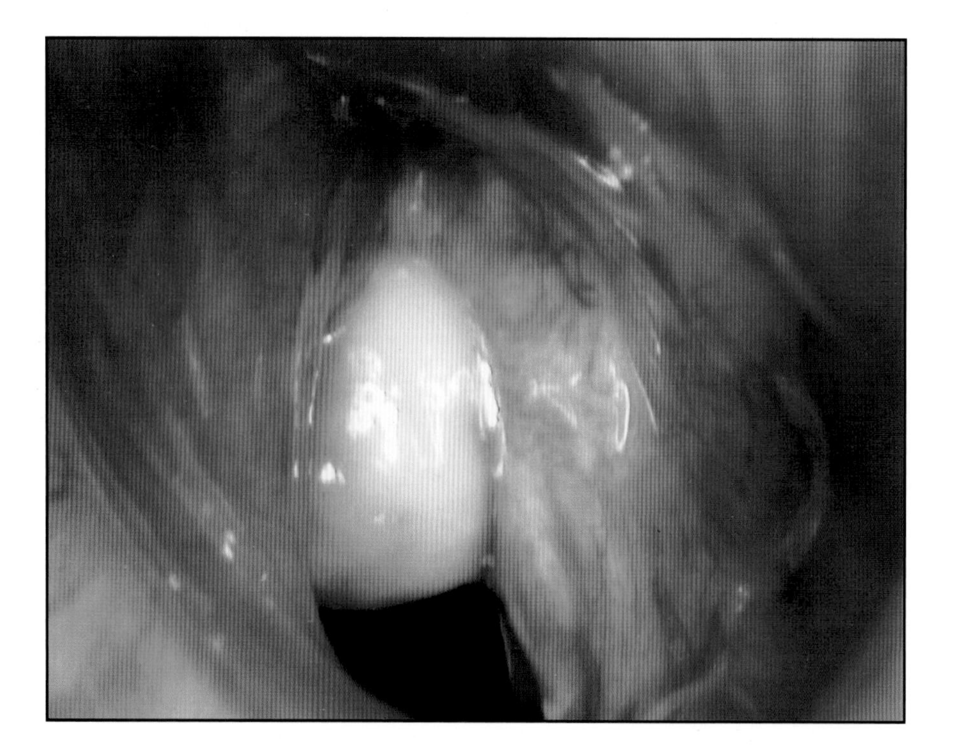

Fig 14–26. Granulomas also can occur in the musculomembranous portion of the vocal fold, although this is relatively uncommon. This large right granuloma occurred following removal of a mass from the right vocal fold. Excision of the granuloma was required.

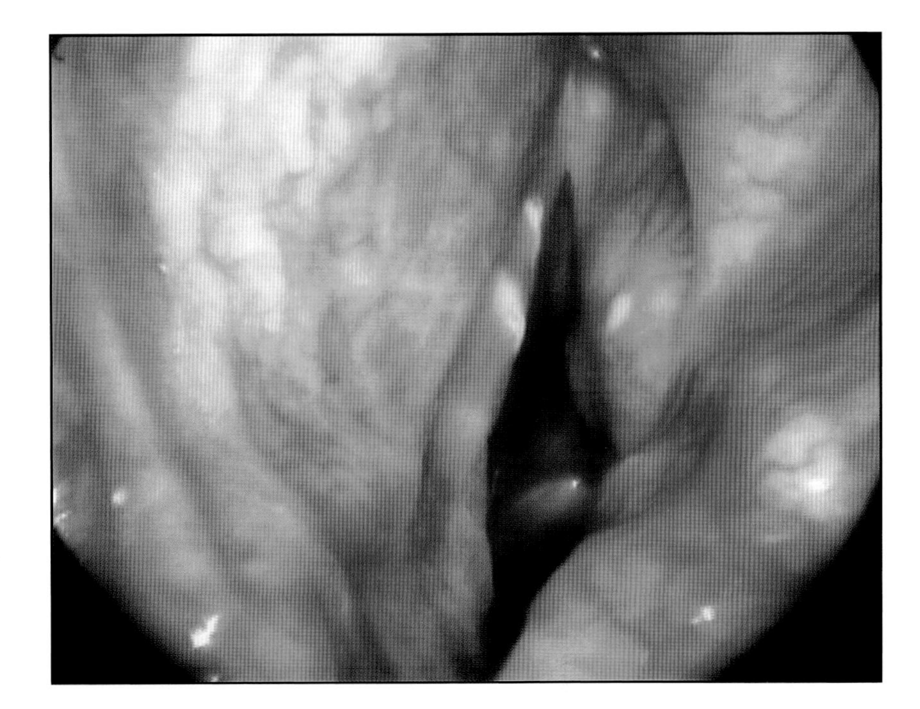

Fig 14–27. Granulomas may be iatrogenic. This videoprint shows a right Teflon granuloma that occurred in a 52-year-old male. He had right recurrent laryngeal nerve paresis. After reviewing all surgical options, he elected Teflon injection in 1988. He was the last patient for whom the author (RTS) utilized Teflon. His voice improved and stayed satisfactory for 2 years. Thereafter, he developed a Teflon granuloma. It was excised with a CO_2 laser resulting in satisfactory voice. However, he has had recurrent Teflon granulomas, requiring surgical re-excision six times over the ensuing 12 years. Teflon granuloma development even long after successful injection is one of the problems that led to the abandonment of this procedure for vocal fold medialization in the late 1980s.

cult patient problems can be solved by chemical tenotomy using Botulinum toxin. Although most other laryngologists have injected Botulinum toxin to the thyroarytenoid (TA) muscle, this author treats the lateral cricoarytenoid (LCA) muscle in most cases. If patients with multiply recurrent granulomas are observed closely using frame-by-frame analysis of strobovideolaryngoscopic images, or using high-speed video, many will make initial contact during adduction near the point of the vocal process, closing the rest of the posterior glottis slightly later. This is a lateral cricoarytenoid-dominant closing pattern, and it is different from the normal closing pattern in which LCA and interarytenoid muscle activity are balanced so that there is a broader area of initial contact. Weakening the LCA with Botulinum toxin prevents this forceful point contact and allows resolution of the granulomas. Usually, only 2.5 mouse units in LCA are necessary. Although this treatment approach has been effective, it is not recommended as initial therapy and is appropriate only for selected recalcitrant cases.

Reinke's Edema

Reinke's edema is characterized by mucoid, gelatinous fluid in the superficial layer of the lamina propria (Reinke's space), creating a typical floppy "elephant ear," polypoid appearance of the vocal fold (Figs 14–1, 14–28, 14–29, 14–30, 14–31). It is generally seen in adults. The condition is more common in women than in men.[24] It was named after Reinke who described the compartment now known as the superficial layer of the lamina propria while studying membraneous edema of the larynx.[25] Reinke's space is defined anteriorly by Broyle's ligament, posteriorly by the arytenoid cartilage; and it is superficial to the vocal ligament. It has been associated with increased subglottic driving pressure in aerodynamic studies by Zeitels et al.[26] It has been suggested that patients with mucosal irritation and muscle tension dysphonia are likely to develop Reinke's edema due to aerodynamically induced unopposed distention of the lamina propria and overlying epithelium.

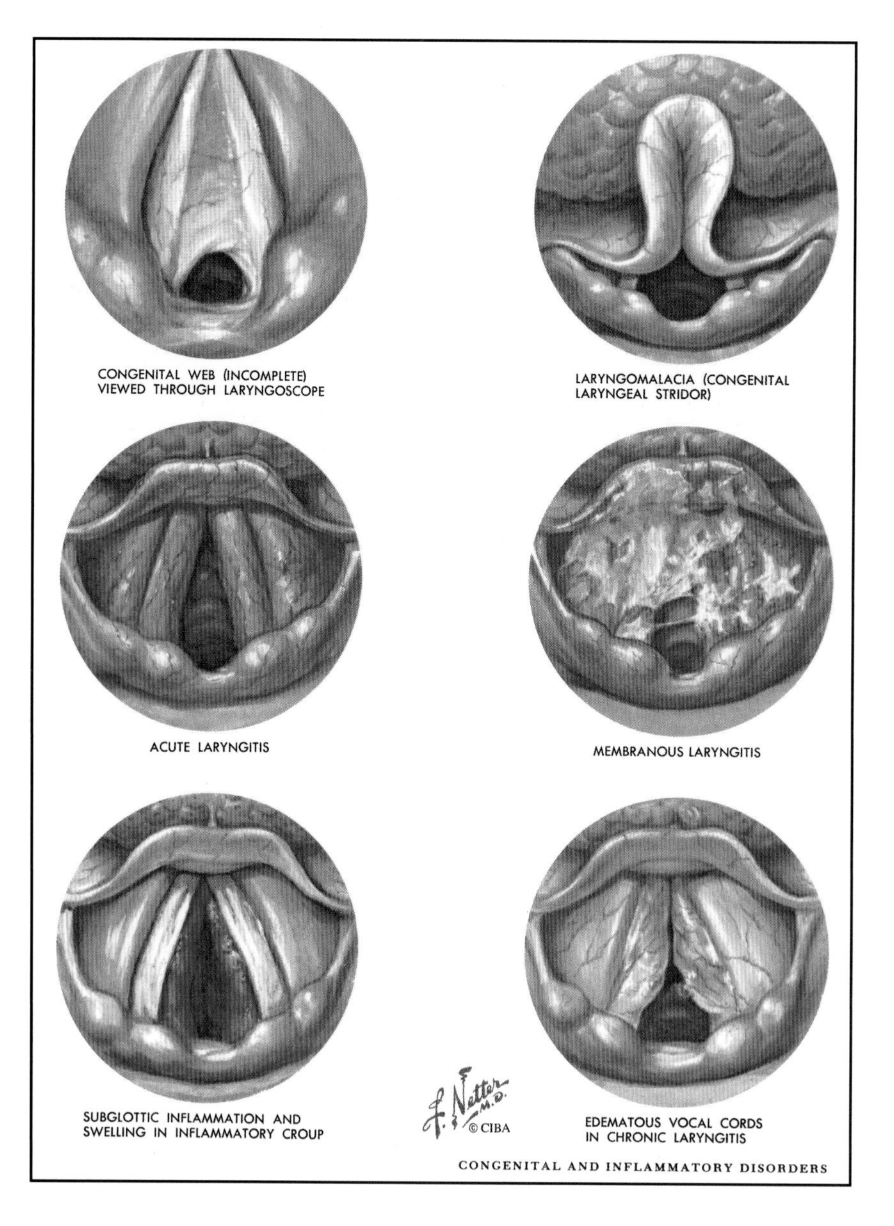

Fig 14–28. Congenital and inflammatory disorders. The erythema, edema, and vascular congestion illustrated in the case of acute laryngitis are typical of a moderate to severe infection. With vocal folds this inflamed, performance could be justified only under the most extraordinary circumstances. The subglottic inflammation illustrated from a case of croup is similar to that seen in adults with severe respiratory infections, which are difficult to control in short periods of time, although in adult performers a lesser degree of inflammation, swelling, and airway compromise is usually present. The edematous vocal folds seen in chronic laryngitis have fluid collections in Reinke's space. Vocal folds with this appearance may be diagnosed as erythematous vocal folds, Reinke's edema, polypoid corditis, or polypoid degeneration. In some cases the edema reverses when the chronic irritant is removed. The congenital web illustrated is extensive. Smaller webs may occur congenitally or following trauma (including surgery). The illustration of laryngomalacia shows an omega-shaped epiglottis. This shape is common in normal larynges before puberty and may persist in some adults, making visualization difficult. Membranous laryngitis is uncommon and severe, necessitating cancellation of performance commitments. (From The larynx. In: *Clinical Symposia.* Summit, NJ: CIBA Pharmaceutical Company; 1964:16[3]: Plate VI. Copyright 1964 Icon Learning Systems, LLC, a subsidiary of MediMedia USA, Inc. Reprinted with permission from ICON Learning Systems, LLC, illustrated by Frank Netter, MD. All rights reserved.)

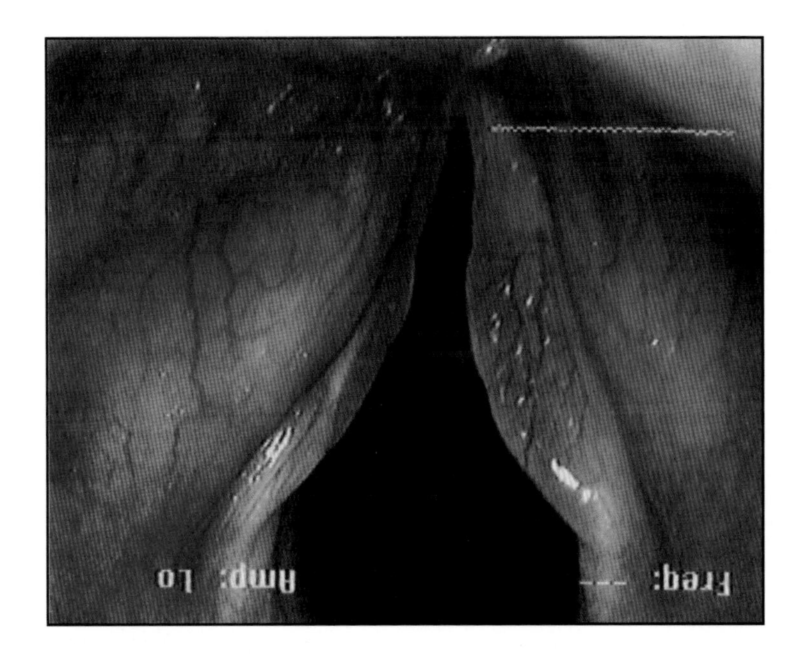

Fig 14–29. Typical appearance of Reinke's edema, worse on the right than on the left. The hypervascularity seen on the superior surface of the right vocal fold is associated with chronic Reinke's edema routinely. This patient was a smoker and had muscle tension dysphonia.

Reike's edema is uncommon in classical professional singers, but it is seen more frequently among pop singers, radio and sports announcers, attorneys, and salespeople. The association of Reinke's edema with voice abuse[27] and smoking[28] dates back more than a half century. Although the etiology is unproven, the condition is almost always related to cigarette smoking and/or other metabolic problems such as hypothyroidism and to voice abuse. Reinke's edema is also known as polypoid degeneration, polypoid corditis, and edematous hypertrophy. It is usually bilateral, involves the entire membranous vocal fold, and may be asymmetrical. Vibration is impaired bilaterally. The mass of the cover is increased, but stiffness is decreased. It causes a low, gruff, husky voice. If it does not resolve after smoking has been discontinued and all irritants (including voice abuse) have been removed, it may be treated surgically. Extreme care must be taken to be certain that the patient wants voice quality restored to normal. Reinke's edema is found commonly in sports announcers, businesswomen, female trial attorneys, and others who may like the low, masculine vocal quality associated with this pathology. When this is the case, and the appearance of the vocal folds does not suggest mailignancy, close follow-up rather than surgery is reasonable.

Unilateral Reinke's edema deserves special attention. The laryngologist should always seek an underlying cause. This condition has not been studied well, but it should be. The author (RTS) has seen malignancy present as unilateral Reinke's edema. More commonly, it occurs secondary to other vocal fold pathology. In some cases, the pathology is obvious, such as a contralateral lesion causing edema in the superficial layer of lamina propria induced by vocal fold contact. However, even more commonly, the pathology is subtler. In the author's (RTS) experience, unilateral Reinke's edema is usually due to vocal paresis, commonly involving the superior laryngeal nerve. The paresis may be on the ipsilateral or contralateral side. Koufman has made similar observations (James A. Koufman, MD, personal communication, 2000) and has termed localized compensatory Reinke's edema that develops in response to paresis a "paresis podule."

Vocal Fold Hemorrhage

Hemorrhage in the vocal folds and mucosal disruption (Fig 14–32) are contraindications to singing, acting, or speaking. When these are observed, the therapeutic course initially includes strict voice rest in addition to correction of any underlying disease. Vocal fold hemorrhage is of such importance that it is discussed in detail in *Professional Voice*.[29]

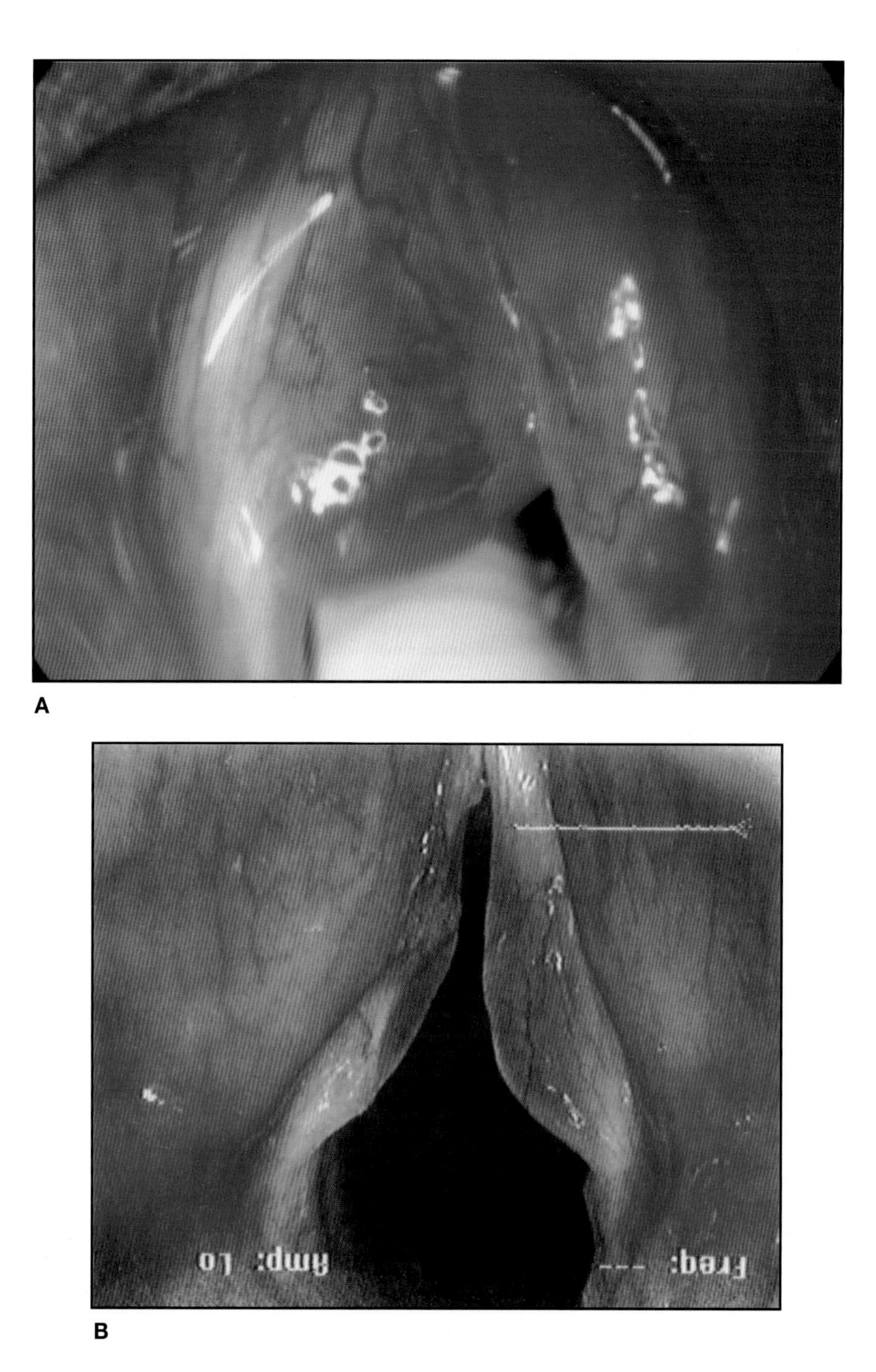

Fig 14–30. A. Reinke's edema can sometimes be severe enough to cause not only dysphonia but also stridor, and occasionally airway obstruction. Surprisingly, the patient whose vocal folds are pictured had a low, masculine voice (she is female), but denied airway difficulties. **B.** This videoprint shows typical, bilateral Reinke's edema. This condition is most often seen in smokers, but it is also often associated with reflux, voice abuse, and sometimes hypothyroidism.

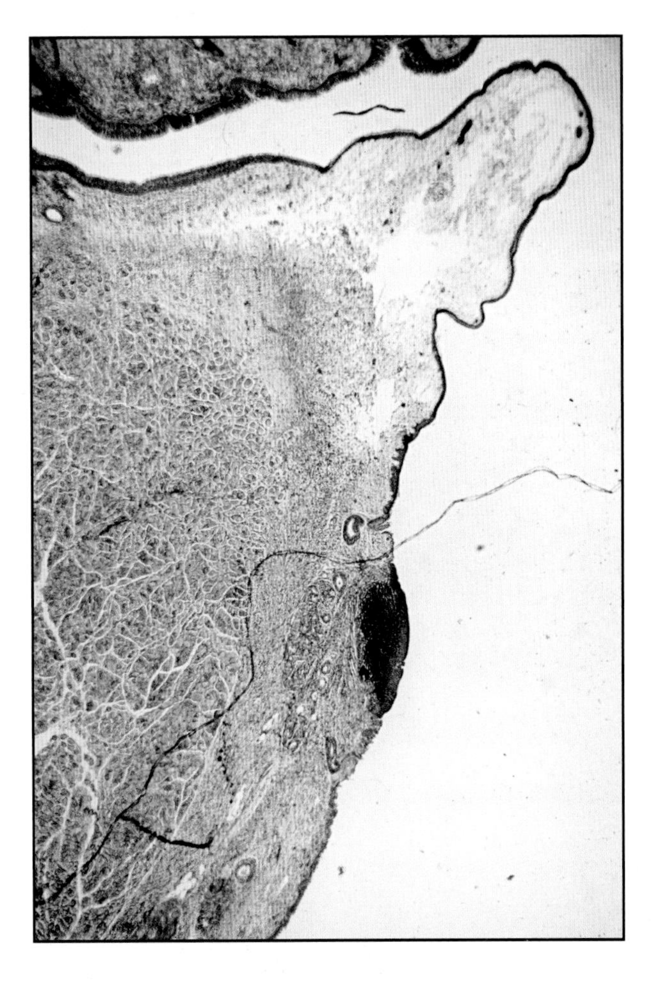

Fig 14–31. Typical appearance of Reinke's edema. There is edema in the superficial layer of the lamina propria. Note that the lesion does not display degeneration, hypertrophy, or inflammation. (Courtesy of Minoru Hirano, MD.)

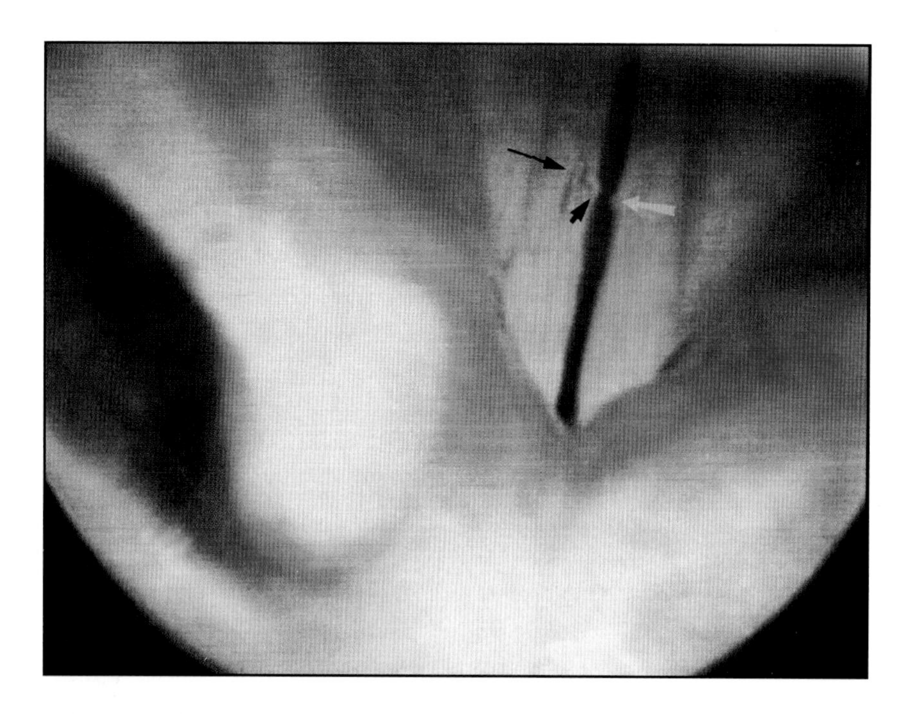

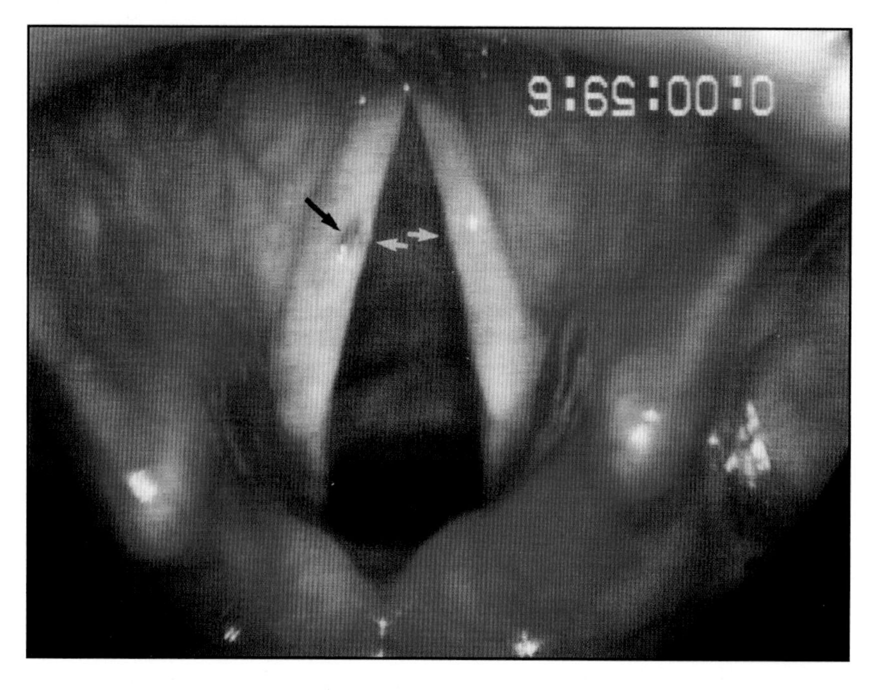

Fig 14–32. Videoprint from a 36-year-old professional singer who developed sudden hoarseness while coughing. Strobovideolaryngoscopy (*top*) revealed an acute right vocal fold tear (*white arrow*) and new left vocal fold varicosities with a surrounding blush of resolving mucosal hemorrhage (*black arrows*) and a small left vibratory margin mass. Re-examination 3 months later (*bottom*) showed smaller residual bilateral vocal fold masses (*white arrows*) and a persistent area of raised, ectatic/varicose vessels (*black arrow*). There was also mild stiffness in the region where the left vocal fold hemorrhage had occurred. (From *ENT J.* 1994;73[9], with permission.)

Sulcus Vocalis

Sulcus vocalis is a groove in the surface of the membranous portion of the vocal fold, usually extending throughout its length (Figs 14–33, 14–34). The lesion is usually bilateral. In sulcus vocalis, the epithelium invaginates through the superficial layer of the lamina propria and adheres to the vocal ligament. This results in a groove running longitudinally along the vocal fold. The apparent groove is actually a sac lined with stratified squamous epithelium, and hyperkeratosis is common near the deepest aspects of the sac or pocket. Some authors believe this represents an open epidermal cyst. There are a deficiency of capillaries and an increase in collagenous fibers in the region of the sulcus. Sulcus vocalis increases the stiffness of the cover layer and is often associated with hoarseness, breathiness, and decreased vocal efficiency. However, it may be asymptomatic if it occurs below the contact edge. The mass of the cover layer is reduced. Invaginated cover layer may adhere to the vocal ligament, causing increased stiffness.

Pseudosulcus vocalis and *sulcus vergeture* may occur in patients with similar dysphonia. Sulcus vergeture has similar appearance, but is not a true sulcus vocalis. Sulcus vergeture is caused by atrophic epithelial changes along the medial margin of the vocal fold. It is often also associated with a bowed appearance. Usually, the superior edge of the groove appears quite mobile, but the inferior edge is generally stiff. The superior layer of the lamina propria is usually deficient, and the epithelium may be closely apposed to the vocal ligament; but it is an atrophic depression of epithelium rather than an invagination of variable thickness and scattered hyperkeratosis, as seen in a true sulcus vocalis. The term pseudosulcus vocalis often is used interchangeably with sulcus vergeture but actually is a different entity. Pseudosulcus is a longitudinal groove that may appear similar to sulcus vocalis or sulcus vergeture, except that it may extend beyond the limit of the musculomembranous portion of the vocal fold, involving the cartilaginous portion, as well. Commonly, it is associated with chronic inflammation and edema, usually caused by laryngopharyngeal reflux. Pseudosulcus vocalis is managed by treating the underlying reflux and any other related conditions. Treatment of sulcus vocalis is controversial and is discussed elsewhere in this book.

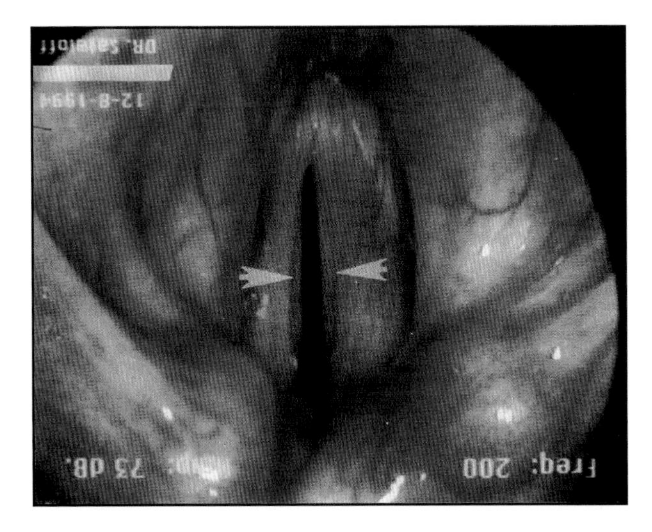

Fig 14–33. Typical appearance of bilateral sulcus vocalis (*arrows*).

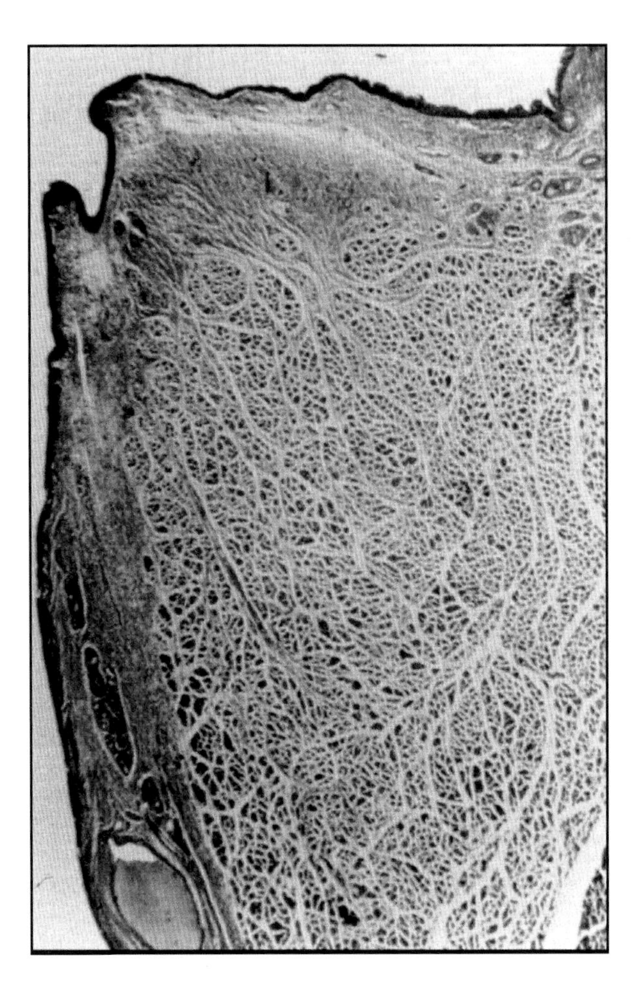

Fig 14–34. Histologically, sulcus vocalis involves the superficial layer of the lamina propria. Dense, collagenous fibers with scant capillaries and thickened epithelium are common. The epithelium may adhere to the vocal ligament, but otherwise the transitional layer is uninvolved. (Courtesy of Minoru Hirano, MD.)

A mucosal bridge involves a longitudinal separation between the mucosa covering the vibratory margin and the rest of the vocal fold (Fig 14–35). Mucosal bridges usually are congenital, but they may be posttraumatic. They have been associated with sulcus vocalis, as well. Ordinarily they are thin strips of mucosa (much less dramatic than the case shown in Fig 14–35), but they are challenging therapeutically. Removal of the mucosal bridge does not always result in improvement in vocal quality. In some cases, there is atrophy of the epithelial surface of the remaining vocal fold, which becomes the vibratory margin after the bridge has been removed. It is often not possible to predict phonatory outcome following excision, rendering intraoperative decision-making difficult.

Laryngeal Webs

Webs connecting the vocal folds may be congenital, or they may follow trauma (Fig 14–36). They are particularly likely to form when mucosa is disrupted in the anterior thirds of both vocal folds simultaneously, especially near the anterior commissure. Posterior glottic webs and stenosis also occur.

Bowed Vocal Folds

The term *bowed vocal fold* is commonly applied when the vocal folds appear to be slightly concave and when glottic closure seems incomplete. Sulcus vergeture is present commonly, as well. Under stroboscopic light, many such cases reveal complete glottic closure but some thinning of the cover. Bowing of this sort is often associated with advanced age. In the past, many patients with this condition have been told either that it is incurable or that surgery to increase vocal fold bulk or tension is advisable. In the author's experience, neither statement is true for most patients. Unless there is neurological damage, the breathiness, slight hoarseness, and voice fatigue associated with apparent bowing in these patients can be corrected with specially designed voice therapy, ideally including both speaking and singing exercises. Such measures result in satisfactory improvement in the vast majority of cases.

True vocal fold bowing occurs with neurologic injury, particularly superior laryngeal nerve paralysis. This condition creates a deficit in longitudinal tension, causing the vocal fold to be at a lower level and to bow laterally. When the condition is unilateral and incom-

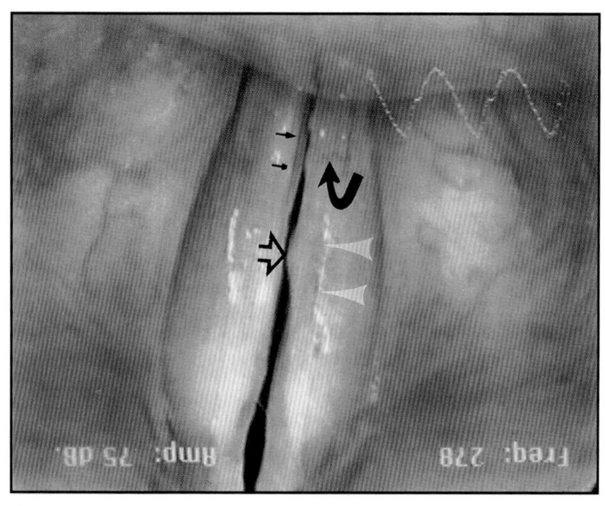

A

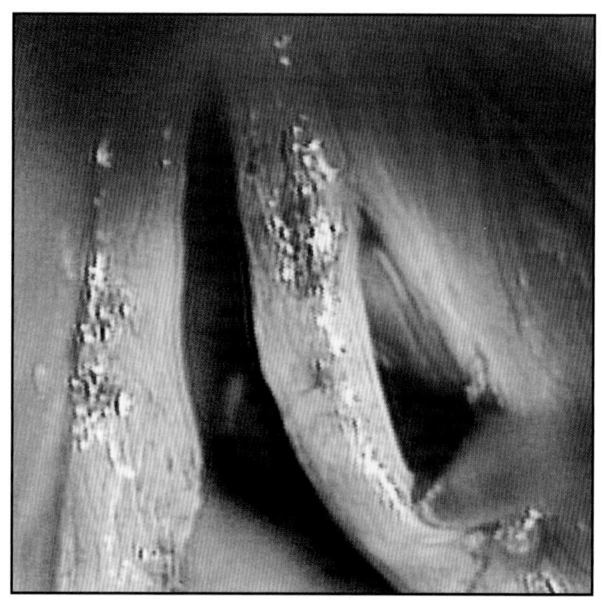

B

Fig 14–35. A. Strobovideolaryngoscopy of this 33-year-old singer revealed bilateral vocal fold stiffness, evidence of previous hemorrhage, left sulcus vocalis (*small arrows*), right vocal fold mass (*open arrow*), ectatic vessels on the superior surfaces of both vocal folds with a prominent vessel running at 90° to the vibratory margin (*curved arrow*), a small anterior glottic web (not shown), and muscular tension dysphonia. The importance of a line on the superior surface of the right vocal fold (*white arrowheads*) was not appreciated preoperatively. It appeared to be simply a light reflex. **B.** Intraoperatively, this was found to be the opening into an unusually large mucosal bridge. The mucosal bridge was removed, and autologous fat was injected laterally to medialize the right vocal fold and improve glottic closure.

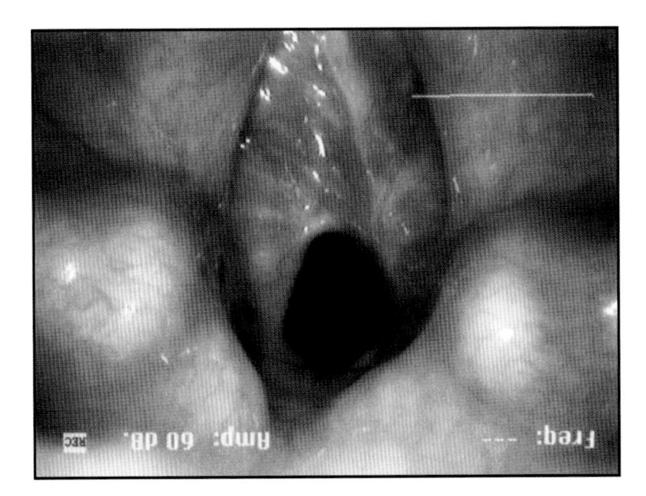

Fig 14–36. Typical appearance of an anterior glottic web.

plete, voice therapy usually is helpful but rarely restores normalcy. When the superior laryngeal nerve is completely paralyzed, treatment is much more difficult. Collagen injections have been advocated for this situation, as have autologous fat injection, thyroplasty, and other procedures.

Laryngeal Trauma

Laryngeal trauma may cause many problems in addition to the webs discussed above. Trauma may be internal or external. It may result in vocal fold hemorrhage or mucosal tears, either of which may produce permanent scars. Trauma may also fracture the laryngeal skeleton, dislocate the arytenoids, or paralyze the laryngeal nerves. The principles of treatment in a professional voice user are the same as those for anyone else, and they are discussed in detail in *Treatment of Voice Disorders*[30] and in other literature. A safe airway should be established. If intubation is required, immediate or early tracheotomy should be performed to minimize the risk of iatrogenic trauma of the vocal folds.

Whenever possible, a complete diagnostic voice evaluation including strobovideolaryngoscopy and objective voice analysis should be carried out to map and document the injury as well as possible. When there is a question as to whether vocal fold motion is impaired because of paralysis or mechanical causes, laryngeal electromyography should be used. High-resolution axial and coronal CT scans are often extremely helpful. High resolution allows not only an excellent view of the larynx, but also clear visualization of the cricoarytenoid and cricothyroid joints.

When major injuries occur in professional voice users, it is advisable to involve a speech-language pathologist in the patient's care as soon as the medical condition permits, preferably prior to surgery. After surgery, the speech-language pathologist should participate in the patient's rehabilitation as soon as the patient is allowed to speak. Early involvement of the patient's professional voice teacher is also helpful, so long as the singing or acting teacher is interested in and comfortable with training of injured voices. Close collaboration among all members of the voice team is particularly important in rehabilitating such patients.

Cricoarytenoid and Cricothyroid Joint Injury

The cricoarytenoid and cricothyroid joints are synovial joints, composed of tissues similar to those that make up knees and elbows. They are also subject to the same afflictions, including infection, arthritis, scarring, subluxation and dislocation, and other maladies. Impairments in laryngeal joint motion may alter phonation during speech and singing. In some cases, joint dysfunction may even prevent the vocal folds from moving at all and cause life-threatening problems such as airway obstruction. Information on this topic can be found in other literature.[31]

Papilloma

Papilloma is a wartlike viral disease that can afflict epithelial surfaces, including the vocal folds. Respiratory papillomatosis is associated typically with frequent recurrences following treatment. Traditionally, treatment has been surgical; and some patients have undergone more than 80 operations for control of their papillomas. New treatments are under investigation to decrease the number of operations required or to treat papillomas nonsurgically. Medications such as indol-3 carbinol (found in cabbage), antiviral agents (such as cidofovir) and others have been tried. Recently, pulsed dye laser therapy has been used. This technique is substantially different from traditional carbon dioxide laser surgery and from resection with cold instruments. Interested readers should consult other literature for more information on laryngeal papilloma.[32]

Precancerous Lesions

Precancerous lesions are discussed in detail in *Professional Voice*.[33] Two common terms are worthy of extra emphasis here, however. The term *leukoplakia* is used for abnormalities that look like white plaques. Patchy white areas may occur anywhere on the mucous membrane, including on the true vocal folds. Although leukoplakia is commonly thought of as premalignant, the term is descriptive and carries no histological implication. Leukoplakia may be caused by cancer, hyperkeratosis, tuberculosis, prolonged ulcerative laryngitis, and other conditions. However, because precancerous lesions and some cancers often present as leukoplakia, white lesions of this sort generally require biopsy if they do not resolve promptly. *Erythroplakic* lesions are red patches, and their implications are similar to those of leukoplakia.

Hyperkeratosis is an abnormality in which keratinized cells build up upon each other in a layered fashion. This causes a mass-effect, and it may cause increased stiffness of the vocal fold cover. It is considered precancerous. However, hyperkeratosis does not generally cause adynamic segments. If hyperkeratosis progresses to invasive carcinoma, the invading tumor essentially attaches the epithelium to the vocal ligament and muscle. This does produce an adynamic region. However, it must also be recognized that early superficial cancers may be present without causing adynamic regions on the vocal fold, so malignancy cannot be ruled out by strobovideolaryngoscopy alone.

Carcinoma of the Vocal Fold

When cancer (Fig 14–37) occurs in professional voice users, a great effort must be made to choose a treatment modality that preserves good voice function while providing the best chance for cure of the cancer. At present, there are no indisputable controlled studies on post-treatment vocal quality to help guide the laryngologist and patient. Initially, it seems as if radiation therapy is "obviously" better for vocal quality than surgery. However, postradiation changes in the mucosa, lubrication, and muscle may be significant. Controlled studies comparing radiation with various surgical techniques are needed, and such studies must consider not only early results, but also vocal quality 5 and 10 years after the treatment. Laser surgery has become popular for treatment of selected vocal lesions including cancer. However, Hirano[22] has pointed out that "tissue is much thicker after laser surgery than after radiation therapy," and critical comparisons of surgery with laser versus traditional instruments also need to be done. For advanced cancer, treatment in professional voice users varies little from that in other patients.

Granular Cell Tumor

Granular cell tumor is a rare neoplasm that may involve the larynx (see Fig 14–38). The tumor can be mistaken easily for a laryngeal granuloma. However, it is important for laryngologists to recognize this neoplasm and treat it appropriately.[34]

Granular cell tumor is rare, usually benign neoplasm that can occur in various parts of the body. Granular cell tumors may be single or multiple. They are most commonly seen in black population and have slightly higher incidence in females. Half of all granular cell tumors occur in the head or neck, with 33% of

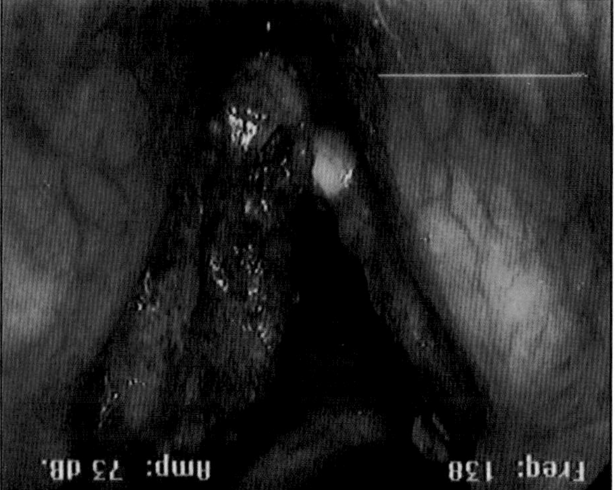

Fig 14–37. $T1_b$ squamous cell carcinoma involving both true vocal folds and the anterior commissure, but not involving cartilage or causing vocal fold fixation.

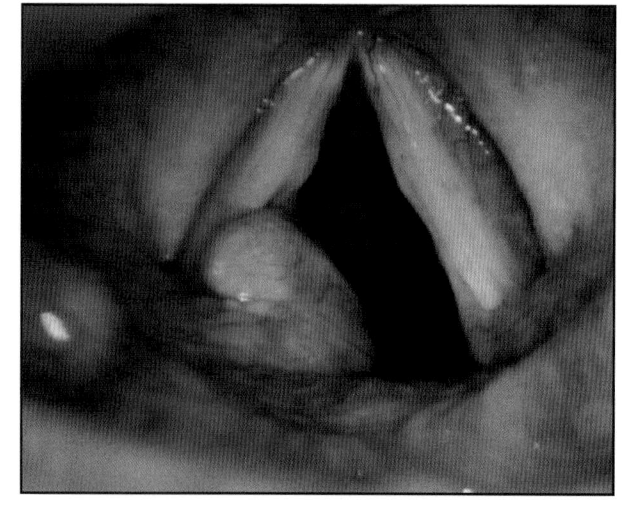

Fig 14–38. Left posterior granular cell tumor.

these occurring in the tongue. Tumors of the larynx are rare, accounting for only 7 to 10% of all reported cases of granular cell tumor.[34] Granular cell tumors present generally between the third and sixth decades of life, with a mean age for laryngeal tumors of 34 years. More than 50% of laryngeal granular cell tumors involve the true vocal folds, but involvement of the arytenoid cartilages, anterior commissure, false vocal folds, subglottis, and posterior cricoid region has been reported.[31] In adults, the posterior portion of the true vocal folds and arytenoid areas are the most common laryngeal sites affected. Although pediatric granular cell tumors are rare, they tend to involve the anterior and subglottic areas.[35]

Granular cell tumors were first described by Abrikossoff in 1926.[36] He called them myoblastomas because he believed that the tumor was of skeletal muscle origin. Since then, it has become evident that the lesion arises more frequently in tissue other than muscle, and there is often a relationship between its cells and peripheral nerves.[37] The research of Sobel and Marquet using microscopic and cytochemical staining techniques[38] has not supported Abrikossoff's theory of muscle origin but rather suggests a derivation from undifferentiated mesenchymal cells or Schwann cells. Although the cause remains unknown, inflammatory, degenerative, regenerative, and congenital etiologies have been proposed. Currently, granular cell tumors generally are accepted to be of neurogenic origin, although it continues to be difficult to confirm the neural origin of some granular cell tumors.[39]

There are two clinicopathologic forms of granular cell tumor in the upper aerodigestive tract. The congenital epulis form occurs in the gum pads of newborns. The nonepulis form is primarily a lesion found in adults. Over 1200 cases have been reported in the literature.[38] However, only 209 of these reported cases occurred in the larynx.[35,39-130]

Macroscopically, granular cell tumors are firm, sessile, and covered with mucosa that usually is intact. They are typically small (<2 cm) and well circumscribed but not encapsulated.[35] A covering of pseudoepitheliomatous hyperplasia overlies the mucosa in 50 to 65% of granular cell tumors. This epithelial finding may lead to the misdiagnosis of squamous cell carcinoma when a shallow biopsy is performed.

Granular cell tumors are distinctive histologically. They are polymorphic and range from polyhedral-shaped cells to a bizarre spindle form. They have abundant pale-staining acidophilic and granular cytoplasm. Cell nuclei are small, densely chromatic, vesicular, and centrally located. The cytoplamic granules react positively to Sudan black B and also to periodic acid-Schiff (PAS). Myelinated nerve fibers commonly are found in granular cell tumors. Ultrastructurally, these tumors have many fragmented, dense cytoplasmic lysosomes that are responsible for the granularity seen by the light microscopy.[127]

The diagnosis of laryngeal granular cell tumor usually is made on the basis of its histopathology. A diagnosis rarely is established preoperatively unless granular cell tumors have occurred in other sites before the development of laryngeal symptoms.[126] Typically, the tumors are painless.[131] The most common presenting symptom is hoarseness, with some patients also reporting dysphasia, otalgia, stridor, or hemoptysis.[131] Larger tumors can present with breathing difficulty.[127] Some tumors also may be asymptomatic and discovered incidentally. Tumor growth usually is slow.[34]

The preferred treatment is local excision using a cold knife or laser. Larger lesions may require laryngofissure or laryngectomy.[35] Treatment usually is curative with a recurrence rate between 2 and 8%.[37] It is possible that some of these "recurrences" actually may be new primary lesions because multiple lesions in various parts of the body occur in approximately 10% of patients.[35] Granular cell tumors are radio-resistant, and therefore radiation therapy generally is not indicated.

Although the literature states that a maximum of 3% of laryngeal granular cell tumors may be malignant, there is actually only one reported case[31] of the 209 (including this study) that the authors have identified. This suggests 0.6% incidence of malignancy in laryngeal granular cell tumors. Considering all sites, only 33 malignant granular cell tumors have been reported, and only 6 of these were in the head and neck.[127] These tumors usually result in death within 2 years of diagnosis, and 5 of the 6 reported patients died within 5 years. Malignancy in granular cell tumor is notoriously difficult to diagnose. There are two types of malignancy in granular cell tumor.[132,133] The first type is histologically and biologically malignant. The second and more common type is biologically malignant but may be histologically impossible to differentiate from benign granular cell tumor. The malignant tumors are typically larger (often over 4 cm), invasive, and grow rapidly. Metastases may occur in regional lymph nodes, lungs, bones, and viscera; and metastasis to areas that are not ordinarily involved with multiple primary granular cell tumors is the only certain criterion for diagnosis of malignancy.[131] To date, the mean age of patients with malignant tumors is 48 years, 16 years older than the mean age of patients with benign tumors at the time of diagnosis.[134]

Granular cell tumors of the larynx are uncommon but not rare. It is important for all otolaryngologists to be familiar with this entity and current concepts in management. Complete surgical resection usually is possible, and in most cases, a serviceable voice can be preserved. Although the length of follow-up has varied substantially in the literature, the author recommends long-term surveillance, including clinical examination and periodic imaging using magnetic resonance imaging (MRI) with gadolinium, at least until additional study has established the natural history and recurrence patterns of granular cell tumor with greater certainty.

Chondroma and Chondrosarcoma

Cartilaginous tumors of the larynx are uncommon. When they occur, they are most likely to be chondromas or low-grade chonodrosarcomas. Three-quarters of these cartilaginous tumors arise from the posterior lamina of the cricoid cartilage on the endolaryngeal surface.[135-138] Twenty percent of tumors or less involve the thyroid cartilage, and only about 10% of tumors involve the body of the arytenoids cartilage.[138] Laryngeal chondromas are extremely uncommon, although the true incidence is difficult to determine from the literature. Chondromas must be placed in a spectrum of cartilaginous lesions including chondroma, chondrometaplasia, chondrosarcoma, and cartilage within a lesion classified otherwise. Chondrosarcomas represent between 30 and more than 50% of cartilaginous tumors in the larynx.[137,140-142] Because the majority of laryngeal chondrosarcomas are histologically low grade and grow slowly, they are misdiagnosed commonly (clinically) as chondromas. Chondromas can occur in children or adults. In general, at the time of presentation they tend to be small (<3 cm in diameter). Chondrosacomas are often larger than 3 cm in diameter and generally are found in adults in the sixth and seventh decades of life. There is a male-to-female preponderance of 3 or 4 to 1.[143] Most cartilaginous tumors arise below the level of the vocal folds. Dyspnea, stridor, and dysphonia are common presenting complaints. In addition to the usual presentations of condrosarcoma, Koufman has described chondrosarcoma of the cricoid cartilage (low grade) presentations as "arytenoids hypertelorism" (excessively wide spacing between the arytenoids cartilages). Treatment with hemicricoidectomy is usually sufficient, although laryngectomy may be required (Jaime Koufman, MD, personal communication, 2003).

Histologically, vascular invasion occurs with both benign chondromas and malignant chondrosarcomas. The differentiation is made based on the presence of many cells with plump nuclei or clumps of chromatin in malignant lesions.[144] The differentiation between chondromas and low-grade chondrosarcomas is difficult, and it is often useful to obtain a second opinion from a pathologist who is expert in these tumors. The increased cellularity and nuclear pleomorphism in high-grade chondrosarcomas make them more distinct. Chondrosarcomas metastasize by hematogenous spread, usually to the lungs, kidney, cervical spine, or as subcutaneous nodules; metastasis occurs in 8% of the cases.[145]

Diagnosis usually is made initially by CT scan. Chondromas typically show coarse calcifications in a smooth soft tissue mass. Chondromas are treated by surgical excision, as well. Low-grade chondrosarcomas usually are treated by conservative surgical excision, as well. Lavertu and Tucker found no difference between radical surgery and conservative surgery followed by salvage therapy.[141] Nevertheless, because local occurrence rates are high and few cases are reported, optimal treatment remains uncertain. High-grade chondrosarcomas are treated by laryngectomy, as are anaplastic tumors, recurrent tumors, and tumors that have destroyed substantial amounts of the laryngeal skeleton.

Osteoma and Osteosarcoma

Osteomas are slow-growing benign neoplasms that form dense, sclerotic bone. They have been described only once in the larynx.[146]

Osteogenic sarcoma of the larynx is also an uncommon tumor.[147] Osteosarcoma will not be discussed in detail in this chapter. It is a potentially lethal tumor that requires aggressive therapy.

Lipoma

Lipoma of the larynx and hypopharynx is rare.[148] These benign fatty tumors can involve hypopharynx or larynx and can be misdiagnosed as laryngoceles, pharyngoceles, or retention cysts. MRI scan is helpful in defining the lesion and in recognizing the typical fatty tissue appearance of a lipoma. Only six cases of laryngeal lipoma have been reported in the literature, five of them in 2000 by Jungehülsing.[148]

Amyloidosis

Amyloidosis is a condition characterized by the accumulation of insoluble fibrillar protein (amyloid) in tissues and organs throughout the body. Some deposition processes are local and some are systemic. Of the several types of amyloidosis, nodular amyloidosis is most commonly found in the larynx and nasopharynx, as well as trachea and lungs.

An illustrative case was reported by Sataloff et al,[149] and is discussed here to highlight the nature of this condition. A 48-year-old basketball coach presented with a 2½-year history of progressive hoarseness, vocal fatigue, loss of high and low range, and pain on speaking. The problems were severe enough to cause his retirement from coaching. His otolaryngologists had diagnosed him recently with amyloidosis of the larynx. Histopathologic evaluation by H&E staining revealed a soft-tissue mass with normal surface squamous epithelium, chronic subepithelial inflammatory infiltrate, and diffuse eosinophilic intercellular deposits (some causing pressure necrosis of surrounding stroma) (Fig 14–39). Congo red dye stained sections showed the characteristic yellow and apple green birefringence caused by cross-beta-pleated configuration of the amyloid fibrils (Fig 14–40).

He was referred to the author (RTS) for further treatment. A thorough system workup showed no evidence of amyloid elsewhere. Physical examination and videostroboscopy revealed a large left supraglottic mass (Fig 14–41) obscuring visualization of the anterior two thirds of the left vocal fold, with partial supraglottic obstruction of the airway and a good subglottic airway, despite evidence of a tracheal mass (Fig 14–42). A pharyngeal mass (Fig 14–43 and a tongue base mass (Fig 14–44) were also found. Surgical resection of the supraglottic mass resulted in an improved voice.

Surgery is the mainstay of treatment for laryngeal amyloidosis. However, the surgeon must guard against the tendency to try to cure the amyloidosis with total resection, unless it is delimited clearly within nonvital structures. Amyloidosis tends to involve areas larger than apparent from clinical inspection (Fig 14–45). Its boundaries can be detected more accurately by CT and MRI. Until better therapy is devised,

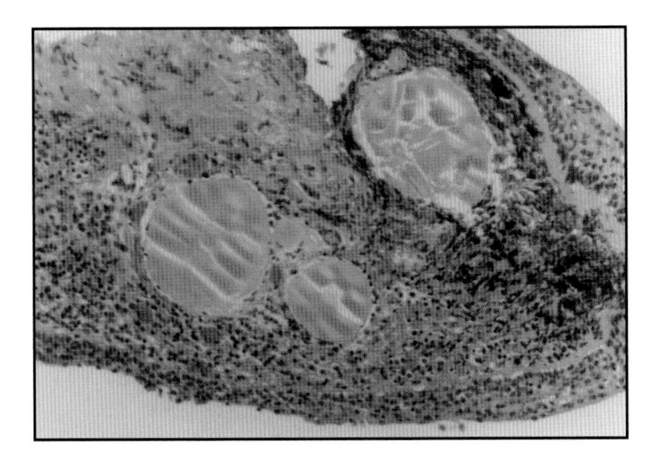

Fig 14–39. Amyloidosis showing normal surface epithelium, with subepithelial inflammatory infiltrate and eosinophilic intracellular deposits.

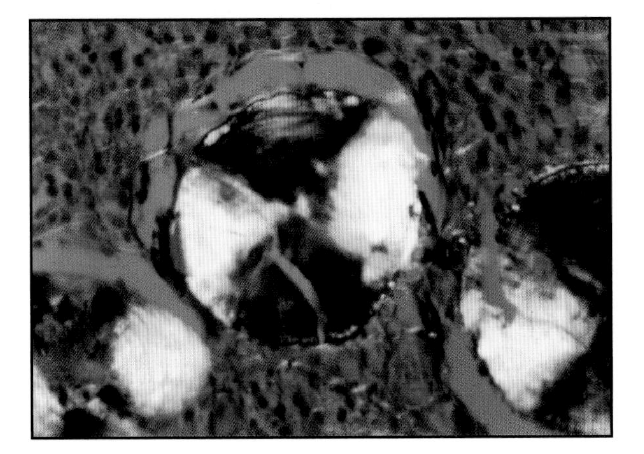

Fig 14–40. Yellow and apple green birefringence typical of amyloidosis stained with Congo red dye.

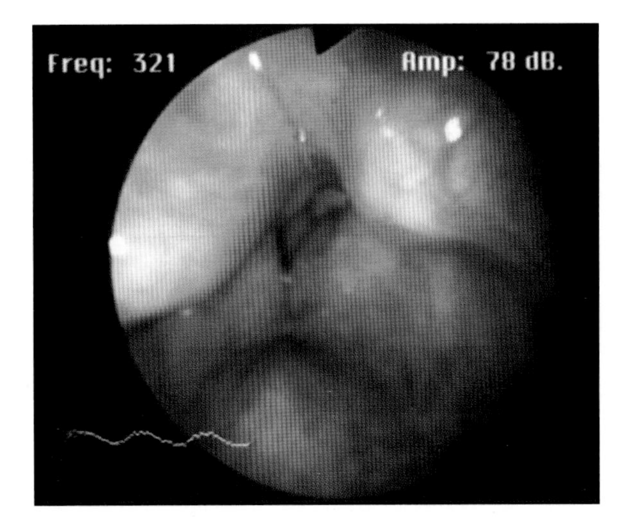

Fig 14–41. Left supraglottic amyloid mass.

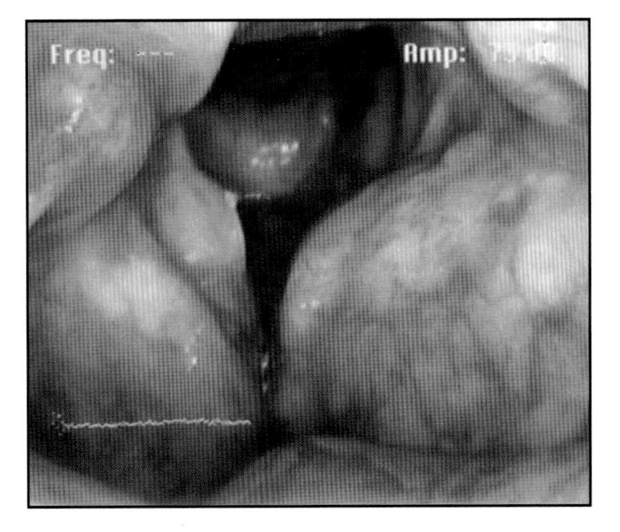

Fig 14–42. Amyloid tracheal mass.

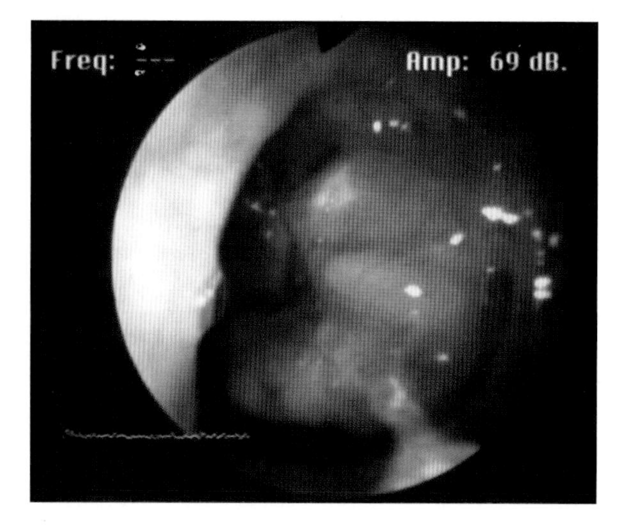

Fig 14–43. Pharyngeal mass of amyloid.

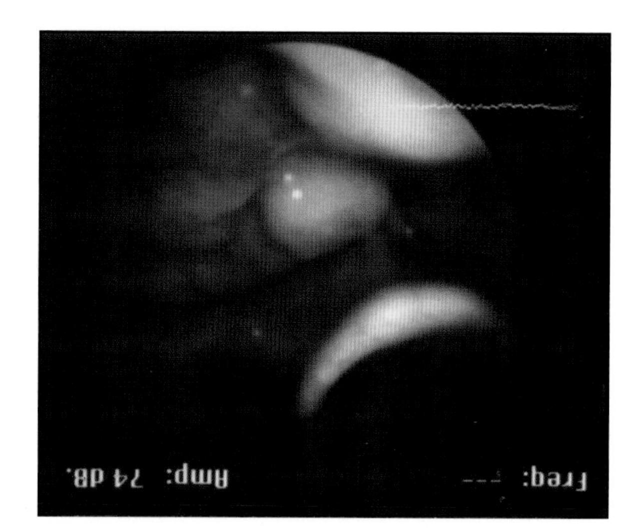

Fig 14–44. Amyloid involving the tongue base.

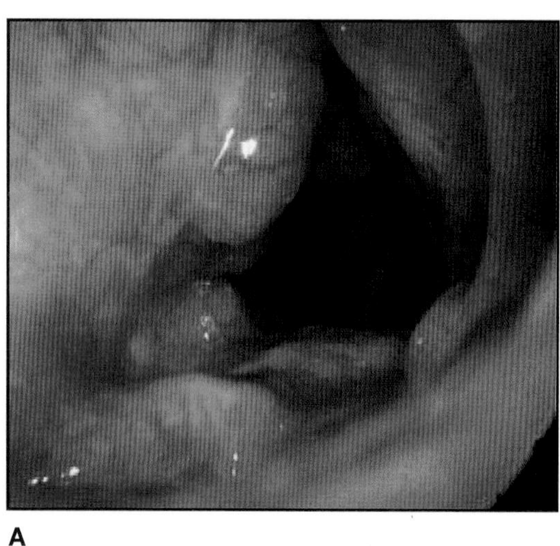

A

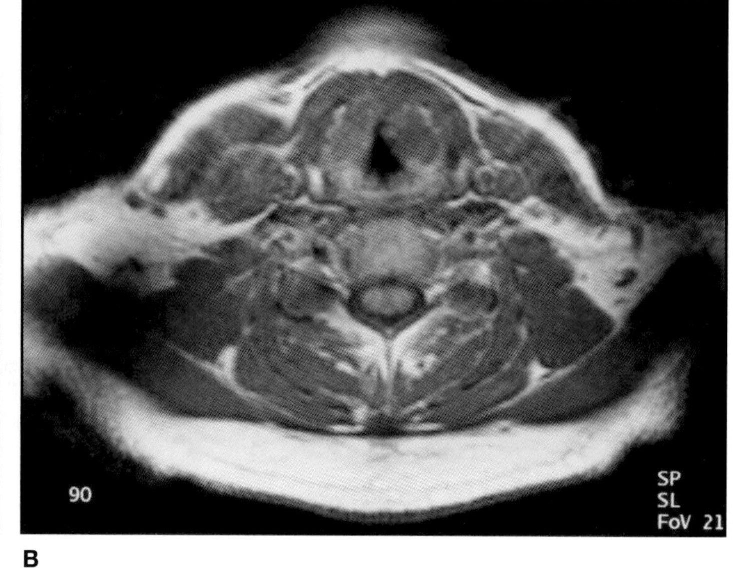

B

Fig 14–45. This patient is a minister who was referred because of severe dysphonia due to supraglottic amyloidosis. The amyloidosis is apparent in the left supraglottic area (**A**) and extending transglottally into the subglottic region. However, CT and MRI (**B**) revealed amyloidosis involving both false vocal folds, and (not shown) extending into tongue base and pharynx. The amyloidosis was resected extensively from the region of the left false vocal fold, removing the bulk of amyloid that was compressing and invading the left true vocal fold. Excellent voice improvement resulted. Additional surgery has been and will be required periodically.

surgery should be directed toward optimizing phonatory and respiratory function in most cases, rather than toward eradication of disease.

Laryngeal amyloidosis has been recognized for many years.[150-152] Laryngeal amyloidosis is most common in the false vocal fold. Amyloid is a substance composed of protein and starch that accumulates in body tissues. Secondary amyloidosis, the more common form, may be associated with multiple myeloma (a malignancy of bone marrow), collagen vascular disease such as rheumatoid arthritis, infections such as chronic osteomyelitis, and other conditions. Primary amyloidosis occurs for no discernible reason. Amyloidosis may affect the heart, kidney, liver, spleen, tongue, stomach, intestines, larynx, and virtually any other body tissue. The involved areas generally enlarge and develop a pink or gray color, and waxy or raised areas are found commonly in the axial, groin, face, and neck. Amyloidosis usually is not hereditary, but there is also an inherited form. Hereditary amyloidosis frequently involves the nervous system, causing peripheral neuropathy, incontinence, decreased sweating, postural hypertension, and renal failure. When the larynx is involved, hoarseness and decreased vocal range are common. Regardless of the tissue affected, diagnosis depends on biopsy with special stains. It is helpful if the surgeon suspects the condition so that the pathologist can be warned to stain the tissues appropriately. In secondary amyloidosis, treatment of the underlying disease often results in stabilization or even reversal of amyloid deposits. However, there is no other specific treatment for secondary amyloidosis and no known treatment for primary amyloidosis other than surgical resection if resectable amyloid deposits cause symptoms.

Miscellaneous Structural Lesions

Other masses, neoplasms, and other structural abnormalities may occur in the larynx. Some of these are covered in *Professional Voice: The Science and Art of Clinical Care.*[153] Others are discussed in other literature. The principles of management for the more uncommon lesions are similar to those discussed in this chapter and in *Professional Voice: The Science and Art of Clinical Care.*[153]

References

1. Curtis HH. The cure of singers' nodules. *NY Med J.* January 8, 1898:37–39.
2. Rubin HJ, Lehrhoff I. Pathogenesis and treatment of vocal nodules. *J Speech Hear Dis.* 1962;27(2):150–161.
3. Brodnitz FS. Goals, results, and limitations of vocal rehabilitation. *Arch Otolaryngol.* 1963;77:148–156.
4. Deal RE, McClain B, Sudderth JF. Identification, evaluation, therapy, and follow-up for children with vocal nodules in a public school setting. *J Speech Hear Dis.* 1976;41(3):390–397.
5. Lancer JM, Sider D, Jones AS, LeBoutillier A. Vocal cord nodules: a review. *Clin Otolaryngol.* 1988;13:43–51.
6. Knight FI. Singer's nodes. *Trans Am Laryngol Assoc.* 1894;16:118–123.
7. Curtis HH. The cure of singers' nodules. *Trans Am Laryngol Rhinol Otolog Soc.* 1897;3:95–101.
8. Zerffi AC. Voice reeducation. *Arch Otolaryngol.* 1948;48: 521–526.
9. Brodnitz FS. *Keep Your Voice Healthy.* New York, NY: Harper & Brothers; 1953.
10. Withers B,. Dawson MH. Treatment of vocal nodule cases: psychological aspects. *Texas J Med.* 1960;56:43–46.
11. Wilson KD. Voice reeducation of adolescents with vocal nodules. *Laryngoscope.* 1962;72:45–53.
12. Wilson KD. Voice reeducation of adults with vocal nodules. *Arch Otol Rhinol Laryngol.* 1962;76:68–73.
13. Fisher HB, Logemann JA. Objective evaluation of therapy for vocal nodules: a case report. *J Speech Hear Dis.* 1970;35:277–285.
14. Fisher HB, Logemann JA. Voice diagnosis and therapy. *Otolaryngol Clin North Am.* 1970;35:639–663.
15. Brodnitz FS. *Vocal Rehabilitation.* Rochester, Minn: American Academy of Ophthalmology and Otolaryngology; 1971.
16. Drudge MK, Philips BJ. Shaping behavior in voice therapy. *J Speech Hear Dis.* 1976;41:398–411.
17. Reed CG. Voice therapy; a need for research. *J Speech Hear Dis.* 1980;45:157–169.
18. Barnes JE. Voice therapy for nodules and vocal polyps. *Rev Laryngol Rhinol.* 1981;102:99–103.
19. Vaughan CW. Current concepts in otolaryngology: diagnosis and treatment of organic voice disorders. *New Engl J Med.* 1982;307:333–336.
20. Sataloff RT, Spiegel JR, Hawkshaw MJ. Strobovideolaryngocopy: results and clinical value. *J Voice.* 1988;1: 359–364.
21. Sataloff RT, Spiegel JR, Hawkshaw MJ. Strobovideolaryngocopy in professional voice users: results and clinical value. *Ann Otol Rhinol Laryngol.* 1991;100:725–757.
22. Hirano M. Surgical anatomy and physiology of the vocal folds. In: Gould WJ, Sataloff RT, Spiegel JR, eds. *Voice Surgery.* New York, NY: Mosby-Yearbook, Inc; 1993: 135–158.
23. Ylitalo R. Clinical studies of contact granuloma in posterior laryngitis with special regard to esophagopharyngeal reflux. Stockholm, Sweden: Karolinska Institute; 2000.
24. Fritzell B, Hertegard S. A retrospective study of treatment of vocal fold edema: a preliminary report. In: Kirchner JA, ed. *Vocal Fold Histopathology: A Symposium.* San Diego, Calif: College-Hill Press; 1986:57–64.
25. Reinke F. Uber die funktionelle Struktur der menschlichen Stimmlippe mit besonderer berucksichtigung des elastischen Gewebes [About the functional structure of the human vocal cord with special reference to the elastic tissue]. *Anat Hefte.* 1897;9:103–117.
26. Zeitels SM, Hillman RE, Bunting GW, Vaughn T. Reinke's edema: phonatory mechanisms and management strategies. *Ann Otol Rhinol Laryngol.* 1997;106: 533–543.
27. Putney FJ, Clerf LH. Treatment of chronic hypertrophic laryngitis. *Arch Otolaryngol.* 1940;31:925–929.
28. Myerson MC. Smoker's larynx. A clinical pathological entity. *Ann Otol Rhinol Laryngol.* 1940;31:925–929.
29. Sataloff RT, Hawkshaw MJ. Vocal fold hemorrhage. In: Sataloff, RT. *Professional Voice: The Science and Art of Clin-*

ical Care. 3rd ed. San Diego, Calif: Plural Publishing, Inc; 2005:1291–1307.
30. Heman-Ackah Y, Sataloff RT. Laryngotracheal trauma. In Sataloff RT. *Treatment of Voice Disorders.* San Diego, Calif: Plural Publishing, Inc: 2005:263–288.
31. Sataloff RT. Cricoarytenoid and cricothyroid joint injury: evaluation and treatment. In: Sataloff RT. *Professional Voice: The Science and Art of Clinical Care.* 3rd ed. San Diego, Calif: Plural Publishing, Inc; 2005:1341–1351.
32. Friedman O, Sataloff RT. Laryngeal papilloma. In: Sataloff RT. *Professional Voice: The Science and Art of Clinical Care.* 3rd ed. San Diego, Calif: Plural Publishing, Inc; 2005:835–844.
33. Dean CM, Sataloff RT. Premalignant lesions of the larynx. In: Sataloff RT. *Professional Voice: The Science and Art of Clinical Care.* San Diego, Calif: 2005:1365–1374.
34. Sataloff RT, Ressue JC, Portell M, et al. Granular cell tumors of the larynx. *J Voice.* 2000;14(1):119–134.
35. Lazar RH, Younis RT, Kluka EA, et al. Granular cell tumor of the larynx: report of two pediatric cases. *Ear Nose Throat J.* 1992:440–443.
36. Abrikossoff AJ. Uber myome. *Virchow Arch* (A). 1926; 260:215–233.
37. Conley SF, Milbrath M, Beste D. Pediatric laryngeal granular cell tumor. *J Otolaryngol.* 1992;21:450–453.
38. Sobel HJ, Marquet E. Granular cells and granular cell lesions. *Pathol Ann.* 1974;9(0):43–79.
39. Batsakis JG. *Tumors of the Head and Neck.* 2nd ed. Baltimore, Md: Williams & Wilkins; 1979:327–331.
40. Dawydow C. Zur Frage der unausgereiften rhabdomyome des kehlkopfes. *Zeitschriff Fur Hals, Nasen und Ohren.* 1931;30:221–227.
41. Derman GL, Golbert ZW. Uber unreife, aus der quergestreifteb muskulatur hervorgehende myome. *Virchows Archiv.* 1931;282:172–180.
42. Glasunow M. Uber nreife, begrenzt und destruierend wachsende rhabdomyoblastome. *Frankf Zeitschr Pathol.* 1933;45:328–345.
43. Geschelin AI. Fall von myoblastom des kehlkopfs. *Zur Klinik Seltener Kehlkopfgeschwulste.* 1934;21:66–70.
44. Kleinfeld L. Myoblastoma of the larynx. *Arch Otolaryngol.* 1934;19:551–555.
45. Kernan JD, Cracovaner AJ. Rhabdomyoma of the vocal cord—report of a case. *Laryngoscope.* 1935;45:891–893.
46. Bobbio A. Mioblastoma ad elementi granulose (mioblastoma di Abrikossoff) della laringe. *Arch Sci Med.* 1936; 61:583–589.
47. Frenckner P. The occurrence of so-called myoblastomas in the mouth and upper air passages. *Acta Otolaryngol* (Stockh). 1938;26:689–701.
48. Iglauer S. Myoblastoma of the larynx. *Ann Otol Rhinol Laryngol.* 1942;51:1089–1093.
49. Fust JA, Custer RP. On the neurogenesis of so-called granular cell myoblastoma. *Am J Clin Pathol.* 1949;19: 522–535.
50. Maguda TA, Young JM. Granular cell myoblastoma of the vocal cord. *Ann Otol Rhinol Laryngol.* 1953;62:1035–1038.
51. Somers K, Farinacci CJ. Granular cell myoblastoma of the vocal cord. *Laryngoscope.* 1953;63:422–429.
52. MacNaughtan IP, Fraser MS. Myoblastoma of the larynx. *J Laryngol Otol.* 1954;68:680–688.
53. Keohane J. Myoblastoma of the larynx: a case report. *J Laryngol Otol.* 1956;70:544–545.
54. Busanny-Caspari W, Hammar CH. Zur malignitat der sogenannten myoblastenmyome. Zentralbl Allg. *Pathol.* 1958;98:401–406.
55. Hinton CD, Weinberger MA. Granular cell myoblastoma of the larynx. *Arch Otolaryngol.* 1958;68:497–500.
56. Bertogalli D. Mioblastoma della corda vocale. *Arch Ital Otol Rinol Laringol.* 1959;70:748–759.
57. Slywanowicz L, Mioduszewska O. Myoblastoma laryngis. *Pol Tyg Lek.* 1959,14:1155–1158.
58. Balshi SF. Myoblastoma of the larynx. *Ann Otol Rhinol Laryngol.* 1960;69:115–120.
59. Beekhuis GJ. Granular-cell myoblastoma of the larynx: report of three cases. *Arch Otolaryngol.* 1960;72:314–320.
60. Walter WL. Granular myoblastoma of the larynx with the presentation of two cases. . *Ann Otol Rhinol Laryngol.* 1960;69:328–340.
61. Chiappe LC. Mioblastoma laringeo. [Laryngeal myoblastoma. Abrikossoff's tumor.] *Prensa Med Argent.* 1961;48:3215–3217.
62. Lyons GD, Haindel C, Blatt IM. Myoblastoma of the larynx. A report of five cases. *Laryngoscope.* 1962;72:909–914.
63. Ward PH, Oshiro H. Laryngeal granular-cell myoblastoma. Appearance with pseudoepitheliomatous hyperplasia. *Arch Otolaryngol.* 1962;76:239–244.
64. Gosavi DK, Bond WM. Granular cell myoblastoma of vocal cord. *J Laryngol Otol.* 1964;78:79–81.
65. Halperin D. Granular cell myoblastoma of the vocal cord. Report of a case. *Ann Otol Rhinol Laryngol.* 1964;73: 184–185.
66. Ottosson BG. Myoblastoma of the larynx. *Acta Otolaryngol* (Stockh). 1964;58:86–93.
67. Von Westernhagen BV. Die sogenannten myoblastenmyome des Kehlkopfes und ihre haufige Fehldeutung als Carcinom. *HNO.* 1964;12:49–50.
68. Pope TH. Laryngeal myoblastoma. *Arch Otolaryngol.* 1965;81:80–82.
69. Andre P. Renault P, Laccourreye H, et al. Tumeur d'Abrikossoff du larynx. *Ann Otolaryngol Chir Cervicofac.* 1966;83(6):437–440.
70. Cracovaner AJ, Opler SR. Granular cell myoblastoma of the larynx. *Laryngoscope.* 1967;77(6):1040–1046.
71. Sedee GA. Granular cell myoblastoma of the larynx. *J Laryngol Otol.* 1967;81:557–559.
72. Guerrier Y, Dejean Y, Galy G, Serrou B. Myoblastome du larynx ou tumeur d'Abrikossoff. *J Fr Otorhinolaryngol Audiophonol Chir Maxillofac.* 1968;17:477–489.
73. Otto HD, Rose AM. Granularzellenmyoblastom mit pseudokarzinomatoser epithelproliferation an der stimmlippe. *Z Laryngol Rhinol Otol.* 1968;47:228–233.
74. Bhatnagar HN, Schawarz HJ. Granular cell myoblastoma of larynx with papillary adenocarcinoma of thyroid. *Arch Otolaryngol.* 1969;90:156–158.
75. Lacomme Y, Galaup J. Volumineuse tumeur d'Abrikossoff du larynx. *J Fr Otorhinolaryngol Audiophonol Maxillofac.* 1969;9:708–712.

76. Piquet JJ, Blondy G, Leduc M, Decroix G. Les tumeurs d'Abrikossoff du larynx. *Ann Otolaryngol Chir Cervicofac.* 1969;86:79–85.
77. Sardana DS, Yadav YC. Granular cell myoblastoma of the laryngopharynx. *J Laryngol Otol.* 1969;83:1023–1025.
78. Schneider C, Gould WJ, Mirani R. Granular cell myoblastoma of larynx. *Arch Otolaryngol.* 1969;89:95–99.
79. Vance SF, Hudson RP. Granular cell myoblastoma. Clinicopathologic study of forty-two patients. *Am J Clin Pathol.* 1969;52:208–211.
80. Booth JB, Osborn DA. Granular cell myoblastoma of the larynx. *Acta Otolaryngol.* 1970;70:279–293.
81. Canalis RF, Cohn AM. Granular cell myoblastoma of the larynx. *Arch Otolaryngol.* 1970; 91:125–127.
82. Goldstein A, Thaler S, Rozycki D. Granular cell myoblastoma and carcinoma of the larynx. *Arch Otolaryngol.* 1971;94:366–368.
83. Miglets AW, Gebhart DE, Gregg LO. Airway obstruction due to a large laryngeal granular cell myoblastoma. *Laryngoscope.* 1971;81:971–978.
84. Wolfowitz BL, Jaffe A. Granular cell myoblastoma of the larynx. *J Laryngol Otol.* 1972;86:643–646.
85. Thawley SE, May M, Oruga JH. Granular cell myoblastoma of the larynx. *Laryngoscope.* 1974;84:1545–1551.
86. Thawley SE, Oruga JH. Granular cell tumor of the trachea. *Arch Otolaryngol.* 1974;100:393–394.
87. Compagno J, Hyams VJ, Ste-Marie P. Benign granular cell tumors of the larynx: a review of 36 cases with clinicopathologic data. *Ann Otol Rhinol Laryngol.* 1975;84: 308–314.
88. Michaels L. Neurogenic tumors, granular cell tumor, and paraganglioma. *Can J Otolaryngol.* 1975;4(2):319–327.
89. Coates HL, Devine KD, McDonald TJ, Weiland LH. Granular cell tumors of the larynx. *Ann Otol Rhinol Laryngol.* 1976;85(4 Pt 1): 504–507.
90. Frable MA, Fisher RA. Granular cell myoblastomas. *Laryngoscope.* 1976;86(1):36–42.
91. Helidonis E, Dokianakis G, Pantazopoulos P. Granular cell myoblastoma of the larynx. *J Laryngol Otol.* 1978; 92:525–528.
92. Kenefick C. Granular cell myoblastoma of the larynx. *J Laryngol Otol.* 1978;92(6):521–523.
93. Agarwal RK, Blitzer A, Perzin KH. Granular cell tumors of the larynx. *Otolaryngol Head Neck Surg.* 1979;87: 807–814.
94. Lulenski GC. Granular cell myoblastoma of the larynx. *Arch Otolaryngol.* 1979;105:296–298.
95. Fechner RE. Pathologic Quiz Case 1. Granular cell tumor. *Arch Otolaryngol.* 1979;105(4):226–228.
96. Lack EE, Worsham GF, Callihan MD, Crawford BE, et al. Granular cell tumor: a clinicopathologic study of 110 patients. *J Surg Oncol.* 1980;13:301–316.
97. Majmudar B, Thomas J, Gorelkin L, Symbas PN. Respiratory obstruction caused by a multicentric granular cell tumor of the laryngotracheobronchial tree. *Hum Pathol.* 1981;12(3):283–286.
98. Shevchenko AM, Egorov VP, Gladkii NI, Miroshnichenko SV. [Abrikosov's granular cell tumor localized on the vocal fold.] *Vestn Otorhinolaringol.* 1981;5:77–78.
99. Tomeckova A, Odehnal F, Cerny K. Abrikosovuv tumor (granularne bunecny myoblastom) lokalozaci v hrtanu. Sdeleni o dvou pripadech. *Cesk Otolaryngol.* 1981;5:296–302.
100. El-Ghazali AMS, El-Ghazali TMS. Granular cell myoblastoma of the larynx. *J Laryngol Otol.* 1982;96:1177–1180.
101. Ivatury R, Shah D, Ascer E, et al. Granular cell tumor of the larynx and bronchus. *Ann Thorac Surg.* 1982;33(1): 69–73.
102. Lapena AM, Caballero T. Mioblastoma de celulas granulosas o tumor de Abrikossof de localizacion laringea. A proposito de un caso. *Acta Otorrinolaringol Esp.* 1982; 164–168.
103. Lopez-Cortijo C, Gonzalez F, Vergara J, Aranda FI. Tumor de celulas granulares (mioblastoma) de la laringe. *Acta Otorrinolaringol Esp.* 1983;34(3):315–320.
104. Garud O, Bostad L, Elverland HH, Mair IW. Granular cell tumor of the larynx in a 5-year-old child. *Ann Otol Rhinol Laryngol.* 1984;93:45–47.
105. Bedbeder P, Gehanno P. Localisations orl des tumeurs d'Abrikossoff a propos de 5 observations une tumeur qui n'est pas toujours anodine. *Ann Otolaryngol Chir Cervicofac.* 1985;102:169–173.
106. Har-El G, Shviro J, Avidor I, et al. Laryngeal granular cell tumor in children. *Am J Otolaryngol.* 1985;6:32–36.
107. Toncini C, Pesce C. Granular cell tumours of the oesophagus and larynx. *J Laryngol Otol.* 1985;99:1301–1304.
108. Broniatowski M. Pathologic Quiz Case 2. Granular cell myoblastoma. *Arch Otolaryngol Head Neck Surg.* 1986; 112:108–109.
109. DeBonis M, Montserrart JR, Mendez R, et al. Mioblastoma de celulas granulosas o tumor de Abrikossoff de localizacion laringea: a proposito de un caso. *Acta Otorrinolaringol Esp.* 1986;37(6):414–417.
110. Gangemi P, Arcidiacono A, Puzzo L. Tumore a cellule granulose (mioblastoma) della corda vocale. *Pathologica.* 1986;78:641–646.
111. Schottenfeld R, Marsh B. Granular cell tumor of the larynx. *Ear Nose Throat J.* 1987;66:415–418.
112. Alessi DM, Zimmerman MC. Granular cells tumors of the head and neck. *Laryngoscope.* 1988;98:810–814.
113. Goldofsky E, Hirschfield LS, Abramson AL. An unusual laryngeal lesion in children: granular cell tumor. *Int J Pediatr Otorhinlaryngol.* 1988;15(3):263–267.
114. Solomons NB. Extensive granular cell tumor of the larynx and trachea (a case of report). *J Laryngol Otol.* 1988; 102(7):658–660.
115. Fliss DM, Puterman M, Zirkin H, Leiberman A. Granular cell lesions in head and neck: a clinicopathological study. *J Surg Oncol.* 1989;42:154–160.
116. Manos PM, Garces GE, Casalots J, et al. Tumor de celulas granulares de laringe. *An Otorrinolaringol Ibero Am.* 1989;16(6):595–606.
117. Robb PJ, Girling A. Granular cell myoblastoma of the supraglottis. *J Laryngol Otol.* 1989;103:328–330.
118. Wight RG, Variend S, Bull PD. Granular cell tumor of the larynx in childhood. *J Laryngol Otol.* 1989;103:880–881.

119. Brandwein M, LeBenger J, Strauchen J, Biller H. Atypical granular cell tumor of the larynx: an unusually aggressive tumor clinically and microscopically. *Head Neck.* 1990;12:154–159.
120. Cree IA, Bingham BJ, Ramesar KC. Granular cell tumor of the larynx. *J Laryngol Otol.* 1990;104:159–161.
121. Falcioni M, Vighi V, Ferri T, Caruana P. Tumore a cellule granulose della laringe: a proposito di un caso. *Acta Biomed Ateneo Parmense.* 1990;61:179–184.
122. Watkins GL, Clark D, Foss D. Pathologic Quiz Case 1. Granular cell tumor of the larynx. *Arch Otolaryngol Head Neck Surg.* 1990;116:1448–1450.
123. Zamarro MT, Lopez JR, Ruiz JV, et al. Tumor de celulas granulosas de laringe. *Acta Otorrinolaringol Esp.* 1990; 41:133–135.
124. Del Toro AJJ, Marques VB, Rocher PF, et al. Tumor de celulas granulares de localizacion glotica. *Acta Otorrinolaringol Esp.* 1991;42(2):117–120.
125. Martinez Martinez CJ, Fogue Calvo L. Tumor de celulas granulares laringeo. *Rev Clin Esp.* 1991;189(4):181–182.
126. Conley SF, Milbrath MM, Beste DJ. Pediatric laryngeal granular cell tumor. *J Otolaryngol.* 1992;21(6):450–453.
127. Zietek E, Ptaszynski K, Jach K, Sienicki J. [Cases of granular cell tumor (myoblastoma) in the larynx.] *Otolaryngol Pol.* 1992;46:71–75.
128. Hamid AM, Alshaikhly A. Granular cell tumor of the larynx in an eight-year-old girl. *J Laryngol Otol.* 1993; 107(10):940–941.
129. Elo J, Arato G, Koppany J. Granular cell (Abrikosov) tumors treated with CO_2 laser. *Orv Hetil.* 1994;135(12): 635–637.
130. Mukherji SK, Castillo M, Rao V, Weissler M. Granular cell tumors of the subglottic region of the larynx: CT and MRI findings. *Am J Roentgenol.* 1995;164:1492–1494.
131. Holland RS, Abaza N, Balsara G, Lesser R. Granular cell tumor of the larynx in a six-year-old child: case report and review of literature. *Ear Nose Throat J.* 1998; 77(8):652–660.
132. Kershisnik M, Batsakis JG, Makay B. Granular cell tumors. *Ann Otol Rhinol Laryngol.* 1994;103:416–419.
133. Batsakis JG, Manning JT. Soft tissue tumors: unusual forms. *Otolaryngol Clin N Am.* 1986;19:659–683.
134. Klima M, Peters J. Malignant granular cell tumor. *Arch Pathol Lab Med.* 1987;111:1070–1073.
135. Neis PR, McMahon MF, Norris CW. Cartilaginous tumors of the trachea and larynx. *Ann Otol Rhinol Laryngol.* 1989;98:31–36.
136. Weise J, Viner T, Rinehart RJ, Dolan K. Imaging case of the month—cartilaginous tumor of the larynx. *Ann Otol Rhinol Laryngol.* 1987;101:617–619.
137. Tiwari RM, Snow GB, Balm AJ, et al. Cartilaginous tumours of the larynx. *J Laryngol Otol.* 1987;101:266–275.
138. Damiani K, Tucker H. Chondroma of the larynx. *Arch Otolaryngol.* 1981;107:399–402.
139. Huizenga C, Balogh K. Cartilaginous tumors of the larynx. *Cancer.* 1979;26:201–210.
140. Cantrell RW, Reibel JF, Jahrsdoerfer RA, Johns ME. Conservative surgical treatment of chondrosarcoma of the larynx. *Ann Otol Rhinol Laryngol.* 1980;89:567–571.
141. Lavertu P, Tucker HM. Chondrosarcoma of the larynx. Case report and management philosophy. *Ann Otol Rhinol Laryngol.* 1984;93:452–456.
142. Neel HB III, Unni KK. Cartilaginous tumors of the larynx: a series of 33 patients. *Otolaryngol Head Neck Surg.* 1982;90:201–207.
143. Franco RA Jr, Singh B, Har-El G. Laryngeal chondroma. *J Voice.* 2002;16(1):92–95.
144. Lichtenstein L, Jaffe HL. Chondrosarcoma of bone. *Am J Pathol.* 1943;19:553–573.
145. Ferlito A, Nicola P, Montaguti A, et al. Chondrosarcoma of the larynx: review of the literature and report of 3 cases. *Am J Otolaryngol.* 1984;5:350–359.
146. Batti JS, Abramson A. First report of a case of osteoma of the larynx. *Ear Nose Throat J.* 2000;79(8):564–566, 568.
147. Pinsolle J, LeChise I, Demeauz H, et al. Osteosarcoma of the soft tissue of the larynx: report of a case with electron microscopic studies. *Otolaryngol Head Neck Surg.* 1990;102:276–280.
148. Jungehülsing M, Fischbach R, Pototschnig C, et al. Rare benign tumors: laryngeal and hypopharyngeal lipomata. *Ann Otol Rhinol Laryngol.* 2000;109:301–305.
149. Sataloff RT, Abaza M, Abaza NA, et al. Amyloidosis of the larynx. *Ear Nose Throat J.* 2001;80(6):369–370.
150. Stark DB, New GB. Amyloid tumors of larynx and trachea or bronchi. *Med Clin North Am.* 1950;34:1145–1150.
151. Epstein SS, Winston P, Friedmann I, Ormerod FC. The vocal cord polyp. *J Laryngol Otol.* 1957;71:673–688.
152. Michaels L, Hyams VJ. Amyloid in localised deposits and plasmacytomas of the respiratory tract. *J Pathol.* 1979;128:29–38.
153. Sataloff RT. *Professional Voice: The Science and Art of Clinical Care.* San Diego, Calif: Plural Publishing, Inc. 2005.

15

Voice Impairment, Disability, Handicap, and Medical-Legal Evaluation

Robert Thayer Sataloff

Medical care of singers and actors inspired the development of voice as a subspecialty of laryngology. Although the interest was originally aesthetic and scientific, the broader practical importance of voice dysfunction soon became apparent. It is intuitively obvious that dysphonia in a great singer is not only an artistic and cultural tragedy, but also a disability that may result in the loss of millions of dollars annually for some performers. However, as our discipline evolved, it became clear that singers are not the only professional voice users. Voice professionals include also actors, clergy, politicians, teachers, sales personnel, secretaries, and anyone else whose ability to make a living is diminished or interrupted by voice disturbance.

As awareness of the importance of the human voice has grown, so too have legal issues surrounding voice dysfunction. Some voice disorders arise out of an individual's employment and may be covered under workers' compensation laws in some jurisdictions. Such cases might include vocal nodules developing in a schoolteacher or dysphonia in a shop foreman who suffers a laryngeal fracture while working and can no longer be heard over the noise at his or her job site. However, workers' compensation statutes are usually quite specific and vary greatly from one jurisdiction to another. The fact that a health problem is causally related to employment does not guarantee that it will be compensable under workers' compensation statutes in any given case. Other legal avenues may be pursued in some cases, such as civil suits under tort law; and physicians should be familiar with their roles in different types of legal proceedings and the financial implications for the patient of the applicable law. Hearing loss illustrates this issue particularly well. A given hearing loss may be compensated at the rate of $18,000 in Rhode Island, $108,940 in Pennsylvania, or at an unlimited level (depending on jury verdict) for a railroad worker subject to the Federal Employer's Liability Act. If a given injury (dysphonia, hearing loss, etc) is covered under workers' compensation law in a given jurisdiction, then compensation is determined by that statute; and the worker is generally prohibited from suing the employer outside the workers' compensation system. If the injury is not covered specifically in the applicable workers' compensation statute, then the employee may be able to file a civil suit and recover a potentially unlimited amount of compensation. Other cases are not causally related to work, such as a patient who develops dysphonia following endotracheal intubation, thoracic surgery, or laryngeal surgery. Yet, such vocal injuries may have profound effects on the patient's earning potential, and redress may be sought under tort law.

It is helpful for physicians to understand the accepted definitions of impairment, disability, and handicap. These terms are defined well by the World Health Organization.[1] An impairment is any loss or abnormality of psychological, physiological, or anatomical structure or function.[1(p47)] The abnormalities or losses that constitute an impairment may be temporary or permanent; and they involve the existence of a defect of a bodily structure, including mental defects. A disability resulting from an impairment is any restriction or lack of ability to perform an activity in the manner or within the range considered normal for a human being.[1(p143)] Disabilities are characterized by abnormalities of customarily expected performance of activities. They may be temporary or permanent; and there may be direct consequences of impairment or individual responses to an impairment (ie, psychological reactions). A handicap is any disadvantage for a given individual, resulting from an impairment or a disability, that limits or prevents the fulfillment of a role that is normal (depending on age, sex, and social and cultural factors) for that individual.[1(p183)] Handicap reflects the consequences for the individual resulting from an impairment and/or disability in terms of social, cultural, environmental, and economic impact.[2]

Voice Impairment, Disability, and Handicap

To help guide fair and reasonable determination of impairment and disability for voice, guidelines developed for other body systems and functions have been helpful. The World Health Organization's *International Classification of Functioning, Disability and Health* provides a classification scheme that is quite useful for many conditions; but it does not furnish specific compensation guidelines for most conditions. In the United States (and in some other countries) the American Medical Association's *Guides to the Evaluation of Permanent Impairment* (referred to as the *Guides*) have become the standard.[2] The *Guides* rate many impairments and disabilities throughout the body in terms of their percentage impairment of the whole person. At present, even the *Guides* do not provide a sufficient and sophisticated approach to the evaluation of voice impairment and disability. Various other publications of international repute also cover voice impairment disability in adequate depth.[2,3] This chapter contains suggestions to modify and improve existing guidelines.[2] Additional information about assessing voice handicap may be found in chapter 8.

For many years, voice and speech were treated by the medical profession (and the first four editions of the AMA *Guides*[2]) as one subject under the heading speech. In the last 20 years, voice and voice science have evolved as independent subspecialties in otolaryngology and speech-language pathology. So, technology and standards of practice now permit appropriate consideration of both aspects of verbal communication. The fifth edition of the AMA *Guides*[2] published in 2001 contains preliminary changes that acknowledge and begin to rectify this problem. *Voice* refers to production of sound of a given quality, ordinarily using the true vocal folds. *Speech* refers to the shaping of sounds into intelligible words. The disability and handicap associated with severe impairment of speech are obvious. If a person cannot speak intelligibly, verbal communication in social environments and the work place is extremely difficult or impossible. However, voice disorders have been underappreciated for so long that their significance may not be as immediately apparent. Nevertheless, if a voice disorder results in hoarseness, breathiness, voice fatigue, decreased vocal volume, or other similar voice disturbances, the worker may be unable to be heard in the presence of even moderate background noise, to carry on telephone conversations for prolonged periods, or to perform other work-related (and social) functions. Communication with hard-of-hearing family members and friends may also be particularly difficult and frustrating.

Numerous conditions, both physical and environmental, can result in voice or speech disturbances. An extensive review of their etiologies, diagnoses, and treatments is beyond the scope of this discussion. Information on this subject is contained elsewhere in this book and in other literature.[4-7] Briefly, voice and speech dysfunction may be due to trauma (brain, face, neck, chest), exposure to toxins and pollution, cerebrovascular accident, voice abuse, cancer, psychogenic disorders, and other causes. This chapter concentrates on the consequences of voice and speech dysfunction and also synthesizes information introduced in previous writings.[2,8,9]

Evaluation

Evaluation of a person with speech or voice complaints begins with a thorough history. Inquiry should include questions regarding the patient's professional and avocational vocal needs and habits, voice use patterns, problems prior to the onset of the current complaint, the time and apparent cause of the onset of voice and speech dysfunction, and any evaluations and interventions that have been tried to improve voice function. It is also essential to obtain information about environmental irritants and pollution, which may impact the voice greatly.[6] The voice may be impaired not only by mucosal irritants and inhalant toxicity, but also by any substances that decrease lung function or neurologic function (including neurotoxins such as heavy metals). However, a thorough history must include information about virtually all body systems, because maladies almost anywhere in the body may be causally related to voice complaints. The details of a comprehensive voice and speech history, and physical examination are beyond the scope of this brief chapter and may be found in other literature[7] and elsewhere in this book. The physical examination should include thorough evaluation of the structures in the head and neck and evaluation of other parts of the body, as appropriate, based on history and physical assessment of the patient. A thorough evaluation of voice and speech is also mandatory.

For the purposes of this chapter, it should be assumed that the evaluation of voice and speech involves an assessment of a person's ability to produce phonation and articulate speech, and does not involve assessment of content, language, or linguistic structure. At the present time, there is no single, universally accepted measure to quantify voice or speech function. Therefore, the standard of practice requires the use of a battery of tests.

Various tests and objective measures of voice have been clinically available since the late 1970s. Tests such as strobovideolaryngoscopy, acoustic analysis, phonatory function assessment, and laryngeal electromyography (EMG) are recognized as appropriate and useful in the evaluation of speech and voice disorders.[10-14] Some or all of these tests may be necessary in selected cases to determine the severity of a voice disorder and establish the presence of organic versus nonorganic voice and/or speech impairment and disability.

Evaluation of voice requires visualization of the larynx by a physician trained in laryngoscopy (usually an otolaryngologist) and determination of a specific medical cause for the voice dysfunction. Assessment of voice quality, frequency range, intensity range and endurance, pulmonary function, and function of the larynx as a valve (airflow regulator) can be performed easily and inexpensively. Normative values for these assessments have been established in the literature and are discussed elsewhere in this book.[7,11,14] More sophisticated techniques to quantify voice function (spectrography, inverse filtering, etc) may be helpful in selected cases. Slow-motion assessment of vocal fold vibration using strobovideolaryngoscopy (an established procedure that was first described more than 100 years ago) is often medically necessary to establish an accurate diagnosis.

In keeping with standard practice to establish the presence and amount of impairment and disability, a battery of tests is required to determine audibility, intelligibility, and functional efficiency of voice and speech. Audibility permits the patient to be heard over background noise. Intelligibility is the ability to link recognizable phonetic units of speech in a manner that can be understood. Functional efficiency is the ability to sustain voice and speech at a rate and for a period of time sufficient to permit useful communication.

Many approaches are available for speech assessment, most of which are described in standard speech-language pathology textbooks.[4] However, for the purposes of determining impairment and disability, the method recommended in the AMA *Guides* is employed most commonly.[2] This assessment protocol uses "The Smith House" reading paragraph, which reads as follows:

Larry and Ruth Smith have been married nearly fourteen years. They have a small place near Long Lake. Both of them think there's nothing like the country for health. Their two boys would rather live here than any other place. Larry likes to keep some saddle horses close to the house. These make it easy to keep his sons amused. If they wish, the boys can go fishing along the shore. When it rains, they usually want to watch television. Ruth has a cherry tree on each side of the kitchen door. In June they enjoy the juice and jelly.

The patient is placed approximately 8 feet from the examiner in a quiet room. The patient is then instructed to read the paragraph so that the examiner can hear him or her plainly and so that the patient can be understood. Patients who cannot read are asked to count to 100 (and should be able to do so in under 75 seconds). Patients are expected to be able to complete at least a 10-word sentence in one breath, sustain phonation for at least 10 seconds on one breath, speak loudly enough to be heard across the room, and maintain a speech rate of at least 75 to 100 words per minute. The advantages of the system described in the *Guides* are simplicity, and wide application for disability determination. However, this approach does not take advantage of many standardized speech evaluation tests, of technology for better quantification, or of techniques available to help identify psychogenic and intentional voice and speech dysfunction. These advanced methods should be used at least when the results of simple confrontation testing are unconvincing or equivocal; ideally they should be used in all cases. In addition, it does not address the issue of workers whose native language is something other than English. No specific passages have been assigned for various languages. However, appropriate passages may be drawn from the phoniatric or speech-language pathology literature of appropriate countries and used by a medical examiner whose command of the specific language is sufficient to permit valid and reliable interpretation of the patient's responses.

In most respects, the medical evaluation of a person sent for medical/legal purposes or independent medical evaluation (IME) is the same thorough examination that should be performed for all patients with voice and speech disorders. However, for medical-legal purposes, it is important for physicians to be certain that they thoroughly understand the occupational needs and demands of the patient. One schoolteacher's professional vocal needs may be very different from those of another schoolteacher, even in the same school district. Similar differences occur among all voice professionals including singers, telephone operators, and many others whose occupations depend on voice and speech. Understanding the individual circumstances is essential in formulating an accurate, rational, and defensible opinion regarding causation and consequences of a voice and/or speech problem. All such information must be thoroughly documented, and the rationale for the physician's conclusions must be apparent.

There is a substantial difference in physician responsibilities for the patient at the conclusion of a medical-legal encounter compared with patients evaluated medically only. Ordinarily, we are accustomed to providing our patients with information, diagnoses, treatment recommendations, and to ordering appropriate studies. Such communication is not appropriate in many medical/legal settings; and the physician, patient, and referring professional (often an attorney) may be better served by having the physician's conclusion communicated in writing in a formal medical-legal report. The physician should be careful not to express opinions until they have been formed to a reasonable degree of medical certainty. This often requires gathering of additional information (eg, work records), which may not be available at the time of the initial examination.

Great care should be taken to avoid expressing opinions prematurely, because retracting them later can be confusing and awkward and can impugn the physician's medical and legal credibility. Formulating accurate conclusions that can be supported is important to help establish what happened and its consequences and, in some cases, to support recommendations for patient assistance. For example, people in vocally intensive occupations (schoolteachers, stockbrokers) who require voice surgery and/or extensive voice therapy may be well served by a leave of absence, acquisition of assistive devices (eg, microphones), and other modifications in performance routine that may have an unexpectedly great impact on their work environment and job security.

Judgments regarding short- and long-term disability issues may have profound effects on both individual lives and businesses; in some cases they may require an employer to pay a disabled worker the equivalent of many years' salary, on top of the cost associated with replacement of the employee. Such recommendations should be made firmly when appropriate and should never be made when they are not truly medically necessary (particularly prolonged leaves of absence). Formulating accurate and fair opinions in these matters requires thorough understanding of all relevant facts and often reflection and review on the part of the physician.

Suggested Criteria for Determining Voice and/or Speech Impairment

An appropriate determination of voice-related disability requires a comprehensive understanding of voice science and medicine, legal definitions and issues, and consideration of the vocal needs of each individual with voice and/or speech impairment.

For the purposes of classifying voice and/or speech impairment and disability, audibility, intelligibility, and functional efficiency must be taken into account. Audibility permits the patient to be heard over background noise. It generally reflects the condition of the voice. Disability determination should be based on subjective and objective assessments of voice and speech, on reports pertaining to the patient's performance in everyday living and occupational situations, and on instruments such as the Vocal Handicap Index.[15] The reports or evidence should be supplied by reliable observers. For the nonprofessional voice user, the standard of evaluation should be the normal speaker's performance in average situations for everyday living. For the professional voice user, the standard of evaluation is the expected performance in professional and everyday situations of comparable voice professionals. Table 15–1 summarizes suggested voice and speech impairment criteria, modified in part from those set forth in the AMA *Guides*. In evaluating functional efficiency, *everyday speech communication* should be interpreted as including activities of daily living and also the routine voice and speech requirements of the patient's profession. A judgment is made regarding the patient's speech and voice capacity with regard to each of the three columns of the classification chart (Table 15–1). The degree of impairment of voice and/or speech is equivalent to the greatest percentage of impairment recorded in any one of the three columns of the classification chart.

For example, a particular patient's voice/speech impairment is judged to be the following: Audibility, 10% (Class 1); Intelligibility, 50% (Class 3), and Functional Efficiency, 30% (Class 2). This patient's voice/speech impairment is judged to be equivalent to the greatest impairment, 50%.

Converting an impairment of voice and speech into impairment of the whole person requires knowledge of the individual's occupational voice and speech requirements. These may be divided into three classes, as follows. (Note that these criteria are this author's recommendations and are not yet accepted AMA guidelines.)

Table 15–1. Voice and Speech Impairment Guide.

Classification	***Audibility***	***Intelligibility***	***Functional Efficiency***
Class 1 0%-14% speech impairment	Can produce voice of intensity sufficient for *most* of the needs of everyday speech communication, although this sometimes may require effort and occasionally may be beyond patient's capacity.	Can perform *most* of the articulatory acts necessary for everyday speech communication, although listeners occasionally ask the patient to repeat, and the patient may find it difficult or impossible to produce a few phonetic units.	Can meet *most* of the demands of articulation and phonation for everyday speech communication with adequate speed and ease, although occasionally the patient may hesitate or speak slowly.
Class 2 15%-34% speech impairment	Can produce voice of intensity sufficient for *many* of the needs of everyday speech communication; is usually heard under average conditions; however, may have difficulty in automobiles, buses, trains, stations, restaurants, etc.	Can perform *many* of the necessary articulatory acts for everyday speech communication. Can speak name, address, etc and be understood by a stranger, but may have numerous inaccuracies; sometimes appears to have difficulty articulating.	Can meet *many* of the demands of articulation and phonation for everyday speech communication with adequate speed and ease, but sometimes gives impression of difficulty, and speech may sometimes be discontinuous, interrupted, hesitant, or slow.
Class 3 35%-59% speech impairment	Can produce voice of intensity sufficient for *some* of the needs of everyday speech communication, such as close conversation; however, has considerable difficulty in such noisy places as listed above; the voice tires rapidly and tends to become inaudible after a few seconds.	Can perform *some* of the necessary articulatory acts for everyday speech communication; can usually converse with family and friends; however, strangers may find it difficulty to understand the patient, who often may be asked to repeat.	Can meet *some* of the demands of articulation and phonation for everyday speech communication with adequate speed and ease, but often can sustain consecutive speech only for brief periods; may give the impression of being rapidly fatigued.
Class 4 60%-84% speech impairment	Can produce voice of intensity sufficient for a *few* of the needs of everyday speech communication; can barely be heard by a close listener or over the telephone, perhaps may be able to whisper audibly but has no louder voice.	Can perform a *few* of the necessary articulatory acts for everyday speech communication; can produce some phonetic units; may have approximations for a few words such as names of own family members; however, unintelligible out of context.	Can meet a *few* of the demands of articulation and phonation for everyday speech communication with adequate speed and ease, such as using single words or short phrases, but cannot maintain uninterrupted speech flow; speech is labored, rate is impractically slow.
Class 5 85%-100% speech impairment	Can produce voice of intensity sufficient for *none* of the needs of everyday speech communication.	Can perform *none* of the articulatory acts necessary for everyday speech communication.	Can meet *none* of the demands of articulation and phonation for everyday speech communication with adequate speed and ease.

Class 1: Voice/speech impairment should not result in significant change in ability to perform necessary occupational functions. Little or no voice/speech required for most daily occupational requirements. Examples: manuscript typist, data-entry clerk, copy editor.

Class 2: Voice/speech is a necessary component of daily occupational responsibilities, but not the principal focus of the individual's occupation. Impairment of voice or speech may make it difficult or impossible for the individual to perform his or her occupation at his or her preimpairment level. Examples: stockbroker, non-trial attorney, supervisor in a noisy shop.

Class 3: Voice/speech is the primary occupational asset. Impairment seriously diminishes the individual's ability to perform his or her job or makes it impossible to do so. Examples: classroom teacher, trial attorney, opera singer, broadcast announcer.

Table 15–2 is intended as a guideline for converting the percentage of voice and/or speech impairment to percentage impairment of the whole person.

The "Worth" of a Voice

Although improved, standardized guidelines for the estimation of vocal impairment and disability such as

Table 15–2. Speech Impairment Related to Impairment of the Whole Person.

% Speech Impairment	*% Impairment of the Whole Person Occupational Class 1*	*% Impairment of the Whole Person Occupational Class 2*	*% Impairment of the Whole Person Occupational Class 3*
0	0	0	0
5	2	4	5
10	4	8	10
15	5	10	15
20	7	14	20
25	9	18	25
30	10	20	30
35	12	24	35
40	14	28	40
45	16	32	45
50	18	36	50
55	19	38	55
60	21	42	60
65	23	46	65
70	24	48	70
75	26	52	75
80	28	56	80
85	30	60	85
90	32	64	90
95	33	66	95
100	35	70	97

those proposed above may be helpful, no such guidelines are universally applicable to each individual case. If such guidelines are accepted by the AMA *Guides*, they may come to govern voice impairment and disability determination in workers' compensation cases and jurisdictions that include speech and voice within their workers' compensation statutes. In other jurisdictions, and in situations in which the vocal impairment is not causally related to employment, legal redress for voice impairment is generally determined under tort law. In these cases, a judge or jury determines the degree of impairment and disability and the value of compensation, generally based on expert testimony. Reference to documents such as the AMA *Guides* may be included, but many other factors are introduced into testimony to help the judge or jury establish whether a loss is compensable (someone was at fault) and, if so, the amount of compensation that is appropriate. Malpractice actions are generally handled in this fashion; and malpractice suits for dysphonia occur frequently. In some cases, they are (arguably) justified. As recently as 2001, this author reviewed actions in which "vocal cord stripping" was used in young professional singers as the first treatment for vocal nodules, and the surgery resulted in profound, bilateral vocal fold scar. In such instances, arguments frequently center on the singer's true artistic skill and potential for life earnings (determination of damages). Other cases involve famous, established singers for whom enormous earning ability is well-documented, and financial losses in the millions are relatively easy to estimate. In such cases, arguments focus on issues of informed consent, accuracy of diagnosis, appropriateness of surgery, and whether the dysphonia was caused by a deviation from the standard-of-care or was simply a recognized complication such as unfavorable scar.

In all such instances, otolaryngologists have an obligation to their profession and the public. As distasteful as medical-legal aspects of voice disorders may be, we must be prepared to evaluate them honestly and dispassionately. Our evaluation should draw on all of the scientific, clinical, and technological advances that have enhanced the practice of laryngology / voice and should be influenced by an awareness of the standard of practice in impairment and disability determination as set forth in publications such as the AMA *Guides*.

We must be prepared to recognize that dysphonia may result in substantial disability and loss of earnings for many of our patients. When such problems occur as an unavoidable consequence of surgery, we must be prepared to help juries and judges understand the unpredictabilities of surgery. However, when they occur because of deviations or violations of the standard-of-care, we must also be willing to recognize that the patient may be entitled to compensation in accordance with our country's legal system. We must also recognize that, to some extent, the pressures exerted by the medical-legal climate have worked to improve the standard-of-care and still exert pressure on our profession to remain current with the latest advances and changes in the state-of-the-art care. Maintaining currency is particularly important in a rapidly evolving discipline such as laryngology / voice.

Case Reports

Case 1 is a 42-year-old, female, former teacher, now an elementary school guidance counselor, who returned to work 7 years ago following a 10-year hiatus. Within the first month, she experienced a sudden onset of hoarseness. She continued to work for several months before seeking medical attention. Initial evaluation by an otolaryngologist revealed inflamed vocal folds and nodules, and relative voice rest for 4 days was recommended. She had no improvement in her voice. She then saw a speech therapist weekly for 2 years with no improvement. She then underwent excision of bilateral vocal fold masses. Her voice improved for 6 months, after which her hoarseness returned. She was again diagnosed with recurrent vocal fold nodules and gastroesophageal reflux disease.

She was referred to this author (RTS) 2 years following surgery with complaints of constant hoarseness and voice fatigue. She was unable to project her voice well and unable to sing, although she would have liked to. She had been treated for gastroesophageal reflux disease for the past year. She had year-round allergy symptoms but stated they were now better controlled since she started receiving injections.

Physical examination revealed a moderately hoarse and breathy voice. Strobovideolaryngoscopy revealed a broad-based, solid, white mass of her right vocal fold with a fibrotic mass of the left vocal fold; arytenoid erythema and edema consistent with gastroesophageal reflux disease; bilateral superior surface varicosities and scarring were apparent on stroboscopic visualization. Laryngeal EMG revealed mild bilateral superior laryngeal nerve paresis. No neuromuscular junction abnormalities were noted. Objective voice evaluations were completed and revealed decreased intensity, phonation time, harmonic-to-noise ratio, acoustic measures, and s / z ratio.

There was no improvement in the appearance of her vocal fold lesions following 6 weeks of aggressive medical treatment for the reflux laryngitis disease.

Voice therapy was unsuccessful over the 6-week period despite excellent compliance by the patient. The patient was taken to the operating room for excision of the bilateral lesions. Biopsy revealed adult-onset laryngeal papillomatosis, not nodules as had been diagnosed by her previous physician.

The patient required two subsequent laryngeal operations within 1 year in an attempt to eradicate disease and improve her phonatory function. She will continue to require ongoing surveillance by a laryngologist for recurrence of papillomata and surveillance for the development of laryngeal carcinoma. She will require ongoing voice therapy and treatment for her reflux disease. When she is able to return to work, she will require a personal amplification system to help with vocal projection. Her vocal prognosis is guarded. Her impairment would be noted as 60% to 84% (Class 4).

Case 2 is a 38-year-old male factory worker who has worked at the same chemical plant for 20 years. He started in the rubber division and 10 years later switched to the plastics and chemical division. He was working in a management position, stating he was responsible for everything that blows up. He suffered an inhalation injury 2 years ago resulting from heavy exposure to vinyl chloride fumes when three reactors malfunctioned. He underwent microlaryngoscopy and excision of bilateral vocal fold polyps 1 year after this injury. His voice improved after surgery, and he remained out of work for approximately 6 weeks following surgery. One month after returning to work, he was exposed to anhydrous ammonia fumes and experienced immediate dyspnea and sudden and severe hoarseness. He underwent a second microlaryngoscopy and vocal fold polypectomy. He attempted to return to work but became aphonic after 3 days.

He reported voice deterioration after voice use and any exposure to fumes, perfumes, smoke, and gasoline and that his hoarseness was now associated with shortness of breath. He also experienced chronic globus sensation. He was undergoing psychological counseling for stress-related problems secondary to his voice problems, and he also had to quit smoking.

His voice was harsh, hoarse, slightly breathy, and pressed. Strobovideolaryngoscopy revealed bilateral vocal fold scarring, decreased mucosal wave, hypervascularity, and mucosal irregularities. Objective voice measures revealed marked abnormalities in harmonic-to-noise ratio, shimmer, and maximum flow rate.

This individual had a mucosal vocal fold injury secondary to inhalation of noxious fumes, initially vinyl chloride, and airway hyperactivity causing dysphonia and dyspnea. Additional surgery was recommended. The vocal fold mucosa had never returned to normal nor had his voice quality. Five years, later he developed progressive dysplastic vocal fold changes (leukoplakia).

This case illustrates the scope of the shortcomings of the *Guides'* current rating system. It does not take into account significant, medically proven symptom fluctuation or specific occupational vocal requirements. When this patient is at home, protected from fumes or pollution, he would be rated Class 3 on the basis of audibility. Once he enters the work environment, or many other everyday settings, his impairment becomes a Class 5. Considering the impact on his life and employability, it is reasonable to assign him a Class 5 rating.

Case 3 is a 28-year-old male singer and songwriter. He developed vocal difficulties 1 year ago while recording an album. He had been singing and performing rock and roll for 10 years with no prior vocal difficulties. While recording his album, he experienced loss of midrange, decreased volume, breathiness, and hoarseness. He was not ill at the time. Three months later he was diagnosed with a left vocal fold polyp, and surgical excision of the lesion was performed the following month. The patient had additional complaints of his voice being worse is the morning, frequent throat clearing, and a globus sensation. He was given advice concerning control of his reflux laryngitis symptoms and placed on a reflux protocol. He remains unhappy with his vocal progress to date.

Strobovideolaryngoscopy revealed a right vocal fold mass, left vocal fold scar, reflux laryngitis, and superior laryngeal nerve paresis. The mass and scar were typical sequelae of hemorrhage, as suggested by his history of sudden voice change while recording. Examination of his singing voice revealed excess tension in the jaw and tongue, hoarseness, and decreased range. Laryngeal EMG was recommended and revealed a 20% decrease in function of the left superior laryngeal nerve. Additionally, he had abnormalities in electroglottography (EGG) quasi-open quotient, AC flow, minimal flow, maximum flow rate, s/z ratio, maximum phonation time, and acoustic measurements.

This case illustrates an important shortcoming of the current rating system. According to the current method, he would be rated Class 2 on the basis of audibility. Yet, as a professional singer, he is totally disabled from this work-related injury. A classification scheme that considered the individual's professional voice needs would classify him as Class 5.

Conclusion

As the field of laryngology/voice evolves over time, considerations of voice impairment and disability also are evolving. All laryngologists should be familiar with these developments, as well as substantive developments in medical, surgical, and post-surgical voice management. Physicians must be extremely diligent about obtaining all of the facts before arriving at a diagnosis and rendering an opinion. Misdiagnoses of voice and speech disorders are common, and somewhat understandably so, because of the dramatic recent advances in the standard of voice and speech care. Nevertheless, misdiagnosis is serious for both medical and medical-legal reasons and can generally be avoided. Information on the latest techniques in voice evaluation is available through The Voice Foundation (1721 Pine Street, Philadelphia, Pa 19103), the literature cited in this article, and many other sources. In medical-legal settings, it is advisable for physicians to consider not only the standard of care, but moreover the state-of-the-art. They should also complement their medical expertise with a reasonable understanding of legal issues, including not only definitions of impairment and disability, but also the legal theories and jurisdiction under which a case is being managed. Such knowledge will enhance our abilities to help not only our patients' voices, but also each patient as a person.

References

1. World Health Organization. *International Classification of Functioning, Disability and Health.* Geneva, Switzerland: WHO; 2001.
2. *Guides to the Evaluation of Permanent Impairment.* 5th ed. Chicago, Ill: American Medical Association; 2001.
3. Sataloff RT. Otolaryngological (ENT) impairment. In: Demeter SL, Andersson GBJ, eds. *Disability Evaluation.* 2nd ed. St. Louis, Mo: Mosby-Yearbook, Inc; 2003:512–530.
4. Aronson A. *Clinical Voice Disorders.* 3rd ed. New York, NY: Thieme Medical Publishers; 1990.
5. Rubin J, Sataloff RT, Korovin G, Gould WJ. *The Diagnosis and Treatment of Voice Disorders.* New York, NY: Igaku-Shoin Medical Publishers, Inc; 1995.
6. Sataloff RT. The impact of pollution on the voice. *Otolaryngol Head Neck Surg.* 1992;106(6):701–705.
7. Rubin JS, Sataloff RT, Korovin GS. *Treatment of Voice Disorders.* 2nd ed. Clifton Park, NY: Delmar Thompson Learning; 2003
8. Sataloff RT. Voice and speech impairment and disability. In: Sataloff RT. *Professional Voice: Science and Art of Clinical Care.* 2nd ed. San Diego, Calif: Singular Publishing Group, Inc; 1997:795–801.
9. Sataloff RT, Abaza MM. Impairment, disability and other medical / legal aspects of dysphonia. *Otolaryngol Clin North Am.* 2000;33:1143–1152.
10. Baken RJ. *Clinical Measurement of Speech and Voice.* Boston, Mass: College-Hill Press; 1987.
11. Hirano M. *Clinical Examination of the Voice.* New York, NY: Springer-Verlag; 1981.
12. Sataloff RT, Spiegel JR, Carroll LM, et al. Strobovideolaryngoscopy in professional voice users: results and clinical value. *J Voice.* 1988;1(4):359–364.
13. Sataloff RT, Spiegel JR, Hawkshaw MJ. Strobovideolaryngoscopy: results and clinical value. *Ann Otol Rhin Laryngol.* 1991;100(9):725–727.
14. Sataloff RT. The human voice. *Sci Am.* 1992;267(6):108–115.
15. Benninger MS, Gardener GM, Jacobson BH, Grywalski C. New dimensions in measuring voice treatment outcomes. In: Sataloff RT. *Professional Voice: The Science and Art of Clinical Care.* 2nd ed. San Diego, Calif: Singular Publishing Group, Inc; 1997:789–794.

Glossary

This glossary has been developed from the author's experience and also from a review of glossaries developed by Johan Sundberg (personal communication, June 1995), Ingo Titze (*Principles of Voice Production*, Englewood, NJ: Prentice-Hall, 1994:330–338), and other sources. It is difficult to credit appropriately contributions to glossaries or dictionaries of general terms, as each new glossary builds on prior works. The author is indebted to colleagues whose previous efforts have contributed to the compilation of this glossary.

AAO–HNS: American Academy of Otolaryngology-Head and Neck Surgery

AIDS: Acquired Immune Deficiency Syndrome

abduct: To move apart, separate

abduction quotient: The ratio of the glottal half-width at the vocal processes to the amplitude of vibration of the vocal fold

abscess: Collection of pus

absolute jitter (Jita): A discrete measure of very short term (cycle-to-cycle) variation of the pitch periods expressed in microseconds. This parameter is dependent on the fundamental frequency of the voicing sample. Therefore, normative data differs significantly for men and women. Higher pitch results in lower Jita

absolute voice rest: Total silence of the phonatory system

acceleration: The rate of change of velocity with respect to time (measured in millimeters per square second mm/s^2)

acoustic power: The physical measure of the amount of energy produced and radiated into the air per second (measured in watts)

acoustical zero decibels: 0.0002 microbar

actin: A protein molecule that reacts with myosin to form actinomysin, the contractile part of a myofilament in muscle

acting-voice trainer: (1) *See* **Voice Coach**; (2) A professional with specialized training who may work with injured voices as part of a medical voice team in an effort to optimize speaking voice performance

Adam's apple: Prominence of the thyroid cartilage, primarily in males

adduct: To bring together, approximate

affricate: Combination of plosive and fricative consonants such as /dʒ/

allergy: Bodily response to foreign substances or organisms

alto: (*See* **Contralto**)

alveolar ridge: The bony ridge of the gum into which the teeth insert

AMA: American Medical Association

amplitude: Maximum excursion of an undulating signal from the equilibrium; the amplitude of a sound wave is related to the perceived loudness; mostly it is expressed as a logarithmic, comparative level measure using the decibel (dB) unit

amplitude perturbation quotient (APQ): A relative evaluation of short term (cycle-to-cycle) variation of peak-to-peak amplitude expressed in percent. This measure uses a smoothing factor of 11 periods

amplitude spectrum: A display of relative amplitude versus frequency of the sinusoidal components of a waveform

amplitude to length ratio: The ratio of vibrational amplitude at the center of the vocal fold to the length of the vocal fold

amplitude tremor: Regular (periodic) long-term amplitude variation (an element of vibrato)

amplitude tremor frequency (Fatr): This measure is expressed in Hz and shows the frequency of the most intensive low-frequency amplitude-modulating component in the specified amplitude-tremor analysis range

amplitude tremor intensity index (ATRI): The average ratio of the amplitude of the most intensive low-frequency amplitude modulating component (amplitude tremor) to the total amplitude of the analyzed sample. The algorithm for tremor analysis determines the strongest periodic amplitude modulation of the voice. This measure is expressed in percent

anabolic steroids: Primarily male hormones, increase muscle mass and may cause irreversible, masculinization of the voice. Anabolic steroids help cells convert simple substances into more complex substances, especially into living matter

anisotropic: Property of a material that produces different strains when identical stresses are applied in different directions

antagonist (muscle): An opposing muscle

anterior: Toward the front

anterior commissure: The junction of the vocal folds in the front of the larynx

antibiotic: Drug used to combat infection (bodily invasion by a living organism such as a bacteria or virus). Most antibiotics have action specifically against bacteria

anticoagulant: Blood thinner; agent that impairs blood clotting

antinodes: The "peaks" in a standing wave pattern

antihistamine: Drug to combat allergic response

aperiodic: Irregular behavior that has no definite period; is usually either chaotic or random

aperiodicity: The absence of periodicity; no portion of the waveform repeats exactly

aphonia: The absence of vocal fold vibration; this term is commonly used to describe people who have "lost their voice" after vocal fold injury. In most cases, such patients have very poor vibration, rather than no vibration; and they typically have a harsh, nearly whispered voice

appendix of the ventricle of Morgagni: A cecal pouch of mucous membrane connected by a narrow opening with the anterior aspect of the ventricle. It sits between the ventricular fold in the inner surface of the thyroid cartilage. In some cases, it may extend as far as the cranial border of the thyroid cartilage, or higher. It contains the openings of 60 to 70 mucous glands, and it is enclosed in a fibrous capsule, which is continuous with the ventricular ligament. Also called *appendix ventriculi laryngis*, and *laryngeal saccule*

aria: Song, especially in the context of an opera

arthritis: Inflammation of joints in the body

articulation: Shaping of vocal tract by positioning of its mobile walls such as lips, lower jaw, tongue body and tip, velum, epiglottis, pharyngeal sidewalls, and larynx

articulators: The structures of the vocal tract that are used to create the sounds of language. They include the lips, teeth, tongue, soft palate, and hard palate

arytenoid cartilages: Paired, ladle-shaped cartilages to which the vocal folds are attached

arytenoid dislocation: A condition frequently causing vocal fold immobility or hypomobility due to separation of the arytenoid cartilage from its joint and normal position atop the cricoid cartilage

ASHA: American Speech-Language-Hearing Association

aspirate: Speech sound characterized by breathiness

aspirate attack: Initiation of phonation preceded by air, producing /h/

aspiration: (1) In speech, the sound made by turbulent airflow preceding or following vocal fold vibration, as in /hɑ/. (2) In medicine, refers to breathing into the lungs substances that do not belong there such as food, water, or stomach contents following reflux. Aspiration may lead to infections such as pneumonia, commonly referred to as *aspiration pneumonia*

asthma: Obstructive pulmonary (lung) disease associated with bronchospasm, and difficulty expiring air

atmospheric pressure: The absolute pressure exerted by the atmosphere, usually measured in millimeters of mercury (mmHg)

atresia: Failure of development. In the case of the larynx, this may result in fusion or congenital webbing of the vocal folds, or failure of development of the trachea

atrophy: Loss or wasting of tissue. Muscle atrophy occurs, for example, in an arm that is immobilized in a cast for many weeks

attractor: A geometric figure in state space to which all trajectories in its vicinity are drawn. The four types of attractors are (1) *point*, (2) *limit cycle*, (3) *toroidal*, and (4) *strange*. A point trajector draws all trajectories to a single point. An example is a pendulum moving toward rest. A limit cycle is characteristic of periodic motion. A toroidal attractor represents quasiperiodic motion (often considered a subset of periodic motion). A strange attractor is associated with chaotic motion

back vowel: A vowel produced by pulling the tongue posteriorly, with relation to its neutral position

bands: Range of adjacent parameter values; a frequency band is an ensemble of adjacent frequencies

band pass filter: Filter that allows frequencies only within a certain frequency range to pass

baritone: The most common male vocal range. Higher than bass and lower than tenor. Singer's formant around 2600 Hz

basement membrane: Anatomic structure immediately beneath the epithelium

bass: (*See* **Basso**)

bass baritone: In between bass and baritone. Not as heavy as basso profundo, but typically with greater flexibility. Must be able to sing at least as high as F_4. Also known as *basso contante* and *basso guisto*. Baritones with bass quality are also called *basse taille*

basso: Lowest male voice. Singer's formant around 2300–2400 Hz

basso profundo: Deep bass. The lowest and heaviest of the bass voices. Can sing at least as low as D_2 with full voice. Singer's formant around 2200–2300 Hz. Also known as *contra-basso*

bel canto: Literally means "beautiful singing." Refers to a method and philosophical approach to singing voice production

benchmark: The standard by which other similar occurrences are judged

benign tumors: Tumors that are not able to metastasize or spread to distant sites

Bernoulli's principle: If the energy in a confined fluid stream is constant, an increase in particle velocity must be accompanied by a decrease in pressure against the wall

bifurcation: A sudden qualitative change in the behavior of a system. In chaos, for example, a small change in the initial parameters of a stable (predominantly linear) system may cause oscillation between two different states as the nonlinear aspects of the system become manifest. This transition is a bifurcation

bilabial covering: Using the lips to constrict the mouth opening and "cover" the sound. This technique is used commonly by young singers in the form of slight vowel distortion to attenuate upper harmonics and make a sound richer and less brash.

bilateral: On both sides

bilateral vocal fold paralysis: Loss of the ability to move both vocal folds caused by neurologic dysfunction

biomechanics: The study of the mechanics of biological tissue

bleat: Fast vibrato, like the bleating of a sheep

body: With regard to the vocal fold, the vocalis muscle

Boyle's law: In a soft-walled enclosure and at a constant temperature, pressure and volume are inversely related

bravura: Brilliant, elaborate, showy execution of musical or dramatic material

break: (*See* **Passagio**)

breathy phonation: Phonation characterized by a lack of vocal fold closure; this causes air leakage (excessive airflow) during the quasi-closed phase, and this produces turbulence that is heard as noise mixed in the voice

bronchitis: Inflammation of the bronchial tubes in the lungs

bronchospasm: Forceful closing of the distal airways in the lungs

bruxism: Grinding of the teeth

bulimia: Self-induced vomiting to control weight

butterfly effect: Refers to the notion that in chaotic (nonlinear dynamics) systems a minuscule change in initial condition may have profound effects on the behavior of the system. For example, a butterfly flapping its wings in Hong Kong may change the weather in New York

cancer: An abnormality in which cells no longer respond to the signals that control replication and growth. This results in uncontrolled growth and tumor formation, and may result in spread of tumor to distant locations (metastasis)

carrier: (1) In physics, a waveform (typically a sinusoid) whose frequency or amplitude is modulated by a signal. (2) In medicine, a person who is colonized by an organism (typically bacteria such as streptococcus or pneumococcus), but who has no symptoms or adverse effects from the presence of the organism.

Nevertheless, that carrier is able to transmit the organism to other people in whom it does cause a symptomatic infection

cartilage: One of the tissues of the skeleton; it is more flexible than bone

cartilage of Wrisberg: Cartilage attached in the mobile portion of each aryepiglottic fold

cartilage of Santorini: Small cartilage flexibly attached near the apex of the arytenoid, in the region of the opening of the esophagus

castrato: Male singer castrated at around age 7 or 8, so as to retain alto or soprano vocal range

category: Voice type classified according to pitch range and voice quality; the most frequently used categories are bass, baritone, tenor, alto, mezzosoprano, and soprano, but many other subdivisions of these exist

caudal: Toward the tail

central vowel: A vowel produced with the tongue at or near neutral position

chaos: A qualitative description of a dynamic system that seems unpredictable, but actually has a "hidden" order. Also a mathematical field that studies fractal geometry and nonlinear dynamics

chaotic behavior: Distinct from random or periodic behavior. A chaotic system *looks* disorganized or random but is actually deterministic, although aperiodic. It has sensitive dependence on initial condition, has definite form, and is bounded to a relatively narrow range (unable to go off into infinity)

chest voice: Heavy registration with excessive resonance in the lower formants

coarticulation: A condition in which one phoneme influences the production of phonemes before and after it, resulting commonly in degradation of the quality and clarity of the surrounding sounds

cochlea: Inner ear organ of hearing

coefficient of amplitude variation (vAm): This measure, expressed in percent, computes the relative standard deviation of the peak-to-peak amplitude. It increases regardless of the type of amplitude variation

coefficient of fundamental frequency variation (vF_0): This measure, expressed in percent, computes the relative standard deviation of the fundamental frequency. It is the ratio of the standard deviation of the period-to-period variation to the average fundamental frequency

collagen: The protein substance of the white (collagenous) fibers of cartilage, bone, tendon, skin, and all of the connective tissues. Collagen may be extracted, processed, and injected into the vocal fold to treat various abnormalities

collagenase: An enzyme that catalyzes the degradation of collagen

coloratura: In common usage, refers to the highest of the female voices, with range well above C_6. May use more whistle tone than other female voices. In fact, coloratura actually refers to a style of florid, agile, complex singing that may apply to any voice classification. For example, the bass runs in Händel's *Messiah* require coloratura technique

complex periodic vibration: A sound that repeats regularly. A pattern of simultaneously sounding partials

complex sound: A combination of sinusoidal waveforms superimposed upon each other. May be complex periodic sound (such as musical instruments) or complex aperiodic sound (such as random street noise)

complex tone: Tone composed of a series of simultaneously sounding partials

component frequency: mathematically, a sinusoid; perceptually, a pure tone. Also called a *partial*

compression: A deformation of a body that decreases its entire volume. An increase in density

concert pitch: Also known as *international concert pitch*. The standard of tuning A_4. Reference pitch has changed substantially over the last 200 to 300 years

condensation: An increase in density

constructive interference: The interference of two or more waves such that enhancement occurs

contact ulcer: A lesion with mucosal disruption most commonly on the vocal processes or medial surfaces of the arytenoids. Caused most commonly by gastroesophageal reflux laryngitis and / or muscular tension dysphonia

contrabasso: (*See* **Basso profundo**)

contraction: A decrease in length

contralto: Lowest of the female voices. Able to sing F_3 below middle C, as well as the entire treble staff. Singer's formant at around 2800–2900 Hz

conus elasticus: Fibroelastic membrane extending inferiorly from the vocal folds to the anterior superior border of the cricoid cartilage. Also called the *cricovocal ligament*. Composed primarily of yellow elastic tissue. Anteriorly, it attaches to the minor aspect of the thyroid cartilage. Posteriorly, it attaches to the vocal process of the arytenoids

convergent: With regard to glottal shape, the glottis narrows from bottom to top

corner vowels: (ɑ), (i), and (u); vowels at the corners of a vowel triangle; they necessitate extreme placements of the tongue

corticosteroid: Potent substances produced by the adrenal cortex (excluding sex hormones of adrenal origin) in response to the release of adrenocorticotropic hormone from the pituitary gland, or related substances. Glucocorticoids influence carbohydrate, fat, and protein metabolism. Mineralocorticoids help regular electrolyte and water balance. Some corticosteroids have both effects to varying degrees. Corticosteroids may also be given as medications for various effects, including anti-inflammatory, antineoplastic, immune suppressive, and ACTH secretion suppressive effects, as well as for hormone replacement therapy

countertenor: Male voice that is primarily falsetto, singing in the contralto range. Most countertenors are also able to sing in the baritone or tenor range. Countertenors are also known as *contraltino* or *contratenor*

cover: (1) In medicine, with regard to the vocal fold, the epithelium and superficial layer of lamina propria. (2) In music, an alteration in technique that changes the resonance characteristics of a sung sound, generally darkening the sound

cranial nerves: Twelve paired nerves responsible for smell, taste, eye movement, vision, facial sensation, chewing muscles, facial motion, salivary gland and lacrimal (tear) gland secretions, hearing, balance, pharyngeal and laryngeal sensation, vocal fold motion, gastric acid secretion, shoulder motion, tongue motion, and related functions

creaky voice: The perceptual result of subharmonic or chaotic patterns in the glottal waveform. According to IR Titze, if a subharmonic is below about 70 Hz, creaky voice may be perceived as pulse register (vocal fry)

crescendo: To get gradually louder

cricoid cartilage: A solid ring of cartilage located below and behind the thyroid cartilage

cricothyroid muscle: An intrinsic laryngeal muscle that is used primarily to control pitch (paired)

crossover frequency: The fundamental frequency for which there is an equal probability for perception of two adjacent registers

cycle: One complete set of regularly recurring events

cysts: Fluid-filled lesions

damp: To diminish, or attenuate an oscillation

damped oscillation: Oscillation in which energy is lost during each cycle until oscillation stops

decibel: One tenth of a bel. The decibel is a unit of comparison between a reference and another point. It has no absolute value. Although decibels are used to measure sound, they are also used (with different references) to measure heat, light, and other physical phenomena. For sound pressure, the reference is 0.0002 microbar (millionths of one barometric pressure). In the past, this has also been referred to as 0.0002 dyne/cm^2, and by other terms

decrescendo: (*See* **Diminuendo**)

deformation: The result of stress applied to any surface of a deformable continuous medium. Elongation, compression, contraction, and shear are examples

dehydration: Fluid deprivation. This may alter the amount and viscosity of vocal fold lubrication and the properties of the vocal fold tissues themselves

destructive interference: The interference of two or more waves such that full or partial cancellation occurs

dialect: A variety of a spoken language, usually associated with a distinct geographical, social, or political environment

diaphragm: A large, dome-shaped muscle at the bottom of the rib cage that separates the lungs from the viscera. It is the primary muscle of inspiration and may be co-activated during singing

diminuendo: To get gradually softer

diphthong: Two consecutive vowels occurring in the same syllable

displacement: The distance between two points in space, including the direction from one point to the other

displacement flow: Air in the glottis that is squeezed out when the vocal folds come together

diuretic: A drug to decrease circulating body fluid generally by excretion through the kidneys

divergent: With regard to the vocal folds, the glottis widens from bottom to top

dizziness: A feeling of imbalance

dorsal: Toward the back

down-regulation: Decreased gene expression, compared with baseline

dramatic soprano: Soprano with powerful, rich voice suitable for dramatic, heavily orchestrated, operatic roles. Sings at least to C_6

dramatic tenor: Tenor with heavy voice, often with a suggestion of baritone quality. Suitable for dramatic roles that are heavily orchestrated. Also referred to as *tenora robusto*, and *helden tenor*. The term helden tenor (literally "heroic" tenor) is used typically for tenors who sing Wagnerian operatic roles

dynamics: (1) In physics, a branch of mechanics that deals with the study of forces that accelerate object(s). (2) In music, it refers to changes in the loudness of musical performance

dysmenorrhea: Painful menstrual cramps

dyspepsia: Epigastric discomfort, especially following meals; impairment of the power or function of digestion

dysphonia: Abnormal voicing

dysphonia plica ventricularis: Phonation using false vocal fold vibration rather than true vocal fold vibration. Most commonly associated with severe muscular tension dysphonia Occasionally may be an appropriate compensation for profound true vocal fold dysfunction

dystonia: A neurological disorder characterized by involuntary movements, such as unpredictable, spasmodic opening or closing of the vocal folds

edema: Excessive accumulation of fluid in tissues, or "swelling"

elastic recoil pressure: The alveolar pressure derived from extended (strained) tissue in the lungs, rib cage, and the entire thorax after inspiration (measured in Pascals)

electroglottograph (EGG): Recording of electrical conductance of vocal fold contact area versus time; EGG waveforms have been frequently used for the purpose of plotting voice source analysis

electromyograph (EMG): Recording of the electric potentials in a muscle, which are generated by the neural system and which control its degree of contraction; if rectified and smoothed the EMG is closely related to the muscular force exerted by the muscle

elongation: An increase in length

embouchure: The shape of the lips, tongue, and related structures adopted while producing a musical tone, particularly while playing a wind instrument

endocrine: Relating to hormones and the organs that produce them

endometriosis: A disorder in which endometrial tissue is present in abnormal locations. Typically causes excessively painful menstrual periods (dysmenorrhea) and infertility

epiglottis: Cartilage that covers over the larynx during swallowing

epilarynx: A region bordered by the rim of the epiglottis and the glottis synonymous with epiglottal tube. This resonating region is considered by some to be the site of origin of the singer's formant

epithelium: The covering, or most superficial layer, of body surfaces

erythema: Redness

esophagus: Tube leading from the bottom of the pharynx to the stomach; swallowed food is transported through this structure

expansion: A deformation of a body such that the entire volume increases

extrinsic muscles of the larynx: The strap muscles in the neck, responsible for adjusting laryngeal height and for stabilizing the larynx

Fach (German): Literally, job specialty. It is used to indicate voice classification. For example, lyric soprano and dramatic soprano are different Fachs

false vocal folds: Folds of tissue located slightly higher than and parallel to the vocal folds in the larynx

falsetto: High, light register, applied primarily to men's voices singing in the soprano or alto range. Can also be applied to women's voices

fibroblasts: Cells responsible in part for the formation of scar in response to tissue injury

fibrosis: Generally refers to a component of scar caused by cross-linking of fibers during a reactive or a reparative process

flat singing: Usually refers to pitch (frequency) lower than the desirable target frequency. Sometimes also used to refer to a singing style devoid of excitement or emotional expression

flow: The volume of fluid passing through a given cross-section of a tube or duct per second; also called volume velocity (measured in liters per second)

flow glottogram: Recording of the transglottal airflow versus time, ie, of the sound of the voice source. Generally obtained from inverse filtering, FLOGG is the acoustical representation of the voice source

flow phonation: The optimal balance between vocal fold adductory forces and subglottic pressure, producing efficient sound production at the level of the vocal folds

flow resistance: The ratio of pressure to flow

fluid: A substance that is either a liquid or a gas

fluid mechanics: The study of motion or deformation of liquids and gases

flutter: Modulation in the 10–12 Hz range

F_0: Fundamental frequency

F_0–tremor frequency (Fftr): This measure is expressed in Hz and shows the frequency of the most intensive low-frequency F_0 modulating component in the specified F_0 tremor analysis range

F_0–tremor intensity index (FTRI): The average ratio of the frequency magnitude of the most intensive low-frequency modulating component (F_0 tremor) to the total frequency magnitude of the analyzed sample. The algorithm for tremor analysis determines the strongest periodic frequency modulation of the voice. This measure is expressed in percent

focal: Limited to a specific area. For example, spasmodic dysphonia may be focal (limited to the larynx), or part of a group of dystonias that affect other parts of the body such as the facial muscles or muscles involved in chewing

force: A push or pull; the physical quantity imparted to an object to change its momentum

forced oscillation: Oscillation imposed on a system by an external source

formant: Vocal tract resonance; the formant frequencies are tuned by the vocal tract shape and determine much of the vocal quality

formant tuning: A boosting of vocal intensity when F_0 or one if its harmonics coincides exactly with a formant frequency

front vowel: A vowel formed by displacing the tongue anteriorly, with regard to its neutral position

functional residual capacity (FRC): Lung volume at which the elastic inspiratory forces equal the elastic expiratory forces; in spontaneous quiet breathing exhalation stops at FRC

fractal: A geometric figure in which an identical pattern or motif repeats itself over and over on an ever-diminishing scale. Self-similarity is an essential characteristic

fractal dimension: Fractal dimensions are measures of fractal objects that can be used to determine how alike or different the objects are. Box counting algorithms and mass-radius measurement are two common approaches to determining fractal dimension. The fractal dimension represents the way a set of points fills a given area of space. It may be defined as the slope of the function relating the number of points contained in a given radius (or its magnification) to the radius itself. For example, an object can be assessed under many magnifications. The coast of Britain can be measured, for example, with a meter stick or a millimeter stick, but the latter will yield a larger measure. As magnification is increased (smaller measuring sticks), a point will be reached at which small changes in magnification no longer significantly affect length. That is, a plot of coastline length versus magnification reaches a plateau. That plateau corresponds to fractal dimension. The more irregular the figure (eg, coastline), the more complex and the more space it occupies, hence, the higher its fractal dimension. A perfect line has a fractal dimension of 1. A figure that fills a plane has a fractal dimension of 2. Fractal dimension cannot be used alone to determine the presence or absence of chaotic behavior

frequency analysis: Same as spectrum analysis

frequency tremor: A periodic (regular) pitch modulation of the voice (an element of vibrato)

fricative: A speech sound, generally a consonant, produced by a constriction of the vocal tract, particularly by directing the airstream against a hard surface, producing noisy air turbulence. Examples include *s* produced with the teeth, *s* produced with the lower lip and upper incisors, and *th* produced with the tongue tip and upper incisors

frontal (or coronal) plane: An anatomic plane that divides the body into anterior and posterior portions; across the crown of the head

functional voice disorder: An abnormality in voice sound and function in the absence of an anatomic or physiologic organic abnormality

fundamental: Lowest partial of a spectrum, the frequency of which normally corresponds to the pitch perceived.

fundamental frequency (F_0): The lowest frequency in a periodic waveform; also called the first harmonic frequency

gas: A substance that preserves neither shape nor volume when acted upon by forces, but adapts readily to the size and shape of its container

gastric: Pertaining to the stomach

gastric juice: The contents of the stomach, ordinarily including a high concentration of hydrochloric acid.

gastroesophageal reflux (GER): The passage of gastric juice in a retrograde fashion from the stomach into the esophagus. These fluids may reach the level of the larynx or oral cavity, and may be aspirated into the lungs

gastroesophageal reflux disease (GERD): A disorder including symptoms and/or signs caused by reflux of gastric juice into the esophagus and elsewhere. Heartburn is one of the most common symptoms of GERD. (*See* also **Laryngopharyngeal reflux**)

genomics: The study of genes (genetic material) made up of DNA, and located in the chromosomes of the nuclei of cells in an organism.

glide: A written consonant that is produced as a vowel sound in transition to the following vowel. Examples include: /j/ and /w/

glissando: A "slide" including all possible pitches between the initial and final pitch sounded. Similar to portamento and slur

globus: Sensation of a lump in the throat

glottal: At the level of the vocal folds

glottal chink: Opening in the glottis during vocal fold adduction, most commonly posteriorly. It may be a normal variant in some cases

glottal resistance: Ratio between transglottal airflow and subglottal pressure; mainly reflects the degree of glottal adduction

glottal stop (or click): A transient sound caused by the sudden onset or offset of phonation

glottal stroke: A brief event in which air pressure is increased behind the occluded glottis and then released, more gently than following a glottal stop. Glottal strokes are used to separate phonemes in linguistic situations in which running them together might result in misunderstanding of the meaning

glottis: Space between the vocal folds. (*See* also **Rima glottitis**)

glottis respiratoria: The portion of the glottis posteriorly in the region of the cartilaginous portions of the vocal folds

glottis vocalis: The portion of the glottis in the region of the membranous portions of the vocal folds

grace days: Refers to a former contractual arrangement, especially in European Opera Houses, in which women were permitted to refrain from singing during the premenstrual and early menstrual portions of their cycles, at their discretion

granuloma: A raised lesion generally covered with mucosa, most commonly in the region of the vocal process or medial surface of the arytenoid. Often caused by reflux and/or muscle tension dysphonia

halitosis: Bad breath

harmonic: A frequency that is an integer multiple of a given fundamental. Harmonics of a fundamental are equally spaced in frequency. Partial in a spectrum in which the frequency of each partial equals n times the fundamental frequency, n being the number of the harmonic

harsh glottal attack: Initiating phonation of a word or sound with a glottal plosive

head voice: A vocal quality characterized by flexibility and lightness of tone. In some classifications, it is used to designate a high register of the singing voice

hemorrhage: Rupture of a blood vessel. This may occur in a vocal fold

hertz: Cycles per second (Hz) (named after Gustav Hertz)

high pass filter: Filter which only allows frequencies above a certain cutoff frequency to pass; the cutoff is generally not abrupt but, rather, gentle and is given in terms of a roll-off value, eg, 24 dB/octave

histogram: Graph showing the occurrence of a parameter value; thus, a fundamental frequency histogram shows the occurrence of different fundamental frequency values, eg, in fluent speech or in a song

Hooke's law: Stress in proportion to strain; or, in simpler form, force is proportional to elongation

hormones: Substances produced within the body that affect or control various organs and bodily functions

hyoid bone: A horseshoe-shaped bone known as the "tongue bone." It is attached to muscles of the tongue and related structures, and to the larynx and related structures

hyperfunction: Excessive muscle effort for example, pressed voice, muscle tension dysphonia

hypernasal: Excessive nasal resonance

hypofunction: Low muscular effort, for example, soft breathy voice

hyponasal: Deficient nasal resonance

hypothyroidism: Lower than normal output of thyroid hormone. This condition is referred to commonly as an "underactive thyroid," and often results in malaise, weight gain, temperature intolerance, irregular menses, muffling of the voice, and other symptoms

Hz: (*See* **Hertz**)

impotence: The inability to accomplish penile erection

in vitro: Outside the living body, for example, an excised larynx

in vivo: In the living body

incompressibility: Property of a substance that conserves volume in a deformation

inertia: Sluggishness; a property of resisting a change in momentum

inferior: Below

infertility: The inability to accomplish pregnancy

infraglottic: Below the level of the glottis (space between the vocal folds). This region includes the trachea, thorax, and related structures

infraglottic vocal tract: Below the level of the vocal folds. This region includes the airways and muscles of support (Infraglottic is synonymous with subglottic)

infrahyoid muscle group: A collection of extrinsic muscles including the sternohyoid, sternothyroid, omohyoid, and thyroid muscles

insertion: The point of attachment of a muscle with a bone that can be moved by the muscle

intensity: A measure of power per unit area. With respect to sound, it generally correlates with perceived loudness

interarytenoid muscle: An intrinsic laryngeal muscle that connects the two arytenoid cartilages

intercostal muscles: Muscles between the ribs

interval: The difference between two pitches, expressed in terms of musical scale

intrinsic laryngeal muscles: muscles within the larynx responsible for abduction, adduction, and longitudinal tension of the vocal folds

intrinsic pitch of vowels: Refers to the fact that in normal speech certain vowels tend to be produced with a significantly higher or lower pitch than other vowels

inverse filtering: Method used for recovering the transglottal airflow during phonation; the technique implies that the voice is fed through a computer filter that compensates for the resonance effects of the supraglottic vocal tract, especially the lowest formants

inverse square law: Sound intensity is inversely proportional to the square of the distance from the sound source

IPA: International Phonetic Alphabet (*See* **Appendix I**)

isometric: Constant muscle length during contraction

iteration: In mathematics, the repetitive process of substituting the solution to an equation back into the same equation to obtain the next solution

jitter: Irregularity in the period of time of vocal fold vibrations; cycle-to-cycle variation in fundamental frequency; jitter is often perceived as hoarseness

jitter percent (Jitt): A relative measure of very short term (cycle-to-cycle) variation of the pitch periods expressed in percent. The influence of the average fundamental frequency is significantly reduced. This parameter is very sensitive to pitch variations

juvenile papillomatosis: A disease of children characterized by the clustering of many papillomas (small blisterlike growths) over the vocal folds and elsewhere in the larynx and trachea. Papillomatosis may also occur in adults, in which case the adjective *juvenile* is not used. The disease is caused by human papilloma virus

keratosis: A buildup of keratin (a tough, fibrous protein) on the surface of the vocal folds

kinematics: The study of movement as a consequence of known or assumed forces

kinetic energy: The energy of matter in motion (measured in joules)

klangfarbe: Tone color, referring to vocal quality

labiodental: A consonant produced by bringing the lower lip in contact with the upper front teeth

lag: A difference in time between one point and another

lamina propria: With reference to the larynx, the tissue layers below the epithelium. In adult humans, the lamina propria consists of superficial, intermediate, and deep layers

laminar: Smooth or layered; in fluid mechanics, indicating parallel flow lines

laminar flow: Airflow in smooth layers over a surface (as differentiated from irregular, or turbulent flow)

laryngeal saccule: (*See* **Appendix of the Ventricle of Morgagni**)

laryngeal sinus: (*See* **Ventricle of Morgagni**)

laryngeal ventricle: Cavity formed by the gap between the true and false vocal folds

laryngeal web: An abnormal tissue connection attaching the vocal folds to each other

laryngectomy: Removal of the larynx. It may be total, or it may be a "conservation laryngectomy," in which a portion of the larynx is preserved

laryngitis: Inflammation of laryngeal tissues

laryngitis sicca: Dry voice

laryngocele: A pouch or herniation of the larynx, usually filled with air and sometimes presenting as a neck mass. The pouch usually enlarges with increased laryngeal pressure as may occur from coughing or playing a wind instrument.

laryngologist: Physician specializing in disorders of the larynx and voice, in most countries. In some areas of Europe, the laryngologist is primarily responsible for surgery, while diagnosis is performed by phoniatricians

laryngomalacia: A condition in which the laryngeal cartilages are excessively soft and may collapse in response to inspiratory pressures, obstructing the airway

laryngopharyngeal reflux (LPR): A form of gastroesophageal reflux disease in which gastric juice affects the larynx and adjacent structures. Commonly associated with hoarseness, frequent throat clearing, granulomas, and other laryngeal problems, even in the absence of heartburn

laryngospasm: Sudden, forceful, and abnormal closing of the vocal folds

larynx: The body organ in the neck that includes the vocal folds. The "voice box"

larynx height: Vertical position of the larynx; mostly measured in relation to the rest position

larynx tube: Cavity formed by the vocal folds and the arytenoid, epiglottis, and thyroid cartilages and the structures joining them

laser: An acronym for *light amplification by stimulated emission of radiation.* A surgical tool using light energy to vaporize or cauterize tissue

lateral: Toward the side (away from the center).

lateral cricoarytenoid muscle: Intrinsic laryngeal muscle that adducts the vocal folds through forward rocking and rotation of the arytenoids (paired)

LD50: In determining drug toxicity, the LD50 is the amount of the substance that will cause death in 50% of test specimens (lethal dose for 50%)

lesion: In medicine, a nonspecific term that may be used for nearly any structural abnormality

legato: Smooth, connected

leukoplakia: A white plaque. Typically, this occurs on mucous membranes, including the vocal folds

level: Logarithmic and comparative measure of sound intensity; the unit is normally dB

lied: Song, particularly art song

lift: (*See* **Passagio**)

ligament: Connective tissue between articular regions of bone

linear system: A system in which the relation between input and output varies in a constant, or linear, fashion

lingual: Related to the tongue

linguadental: A consonant produced by bringing the tongue in contact with the teeth

linguapalatal: A consonant produced by bringing the tongue in contact with the hard palate

lip covering: Altering lip shape to make a sound less brash or bright, and "rounder" or more "rich"

liquid: A substance that assumes the shape of its container, but preserves its volume

loft: A suggested term for the highest (loftiest) register; usually referred to as *falsetto voice*

logistic map: A simple quadratic equation that exhibits chaotic behavior under special initial conditions and parameters. It is the simplest chaotic system

Lombard effect: Modification of vocal loudness in response to auditory input. For example, the tendency to speak louder in the presence of background noise

long-term average spectrum (LTAS): Graph showing a long-time average of the sound intensity in various frequency bands; the appearance of an LTAS is strongly dependent on the filters used

longitudinal: Along the length of a structure

longitudinal tension: With reference to the larynx, stretching the vocal folds

loudness: The amount of sound perceived by a listener; a perceptual quantity that can only be assessed with an auditory system. Loudness corresponds to intensity, and to the amplitude of a sound wave

low pass filter: Filter which allows only frequencies below a certain frequency to pass; the cutoff is generally not at all abrupt but gentle and is given in terms of a roll-off value, eg, 24 dB/octave

LTAS: An acronym for long-term-averaged spectrum

lung volume: Volume contained in the subglottic air system; after a maximum inhalation following a maximum exhalation the lung volume equals the vital capacity

lyric soprano: Soprano with flexible, light vocal quality, but one who does not sing as high as a coloratura soprano

lyric tenor: Tenor with a light, high flexible voice

malignant tumor: Tumors that have the potential to metastasize, or spread to different sites. They also have the potential to invade, destroy, and replace adjacent tissues. However, benign tumors may have the capacity for substantial local destruction, as well

Mandelbrot's set: A series of two equations containing real and imaginary components that, when iterated and plotted on a two-dimensional graph, depict a very complex and classic fractal pattern

mandible: Jaw

marcato: Each note accented

marking: Using the voice gently (typically during rehearsals) to avoid injury or fatigue

masque (mask): "Singing in the masque" refers to a frontal tonal placement conceptualized by singers as being associated with vibration of the bones of the face. It is generally regarded as a healthy placement associated with rich resonant characteristics and commonly a strong singer's formant (or "ring")

mechanical equilibrium: The state in which all forces acting on a body cancel each other out, leaving a zero net force in all directions

mechanics: The study of objects in motion and the forces that produce the motion

medial (or mesial): Toward the center (midline or midplane).

melisma: Two or more notes sung on a single syllable

menopause: Cessation of menstrual cycles and menstruation. Associated with physiologic infertility

menstrual cycle: The normal, cyclical variation of hormones in adult females of child-bearing age, and bodily responses caused by those hormonal variations

menstrual period: The first part of the menstrual cycle, associated with endometrial shedding and vaginal bleeding

messa di voce: Traditional exercise in Italian singing tradition consisting of a long prolonged crescendo and diminuendo on a sustained tone

metastasis: Spread of tumor to locations other than the primary tumor site

mezza voce: Literally means "half voice." In practice, means singing softly, but with proper support

mezzo soprano: Literally means "half soprano." This is a common female range, higher than contralto but lower than soprano

middle (or mixed): A mixture of qualities from various voice registers, cultivated in order to allow consistent quality throughout the frequency range

middle C: C_4 on the piano keyboard, with an international concert pitch frequency of 261.6 Hz

millisecond: One thousandth of a second; usually noted ms. or msec

modulation: Periodic variation of a signal property; for example, as vibrato corresponds to a regular variation of fundamental frequency, it can be regarded as a modulation of that signal property

motor: Having to do with motion. For example, motor nerves allow structures to move

motor unit: A group of muscle fibers and the single motor nerve that activates the fibers

mucocele: A benign lesion filled with liquid mucus

mucolytic: A substance that thins mucous secretions

mucosa: The covering of the surfaces of the respiratory tract, including the oral cavity and nasal cavities, as well as the pharynx, larynx, and lower airways. Mucosa also exits elsewhere, such as on the lining of the vagina

mucosal tear: With reference to the vocal folds, disruption of the surface of the vocal fold. Usually caused by trauma

mucosal wave: Undulation along the vocal fold surface traveling in the direction of the airflow

modulation: The systematic change of a cyclic parameter, such as amplitude or frequency

momentum: Mass times velocity; a quantity that determines the potential force that an object can impart to another object by collision

muscle fascicles: Groups of muscle fibers enclosed by a sheath of connective tissue

muscle fibers: A long, thin cell; the basic unit of a muscle that is excited by a nerve ending

muscle tension dysphonia: Also called muscular tension dysphonia. A form of voice abuse characterized by excessive muscular effort, and usually by pressed phonation. A form of voice misuse

mutational dysphonia: A voice disorder. Most typically, it is characterized by persistent falsetto voice after puberty in a male. More generally, it is used to refer to voice with characteristics of the opposite gender

myasthenia gravis: A neuromuscular junction disease associated with fatigue

myoelastic-aerodynamic theory of phonation: The currently accepted mechanism of vocal fold physiology. Compressed air exerts pressure on the undersurface of the closed vocal folds. The pressure overcomes adductory forces, causing the vocal folds to open. The elasticity of the displaced tissues (along with the Bernoulli effect) causes the vocal folds to snap shut, resulting in sound.

myofibril: A subdivision of a muscle fiber; composed of a number of myofilaments

myofilament: A microstructure of periodically arranged actin and myosin molecules; a subdivision of a myofibril

myosin: A protein molecule that reacts with actin to form actinomycin, the contractile part of a myofilament

nasal tract: Air cavity system of the nose

NATS: National Association of Teachers of Singing

natural oscillation: Oscillation without imposed driving forces

neoplasm: Abnormal growth. May be benign or malignant

nervous system: Organs of the body including the brain, spinal cord, and nerves. Responsible for motion, sensation, thought, and control of various other bodily functions

neurotologist: Otolaryngologist specializing in disorders of the ear and ear-brain interface (including the skull base), particularly hearing loss, dizziness, tinnitus, and facial nerve dysfunction

neutral vowel: A vowel produced in the center of the oral cavity.

nodes: The "valleys" in a standing wave pattern

nodules: Benign growths on the surface of the vocal folds. Usually paired and fairly symmetric. They are generally caused by chronic, forceful vocal fold contact (voice abuse)

noise: Unwanted sound

noise-to-harmonic ratio (NHR): A general evaluation of noise percent in the signal and includes jitter, shimmer, and turbulent noise

nonlinear dynamics: (*See also* **Chaos** and **Chaotic Behavior**) The mathematical study of aperiodic, deterministic systems that are not random and cannot be described accurately by linear equations. The study of nonlinear systems whose state changes with time

nonlinear system: Any system in which the output is disproportionate to the input

objective assessment: Demonstrable, reproducible, usually quantifiable evaluation, generally relying on instrumentation or other assessment techniques that do not involve primarily opinion, as opposed to subjective assessment

octave: Interval between two pitches with frequencies in the ratio of 2:1

off-glide: Transition from a vowel of long duration to one of short duration

olfaction: The sense of smell, mediated by the first cranial nerve

on-glide: Transition from a sound of short duration to a vowel of longer duration

onset: The beginning of phonation

open quotient: The ratio of the time the glottis is open to the length of the entire vibratory cycle

oral contraceptive: Birth control pill

organic disorder: A disorder due to structural malfunction, malformation, or injury, as opposed to psychogenic disorders

organic voice disorder: Disorder for which a specific anatomic or physiologic cause can be identified, as opposed to psychogenic or functional voice disorders

origin: The beginning point of a muscle and related soft tissue

oscillation: Repeated movement, back and forth

oscillator: With regard to the larynx, the vibrator that is responsible for the sound source, specifically the vocal folds

ossicle: Middle ear bone

ossify: To become bony

ostium: Opening

otolaryngologist: Ear, nose, and throat physician

otologist: Otolaryngologist specializing in disorders of the ear

overtone: Partial above the fundamental in a spectrum

ovulation: The middle of the menstrual cycle, associated with release of an ovum (egg), and the period of fertility

palatal: Related to the palate (*See* also **Linguapalatal**)

papillomas: Small benign epithelial tumors that may appear randomly or in clusters on the vocal folds, larynx, and trachea and elsewhere in the body. Believed to be caused by various types of human papillomavirus (HPV), some of which are associated with malignancy

parietal pleura: The outermost of two membranes surrounding the lungs

partial: Sinusoid that is part of a complex tone; in voiced sounds, the partials are harmonic implying that the frequency of the nth partial equals n times the fundamental frequency

particle: A finite mass with zero dimensions, located at a single point in space

pascal (Pa): International standard unit of pressure; one newton (N) per meter squared (m^2)

Pascal's law: Pressure is transmitted rapidly and uniformly throughout an enclosed fluid at rest

pass band: A band of frequencies minimally affected by a filter

passaggio (Italian): The break between vocal registers

period: (1) In physics, the time interval between repeating events; shortest pattern repeated in a regular undulation; a graph showing the period is called a waveform. (2) In medicine, the time during the menstrual cycle associated with bleeding and shedding of the endometrial lining

period doubling: One form of bifurcation in which a system that originally had x period states now has 2x periodic states, with a change having occurred in response to a change in parameter or initial condition

period time: In physics, duration of a period

periodic behavior: Repeating over and over again over a finite time interval. Periodic behavior is governed by an underlying deterministic process

peristalsis: Successive contractions of musculature, which cause a bolus of food to pass through the alimentary tract

perturbation: Small disturbances or changes from expected behavior

pharyngocele: A pouch or herniation of part of the pharynx (throat), commonly fills with air in wind players

pharynx: The region above the larynx, below the velum and posterior to the oral cavity

phase: (1) The manner in which molecules are arranged in a material (gas, liquid, or solid); (2) the angular separation between two events on periodic waveforms

phase plane plot: Representation of a dynamic system in state space

phase space: A space created by two or more independent dynamic variables, such as positions and velocities, utilized to plot the trajectory of a moving object

phase spectrum: A display of the relative phases versus frequency of the components of a waveform

phonation: Sound generation by means of vocal fold vibrations

phoneme: A unit of sound within a specific language

phonetics: The study of speech sounds

phonetogram: Recording of highest and lowest sound pressure level versus fundamental frequency that a voice can produce; phonetograms are often used for describing the status of voice function in patients. Also called *voice range profile*

phoniatrician: A physician specializing in diagnosis and nonsurgical treatment of voice disorders. This specialty does not exist in American medical training, where the phoniatrician's activities are accomplished as a team by the laryngologist (responsible for diagnosis and surgical treatment when needed) and speech-language pathologist (responsible for behavioral voice therapy)

phonosurgery: Originally, surgery designed to alter vocal quality or pitch. Now used commonly to refer to all delicate microsurgical procedures of the vocal folds

phonotrauma: Vocal fold injury caused by vocal fold contact during phonation, associated most commonly with voice abuse or misuse

phrenic nerve: The nerve that controls the diaphragm. Responsible for inspiration. Composed primarily of fibers from the third, fourth, and fifth cervical roots

piriform sinus: Pouch or cavity constituting the lower end of the pharynx located to the side and partially to the back of the larynx. There are two, paired pyriform sinuses in the normal individual

pitch: Perceived tone quality corresponding to its fundamental frequency

pitch matching: Experiment in which subjects are asked to produce the pitch of a reference tone

pitch period perturbation quotient (PPQ): A relative evaluation of short term (cycle-to-cycle) variation of the pitch periods expressed in percent

pleural space: The fluid-filled space between the parietal and visceral pleura

plosive: A consonant produced by creating complete blockage of airflow, followed by the buildup of air pressure, which is then suddenly released, producing a consonant sound

Poincaré section: A graphical technique to reveal a discernable pattern in a phase plane plot that does not have an apparent pattern. There are two kinds of Poincaré sections

polyp: A sessile or pedunculated growth. Usually unilateral and benign, but the term is descriptive and does not imply a histological diagnosis

posterior: Toward the back

posterior cricoarytenoid muscle: An intrinsic laryngeal muscle that is the primary abductor of the vocal folds (paired)

power: The rate of delivery (or expenditure) of energy (measured in watts)

power source: The expiratory system including the muscles of the abdomen, back, thorax, and the lungs. Responsible for producing a vector of force that results in efficient creation and control of subglottal pressure

power spectrum: Two-dimensional graphic analysis of sound with frequency on the x axis and amplitude on the y axis

prechaotic behavior: Predictable behavior prior to the onset of chaotic behavior. One example is period doubling

pressed phonation: Type of phonation characterized by small airflow, high adductory force, and high subglottal pressure. Not an efficient form of voice production. Often associated with voice abuse, and common in patients with lesions such as nodules

pressure: Force per unit area

prevoicing: Phonation that occurs briefly before phonation of a stop consonant

prima donna: Literally means "first lady." Refers to the soprano soloist, especially the lead singer in an opera

primo passaggio: "The first passage"; the first register change perceived in a voice as pitch is raised from low to high

proteomics: The study of proteins

psychogenic: Caused by psychological factors, rather than physical dysfunction. Psychogenic disorders may result in physical dysfunction or structural injury

pulmonary system: The breathing apparatus including the lungs and related airways

pulse register: The extreme low end of the phonatory range. Also know as *vocal fry* and *Strohbass*, characterized by a pattern of short glottal waves alternating with larger and longer ones, and with a long closed phase

pure tone: Sinusoid. The simplest tone. Produced electronically. In nature, even pure-sounding tones like bird songs are complex

pyrotechnics: Special effects involving combustion and explosion, used to produce dramatic visual displays (similar to fireworks), indoors or outdoors

pyrosis: Heartburn

quadrangular membrane: Elastic membrane extending from the sides of the epiglottic cartilage to the corniculate and arytenoid cartilages. Mucosa covered. Forms the aryepiglottic fold and the wall between the piriform sinus and larynx

quasiperiodic: A behavior that has at least two frequencies in which the phases are related by an irrational number

radian: The angular measure obtained when the arc along the circumference of the circle is equal to the radius

radian frequency: The number of radians per second covered in circular or sinusoidal motion

random behavior: Action that never repeats itself and is inherently unpredictable

rarefaction: A decrease in density

recurrent laryngeal nerves: The paired branches of the vagus nerve that supply all of the intrinsic muscles of the larynx except for the cricothyroid muscles. The recurrent laryngeal nerves also carry sensory fibers (feeling) to the mucosa below the level of the vocal folds

reflux: (*See* **Gastroesophageal Reflux** and **Laryngopharyngeal Reflux**)

reflux laryngitis: Inflammation of the larynx due to irritation from gastric juice

refractive eye surgery: Surgery to correct visual acuity

registers: Weakly defined term for vocal qualities; often, register refers to a series of adjacent tones on the scale that sound similar and seem to be generated by the same type of vocal fold vibrations and vocal tract adjustments. Examples of register are vocal fry, modal, and falsetto; but numerous other terms are also used

regulation: The events by which a protein is produced or destroyed, and the balance between these two conditions

Reinke's space: The superficial layer of the lamina propria

relative average perturbation (RAP): A relative evaluation of short-term (cycle-to-cycle) variation of the pitch periods expressed in percent

relative voice rest: Restricted, cautious voice use

resonance: Peak occurring at certain frequencies (resonance frequencies) in the vibration amplitude in a system that possesses compliance, inertia, and reflection; resonance occurs when the input and the reflected energy vibrate in phase; the resonances in the vocal tract are called *formants*

resonator: With regard to the voice, refers primarily to the supraglottic vocal tract, which is responsible for timbre and projection

restoring force: A force that brings an object back to a stable equilibrium position

return map: Similar to phase plane plot, but analyzed data must be digital. This graphic technique represents the relationship between a point and any subsequent point in a time series

rhinorrhea: Nasal discharge; runny nose

rhotic: A vowel sound produced with r-coloring.

rima glottitis: The space between the vocal folds. Also known as the glottis

roll-off: Characteristics of filters specifying their ability to shut off frequencies outside the pass band; for example, if a low pass filter is set to 2 kHz and has a roll-off of 24 dB/octave, it will alternate a 4 kHz tone by 24 dB and a 8 kHz tone by 48 dB

rostral: Toward the mouth (beak)

sagittal: An anatomic plane that divides the body into left and right sides

sarcoplasmic reticulum: Connective tissue enveloping groups of muscle fibers

scalar: A quantity that scales, or adjusts size; a single number

second passaggio: "The second passage"; the second register change perceived in a voice

semicircular canal: Inner ear organ of balance

semi-vowel: A consonant that has vowel-like resonance

sensory: Having to do with the feeling or detection of other nonmotor input. For example, nerves responsible for touch, proprioception (position in space), hearing, and so on

sharp singing: Singing at a pitch (frequency) higher than the desirable target pitch

shimmer: Cycle-to-cycle variability in amplitude

shimmer percent: Is the same as shimmer dB but expressed in percent instead of dB. Both are relative evaluations of the same type of amplitude perturbation but they use different measures for this result: either percent or dB

simple harmonic motion: Sinusoidal motion; the smoothest back and forth motion possible

simple tone: (*See* **Pure Tone**)

singer's formant: A high spectrum peak occurring between about 2.3 and 3.5 kHz in voiced sounds in Western opera and concert singing. This acoustic phenomenon is associated with "ring" in a voice, and with the voices ability to project over background noise such as a choir or an orchestra. A similar phenomenon may be seen in speaking voices, especially in actors. It is known as the *speaker's formant*

singing teacher: Professional who teaches singing technique (as opposed to Voice Coach).

singing voice specialist: A singing teacher with additional training, and specialization in working with injured voices, in conjunction with a medical voice team

sinus of Morgagni: Often confused with ventricle of Morgagni. Actually, the sinus of Morgagni is not in the larynx. It is formed by the superior fibers of the superior pharyngeal constrictor as they curve below the levator veli palatini and the eustachian tube. The space between the upper border of the muscle and the base of the skull is known as the sinus of Morgagni, and is closed by the pharyngeal aponeurosis

sinusitis: Infection of the paranasal sinus cavities

sinusoid: A graph representing the sine or cosine of a constantly increasing angle; in mechanics, the smoothest and simplest back-and-forth movement, characterized by a single frequency, an amplitude, and a phase; tone arising from sinusoidal sound pressure variations

sinusoidal motion: The projection of circular motion (in a plane) at constant speed onto one axis in the plane

skeleton: The bony or cartilaginous framework to which muscle and other soft tissues are attached

smoothed amplitude perturbation quotient (sAPQ): A relative evaluation of long-term variation of the peak-to-peak amplitude within the analyzed voice sample, expressed in percent

smoothed pitch perturbation quotient (sPPQ): A relative evaluation of long-term variation of the pitch period within the analyzed voice sample expressed in percent

soft glottal attack: Gentle glottal approximation, often obtained using an imaginary /h/

soft phonation index (SPI): A measure of the ratio of lower frequency harmonic energy to higher frequency harmonic energy. If the SPI is low, then the spectral analysis will show well-defined higher formants

solid: A substance that maintains its shape, independent of the shape of its container

soprano acuto: High soprano

soprano assoluto: A soprano who is able to sing all soprano roles and classifications

sound level: Logarithmic, comparative measure of the intensity of a signal; the unit is dB

sound pressure level (SPL): Measure of the intensity of a sound, ordinarily in dB relative to 0.0002 microbar (millionths of 1 atmosphere pressure)

sound propagation: The process of imparting a pressure or density disturbance to adjacent parts of a continuous medium, creating new disturbances at points farther away from the initial disturbance

source-filter theory: A theory that assumes the time-varying glottal airflow to be the primary sound source and the vocal tract to be an acoustic filter of the glottal source

source spectrum: Spectrum of the voice source

spasmodic dysphonia: A focal dystonia involving the larynx. May be of adductor, abductor, or mixed type. Adductor spasmodic dysphonia is characterized by strain-strangled interruptions in phonation. Abductor spasmodic dysphonia is characterized by breathy interruptions

speaker's formant: (*See* **Singer's formant**)

special sensory nerves: Nerves responsible for hearing, vision, taste, and smell

spectrogram: Three-dimensional graphic representation of sound with time on the x axis, frequency on the y axis, and amplitude displayed as intensity of color

spectrograph: The equipment that produces a spectrogram

spectrum: Ensemble of simultaneously sounding sinusoidal partials constituting a complex tone; a display of relative magnitudes or phases of the component frequencies of a waveform

spectrum analysis: Analysis of a signal showing its partials

speech-language pathologist: A trained, medically affiliated professional who may be skilled in remediation of problems of the speaking voice, swallowing, articulation, language development, and other conditions

speed: The rate of change of distance with time; the magnitude of velocity

spinto: Literally means *pushed* or *thrust*. Usually applies to tenors or sopranos with lighter voice than dramatic singers, but with aspects of particular dramatic excitement in their vocal quality. Enrico Caruso was an example

spirometer: A device for measuring airflow

stable equilibrium: A unique state to which a system with a restoring force will return after it has been displaced from rest

staccato: Each note accented and separated

standard deviation: The square root of the variance

standing wave: A wave that appears to be standing still; it occurs when waves with the same frequency (and wavelength) moving in opposite directions interfere with each other

state space: In abstract mathematics, the area in which a behavior occurs

stent: A device used for shape, support, and maintenance of patency during healing after surgery or injury

steroid: Steroids are potent substances produced by the body. They may also be consumed as medications. (*See* **Anabolic steroids, Corticosteroids**)

stochastic: Random from a statistical, mathematical point of view

stop band: A band of frequencies rejected by a filter; it is the low region in a filter spectrum

strain: Deformation relative to a rest dimension, including direction (eg, elongation per unit length)

strain rate: The rate of change of strain with respect to time

stress: Force per unit area, including the direction in which the force is applied to the area

striking zone: The middle third of the musculomembranous portion of the vocal fold; the point of maximum contact force during phonatory vocal adduction

stroboscopy: A technique that uses interrupted light to simulate slow motion. (*See* also **Strobovideolaryngoscopy**)

strobovideolaryngoscopy: Evaluation of the vocal folds utilizing simulated slow motion for detailed evaluation of vocal fold motion

Strohbass (German): "Straw bass"; another term for *pulse register* or *vocal fry*

subglottal: Below the glottis

subglottal pressure: Air pressure in the airway immediately below the level of the vocal folds. The unit most commonly used is centimeters of water. That distance in centimeters that a given pressure would raise a column of water in a tube

subglottic: The region immediately below the level of the vocal folds

subharmonic: A frequency obtained by *dividing* a fundamental frequency by an integer greater than 0

subjective assessment: Evaluation that depends on perception and opinion, rather than independently reproducible quantifiable measures, as opposed to objective assessment

sulcus vocalis: A longitudinal groove, usually on the medial surface of the vocal fold

superior: above

superior laryngeal nerves: Paired branches of the vagus nerve that supply the cricothyroid muscle and supply sensation from the level of the vocal folds superiorly

support: Commonly used to refer to the power source of the voice. It includes the mechanism responsible for creating a vector force that results in efficient subglottic pressure. This includes the muscles of the abdomen and back, as well as the thorax and lungs; primarily the expiratory system

supraglottal: Above the glottis, or level of the vocal folds

supraglottic: (1) Above the level of the vocal folds. This region includes the resonance system of the vocal tract, including the pharynx, oral cavity, nose, and related structures. (2) Posterior commissure. A misnomer. Used to describe the posterior aspect of the larynx (interarytenoid area), which is opposite the anterior commissure. However, there is actually no commissure on the posterior aspect of the larynx

suprahyoid muscle group: One of the two extrinsic muscle groups. Includes the stylohyoid muscle, anterior and posterior bellies of the digastric muscle, geniohyoid, hyoglossus, and mylohyoid muscles

temporal gap transition: The transition from a continuous sound to a series of pulses in the perception of vocal registers

temporomandibular joint: The jaw joint; a synovial joint between the mandibular condyle and skull anterior to the ear canal

tenor: Highest of the male voices, except countertenors. Must be able to sing to C_5. Singer's formant is around 2800 Hz

tenore serio: Dramatic tenor

testosterone: The hormone responsible for development of male sexual characteristics, including laryngeal growth

thin voice: A term used by singers to describe vocal weakness associated with lack of harmonic richness. The voice often also has increased breathiness, noise, and weakness and is commonly also described as "thready"

thoracic: Pertaining to the chest

thorax: The part of the body between the neck and abdomen

thready voice: (*See* **Thin voice**)

thyroarytenoid muscle: An intrinsic laryngeal muscle that comprises the bulk of the vocal fold (paired). The medial belly constitutes the body of the vocal fold

thyroid cartilage: The largest laryngeal cartilage. It is open posteriorly and is made up of two plates (thyroid laminae) joined anteriorly at the midline. In males, there is a prominence superiorly known as the "Adam's apple"

tidal volume: The amount of air breathed in and out during respiration (measured in liters)

timbre: The quality of a sound. Associated with complexity, or the number, nature, and interaction of overtones

tonsil: A mass of lymphoid tissue located near the junction of the oral cavity and pharynx (paired)

tonsillitis: Inflammation of the tonsil

tracheal stenosis: Narrowing in the trachea. May be congenital or acquired

tracheoesophageal fistula: A connection between the trachea and esophagus. May be congenital or acquired

trajectory: In chaos, the representation of the behavior of a system in state space over a finite, brief period of time. For example, one cycle on a phase plane plot

transcription: Converting the message in DNA to messenger RNA

transfection: Infection by naked viral nucleic acid

transglottal flow: Air that is forced through the glottis by a transglottal pressure

transition: With regard to the vocal fold, the intermediate and deep layers of lamina propria (vocal ligament)

translation: Using messenger RNA to make proteins

transverse: Refers to an anatomic plane that divides the body across. Also used to refer to a direction perpendicular to a given structure or phenomenon such as a muscle fiber or airflow

tremolo: An aesthetically displeasing, excessively wide vibrato (*See* **Wobble**). The term is also used in music to refer to an ornament used by composers and performers

tremor: A modulation in activity

trill: In early music (Renaissance) where it referred to an ornament that involved repetition of the same note. That ornament is now referred to as a *trillo*

trillo: Originally a trill, but in recent pedagogy a rapid repetition of the same note, which usually includes repeated voice onset and offset

triphthong: Three consecutive vowels that make up the same syllable

tumor: A mass or growth

turbulence: Irregular movement of air, fluid, or other substance, which causes a hissing sound. White water is a typical example of turbulence

turbulent airflow: Irregular airflow containing eddies and rotating patterns

tympanic membrane: Eardrum

unilateral vocal fold paralysis: Immobility of one vocal fold, due to neurological dysfunction

unstable equilibrium: The state in which a disturbance of a mechanical system will cause a drift away from a rest position

unvoiced: A sound made without phonation, and devoid of pitch; voiceless

upregulation: Increased gene expression, compared with baseline

variability: The amount of change, or ability to change

variance: The mean squared difference from the average value in a data set

vector: A quantity made up of two or more independent items of information, always grouped together

velar: Relating to the velum or palate

velocity: The rate of change of displacement with respect to time (measured in meters per second, with the appropriate direction)

velopharyngeal insufficiency: Escape of air, liquid or food from the oropharynx into the nasopharynx or nose at times when the nasopharynx should be closed by approximation of the soft palate and pharyngeal tissues

velum: The area of the soft palate and adjacent nasopharynx.

ventral: Toward the belly

ventricle of Morgagni: Also known as *laryngeal sinus*, and *ventriculus laryngis*. The ventricle is a fusiform pouch bounded by the margin of the vocal folds, the edge of the free crescentic margin of the false vocal fold (ventricular fold), and the mucous membrane between them that forms the pouch. Anteriorly, a narrowing opening leads from the ventricle to the appendix of the ventricle of Morgagni

ventricular folds: The "false vocal folds," situated above the true vocal folds

ventricular ligament: A narrow band of fibrous tissue that extends from the angle of the thyroid cartilage below the epiglottis to the arytenoid cartilage just above the vocal process. It is contained within the false vocal fold. The caudal border of the ventricular ligament forms a free crescentic margin, which constitutes the upper border of the ventricle of Morgagni

ventricular phonation: (*See* **Dysphonia plica ventricularis**)

vertical phase difference: With reference to the vocal folds, refers to the asynchrony between the lower and upper surfaces of the vibratory margin of the vocal fold during phonation

vertigo: Sensation of rotary motion. A form of dizziness

vibrato: In classical singing, vibrato is a periodic modulation of the frequency of phonation. Its regularity increases with training. The rate of vibrato (number of modulations per second) is usually in the range of 5–6 per second. Vibrato rates over 7–8 per second are aesthetically displeasing to most people, and sound "nervous." The extent of vibrato (amount of variation above and below the center frequency) is usually one or two semitones. Vibrato extending less than ±0.5 semitone are rarely seen in singers although they are encountered in wind instrument playing. Vibrato rates greater than two semitones are usually aesthetically unacceptable, and are typical of elderly singers in poor artistic vocal condition, in whom the excessively wide vibrato extent is often combined with excessively slow rate

viscera: The internal organs of the body, particularly the contents of the abdomen

visceral pleura: The innermost of two membranes surrounding the lungs

viscoelastic material: A material that exhibits characteristics of both elastic solids and viscous liquids. The vocal fold is an example

viscosity: Property of a liquid associated with its resistance to deformation. Associated with the "thickness" of a liquid

vital capacity: The maximum volume of air that can be exchanged by the lungs with the outside; it includes the expiratory reserve volume, tidal volume, and inspiratory reserve volume (measured in liters)

vocal cord: Old term for vocal fold

vocal fold (or cord) stripping: A surgical technique, no longer considered acceptable practice under most circumstances, in which the vocal fold is grasped with a forceps, and the surface layers are ripped off

vocal fold stiffness: The ratio of the effective restoring force (in the medial-lateral direction) to the displacement (in the same direction)

vocal folds: A paired system of tissue layers in the larynx that can oscillate to produce sound

vocal fry: A register with perceived temporal gaps; also known as *pulse register* and Strohbass. (*See* **Pulse register**)

vocal ligament: Intermediate and deep layers of the lamina propria. Also forms the superior end of the conus elasticus

vocal tract: Resonator system constituted by the larynx, the pharynx and the mouth cavity

vocalis muscle: The medial belly of the thyroarytenoid muscle

vocalise: A vocal exercise involving sung sounds, commonly vowels on scales of various complexity

voce coperta: "Covered registration"

voce mista: Mixed voice (also voix mixed)

voce di petto: Chest voice

voce sgangherata: "White" voice. Literally means immoderate or unattractive. Lacks strength in the lower partials

voce di testa: Head voice

voce piena: Full voice

voice abuse: Use of the voice in specific activities that are deleterious to vocal health, such as screaming

voice box: (*See* **Larynx**)

voice coach: (1) In singing, a professional who works with singers, teaching repertoire, language pronunciation, and other artistic components of performance (as opposed to a singing teacher, who teaches technique); (2) The term voice coach is also used by acting-voice teachers who specialize in vocal, bodily, and interpretive techniques to enhance dramatic performance

voice misuse: Habitual phonation using phonatory techniques that are not optimal and then result in vocal strain. For example, speaking with inadequate support, excessive neck muscle tension, and suboptimal resonance. Muscular tension dysphonia is a form of voice misuse

voice range profile: (*See* **Phonetogram**)

voice rest: (*See* **Absolute voice rest, relative voice rest**)

voice source: Sound generated by the pulsating transglottal airflow; the sound is generated when the vocal fold vibrations chop the airstream into a pulsating airflow

voice turbulence index (VTI): A measure of the relative energy level of high frequency noise

voiced: A language sound made with phonation, and possessing pitch.

voiceless: (*See* **Unvoiced**)

volume: "Amount of sound," best measured in terms of acoustic power or intensity

vortex theory: Holds that eddys, or areas of organized turbulence, are produced as air flows through the larynx and vocal tract

Vowel color: refers to vowel quality, or timbre, and is associated with harmonic content

Waldeyer's ring: An aggregation of lymphoid tissue in the pharynx, including the tonsils and adenoids

waveform: A plot of any variable (eg, pressure, flow, or displacement) changing as time progresses along the horizontal axis; also known as a time-series

wavefront: The initial disturbance in a propagating wave

wavelength: The linear distance between any point on one vibratory cycle and a corresponding point of the next vibratory cycle

whisper: Sound created by turbulent glottal airflow in the absence of vocal fold vibration

whistle register: The highest of all registers (in pitch). It is observed only in females, extending the pitch range beyond F_6

wobble: Undesirable vibrato, usually with vibrato rate of 2 to 4 Hz, and extent greater than ± 0.5 semitone (*See also* **Tremolo**)

xerostomia: Dry mouth

Young's modulus: The ratio between magnitudes of stress and strain

Appendix Ia

PATIENT HISTORY: SINGERS
Robert Thayer Sataloff, M.D., D.M.A.
1721 Pine Street
Philadelphia, PA 19103

NAME ______________________________ AGE ______ SEX ______ RACE ____________________
HEIGHT ___________________________ WEIGHT ________________ DATE ____________________
VOICE CATEGORY: _______ soprano _______ mezzo-soprano _______ alto
_______ tenor _______ baritone _______ bass

(If you are not currently having a voice problem, please skip to Question #3.)

PLEASE CHECK OR CIRCLE CORRECT ANSWERS

1. How long have you had your present voice problem?

   Who noticed it?

   [self, family, voice teacher, critics, everyone, other _______]

   Do you know what caused it? Yes _______ No _______

   If yes, what?

   Did it come on slowly or suddenly? Slowly _______ Suddenly _______
   Is it getting: Worse: _______, Better _______, Same _______

2. Which symptoms do you have? (Please check all that apply.)
   _______ Hoarseness (coarse or scratchy sound)
   _______ Fatigue (voice tires or changes quality after singing for a short period of time)
   _______ Volume disturbance (trouble singing) softly _______ loudly _______
   _______ Loss of range (high _______ low _______)
   _______ Change in classification (example: voice lowered from soprano to mezzo)
   _______ Prolonged warm-up time (over ½ hr to warm up voice)
   _______ Breathiness
   _______ Tickling or choking sensation while singing
   _______ Pain in throat while singing
   _______ Other: (Please specify)____
   ____
   ____

3. Do you have an important performance soon? Yes _______ No _______
   Date(s): ____

4. What is the current status of your singing career?
   Professional _______ Amateur _______

5. What are your long-term career goals in singing?
   [ ] Premier operatic career
   [ ] Premier pop music career
   [ ] Active avocation
   [ ] Classical
   [ ] Pop
   [ ] Other (___________________________)
   [ ] Amateur performance (choral or solo)
   [ ] Amateur singing for own pleasure

6. Have you had voice training? Yes _______ No _______
   At what age did you begin?

7. Have there been periods of months or years without lessons in that time? Yes _______ No _______

8. How long have you studied with your present teacher?

   Teacher's name:
   Teacher's address:

   Teacher's telephone number:

9. Please list previous teachers and years during which you studied with them.

10. Have you ever had training for your speaking voice? Yes _______ No _______
    Acting voice lessons? Yes _______ No _______
    How many years?
    Speech therapy? Yes _______ No _______
    How many months?

11. Do you have a job in addition to singing? Yes _______ No _______

    If yes, does it involve extensive voice use? Yes _______ No _______

    If yes, what is it? [actor, announcer (television/radio/sports arena), athletic instructor, attorney, clergy, politician, physician, salesperson, stockbroker, teacher, telephone operator or receptionist, waiter, waitress, secretary, other _________________

12. In your performance work, in addition to singing, are you frequently
    required to speak? Yes _______ No _______
    dance? Yes _______ No _______

13. How many years did you sing actively before beginning voice lessons initially?

14. What types of music do you sing? (Check all that apply.)
_______ Classical _______ Show
_______ Nightclub _______ Rock
_______ Other: (Please specify.) ____________________

15. Do you regularly sing in a sitting position (such as from behind a piano or drum set)?
Yes _______ No _______

16. Do you sing outdoors or in large halls, or with orchestras? (Circle which one.) Yes _______ No _______

17. If you perform with electrical instruments or outdoors, do you use monitor speakers? (Circle which one).
Yes _______ No _______

If yes, can you hear them? Yes _______ No _______

18. Do you play a musical instrument(s)? Yes _______ No _______
If yes, please check all that apply:
_______ Keyboard (piano, organ, harpsichord, other _______________)
_______ Violin, viola
_______ Cello
_______ Bass
_______ Plucked strings (guitar, harp, other _______________)
_______ Brass
_______ Wind with single reed
_______ Wind with double reed
_______ Flute, piccolo
_______ Percussion
_______ Bagpipe
_______ Accordion
_______ Other: (Please specify)._______________

19. How often do you practice?
Scales: [daily, few times weekly, once a week, rarely, never]

If you practice scales, do you do them all at once, or do you divide them up over the course of a day?
[all at once, two or three sittings]

On days when you do scales, how long do you practice them?
[15 ,30,45,60,75 ,90,105,120, more] minutes

Songs: [daily, few times weekly, once a week, rarely, never]

How many hours per day?
[½,1,1½,2,2½,3,more]

Do you warm up your voice before you sing? Yes _______ No _______

Do you cool down your voice when you finish singing? Yes _______ No _______

20. How much are you singing at present (total including practice time) (average hours per day)?
    Rehearsal: _________________________
    Performance: _________________________

21. Please check all that apply to you:
    _______ Voice worse in the morning
    _______ Voice worse later in the day, after it has been used
    _______ Sing performances or rehearsals in the morning
    _______ Speak extensively (e.g., teacher, clergy, attorney, telephone work)
    _______ Cheerleader
    _______ Speak extensively backstage or at postperformance parties
    _______ Choral conductor
    _______ Frequently clear your throat
    _______ Frequent sore throat
    _______ Jaw joint problems
    _______ Bitter or acid taste, or bad breath first thing in the morning
    _______ Frequent "heartburn" or hiatal hernia
    _______ Frequent yelling or loud talking
    _______ Frequent whispering
    _______ Chronic fatigue (insomnia)
    _______ Work around extreme dryness
    _______ Frequent exercise (weight lifting, aerobics)
    _______ Frequently thirsty, dehydrated
    _______ Hoarseness first thing in the morning
    _______ Chest cough
    _______ Eat late at night
    _______ Ever used antacids
    _______ Under particular stress at present (personal or professional)
    _______ Frequent bad breath
    _______ Live, work, or perform around smoke or fumes
    _______ Traveled recently: When: _________________________
    Where: _________________________

    Eat any of the following before singing?

    _______ Chocolate _______ Coffee
    _______ Alcohol _______ Milk or ice cream
    _______ Nuts _______ Spiced foods

    Other: (Please specify.)

    _______ Any specific vocal technical difficulties? [trouble singing soft, trouble singing loud, poor pitch control, support problems, problems at register transitions, other] Describe other:

    _______ Any problems with your singing voice recently prior to the onset of the problem that brought you here? [hoarseness, breathiness, fatigue, loss of range, voice breaks, pain singing, other] Describe other:

_______ Any voice problems in the past that required a visit to a physician? If yes, please describe problem(s) and treatment(s): [laryngitis, nodules, polyps, hemorrhage, cancer, other]
Describe other:

22. Your family doctor's name, address, and telephone number

23. Your laryngologist's name, address, and telephone number:

24. Recent cold? Yes _______ No _______

25. Current cold? Yes _______ No _______

26. Have you been exposed to any of the following chemicals frequently (or recently) at home or at work? (Check all that apply.)
_______ Carbon monoxide
_______ Mercury
_______ Insecticides
_______ Lead
_______ Arsenic
_______ Aniline dyes
_______ Industrial solvents (benzene, etc.)
_______ Stage smoke

27. Have you been evaluated by an allergist? Yes _______ No _______

If yes, what allergies do you have:
[none, dust, mold, trees, cats, dogs, foods, other]
(Medication allergies are covered elsewhere in this history form.)
If yes, give name and address of allergist:

28. How many packs of cigarettes do you smoke per day?

Smoking history
_______ Never
_______ Quit. When? _________
_______ Smoked about _________ packs per day for _________ years.
_______ Smoke _________ packs per day. Have smoked for _________ years.

29. Do you work or live in a smoky environment? Yes _______ No _______

30. How much alcohol do you drink? [none, rarely, a few times per week, daily]
If daily, or few times per week, on the average, how much do you consume? [1,2,3,4,5,6,7,8,9,10, more] glasses per [day, week] of [beer, wine, liquor].

Did you formerly drink more heavily? Yes _______ No _______

31. How many cups of coffee, tea, cola, or other caffeine-containing drinks do you drink per day?

32. List other recreational drugs you use [marijuana, cocaine, amphetamines, barbiturates, heroin, other]:

33. Have you noticed any of the following? (Check all that apply)

_______ Hypersensitivity to heat or cold
_______ Excessive sweating
_______ Change in weight: gained / lost _______ lb in _______ weeks / _______ months
_______ Change in skin or hair
_______ Palpitation (fluttering) of the heart
_______ Emotional lability (swings of mood)
_______ Double vision
_______ Numbness of the face or extremities
_______ Tingling around the mouth or face
_______ Blurred vision or blindness
_______ Weakness or paralysis of the face
_______ Clumsiness in arms or legs
_______ Confusion or loss of consciousness
_______ Difficulty with speech
_______ Difficulty with swallowing
_______ Seizure (epileptic fit)
_______ Pain in the neck or shoulder
_______ Shaking or tremors
_______ Memory change
_______ Personality change

For females:

Are you pregnant? Yes _______ No _______
Are your menstrual periods regular? Yes _______ No _______
Have you undergone hysterectomy? Yes _______ No _______
Were your ovaries removed? Yes _______ No _______
At what age did you reach puberty? ____________________
Have you gone through menopause? Yes _______ No _______
If yes, when?

34. Have you ever consulted a psychologist or psychiatrist? Yes _______ No _______

Are you currently under treatment? Yes _______ No _______

35. Have you injured your head or neck (whiplash, etc.)? Yes _______ No _______

36. Describe any serious accidents related to this visit.
None _______

37. Are you involved in legal action involving problems with your voice? Yes _______ No _______

38. List names of spouse and children:

39. Brief summary of ear, nose, and throat (ENT) problems, some of which may not be related to your present complaint.

PLEASE CHECK ALL THAT APPLY

_______ Hearing loss
_______ Ear noises
_______ Dizziness
_______ Facial paralysis
_______ Nasal obstruction
_______ Nasal deformity
_______ Mouth sores
_______ Jaw joint problem
_______ Eye problem
_______ Other: (Please specify.)
_______ Ear pain
_______ Facial pain
_______ Stiff neck
_______ Lump in neck
_______ Lump in face or head
_______ Trouble swallowing
_______ Excess eye skin
_______ Excess facial skin

40. Do you have or have you ever had:

_______ Diabetes
_______ Hypoglycemia
_______ Thyroid problems
_______ Syphilis
_______ Gonorrhea
_______ Herpes
_______ Cold sores (fever blisters)
_______ High blood pressure
_______ Severe low blood pressure
_______ Intravenous antibiotics or diuretics
_______ Heart attack
_______ Angina irregular heartbeat
_______ Other heart problems
_______ Rheumatic fever
_______ Tuberculosis
_______ Glaucoma
_______ Multiple sclerosis
_______ Other illnesses: (Please specify.)
_______ Seizures
_______ Psychiatric therapy
_______ Frequent bad headaches
_______ Ulcers
_______ Kidney disease
_______ Urinary problems
_______ Arthritis or skeletal problems
_______ Cleft palate
_______ Asthma
_______ Lung or breathing problems
_______ Unexplained weight loss
_______ Cancer of (_______________________)
_______ Other tumor (_______________________)
_______ Blood transfusions
_______ Hepatitis
_______ AIDS
_______ Meningitis

41. Do any blood relatives have:

_______ Diabetes
_______ Hypoglycemia
_______ Cancer
_______ Heart disease
_______ Other major medical problems such as those above. Please specify:

42. Describe serious accidents unless directly related to your doctor's visit here.
    _______ None
    _______ Occurred with head injury, loss of consciousness, or whiplash
    _______ Occurred without head injury, loss of consciousness, or whiplash
    Describe:

43. List all current medications and doses (include birth control pills and vitamins).

44. Medication allergies
    _______ None
    _______ Penicillin
    _______ Sulfa
    _______ Tetracycline
    _______ Erythromycin
    _______ Keflex/Ceclor/Ceftin
    _______ Other: (Please specify.)
    _______ Novocaine
    _______ Iodine
    _______ Codeine
    _______ Adhesive tape
    _______ Aspirin
    _______ X-ray dyes

45. List operations
    _______ Tonsillectomy (age _______)
    _______ Appendectomy (age _______)
    _______ Adenoidectomy (age _______)
    _______ Heart surgery (age _______)
    _______ Other: (Please specify.)

46. List toxic drugs or chemicals to which you have been exposed:
    _______ Lead
    _______ Streptomycin, Neomycin, Kanamycin
    _______ Mercury
    _______ Other: (Please specify.)

47. Have you had x-ray *treatments* to your head or neck (including treatments for acne or ear problems as a child, treatments for cancer, etc.)?
    Yes _______ No _______

48. Describe serious health problems of your spouse or children.
    _______ None

Appendix Ib

PATIENT HISTORY: PROFESSIONAL VOICE USERS

Robert Thayer Sataloff, M.D., D.M.A.
1721 Pine Street
Philadelphia, PA 19103

NAME ______________________ AGE _____ SEX _____ RACE ______________

HEIGHT ____________________ WEIGHT ____________ DATE ______________

1. How long have you had your present voice problem? ______________________________

   Who noticed it?

   Do you know what caused it? Yes _______ No _______

   If so, what?

   Did it come on slowly or suddenly? Slowly _______ Suddenly _______

   Is it getting: Worse _______, Better _______, Same _______

2. Which symptoms do you have? (Please check all that apply.)

   _______ Hoarseness (coarse or scratchy sound)
   _______ Fatigue (voice tires or changes quality after speaking for a short period of time)
   _______ Volume disturbance (trouble speaking) softly _______ loudly _______
   _______ Loss of range (high _______, low _______)
   _______ Prolonged warm-up time (over ½ hr to warm up voice)
   _______ Breathiness
   _______ Tickling or choking sensation while speaking
   _______ Pain in throat while speaking
   _______ Other: (Please specify.)______________________________________
   ____
   ____

3. Have you ever had training for your speaking voice?

   Yes _______ No _______

4. Have there been periods of months or years without lessons in that time? Yes _______ No _______

5. How long have you studied with your present teacher?
   Teacher's name: ____
   Teacher's address: ____
   Teacher's telephone number:____

6. Please list previous teachers and years during which you studied with them:

7. Have you ever had training for your singing voice? Yes _______ No _______
   If so, list teachers and years of study:

8. In what capacity do you use your voice professionally?
   _______ Actor
   _______ Announcer (television / radio / sports arena)
   _______ Attorney
   _______ Clergy
   _______ Politician
   _______ Salesperson
   _______ Teacher
   _______ Telephone operator or receptionist
   _______ Other: (Please specify.)

9. Do you have an important performance soon? Yes _______ No _______
   Date(s): ____________________________

10. Do you do regular voice exercises? Yes _______ No _______
    If yes, describe:

11. Do you play a musical instrument? Yes _______ No _______
    If yes, please check all that apply:
    _______ Keyboard (piano, organ, harpischord, other _______)
    _______ Violin, viola
    _______ Cello
    _______ Bass
    _______ Plucked strings (guitar, harp, other _______)
    _______ Brass
    _______ Wind with single reed
    _______ Wind with double reed
    _______ Flute, piccolo
    _______ Percussion
    _______ Bagpipe
    _______ Accordion
    _______ Other: (Please specify.) ____________________________

12. Do you warm up your voice before practice or performance? Yes _______ No _______

    Do you cool down after using it? Yes _______ No _______

13. How much are you speaking at present (average hours per day)?
    _______ Rehearsal _______ Performance _______ Other

14. Please check all that apply to you:
    _______ Voice worse in the morning
    _______ Voice worse later in the day, after it has been used
    _______ Sing performances or rehearsals in the morning
    _______ Speak extensively (e.g., teacher, clergy, attorney, telephone work)
    _______ Cheerleader
    _______ Speak extensively backstage or at postperformance parties
    _______ Choral conductor
    _______ Frequently clear your throat
    _______ Frequent sore throat
    _______ Jaw joint problems
    _______ Bitter or acid taste; bad breath or hoarseness first thing in the morning
    _______ Frequent "heartburn" or hiatal hernia
    _______ Frequent yelling or loud talking
    _______ Frequent whispering
    _______ Chronic fatigue (insomnia)
    _______ Work around extreme dryness
    _______ Frequent exercise (weight lifting, aerobics)
    _______ Frequently thirsty, dehydrated
    _______ Hoarseness first thing in the morning
    _______ Chest cough
    _______ Eat late at night
    _______ Ever used antacids
    _______ Under particular stress at present (personal or professional)
    _______ Frequent bad breath
    _______ Live, work, or perform around smoke or fumes
    _______ Traveled recently: When: _______
    Where: _______

15. Your family doctor's name, address, and telephone number:

16. Your laryngologist's name, address, and telephone number:

17. Recent cold? Yes _______ No _______

18. Current cold? Yes _______ No _______

19. Have you been evaluated by an allergist? Yes _______ No _______
If yes, what allergies do you have:
[none, dust, mold, trees, cats, dogs, foods, other, ____________________________]
(Medication allergies are covered elsewhere in this history form.)
If yes, give name and address of allergist:

20. How many packs of cigarettes do you smoke per day?
Smoking history
_______ Never
_______ Quit. When? _________________________
_______ Smoked about ____ packs per day for ____ years.
_______ Smoke ____ packs per day. Have smoked for ____ years.

21. Do you work or live in a smoky environment? Yes _______ No _______

22. How much alcohol do you drink? [none, rarely, a few times per week, daily] If daily, or few times per week, on the average, how much do you consume? [1, 2, 3, 4, 5, 6, 7, 8, 9, 10, more] glasses per [day, week] of [beer, wine, liquor]

Did you formerly drink more heavily? Yes _______ No _______

23. How many cups of coffee, tea, cola, or other caffeine-containing drinks do you drink per day?

24. List other recreational drugs you use [marijuana, cocaine, amphetamines, barbiturates, heroin, other ______ ______________________]

25. Have you noticed any of the following? (Check all that apply)
_______ Hypersensitivity to heat or cold
_______ Excessive sweating
_______ Change in weight: gained/lost _______ lb in _______ weeks/ _______ months
_______ Change in your voice
_______ Change in skin or hair
_______ Palpitation (fluttering) of the heart
_______ Emotional lability (swings of mood)
_______ Double vision
_______ Numbness of the face or extremities
_______ Tingling around the mouth or face
_______ Blurred vision or blindness
_______ Weakness or paralysis of the face
_______ Clumsiness in arms or legs
_______ Confusion or loss of consciousness
_______ Difficulty with speech
_______ Difficulty with swallowing

_______ Seizure (epileptic fit)
_______ Pain in the neck or shoulder
_______ Shaking or tremors
_______ Memory change
_______ Personality change

For females:

Are you pregnant?	Yes _______	No _______
Are your menstrual periods regular?	Yes _______	No _______
Have you undergone hysterectomy?	Yes _______	No _______
Were your ovaries removed?	Yes _______	No _______
At what age did you reach puberty?	__________	
Have you gone through menopause?	Yes _______	No _______

26. Have you ever consulted a psychologist or psychiatrist?
    Yes _______ No _______

    Are you currently under treatment? Yes _______ No _______

27. Have you injured your head or neck (whiplash, etc.)?
    Yes _______ No _______

28. Describe any serious accidents related to this visit.
    None _______

29. Are you involved in legal action involving problems with your voice?
    Yes _______ No _______

30. List names of spouse and children:

31. Brief summary of ear, nose, and throat (ENT) problems, some of which may not be related to your present complaint.

_______ Hearing loss
_______ Ear noises
_______ Dizziness
_______ Facial paralysis
_______ Nasal obstruction
_______ Nasal deformity
_______ Nose bleeds
_______ Mouth sores
_______ Excess facial skin
_______ Jaw joint problem
_______ Other (Please specify.)
_______ Ear pain
_______ Facial pain
_______ Stiff neck
_______ Lump in neck
_______ Lump in face or head
_______ Trouble swallowing
_______ Trouble breathing
_______ Excess eye skin
_______ Eye problem

32. Do you have or have you ever had:
    _______ Diabetes
    _______ Hypoglycemia
    _______ Thyroid problems
    _______ Syphilis
    _______ Gonorrhea
    _______ Herpes
    _______ Cold sores (fever blisters)
    _______ High blood pressure
    _______ Severe low blood pressure
    _______ Intravenous antibiotics or diuretics
    _______ Heart attack
    _______ Angina
    _______ Irregular heartbeat
    _______ Other heart problems
    _______ Rheumatic fever
    _______ Tuberculosis
    _______ Glaucoma
    _______ Multiple sclerosis
    _______ Other illnesses: (Please specify.)
    _______ Seizures
    _______ Psychiatric therapy
    _______ Frequent bad headaches
    _______ Ulcers
    _______ Kidney disease
    _______ Urinary problems
    _______ Arthritis or skeletal problems
    _______ Cleft palate
    _______ Asthma
    _______ Lung or breathing problems
    _______ Unexplained weight loss
    _______ Cancer of (_______)
    _______ Other tumor (____________________)
    _______ Blood transfusions
    _______ Hepatitis
    _______ AIDS
    _______ Meningitis

33. Do any blood relatives have:
    _______ Diabetes
    _______ Hypoglycemia
    _______ Other major medical problems such as those above. Please specify:
    _______ Cancer
    _______ Heart disease

34. Describe serious accidents *unless* directly related to your doctor's visit here.
    _______ None
    _______ Occurred with head injury, loss of consciousness, or whiplash
    _______ Occurred without head injury, loss of consciousness, or whiplash
    Describe:

35. List all current medications and doses (include birth control pills and vitamins).

36. Medication allergies
    _______ None
    _______ Penicillin
    _______ Sulfa
    _______ Novocaine
    _______ Iodine
    _______ Codeine

_______ Tetracycline
_______ Erythromycin
_______ Keflex/Ceclor/Ceftin
_______ Other: (Please specify.)
_______ Adhesive tape
_______ Aspirin
_______ X-ray dyes

37. List operations:
_______ Tonsillectomy
(age _______)
_______ Appendectomy
(age _______)
Other: (Please specify.)
_______ Appendectomy
(age _______)
_______ Heart surgery
(age _______)

38. List toxic drugs or chemicals to which you have been exposed:
_______ Lead
_______ Mercury
_______ Streptomycin, Neomycin, Kanamycin
_______ Other: (Please list.)

39. Have you had x-ray *treatments* to your head or neck (including treatments for acne or ear problems as a child), treatments for cancer, etc.?
Yes _______ No _______

40. Describe serious health problems of your spouse or children.
_______ None

Appendix IIa

Reading Passages

A classic passage including all the speech sounds of English.

The Rainbow Passage

When the sunlight strikes raindrops in the air, they act like a prism and form a rainbow. The rainbow is a division of white light into many beautiful colors. These take the shape of a long round arch, with its path high above, and its two ends apparently beyond the horizon. There is, according to legend, a boiling pot of gold at one end. People look but no one ever finds it. When a man looks for something beyond his reach, his friends say he is looking for the pot of gold at the end of the rainbow.

An all voiced passage.

Marvin Williams

Marvin Williams is only nine. Marvin lives with his mother on Monroe Avenue in Vernon Valley. Marvin loves all movies, even eerie ones with evil villains in them. Whenever a new movie is in the area, Marvin is usually an early arrival. Nearly every evening Marvin is in row one, along the aisle.

A general purpose passage useful for evaluating hard glottal attack, phrasing, and nasal resonance.

Towne-Heuer Vocal Analysis Reading Passage

If I take a trip this August, I will probably go to Austria. Or I could go to Italy. All of the places of Europe are easy to get to by air, rail, ship or auto. Everybody I have talked to says he would like to go to Europe also.

Every year there are varieties of festivals or fairs at a lot of places. All sorts of activities, such as foods to eat, sights to see occur. Oh, I love to eat ices seated outdoors! The people of each area are reported to like us . . . the people of the U.S.A. It is said that that is true except for Paris.

Aid is easy to get because the officials are helpful. Aid is always available if troubles arise. It helps to have with you a list of offices or officials to call if you do require aid. If you are lost, you will always be helped to locate your route or hotel. The local police will assist you, if they are able to speak as you do. Otherwise a phrase book is useful.

I have had to have help of this sort each trip abroad. However, it was always easy to locate. Happily, I hope, less help will be required this trip. Last trip every hotel was occupied. I had to ask everywhere for flats. Two earlier trips were hard because of heat or lack of heat at hotels.

On second thought, I may want to travel in autumn instead of in August. Many countries can be expensive in the summer months and much less so in autumn. November and December can make fine months for entertainment in many European countries. There may be concerts and musical events more often than during the summer. Milan, Rome, and Hamburg, not to mention Berlin, Vienna, and Madrid are most often mentioned for music.

Most of my friends and I wouldn't miss the chance to try the exciting, interesting, and appetizing menus at most continental restaurants. In many European countries food is inexpensive and interestingly prepared. Servings may be small but meals are taken more often so that there is no need to go hungry.

Maritime countries make many meals of seafood, such as mussels, clams, shrimp, flounder, and salmon or herring. Planning and making your own meals cannot be done even in most small, inexpensive hotels. One must eat in the dining room or in restaurants. Much fun can be had meeting the local natives during mealtimes. Many of them can tell you where to find amusing and interesting shops and sights not mentioned in tour manuals.

Appendix IIb

Laryngeal Examination

Speaking Voice

Range:	____Soprano	____Alto	____Tenor	____Baritone	____Bass
Pitch variability:	____Normal	____Decreased	____Increased		
Excess tension:	____Normal	____Minimal	____Moderate	____Severe	
	____Tongue				
	____Neck				
	____Face				
Support:	____Good	____Deficient			
Volume:	____Appropriate	____Soft	____Loud		
Volume variability:	____Appropriate	____Diminished	____Excessive		
Quality:	____Normal	____Hoarse	____Breathy		
	____Fatiguable	____Diplophonic			
Rhythm:	____Normal	____Slow	____Fast	____Spasmodic	
	____Stuttering	____Dysarthric			
Habits:	____Throat clearing	____Coughing			
Other:					

Singing Voice

Stance:	____Balanced, proper	____Balanced, weight back	____Unbalanced		
	____Knees locked				
Breathing:	____Nasal, unobstructed				
	____Nasal, partially obstructed				
	____Oral Chest (excessive)				
	____Abdominal (proper)				
Excess tension:	____Face	____Lip	____Jaw	__Neck	____Shoulders	____Tongue
Tongue tension:	____Corrects easily	____Does not correct easily			
Support:	____Present	____Practically absent			
	____Effective	____Ineffective			
	____Initiated after the tone				
Laryngeal position:	____Stable	____Alters		____High	____Low
Mouth opening:	____Appropriate	____Decreased		____Excessive	
Vibrato:	____Regular	____Irregular		____Rapid	____Tremolo
Range:	____Soprano	____Alto	____Tenor	____Baritone	____Bass
Register changes:	____Controlled	____Uncontrolled			
Quality:	____Premier	____Professional		____Amateur	____Pathologic
	____Hoarse	____Breathy		____Fatiguable	____Diplophonic
Technical errors present:	____In all registers	____Low		____Middle	____High
Pitch:	____Accurate	____Inaccurate			

Appendix IIIa

Laryngologist's Report

PATIENT OFFICE
(215) 545-3322
FAX: (215) 790-1192
office@phillyent.com

Sataloff Institute for Voice & Ear Care

ADMINISTRATIVE OFFICE
(215) 732-6100
FAX: (215) 545-3374
rtsataloff@phillyent.com

February 10, 2004

Re: John Doe

To Whom It May Concern:

I had the pleasure of seeing John Doe in the office today. He is a 25-year-old actor performing the lead role with a national touring company now performing at the Walnut Street Theater. He is concerned about his voice. He denies any voice loss but complains of frequent sore throat and voice fatigue. Recently he has found his voice is gravelly and lower than his normal range. He is concerned about "crackling sounds." One month ago, he saw a physician who diagnosed him with laryngopharygeal reflux and started him on Aciphex twice daily. Last week he developed a globus sensation that lasted all day. He also reports a bitter taste upon awakening, throat clearing and "post nasal drip." He has been seen by several other physicians over the past two years and has been told he has dust allergy and reflux. He wants reassurance that he is not "destroying" his voice. He is not singing at this time and is acting full-time. He has had acting training in college and some singing training, as well. However, the singing training in college left him with a sore throat, and he reports that he has discounted his training from college because he does not believe it was of high quality. He has also had acting lessons in school and some after graduation. He is currently performing eight shows per week. He is on stage for the entire two and one half hours. He has been performing in this show since Christmas 2003. He does not play musical instruments, and he is not exposed to noxious fumes.

Mr. Doe reports a past medical history of microhematuria in childhood, prostratitis, depression and intermittent tightness in his chest for many years. He finds the chest tightness can last for two days at a time and then abates for as long as two years.

Mr. Doe reports a past surgical history of extraction of four impacted wisdom teeth five years ago.

His current medications include Aciphex twice daily, Zyrtec and Nasonex. He denies any medication allergies but reports environmental allergies to mold, dust and dogs. He is a lifelong non-smoker, drinks no caffeinated beverages and consumes one alcoholic beverage per week.

Page 2
February 10, 2004
Re: John Doe

His tympanic membranes and hearing were normal. Examination of the nose was normal. Examination of the oral cavity and pharynx revealed diminished gag reflex on the left. Examination of the neck was normal. Laryngeal examination was completed by strobovideolaryngoscopy and a copy of that report is attached. FEEST revealed slightly decreased sensation side of the larynx on the left. During conversational speech, his voice was pressed but not hoarse. During speaking, he had jaw and tongue tension and inadequate support. Brief singing evaluation revealed excessive tension in the tongue and jaw and suboptimal support technique. Voice team evaluation will be performed, and reports will be attached to this letter.

I have asked Mr. Doe to continue on his Aciphex twice daily for control of his laryngeal reflux and have added Zantac 300 mg at bedtime to his regimen. I have given him prescriptions for selected blood tests and referred him to Dr. Steven Mandel for a laryngeal EMG. He will be evaluated by my voice team, and I have asked him to follow up with me after completion of his testing for his reflux, paresis, vocal fold mass, and muscle tension dysphonia.

With best regards.

Very truly yours.

Robert T. Sataloff, M.D., D.M.A.

RTS/jb

Enclosure

cc: Mr. John Doe

Appendix IIIb
Strobovideolaryngoscopy Report

PATIENT OFFICE
(215) 545-3322
FAX: (215) 790-1192
office@phillyent.com

Sataloff Institute for Voice & Ear Care

ADMINISTRATIVE OFFICE
(215) 732-6100
FAX: (215) 545-3374
rtsataloff@phillyent.com

REPORT OF OPERATION: John Doe

DATE: February 10, 2004

PRE-OPERATIVE DIAGNOSIS:	1. Dysphonia
POST-OPERATIVE DIAGNOSIS:	1. Left vocal fold paresis 2. Left vocal fold fibrotic mass 3. Right vocal fold contact cyst or pseudocyst 4. Laryngopharyngeal reflux
PROCEDURE:	Laryngoscopy with magnification, strobovideolaryngoscopy, and complex voice analysis and synchronized electroglottography including sensory testing.
SURGEON:	Robert T. Sataloff, M.D., D.M.A.

Anesthesia: Topical
Rigid Endoscope: Kay-70

Flexible Laryngoscope: Olympus ENF-L3

Stroboscope: Kay-4

Procedure: The patient was taken to the special procedure room and prepared in the usual fashion. The laryngoscope was inserted, and suspended from the video system for magnification and documentation. Testing was performed at several frequencies and intensities. Initial examination was performed using continuous light. The findings were as follows:

Voice: Normal

Page 2
February 10, 2004
Re: John Doe

Supraglottic Hyperfunction: Moderate with decreased anterior-posterior distance and decreased lateral distance. It did improve with voluntary increase in pitch.

Right vocal fold abduction, adduction and longitudinal tension: Normal

Left vocal fold abduction was normal; adduction was slightly sluggish; and longitudinal tension was mildly decreased.

Arytenoid Joint Movement: Normal

Dysdiadochokinesis: Absent

Laryngeal EMG: Was recommended

CT: Not recommended

MRI: Not recommended

Arytenoids: Moderately erythematous and mildly edematous, right greater than left.

Posterior laryngeal cobblestoning (pachydermia): Absent

Right true vocal fold color: Normal, without significant varicosities.

Left true vocal fold color: Normal, without significant varicosities.

Masses and other Vibratory Margin Irregularities: The patient has a left vocal fold paresis and a left fibrotic mass in the striking zone that is about 3 mm in length at its base and has mild underlying stiffness. He also has a right contralateral cyst verses pseudocyst at the contact point. There is also stiffness at its base.

Other Significant Structural Lesions: Absent

Vocal Fold Vibrations: Symmetric in amplitude and phase

Periodicity: Regular

Glottic Closure: Intermittently incomplete anterior and posterior to the mass(es).

Vocal process height: Equal

Page 3
February 10, 2004

Amplitude of Right Vocal Fold: Minimally decreased
Amplitude of Left Vocal Fold: Mildly decreased
Minimally-to-mildly decreased

Wave Form of Right Vocal Fold: Minimally-to-mildly decreased
Wave Form of Left Vocal Fold: Mildly decreased

Right musculomembranous vocal fold vibratory function: Slightly hypodynamic in the middle one-third.

Left musculomembranous vocal fold vibratory function: Hypodynamic in the middle one-third

EGG: Revealed peak skewing. This indicates increased adduction, suggestive of pressed phonation.

The procedure concluded without complication

Robert T. Sataloff, M.D., D.M.A.

RTS/jb

Appendix IIIc

Objective Voice Analysis and Laryngeal Electromyography

Robert Thayer Sataloff, MD, DMA

Objective Voice Assessment

Patient: John Doe **Date of Birth**: xx-xx-xx **Age**: 25
Occupation: actor **Date of Evaluation**: 02-10-04 **Physician**: Dr. RTS
Diagnosis: Left vocal fold paresis, Laryngeal reflux, Small bilateral masses of the vocal folds, MTD
Hoarseness rating:Grade: 4 mm Roughness: 6.5 mm Breathiness: 3.5 mm Asthenia: 2.5 mm Strain: 4 mm

Acoustic Assessment

Conversation (name, date, age)
Mean Frequency: 107.23 Hz
Mean Intensity: 73.21 dBSPL
Reading Time: 17.91 sec Total Voiced Time: 11.25sec

Reading (M. Williams Passage)
Mean Frequency: 105.55 Hz
Mean Intensity: 73.58 dBSPL
% voiced: 62.814 %

Physiological Frequency Range of Phonation
Low = 73.5 Hz (*1/period*)
High= 412.15 Hz (*1/period*)
Semitone Range (STR) = 29.84589 ST

Singing Frequency Range
Low = Hz (*1/period*)
High= Hz (*1/period*)
Norm = 33-36 ST, (Hollien, Dew, Philips 1971)

Perturbation Measures

5 Token /a/: **Please see attached printout with graph.**
Fo(M85-155Hz;F143-235Hz)-108.375 Hz;**Jitter%**(M0.5389;F0.633)-0.447%;**RAP%**(M 0.345; F 0.378)-0.267%;
Shimmer% (M 2.523; F 1.977)- 1.288 %; **NHR** (M 0.122; F 0.112)- 0.147 ; **STD** (M 3.3; F 2.5)- 0.992

Spectrography

Sustained /i/ (Spectrogram) ; Yanagihara Hoarseness Rating Type: Type I
Type I= harmonic components mixed with noise in F1 and F2

Aerodynamic assessment

Spirometry: FVC = 115(%) FEV 1.0 = 75(%) FEF (25%-75%) = 33(%)
Mean Flow Rate (MFR): 329.4376 mls/sec
Maximum Phonation Time /a/ = 16.36 sec (mean); the best- 18.84 sec
(WNL females= 25.7 sec; WNL males=34.6 sec)

S/Z ratio: 1.1763034
(WNL range 0.8-1.29)

Glottal Efficiency Profile

Mean Flow Rate

49 69 89-------------112--------------136 156 256**...............X**

S/Z RATIO

0.2 0.4 0.8------------1.07------**X**-------1.29 2.2 4.4

Maximum Phonation Time

40 33 28.7-----------25.7-------------22.5 **X** 15 9.0

Recording/Analysis Equipment: TASCAM DAP1 DAT recorder, KAY model 4302 head-mount microphone at 15 cm., KAY Multi-Speech Model 3700 (MDVP Advanced 5105, Real-Time Spectrogram 5121) Schiller SP-10 Spirometer).

Page 2
February 10, 2004
Operative Report (cont'd)
Robert Thayer Sataloff, M.D., D. M. A.
re: John Doe

ACOUSTIC PROFILE (SPOKEN) /ɑ/

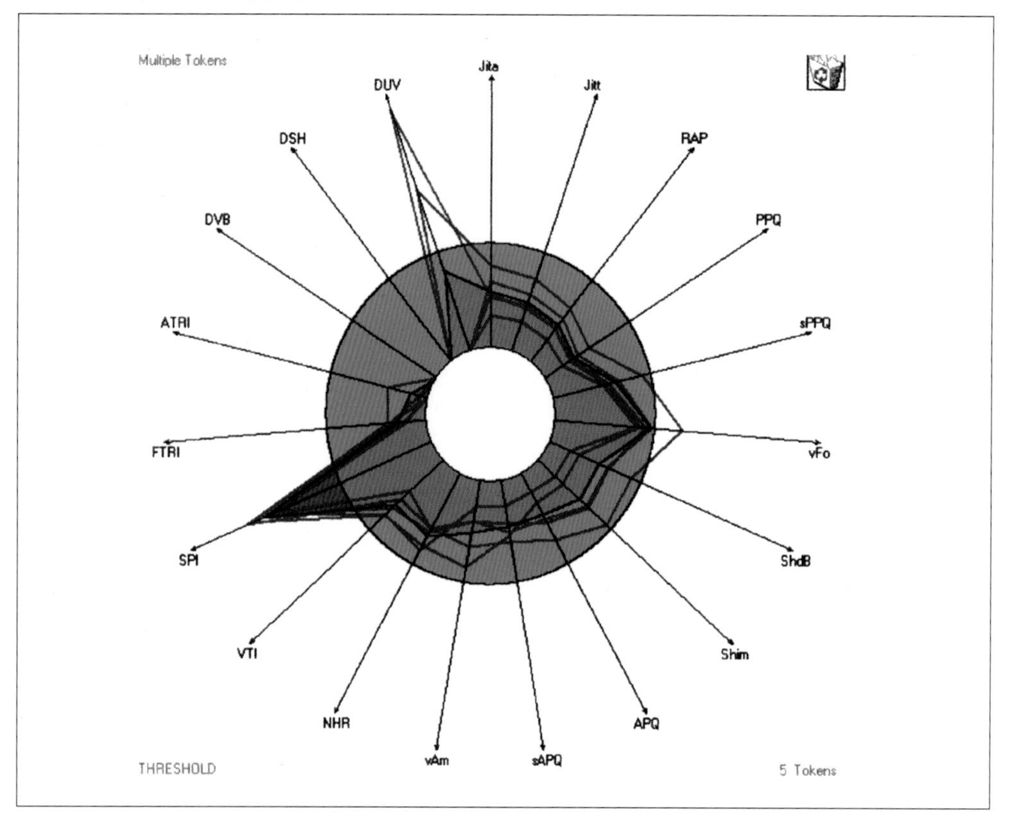

Page 3
February 10, 2004
OBJECTIVE VOICE ANALYSIS: John Doe

MDVPreport: Voice Report

Token 2

Parameter	Name	Value	Unit	Norm(f)	STD(f)	Thresh
Average Fundamental Frequency	**Fo**	**108.375**	**Hz**	**243.973**	**27.457**	
Mean Fundamental Frequency	**MFo**	**108.366**	**Hz**	**241.080**	**25.107**	
Average Pitch Period	To	9.228	ms	4.148	0.432	
Highest Fundamental Frequency	Fhi	111.164	Hz	252.724	26.570	
Lowest Fundamental Frequency	Flo	105.204	Hz	234.861	28.968	
Standard Deviation of Fo	STD	0.992	Hz	2.722	2.115	
Phonatory Fo-Range in semi-tones	PFR	2		2.250	1.060	
Fo-Tremor Frequency	Fftr	4.167	Hz	3.078	1.964	
Length of Analyzed Sample	Tsam	3.750	s	3.000	0.000	
Absolute Jitter	Jita	41.230	us	26.927	16.654	83.200
Jitter Percent	Jitt	0.447	%	0.633	0.351	1.040
Relative Average Perturbation	RAP	0.267	%	0.378	0.214	0.680
Pitch Perturbation Quotient	PPQ	0.253	%	0.366	0.205	0.840
Smoothed Pitch Perturbation Quotient	sPPQ	0.553	%	0.532	0.220	1.020
Fundamental Frequency Variation	vFo	0.916	%	1.149	1.005	1.100
Shimmer in dB	ShdB	0.113	dB	0.176	0.071	0.350
Shimmer Percent	Shim	1.288	%	1.997	0.791	3.810
Amplitude Perturbation Quotient	APQ	0.986	%	1.397	0.527	3.070
Smoothed Ampl. Perturbation Quotient	sAPQ	2.212	%	2.371	0.912	4.230
Peak-to-Peak Amplitude Variation	vAm	6.847	%	10.743	5.698	8.200
Noise to Harmonic Ratio	NHR	0.147		0.112	0.009	0.190
Voice Turbulence Index	VTI	0.047		0.046	0.012	0.061
Soft Phonation Index	SPI	27.227		7.534	4.133	14.120
Fo-Tremor Intensity Index	FTRI	0.333	%	0.304	0.156	0.950
Degree of Voice Breaks	DVB	0.000	%	0.200	0.100	1.000
Degree of Sub-harmonics	DSH	0.000	%	0.200	0.100	1.000
Degree of Voiceless	DUV	0.000	%	0.200	0.100	1.000
Number of Voice Breaks	NVB	0		0.200	0.100	0.900
Number of Sub-harmonic Segments	NSH	0		0.200	0.100	0.900
Number of Unvoiced Segments	NUV	0		0.200	0.100	0.900
Number of Segments Computed	SEG	124		92.594	0.000	
Total Number Detected Pitch Periods	PER	405		713.188	0.000	

Report Date: Feb. 10, 2004 Tuesday Name: John Doe Age & Gender: 25 years, male

Page 4
April 27, 1995
OBJECTIVE VOICE ANALYSIS: John Doe

<u>SPECTROGRAPHIC ANALYSIS</u>
<u>KAY ELEMETRICS</u>
<u>DSP SONA-GRAPH 5500</u>

POWER SPECTRUM (TOP) AND NARROW BAND SPECTRUM (BOTTOM) FOR /ɑ/:

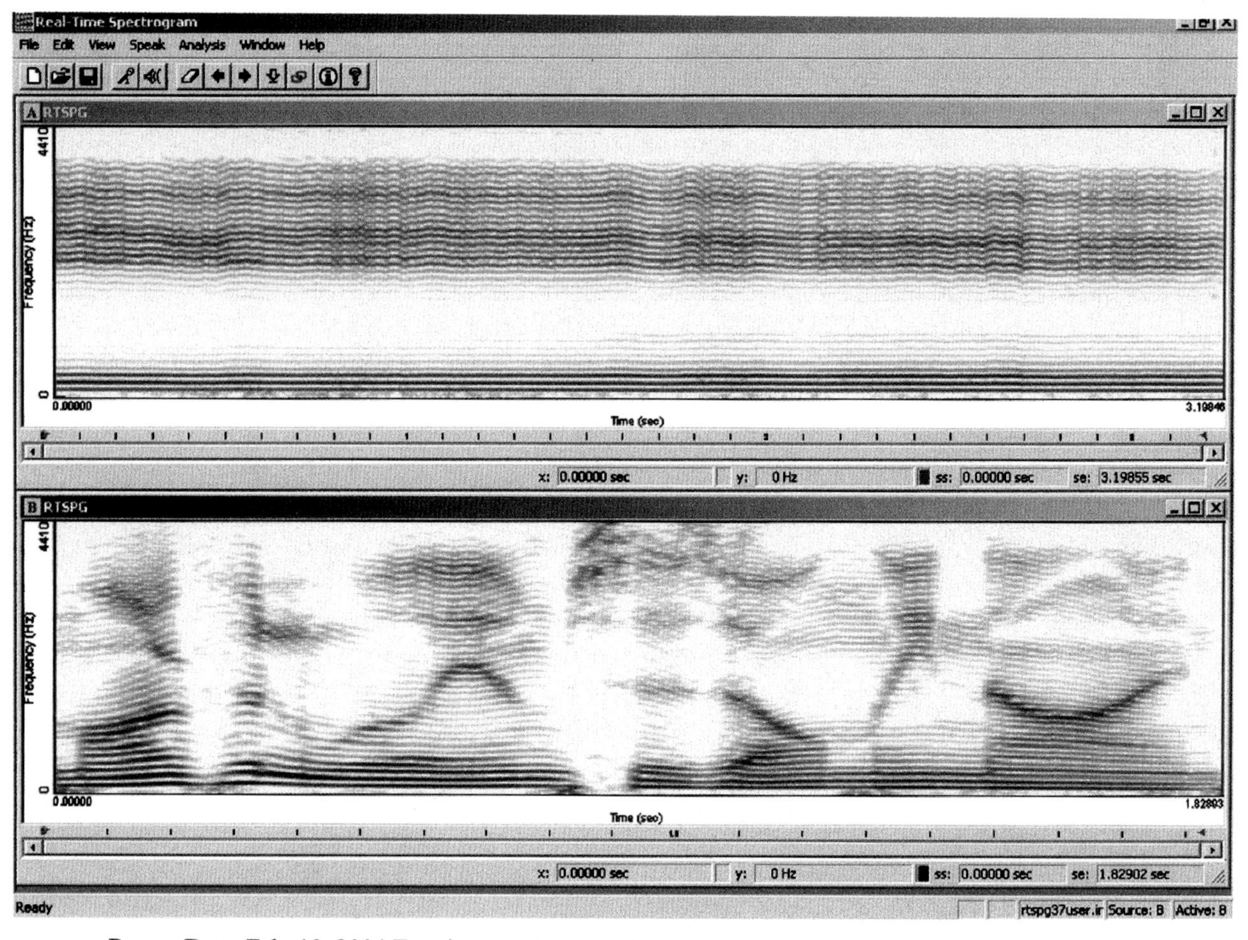

Report Date: Feb. 10, 2004 Tuesday Name: John Doe Age & Gender: 25 years, male

Page 5
OBJECTIVE VOICE ANALYSIS: John Doe

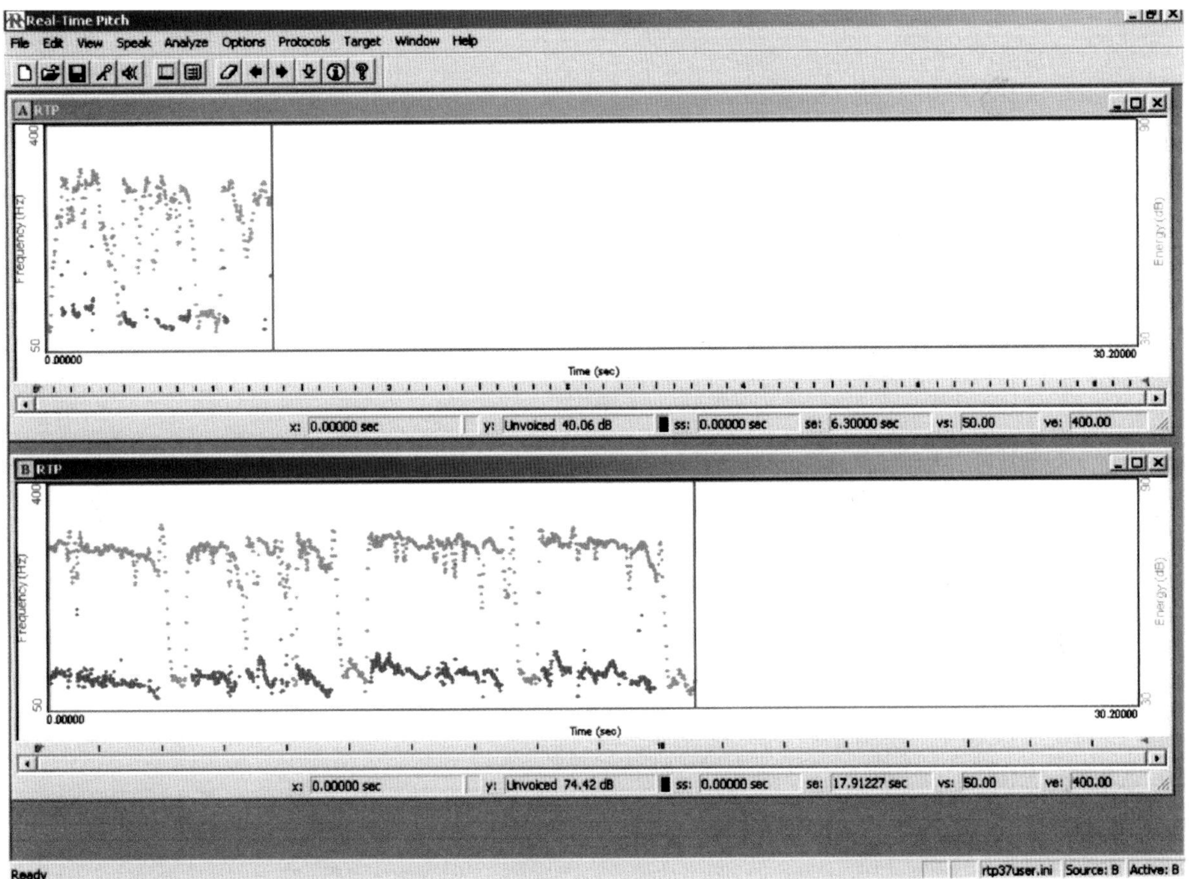

Report Date: Feb.10, 2004 Tuesday Name: John Doe Age & Gender: 25 years, male

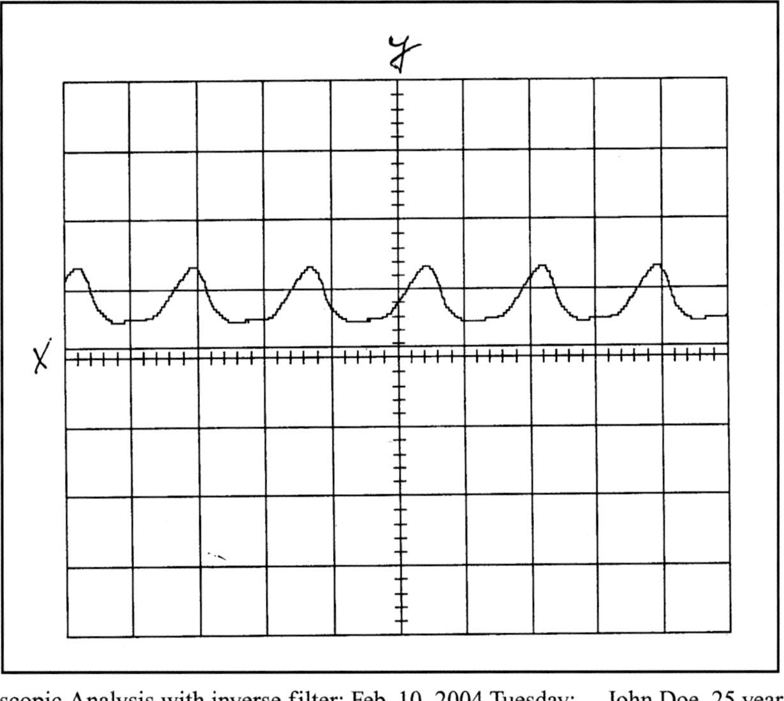

Oscilloscopic Analysis with inverse filter: Feb. 10, 2004 Tuesday; John Doe, 25 years, male

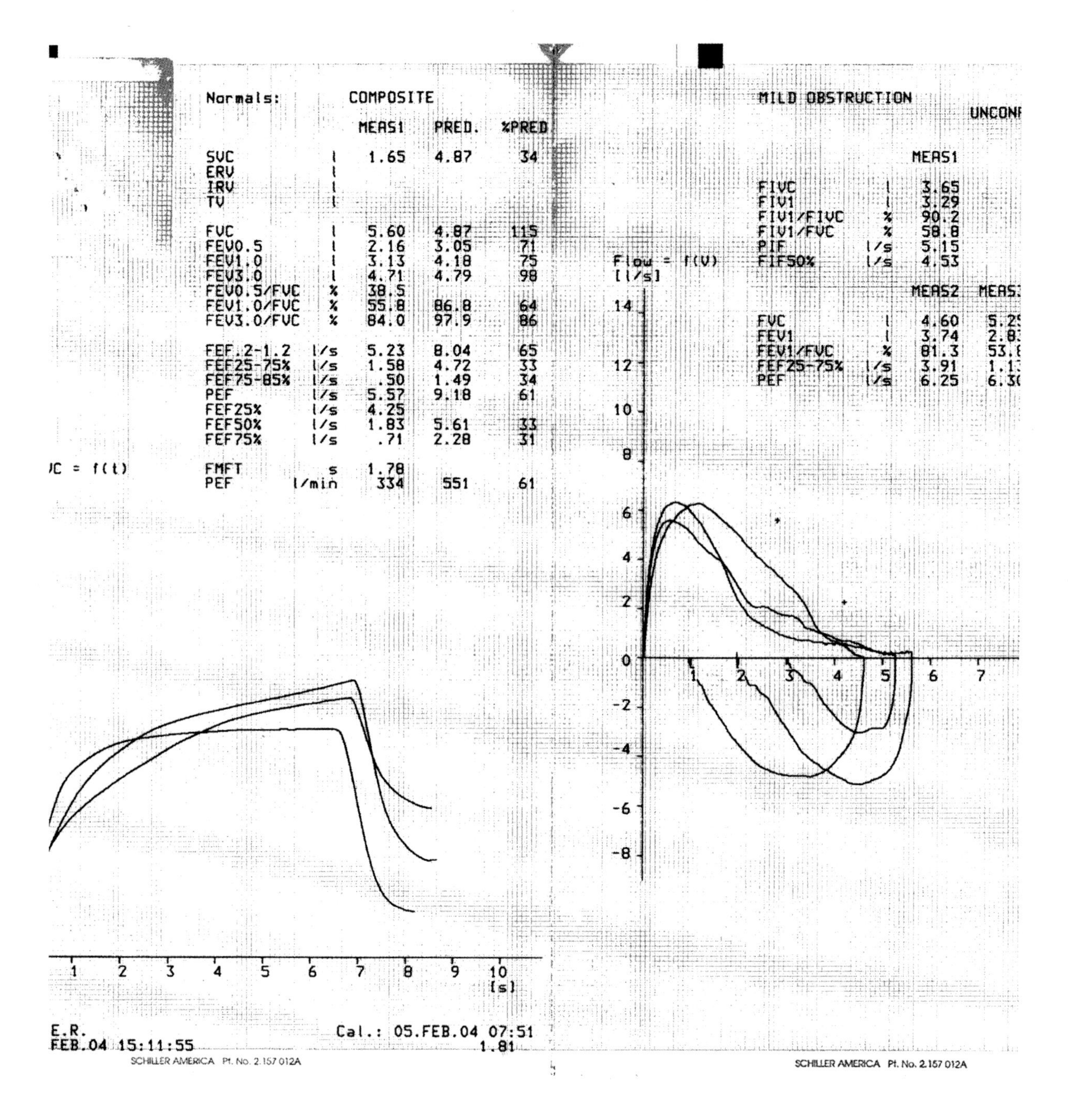

Normals: COMPOSITE
MEAS1 PRED. %PRED
SVC l 1.65 4.87 34
ERV l
IRV l
TV l
FVC l 5.60 4.87 115
FEV0.5 l 2.16 3.05 71
FEV1.0 l 3.13 4.18 75
FEV3.0 l 4.71 4.79 98
FEV0.5/FVC % 38.5
FEV1.0/FVC % 55.8 86.8 64
FEV3.0/FVC % 84.0 97.9 86
FEF.2-1.2 l/s 5.23 8.04 65
FEF25-75% l/s 1.58 4.72 33
FEF75-85% l/s .50 1.49 34
PEF l/s 5.57 9.18 61
FEF25% l/s 4.25
FEF50% l/s 1.83 5.61 33
FEF75% l/s .71 2.28 31
FMFT s 1.78
PEF l/min 334 551 61
1 2 3 4 5 6 7 8 9 10
[s]
E.R.
FEB.04 15:11:55
Cal.: 05.FEB.04 07:51
1.81
SCHILLER AMERICA Pt. No. 2.157 012A
MILD OBSTRUCTION
MEAS1
FIVC l 3.65
FIV1 l 3.29
FIV1/FIVC % 90.2
FIV1/FVC % 58.8
PIF l/s 5.15
FIF50% l/s 4.53
MEAS2
FVC l 4.60
FEV1 l 3.74
FEV1/FVC % 81.3
FEF25-75% l/s 3.91
PEF l/s 6.25
Flow = f(V)
[l/s]
14
12
10
8
6
4
2
0
-2
-4
-6
-8
1 2 3 4 5 6 7
SCHILLER AMERICA Pt. No. 2.157 012A

Robert Thayer Sataloff, M.D., D.M.A.
1721 Pine Street
Philadelphia, PA 19103-6771

Graduate Hospital
Tenet

Professor, Otolaryngology-Head & Neck Surgery
Director, Jefferson Arts Medicine Center
Conductor, Thomas Jefferson University Choir
Thomas Jefferson University

SIVEC

Chairman, Otolaryngology-Head & Neck Surgery
Graduate Hospital
Adjunct Professor, Otorhinolaryngology-HNS
The University of Pennsylvania

PATIENT OFFICE
(215) 545-3322
FAX: (215) 790-1192
office@phillyent.com

Sataloff Institute for Voice & Ear Care

ADMINISTRATIVE OFFICE
(215) 732-6100
FAX: (215) 545-7813
rtsataloff@phillyent.com

Interpretations of Findings:

Objective voice assessment reveals the following: Values of NHR (noise to harmonic ratio), SPI (soft phonation index), and MFR (mean flow rate) were all noticeably above the accepted normal limits, while Jitter %, RAP % (relative average perturbation), Shimmer %, STD (standard deviation of fundamental frequency), MPT (maximum phonation time), and mean frequencies of both conversational and reading voice samples as well as semitone range for the physiologic frequency, fell bellow or at the lowest possible level of the appropriate amplitude for these parameters. Oscilloscopic analysis with inverse filter demonstrates an epiglottic gap in the amount of 200 mls of escaping air. Spectrography reveals increase noise above 2.2 kHz in the area of F1 and F2.

Acoustic measures demonstrate moderately low mean Fundamental frequencies of conversational and reading (Marvin Williams's passage) voice samples and reduced semi-tone range. The combination of decreased perturbation measures of Jitter %, RAP %, Shimmer %, and STD as well as increased SPI and NHR reveals the existence of moderate irregularity of vocal fold vibration in sustained phonation and are consistent with the diagnosis of tension dysphonia due to unilateral vocal fold paresis and small, bilateral masses on the vocal folds. Spectrographic analyses of sustain vowel /i/ reveal decreased intensity of harmonics and increased noise elements chiefly in the formant region of the vowels. This correlates to perceptual measures of decreased oral resonance and is consistent with acoustic measures showing mild to moderate irregularity of vocal fold vibration.

Low MPT measures and abnormally high mean Flow rate denote inadequate glottal closure. This correlates with the diagnosis of unilateral vocal fold paresis. Oscilloscope measures with inverse filter further indicate insufficient glottal closure.

Decreased physiologic frequency range (pitch range) and low-average speaking F0 correlates with perceptual measures of increased strain and supports the diagnosis of muscle tension dysphonia. In addition, a few short, irregular periods of contraction and instability are seen on the spectrographic representation of sustained phonation. This finding is consistent with the diagnosis of muscle tension dysphonia as well.

Pulmonary function measurements demonstrate lung capacity at the upper levels of normal limits for this age, gender, height, and weight. However, low levels of FEV1.0/FVC and FEF25-75% at 64% and 33%, respectively, indicate mild obstructive changes at the end of expiration.

Dimiter Dentchev (M.D., Ph.D)

Chairman, Board of Directors
The Voice Foundation
Editor-in-Chief
Journal of Voice
215-735-7999

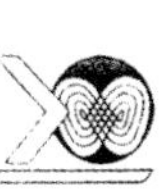

Chairman, Board of Directors
American Institute for Voice and Ear Research
215-735-7487

Philadelphia Ear, Nose & Throat Associates
Robert Thayer Sataloff, M.D., D.M.A.
Joseph R. Spiegel, M.D., F.A.C.S.
Karen M. Lyons, M.D.
web: www.phillyent.com

NEUROLOGY AND NEUROPHYSIOLOGY ASSOCIATES, P.C.

Ramon Mañon-Espaillat, M.D.
Clinical Professor of Neurology
Jefferson Medical College
Epilepsy and Sleep Disorders

Steven Mandel, M.D.
Clinical Professor of Neurology
Jefferson Medical College
Neuromuscular Diseases

Olga A. Katz, M.D., PhD.
Instructor of Neurology
Jefferson Medical College
Clinical Neurophysiology

xx/xx/xx

Robert Sataloff, M.D.
1721 Pine Street
Philadelphia, PA 19103

Reference: **John Doe**
DOB: xx/xx/xxxx
Evaluation Date: x/x/xx

Dear Dr. Sataloff:

HISTORY: I had the pleasure of seeing John Doe in the office on xx/xx/xx for a neurological consultation and electrodiagnostic studies.

He is a 25-year-old gentleman who reports difficulty with his voice. He has noted some hoarseness and projection difficulties.

He has been on a number of medications, including Zyrtec, Aciphex, Nasonex, and ranitidine.

He does not drink alcohol and does not smoke cigarettes. He is not receiving any therapy.

He has a history of hayfever.

Family history is noncontributory for neurological disease.

The patient has completed a patient history form and this form was reviewed in the presence of the patient as this note was being dictated.

1015 Chestnut Street • Suite 810 • Philadelphia, PA 19107
151 Fries Mill Road • Suite 506 • Turnersville, NJ 08012
Phone: (215) 574-0075 Fax: (215) 627-8208 • NJ Phone: (856) 228-0006
E-Mail: steven.mandel@mail.TJU.EDU

Page 2
John Doe
Evaluation Date: x/x/xx

EXAMINATION: He was awake and alert, answering appropriately. He had no obvious aphasia or dysarthria. He had no motor deficits. No tremors, dysmetria, or bruits were detected. Position and vibratory sense were normal.

Based upon his complaints, electrodiagnostic studies were obtained.

Prior to performing electrodiagnostic studies, "Consent for Electrodiagnostic Testing" was signed by the patient in my presence with the consent form present in the patient's chart.

LARYNGEAL EMG: Accessory nerve stimulation revealed normal latency and amplitude responses with repetitive stimulation study being normal. Needle EMG examination demonstrated approximately 80-90% recruitment response from left cricothyroid. Right cricothyroid, vocalis, and posterior cricoarytenoid muscles appeared to be normal. There was poor relaxation at rest and findings consistent with muscular tension dysphonia.

IMPRESSION: The above electrical studies indicate mild left superior laryngeal nerve paresis with muscular tension dysphonia. There is no evidence to indicate any neuromuscular junction abnormalities.

This note was dictated in the presence of the patient so as to insure the accuracy of the history provided by the patient. The patient has verbalized understanding as to the contents of this letter.

Thank you for allowing me to participate in the care of your patient. If you have any questions regarding the contents of this report or any other issues related to the care of this patient, please do not hesitate to contact me.

Sincerely,

Steven Mandel, M.D.

SM/ac

Patient Name: John Doe **Date:** 2/10/04

Voice Handicap Index (VHI)

(Jacobson, Johnson, Grywalski, et al.)

Instructions: These are statements that many people have used to describe their voices and the effects of their voices on their lives. Check the response that indicates how frequent you have the same experience.

Never=0 points; Almost never=1point; Sometimes=2 points; Almost Always=3 points; Always=4 points	**Never**	**Almost Never**	**Sometimes**	**Almost Always**	**Always**
F1. My voice makes it difficult for people to hear me.	✓				
P2. I run out of air when I talk.	✓				
F3. People have difficulty understanding me in a noisy room.	✓				
P4. The sound of my voice varies throughout the day.				✓	
F5. My family has difficulty hearing me when I call them throughout the house.	✓				
F6. I use the phone less often than I would like.			✓		
E7. I'm tense when talking with others because of my voice.			✓		
F8. I tend to avoid groups of people because of my voice.	✓				
E9. People seem irritated with my voice.		✓			
P10. People ask, "What's wrong with your voice?"	✓				
F11. I speak with friends, neighbors, or relatives less often because of my voice.	✓				
F12. People ask me to repeat myself when speaking fact-to-face.	✓				
P13. My voice sounds creaky and dry.			✓		
P14. I feel as through I have to strain to produce voice.			✓		
E15. I find other people don't understand my voice problem.				✓	
F16. My voice difficulties restrict my personal and social life.			✓		
P17. The clarity of my voice is unpredictable.		✓			
P18. I try to change my voice to sound different.			✓		
F19. I feel left out of conversations because of my voice.	✓				
P20 I use a great deal of effort to speak.		✓			
P21. My voice is worse in the evening.			✓		
F22. My voice problem causes me to loss income.	✓				
E23. My voice problem upsets me.				✓	
E24. I am less out-going because of my voice problem.		✓			
E25. My voice makes me feel handicapped.		✓			
P26. My voice "gives out" on me in the middle of speaking.	✓				
E27. I feel annoyed when people ask me to repeat.	✓				
E28. I feel embarrassed when people ask me to repeat.	✓				
E29. My voice makes me feel incompetent.		✓			
E30. I'm ashamed of my voice problem.				✓	

P Scale 23 F Scale 14 E Scale 25 Total Scale 62

Please **Circle** the word that matches how you feel your voice is today. 1. Normal (2. Mild 3. Moderate) 4. Severe

Appendix IIId

Speech-Language Pathologist's Report

INITIAL VOICE EVALUATION

Name: John Doe

Date of evaluation: 2/10/04

D.O.B.: XX/XX/XX

History: John Doe is a 25-year-old professional actor, currently performing the lead role in a touring company of "XXXXX XXXXX" at the Walnut Street Theatre in Philadelphia. He comes to this office with complaints of gravelly vocal quality, loss of range, and vocal fatigue. Mr. Doe reports that he has experienced voice problems since college, where he majored in theatre, but indicates that his problems have become more evident now that he has been cast in several major roles. He reports that the show opened in December of 2003, and adds that he is onstage for almost the entire 2_ hour duration of this show. Mr. Doe relates that he uses physical warm-ups for prior to performing, but that he is not confident in the vocal training he has received and avoids using vocal warm-ups for fear of fatiguing his voice before going onstage. Mr. Doe adds that he recently saw a physician who made a diagnosis of reflux and prescribed Aciphex twice daily.

Laryngovideostroboscopy performed by Dr. Robert Sataloff today revealed left vocal fold paresis, a left vocal fold fibrotic mass, a right vocal fold cyst vs. pseudocyst, and reflux. Laryngeal EMG was ordered to confirm vocal fold paresis. Dr. Sataloff asked Mr. Doe to continue Aciphex for symptoms of reflux and added Zantac 300 mg at bedtime. Mr. Doe's medical history is reportedly otherwise significant for microhematuria in childhood, prostatisis, allergies, and depression.

Medications: Aciphex, Zantac, Zyrtec, Nasonex

Allergies:

Vocal Hygiene: Mr. Doe reportedly drinks 8 glasses of water daily. He reports occasional consumption of caffeinated soda and frequent consumption of cranberry juice. He denies tobacco use. Mr. Doe admits to frequent throat clearing. He indicates that he avoids using his voice in an extreme fashion when he is not on stage, but is concerned that he may be forced to yell frequently if he has to return to waiting tables between acting jobs. He received some acting voice training as an undergraduate theatre major, but indicates that he had not found the training to be helpful,

Oral Mechanism Exam: The oral mechanism exam was unremarkable

Objective Evaluation: May be found under separate cover.

Subjective Evaluation: During conversational speech, Mr. Doe presented with intermittent hoarseness and occasional glottal fry and posterior tone placement at the ends of sentences. Tone placement was otherwise anterior, and occasionally hypernasal. Excessive tension was visible in the jaw, and his tone quality was suggestive of decreased pharyngeal space and tongue base tension. Mr. Doe demonstrated a tendency to sit with his sternum depressed and to utilize a shallow abdominal breathing technique with minimal rib cage expansion. Breath support was judged to be insufficient to promote maximal vocal resonance and freedom. On reading the Towne-Heuer Vocal Analysis reading passage, he produced 18% of hard glottal attacks (7-23% is considered to be in the normal range).

Doe, John
Voice Evaluation
Page 2 of 2

Trial Therapy: Vocal hygiene issues were discussed with an emphasis on adherence to a reflux protocol. Trial therapy focused on the reduction of excessive tension in the jaw and tongue and more efficient use of abdominal breath support. Jaw massage and relaxation exercises were introduced and resulted in increased volume and resonance during the production of open-vowel words. Tongue stretches and speech with tongue extension were practiced, and subsequent cueing for anterior tongue placement resulted in a more anterior, less pressed technique. Instruction in abdominal breath support was initiated. The patient accessed a much freer vocal production when encouraged to allow expansion of the rib cage upon inhalation rather than attempting to hold his rib cage fixed in place while breathing abdominally. An audiotape of these exercises was provided to the patient for home practice.

Impressions and Recommendations: John Doe is a professional actor who presents with intermittent hoarseness, decreased range, and vocal fatigue secondary to bilateral vocal fold masses, vocal fold paresis, and lack of adequate vocal technique to allow for successful compensation. Mr. Doe would benefit from voice therapy to promote the reduction of his vocal fold masses and improved voice quality and endurance through the establishment of a more efficient, well-supported vocal technique.

The following are the projected goals of the aforementioned therapy:

1. Establishment of improved posture and spinal alignment to promote greater efficiency of breathing and support.
2. More effective use of abdominal breathing and support in conversational speech.
3. Consistent use of frontal tone focus and increased oropharyngeal space to improve vocal tone quality, ease, and efficiency.
4. Elimination of excessive muscle tension in jaw and tongue.
5. Practice of exercises designed to address laryngeal nerve paralysis.

A course of 8 voice therapy sessions, 60 minutes in duration, is recommended to address these goals. Prior to the completion of such therapy, Mr. Doe will be referred back to Dr. Sataloff for re-evaluation and the need for further treatment assessed. Mr. Doe is an intelligent and motivated patient. Based upon his response to trial therapy, the prognosis for improved voice quality and function with compliance to a course of voice therapy is considered good.

Shirley Gherson, CCC-SLP

Appendix IIIe

Singing Voice Specialist's Report

VOCAL STRESS ASSESSMENT

Patient: John Doe
Date of Evaluation: February 18, 2004

John Doe is a 25-year-old professional actor who has been experiencing his current vocal complaints of vocal fatigue, a "gravelly-sounding" vocal quality, loss of vocal range and general vocal unreliability during the recent run of a high-level professional play in which he plays the lead role. Mr. Doe states that he has a history of these vocal complaints dating back to college, and he believes that they are now more evident as the demands of his career have increased. His recent lead role requires extensive voice use for most of the show, approximately 3 hours. He was examined by an ENT physician who diagnosed reflux and prescribed Aciphex. Mr. Doe was evaluated by Dr. Robert T. Sataloff on February 10, 2004 who diagnosed left vocal fold paresis, a left vocal fold fibrotic mass, a right vocal fold contact cyst or pseudocyst and laryngopharyngeal reflux.

Mr. Doe has been acting since childhood but does not believe that he has ever received adequate training in voice production and vocal health for his speaking voice. He is not a singer and has had no significant training for his singing voice. For the past two years, when not involved in a production, he has been supplementing his income by working about 20 hours a week in the kitchen of a Hard Rock Café. He acknowledges talking on the phone "a lot."

Mr. Doe denies using tobacco products and rarely drinks alcoholic beverages. He exercises regularly and considers his general health to be good. His regular medications include daily Zyrtec and Nasonex for allergies, as well as Aciphex BID and 300 mg of Zantac at night for his reflux.

During the intital singing evaluation, Mr. Doe demonstrated the following technical patterns: mid-abdominal inhalation and breath support efforts; excessive muscular tension in the regions of the jaw and tongue; reduced oral resonance space; audibly suggested muscle tension in the region of the pharynx. His approximate singing range was C2-C5, with only falsetto present above E4. Mr. Doe presented with an average bari-tenor singing voice that matched pitch well and was pleasant in quality. His conversational speaking voice was moderately pressed with a generally posterior tone placement.

This session continued with efforts to release some of the counterproductive compensatory muscle tension in Mr. Doe's jaw and tongue. Gentle tongue stretching

Page 2
February 18, 2004
Vocal Stress Assessment (continued)
Re: John Doe

exercises as well as verbal cues with tactile jaw massage proved effective. We then focused on utilizing this more relaxed musculature on simple singing exercises (5-1, 1-5-1 and 135875421 on lip trills, A2-D#4 and 3-1 on \baɪbaɪ\ with the resulting voice showing more freedom of production as well as a more balanced resonance quality. Mr. Doe recognized these changes and will practice daily with a cassette tape of this session until he can return for a follow-up session, hopefully in one week.

Mr. Doe is an extremely intelligent and compliant patient who appears highly motivated to improve his vocal quality and endurance. It is likely that his current vocal complaints are related to a combination of causes including reflux, vocal fold masses, vocal fold paresis and a less-than-optimum level of vocal technique and conditioning necessary to meet the rigorous vocal demands of a busy acting career. Regular singing voice sessions (in conjunction with voice therapy) focused on identifying and eliminating counterproductive compensatory muscle tension, establishing a more efficient and reliable breath management system and encouraging more anterior tonal placement may allow Mr. Doe to access more of his vocal potential with less strain. More efficient vocal production may lead to some spontaneous reduction of his vocal fold masses. Strict reflux control may also prove to be a necessary component to his recovery strategy.

Thank you for allowing me to participate in his care.

Sincerely yours,

Margaret Baroody, M.M.
Singing Voice Specialist

Appendix IIIf

Acting Voice Specialist's Report

ACTING VOICE EVALUATION

Name: John Doe

Date of evaluation: 2/10/04

Date of birth:

History: John Doe is a 25-year-old professional actor, currently performing the lead role in a touring company of "XXXXX XXXXX" at the Walnut Street Theatre in Philadelphia. He comes to this office with complaints of a gravelly voice quality, loss of range, and vocal fatigue. Mr. Doe reports that he has experienced vocal problems since college, where he majored in theatre, but indicates that his problems have become more evident now that he has been cast in several major roles. He reports that he is onstage for almost the entire 2_ hour duration of this show, and that his character often serves as narrator or to comment on the action of the play to the audience. He adds that the show opened in December of 2003. Mr. Doe relates that he uses physical warm-ups prior to performing, but that he is not confident in the vocal training he has received and avoids using vocal warm-ups for fear of fatiguing his voice before going onstage. Mr. Doe adds that he recently saw a physician who made a diagnosis of reflux and prescribed Aciphex twice daily.

Laryngovideostroboscopy performed by Dr. Robert T. Sataloff today revealed left vocal fold paresis, a left vocal fold fibrotic mass, a right vocal fold cyst vs. pseudocyst, and reflux. Laryngeal EMG was ordered to confirm the vocal fold paresis. Dr. Sataloff asked Mr. Doe to continue Aciphex for symptoms of reflux and added Zantac 300 mg at bedtime. Mr. Doe's medical history is reportedly otherwise significant for microhematuria in childhood, prostatitis, and depression.

Evaluation of Vocal Technique: During conversational speech, Mr. Doe demonstrated a mildly pressed, posteriorly placed voice produced with inadequate breath support and reduced oropharyngeal space. When asked to demonstrate his vocal production for this particular role (and when observed in performance at the theatre), he demonstrated a more anteriorly placed, but mildly nasal and pressed voice. The use of a "Brooklynese" accent in his current role intensified hypernasality. Vocal hyperfunction was judged to be exacerbated by jaw tension, restricted rib cage expansion, laryngeal tension, head/neck misalignment, and decreased oropharyngeal space.

Vocal Exercises Given: Because the patient was evaluated in the afternoon prior to a performance, today's work focused primarily on introducing a vocal warm-up combining physical movement to free the upper body and rib movement and vocal work to promote increased airflow and space. An arm-swing warm-up utilizing lip trills on glides and lip trills elided into spoken words and text resulted in freer, more resonant vocal production. The patient reported that his voice felt easier to produce and yet stronger than it has recently. These exercises were recorded on audiotape and provided to the patient for home practice.

Doe, John
Acting Voice Evaluation
Page 2 of 2

Impressions and Recommendations: John Doe is a 25-year-old actor, who presents with a pressed, inadequately supported voice, secondary to bilateral vocal fold masses, left vocal fold paresis, and reflux. His vocal training has not prepared him to effectively compensate for laryngeal weakness or injury. He would benefit from acting voice sessions designed to assist the patient in preparing himself for performance with warm-ups to promote the reduction of upper body tension, improved alignment, and increased jaw relaxation and oropharyngeal space during voice production. It has also been recommended that the patient receive concurrent speaking voice therapy

and singing voice sessions to address vocal techniques in conversational speech and promote greater vocal endurance and strength.

Mr. Doe is a very pleasant and motivated patient. It is a privilege to participate in his care.

Michelle Horman, CCC-SLP
Acting Voice Specialist

Index

D

E

F

G

H

M

N

Q

R

S

W

X

Z